D0903184

29.64

LOVE
MARRIAGE
FAMILY

A Developmental Approach

LOVE
MARRIAGE
FAMILY

A Developmental Approach

Marcia E. Lasswell
California State Polytechnic University

Thomas E. Lasswell
University of Southern California

Scott, Foresman and Company
Glenview, Illinois   Brighton, England

Library of Congress Catalog Card Number: 72–93545
ISBN: 0–673–07523–0

Copyright © 1973 Scott, Foresman and Company, Glenview, Illinois.
Philippines Copyright 1973 Scott, Foresman and Company.
All Rights Reserved.
Printed in the United States of America.

Regional offices of Scott, Foresman and Company are located in Dallas, Texas;
Glenview, Illinois; Oakland, New Jersey; Palo Alto, California; Tucker, Georgia;
and Brighton, England.

HQ
728
.L398

Acknowledgments

1. Excerpted from "Interpersonal Relationships—Crux of the Sexual Renaissance," by Lester A. Kirkendall and Roger W. Libby from *The Journal of Social
Issues*, Vol. 22, No. 2 (April 1966). Reprinted by permission of the authors and
the Society for the Psychological Study of Social Issues.

2. "Prospective Changes in Marriage and the Family," by Robert Parke, Jr., and
Paul C. Glick from *Journal of Marriage and the Family*, Vol. 29, No. 2 (May
1967). Reprinted by permission of the authors and the National Council on
Family Relations.

3. "An Informal History of Love, U.S.A." by Arthur Schlesinger, Jr., from *The
Saturday Evening Post* (December 31, 1966). © 1966 The Curtis Publishing Company. Reprinted with permission from *Saturday Evening Post*.

4. "The Process of Learning Parental and Sex-Role Identification," by David
B. Lynn from *Journal of Marriage and the Family*, Vol. 28 (November 1966).
Reprinted by permission of the author and the National Council on Family Rela-
tions.

5. "Identification" in *Psychology in Women: A Study of Bio-Cultural Conflicts*
by Judith M. Bardwick. Copyright © 1971 by Judith M. Bardwick. Reprinted by
permission of Harper & Row Publishers, Inc.

6. Orville Brim, "Family Structure and Sex Role Learning by Children," *Sociometry*, Vol. 21, 1958, pp. 1–16. Reprinted by permission of the author and the
American Sociological Association.

7. "Sexual Behavior Among Preadolescents," by Carlfred B. Broderick from
The Journal of Social Issues, Vol. 22, No. 2 (April 1966). Reprinted by permission
of the author and the Society for the Psychological Study of Social Issues.

8. "Helping Children Grow Up Sexually: How? When? By Whom?" by Eleanore
Braun Luckey from *Children*, Vol. 14, No. 4 (July-August 1967). Reprinted by
permission.

9. "Sexuality and Its Implications for Personal Identity and Fulfillment" by
Morton S. Eisenberg from *Sex Education and the New Morality: A Search for
a Meaningful Ethic:* Child Study Association of America © 1967. Reprinted by
permission.

10. "'Anatomy Is Destiny': Psychological Implications of Adolescent Physical
Changes in Girls" by Ellen Rothchild from *Pediatrics*, Vol. 39 (April 1967). Reprinted by permission of the author and the American Academy of Pediatrics.

11. "Self-Perceived Rate of Physical Maturation and Personality in Late Adolescence" by Donald Weatherley from *Child Development*, Vol. 35, 1964. Reprinted by permission of The Society for Research in Child Development, Inc., and the author.

12. "Youth Looks at Sex" by Gertrude B. Couch from *Adolescence*, Vol. 2, No. 6, 1967. Reprinted by permission of Libra Publishers, Inc.

13. "The Perceptual Context of Boy-Girl Communication" by Carlfred B. Broderick and Jean Weaver from *Journal of Marriage and the Family*, Vol. 30, No. 4 (November 1968). Reprinted by permission of the authors and the National Council on Family Relations.

14. "Adolescent Love as a Reflection of Teen-Agers' Search for Identity" by Evelyn Millis Duvall from *Journal of Marriage and the Family*, Vol. 26, No. 2 (May 1964). Reprinted by permission of the author and the National Council on Family Relations.

15. "To Both Their Own" from *Male and Female*, Apollo Edition by Margaret Mead. Reprinted by permission of William Morrow & Company, Inc., and Victor Gollancz Ltd. Copyright 1949 by Margaret Mead.

16. "The Young Adult" from Chapter 11 of *The Person: His Development Throughout the Life Cycle* by Theodore Lidz, © 1968 by Theodore Lidz, Published by Basic Books, Inc., Publishers, New York. Reprinted by permission.

17. Reprinted by permission of Coward, McCann & Geoghegan, Inc. and The Foley Agency from *The American Male* by Myron Brenton. Copyright © 1966 by Myron Brenton.

18. "The New Woman: Out to Finish What the Suffragette Started," by Caroline Bird from *Think*, Vol. 36, No. 4 (July-August 1970). Reprinted by permission from *Think* Magazine, published by IBM, Copyright 1970 by International Business Machines Corporation.

19. "The Changing Role of the Black Woman" by Barbara Rhodes from *The Black Family: Essays and Studies* by Robert Staples. © 1971 by Wadsworth Publishing Company, Inc., Belmont, California 94002. Reprinted by permission of the publisher and Professor Rhodes.

20. "Dating Behavior: A Framework for Analysis and an Illustration" by James A. Skipper, Jr., and Gilbert Nass from *Journal of Marriage and the Family*, Vol. 28, No. 4 (November 1966). Reprinted by permission of the authors and the National Council on Family Relations.

21. "Role Definition in the Unarranged Date," by Jack O. Balswick and James A. Anderson from *Journal of Marriage and the Family*, Vol. 31, No. 4 (November 1969). Reprinted by permission of the authors and the National Council on Family Relations.

22. From *The World of the Formerly Married* by Morton Hunt. Copyright © 1966 by Morton Hunt. Used with permission of McGraw-Hill Book Company.

23. "Teen-Age Interracial Dating" by Frank A. Petroni. Published by permission of the author and Transaction Inc. from *transaction*, Vol. 8 (September 1971). © 1971 by Transaction Inc.

24. "Research in Interreligious Dating and Marriage" by Larry D. Barnett from *Marriage and Family Living* (May 1962). Reprinted by permission of the author and the National Council on Family Relations.

25. Copyright © 1970 by George R. Bach and Ronald M. Deutsch. From the book *Pairing*, published by Peter H. Wyden, Inc. Reprinted by permission of the publisher.

ALMA COLLEGE
MONTEITH LIBRARY
ALMA, MICHIGAN

26. "The Theoretical Importance of Love," by William J. Goode from *American Sociological Review*, Vol. 24, No. 1 (February 1959). Reprinted by permission of the author and the American Sociological Association.

27. "Toward a Sociology of the Heterosexual Love Relationship" by Ira L. Reiss from *Marriage and Family Living*, Vol. 22, No. 1 (February 1960). Reprinted by permission of the author and the National Council on Family Relations.

28. "Some Correlates of Romantic Love" by William M. Kephart from *Journal of Marriage and the Family*, Vol. 29 (August 1967). Reprinted by permission of the author and the National Council on Family Relations.

29. "Love or Marriage?" by Ernest Van Den Haag. Copyright © 1962, by Minneapolis Star and Tribune Co., Inc. Reprinted from the May 1962 issue of *Harper's Magazine* by permission of the author. "The Lady's First Song" by William Butler Yeats. Reprinted with permission of The Macmillan Company, Mr. M. B. Yeats, Macmillan London Ltd. and the Macmillan Company of Canada Ltd., from *Collected Poems* by William Butler Yeats. Copyright 1940 by Georgie Yeats, renewed 1968 by Bertha Georgie Yeats, Michael Butler Yeats and Anne Yeats.

30. "Understanding Sexual Attraction" from *Story of Life*. Reprinted by permission of Michael Cavendish Ltd., London.

31. "A Comparison of Sexual Attitudes and Behavior in an International Sample" by Eleanore B. Luckey and Gilbert D. Nass from *Journal of Marriage and the Family*, Vol. 31, No. 2 (May 1969). Reprinted by permission of the authors and the National Council on Family Relations.

32. " 'The Arrangement' at College" Part I, by William A. McWhirter from *Life* (May 31, 1968), pp. 56–62. Copyright *Life* Magazine, © 1968 Time Inc.

33. " 'The Arrangement' at College" Part II, by Albert Rosenfeld from *Life* (May 31, 1968), p. 68. Copyright *Life* Magazine, © 1968 Time Inc.

34. "The Pleasures and Pain of the Single Life." Reprinted by permission from *Time*, The Weekly Newsmagazine; Copyright Time Inc.

35. "Abortion—or Compulsory Pregnancy?" by Garrett Hardin from *Journal of Marriage and the Family*, Vol. 30, No. 2 (May 1968). Reprinted by permission of the author and the National Council on Family Relations.

36. From "The Law and Sexual Relationships," by Robert Veit Sherwin, J.D., from *The Journal of Social Issues*, Vol. 22, No. 2 (April 1966). Reprinted by permission of the author and the Society for the Psychological Study of Social Issues.

37. "Attitudes: A Study of Homogamy and Marital Selectivity," by Eloise C. Snyder from *Journal of Marriage and the Family*, Vol. 36, No. 3 (August 1964). Reprinted by permission of the author and the National Council on Family Relations.

38. "Theories of Mate Selection" by Bruce K. Eckland from *Eugenics Quarterly*, Vol. 15, 1968. Reprinted by permission of The University of Chicago Press. Copyright © *Eugenics Quarterly*, 1968.

39. Bernard I. Murstein, "Self–Ideal-Self Discrepancy and the Choice of Marital Partner," *Journal of Consulting and Clinical Psychology*, Vol. 27 (1971), pp. 47–52. Copyright © 1971 by the American Psychological Association, and reproduced by permission.

40. "The Transition from Engagement to Marriage" by Rhona Rapoport from *ACTA Sociologica*, Vol. 8. Reprinted by permission of Journal of The Scandinavian Sociological Association.

41. "Trial Marriage: Harnessing the Trend Constructively" by Miriam E. Berger from *The Family Coordinator*, Vol. 20, No. 1 (January 1971). Reprinted by permission of the author and the National Council on Family Relations.

42. "The Clinical Implications of Perceptual Distortions in Forced Marriages," by Dean H. Hepworth from *Social Casework*, Vol. 45, No. 10 (December 1964). Reprinted by permission of the Family Service Association of America.

43. "Making a Marriage" from *Story of Life*. Reprinted by permission of Michael Cavendish Ltd., London.

44. From *Youth, Marriage and the Seductive Society*. Reprinted by permission of Wm. C. Brown Company Publishers.

45. "Patterns of Newlywed Marriage" by Wells Goodrich, Robert G. Ryder, and Harold L. Raush from *Journal of Marriage and the Family*, Vol. 30, No. 3 (August 1968). Reprinted by permission of the authors and The National Council on Family Relations.

46. "Initial Adjustment Processes in Young Married Couples" by Beverly R. Cutler and William G. Dyer from *Social Forces*, Vol. 44, No. 2 (December 1965). Reprinted by permission of The University of North Carolina Press.

47. "The Politics of Marriage: A Delicate Balance" by Vivian Cadden. Reprinted from *Redbook* Magazine, July 1971, copyright © 1971 The McCall Publishing Company.

48. Reprinted from *The Mirages of Marriage* by William J. Lederer and Don D. Jackson, M.D. By permission of W. W. Norton & Company, Inc. Copyright © 1968 by W. W. Norton & Company, Inc.

49. "Housewife and Woman? The Best of Both Worlds?" from *Man and Civilization: The Family's Search for Survival*, Edited by Farber, Mustacchi & Wilson. Copyright © 1965 by McGraw-Hill, Inc. Used with permission of McGraw-Hill Book Company.

50. "Motherhood: Who Needs It?" by Betty Rollin from *Look*, September 22, 1970. Copyright © Cowles Communications, Inc., 1970. Reprinted by permission.

51. Adapted with permission of The Macmillan Company and Parents' Magazine from *Birth Control and Love* by Alan F. Guttmacher, Winfield Best and Frederick Jaffe. Copyright © 1961, 1964, 1968, 1969 by Alan F. Guttmacher, Winfield Best and Frederick Jaffe.

52. "Transition to Parenthood," by Alice S. Rossi from *Journal of Marriage and the Family*, Vol. 30, No. 1 (February 1968). Reprinted by permission of the author and the National Council on Family Relations.

53. "Children in the Family: Relationship of Number and Spacing to Marital Success" by Harold T. Christensen from *Journal of Marriage and the Family*, Vol. 30, No. 2 (May 1968). Reprinted by permission of the author and the National Council on Family Relations.

54. "The Father in Contemporary Culture and Current Psychological Literature" by John Nash from *Child Development*, 1965, *36*, 261–297. Reprinted by permission of The Society for Research in Child Development, Inc.

55. Marian Radke Yarrow, Phyllis Scott, Louise de Leeuw and Christine Heinig, "Child-Rearing in Families of Working and Nonworking Mothers," *Sociometry*, Vol. 25 (June 1962). Reprinted by permission of the authors and the American Sociological Association.

56. "Role Perception and Marital Satisfaction—A Configurational Approach," by Robert P. Stuckert from *Journal of Marriage and the Family*, Vol. 25 (November 1963). Reprinted by permission of the author and the National Council on Family Relations.

57. "Marital Satisfaction Over the Family Life Cycle," by Boyd C. Rollins and Harold Feldman from *Journal of Marriage and the Family,* Vol. 32, No. 1 (February 1970). Reprinted by permission of the authors and the National Council on Family Relations.

58. "Working Wives and Marriage Happiness" by Susan Orden and Norman Bradburn from *American Journal of Sociology,* Vol. 74 (January 1969). Reprinted by permission of the authors and The University of Chicago Press.

59. "Correlates of Dissatisfaction in Marriage," by Karen S. Renne from *Journal of Marriage and the Family,* Vol. 32 (February 1970). Reprinted by permission of the author and the National Council on Family Relations.

60. "Conjugal Organization and Health" by Lois Pratt from *Journal of Marriage and the Family,* Vol. 34, No. 1 (February 1972). Reprinted by permission of the author and the National Council on Family Relations. This investigation was supported by the National Center for Health Services Research and Development (PHS Grant Number HS 00065).

61. "A Marriage in Trouble" by Richard Meryman from *Life,* Vol. 72, No. 16 (April 28, 1972). Copyright: *Life* Magazine, © 1972 Time Inc. Reprinted by permission of Time/Life Syndication Service.

62. "A Radical Guide to Wedlock" adapted from *Uncoupling: The Art of Coming Apart* by Norman Sheresky and Marya Mannes. Copyright © 1972 by Norman Sheresky and Marya Mannes. Reprinted by permission of The Viking Press, Inc., and Harold Ober Associates, Incorporated.

63. "Mate Swapping: The Family That Swings Together Clings Together" by Duane Denfeld and Michael Gordon from *Journal of Sex Research,* Vol. 7, No. 2 (May 1970). Reprinted by permission of *The Journal of Sex Research.*

64. "Ethical and Ideological Problems for Communal Living: A Caveat" by Joy G. Schulterbrandt and Edwin J. Nichols from *The Family Coordinator* (October 1972). Reprinted by permission of the National Council on Family Relations.

65. "The Group Marriage" by Larry L. and Joan M. Constantine from *The Nuclear Family in Crisis* by Michael Gordon. Copyright © 1972 by Michael Gordon. Reprinted by permission of the authors.

66. "Widowhood Status in the United States: Perspective on a Neglected Aspect of the Family Life-Cycle," by Felix M. Berardo from *The Family Coordinator,* Vol. 17, No. 3 (July 1968). Reprinted by permission of the author and the National Council on Family Relations.

67. From "Divorce Is a Family Affair" by Jack C. Westman and David W. Cline from *Family Law Quarterly,* Vol. 5, No. 1 (March 1971). Reprinted by permission of *Family Law Quarterly.*

68. "Parents Without Partners" from *Parents in Modern America* by E. E. LeMasters. Reprinted by permission of The Dorsey Press.

69. "The Six Stations of Divorce" from *Divorce and After* by Paul Bohannan. Copyright © 1970 by Paul Bohannan. Reprinted by permission of Doubleday & Company, Inc.

70. "The American Way of Marriage: Remarriage" by Betty Rollin from *Look,* September 21, 1971. Copyright © Cowles Communications, Inc., 1971. Reprinted by permission.

71. "Some Relationships of Stepchildren to Their Parents," by C. E. Bowerman and D. P. Irish from the *Journal of Marriage and the Family* (May 1962). Reprinted by permission of the authors and the National Council on Family Relations.

72. "The Changing American Grandparent," by Bernice L. Neugarten and Karol K. Weinstein from *Journal of Marriage and the Family*, Vol. 26, No. 2 (May 1964). Reprinted by permission of the authors and the National Council on Family Relations.

73. "Socialization for Postparental Life" by Irwin Deutscher from *Human Behavior and Social Processes*, ed. Arnold Rose. Reprinted by permission of Houghton Mifflin Company and Routledge & Kegan Paul Ltd.

74. "Looking Ahead in Aging: Love After Fifty" by Marcia E. Lasswell. Previously unpublished paper delivered at the University of California, San Diego, October 29, 1971.

75. "Anticipation of Things to Come" in *Married Love in the Middle Years* by James A. Peterson. Copyright © 1968 by The National Board of the Young Men's Christian Associations. Reprinted by permission of Association Press.

76. "Older Families and Their Troubles: Familial and Social Responses," by Gordon F. Streib from *The Family Coordinator*, Vol. 21, No. 1 (Jan. 1972). Reprinted by permission of the author and the National Council on Family Relations.

77. Reprinted by permission of G. P. Putnam's Sons, Andre Deutsch Limited and George Weidenfeld & Nicolson Ltd. from *The Coming of Age* by Simone de Beauvoir. English translation by Patrick O'Brian copyright © 1972 by Andre Deutsch, Weidenfeld and Nicolson and G. P. Putnam's Sons.

78. "Toward a Hundred Years" by Emory S. Bogardus. Used by permission of the author.

To Emory Stephen Bogardus, Ph.D.
Eminent sociologist, good friend,
and a model for living to be one hundred years old.

Preface

Nearly every college and university offers one or more courses dealing with the family and preparation for family life. In addition, community organizations offer countless study courses pertinent to this area. Junior college, four-year college, and university courses range from what has been termed a "cookbook" course to a theoretical approach concerning itself with the historical and cultural emphases of family life.

Currently, colleges and universities seem to be moving away from the "how-to" approach toward the broader foundation of the study and understanding of male-female relationships. The college-aged person today seeks facts and objectivity, as well as practical knowledge and solutions to everyday problems. There is a growing interest in the dynamics of love, marriage, and family relationships and in the foundation upon which these dynamics are based.

Marriage and family courses are taught by instructors with a wide range of backgrounds—sociologists, psychologists, home economists, ministers, social workers, and physicians, to name but the major orientations. Some instructors specialize in this area and are experts in nearly all aspects of family-life preparation and male-female relationships; others may teach the course because of a special kind of interest in a particular phase. Regardless of the approach, the courses are usually popular ones, for they deal with a popular subject.

Students enrolling in these courses are also from diverse backgrounds. Since they may come from any college major, and since the course is usually an elective subject, a large number of the readers of this book will have no specialized academic background in marriage and family living to bring to the course and will be relying on personal experience, current interests, and perhaps an ample exposure to the popular treatment of the topics through periodicals and certain trade books.

Obviously, no book of readings can be all things to all readers. Each male-female relationship is unique, and providing a broad framework for an understanding of how such relationships can develop seems to be a better approach than does giving advice based on our opinions or describing the popular varieties of roles, for instance. The research we present to help build this broad framework primarily concerns middle-class men and women, although, when possible, a broader treatment is given. At this point in time, while there are some good studies other than middle-class ones, they are somewhat isolated and do not provide as clear a picture as does the majority of the research on middle-class heterosexual relationships.

This book takes a developmental approach, which is but one of many approaches. As with the middle-class orientation, we have chosen to stick with one approach for the sake of continuity. The early part of the book is devoted to a discussion of the development of masculinity and femininity as a result of environmental forces; the sequences of dating, marrying, and maintaining heterosexual relationships follow a chronological pattern. We then follow marriage and family life from the childbearing years through the time when the children leave home and the couple faces old age. As the table of contents indicates, the emphasis of the readings is to provide a broad perspective on the problems and pleasures of being a man or a woman and relating to the opposite sex. To this aim, the book is dedicated; and it is hoped that the reader can use the articles to develop a better grasp of where he or she stands in the total spectrum of being a man or a woman in today's world.

M. E. L. and T. E. L.

Contents

A Look at the Changing Patterns of Love and Marriage in the Second Half of the Twentieth Century

Scholars and laymen alike have long been interested in the topics of love, marriage, sex, and family life. Because they deal with living and self-fulfillment, these topics never seem to grow stale or uninteresting. It is difficult to pick up a newspaper or to glance through a magazine without finding several articles which point to the continued amount of attention being paid to how we love and how we live, in and out of marriage and in family situations. Particularly in the United States, we seem to be preoccupied with these aspects of our lives; and we have been criticized for devoting too much attention to romanticism, love, and sex, and for seeking our happiness and satisfaction from marriage and from the children in our small nuclear families.

There is little doubt that these interests are widely shared by a large percentage of the population. However, the problem is not necessarily that there is too much time and concern devoted to them; perhaps the criticism should rather be directed toward the quality of the concern and whether the concern is producing the desired results. Probably, no other field of interest has so many self-styled "experts" who disseminate advice and information ranging from the solid research conducted by behavioral scientists to the "love magazine" stories with headlines calculated to startle.

While some of the advice given in newspaper and magazine columns should probably be ignored, the popularity of such columns does indicate that problems are being aired and answers being sought to conditions which might have been allowed to develop unchecked in times past. This openness in discussing the various aspects of male-female relationships may, in fact, be one of the most significant changes in the patterns of love and marriage in the second half of the twentieth century. Indeed, the openness is a positive quality of the change; on the negative side are some of the kinds of discussions taking place within the newfound freedom to explore the patterns.

When a topic as intimate as the one of male-female relationships is opened to wide and popular analysis, it is not surprising that the discussion ranges from the totally scientific to the sensational. The issues involved are personal, so there tends to be much individual and subjective involvement. Thus, scientific research is called upon to help explain the varieties of conduct, and the sensationalists then intrude to exploit the interest and even to twist the facts.

To understand the trends and to evaluate the changes, the student of male-female relationships must look for the roots of present practices and attitudes. Such a perspective gives a special understanding of the present that cannot be gained from the vantage point of the here-and-now alone. It is important to know how we got where we are, to understand where we presently are, and to be able to predict with some measure of success where we are going.

The readings selected for Part One give an overview of contemporary male-female relationships—both in and out of marriage —and stress the relationship of the present to the past. The first selection, by Lester Kirkendall and Roger Libby, considers what makes the sexual norms different for various cultures. By looking beyond one's own immediate world and realizing the almost unlimited patterns possible, one becomes able to weave together this knowledge into some fabric of understanding.

The Robert Parke and Paul Glick article is a comprehensive review of recent trends in marriage and family statistics. Some people have seen in these patterns the deterioration of the stable relationships of the past, while others find in them new hope for more stable relationships in the future. The authors have given careful and thoughtful consideration to the changes, and they predict possible future developments which are useful to an understanding of marriage and family trends.

Arthur Schlesinger's history of love in the United States is a popular treatment of the much discussed topic, which only recently has been approached by behavioral scientists. It has been pointed out by many social critics that science seems to be the only social institution presently credited with the authority to speak out decisively on matters relating to relationships between men and women. The popularity of the scientifically oriented work of Masters and Johnson seems to support this contention. However, this is not the case with the topic of love, and many of the most enlightening and respected comments on this all-important subject come from outside the laboratory.

1

INTERPERSONAL RELATIONSHIPS— CRUX OF THE SEXUAL RENAISSANCE

Lester A. Kirkendall and Roger W. Libby

A debate over whether sexual morality is declining, or whether we are experiencing a sexual revolution, has broken into the open. The controversy, which has been brewing for over a decade, has been mulled by news media, magazines, books, and professional conferences. Varying views have been expressed, but one thing is clear—the very foundations upon which sexual morality has rested, and which have governed the exercise of sexual behavior, are being challenged. This, of course, is characteristic of a renaissance.

Many influential people are moving away from the view that sexual morality is defined by abstinence from nonmarital intercourse toward one in which morality is expressed through responsible sexual behavior and a sincere regard for the rights of others. While these people do not advocate nonmarital sexual relations, this possibility is clearly seen as more acceptable if entered in a responsible manner, and contained within a relationship characterized by integrity and mutual concern. In other words, the shift is from emphasis upon an act to emphasis upon the quality of interpersonal relationships. . . .

Liberal religious leaders probably provide the most striking illustration of this change. Selections from their writings and pronouncements could be extended considerably beyond the following quotations, but these three are indicative of the changing emphasis.

Douglas Rhymes, Canon Librarian of Southwark Cathedral, writes:

We are told that all sexual experience outside marriage is wrong, but we are given no particular rulings about sexual experience within marriage. Yet a person may just as easily be treated as a means to satisfy desire and be exploited for the gratification of another within marriage as outside it. It is strange that we concern ourselves so much with the morality of premarital and extramarital sex, but seldom raise seriously the question of sexual morality within marriage. . . . (11, p. 25)

John A. T. Robinson, Bishop of Woolwich, in his controversial book asserts:

. . . nothing can of itself always be labelled "wrong." One cannot, for instance, start from the position "sex relations before marriage" or "divorce" are wrong or sinful in themselves. They may be in 99 cases or even 100 cases out of 100, but they are not intrinsically so, for the only intrinsic evil is lack of love (12, p. 118).

Harvey Cox, who is a member of The Divinity School faculty at Harvard University comments:

To refuse to deliver a prepared answer whenever the question of premarital intercourse pops up will have a healthy influence on the continuing conversation that is Christian ethics. . . . It gets us off dead-end arguments about virginity and chastity, forces us to think about fidelity to persons. It exposes the . . . subtle exploitation that poisons even the most immaculate Platonic relationships.

By definition premarital refers to people who plan to marry someone some day. Premarital sexual conduct should therefore serve to strengthen the chances of sexual success and fidelity in marriage, and we must face the real question of whether avoidance of intercourse beforehand is always the best preparation (4, p. 215).

What is common to these quotes is readily seen. In each the focus is on what happens to persons within the context of the interpersonal relationship matrix in which they find themselves. Morality does not reside in complete sexual abstinence, nor immorality in having had nonmarital experience. Rather, sex derives its meaning from the extent to which it contributes to or detracts from the quality and meaning of the relationship in which it occurs, and relationships in general.

This changing emphasis is also reflected in marriage manuals—those books purporting to help couples toward an adequate sexual adjustment. One of the earliest to appear in the United States (1926) was *The Ideal Marriage* by Theodore Van de Velde. The physiological aspect predominates in this 320-page book. Thus 310 pages of the 320 are devoted to detailed descriptions of the genital organs and the reproductive system, their hygiene and care. The last 10 pages (one chapter) are devoted to the psychic, emotional, and mental hygiene of the ideal marriage.

To say that the psychological and emotional aspects are completely ignored except for this chapter is not wholly fair, but the book, written by a physician, carries the vivid imprint of the medical profession with its concentration on physiology. At the time of its publication it was a forward-looking book.

The rising concern for interpersonal relationships, however, can be seen in another book written by a physician, Dr. Mary Calderone, in 1960. Dr. Calderone tries to create for her readers a perception of sexuality which is embedded firmly in the total relationship. At one point she comments:

Sex responsiveness comes to those who not only view sex as a sacred and cherished factor in living, but who also retain good perspective about it by being sensitive to the needs of their partners and by taking into account the warmth, graciousness, and humor inherent in successful marital sex (3, p. 163).

The historical preoccupation with sex as an act has also been reflected in the character of sex research. Until recently it has concentrated on incidences and frequencies of various forms of sexual behavior. Some of the more pretentious studies broke incidences and frequencies of the total research population into smaller groups, e.g., Kinsey (6, 7). He looked for possible differences in sex behavior in subgroups distinguished by such factors as religious affiliations, socioeconomic levels, rural or urban residence, adequacy of sex education, and similar factors. This analysis, of course, took into account situational factors which could and do influence interpersonal relationships. Strictly speaking, however, the research still remained outside the interpersonal relationships framework. . . .

If an increasing concern for sex as an interpersonal relationship is the trend of the sexual renaissance, and we think it is, then clearly we must know how sex and sexual functioning are affected by relationships and vice versa. An extensive psychological literature has been developed to explain individual functioning; individual differences, individual growth patterns, individual cognitive development have all been explored. But relatively little is known about *relationships* as such—their components, or what precisely causes them to flourish, or to wither and die. A psychology more concerned with interpersonal relationships is now much needed. This also suggests the need to develop a field of research devoted to understanding sex and interpersonal relationships.

Finally, as a psychology and a sociology of relationships is developed, and as research findings provide a tested body of content for teaching, parents and educators may find a new stance. They can become less concerned with interdicting sexual expression of any kind, and more concerned with building an understanding of those factors which facilitate or impede the development of interpersonal relationships. . . .

It is only within the last few years that some research has come to focus on interpersonal aspects of sexual adjustment.

That this is a fruitful approach is already evident from the results of some of the recent studies. Such research is still meager in scope and its methods and procedures will undoubtedly be much improved with experience. Much still remains in the realm of speculation and conjecture. But a beginning has been made, and the findings are enlightening and exciting.

One generalization growing out of the studies can be advanced at this point. *A sexual relationship is an interpersonal relationship, and as such is subject to the same principles of interaction as are other relationships.* It too is affected by social, psychological, physiological, and cultural forces. The effort, so characteristic of our culture, to pull sex out of the context of ordinary living, obscures this simple but important generalization. Yet research findings constantly remind us of it. . . .

The data which have emerged from various studies . . . make it clear that a tremendous range of factors can influence the quality of relationships which contain sexual expression; that these factors can and do change from time to time in the course of the relationship; and that almost an unlimited range of consequences can result.

Thus, one of the very important factors influencing the meaning of sex in a relationship is the degree of fondness which a couple have for one another. . . . Kirkendall (9) in his study utilized a continuum of affectional involvement. He found that the character of motivation and communication, and the readiness of men to assume responsibility for the consequences of intercourse changed with the degree of emotional involvement. For example, as the length of elapsed time in a dating relationship prior to intercourse increased, there was an increase in the amount of communication devoted to understanding and a decrease in the amount of argumentative-persuasive communication. . . .

Maturity and developmental level represent still other factors. Broderick (1, 2) has made some interesting studies on the appearance and progressive development of various sexual manifestations with age. In a study of children in a suburban community he found that for many children interest in the opposite sex begins in kindergarten or before. Kissing "which means something special" is found among boys and girls as early as the third and fourth grades. In some communities dating begins for a substantial number of children in the fifth and

sixth grades, while "going steady" is common at the junior high school level.

Schofield (13) also found that "those who start dating, kissing, and inceptive behavior at an early age are also more likely to have early sexual intercourse." (13, p. 73) In an analysis of family backgrounds he also found that

. . . *girls who got on very well with their fathers were far less likely to be sexually experienced.* . . .

. . . *boys who did not get on well with their mothers were more likely to be sexually experienced.* . . .

. . . *girls who got on well with their mothers were less likely to be sexually experienced* . . . (13, p. 144).

Role concepts, which in turn may be influenced by other factors and conditions, influence the interplay between sexual behavior and interpersonal relationships. . . .

The interaction becomes extremely complex as role concepts, sexual standards, cultural changes, sheer biology, and still other factors all become involved in a single situation.

Reiss' work (10), especially his discussion of the interplay between role concepts and the double standard, makes this point most vividly. He shows clearly how adherence to the double standard conditions the individual's concept of his own role and the role of his sexual partners. Thus what the individual may conceive of as freely willed and consciously chosen behavior is actually controlled by concepts deeply rooted in a long-existing cultural pattern.

The complexity is further emphasized as the origins of the double standard are studied. Reiss sees the roots of the double standard as possibly existing in "man's muscular strength, muscular coordination, and bone structure. . . ." These "may have made him a better hunter than woman; it may have made him more adept at the use of weapons. Couple this hunting skill with the fact that women would often be incapacitated due to pregnancy and childrearing, and we have the beginning of male monopoly of power." (10, p. 92)

Reiss feels that "The core of the double

standard seems to involve the notion of female inferiority." (10, p. 192)

Once the double standard became embedded in the mores, however, cultural concepts reinforced it and helped embed it still more deeply. Now, however, cultural developments have begun to weaken the power of the double standard. The declining importance of the physical strength of the male in the modern economy; the ability to make reproduction a voluntary matter; emphasis on freedom, equality, and rationality —these and other forces have been eroding the power of the double standard, and in the process have been altering the association between sexual behavior and interpersonal relationships.

Shuttleworth (14) made an incisive critique of Kinsey's views on masculine-feminine differences in interest in sex as a function and as a physical experience. In the process, he advanced a theoretical position of his own which suggests that much role behavior is inherent in the biological structures of the sexes. He argues that their respective biology disposes male and female to regard their sexual functioning differently. Males, for example, can experience the erotic pleasures of sex more easily and with less likelihood of negative repercussions than can females. This fact, then, has helped to formulate both male and female sex roles, the attitudes of men and women toward sex and themselves, and to condition their sexual behavior. If this theoretical view can be established, it definitely has implications for a better understanding of the kind of interpersonal behavior which can be expected to involve the sexes, and how it may develop.

Vincent's (17) study of unwed mothers helped demonstrate that a wide range of outcomes in interpersonal relationships can arise from the circumstances of premarital pregnancy. The attitudes of unwed mothers ranged from those who found the pregnancy a humiliating and terrifying experience to those who found it maturing and satisfying, from those who rejected their child to those who found great satisfaction in having it, from those who rejected and hated the father to those who accepted him fully. When considering the interpersonal reac-

tions of unwed mothers, no stereotype is possible.

Sexual intercourse in our culture has been invested with so many meanings and such strong emotions have been tied to it that nonparticipation may have as many consequences for interpersonal relations as participation. Tebor (15) studied 100 virgin college males and found that a large proportion of them felt insecure about their virginity and pressured by their peers to obtain experience. At the same time significant adults—teachers and parents—were quite unaware of what sexual pattern these men were following, and provided them no support in their pattern of chastity. . . .

The theme of this article has been that a concern for interpersonal relationships as the central issue in the management of sexuality is displacing the traditional emphasis on the avoidance or renunciation of all nonmarital sexual experience. Only as a shift of this sort occurs are we in any way justified in speaking of a sexual renaissance.

Some requirements, however, face social scientists who wish to understand this shift. We have four to suggest.

1. *It will be necessary to commit ourselves fully to the study of relationships rather than simply reflecting on them occasionally.* In the area of sex, concern has been overfocused on the physical acts of sex. Thus the senior author, while doing the research for his book, *Premarital Intercourse and Interpersonal Relationships,* became aware that he was giving undue attention to the act of premarital intercourse, even while trying to set it in an interpersonal relationship context. As a consequence, crucial data were ignored. For example, in selecting subjects, if one potential subject had engaged in much caressing and petting, but had renounced the opportunity for intercourse many times, while another possible subject had merely gone through the physical act of copulation a single time, the latter one was defined as a subject for the research and the first was bypassed as though he had engaged in no sexual nor any interpersonal behavior.

With this realization came a decision to do research on decisions made by individuals concerning sexual behavior, regardless of whether they had had intercourse. The result is a recently completed preliminary study in which 131 nonrandomly selected males were interviewed. (8) Of this group 72 (55 percent) had not had intercourse, but apparently only 17 (13 percent) had not been in a situation which required a decision. Eleven of these had made a firm decision against intercourse, quite apart from any decision-requiring situation, thus leaving only six who had never faced the issue of decision-making. In other words, when one thought of sexual decision-making as an aspect of interpersonal relationships, rather than continuing to focus on whether or not an act had occurred, one greatly increased the number who were potential subjects, and vastly increased the range of interpersonal behavior available for study.

We offer one further illustration of the reorientation in thinking necessary as we come to accept a concern for relationships as the central issue. The view which emphasizes the quality of interpersonal relationships as of foremost concern is often labelled as "very permissive" when sex standards and behavior are under discussion. This conclusion is possible when concern is focused solely on whether the commission of a sexual act is or is not acceptable. Certainly the emphasis on interpersonal relationships diverts attention from the act to the consequences. But having moved into this position, one finds himself in a situation which is anything but permissive. Relationships and their outcome seem to be governed by principles which are unvarying and which cannot be repealed. The fiat of parents or the edicts of deans can be softened, but there is no tempering of the consequences of dishonesty, lack of self-discipline, and lack of respect for the rights of others upon interpersonal relationships. If one wishes warm, accepting interpersonal relationships with others he will be defeated by these practices and no one, regardless of his position of authority, can change this fact. Proclamations and injunction will be of no avail. There is no permissiveness here!

2. *Conceptual definitions of relationships will have to be developed.* Several social scientists have initiated work on this. For example, Foote and Cottrell (5) have identified six components of interpersonal competence—health, intelligence, sympathy, judgment, creativity, and autonomy. . . . As has been noted, Kirkendall (9) centered his study around three components—motivation, communication, and readiness to assume responsibility. Communication and motivation have both been frequently recognized aspects of interpersonal relationships.

However, the conceptualization of relationships in a manner which will permit effective research is still at an embryonic level. The numerous (for there are undoubtedly many) components of relationships have still to be determined, and methods and instruments for their measurement must be developed and perfected. Interpersonal relationships as a field of psychological study should be developing concurrently, for only in this way can we gain the needed broadening of our horizons.

3. *Methods and procedures will have to be devised which will enable us to study relationships.* The perceptive reader will have noted that while studies have been cited because, in our estimation, they bore on interpersonal relationships, all of them . . . obtained their information on interpersonal relationships by using individuals rather than pairs or groups as subjects. This is quite limiting. Would we not get a different view of premarital intercourse if we could interview both partners to the experience rather than one?

Methods of dealing with couples and groups, and research procedures which can zero in on that subtle, intangible, yet real tie which binds two or more people in an association are needed. Some work has already been done in this direction, but it has not been applied to sex and interpersonal relationships.

4. *The isolation of the most important problems for research is a requirement for progress.* Opinions would naturally differ in regard to what these problems are. We would suggest, however, that since sex relationships *are* interpersonal relationships, the whole field of interpersonal relationships with sex as an integral part needs to be attacked.

Kirkendall (9) has suggestions for further research scattered throughout his book. He suggests such problems as an exploration of the importance of time spent and emotional involvement in a relationship as a factor in determining whether a relationship can sustain intercourse, the factors which produce "loss of respect" when sexual involvement occurs, the meaning of sexual noninvolvement for a relationship, factors which impede or facilitate sexual communication, and the relation of knowledge of various kinds of success or failure in sexual relationships.

His study poses many questions which merit answering. How do the emotional involvements of male and female engaged in a sexual relationship differ, and how do they change as the relationship becomes more (or less) intense? How nearly alike, or how diverse, are the perceptions which male and female hold of the total relationship and of its sexual component at various stages in its development? How does the rejection of a proffered sexual relationship by either partner affect the one who ex-tended the offer? And what are the reactions and what produced them in the person receiving it? If there are no sexual overtures, how does this affect relationships?

Which value systems make it most (and least) possible for a couple to communicate about sex? To adjust to tensions which may accompany intercourse or its cessation? Which enable a couple to cope most effectively to the possible traumas of having their relationship become public knowledge, or of pregnancy?

In what diverse ways do premarital sexual experiences affect marital adjustments? What enables some couples who have been premarital sexual partners to separate as friends? Why do others separate with bitterness and hostility? What relation has maturity in other aspects of life to maturity in assessing the meaning of and coping with sexual manifestations of various kinds in the premarital period?

The questions could go on endlessly, yet the isolation of important areas for research remains one of the important tasks before us.

REFERENCES

1. Broderick, Carlfred B. *Socio-Sexual Development in a Suburban Community.* University Park: Pennsylvania State University. Unpublished manuscript (mimeographed) 1963.

2. Broderick, Carlfred B., and S. E. Fowler. "New Patterns of Relationships Between the Sexes Among Preadolescents." *Marriage and Family Living,* 1961, 23, 27–30.

3. Calderone, Mary. *Release from Sexual Tensions.* New York: Random House, 1960.

4. Cox, Harvey. *The Secular City.* New York: Macmillan, 1965.

5. Foote, Nelson, and Leonard S. Cottrell, Jr. *Identity and Interpersonal Competence.* Chicago: University of Chicago Press, 1955.

6. Kinsey, Alfred C., et al. *Sexual Behavior in the Human Female.* Philadelphia: W. B. Saunders, 1953.

7. Kinsey, Alfred C., et al. *Sexual Behavior in the Human Male.* Philadelphia: Saunders, 1948.

8. Kirkendall, Lester A. "Characteristics of Sexual Decision-Making." To be published in *The Journal of Sex Research.*

9. Kirkendall, Lester A. *Premarital Intercourse and Interpersonal Relationships.* New York: Julian Press, 1961.

10. Reiss, Ira L. *Premarital Sexual Standards in America.* Glencoe, Illinois: The Free Press, 1960.

11. Rhymes, Douglas. *No New Morality.* Indianapolis: Bobbs-Merrill, 1964, p. 25.

12. Robinson, John A. T. *Honest to God.* Philadelphia: Westminster Press, 1963, p. 118.

13. Schofield, Michael. *The Sexual Behavior of Young People.* London: Longmans, Green, 1965.

14. Shuttleworth, Frank. "A Biosocial and Developmental Theory of Male and Female Sexuality." *Marriage and Family Living,* 1960, 21, 163–170.

15. Tebor, Irving. "Selected Attributes, Interpersonal Relationships and Aspects of Psychosexual Behavior of One Hundred College Freshmen, Virgin Men." Unpublished Ph.D. Thesis, Oregon State College, 1967.

16. Van de Velde, Theodore H. *Ideal Marriage.* New York: Random House, 1926.

17. Vincent, Clark E. *Unmarried Mothers.* New York: Free Press of Glencoe, 1961.

2

PROSPECTIVE CHANGES IN MARRIAGE AND THE FAMILY

Robert Parke, Jr., and Paul C. Glick

Consideration of prospective changes in American families can begin with no more appropriate issue than what is happening to the age at marriage. This subject is of interest in its own right, partly because of concern over the number of teen-age marriages. In addition, the age at marriage significantly influences events in the middle and late stages of the family life cycle; it determines, in part, the age at which the wife's responsibilities for child-care have declined to the point where she is free to seek full-time employment and the probability that she and her husband will survive to enjoy life together after the husband retires. . . .

For several years Americans have married at an exceptionally young average age for an industrial society. Furthermore, American women marry men who are more nearly their own ages than is generally true elsewhere.

One of the striking features of recent trends in American marriage is the extent to which marriage patterns are becoming standardized.

First, nearly everyone gets married nowadays. . . . As few as three percent of the men and women now in their late twenties may enter middle age without having married. These proportions are one-third of the corresponding proportions actually experienced by persons who are now in late middle age.

Second, to a greater extent than before, young persons are getting married at about the same age. The reduction in the age at marriage has been accompanied by a compressing of marriages into a narrower age range than before. . . . Among the ever-married men now in late middle age, about eight years elapsed between the age by which the first one-fourth of the men had married and the age by which three-fourths had married. For men who are now in their late twenties, the corresponding figure is expected to be about five years. . . . A corresponding trend has occurred among women. The interquartile range of age at first marriage experienced by the women who are now in late middle age was about seven years. This is expected to contract to about four years by the time the women who are now in their late twenties reach middle age.

Third, women are marrying men who are closer to their own ages. This observation is suggested by the declining difference between the median ages at first marriage for men and women . . . and is confirmed by data from the 1960 Census, which showed the median difference between the age of the husband and the age of the wife for married couples in which both partners were married only once. Husbands over 55 years old in 1960 were 3.6 years older than their wives, on the average; while husbands under 35 were only 1.9 years older on the average. Forty-two percent of the older husbands were at least five years older than their wives, as compared with only 17 percent of the younger husbands. . . .

The lessening of the difference between the ages of the husband and wife causes a significant improvement in the chances of joint survival of the married couple. Under mortality conditions prevailing in 1960, a woman who was married at age 20 to a man four years her senior ran a 42-percent chance of being widowed before age 65, assuming that she survived to that age. If she married a man only two years older than herself, her chances of widowhood before reaching 65 would be only 37 percent, and, if her husband were the same age as she, her chances of widowhood would be only 33 percent.

The joint survival of a married couple depends, of course, on a number of factors besides the difference between their ages. The foregoing figures assume no divorce, a fact which would not affect the interpretation if there is no fundamental change in the trend of the divorce rate; and the foregoing figures assume constant mortality conditions, whereas mortality conditions will likely change somewhat though probably not enough to negate the points being made. Nor do they take into account the effect of separation and desertion on the population of married couples; but, as indicated below, there seems actually to be a real likelihood that desertions will diminish, assuming that the educational and economic levels of the population improve over time.

However, the net effect of these factors over the past ten years has been such as to suggest substantial future increases in the proportion of persons living with their spouses in late middle age and in old age. For example, 64 percent of all women 55 to 64 years old were married and living with their (first or subsequent) husbands in 1965. According to experimental projections, the corresponding figure may increase eight

points to 72 percent by 1985. The smaller increase of about three points that is projected for women over 65 nonetheless represents a substantial relative improvement over the current level of 34 percent in this age range. . . .

The public concern over the number of teen-age marriages has arisen because of the notorious instability of these marriages. The 1960 Census showed that, among the men who first married at age 18 during the period five to 15 years prior to the census, the first marriage was not intact at the time of the census in about 21 percent of the cases. This was twice as high as the proportion of not intact first marriages among men who first married at ages 23 to 24. A similar relationship was evident in the data for females. (Nearly all such persons with first marriage not intact were divorced, separated, or remarried at the time of the census.)

Actually, however, figures that have recently become available . . . show that the marriage rate among very young women reached a peak perhaps ten to 15 years ago and is now on the decline. Twenty-three percent of all the women who are currently 30 to 34 years old married before age 18. The rate of early teen-age marriages is successively smaller for each younger group of women. Only 15 percent of all the women who are currently 18 and 19 years old married before age 18.

Extremely young age at marriage has never been very widespread among men. Thus, the proportion of men who married before age 18 appears to have been no greater than four percent for any of the age groups. . . . Even so, the percent of very young marriages among men who are now in their late twenties was twice as high as it was among men now in their forties, and there is evidence of a recent downturn in this percent among men who are now in their late teens.

This may or may not portend a downturn in the percent of all men who marry under age 20, which rose in recent years from nine percent for the men who are now in their late forties to a stable level of around 18 percent for the men who are now under 35.

The recent downward trend in teen-age marriages among women may be in part a response to the changing ratio of males to females in the marriageable ages. If so, this has interesting implications for the pattern of age at marriage in the next few years. . . .

Because of past changes in the annual number of births and because women marry men who are two or three years their senior, on the average, there has been, in the past few years, a drop in the number of males per 100 females in the main marrying ages. By the main marrying ages, the authors mean those between the first and third quartile ages at first marriage according to recent experience, or approximately ages 18 to 22 for females and 20 to 24 for males.

In the early 1950's there were, in the average year, about 104 males per 100 females in the main marrying ages. In the late 1950's this ratio had dropped to 99 per 100, and in the early 1960's it was only 94. In the latter half of the 1960's, it [averaged] only about 93 and will subsequently return to 99 per 100 in the [middle] 1970's.

These figures describe, in broad terms, the "marriage squeeze" that has resulted from the fact that the girls born in the postwar baby boom have come of age (for purposes of marriage) sooner than the boys.

Generally speaking, the squeeze can be resolved in any or all of several ways: by the boys marrying for the first time at younger ages or by the girls marrying for the first time at older ages or marrying older widowed and divorced men or older single men who might not otherwise have married. Or it is possible that more girls will ultimately not marry at all.

Any of these ways out of the squeeze involves a sequence of changes in age at marriage and in the difference between the ages of the husband and wife. The evidence so far available suggests that, in the first half of the 1960's, the marriage squeeze was resolved in large part by changes in the marriage patterns of the women and not by alteration of the trend of ages at first marriage for men. The data . . . show no acceleration in the downward trend of male ages at first marriage. This fact may be construed as implying that, up to now, the

young men have been successfully warding off any pressure from the mounting numbers of marriageable young women.

The marriage squeeze will continue for perhaps a decade. If the pattern of ages for men at marriage from 1965 to 1975 is like that observed in the first half of the 1960's, then about a million women will have to postpone getting married. . . . This figure represents the difference between (a) the number of women who would get married if marriages followed the rates observed for females from 1959 to 1964 and (b) the number who would marry if the number of marriages were governed by the observed marriage rates for males. If such a postponement occurred, it would force the lifetime age at first marriage up about one-third of a year for the women who enter the marriage ages during this period. Such an increase would represent a continuation of the rise in the female age at first marriage that has been observed since the late 1950's.

Of course, in the next few years the tide may turn so that the women, rather than the men, will have their way. Thus, if the girls persuade the boys to marry prematurely, by the standards of recent years, there will be more marriages and more young husbands than otherwise. . . .

The preceding discussion already suggested the extent to which marital dissolution due to widowhood will be reduced by recent reductions in the difference between the ages of the husband and wife. Additional changes toward more marriages remaining intact may be expected as a natural result of the anticipated continuation in the upgrading of the population with respect to income inasmuch as separation and divorce are less extensive among the affluent than among the poor.

Hollywood to the contrary notwithstanding, statistics from the 1960 Census provide further confirmation of the fact that stability of marriage is a condition that is shared less by the lower-status segments of the population than by the rest.

The special reports of the 1960 Census on *Marital Status* and *Age at First Marriage* devoted much attention to social and economic analysis of the patterns of marriage and dissolution of marriage among men 45 to 54 years old, a group that has reached its peak earning capacity and among whom few additional first marriages will occur. There were one and a half million ever-married white men in this age group with incomes of less than $3,000, and more than two million with incomes of $10,000 or more. Fully 29 percent of the poor men, but only 16 percent of the affluent men, were no longer living with their first wives at the time of the census. The corresponding relationship was even more striking among nonwhites than it was for whites. These differences are too great to be attributed solely to socioeconomic differences in the proportion of men whose wives have died. It follows that these differences reflect, in part, socioeconomic differences in divorce and separation. Barring a rise in the divorce rate or major changes in the pattern of divorce and separation by socioeconomic status, the reduction of poverty should result in a substantial long-term improvement in the average stability of marriages.

This expectation is expressed with slight reservations in view of the increases over the past few years in the percent of the population who are divorced. A recent Census Bureau report shows the following age-standardized percentages of divorced persons in the population 14 years old and over:

Year	Male	Female
1966	2.2	3.1
1965	2.2	2.9
1960	1.9	2.6
1955	1.8	2.3

However, these increases do not necessarily imply the existence of a rising divorce rate, nor is there independent evidence of such. A stable divorce rate may produce an increasing accumulation of divorced persons in the population unless remarriage is universal and instantaneous. This it is not, although remarriage rates for divorced persons are high. . . .

Results indicate a continued decline in the average number of adults per household and family and little change in the average number of children. The figures express the average size of households and families in terms of the number of persons living together at any one point in time. The 1966 figures on children, for instance, refer to the average number now living in the household or family and not to the number born. Furthermore, the numbers of households and families include those with no children as well as those with children.

The 1985 estimate of 2.2 adults per family is very close to a minimum average. It is subject to substantial further reduction only by further reducing the number of offspring over the age of 17 who live with their parents. The average number of adults per family cannot fall much below two, since nearly nine out of ten families include a husband and wife. . . .

The average size of household is smaller to begin with because it takes into account persons who live alone and maintain their own home. This average is subject to greater potential decline than the average family size, because there are still many people who potentially might set up housekeeping by themselves who have not yet done so. Moreover, there is a strong prospect for further household formation from this source if the projections . . . prove to be well founded. . . .

In 1965 about 78 percent of the married couples and individuals who might have maintained their own household were actually doing so. An *individual* who might maintain his own household is defined, for present purposes, as anyone 20 years old and over who is not "married with spouse present" and is not an inmate of an institution. The category includes heads of broken families, persons living alone, adult children and relatives in the home, lodgers, and other persons who live with a relative or share the living accommodations of someone else, and persons in rooming houses and other group quarters.

No substantial increase in the number of separate households can result from an increase in the propensity of married couples to maintain their own households, since 98 percent already do so. However, only half the eligible individuals were maintaining their own households in 1965. Recent trends suggest that this figure may rise to two-thirds of the eligible individuals by 1985.

The increase anticipated among individuals at age 65 and over is fairly striking, rising as it does from 66 to 84 percent of the eligibles. Medicare and other social programs may cause this to rise even further by making it possible for higher proportions of aged relatives who now share the homes of children to be self-sustaining or to remove themselves from the population of eligibles, as here defined, by entering a nursing home.

CONCLUSION

A review of recent trends in marriage and family statistics provides a basis for the following expectations, if one keeps in mind the foregoing qualifications:

1. Persons now in their late twenties and their early thirties are more likely to marry at some time in their lives than any other group on record.

2. The rate of teen-age marriage, which is now on the decline, will continue to go down for a while, then level off.

3. The relative oversupply of young women will tend to produce a further rise in the next ten years in the age at which women marry for the first time.

4. The compression of marriages into a narrow age range will cause marriage and household formation to be somewhat more responsive than before to changes in the number of past births from which the marrying population comes.

5. Over and above any general decline in mortality, the declines in the difference between the ages of the husband and wife will reduce the frequency of the widowhood and increase the proportion of couples who survive jointly to retirement age.

6. Declines in the relative frequency of divorce and separation should result to the extent that there are reductions in poverty and general improvements in the socioeconomic status of the population.

7. The small average size of American families (in terms of related persons sharing the same living quarters) will not change very much, but the average number of adult members may come very close to a minimum size. Greater changes are likely to develop only if there are major changes in the average number of children in the home.

8. Nearly all married couples now maintain their own households. In addition, there is a good prospect that within the next 20 years five out of every six aged individuals not in institutions will keep house on their own, and more than half the adult individuals of other ages will do so.

In closing, it is acknowledged that here and there the observations presented have gone a step or two beyond the projections. Furthermore, the future patterns could actually veer off in new directions not anticipated in the projections. However, there is reason to expect that further development of the program for preparing marriage and family projections, and improvements in the data available, will make it possible to reduce the area of uncertainty and to provide prompt corrections of future readings so as to bring them in line with current developments.

3

AN INFORMAL HISTORY OF LOVE, U.S.A.

Arthur Schlesinger, Jr.

The Founding Fathers dedicated this republic to the agreeable proposition that all men, and all Americans especially, were endowed by their Creator with unalienable rights to life, liberty, and the pursuit of happiness. Their descendants have been trying to claim these rights for themselves ever since. We have, on the whole, caught up with life and liberty. But, so far as the third item is concerned, we appear to have had a good deal more pursuit than happiness.

"This people is one of the happiest in the world," wrote Alexis de Tocqueville a century and a quarter ago. Would anyone say this so confidently today? The pursuit of happiness has never ceased, but we seem to be falling farther and farther behind our goal. George and Martha were once the father and mother of their country. Now they revile each other in a thousand movie houses in *Who's Afraid of Virginia Woolf?* The passion for happiness carries us everywhere—to the neighborhood saloon and the psychoanalyst's couch, to the marriage counselor and the divorce lawyer, to promiscuity, homosexuality, and impotence, to mom or to marijuana and amphetamines—everywhere, evidently, except to happiness itself.

What has happened to the American theory of happiness? We have always construed that theory in private terms—in terms of individual success and individual fulfillment. And if, for some, such success and fulfillment can come from acquiring power or money, for very many Americans it comes ultimately from the triumphs and consolations of personal relations—above all, the relation of love. As a nation we have inherited the dream of love brought to our shores by the earliest colonists, a dream nourished by our fantasies but often negated by facts.

So fundamental is the romantic dream to our lives that we do not realize how small a part of mankind through history has shared it. All ages and cultures, of course, have known marriage and family. Some peoples, like the old Romans or the Indians of the *Kamasutra,* have thought deeply and ingeniously about sex. But the idea of romantic love as cherished by Americans—the belief in passion and desire as the key to happy marriage and the good life—is relatively new and still largely confined to the Christian world. "In China," Francis L. K. Hsu has reminded us, "the term 'love,' as it is used by Americans, has never been respectable. Up to modern times the term was scarcely used in Chinese literature." (If the Red Guards have their way, it will not be used again.) And even on the continent of Europe, except as the young in recent years have succumbed to the processes of Americanization, passion has generally kept distinct from marriage and family. There romantic love, that ennobling emotional experience, has remained an improbable hope, to be pursued outside the normal conventions of life and doomed to tragedy. Only the Americans have assumed that passion is destined to fulfillment. Only the Americans have attempted on a large scale the singular experiment of trying to incorporate romantic love into the staid and stolid framework of marriage and the family.

This was true from the start—in spite of misconceptions we still have about the 17th century Puritans. Stern and God-fearing, the first settlers no doubt rejected the licentiousness of the Old World for the austerity of the New. Yet, for all their condemnation of playing cards, the theater, fancy clothes, and other lures of the devil, for all the repression wrought by their dogmatic Calvinism, the Puritans were surprisingly open and frank about sex. Hawthorne's prim moralistic Puritans were characters more of the 19th than of the 17th century. In extreme cases, the elders issued their scarlet letters, they insisted on confessions of fornication in open church (and these became so common that they were almost routine); and they rebuked outspoken hussies, like Abigail Bush of Westfield who said in 1697 that her new stepmother was "hot as a bitch." But, if one might expect John Rolfe to go off with Pocahontas in hot-blooded Virginia, one must not forget that Priscilla Mullens and John Alden lived and loved in rockbound Plymouth. Gov. William Bradford in his *History of Plymouth Plantation,* after roundly deploring the sexual excesses of his flock, concluded philosophically:

It may be in this case as it is with waters when their streams are stopped or dammed up; when they get passage they flow with more violence and make more noise and disturbance, than when they are suffered to run quietly in their own channels.

The elders expelled James Mattock from the First Church of Boston for declining to sleep with his wife; and town records show that Puritan ministers cheerfully married an astonishing number of New England maidens already well along with their first babies.

After all, if the Puritans put people into stocks, they also bundled. No doubt this was because houses were small and winters cold, and young men and women could find privacy and warmth only in bed. "Why it should be thought incredible," wrote the Rev. Samuel Peters "for a young man and young woman innocently and virtuously to lie down together in a bed with a great part of their clothes on, I cannot conceive." If the Reverend Peters could not conceive, some of the young bundlers evidently did. One thing sometimes led to another, then as now; and still the practice continued in Puritan New England for nearly two centuries.

The Puritans thus in their way saw sex as a natural and joyous part of marriage, to be plainly discussed and freely accepted. A Marylander visiting Boston in 1744 could report "this place abounds with pretty women who appear rather more abroad than they do at (New) York and dress elegantly. They are, for the most part, free and affable as well as pretty. I saw not one prude while I was there." He would not

have been so fortunate a century later. For, though passion and marriage continued together in the romantic dream, circumstances were conspiring to separate them in American reality.

For one thing the very proclamation of independence and the formation of the new democratic republic contained a deep and a subtle challenge to the ideals of romantic love. Romance, after all, had sprung up in the feudalism of medieval Europe, as the pastime of the nobility. The American colonies had no nobility, no feudal institutions, and the new republic pledged itself to liberty, equality, and rationality. The bright, clear light of the young nation was hard on passion. "No author, without a trial," observed Hawthorne, "can conceive of the difficulty of writing a romance about a country where there is no shadow, no antiquity, no mystery, no picturesque and gloomy wrong, nor anything but a commonplace prosperity, in broad and simple daylight, as is happily the case with my dear native land."

The French writer Stendhal, reflecting on romantic love half a century after the Declaration of Independence, predicted sorrowfully that it has no future in America. "They have such a *habit of reason* in the United States," he wrote, "that 'crystallization' [by which he meant the moment of abandonment to love] has become impossible. . . . Of the pleasure that passion gives I see nothing." In Europe, "desire is sharpened by restraint; in America it is blunted by liberty."

In America desire was blunted too by the role of marriage in a new country. For the incessant demand for population and labor was transforming marriage into a service institution, and this utilitarian motive was fundamentally at conflict with the old ideals of romantic love. Benjamin Franklin, an instinctive anti-romantic, made the point with characteristic pungency in 1745: "A single man has not nearly the value he would have in [a] state of union. He is an incomplete animal. He resembles the odd half of a pair of scissors." When a good colonist met and married a girl right off the boat, it was probably less a case of love at first sight than of an overweening practical need for a wife—if only to escape the bachelors' tax. And when a man instructed his wife to dress only in a shift at the wedding ceremony, it was less because of concupiscence than of computation; for a widow, by thus symbolizing her poverty, could spare her new husband responsibility for the debts of his predecessor. So South Kingstown, R.I., February, 1720:

Thomas Calverwell was joyned in marriage to Abigail Calverwell his wife. . . . He took her in marriage after she had gone four times across the highway in only her shift and hair-lace and no other clothing. Joyned together in marriage by me
                    GEORGE HAZARD, *Justice*

Men absorbed in building a new land in the wilderness had little time or energy left for the cultivation of romantic passions. And, as the new nation grew, they seemed to have even less time. By the early part of the 19th century the making of money was becoming an obsessive masculine goal. Tocqueville, visiting the United States in 1831–32, noted that American men had contracted "the way of thinking of the manufacturing and trading classes." This constituted another blow to romance. Few American men, Tocqueville said, were "ever known to give way to those idle and solitary meditations which commonly precede and produce the great emotions of the heart."

If American men were becoming too preoccupied for passion, American women were becoming too rational. Scarcity gave women in the early colonies and, later, on the ever-receding frontier a measure of bargaining power they could never have expected in the homeland, and they happily seized every opportunity for self-assertion. One finds even George Washington commenting ruefully on female independence. He wrote in 1783:

I never did, nor do I believe I ever shall, give advice to a woman who is setting out on a matrimonial voyage; first, because I never could advise one to marry without her consent; and, secondly, because I know it is to no purpose to advise her to refrain when she has obtained it. A woman very rarely asks an opinion or requires advice on such an occasion, till her resolution is formed; and then it is with the hope and expectation of obtaining a sanction, not that she means to be governed by your disapprobation.

This is one of the first descriptions of the clear-eyed, rational American girl who would grow in glory through the 19th century and have her final triumph as the heroine of the novels of Henry James and in the drawings of Charles Dana Gibson. From the start she was a source of wonder to foreigners. Young Tocqueville, encountering her wherever he went, confessed himself "almost frightened at her singular address and happy boldness." She rarely displayed, he said, "that virginal bloom in the midst of young desires or that innocent and ingenuous grace" characteristic of the girls he knew in Europe, but she was far more formidable, thinking for herself, speaking with freedom, acting on her own impulse, surveying the world with "firm and calm gaze," viewing the vices of society "without illusion" and braving them "without fear." Above all there was her remarkable, her terrible self-control: "She indulges in all permitted pleasures without yielding herself up to any of them, and her reason never allows the reins of self-guidance to drop." The result, the young Frenchman decided, was "to make cold and virtuous women instead of affectionate wives and agreeable companions to men. Society may be more tranquil and better regulated, but domestic life has often fewer charms."

So as America entered the 19th century, love was lost between the preoccupied male and the cool female. The memory of passion lingered, the haunting hope of romantic fulfillment. "Give all to love," sang Emerson:

Obey thy heart;
Friendship, kindred, days,
Estate, good fame,
Plans, credit, and the Muse—
Nothing refuse.

The sentimental popular novel dilated endlessly on romance. The new middle class reveled in the fantasy of love. But in practice not many (not Emerson himself) gave all to love—and least of all estate, fame, plans, or credit. When Alexander Hamilton as Secretary of the Treasury was accused of having connived with a minor official in crooked financial dealings, he triumphantly proved that his payments to Mr. Reynolds involved no corruption at all; they were simply in exchange for the favors of Mrs. Reynolds. This was the pattern of priority in the new republic.

The growing conflict between romantic dream and bourgeois circumstance set the pursuit of happiness on its path of frustration. Passion and marriage, which the American experiment in love had tried to bring together, were now in the 19th century thrust asunder. Sex once again became a matter of physical gratification, which man warily pursued on his own. "If ye touch at the islands, Mr. Flask," shouted Captain Bildad in his farewell to the *Pequod* in *Moby Dick*, "beware of fornication. Good-bye, good-bye!" Marriage was to be a higher union of souls, with sexual emotion strictly confined to its procreative goal. Such was the accepted view. But the strain between the theory and reality now introduced a deep and disabling confusion into the American attitude toward love.

Tocqueville commented on "the great change which takes place in all the habits of women in the United States as soon as they are married." He attributed this to their "cold and stern reasoning power" which taught them that "the amusements of the girl cannot become the recreations of the wife," banished their "spirit of levity and independence" and dedicated them to the notion that "the sources of a married woman's happiness are in the home of her husband." For his part the 19th-century American husband placed his wife on a pedestal as one above the temptations of physical passion. So the cool girl tended to become the frigid wife, sentimentality replaced sexuality, and the 19th-century marriage lost the sense of easy companionship between man and woman. "In America," wrote Mrs. Frances Trollope, a traveler from England, "with the exception of dancing, which is almost wholly confined to the unmarried of both sexes, all the enjoyments of the men are found in the absence of the women. They dine, they play cards, they have musical meetings, they have suppers, all in large parties, but all without women. . . . The two sexes can hardly mix for the greater part of a day without great restraint and ennui."

Soon, the 19th-century marriage, as it divorced itself from passion, began to acquire an appalling gentility. The plain speaking of the early Puritans was long since forgotten. Soon the shadow of Queen Victoria was to fall almost more heavily on America than on her native land. Mrs. Trollope was exasperated to discover, for example, that men and women could visit the art gallery in Philadelphia only in separate groups, lest exposure to classical statues cause embarrassment in mixed company. Often statues were draped to spare the female sensibility. Captain Marryat, the sturdy British novelist, asked a young American lady who had fallen off a rock whether she had hurt her leg. To his total bafflement, she appeared deeply offended. Finally, she instructed him that the word "leg" was never used before ladies in a mixed company, she said, the word was "limb." Later, visiting a ladies' seminary, Marryat was stunned to see a square piano with four limbs, each of which, to protect the pupils, had been dressed in little trousers with frills at the bottom.

The sickness of prudery grew in the course of the century. By the '80's the public library of Concord, Mass., was banning *The Adventures of Huckleberry Finn* as a dirty book. By the '90's tracts like *From the Ball Room to Hell* explained how the waltz led young ladies to ruin. According to Thomas Beer in *The Mauve Decade*, ladies of gentle breeding were specifying in the premarital contracts with their well-bred fiancés that the terminology of the wedding ceremony did not imply the right of consummation.

As marriage expelled passion, it was tacitly agreed that men were entitled to an outlet for the base drives of their lower natures, and sex acquired its own separate and accepted domain. This was the heyday of flamboyant prostitution and the "double standard." When Gov. Grover Cleveland of New York, running as the Democratic candidate for President in 1884, was accused of having fathered an illegitimate child 10 years before, it was readily admitted that he had had an affair with Maria Halpin and had assumed responsibility for her child. The Republicans chanted sarcastically in the streets:

Ma! Ma! Where's my pa?
Gone to the White House,
Ha! Ha! Ha!

But the voters elected Cleveland, and on Election Night the Democrats sang:

Hurrah for Maria,
Hurrah for the kid.
We voted for Grover,
And we're damned glad we did.

Cleveland thus benefited from the separation between passion and marriage in the public mind. Eighty years later, when the two had been once again brought together, the electorate snuffed out the presidential ambitions of another governor of New York who had committed the offense, not of illicit romance, but of behaving with splendid legality in divorcing one wife and marrying another.

An even more notorious Victorian case involved the most popular preacher of the day. Here too the separation between passion and marriage enabled the Rev. Henry Ward Beecher to ride out a scandal that would very possibly have destroyed his career in a presumably more sophisticated age. A man of magnetic charm and robust appetite, Beecher seduced pretty Elizabeth Tilton, who taught Sunday school at his church. In time the story reached Victoria Woodhull, a leading feminist of the day, who published it in her weekly magazine, rejoicing in this ministerial recognition of the power of sex: "The immense physical potency of Mr. Beecher, and the indomitable urgency of his great nature for the intimacy and embraces of the noble and cultured women about him, instead of being a bad thing, as the world thinks, . . . is one of the noblest and grandest endow-

ments of this truly great and representative man."

Elizabeth Tilton, who had earlier confessed her relations with Beecher to her husband, now rushed to Beecher's defense and denied the charge. Theodore Tilton sued Beecher for the alienation of his wife's affections. While the whole nation watched with palpitant and prurient curiosity, the case ended with a hung jury. Three years later Elizabeth Tilton said, "The charge, brought by my husband, of adultery between myself and the Reverend Henry Ward Beecher was true. . . . The lie I had lived so well the last four years had become intolerable to me." But none of this perceptibly lessened the size of Beecher's congregation or his popularity and moral influence with it.

For most Americans, of course, life went on. Young men and women met, flirted, skated together, or went on hayrides, kissed, married, made love, had children, and placidly completed the cycle of life. When they thought about love at all, they thought about it with the sentimentality they found in the saccharine popular fiction of the day, or else with overpowering moral gravity. "I lose my respect," said Thoreau, "for the man who can make the mystery of sex the subject of a coarse jest, yet, when you speak earnestly and seriously on the subject, is silent."

Still the schism between passion and marriage, between sacred and profane love, created a pervasive tension in the American consciousness. The expulsion of sex from Victorian marriage led to much agony beneath the respectable surface: sick headaches, neurasthenia, nervous breakdowns, addiction to patent medicines (often containing large admixtures of alcohol or morphine), frigidity, impotence, homosexuality. The more extreme feminists raged at the proposition that women were not expected to find pleasure in the sexual act.

"Yes, I am a free lover!" cried Victoria Woodhull in a public lecture. "I have an inalienable, constitutional, and natural right to love whom I may, to love as long or as short a period as I can, to change that love every day if I please!"

Sensitive individuals, unable to join the

conspiracy to sweep passion under the rug, grew deeply concerned about sex, fearful of its power, anxious to bring it under control.

Sex became, for example, a central issue in many of the communities founded in mid-century by men and women abandoning contemporary society in search of a more perfect way of living together. Thus one of the older utopian groups, the Shakers, solved the problem of sex by abolishing it. Sworn to celibacy, they kept their communities going by recruitment. Yet as old Governor Bradford had said, water dammed up flows with the greater violence. Visitors noted that while the Shakers abstained from sexual relations, they indulged instead in ecstatic dances carried on at increasing tempo till they dropped in dazed exhaustion.

At the other extreme was the sexual experimentation of John Humphrey Noyes at the Oneida Community. Theologically, Noyes was a Perfectionist; he believed that Christ had long since returned to earth and that men of faith were now sinless. His community avowed the principles of complex marriage and male continence. Normal marriage seemed to him a selfish limitation on the biblical commandment to love. At Oneida, therefore, couples could have sexual relations as they wished. But having children was another matter. Here Noyes proposed an early form of eugenics—of selective mating—which he called "stirpiculture." To assure the separation of intercourse and breeding, Noyes advised methods of sexual restraint. Noyes was himself a man of considerable presence and ability. The community prospered far longer than other similar communities, eventually disbanding without having made a permanent contribution to the solving of mankind's ancient riddles of love and sex.

The tension about sex was also reflected in American literature. For the striking fact about the American novel in the 19th century was its avoidance of love—that is, of heterosexual love between consenting adults. Among major writers only Hawthorne hinted at the subject toward the middle of the century, and James and Howells toward the end, and all so cryptically that a great part of their audience hardly understood what they were saying. While European novels described mature passion between men and women—*Wuthering Heights* or *Madame Bovary* or *Anna Karenina*—American novelists wrote about men by themselves in the forest or on a whaling ship, or boys lazily drifting down the river on a raft. When women appeared, they generally represented a contrast between symbolic abstractions: the ethereal fair girl and the passionate, and therefore dangerous, dark girl. The women in Cooper were waxworks; there were no women in *Moby Dick;* in Poe they were generally symbols of death; Whitman's invocation of women was of men in disguise; Mark Twain fled from adult love like the plague. Unable to deal with the fact of heterosexual love, American literature in the 19th century suppressed it.

In the 19th century American society thus twisted itself into a torment of contradiction and uncertainty in its attitudes toward love. I do not mean that most Americans did not achieve a tolerable happiness with their wives; of course they did; and they conserved the family—at least in the middle classes—as the basic social unit. Yet the pursuit of happiness through a passionless marriage was generating a lurking, nagging frustration. By barring the joy of sex from wedlock, the Victorian code at once degraded the sexual impulse and weakened the marital tie. By transferring romantic love to the fantasy world of the sentimental novel and emptying serious literature of adult sexual content, it misled the national imagination and impoverished the national sensibility. The Victorians' unsatisfactory pursuit of happiness thus ended half on Main Street and half on Back Street, with marriage denied passion and passion denied legitimacy.

But the Victorian code corresponded neither to the emotional nor the physical realities of an increasingly urban and cosmopolitan society. Its collapse was inevitable. How shocking at the time were the first intimations of sexual liberation just before the First World War; how innocent they seem in retrospect! War itself hastened the disappearance of the old inhibitions, bringing back from France a new generation determined to live life to the full. The success of the feminist movement increased the pressure against the double standard. The psychology of Sigmund Freud gave the role of sex in life a fresh legitimacy. Then the prosperity of the '20's began to free the American people for the first time on a large scale from the acquisitive compulsions which Tocqueville had noted a century earlier. And, as the new psychology and the new leisure encouraged romantic love, so the new technology simplified life for romantic lovers. The automobile offered lovers mobility and privacy at just the time that contraceptives, now cheap and available, offered them security. Advertising and popular songs incessantly celebrated the cult of sex. Above all, the invention of the movies gave romantic love its troubadours and its temples of worship.

Living life to the full was still relatively innocuous in the '20's. "None of the Victorian mothers—and most of the mothers were Victorian—had any idea how casually their daughters were accustomed to be kissed," Scott Fitzgerald wrote in *This Side of Paradise* at the start of the decade.

. . . Amory saw girls doing things that even in his memory would have been impossible: eating three-o'clock, after-dance suppers in impossible cafés, talking of every side of life with an air half of earnestness, half of mockery, yet with a furtive excitement.

Skirts grew shorter; women bobbed their hair and smoked cigarettes; men packed hip flasks in their raccoon coats; and together they danced the Charleston, saxophones wailing in the background, or waded fully clothed into the fountain at the Plaza. Skeptics scorned the romantic dream. "Love," said H. L. Mencken, "is the delusion that one woman differs from another." But the contagion was irresistible.

Thus the Victorian schism was repaired and passion came back into marriage. "All societies recognize that there are occasional violent attachments between persons of opposite sex," Ralph Linton, the anthropologist, observed in 1936, "but our present American culture is practically the only one which has attempted to capitalize these and make them the basis for marriage." The American experiment was at last in full tide. "No other known civilization, in the 7,000 years that one civilization has been succeeding another," wrote the historian Denis de Rougemont, "has bestowed on the love known as *romance* anything like the same amount of daily publicity. . . . No other civilization has embarked with anything like the same ingenuous assurance upon the perilous enterprise of making marriage coincide with love thus understood, and of making the first depend upon the second." The Age of Love, in Morton Hunt's phrase, had begun—and it is still going strong.

But the Age of Love has hardly turned out to be an age of fulfillment. If sexual repression failed to produce happiness in the 19th century, sexual liberation appears to have done little better in the 20th. More than that, while repression at least preserved the family, if at times by main force, the pursuit of happiness through love is now evidently weakening the family structure itself. Divorce, of course, is an expression of the determination to make romance legal at any cost; so, if one marriage fails, another must be promptly started; and the steady increase in divorce in these years—the rate trebled from 1900 to 1960—suggests how the pursuit of love is paradoxically leading to the breakdown of marriage. Freedom, instead of resolving the dilemmas of love, is only heightening anxiety. Another of those observant Frenchmen, Raoul de Roussy de Sales, noted in 1938: "America appears to be the only country in the world where love is a national problem."

It remains a national problem today. The Second World War and its aftermath swept away whatever remained of the Victorian code; and the postwar years have seen the pursuit grow ever more complex. Most young Americans have adapted themselves to the new folkways. Like their ancestors, they meet and marry and live out their lives in quiet content. But in the margins of American society the search for love, having broken out of the old channels, is being driven more and more by frustration to sensation. Amory Blaine, the hero of *This Side of Paradise*, was dismayed by the '20's. He would have been appalled by the '60's. Among the seekers of sensation, drink has given way to drugs, fraternity hops to Sexual Freedom Leagues, petting to orgies, experiment to perversion. For some, sensation leads on to violence.

Denis de Rougemont has argued that the whole idea of romantic love manifested a repressed longing for suffering and tragedy. No doubt this is an exaggeration. But poets have long sensed a kinship between love and death. "Come lovely and soothing death," wrote Walt Whitman:

Undulate round the world, serenely arriving, arriving,
In the day, in the night, to all, to each,
Sooner or later delicate death.

If the suppression of sex in our 19th-century literature resulted in the Gothic obsessions of American fiction—the tormented allegories of Hawthorne, the necrophilia of Poe, the hallucinated terror of the later Mark Twain—the age of sexual liberation has produced the dark violence of Faulkner and the erotomegalomania of Mailer. Gershon Legman has underlined the irony that sexual congress is legal, but describing it (at least until very recently) is not; while murder is illegal but describing it has long been acceptable.

Is our literary violence in some sense a surrogate for sex? Is novelist and critic Leslie Fiedler right in suggesting that "the death of love left a vacuum at the affective heart of the American novel into which there rushed the love of death"? Our literature at least raises the possibility that the compulsive pursuit of love reinforces destructive tendencies already deep in our national character. The Measuring Man, entering girls' apartments under the pretense of inspecting them for a model agency, is revealed to be the Boston Strangler.

The American experiment in love has not yet proved itself. The national attempt to unite passion and marriage led many Americans into hypocrisy in the 19th century and into hysteria in the 20th. Must the conclusion be that we have essayed a human impossibility?—that the attempt to combine the tumult of romance with the permanence of marriage places a greater burden on marriage than it can bear? Some sociologists have even speculated that we may be moving toward a society of "progressive polygamy," as more and more Americans marry several spouses in the course of life.

No doubt Americans ask a great deal of marriage. Yet the probability is that the attempt to combine romance and monogamy will continue. When this works, it is the highest felicity. "The happiness of the domestic fireside," wrote Jefferson, "is the first boon of heaven." As for the less blessed in American society, they would perhaps do better to concentrate on the deflation of undue expectations, the recovery of discipline, and the recognition that romantic love, while the most beautiful of human experiences, is not a divinely guaranteed way of life.

Part Two

The Family Years
and Their Impact
on Human Sexuality

Archaeologists report that the institution of the family has existed for more than a million years, and that there are traceable forms of mammalian family life for the last seventy million years. Since men and women begin life and, in most instances, end life as a part of some kind of family unit, family relationships determine in large measure the quality of male-female relationships for most people. Hence, the family is not merely a unit produced by such relationships but is instead the framework in which such interactions are rooted.

Although the patterns that were taken by early male-female relationships are poorly understood, there are records dating back more than four thousand years. Furthermore, elaborate studies have been made on the origins and early forms of the family and on interactions between men and women from earliest recorded history. Such studies can help the individual see how he or she fits into the total scheme. For example, the way that early Hebrew families lived is important historically to the family structure in the contemporary United States; and studies dealing with this subject can be used to help the student bring his or her own life into focus, for they shed light on such topics as roles of men and women, sex laws, and property settlements in families. Similarly, the current customs of citizens of Japan or Russia or Tanzania, which are often considered quaint, irrelevant oddities, may help the student understand his or her own life more meaningfully by offering means of comparisons of various life-styles.

Just as the historical and the cross-cultural material may be relevant to contemporary society, the developmental approach —which traces life from birth to death— can be applied to the reader's life. Such material, when individualized and made practical, helps the student deal with questions and problems that arise in daily living. Hence, the effects of the diverse influences of the home on the child should be examined in terms of their impact on the child's search for identity, for the sexual identity of the adult is directly dependent upon these influences, at least in part. The importance of such factors as sibling relations, size of family, order of birth in the family, and the stability of the parents' marriage is best judged by becoming familiar with research on such matters.

What a child learns in the home becomes a major part of the foundation upon which the rest of life is built. However, the interplay of these influences is a complex process; the reader should not accept the research as precise evidence of just how the various influences shape identity. Rather, the evidence should be viewed as suggesting ways for the reader to apply the findings to his or her own life and to gain a fuller understanding of the early years and how they have molded individual adult sexual identity.

Many investigations into the influence of family organization upon the family members have stressed the principle of identification. The process of identification is important in that it enables the child to pattern his or her behavior after other family members. In particular, identification with the parent of the same sex is influential in forming the young person's sex-role identity as he or she matures. The first selection in Part Two, by David Lynn, hypothesizes that there are definite differences between the process of identification which boys go through and that which exists for girls. The article stresses how important identification is in the life of a child and how adult sex roles are derived from imitating parents and other significant adults. The pressures on children to behave in sex-appropriate ways begins to be felt early in their lives, and their responses to such pressures carry over to other areas as well.

Much has recently been written about the way early socialization limits the development of men and, particularly, women. The emphasis on sex differences and the concomitant casting of males and females into rather rigid roles at an early age more often than not causes a restriction of total growth. Young people come to accept such restrictions, as well as the roles themselves, as both necessary and desirable. In the second reading in this section, Judith Bardwick takes a careful look at

how the basic differences between the sexes develop and points out how complicated the process really is.

Role-interaction theory points out more than just how identification with the parents affects the kind of man or woman each person turns out to be. In a family, a child learns about others' roles as well as his or her own by daily interaction, and, in so doing, assimilates a certain amount of the others' behavior. Parental influence is of paramount importance, of course, but sibling interaction also plays a significant part in the determination of sexual identity. Orville Brim's article gives an analysis of the research supporting the role-interaction theory and illustrates the complexity of the influence of family members on each other.

Continuing family influences, peer-group experience, the school, and other socialization influences have their impact on boy-girl relationships and lay important foundations for future roles as men and women. The fourth article in this section, by Carlfred Broderick, considers the sexual behavior of preadolescent children and discusses how this behavior is molded by the experiences afforded by the environment. The article explores the psychoanalytic theory of sexual development, as well as other theories of childhood sexuality. Broderick emphasizes the point that the foundation for later male-female relationships is formed in early childhood—that the child is constantly being shaped by his or her environment during these early years for his role as a man or her role as a woman.

Broderick concludes his article by questioning how children can best be helped to deal with sexual experiences in these early years. The thoughtful reader may well reflect on his or her own childhood at this point to ask how childhood experiences concerning sexuality have helped or hindered his or her present ability to understand and deal with his or her sexual nature. The last reading in this section focuses on ways to help children grow up sexually. The author, Eleanore Luckey, stresses the importance of a better understanding of both the biological and the psychological aspects of sexuality. During each stage of development, the child receives certain information which aids in coming to grips with the total picture of what it means to be a boy or girl and later a man or woman in the contemporary world. The child's interest in his or her body and sexuality develops early, and his or her education for male-female relationships is a continuous process. Sexual fears and misinformation that cause serious adjustment problems later in life are frequently based on an improper handling of children's curiosity about themselves.

Before the onset of puberty, just as afterwards, sexuality is an important part of each person's life. Because of the importance of these early sexual experiences, the possibility of success as a marriage partner and as a parent begins to be determined for each individual as soon as he or she is born.

4

THE PROCESS OF LEARNING PARENTAL AND SEX-ROLE IDENTIFICATION

David B. Lynn

. . . Before developing specific hypotheses, one must briefly define identification as it is used here. *Parental identification* refers to the internalization of personality characteristics of one's own parent and to unconscious reactions similar to that parent. This is to be contrasted with *sex-role identification,* which refers to the internalization of the role typical of a given sex in a particular culture and to the unconscious reactions characteristic of that role. Thus, theoretically, an individual might be thoroughly identified with the role typical of his own sex generally and yet poorly identified with his same-sex parent specifically. This differentiation also allows for the converse circumstances wherein a person is well identified with his same-sex parent specifically and yet poorly identified with the typical same-sex role generally. In such an instance the parent with whom the individual is well identified is himself poorly identified with the typical sex role. An example might be a girl who is closely identi-

fied with her mother, who herself is more strongly identified with the masculine than with the feminine role. Therefore, such a girl, through her identification with her mother, is poorly identified with the feminine role.[1] . . .

It is postulated that the initial parental identification of both male and female infants is with the mother. Boys, but not girls, must shift from this initial mother identification and establish masculine-role identification. Typically in this culture the girl has the same-sex parental model for identification (the mother) with her more hours per day than the boy has his same-sex model (the father) with him. Moreover, even when home, the father does not usually participate in as many intimate activities with the child as does the mother, e.g., preparation for bed, toileting. The time spent with the child and the intimacy and intensity of the contact are thought to be pertinent to the process of learning parental identification.[2] The boy is seldom if ever with the father as he engages in his daily vocational activities, although both boy and girl are often with the mother as she goes through her household activities. Consequently, the father, as a model for the boy, is analogous to a map showing the major outline but lacking most details, whereas the mother, as a model for the girl, might be thought of as a detailed map.

However, despite the shortage of male models, a somewhat stereotyped and conventional masculine role is nonetheless spelled out for the boy, often by his mother and women teachers in the absence of his father and male models. Through the reinforcement of the culture's highly developed system of rewards for typical masculine-role behavior and punishment for signs of femininity, the boy's early learned identification with the mother weakens. Upon this weakened mother identification is welded the later learned identification with a culturally defined, stereotyped masculine role. (1)* *Consequently, males tend to identify with a culturally defined masculine role, whereas females tend to identify with their mothers.*

Although one must recognize the contribution of the father in the identification of males and the general cultural influences in the identification of females, it nevertheless seems meaningful, for simplicity in developing this formulation, to refer frequently to *masculine-role identification* in males as distinguished from *mother identification* in females.

Some evidence is accumulating suggesting that (2) *both males and females identify more closely with the mother than with the father.* Evidence is found in support of this hypothesis in a study by Lazowick[3] in which the subjects were 30 college students. These subjects and their mothers and fathers were required to rate concepts, e.g., "myself," "father," "mother," etc. The degree of semantic similarity as rated by the subjects and their parents was determined. The degree of similarity between fathers and their own children was not significantly greater than that found between fathers and children randomly matched. However, children did share a greater semantic similarity with their own mothers than they did

when matched at random with other maternal figures. Mothers and daughters did not share a significantly greater semantic similarity than did mothers and sons.

Evidence is also found in support of Hypothesis 2 in a study by Adams and Sarason[4] using anxiety scales with male and female high school students and their mothers and fathers. They found that anxiety scores of both boys and girls were much more related to mothers' than to fathers' anxiety scores.

Support for this hypothesis comes from a study in which Aldous and Kell[5] interviewed 50 middle-class college students and their mothers concerning childrearing values. They found, contrary to their expectation, that a slightly higher proportion of boys than girls shared their mothers' childrearing values. . . .

It is hypothesized that the closer identification of males with the mother than with the father will be revealed more clearly on some measures than on others. (3) *The closer identification of males with their mothers than with their fathers will be revealed most frequently in personality variables which are not clearly sex-typed.* In other words, males are more likely to be more similar to their mothers than to their fathers in variables in which masculine and feminine role behavior is not especially relevant in the culture.

There has been too little research on tested similarity between males and their parents to presume an adequate test of Hypothesis 3. In order to test it, one would first have to judge personality variables as to how typically masculine or feminine they seem. One could then test to determine whether a higher proportion of males are more similar to their mothers than to their fathers on those variables which are not clearly sex-typed, rather than on those which are judged clearly to be either masculine or feminine. To this writer's knowledge, this has not been done.

It is postulated that the task of achieving these separate kinds of identification (masculine role for males and mother identification for females) requires separate methods of learning for each sex. These separate methods of learning to identify seem to be problem-solving for boys and lesson-learning for girls. Woodworth and Schlosberg differentiate between the task of solving problems and that of learning lessons in the following way:

With a problem to master the learner must explore the situation and find the goal before his task is fully presented. In the case of a lesson, the problem-solving phase is omitted or at least minimized, as we see when the human subject is instructed to memorize this poem or that list of nonsense syllables, to examine these pictures with a view to recognizing them later.[6]

Since the girl is not required to shift from the mother in learning her identification, she is expected mainly to learn the mother-identification lesson as it is presented to her, partly through imitation and through the mother's selective reinforcement of mother-similar behavior. She need not abstract principles defining the feminine role to the extent that the boy must in defining the masculine role. Any bit of behavior on the mother's part may be modeled by the girl in learning the mother-identification lesson.

However, finding the appropriate identification goal does constitute a major problem for the boy in solving the masculine-role identification problem. When the boy discovers that he does not belong in the same sex category as the mother, he must then find the proper sex-role identification goal. Masculine-role behavior is defined for him through admonishments, often negatively given, e.g., the mother's and teachers' telling him that he should not be a sissy without precisely indicating what he *should* be. Moreover, these negative admonishments are made in the early grades in the absence of male teachers to serve as models and with the father himself often unavailable as a model. The boy must restructure these admonishments in order to abstract principles defining the masculine role. It is this process of defining the masculine-role goal which is involved in solving the masculine-role identification problem.

One of the basic steps in this formulation can now be taken. (4) *In learning the sex-typical identification, each sex is thereby acquiring separate methods of learning which are subsequently applied to learning tasks generally.*[7]

The little girl acquires a learning method which primarily involves (a) a personal relationship and (b) imitation rather than restructuring the field and abstracting principles. On the other hand, the little boy acquires a different learning method which primarily involves (a) defining the goal, (b) restructuring the field, and (c) abstracting principles. There are a number of findings which are consistent with Hypothesis 4, such as the frequently reported greater problem-solving skill of males and the greater field dependence of females.[8]

The shift of the little boy from mother identification to masculine-role identification is assumed to be frequently a crisis. It has been observed that demands for typical sex-role behavior come at an earlier age for boys than for girls. These demands are made at an age when boys are least able to understand them. As was pointed out above, demands for masculine sex-role behavior are often made by women in the absence of readily available male models to demonstrate typical sex-role behavior. Such demands are often presented in the form of punishing, *negative* admonishments, i.e., telling the boy what not to do rather than what to do and backing up the demands with punishment. These are thought to be very different conditions from those in which the girl learns her mother-identification lesson. Such methods of demanding typical sex-role behavior of boys are very poor methods for inducing learning.

(5) *Therefore, males tend to have greater difficulty in achieving same-sex identification than females.*[9]

(6) *Furthermore, more males than females fail more or less completely in achieving same-sex identification, but they rather make an opposite-sex identification.*[10]

Negative admonishments given at an age when the child is least able to understand them and supported by punishment are thought to produce anxiety concerning sex-role behavior. In Hartley's words:

This situation gives us practically a perfect combination for inducing anxiety—the demand that the child do something which is not clearly defined to him, based on reasons he cannot possibly appreciate, and enforced with threats, punishments, and anger by those who are close to him.[11]

(7) *Consequently, males are more anxious regarding sex-role identification than females.*[12] It is postulated that punishment often leads to dislike of the activity that led to punishment.[13] Since it is "girl-like" activities that provoked the punishment administered in an effort to induce sex-typical behavior in boys, then, in developing dislike for the activity which led to such punishment, boys should develop hostility toward "girl-like" activities. Also, boys should be expected to generalize and consequently develop hostility toward all females as representatives of this disliked role. There is not thought to be as much pressure on girls as on boys to avoid opposite-sex activities. It is assumed that girls are punished neither so early nor so severely for adopting masculine sex-role behavior.

(8) *Therefore, males tend to hold stronger feelings of hostility toward females than females toward males.*[14] The young boy's same-sex identification is at first not very firm because of the shift from mother to masculine identification. On the other hand, the young girl, because she need make no shift in identification, remains relatively firm in her mother identification. However, the culture, which is male-dominant in orientation, reinforces the boy's developing masculine-role identification much more thoroughly than it does the girl's developing feminine identification. He is rewarded simply for having been born masculine through countless privileges accorded males but not females. As Brown pointed out:

The superior position and privileged status of the male permeates nearly every aspect, minor and major, of our social life. The gadgets and prizes in boxes of breakfast cereal, for example, commonly have a strong masculine rather than feminine appeal. And the most basic social institutions perpetuate this pattern of masculine aggrandizement. Thus, the Judeo-Christian faiths involve worshipping God, a "Father," rather than a "Mother," and Christ, a "Son," rather than a "Daughter."[15]

(9) *Consequently, with increasing age, males become relatively more firmly identified with the masculine role.*[16]

Since psychological disturbances should, theoretically, be associated with inadequate same-sex identification and since males are postulated to be gaining in masculine identification, the following is predicted: (10) *With increasing age males develop psychological disturbances at a more slowly accelerating rate than females.*[17]

It is postulated that as girls grow older, they become increasingly disenchanted with the feminine role because of the prejudices against their sex and the privileges and prestige offered the male rather than the female. Even the women with whom they come in contact are likely to share the prejudices prevailing in this culture against their own sex.[18] Smith[19] found that with increasing age girls have a progressively better opinion of boys and a progressively poorer opinion of themselves. (11) *Consequently, a larger proportion of females than males show preference for the role of the opposite sex.*[20]

Note that in Hypothesis 11 the term "preference" rather than "identification" was used. It is *not* hypothesized that a larger proportion of females than males *identify* with the opposite sex (Hypothesis 6 predicted the reverse) but rather that they will show *preference* for the role of the opposite sex. *Sex-role preference* refers to the desire to adopt the behavior associated with one sex or the other or the perception of such behavior as preferable or more desirable. *Sex-role preference* should be contrasted with *sex-role identification*, which, as stated previously, refers to the actual incorporation of the role of a given sex and to the unconscious reactions characteristic of that role.

Punishment may suppress behavior without causing its unlearning.[21] Because of the postulated punishment administered to males for adopting opposite-sex role behavior, it is predicted that males will repress atypical sex-role behavior rather than unlearn it. One might predict, then, a discrepancy between the underlying sex-role identification and the overt sex-role behavior of males. For females, on the other hand, no comparable punishment for adopting many aspects of the opposite-sex role is postulated. (12) *Consequently, where a discrepancy exists between sex-role preference and identification, it will tend to be as follows: Males will tend to show same-sex role preference with underlying opposite-sex identification. Females will tend to show opposite-sex role preference with underlying same-sex identification.*[22] Stated in another way, where a discrepancy occurs both males and females will tend to show masculine-role preference with underlying feminine identification.

Not only is the masculine role accorded more prestige than the feminine role, but males are more likely than females to be ridiculed or punished for adopting aspects of the opposite-sex role. For a girl to be a tomboy does not involve the censure that results when a boy is a sissy. Girls may wear masculine clothing (shirts and trousers), but boys may not wear feminine clothing (skirts and dresses). Girls may play with toys typically associated with boys (cars, trucks, erector sets, and guns), but boys are discouraged from playing with feminine toys (dolls and tea sets). (13) *Therefore, a higher proportion of females than males adopt aspects of the role of the opposite sex.*[23]

Note that Hypothesis 13 refers to *sex-role adoption* rather than *sex-role identification* or *preference*. *Sex-role adoption* refers to the overt behavior characteristic of a given sex. An example contrasting sex-role adoption with preference and identification is an individual who *adopts* behavior characteristic of his own sex because it is expedient, not because he *prefers* it nor because he is so *identified*.

SUMMARY

The purpose of this paper has been to summarize the writer's theoretical formulation and to place it in a more comprehensive and coherent framework. The following hypotheses were presented and discussed:

1. Males tend to identify with a culturally defined masculine role, whereas females tend to identify with their mothers.

2. Both males and females identify more closely with the mother than with the father.

3. The closer identification of males with their mothers than with their fathers will be revealed most frequently in personality variables which are not clearly sex-typed.

4. In learning the sex-typical identification, each sex is thereby acquiring separate methods of learning which are subsequently applied to learning tasks generally.

5. Males tend to have greater difficulty in achieving same-sex identification than females.

6. More males than females fail more or less completely in achieving same-sex identification but rather make an opposite-sex identification.

7. Males are more anxious regarding sex-role identification than females.

8. Males tend to hold stronger feelings of hostility toward females than females toward males.

9. With increasing age, males become relatively more firmly identified with the masculine role.

10. With increasing age, males develop psychological disturbances at a more slowly accelerating rate than females.

11. A larger proportion of females than males show preference for the role of opposite sex.

12. Where a discrepancy exists between sex-role preference and identification, it will tend to be as follows: Males will tend to show same-sex role preference with underlying opposite-sex identification. Females will tend to show opposite-sex role preference with underlying same-sex identification.

13. A higher proportion of females than males adopt aspects of the role of the opposite sex.

NOTES

[1] D. B. Lynn, "Sex-Role and Parental Identification," *Child Development,* 33:3 (1962): 555–564.

[2] B. A. Goodfield, "A Preliminary Paper on the Development of the Time Intensity Compensation Hypothesis in Masculine Identification," paper read at the San Francisco State Psychological Convention, April, 1965.

* Specific hypotheses are numbered and in italics.

[3] L. M. Lazowick, "On the Nature of Identification," *Journal of Abnormal and Social Psychology,* 51 (1955): 175–183.

[4] E. B. Adams and I. G. Sarason, "Relation Between Anxiety in Children and Their Parents," *Child Development,* 34:1 (1963): 237–246.

[5] J. Aldous and L. Kell, "A Partial Test of Some Theories of Identification," *Marriage and Family Living,* 23:1 (1961): 15–19.

[6] R. S. Woodworth and H. Schlosberg, *Experimental Psychology* (New York: Holt, 1954), p. 529.

[7] D. B. Lynn, "Sex-Role and Parental Identification," op. cit.

[8] Ibid.

[9] D. B. Lynn, "Divergent Feedback and Sex-Role Identification in Boys and Men," *Merrill-Palmer Quarterly,* 10:1 (1964): 17–23.

[10] D. B. Lynn, "Sex Differences in Identification Development," *Sociometry,* 24:4 (1961): 372–383.

[11] R. E. Hartley, "Sex-Role Pressures and the Socialization of the Male Child," *Psychological Reports,* 5 (1959): 458.

[12] D. B. Lynn, "Divergent Feedback and Sex-Role Identification in Boys and Men," op. cit.

[13] E. R. Hilgard, *Introduction to Psychology* (New York: Harcourt, Brace, and World), 1962.

[14] D. B. Lynn, "Divergent Feedback and Sex-Role Identification Boys and Men," op. cit.

[15] D. G. Brown, "Sex-Role Development in a Changing Culture," *Psychological Bulletin,* 55 (1958): 235.

[16] D. B. Lynn, "A Note on Sex Differences in the Development of Masculine and Feminine Identification," *Psychological Review,* 66:2 (1959): 126–135.

[17] D. B. Lynn, "Sex Differences in Identification Development," op. cit.

[18] P. M. Kitay, "A Comparison of the Sexes in Their Attitudes and Beliefs About Women: A Study of Prestige Groups," *Sociometry,* 3 (1940): 399–407.

[19] S. Smith, "Age and Sex Differences in Children's Opinion Concerning Sex Differences," *Journal of Genetic Psychology,* 54 (1939): 17–25.

[20] D. B. Lynn, "A Note on Sex Differences in the Development of Masculine and Feminine Identification," op. cit.

[21] Hilgard, op. cit.

[22] D. B. Lynn, "Divergent Feedback and Sex-Role Identification in Boys and Men," op. cit.

[23] D. B. Lynn, "A Note on Sex Differences in the Development of Masculine and Feminine Identification," op. cit.

5

IDENTIFICATION

Judith M. Bardwick

The term "identification" is used in psychology to explain everything from intense guilt about moral standards to the 2-year-old's imitation of hammering and sweeping. Basically, the term describes the incorporation of the model into oneself, in which there is no boundary between the self and the model. However, a person's *identity* is larger than the sum of his identifications. . . .

One of the studies I recently read reported that in a testing situation boys between the ages of 2 and 8 were more upset than girls of the same age when they were separated from their mothers. That made me wonder whether the affectional tie of the boy to the mother was greater and whether the girls might not be more ambivalent in their relationships with their mothers—loving, aggressive, and a little independent. I was also reminded of other cultures where the training-discipline roles are held by the biological parents and the affectional-noncritical roles by aunts and uncles, and I wondered whether something similar might be happening here. Not only may the child be identifying with the parent of the same sex, but the like-sexed parent may be identifying with the child and assuming the responsibility for role training and the creation of role expectations in the child. Training necessarily requires some discipline, some frustration, and therefore some (mutual) aggression. The parent of the opposite sex, although not totally removed from disciplining (especially for personality qualities rather than role characteristics), is likely to act with less discipline and aggression and is therefore likely to be perceived by the child as the good guy, affectionate, supportive, and permissive. This will also affect the child's expectation that those of the opposite sex can love and be loved in a relatively unambivalent relationship and be trusted with intimacy. Indeed, if you think about it, "femininity" is really a relative term and is probably first learned by girls in their relationships with their fathers —as "masculinity" is a relative term and is probably first learned by boys in relationships with their mothers. The sex-linked differences in parental behaviors are not absolute. But later there will be reinforcement for the original percepts as boys scramble for peer dominance and compete aggressively, and the boy will see males as potentially hostile, thwarting, and competitive—as well as affectionate. These are the same ambivalent sentiments they have toward their fathers. A girl will have similar experiences. In the single-sex play groups prior to adolescence the ambivalence of a girl's relationship to her mother will be repeated in her experiences with girlfriends. (Of course the intrusion of sex into adolescent relationships will result in strong ambivalence to persons of the opposite sex, but there the goal will be the establishment of an honest, trusting, and mutually dependent relationship.)

In much of the literature the mother is described as *expressive*, which means she is primarily concerned with affects, with the establishment of warm, rather uncritical relationships with her children. The father is described as *instrumental*, largely preoccupied with the long-term goals and accomplishments of the family and the children in the world outside of the home. I think it is an error to view the mother as only expressive and not instrumental. Compared with the father, she is likely to be more expressive, but she is also likely to be rather instrumental toward her daughter and rather expressive toward her son. In terms of instrumental behavior she may discriminate little when compared with the father, but discrimination should increase as the children grow older and she no longer perceives them as babies. Dependency on the part of the children, especially daughters, which evoked expressive, affectionate, supportive behavior from her, should decrease as the children grow older. The father, in a like way, should be more instrumental than the mother in general—but more so to his son than to his daughter. Thus it may be normal and beneficial when children can perceive one parent as rather uncritical and unambivalent and the other as more directive. Of course it may also be dangerous in the sex identity of the child when the instrumental, critical parent is not expressive and supportive at all. In that case, the child may be drawn or driven to the parent of the opposite sex, with whom he may identify.

Although children receive both instrumental and expressive responses from both parents, I think that

1. The mother is more expressive than the father, but especially to her son;
2. The mother is less instrumental than the father, but more so to her daughter;
3. The father is more instrumental than the mother, but especially to his son;
4. The father is less expressive than the mother, but more so to his daughter.

Philip Slater (1961) has written a paper on identification which I thoroughly enjoy because he has returned warmth to the parent-child relationship and because he also feels that children must identify with both parents in order to be psychologically healthy. Slater distinguished between *personal* and *positional* identification. In personal identification, the child identifies with the role model and adopts the values, attitudes, and personality traits of the model. This kind of identification is motivated primarily by the child's love and admiration. Slater writes that the child is, in effect, saying: "I want to be like you. If I were, I would have you (and your virtues) with me all the time, and I would love myself as much as I love you. To achieve this I will incorporate your qualities and your values and ideals. I will view and judge myself through your eyes" (p. 113). This kind of identification is the result of parental warmth, affection, and support; it

seems to be an intervening variable between a supportive relationship and the child's internalization of parental values.

In positional identification, the child identifies with the position or role of the model. Instead of an empathic personal relationship, there is a fantasied projection into the situation of the model and the role behavior of the model. Slater tells us that this child is saying: "I wish I were in your shoes. If I were, I would not be in the unpleasant position I am in now. If I wish hard enough and act like you do, I may after all achieve your more advantageous status" (p. 113). The motives involved are identification with the aggressor ("I will be strong, powerful, and menacing instead of weak, powerless, and menaced") and the Oedipal wish ("Mother or Father will love me and not you"). In positional identification there is a wish for the destruction and replacement of the model by the identifier. Slater conceives of this kind of identification as a defensive reaction to the frustration of a lack of parental warmth, support, and affection. For children of both sexes, both kinds of identification will occur at the same time and, I would add, with both parents.

Insofar as the model commands because of positive qualities in his personality, the identification will be personal; if the model commands because of his role or status, the identification will be positional. "Positional identification, then, will occur insofar as personal identification has failed to occur" (Slater, p. 118). It should be clear that interaction is probable—even warm and supportive child relationships are ambivalent, and the parent is always in a more powerful status than the child. (And the child's percept of parental power is greater than the actual power the parent commands.)

I suggest that both parents are a source of love to children of both sexes, and they are also a source of rejection. The mother's relationship to the daughter, especially insofar as the female role is concerned, is largely instrumental; in Slater's terms, the identification is positional. But to the extent that the mother is also a nurturant, warm human being, the identification is simultaneously personal. Insofar as the mother pushes the daughter to the assumption of role responsibilities, she will be perceived as manipulative and powerful. The girl is also aware that she is expected to learn role behaviors and that she will receive reinforcement for learning. In the analytic model, she has an unconscious identification with the mother; she has a learning-theory identification with the mother insofar as she perceives similarities in personality between herself and her mother and insofar as she sees herself in the female role. She has a personal identification with the father because that relationship is warmer and less ambivalent than the relationship with the mother. She may also have a positional identification with the father because she perceives that his roles, especially economically, are sources of money, power, and prestige, which are generally valued by the culture. Thus the girl identifies with the personal qualities of the mother and with the role of the mother, and simultaneously, in a reciprocal role relationship, she identifies with the father because she loves him and because she is loved by him.

If the daughter rejects the maternal role, or if her mother is more rejecting than supportive, or if her relationship with her father is the only source of love and support, she may well identify with his role activities, especially because this culture values the achievements that come from successful competition in nonfeminine roles. These relationships may change over time so that, for example, the sexuality of the adolescent girl and her dating activity arouse anxiety in the father. He now becomes more restrictive and less supportive than the mother, who can identify with the daughter and enjoy her daughter's social successes. At that point, the identification with the mother may be less ambivalent than it had been, and the daughter can empathize with and desire the role and the femininity of the mother.

The psychoanalysts . . . conceive of identification as an all-or-nothing proposition with only one parent. We are suggesting that identification is also a developmental process and involves both parents. Slater writes, "When measured independently and correlated (as they rarely are), paternal and maternal identification are strongly and positively related" (Slater, 1955, p. 119). One can identify with the roles of both parents, one can identify with the concept of the appropriate role, and one can personally identify with the model and reject the appropriate role. There are basic and unconscious core identifications, there are learned identifications that reflect one's age and status, there are identifications with one's own parents, and there are identifications with cultural models. There are internalized expectations and standards and there are reactions from others. All of these combine in complex ways and probably reflect the strengths and pressures in individual family situations as well as in general cultural patterns.

Rothbart and Maccoby (1966) have to some extent verified the cross-sex interaction that we have been describing. (That's very pleasing to me, of course, and doubly so because they didn't expect the results they got.) In a previous study (1957), Sears, Maccoby, and Levin[1] had found that mothers were tolerant of aggression from sons while fathers took the major responsibility for disciplining sons when both parents were at home. The 1966 study was designed to explore a rather traditional hypothesis: both parents would reinforce aggression in sons and dependency in daughters.

The experimenters taped the voice of a 4-year-old who made 12 statements like "Daddy, help me," or "I don't like this game . . . I'm gonna break it." Sixty mothers and 21 fathers were told that the voice was a girl's; 38 mothers and 11 fathers were told that it was a boy's. Contrary to expectations from Maccoby's original study, mothers tended to be more permissive when the voice was identified as a boy's, fathers when the voice was a girl's. Fathers showed more permissiveness and positive attention to their daughters, and allowed them more autonomy. Mothers were more restrictive and negative to their daughters. Confounding the sex-role stereotype, parents were not warm to girls and harsh to boys but showed cross-sexed responses.

Maccoby and Rothbart felt that these were unexpected results because in this study the sex of the parent was a better predictor of the response to a girl or boy than the sex-role stereotype. These authors suggested that parents shift their reinforcements of behavior as the children grow older—an idea we have also suggested. . . .

Mussen and Rutherford (1963) suggest that the interactive variables which are usually omitted in studies of identification include the personality qualities of the parents and the general cultural sex-role values. They found that the feminization of daughters was dependent upon a warm relationship between the mother and daughter (personal identification). They also found that those mothers whose daughters were most feminine were not more feminine themselves, nor did they particularly encourage their daughters to participate in feminine activities, but were themselves clearly more self-accepting and self-confident. The fathers of very feminine girls tended to be masculine and tended to encourage their daughters to participate in feminine activities. They found that the mother's personality and interactions with the son tended to have little influence on his sex-role preference, but the father's personality and interest and his encouragement of his daughter's femininity were crucial in the girl's development of an appropriate sex-role preference. Feminization of the daughter depended upon a warm relationship with a mother who held herself in esteem and with a father who encouraged and responded to his daughter's emerging femininity.

Mussen and Rutherford feel that the family is more critically important in the daughter's sex-role socialization than the son's. The male role in this culture is more highly valued and more clearly defined, and for the son there is a consistency of role expectation over his lifetime and a consistency in the portrait of that role in the entire culture. Therefore the boy receives assistance, support, and criticism from all of the culture's socialization agents, while the girl does not. Indeed, because the feminine role is devalued, a daughter is likely to have a mother who is experiencing conflicts about her own femininity and who therefore cannot support her daughter's self-esteem or serve as a successful role model. . . .

The culture values masculine roles, goals, and success. What effect does this have upon the female's identification? We find a peculiar state of affairs in which the roles of both parents are changing, girls are permitted (and sometimes encouraged) to succeed in traditionally masculine pursuits at least until adolescence, 38.5 percent of American women are working, and children still perceive the sex roles traditionally.

Many of the personality and identification studies have been done with very young children in nursery schools. This has led to the idea that, unlike fathers, mothers do not discriminate among their children in terms of any variable, including the sex of the child. This may be true with very young children who evoke nurturant, protective responses in the mother, and to a lesser extent, in the father.[2] As children grow older the instrumentality of both parents' responses would be expected to increase. Goodenough (1957) interviewed upper-status parents of nursery-school children about their ideas of masculinity and femininity and found that the mothers were not nearly so concerned with the appropriate sex-typing in their children as were the fathers. The fathers were already actively involved in the sex-typing of their children, and while the mothers were aware of what the fathers were doing they did not actively participate. "It almost seems as if sex-typing goes on in boys independent of maternal influence, and goes on in girls with very little effort from the mother to exclude masculine influence" (p. 312). That is not surprising if one recalls that as the son emerges from infancy his dependent behavior will be perceived by the father as effeminate and he will be pressured to behave in a more masculine, independent, or aggressive way. One should also anticipate that any perceived effeteness in the son arouses more anxiety in the father than in the mother. The masculine influences on the young girl probably have two components: one is reciprocal femininity in her relations with her father, in which he responds to her feminine qualities, and the other is permission to engage in competitive sports or competitive academics or leadership roles, which will *later* be associated with the male role or masculine traits. The girl's early participation and possible success in activities which will later be defined as masculine provide the underpinnings for what I call a "bisexual" identification. By that I mean that the normal girl will identify herself as female and perceive herself as feminine but she may have also learned that she is capable of achieving success and self-esteem in the competitive and aggressive modes of scholastic achievement or athletics that are precursors of professional achievement. Since the culture is essentially masculine and masculine activities are more valued than traditional feminine ones, . . . and since females are permitted masculine-role participation, it is likely that a part of the girl's self-percept evolves in relation to the more highly valued activities. At the same time, since many of her peers are also engaged in these activities and since there are no negative repercussions, she can still feel unambivalently female. This apparent role contradiction will not become important until adolescence, when achievement success can be seen as threatening affiliative (dating) success; at that time it will be an important conflict if the girl cannot gratify both her traditionally feminine needs and her achievement needs. . . .

By the age of 3, children are able to tell you what sex they belong to and also which jobs are done by women and which by men. The 3-year-old generalizes to the sexes from his perception of his parents, and he imposes the traditional sex-role functions even though his mother may be working: mothers take care of the house and children, fathers work; mothers are "nicer" and fathers are more competent and punitive. . . . When I look at my own children I think the imposition of the traditional roles is a cognitive simplification by young children who are uncertain of their status. The simplification is clearly aided by the content of children's books and television programs.

Young children are terribly pragmatic, literal, concrete. They are highly motivated to achieve some kind of stable self-definition, and one of the components of that self-definition is sex. One's sex is a "given," not subject to change as one grows older. From that point of view it is one of the few variables the child can grasp as a stable

part of himself. Sex for 3-year-old children doesn't even involve the genitals (that comes when they are 5). My youngest daughter, wearing slacks, tells me that she knows another child is a girl "because she wears a dress." Their early interest in sex identity generally reveals curiosity about their future adult roles, but they have no uncertainty about their own sex. I don't think that sex identity, for girls, is an important part of self-esteem. The major tasks that children set for themselves are the mastery of cognitive, physical, verbal, and interpersonal skills, and in the early years age is the important variable, not sex. Whether behavior is appropriate, what goals the child sets for himself, the way he perceives himself, what parents expect of him, are more determined by age than by sex. . . .

But the pressure to become masculine, to grow up, begins early for boys, about the age of 5, and sex-identity becomes a crucial issue. By this time the boy has learned that he has to earn his masculinity. It is no longer given. By the time he reaches adolescence the psychologically healthy boy, helped by the power and the clarity of the male sex-role in the culture, will be certain of his masculinity and of his future role. Of course the new role-demands of adolescence will generate anxiety about whether he can be successful in his new responsibilities, but the bases of his male identity will have developed in the so-called latency years. The identification pressures on girls to become really feminine, to inhibit their freedom, and to inhibit masculine behaviors or personality traits do not occur until adolescence. Prepubertal girls are aware of their sex, they practice certain housekeeping roles, sometimes they baby-sit, and they can tell you what their future responsibilities as women will be. But this is all still playing, anticipating. When the pubertal development creates the extraordinary physical changes of the menstrual cycle and the secondary sex characteristics, the girl's status now depends upon her feminine desirability, and her psyche depends upon her acceptance of these happy and threatening changes. Anxiety can come from external parental or cultural pressures or from changes within oneself and one's own body.

Early adolescence is probably the first critical identity period for girls. There is likely to be a somewhat dangerous consequence of this identity delay—the girl has had many years in which she has been permitted to participate in what will be perceived as masculine activities, and to the extent that success in these activities, especially individual competitive ones, form a core part of her self-esteem, it will be difficult for her to assume a clearly feminine sex-role identity and a preference for the feminine role. This ambiguity does not exist for boys, and in this sense their sex-role identity is both clearer and easier.

In adolescence the evaluative importance of parents probably diminishes proportionately to the increased importance of peer evaluation. The adolescent's behavior is guided by internalized values, responses of the parents, and the real or anticipated reactions of peers. Girls will be able to perceive themselves as feminine in spite of academic success or other male-associated activity, unless they are so tomboyish that they cannot interact with girls and the girls reject them, or unless they fail in the competition of adolescent dating, or, later on, unless they fail to marry and have a child. In other words, the more permissive identification process in girls allows them to perceive themselves as feminine even while they are competitive, verbally aggressive, or independent, if they are also able to succeed in the distinctly feminine tasks appropriate to their age. In that special sense the identification of girls is bisexual. (Life is not really so simple of course, and in adolescence a girl is likely to feel anxiety about ambitions or personality characteristics closer to the male model if her parents or peers react to such qualities as real or potential threats to success in the female role. For many girls the solution is a self-conscious deference to the male, a role played with tongue-in-cheek.) But the data . . . gives support to the idea that the majority of girls are not aggressive, active, or independent, and along with their feminine personality characteristics the physical changes of puberty and the joys of successful courtship will make their assumption of a feminine-role identity and feminine-role prefer-

ence relatively easy. Most books on the subject written by women are by the achieving woman who is probably dissatisfied with the feminine role. Most of the studies are done on female college students who have competed successfully enough to get into college. The majority has been relatively silent and satisfied.

Since masculine behaviors are valued, since girls frequently say they envy boys, since masculine characteristics are highly rated by children and adults of both sexes, we may assert that the culture strongly motivates the boy to become masculine and rewards him when he does. The girl is not as highly motivated to become feminine, and when she does succeed she is not as highly rewarded. Even in very young children, the acceptable behaviors for boys are very clearly defined, and if a boy crosses the sex-line in behavior he is likely to be rejected by parents, friends, and teachers. Not so with girls. Unless they are grotesquely masculine in dress and play, they are permitted masculine activities (the number of tomboys is greater than the number of sissies). We might expect that the specific family of the girl is crucially important in inducing motivation for her to become feminine and in presenting behaviors acceptable as feminine. We might also expect a greater diversity in women, a wider range of feminine sex-role attributes and personality qualities than is true for the male in his sex-role, because the culture, by not defining the female role as rigidly as the male, permits greater variance. Female role expectations become more specific in adolescence, but by that time it is rather late to impose stringent criteria for acceptable personality traits and behaviors. Many personality qualities, motives, and behaviors are formed in childhood and latency, and the sudden pressure for the girl to conform to a rather specific sex-role stereotype is bound to induce some role-conflict and anxiety about her femininity. Fortunately, I think two things mitigate the new demands: In their relationships with boys, the girls use a self-conscious adaptation pattern of deference and seduction, and . . . girls tend to be basically more passive, less active, less sexy, and more dependent than boys. There should be relatively little conflict, but for some percentage of girls conflict is probably inevitable. Lynn (1966) predicts that because girls are not punished as much for masculine behavior as boys are for feminine, and because the masculine role has more prestige, a higher proportion of American females will adopt aspects of the opposite sex:

Despite the overrepresentation of women in the boy's world and the concomitant shortage of male models a somewhat stereotyped and conventional masculine role is clearly spelled out for him, positively reinforced if he complies and negatively reinforced if he does not behave in a masculine-stereotyped fashion. Moreover, he is rewarded simply for being born male through countless privileges accorded males and not females. Thus, through the reinforcement of the culture's highly developed system of rewards and punishment, the boy's early learned identification with the mother eventually weakens and becomes more or less replaced by the later learned identification with a culturally defined, somewhat stereotyped masculine role. . . .

The development of the appropriate sex-role identification for the girl is converse that for the boy. She moves from a same-sex-oriented to an opposite-sex-oriented world. Upon leaving infancy she is, in a sense, punished for being female (does not benefit from the same advantages and privileges as the boy) nor is she given the degree of negative reinforcement for adopting certain aspects of the opposite-sex role. The result of these forces is a weakening of the girl's feminine identification. The girl learns to prefer the masculine role because of its many advantages and since while she is unmarried she is barred from playing her primary role of wife and mother she is unclear about what her role really is.

In a sense Lynn is repeating the phallocentric position, although he has shorn it of the psychoanalytic terms.

We know from simple observation as well as from complex psychological reasoning that the rewards of competitive success in the marketplace are status, money, power, self-esteem, heart attacks, and ulcers. We assume that women have internalized the same set of values, and in part they have. Realistically, most women participate in the success of men in their roles as wives, and for most women that appears to be enough. Simultaneously, women have also internalized a set of discretely feminine values which receive less public attention and reward. They conceive of their achievements differently than men, and they evaluate their success as women and as persons in terms of feminine criteria as well as the more obvious masculine values. Women do not perceive rearing children as a secondary accomplishment and they do perceive themselves as successful when they enjoy love (and power and status) from their husbands and children and when they give love and support. They conceive of this as their major function, and their success in affiliative relationships defines their personal success. Although we have a tendency to ignore it or claim that it is a defensive solution to frustrated masculine aspirations, the apparent truth is that this is the primary role and source of gratification for the majority of middle-class American women.

Feminism is not and actually never has been a widespread movement among American women, and the goals and values held by most women are gratified primarily in the traditional feminine activities. Given the extent of the preference in the culture for masculine activities, one must ask why this is so, why so few women are motivated to achieve professionally. Most women may never have developed a strong achievement motivation as children and adolescents, they may fear failure because they fear competition and the implications of public failure, and they may fear that success will make them less feminine.

We are rather glib in assuming that girls are second-class citizens; until a girl marries and has the responsibility of home and children she is more likely to be pampered. Indeed, if she has been successful as a female, she is courted. In these affluent times I think that there are very few privileges that middle-class girls are cheated of in comparison with their brothers. Only in terms of freedom does the adolescent girl feel a measure of sex-linked restriction, and little in her life prepares her for the restrictions she will encounter later as a mother, for the unending responsibility and the myriad of unfinished details that accompany raising children. This is a peculiar situation. If the woman is barren she is regarded and regards herself as a failure; on the other hand, having children does not bestow status. When we see women returning to work when their children are all in school, we see not so much a running *to* express oneself as much as a reaction *from* the closed and inhibiting world of small children. But identification remains feminine; in a primary sense and as a reaction to guilt the motive for the return to work is to increase the standard of living for the family. It is also my feeling that when women have achieved security in their relationships with their husbands, they can permit the re-emergence of achievement motives they had as girls. I also think that women feel the need to perceive themselves as able and independent, although this need develops later than it does in men, and after awhile they reject their total dependency on their husbands and search for a more individual feeling of identity and a feeling of direct participation in the real world.[3] Because they are still expressive or nurturant or attuned to the well-being of people instead of abstract ideas, they may also find a real commitment to welfare or voluntary organizations very gratifying. . . .

What are the effects upon the daughter's sex-role identity and aspirations when her mother works? Hartley (1960) found that not only do the children perceive the mother's role as an extension of her traditional responsibilities but most of the working mothers also perceived their work as an extension of their nurturant role. A very large percentage of American women work, but a real revolution would occur only if women worked not particularly to maximize the welfare of their families but to enhance their own self-esteem, to gratify their own ambitions. Most working mothers and their children continue to perceive the father as responsible for the economic support of the family, and the working mother is seen as adding this extra duty to all of her other role responsibilities. Hartley writes that the sex-role changes in American adults are more a matter of a change in form than function (the apparent change is an extension of the older responsibilities into another place); for this reason, and also because children do not perceive social changes that occur over a long time-span, the children of working mothers do not perceive any real change in the sex roles. The professional women, the small minority of American women who work in order to use all of their potential and who need achievements for self-esteem, probably create a somewhat different picture for their children; even so, if we look closely at the families of these women, we find that the major responsibility for the home and the children is still assumed by the mother.

Hartley found that children of mothers who work tend to perceive their mothers as enjoying work and anticipate similar roles when they grow up. . . . Working mothers [are] warmer, more helpful, supportive, and mild, more relaxed and satisfied with themselves as people, than nonworking mothers. They are successful in the traditional mothering responsibilities and as active participants in the economy. This means that the working mother is a likelier model for personal identification. It is logical for daughters of these mothers to have an anticipatory self-concept that is both traditionally female and nontraditional. If the woman is successful in the basic female responsibilities, participation in a job does not necessarily mean a profound role conflict. Conflict in that case is only pragmatic and comes down to a question of which traditional female role-responsibilities need to be shared with other family members.

Since most working women are content with an agreeable job that makes limited demands, and since they are not striving for positions of economic power or large monetary success, there has not really been a radical reversal of the traditional sex-role functions in the United States. This is probably an evolutionary period. For some women with high achievement aspirations there is likely to be profound role conflict touching not only behaviors but acceptable personality traits, but these women are still in the minority. Most of the overt sex-typed responses that girls make require a response from someone else, and most children and adults expect more dependence, passivity, and nurturance from females than males. These expectations and responses and the personality qualities of most women make their job selections of nurse, secretary, teacher, pediatrician, and psychologist understandable. . . .

Between Simone de Beauvoir's *The Second Sex* and Betty Friedan's *The Feminine Mystique*, the college students who serve as subjects in psychological experiments, and the return of women to work after their children are in school we tend to forget that most adolescent girls are motivated to achieve within the traditional feminine role. One of the most interesting studies on sex differences in adolescence is Douvan and Adelson's *The Adolescent Experience* (1966). In 1955–1956 they interviewed in depth 1045 boys aged 14 through 16 and 2005 girls aged 11 through 18. Their major theoretical assumption was that as a result of the diffuse sexual impulses of the adolescent girl, her previous ego development, her high degree of compliance, and the controls imposed upon her from external sources, the development of internal controls would be less salient and pressing than for boys.[4] They therefore hypothesized that girls would show more compliant relationships with their parents, would identify with their parents' standards, would be less consciously concerned with the control of their impulses, and would tend not to differentiate between parental standards and controls and their own. In other words, adolescent girls would be less concerned with the development of personal values and internal controls of behavior than boys. A girl's sensitivity and skill in her interpersonal relationships are the critical variables in her personal adjustment, and in general the feminine character —in terms of personal standards, controls, and an individual sense of self—develops after adolescence. Adolescence is more dramatic and probably crucial for boys. . . . Insofar as the girl's self-percept is dependent upon reflected appraisals in interpersonal relationships, adolescence will be

a critical period in her development too, but it will not result in an individual sense of identity.

What did Douvan and Adelson find in their interviews? During the ages of 14 through 16 boys consistently view their relations with their families as combative, with the major battles over independence, behavior control, and an individual sense of autonomy. In terms of the actual development of internal controls and values, the boys have developed much further than the girls. Boys think of their future in an instrumental way. Their plans are rather concrete, crystallized, and tied to reality, especially concerning their future vocation. A boy's hopes for adult status reflect his faith in himself, and the goal he chooses is realistic in terms of his talents and opportunities. He is highly motivated to be independent, and his identity and capacity for erotic ties depend upon autonomy and separation from the parents. To achieve status as an adult he particularly severs his ties with his father and clarifies (and achieves) his vocational goals. His vocational identity and his sexual identity are separate.

Douvan and Adelson found the adolescent girl very different: While boys rebel, girls remain compliant, continue dependency relationships with their parents, and do not express an intense internal need to break the old familial bonds. While the boy's preoccupation and development of internal standards allowed one to predict his ego strength, only the girl's interpersonal relationships related to her ego strength. In social relations girls are very much more mature than boys. The girl's identity is critically dependent upon the man she marries and the children she has. She perceives her major task as assuring her acceptability as a person who will be loved, a person someone will marry.

The adolescent girls interviewed focused on the interpersonal aspects of their future life, on their roles as wives and mothers. They anticipated their future roles in fantasy, and this imagining allowed a clear concept of their adult femininity and goals. Up until the age of 18 (the oldest girls in this study), girls showed no urge to develop independent beliefs, standards, or controls.

They were compliant, dependent upon authority, and progressing in all areas except those of achievement and moral autonomy. They used authority, especially parental, as a means of controlling their impulses and as a source of self-identity. (You may recall our suggestion that the impulse levels of girls are originally lower than those of boys and necessitate less control while, simultaneously, the culture permits female dependence upon adults for impulse control.) The quality of dependence changes over the years, becoming more rational and sophisticated. Thus the 11-year-old girl says that one obeys parental rules because it is expected and because the rules help kids, but the 18-year-old says that one obeys so as not to worry one's parents or because the rules reflect standards and guidelines for behavior (which, presumably, everyone should agree with).

For the adolescent girl, the interpersonal sphere is pivotal. Her sensitivity and skill in interpersonal relations express her developing eroticism, and her efforts to gain popularity express her erotic needs and her skills in winning and maintaining love. I believe that this takes a competitive form marked by a good deal of achievement motivation—that instead of an academic or vocational achievement goal, the adolescent girl has an affiliative achievement goal. What the boy achieves through separation and autonomy the girl achieves through intimate connections with others because her identity is defined through her attachments to others. Douvan and Adelson found that the girl's vocational identity and her sexual identity were interlaced, her vocational ideas were infused with sexual and sex-role themes, and her goals were closely tied to the objects she identified with. This served to continue her tendency to be dependent, compliant, and conformist. An independent sense of self is not accomplished without severance of old interpersonal ties, without the establishment of internal, individual criteria for achievement, without a sense of identity that is relatively independent of other people.

In a book like this there is an exaggeration of the differences between sexes and a minimizing of the differences within one sex. Obviously not all girls, adolescent or otherwise, are the same in traits or ambitions. In this context it is useful to briefly summarize the different types of female development that Douvan and Adelson found in their study.

Feminine Patterns

1. *Unambivalent, feminine girls.* Most thoroughly focused on the social and personal aspects of reality. These girls gain self-esteem from helping others and being succorant. They show little motivation for personal achievement and prefer security to success; they daydream about popularity, marriage, and family goals. Their educational goals are relatively low. They have a compliant, dependent relationship to their parents.

2. *Ambivalent, feminine girls.* While these girls are also concerned with marriage, motherhood, and social development, they are also interested in personal achievements and individual development. They are interested in jobs and real (versus social) skills. They select as models masculine figures or women who are nonfamily figures. Their family milieu emphasizes autonomy, and their parents encourage self-reliance and independence to a greater extent than the parents of feminine, unambivalent girls.

Nonfeminine Patterns

1. *Achievement-oriented girls.* These girls want to marry, but they do not make marriage and feminine goals central to their future plans. Their ideas about marriage are less detailed and less mature than those of the feminine girls. These girls are less socially developed, less mature in their attitudes about friendship, and less concerned with boys and popularity than the feminine girls. Their relationships with their parents are pleasant.

2. *Boyish girls.* These girls emphasize current interests and boyish activities. They feel important and useful when they are in competitive sports and games. They have a more limited time-perspective and are worried about their current adolescent problems, but they do want to marry ultimately. While their parents are not unduly strict, these girls perceive their parents

as very restrictive. This is felt to be a slow-developing group.

3. *Neutral girls*. These girls are nonfeminine in the sense that their future plans and their current activities are not focused on marriage or feminine roles. The authors also consider this group slow-developing.

4. *Antifeminine girls*. This group includes all the girls in the sample who said they did not want to marry. These girls showed psychological deviance and signs of severe pathology. They have little awareness of their internal selves, have limited fantasy, and give the impression of having constructed a wall about their internal world. They are all from large families and are often the first-born. Their parents tend to be traditional, restrictive, and punitive. All of these girls wish to be boys, and it is probably not accidental that they tend to menstruate later than the other girls.

Girls who scored high on measures of femininity were more explicitly interested in boys and popularity with boys and were preoccupied with thoughts of marriage and family life. Their concepts about marriage were more detailed and sophisticated than other girls. The feminine girl is not passive in the ordinary sense; she is passive only in interpersonal situations and only at the level of overt activity. She is active on a psychological level trying to handle problems and conflicts by absorbing some of these conflicts rather than using aggressive assertion. She has a love of social activity, an extended time-perspective, greater poise and social skill, more sources of self-esteem, and an integrated ego ideal (she can name an adult she would like to be like, while nonfeminine girls tend to reject all adults as models).

Douvan and Adelson found that the most typical pattern of identity formation was that of the unambivalent, feminine girl. In an adolescent girl this is the most functional for her future success as a wife and mother. Since the girl remains tied to others, she never really achieves a strong sense of identity with strong values and criteria, and this allows her to identify with the man she marries and adapt herself to the needs of the marriage relationship.

I have also found the unambivalent, feminine girl to be most typical, and agree that she will function successfully in the marital role, yet I find this a disquieting observation. I think it is dangerous for a woman's sense of worth to be enormously dependent upon her husband's reactions to her and to her contributions to his welfare. As husbands become more and more involved in their vocational efforts, as children grow and go to school and as they need to become independent, the value of the traditional female role declines. The return of women to the work force when children go to school can be a time of crisis. While the middle-class college-educated woman's adolescence is typically preoccupied with questions of feminine interpersonal achievement, she also has a secondary identity component which is related to vocational success. In a very real way, girls achieve identity when they marry and when they have children—but when their most important functions in that role dissolve, they have an identity crisis.

Adherence to the traditional sex-role behaviors is breaking down in the middle class and this is strongly correlated with educational levels. Perhaps the confidence which accrues from being well-educated with a high-status vocation allows one to relax about conforming to other persons' expectations, which would include role expectations. . . . Lower-class mothers encourage sex-typing more vigorously and consistently than middle-class mothers, . . . and the class difference in pressures is greater for girls. . . . The higher the educational level of the parents, the more a daughter is permitted to participate in masculine activities. Middle-class boys, like lower-class children of both sexes, are fairly restricted in sex-appropriate behaviors.

There are other differences which will prove to be important when we look at academic achievement as used for conflict resolution or as the preliminary for vocational success. While the boys of both classes reject the effeminate boy, the middle-class boy accepts the academically studious boy. Both lower- and middle-class girls accept the academically serious girl. But the middle-class girl rejects the girl who displays an early and excessive interest in dating, while the lower-class girl accepts her. The lower-class girl who accepts the traditional sex-role earlier and with more enthusiasm than the middle-class girl is more concerned with dating, with personal attractiveness, and with her feminine success earlier than the middle-class girl. In terms of Douvan and Adelson's typology, I would anticipate that increasing numbers of middle-class girls can be characterized as ambivalent feminine girls or achievement-oriented girls. This is a logical evolution of their histories and does not indicate a rejection of femininity; it is normal and not pathological. To the extent that the girl does not perceive academic or vocational achievements as a route to independence and esteem, she will continue to depend upon the reactions of others to assure her that she is attractive and an object to love, and her personality qualities will conform to the traditional female model.

The feminine girl who is nonetheless achievement-oriented will have anxieties that the less ambitious girl does not have: fear that men may reject her for her intelligence, her competitiveness, or her success; anger over the dominance of men at work and anxiety about the place of women in the home; real conflicts between the demands of family and work upon her time and her psychological energy; ambivalence about when to marry or have children; some possible difficulty in accepting the general responsibilities of the female role; and possible difficulties in shifting from the interpersonal demands of her different roles as wife, mother, and professionally committed worker. She is not a man and she is still vulnerable to being rejected. Fear that she may lose love or guilt that she may fail her family will coexist with ambitions to succeed and fears of failing. . . .

We usually assume that this message comes down from the parents, but we ought not to ignore the fact that the peer-group has enormous influence at this time, . . . and the pressure on the girl comes not only from the parents (whom she may relatively easily reject as "not understanding"), but from her girlfriends. The values of peers are not easily shrugged off. I don't know what it is called in other schools but at the University of Michigan we call it the "senior slump," and it refers to a great increase in the anxiety levels of senior girls who have not become engaged, pinned, or married. Most of the women who go to graduate school tend to express a feeling that not having found a husband their identities are not yet settled, and staying in school rather than working allows them to continue to slowly evolve a sense of self-identity. (It is no wonder that the woman in graduate school who is married tends to do better in academics—she has achieved an acknowledged love relationship, she has settled a sense of identity in terms of the man she married, and he has accepted her abilities and ambitions.) In my interviews with graduate-school students I find many of them consciously rejecting an identification with their mother's traditional sex-role. When I ask them why they are going to graduate school many reply that they have looked at their mothers and at their mothers' lives, and while they do not really know what they want to do, they do not want to spend their lives as their mothers did. It is my impression that the mothers share these views and are in sympathy with their daughters. . . .

Our women tend not to participate fully in activities outside of the traditional spheres. The critical question . . . is whether this is because they are not highly motivated to do so in the first place or because such motives are seen as destructive of their success as women.

NOTES AND REFERENCES

[1] R. R. Sears, E. E. Maccoby, and H. Levin, *Patterns of Child Rearing* (New York: Harper & Row, 1957).

[2] I wonder if we can appreciate to what extent the father's role in rearing his children has changed in a single generation. There is a classic story in my husband's family about a family friend who went so far as to baby-sit with his infant for a few hours while his wife was shopping. When she returned the baby was in the buggy in front of an open window. "Clara," he said, "your baby smells." Contrast that with the suburban ideal in which the father spends most of his free time in the Little League and other child-centered activities. The father who does not take an important share in the rearing of his children, with the assumption that he enjoys it, is now considered abnormal. This reflects the extent to which we have become a child-centered culture. The value of *that* is debatable.

[3] A clinician told me of a meeting at which a breast-feeding mother said, "Sometimes I feel as if the top of me is the baby's and the bottom is my husband's and nothing is left for me at all" (Mary McCaulley, personal communication, 1970).

[4] A follow-up study is in preparation and it will be interesting to see whether significant changes have occurred in these 15 years. Current data on college students do not suggest that the main ideas discussed here have altered significantly. On the other hand, college students seem more aware of role conflicts than my generation was in the 1950s.

Douvan, Elizabeth, and J. Adelson. *The Adolescent Experience.* New York: Wiley, 1966.

Goodenough, E. W. "Interest in Persons as an Aspect of Sex Difference in the Early Years." *Genetic Psychology Monographs,* 55 (1957): 287–323.

Hartley, Ruth E. "Children's Concepts of Male and Female Roles." *Merrill-Palmer Quarterly,* 6 (1960): 153–163.

Kagan, J. "The Concept of Identification." *Psychology Review,* 65 (1958): 296–305.

Lynn, D. B. "The Process of Learning Parental and Sex-Role Identification." *Journal of Marriage and the Family,* 28 (1966): 446–470.

Mussen, P., and E. Rutherford. "Parent-Child Relations and Parental Personality in Relation to Young Children's Sex-Role Preferences." *Child Development,* 34 (1963): 589–607.

Parsons, T. "Social Structure and the Development of Personality: Freud's Contribution to the Integration of Psychology and Sociology." *Psychiatry,* 21 (1958): 321–340.

Rothbart, Mary, and Eleanor E. Maccoby. "Parents' Differential Reactions to Sons and Daughters." *Journal of Personality and Social Psychology,* 4 (1966): 237–243.

Sears, R. R., E. E. Maccoby, and H. Levin. *Patterns of Child Rearing.* New York: Harper & Row, 1957.

Slater, P. E. "Psychological Factors in Role Specialization." Ph.D. dissertation, Harvard University, unpublished, 1955.

Slater, P. E. "Toward a Dualistic Theory of Identification." *Merrill-Palmer Quarterly,* 7 (1961): 113–126.

6

FAMILY STRUCTURE AND SEX ROLE LEARNING BY CHILDREN

Orville G. Brim, Jr.

The structure of a social group, delineated by variables such as size, age, sex, power, and prestige differences, is held to be a primary influence upon the patterns of interaction within the group, determining in major part the degree to which any two group members interact. It is held, second, that social roles are learned through interaction with others, such interaction providing one with the opportunity to practice his own role as well as to take the role of the other. On this basis one may hypothesize that group structure, by influencing the degree of interaction between group members, would be related to the types of roles learned in the group: one would learn most completely those roles which he himself plays, as well as the roles of the others with whom he most frequently interacts. This argument is applied in this paper specifically to the relation between family structure, described in terms of age, sex, and ordinality of children, and the sex role learning by the children.

The process of role learning through interaction, which has been described in detail by Mead (15), Cottrell (2), and others, can be sketched as follows. One learns the behavior appropriate to his position in a group through interaction with others who hold normative beliefs about what his role should be and who are able to reward and punish him for correct and incorrect actions. As part of the same learning process, one acquires expectations of how others in the group will behave. The latter knowledge is indispensable to the actor, in that he must be able to predict what others expect of him, and how they will react to him, in order to guide his own role performance successfully. Accurate or erroneous understanding and prediction are respectively rewarding and punishing to the actor, and learning proceeds systematically

through the elimination of incorrect responses and the strengthening of correct ones.

It has been the distinctive contribution of sociology to demonstrate that learning the role of others occurs through the actor's taking the role of the other, i.e., trying to act as the other would act. While this role-taking of the other can be overt, as with children who actively and dramatically play the role of the parent, it is commonly covert in adults, as with the husband who anticipates what his wife will say when he returns home late, or the employee who tries to foresee his employer's reaction when he asks for a raise.

It follows that, whether taking the role of others is overt or covert, certain responses (belonging to the role of the other) are in fact made, run through, completed, and rewarded if successful, i.e., accurate, and that this process adds to the repertoire of possible actions of a person those actions taken by others in their own roles. Such actions, as part of one's repertoire or pool of learned responses, are available for performance by an actor, not now simply in taking the role of the other, but as resources which he can use as part of his *own* role performances. . . .

Turning now to a consideration of sex-role learning specifically, pertinent reviews (1, 17) of the data show that sex-role prescriptions and actual performance begin early. The accepted position is that children in a family learn their appropriate sex roles primarily from their parents. There is remarkably little data, other than clinical materials, on this topic, perhaps because of its obviousness. . . . Sears, Pintler, and Sears (14) have shown that in families where the father is absent the male child is slower to develop male sex-role traits than in families where the father is present, a finding predictable from the fact that there is no father whose role the child needs to take. Both Sears (13) and Payne and Mussen (12) have shown that father role-playing, identification with the father, and masculinity of attitudes are positively related to the father's being warm, affectionate, and rewarding. This strikes one as the same type of finding as the first, but at the other end of the interaction range; insofar as warm, affectionate, and rewarding fathers interact more with their sons, or are perceived as such because they interact more, it follows that the sons have more experience in taking their role.

In regard to the effects of sibling characteristics upon sex-role learning, there is again almost no information. Fauls and Smith (3) report that only children choose sex-appropriate activities more often than do children with older same-sex siblings, a finding which seems to fit none of our role-learning propositions. While one might hold that the only child has more interaction, because of sibling absence, with his same-sex parent, hence learns his sex role better, one might equally say, especially for the young boys, that it is the cross-sex parent with whom the child interacts and hence the only child should not learn his sex role well. In any case, the finding serves to stress the limitations of the data we are to report, namely, that they pertain to variations within two-child families, and that generalization to families of varying sizes is unwarranted. We return to this point later.

Even with respect to theory concerning the effects of siblings on sex-role learning, we have not noted any systematic predictions in the literature. It seems to us implicit in Parsons' recent analysis (11) of sex-role learning in the nuclear family that when the child begins his differentiation between the father and mother sex roles he would be helped in making the differentiation if he had a cross-sex sibling; this is not formally stated, however, and we may be guilty of misinterpretation.

It is against this background of comparative absence of research and theory on the effects of siblings on sex-role learning that our own report must be viewed. The very valuable data on personality traits of chil-dren presented in recent publications by Helen Koch (4, 5, 6, 7, 8, 9, 10) provide the opportunity to apply several of the general hypotheses set forth above to the substantive area of sibling effects on sex-role learning. The specific application of these hypotheses can be summarized as follows:

First, one would predict that cross-sex, as compared with same-sex, siblings would possess more traits appropriate to the cross-sex role. When taking the role of the other in interaction, cross-sex siblings must take the role of the opposite sex, and the assimilation of roles as delineated above should take place.

Second, one would predict that this effect would be more noticeable for the younger, as compared with the older, sibling in that the latter is more powerful and is more able to differentiate his own from his sibling's role.

Third, on the assumption that siblings close in age interact more than those not close in age, one would predict that this effect would be more noticeable for the siblings who are closest together in age. This is in essence an extension of the first hypothesis to deal with variations in interaction within the cross-sex sibling groups. . . .

With respect to our first hypothesis, that through interaction and taking the role of the other the cross-sex sibs would have more traits of the opposite sex than would same-sex sibs, . . . this is clearly the case. Controlling for ordinality, the older girl with a younger brother has more high masculinity traits and fewer low masculinity traits, than does her counterpart, the older girl with a younger sister. This distribution of traits is even more pronounced for the girls in the second ordinal position, the younger girl with older brother being substantially higher on masculinity than her counterpart with an older sister. One will note that the acquisition of male traits does not seem to reduce the number of feminine traits of the girls with brothers. The more accurate interpretation is that acquisition of such traits adds to their behavioral repertoire, probably with a resultant dilution of their femininity in behavior, but not a displacement. . . .

It holds for boys also. While not pronounced for the boys in the eldest child position, the boy with the sister is feminine to a greater degree than the boy with the brother. For the boys who are second-born, the difference is clear: the boy with the elder sister is substantially more feminine than his counterpart with an older brother. For the boy with the older sister the acquisition of feminine traits would seem to have displaced, rather than simply diluted, his masculinity and he thus contrasts with the girls for whom this did not occur. We can offer no explanation for this, but it may provide a lead for further study in this area.

In connection with this result, the role of the parent requires attention. While all would agree that parents actively assist cross-sex sibs in separating their sex roles, the data show they are unsuccessful in completely arresting the process of assimilation. Perhaps in earlier times, when children's sex roles were stressed more strongly, and perhaps today for some parents making an extreme effort, the effects of interaction would be reduced. However, it certainly appears that the average parent today cannot completely avoid the effects of such sib interaction. Even were more attention given by parents to cross-sex as opposed to same-sex sibs in this matter, we believe that the tremendously greater cross-sex interaction of the former would leave its mark.

With respect to our second hypothesis, that because of differences in control of rewards and punishments and in ability to discriminate between self and other roles the effects of role-taking would be more pronounced for the younger child, an examination . . . seems to support the hypothesis. While the younger, as contrasted with the older, girl with a brother manifests only a slightly greater degree of masculinity, this difference for boys is quite striking: the younger, as contrasted with the older, boy with a sister is substantially more feminine.

With respect to our third hypothesis, that on the assumption of interaction varying inversely with age-gap and greater interaction producing greater role-taking, the effects of role-taking would be largest for the sibs closest in age, the results . . . are neg-

ligible. One might discern some such relationship for the boy with an older sister, and the girl with an older brother, but even here it is tenuous. Because the assumption that interaction varies with sib age differences may in fact be untenable, we cannot in this instance say we have made a direct test of the hypothesis that more frequent interaction produces more role assimilation. Since the first hypothesis, which in essence states the same point, was so strongly confirmed, our inclination is to reject our assumption that interaction varies with age difference, at least to a degree sufficient to produce differences in role-taking. . . .

To conclude, our . . . data indicate that cross-sex siblings tend to assimilate traits of the opposite sex, and that this effect is most pronounced in the younger of the two siblings. These findings support the role-learning theory presented here, and also stand as a substantive contribution to the area of sex-role learning. We wish now to stress two points mentioned earlier.

First, these findings must be subject to strict limitations to two-child families. Not only does the Fauls and Smith study demonstrate this limitation with regard to only-child families, but observation suggests that in larger families other variables come into play; e.g., in the four-child family with a three and one sex split, parents may actively help the solitary child in differentiating sex roles; or in the four-child family with a two and two split, siblings may pair off by sex and the cross-sex role-taking effect is minimized.

Second, with respect to the substantive value of these results, we would point out that even though parents must remain as the major source of sex-role learning, almost every child has a mother and father to learn from. Hence the *variations* in type and amount of sex-role learning occur on top of this base, so to speak, and in this variability the effect of a same or a cross-sex sib may play as large or larger a role than variations in parental behavior, mixed versus single-sexed schooling, sex of neighborhood playmates, and the like. Speculations on the durable and considerable effects of sex of sib on sex-role learning thus seem warranted and lead one to consider problems such as the effect of sex of sibling on one's later role in the marital relation, on career choices, and on other correlates of the adult sex role. . . .

This paper reports some relations between ordinal position, sex of sibling, and sex-role learning by children in two-child families. The findings are based on a further analysis of Helen Koch's data relating personality traits of children to their sex, sex of sibling, ordinal position, and age difference from sibling. In this analysis the personality traits were classified as pertaining either to the instrumental (masculine) role or the expressive (feminine) role. The distribution of such traits in children as a correlate of family structure was then assessed.

General propositions describing role learning in terms of interaction with others, including taking the role of the other, leads to hypotheses that cross-sex siblings will have more traits of the opposite sex than will same-sex siblings, and that this effect will be greater for the younger, as contrasted with the older, sibling. Both hypotheses are confirmed by the data presented.

REFERENCES

1. Brim, O. G., Jr., "The Parent-Child Relation as a Social System: I. Parent and Child Roles," *Child Development*, 1957, 28, 344–364.
2. Cottrell, L. S., Jr., "The Analysis of Situational Fields in Social Psychology," *American Sociological Review*, 1942, 7, 370–382.
3. Fauls, L. B., and W. D. Smith, "Sex Role Learning of Five-Year-Olds," *Journal of Genetic Psychology*, 1956, 89, 105–117.
4. Koch, H. L., "The Relation of 'Primary Mental Abilities' in Five- and Six-Year-Olds to Sex of Child and Characteristics of His Sibling," *Child Development*, 1954, 25, 210–223.
5. Koch, H. L., "Some Personality Correlates of Sex, Sibling Position, and Sex of Sibling Among Five- and Six-Year-Old Children," *Genetic Psychology Monographs*, 1955, 52, 3–50.
6. Koch, H. L., "The Relation of Certain Family Constellation Characteristics and the Attitudes of Children Toward Adults," *Child Development*, 1955, 26, 13–40.
7. Koch, H. L., "Attitudes of Children Toward Their Peers as Related to Certain Characteristics of Their Sibling," *Psychological Monographs*, 1956, 70, No. 19 (whole No. 426).
8. Koch, H. L., "Children's Work Attitudes and Sibling Characteristics," *Child Development*, 1956, 27, 289–310.
9. Koch, H. L., "Sibling Influence on Children's Speech," *Journal of Speech and Hearing Disorders*, 1956, 21, 322–328.
10. Koch, H. L., "Sissiness and Tomboyishness in Relation to Sibling Characteristics," *Journal of Genetic Psychology*, 1956, 88, 231–244.
11. Parsons, T., "Family Structure and the Socialization of the Child," in T. Parsons and R. F. Bales, *Family, Socialization and Interaction Process*, Glencoe, Illinois: Free Press, 1955.
12. Payne, D. E., and P. H. Mussen, "Parent-Child Relations and Father Identification Among Adolescent Boys," *Journal of Abnormal and Social Psychology*, 1956, 52, 359–362.
13. Sears, P. S., "Child-Rearing Factors Related to Playing of Sex-Typed Roles," *American Psychologist*, 1953, 8, 431 (abstract).
14. Sears, R. R., M. H. Pintler, and P. S. Sears, "Effect of Father Separation on Preschool Children's Doll Play Aggression," *Child Development*, 1946, 17, 219–243.
15. Strauss, A., *The Social Psychology of George Herbert Mead*, Chicago: Phoenix Books, University of Chicago Press, 1956.
16. Strodtbeck, F. L., and R. D. Mann, "Sex Role Differentiation in Jury Deliberations," *Sociometry*, 1956, 19, 3–11.
17. Terman, L. M., and L. E. Tyler, "Psychological Sex Differences," in L. Carmichael (ed.), *Manual of Child Psychology* (2d ed.), New York: Wiley, 1954.
18. Zelditch, M., Jr., "Role Differentiation in the Nuclear Family: A Comparative Study," in T. Parsons and R. F. Bales, *Family, Socialization and Interaction Process*, Glencoe, Illinois: Free Press, 1955.

7

SEXUAL BEHAVIOR AMONG PREADOLESCENTS

Carlfred B. Broderick

It is a part of popular belief about the sexual instinct that it is absent in childhood and that it first appears in the period of life known as puberty. This, though a common error, is serious in its consequences and is chiefly due to our ignorance of the fundamental principles of the sexual life.

With this statement in 1905 Freud introduced his essay on Infantile Sexuality (5), and opened the doors to a modern reevaluation of the place of sex in children's development. It is entirely possible that the social historians of the future may view this revolutionary doctrine as the most significant landmark of the sexual renaissance. It challenged both the traditional concept of childhood and the traditional concept of sexuality.

Freud's pivotal portion in the eventual establishment of this point of view did not grow out of his being the first to observe sexuality in children. Others before him, especially medical writers, had challenged the prevailing doctrine of asexual childhood.[1] Freud, however, was the first to develop a systematic theory of human development which included infantile sexuality as an integral element. Moreover, because of the attention which his entire method and theory of psychoanalysis attracted, his views could not be ignored.

Freud's basic contentions could be separated into three main points:

1) Libidinal (sexual) energy is not a product of puberty but a basic life force that manifests itself from birth onwards.

2) The process of channelling this libidinal energy is essentially social rather than merely instinctual. That is, appropriate sexual aims (modes of sexual gratification) and sexual objects are learned.

3) The process of psychosexual development typically involves sequential progress through a series of more or less uniform stages.

The remainder of this paper will address itself to the evaluation of these contentions, first looking more closely at Freud's original observations and then assessing the subsequent research bearing on the validity of the assertions. It should be admitted at the beginning, however, that the sixty years which have intervened since Freud's original essay have not produced as much research as the significance of the subject warrants. Cultural sanctions against sexual investigations of any kind are compounded in the case of children. By cultural definition preadolescents are held to be without sexual interest or capacity, and the investigator is liable at least to ridicule for attempting to find what is not there and at worst to persecution for imperiling the morals of children by putting unnatural ideas into their heads. Ironically, public prejudice has been abetted as a deterrent to research by the too-ready acceptance of Freud's theories by many professionals in the field. As the body of the paper will show, both of these impediments are beginning to yield, and it seems likely that we are on the threshold of a great expansion of research on the process of sexual development in children.

THE SEXUAL RESPONSIVENESS OF CHILDREN

One cannot go far in the literature on children's sexual responsiveness without becoming involved in the question of definitions. What are the criteria of sexuality against which the behavior of children can be evaluated? Opinions range from those of

Freud, who came to accept all pleasure seeking as libidinal by definition, to those more austere authorities who dismiss all prepubertal behavior as nonsexual by definition.

For the present purpose it seems justified to apply the following standards of judgment: behavior will be judged as sexual 1) if it involves the stimulation of one's own or another's genitals for pleasure, or 2) if it involves a response to genital stimulation by one's self or another which in an adult would unambiguously indicate a high level of sexual excitement.

The Psychoanalytic Development of a Theory of Infantile Sexuality

Freud himself came to his theory of infantile sexuality only after a long and painful series of theoretical revisions. His first inkling of the role of sex in childhood came when, in the course of analysis, several of his hysteric patients reported traumatic childhood seductions by adults. He was so struck by the frequency of this report that for four years he maintained that childhood seduction was the principal cause of hysteria. Gradually, however, he came to doubt this interpretation. In the first place, the principal offenders in most of these reported cases were the fathers of his clients, some of whom he knew well enough to find this allegation incredible. Secondly, he could see hysteric symptoms in his own brother and several sisters and he found the idea of his own father performing such a series of seductions unbelievable. Thirdly, about this same time he entered into a period of intense self-analysis and discovered incestuous longings for his mother inside himself. These factors gradually led him to the conclusions that he was dealing principally with children's phantasies rather than adults' depravity. As his chief biographer, Ernest Jones, has put it, ". . . irrespective of incest wishes of parents toward their children, and even of occasional acts of this kind, what he had to concern himself with was the general occurrence of incest wishes of children toward their parents, characteristically toward the parent of the opposite sex" (8, Vol. 1, p. 322).

Thus Freud's initial convictions on the subject of infantile sexuality grew out of his discovery of the Oedipus complex in himself and in several of his patients. Once the basic concept of children's capacity for sexual desire was established in his mind, many other things began to fall into place. For example, he had previously noted that an unexpectedly high proportion of phantasized seductions had involved perverted sexual practice; that is, the child's mouth or anus rather than his genitals were involved. Since Freud had come to believe that all dreams and phantasies were based on the principle of wish fulfillment, this pointed to the oral and anal orifices as major source of childhood erotic satisfaction. From there it was a short step to the reinterpretation of the common observation that young children were indeed more concerned with their mouths and anuses than with their genitals. Thus the concept of erogenous zones developed, and the main elements of Freud's theory of preadolescent development began to fall into place.

That theory will be more fully considered in a later section of the paper. For the present purpose it is enough to note that the first systematic investigation of childhood sexuality consisted of the analysis of adult recall and deductions from adult dreams and phantasies.

The limitations of such techniques of investigation are obvious and, of course, were immediately and legitimately pointed out by critics of psychoanalytic theory. Freud was unperturbed by their criticism, retaining the greatest faith in his methodology. Others, including some of the British analysts, attempted to meet these criticisms by getting data closer to the source through child analysis, but neither Freud nor his critics had much confidence in this approach (8, Vol. 3, pp. 137, 197). It is probable that the impasse could not have been resolved except for the introduction of an entirely independent set of observations: those of the anthropologists.

The Anthropological Evidence

If there is a potential for sexual response in children, surely the best place to observe it would be in a sexually permissive society rather than in a sexually restrictive society such as the society in which Freud practiced. The classic example of this approach, Malinowski's *The Sexual Life of Savages in North Western Melanesia,* was published in 1929 (12). By 1951 Ford and Beach were able, with the help of the Human Relations Area Files, to find data on 32 societies which were permissive in their attitude toward children's sexuality (4).

What type of childhood behavior was found in these permissive societies? The Ford and Beach data seem to indicate two important facts about the development of sexual behavior in children. First, if it is permitted, most boys and girls will progress from absent minded fingering of the genitals in the very early years to systematic masturbation by the age of 6 to 8 (4, p. 195). (Of course it cannot be ascertained how much of this is self discovery and how much of it is peer- or even adult-initiated behavior originally.) Secondly, where children are permitted to watch adult love making, oral-genital and copulatory attempts will be made very early in childhood. Among some groups such as the Trobrianders of Melanesia, the Chewa of Africa, and the Lepcha of India it is common for girls and boys to be active participants in full sex relations several years before puberty and in some cases as early as 6 or 7 years of age (4, pp. 197–8). In these societies, however, it should be noted that there is active instruction in these matters by older members of the group. In any case these anthropological studies seem to have established beyond question the fact that prepubertal children are capable of learning to respond sexually several years prior to puberty.

The Evidence of the Surveyors

The conclusions of anthropologists based on observation in permissive primitive societies have been reinforced in recent years by the finding of sex researchers in our own society. These studies have addressed themselves to at least two different questions: first, what is the actual incidence of the various types of prepubertal sexual behavior in our culture? secondly, what is the innate species-potential for sexual response at early ages?

Sexual Experience. Unfortunately the findings of various researchers on preadolescent sexual behavior do not present a consistent picture. The two best surveys, those of Ramsey (15) and Kinsey and his coworkers (10, 11) are particularly divergent in their findings. This is true despite the fact that Ramsey was an early associate of Kinsey's at the Institute for Sex Research and used an interview similar to Kinsey's in collecting his data. There were some important differences in their samples, however. Ramsey interviewed 291 boys in a middle-sized midwestern city. They were predominantly white, middle class, and Protestant. Kinsey's national sample involved adults primarily including many who were middle-aged and older. It seems probable, therefore, that the differences may be due primarily to three factors: 1) As Kinsey himself observed with respect to his data on preadolescent masturbation "these are minimum data, derived chiefly from the memories of adults, and adults sometimes forget their childhood experiences" (10, p. 501); 2) apart from differential recall there may be real generational differences; and 3) it may be that Ramsey's data were drawn from a community with a particularly precocious group of young boys. This last explanation is consistent with the present writer's observation from his own data that the incidence of such sociosexual behavior as kissing, for example, varies considerably from community to community and from one region to another.[2] . . .

Some boys and girls [seem to be] capable of orgasm at very young ages indeed. Kinsey reports observations of orgasm-like responses[3] in babies of both sexes at 4 or 5 months of age. Of the selected sample on which he has data he reports about one third of the boys were capable of orgasm within the first year and that this proportion increased steadily until it reached 80 percent just before puberty. The sample of girls is much too small to make any general statements about, but the data were consistent with the more systematic observations of the boys.

In addition to these observational data Kinsey cites a number of male and female adults who retrospectively reported their own prepubertal orgasms. All of this falls far short of establishing the proportion of children capable of this experience at various ages, but it does indicate that the capacity for prepubertal orgasm is present in some children, at least.

Together with the anthropological data, the work of the surveyors has probably laid to rest once and for all the theory that preadolescent children are, by definition, asexual. To this extent Freud's first general contention is supported by auxiliary data.

THE PROCESS
OF SEXUAL SOCIALIZATION

Freud conceptualized development toward sexual maturity as a process of differentiation. He viewed the infant as possessed of diffuse libidinal energy which lacked any attachment to specific objects and which was completely unchannelled in its forms of expression. Psychosexual development occurred as biology and society conspired to focus the libido of this "polymorphous pervert" onto a culturally approved sex object and sex aim or mode of gratification (5).

Freud divided preadolescence into three primary stages. Of the first or pre-Oedipal stage (age 0–3), he had to admit that little was actually known (6, p. 188). It was his surmise, however, that two important developmental sequences took place during this period. First the mother typically became differentiated out of the psychic universe as the first libidinal object of both boys and girls. Second the sexual aim gradually shifted from gratification through the infantile alimentary orifices to gratification through the stimulation of the penis and the clitoris.

The intersection of these two developments in the male was held to lead him more or less inexorably into sexual competition with his father in stage 2 (age 4 to 5), the period of the so-called Oedipus complex. In order to escape the consequences of this competition the boy lapsed into the latency period, stage 3 (ages 6–12), repudiating his mother and with her all other females as sexual objects.

In the case of the girl what happened was less clearly developed, but basically it involved a shift to the father as a more adequate sex object than the mother. Freud expressed doubt that girls experienced either the Oedipus complex or latency with the regularity or intensity that boys did (6, 7).

The final step in this process was the move toward adult genital sexuality which was initiated by puberty. The love object now became an extra-familial member of the opposite sex, and the chief sexual aim became full genital intercourse.

Over the years this model of psychosexual development has been criticized from many sources on both empirical and theoretical grounds. Perhaps the two most systematic attacks have come from the learning theorists and from the anthropologists. The learning theorists believe that the whole theory is unnecessarily complex. To them it seems apparent that sex role learning, like any other type of learning, is simply a process of reinforcing socially approved behavior and punishing undesirable behavior. A substantial body of research on sex role learning has grown up, based on this theoretical position.

Anthropologists have also attacked the idea that each of these stages, and particularly the stage of the Oedipal conflict, is necessary to normal personality development. These objections were based on the observation of societies in which a very different pattern of psychosexual development seemed to occur. See for example Malinowski's classic attack on the universality of the Oedipus complex (13). Several more or less successful attempts have been made to integrate these various points of view and it is beyond the scope of this paper to add another to the list. It may be useful, however, to indicate a few of the cardinal principles of heterosexual development for which there is research support and general theoretical agreement. In addition, the findings from an on-going study of the present writer will be introduced where they throw light on the subject under question.

Early Childhood: The Period of Basic Heterosexual Orientation

In simplest terms, it is universally agreed that the foundation for later heterosexual attachments is laid in early childhood in the interactions between the child and his parents. There seem to be three primary conditions for normal heterosexual development. First, the parent or parent-surrogate of the same sex must not be so punishing on the one hand or so weak on the other hand as to make it impossible for the child to identify with him. Second, the parent or parent-surrogate of the opposite sex must not be so seductive, or so punishing, or so emotionally erratic as to make it impossible for the child to trust members of the opposite sex. Third, the parents or parent-surrogates must not systematically reject the child's biological sex and attempt to teach him cross-sex role behavior. A number of studies and clinical reports support these generalizations. There is not sufficient space to do an adequate review of the literature here. Kagan's recent summary of the effects of various family patterns on sex role identification does a good job of reviewing the studies based on normal populations (9). The literature on homosexuality is still divided on the question of causes. Increasingly, however, the central significance of the family as a factor in the etiology of homosexuality is being accepted. For a good current review representing this point of view see Bieber (2).

A fourth factor in normal heterosexual development is the necessity of establishing a positive conception of marriage as an eventual goal. Data from a current study of sociosexual development in children have led the present writer to conclude that the significance of this factor has been underestimated in previous explanations of the mechanisms of heterosexual socialization. Long before most children have any concept of the nature of adult coital sexuality (much less any commitment to it as a sexual aim) they have begun to accept the inevitability and desirability of the heterosexual marital arrangement.

These unpublished data show that five-year-olds have a good idea of the field of eligibles from which they must select an eventual mate (cross-sex peers of the same generation but not of the same family). They are also aware of most of the non-coital content of the marital relationship. But more to the point, the majority of them are already committed to their own eventual marriage. This majority increases at each age throughout childhood. The significance of this positive attitude toward marriage is underscored by the findings that achievement of this attitude seems to be almost a prerequisite to further heterosexual progress during the next stage of development.

Middle Childhood: The Period of Transition

It seems probable that there has been more confusion over the course of heterosexual socialization during the period of middle childhood than during any other period. Freud and the great majority of subsequent writers have referred to this stage as a period of sexual latency. Many have viewed it as a step backward away from heterosexuality into a haven of monosexual attachments and interactions. We have already seen however that both the anthropologists and the surveyors have produced evidence that this is not a sexually stagnant period, and data from the present writer's study indicate that a great deal of significant progress toward eventual full-fledged heterosexuality takes place during these years.[4]

The data were taken from questionnaires administered to all 10- and 11-year-olds attending fifth and sixth grades in ten elementary schools throughout central Pennsylvania. Urban, suburban, and rural schools were included and the full range of social classes was involved. The full report of the analysis is still in manuscript form but the results can be summarized here.

The most significant finding was that progress toward heterosexuality appears to be achieved in a series of steps, with achievement at one level preparing the way for the next. As indicated in the previous section the foundation of subsequent progress seems to be one's attitude toward his own eventual marriage. Next came an emotional attachment to a member of the opposite sex as evidenced by reporting having a special girlfriend (or a boyfriend if it was a girl). The next step was to confess having been in love. After that came an expression of preference for a cross-sex companion rather than a same sex companion when going to a movie. And finally the most advanced step for these preadolescents was actually going out on a date.

Each step, of course, is not an absolute prerequisite to the other, but the nature of the relationships can be indicated by the following sets of comparisons: 74 percent of those who wanted to get married some day reported a boyfriend or girlfriend, but only 34 percent of the others did; 66 percent of those who reported having a girlfriend or boyfriend also reported having been in love, but only 19 percent of the others did so; 43 percent of those who had been in love said they would prefer a cross-sex companion at the movies but only 21 percent of the others expressed this preference; and finally 32 percent of those who would prefer a companion of the opposite sex had actually gone out on a date, while only 11 percent of the others had done so.

Each of these differences was significant beyond the .05 level when tested by chi-square and the entire series met the criteria of a Guttman scale.[5]

It may be true that these specific items are not of any great theoretical significance in and of themselves, and that a similar list of different items could be developed which would represent the process of heterosexual socialization equally well. The significant point is that middle childhood is actually a period of great importance in the process of becoming a fully heterosexual adult. It seems logical to assume that the steps typical of this period build upon the experiences of early childhood and in turn determine the course of development during adolescence.

SUMMARY AND DISCUSSION

The sexual behavior of preadolescents first became an area of systematic scientific interest when Freud published his theory of infantile sexuality sixty years ago. Since then the amount of research done has not been very great but such data as there are support at least the major points of Freud's original observations.

There is still a great deal of uncertainty as to the actual incidence of various sexual behaviors among children, but it would seem to be conclusively demonstrated that many children are capable of sexual arousal and even orgasm from a very early age.

Data on the process of sexual socialization are even more scarce than those on sexual behavior. Various aspects of the particular developmental sequence which Freud postulated have been seriously challenged. Nevertheless his main contention, that normal heterosexual development is determined by a child's familial relationships and social experiences rather than by simple biological factors, seems to be borne out by the available data. Before much progress can be made in specifying the precise stages and critical points in development, longitudinal research will have to be designed to plot the process.

Whatever the course of future research in this area, however, enough is already established to make it unlikely that the conceptualization of sex or of childhood will ever revert to its pre-Freudian state. This observation leads us to challenge, in the last analysis, the accuracy of the title of this issue of the *Journal*. Implicit in the phrase "sexual renaissance" is the notion that we are experiencing a rebirth of what was once before. It suggests that this new era of understanding and openness with respect to sex is not really new, but only seems so because it is separated from an earlier edition of itself by an intervening period of great sexual prudery and repression.

It is doubtful whether this point of view is valid for any aspect of sexual behavior but it is certainly an inadequate interpretation of the historical facts about views of childhood sexuality. It is true that in the 13th to 16th centuries records indicate that children were not sheltered from sexual information and stimulation as they have been since the 17th century Reformation, but it is not true that this carefree attitude was evidence of the acceptance of preadolescent sexuality—quite the opposite. As Philippe Ariés has written in his *Centuries of Childhood:*

> . . . *gestures and physical contacts were freely and publicly allowed which were forbidden as soon as the child reached the age of puberty, or in other words was practically adult. There were two reasons for this. In the first place the child under the age of puberty was believed to be unaware of or indifferent to sex. Thus gestures and allusions had no meaning for him; they became purely gratuitous and lost their sexual significance. Secondly, the idea did not yet exist that references to sexual matters, even when virtually devoid of dubious meanings, could soil childish innocence, either in fact or in the opinion people had of it: nobody thought this innocence really existed.* (1, p. 106)

The modern view of childhood sexuality is, as far as this author has been able to determine, unique in the history of Western civilization. In contrast to the conceptualizations of any previous century it assumes the capacity of children to experience sexual sensations and emotions and to learn attitudes and behavior patterns with respect to sex. It changes fundamentally the range of questions which society must ask itself concerning the upbringing of children. Formerly one might ask: "At what age should a parent first begin trying to mold the child's ideas about sex?" It is clear that the appropriate question is rather "How shall a parent best deal with the sexual experiences and potentials at each age?" Formerly one might ask "How can a parent protect his child from the intrusion of sexuality until he is old enough to handle it?" Today one might better ask "How can a parent help his child to understand and manage his own sexual nature from infancy onward?" Whatever one's value position, from the most permissive to the most restrictive, the question can never again be "Whether?" or "When?" but rather "How?"

In the matter of attitudes toward the sexual nature of children we are dealing, it seems to me, not with a renaissance, but with a revolution.

NOTES AND REFERENCES

[1] It is not the purpose of the present paper to trace the history of this idea in any great detail. For such treatment see Albert Moll's early (1912) but comprehensive review of the subject (14). For a more recent review giving additional references see William Reevy's article in *The Encyclopedia of Sexual Behavior* (16).

[2] Compare kissing data in Broderick, Carlfred B., and Fowler, Stanley E. "New Patterns of Relationships Between the Sexes Among Preadolescents." *Marriage and Family Living*, 1961, 23, 27–30, based on a middle class white Georgia sample of preadolescents, with the data on various groups of Pennsylvania children reported in Broderick, Carlfred B. "Social Heterosexual Development Among Urban Negroes and Whites." *Journal of Marriage and the Family*, 1965, 27, 200–4, and "Socio-Sexual Development in a Suburban Community." *Journal of Sex Research*, 1966, 2, 1–24.

[3] "The orgasm in an infant or other young male is, except for the lack of ejaculation, a striking duplicate of orgasm in an older adult . . . [T]he behavior involves a series of gradual physiologic changes, the development of rhythmic body movements with distinct penis throbs and pelvic thrusts, an obvious change in sensory capacities, a final tension of muscles, especially of the abdomen, hips, and back, a sudden release with convulsions, including rhythmic anal contractions—followed by the disappearance of all symptoms." (10, p. 177). A similar clinical description of orgasm in a female infant can be found in the Kinsey Female volume (11, p. 104).

[4] The fullest development of the relevant data from the present writer's study is a manuscript, Broderick, Carlfred B. "A Scale of Preadolescent Heterosexuality" which will probably appear in print next year. For a list of published reports on this project see footnote 2.

[5] Ibid.

1. Ariés, Philippe. *Centuries of Childhood: A Social History of Family Life*. (Robert Baldick, translator), New York: Alfred A. Knopf, 1962.

2. Bieber, Irving. "Clinical Aspects of Male Homosexuality." In *Sexual Inversion* (Judd Marmor, Ed.). New York: Basic Books, 1965.

3. Ellis, Havelock. *Studies in the Psychology of Sex*. New York: Random House, 1942. 2 vol. (Original in 1905).

4. Ford, Cellan S., and Beach, Frank A. *Patterns of Sexual Behavior*. New York: Harper & Brothers, 1951.

5. Freud, Sigmund. "Three Contributions to the Theory of Sex." In *The Basic Writings of Sigmund Freud* (A. A. Brill, Ed.). New York: The Modern Library, 1938 (Original in 1905).

6. ———. "Some Psychological Consequences of the Anatomical Distinction Between the Sexes." In *Collected Papers* (James Strachey, Ed.). New York: Basic Books, 1959 (Original in 1925), Vol. 5, 186–197.

7. ———. "Female Sexuality." In *Collected Papers* (James Strachey, Ed.). New York: Basic Books, 1959 (Original in 1931), Vol. 5, 252–272.

8. Jones, Ernest. *The Life and Works of Sigmund Freud*. New York: Basic Books, 1953. 3 vol.

9. Kagan, Jerome. "Acquisition and Significance of Sex Typing and Sex Role." In *Child Development Research: Vol. I*. (Martin L. Hoffman and Lois W. Hoffman, Eds.) New York: Russell Sage Foundation, 1964, pp. 137–167.

10. Kinsey, Alfred C. et al. *Sexual Behavior in the Human Male*. Philadelphia: W. B. Saunders, 1948.

11. ———. *Sexual Behavior in the Human Female*. Philadelphia: W. B. Saunders, 1953.

12. Malinowski, Bronislaw. *The Sexual Life of Savages in North-Western Melanesia*. New York: Harcourt, Brace, & World, 1929.

13. ———. *Sex and Repression in Savage Society*. New York: The World Publishing Co., 1955 (Original in 1927).

14. Moll, Albert. *The Sexual Life of the Child*. New York: Macmillan, 1923 (Original in 1912).

15. Ramsey, Glenn V. "The Sexual Development of Boys." *American Journal of Psychology*, 1943, 56, 217–233.

16. Reevy, William R. "Child Sexuality." In *The Encyclopedia of Sexual Behavior* (Albert Ellis and Albert Abarbanel, Eds.), New York: Hawthorn Books, 1961, Vol. 1, 258–267.

8

HELPING CHILDREN GROW UP SEXUALLY: HOW? WHEN? BY WHOM?

Eleanore Braun Luckey

Today many parents who themselves were reared by mothers and fathers afraid to educate their children in sexual matters are now afraid *not* to educate their own children regarding sex. Social pressures on young people different from the kind they experienced when young, prevalent attitudes toward sex that reflect a changing value system in society as a whole, and behavior among many young people that they do not understand have left today's parents perplexed and anxious. As a result they are eagerly seeking help for themselves and for their children, whom they want to achieve "normal sexual maturity."

Community agencies, youth organizations, churches, and schools are all scurrying to initiate programs of sex education—sometimes called family life education, boy-girl relationships, or interpersonal development. Inservice training programs, workshops, and institutes are being organized for nurses, social workers, clergymen, teachers, counselors, health educators, community youth leaders, and parents. After a long period of being treated with silence or half-truths, blushes, and snickers, the subject of sex can openly be talked about in "respectable" society. Young people's attitudes and behavior toward the opposite sex—and the consequences—are the subject of serious concern not just to adolescents and their parents but also to persons in the teaching and helping professions.

Nevertheless, the goals of sex education are not altogether clear. Nor is it clear just whose responsibility it is to give sex information to children and adolescents and to try to shape the attitudes that determine their moral values and sexual behavior. Dealing with the sexual problems of young people is especially difficult for adults brought up in a society confused about sex, one that has been filled with sexual stimuli and at the same time with harsh taboos against sexual expression. Social scientists are not surprised that the combination of stimulation and repression has resulted in a demand for a "better way" of dealing with sex.

In response to the demand, persons who work professionally with children, adolescents, and parents are seeking *the* way (if there is *one*) or *a* way (if there are *many*) to help children grow toward "sexual maturity." This goal in itself is difficult to define, and to chart a course leading to its achievement is even more challenging.

Sexual behavior among men and women and sexuality as it is manifested in masculinity and femininity vary from culture to culture. Anthropologists tell us that there is no sexual practice that has been universally sanctioned or prohibited; even incest, the sexual behavior that comes nearest to being universally tabooed, has been approved in some societies in some periods of history.

In any culture, what is "normal" depends upon the practices of the majority. Many behavior patterns that are quite objectionable in our society are sanctioned in others; for example, homosexual practices, sexual relationships between children, premarital sexual promiscuity, and wife swapping and borrowing are approved forms of behavior in some societies. It is not possible to speak of what is or is not "normal" unless we specify the society to which we refer. . . .

Even in this country alone the wide range of sexual behavior and values existing today make "the norm" impossible to define. At one extreme are those people who advocate complete sexual freedom amounting to anarchy; at the other extreme are those who condone the use of sex only for reproduction. Between these extremes lies immense variation in attitude and practice.

For example, chastity before marriage is held to be a supreme value; it is considered "a good thing"; it is thought not to be very important; it is valued not at all; it is considered a poor thing. Masturbation is valued as a means of releasing sexual tension; it is considered an acceptable adolescent pastime; it is thought to be a shameful practice or a sin. Marital practices vary: there is no consensus on how frequently coitus should take place, nor on the appropriate position, nor on the amount or kind of foreplay that is acceptable. Most social scientists agree that it would be difficult if not impossible to define the norm of sexual behavior in contemporary American society. Even if such a norm could be defined, the definition would be meaningless, for sexual expression is a highly individual matter, an integral part of the total personality.

Sexual maturity rather than sexual normality may be a better goal for sex education. Even so, we must make assumptions that cannot be validated about the nature of man and the patterns of his maturing. By careful measurement and observation we have learned a great deal about the physical growth and development of boys and girls; we know about many of the factors that contribute to or detract from soundness and roundness of body; we have been able to trace general developmental patterns from the prenatal period to maturity and then to decadence. Intellectual growth has been more difficult to discover and predict in a sequential pattern, but in general we know a good deal about such aspects of growth as language development, concept development, learning, and creativity.

What we know of emotional growth is still largely theory or educated guesses; and social patterns that propel a child on to becoming a socially mature adult are known to vary from generation to generation. Even so, through keen observation, crude but persistent evaluation, and creative speculation, we can draw at least some tentative conclusions about the emotional and social development of the human being.

When we realize that sexual growth includes factors that are physical, intellectual, emotional, and social, it becomes clear that with the incompleteness of our knowledge it is impossible to trace a sequential pattern of sexual development and to predict maturity with any degree of precision. This is a task to be explored by scientific research. We cannot wait for the results, however, to define our social goals in broad terms and to plan the practical steps toward their achievement. . . .

As with other social goals, the consideration of educational goals requires two foci: the individual and the group in which he lives. Managing these two compatibly is a constant challenge for a democratic society. It is a greater challenge today than ever before, for in our rapidly changing society young people are demanding greater freedom in individual behavior than in any previous generation.

Our society has not yet provided an adequate way of caring for children born out of wedlock; it is therefore desirable today to discourage out-of-wedlock births. This is one social goal on which we can secure a great deal of agreement. Another is the elimination of venereal disease. So far, we have found no medically satisfactory way of preventing venereal infection. Both of these goals are served when premarital, promiscuous intercourse is avoided. Thus, at this point in our social development, it is reasonable to want to restrict premarital coitus.

However, with the increased effectiveness and availability of contraceptives and with the possible future development of immunizations against venereal diseases, the social consequences of promiscuous premarital sexual relationships will change. Insofar as morality is based on social consequences, when the consequences change the moral values change. What is immoral in today's society may be moral in tomorrow's. And what is right for today's generation of young people may be wrong for a generation to come.

One way to avoid getting hopelessly involved in dilemmas is to go beyond what is presently called "sexual morality" to a broader concept of morality, one based on the use of self and one's personal freedom for the benefit of others.

Broader definitions of goals are appropriate, too, in considering the individual's personal growth and satisfaction. Here the goal is not only a sexually fulfilled person but also one who accepts and values his total self—a person who understands himself, his behavior, and his value system and who has the integrity to defend his principles. The ultimate goal is a person who can communicate with others without fear, who can reveal himself, and who can listen to and be concerned about the welfare of others.

Sexuality can never be separated from personality, nor can sexual morality be separated from social morality. For this reason the term "sex education" tends to be misleading. By emphasizing sex it pulls the subject out of a total context. Unfortunately, our culture has for a long time treated a sexual relationship as a special and separate part of personal and social relationships rather than a normal, natural use of self in relating meaningfully to a person of the opposite sex.

Now, because of the need to provide information, to correct misconceptions, and to break the spell of silence, it will be hard for any program of sex education to avoid further isolating and emphasizing the sexual components of personality and interpersonal relationships. Nevertheless, the real goal of any program must be to help in the total development of young people so that they will become the kind of secure persons described above. If we can achieve this goal, we will not have to worry about sexual behavior. . . .

The questions of *how* and *when* are better dealt with together, because, except for always giving children frank, honest answers and explanations, the most important point about sex education is to provide the information in a normal context. Sexual matters need to be dealt with as the natural part of a total picture, whatever that picture may be. When children are curious about their own bodies—hands, feet, elbows, and "tummies"—they are also interested in their genitals and need to know proper terms for them. When children are interested in what happens to food in the human body and in why and how we breathe, they are also interested in the excretory functions and need proper explanations about them.

Most of a child's early questions about sex are occasioned by exposure to a situation that is new to him. He sees an adult body and notes that it is different from his own; he wants to know more about it. He sees a child of the other sex and notes that the genitals are different; he wants an explanation. He sees a pregnant woman and wants to know why her stomach is swollen, and he also may want to know how this came about. The child usually brings these questions to his mother because they occur to him before he reaches school age.

The way in which these early questions are answered largely determines what other questions the child will ask, how he will feel about asking them, and how he will feel about the answers. A parent reveals his own feelings about sex through common, everyday events in many ways. His attitudes will be regarded by his child as those of all adults, so that what questions the child asks or does not ask the teacher at school depend a great deal on the kind of reception they would get if asked at home.

In the school the teacher has continuous opportunities to answer questions bearing on sex that come up in the ordinary events of the day and in the content of every subject. From kindergarten through 12th grade, the child can be encouraged to develop a normal progression of interest in and an increasing body of information about family relationships and sex differences and functions and, in doing so, to form values and make decisions about behavior. In the elementary grades imparting information about animal and human reproduction is becoming a routine part of instruction. However, helping children understand their own developing masculinity or femininity is more difficult for the teacher because it involves a personal concept that can be discussed more naturally in the home than in the schoolroom; nonetheless, much thought about the meaning to oneself of one's sex can be stimulated at school through units in self-understanding and personality growth.

Many persons believe that the school has

a better opportunity than the home to present the child with *information* regarding sex. This is partly true, at least, because teachers tend to be more knowledgeable than many parents about physiology, anatomy, health, psychology, and social problems. It is true, also, because as the child progresses through the grades the teaching becomes concentrated into subject areas, many of which relate specifically to sex and reproduction, to social-sexual-psychological development, and to social problems and health. Thus information about sex is not only a normal part of the subject matter in junior and senior high schools but is also an integral part that has to be conspicuously avoided if it is *not* to be included.

Every school subject, even one not directly concerned with sex information, has its contribution to make in helping children and young people understand interpersonal relationships, familial roles, and the relation of one's sex to these. Literature, music, art, history, and the social sciences especially offer such opportunities.

The home and the school are not alone in having opportunities to help the child develop a mature understanding of sex. Groups such as the Boy Scouts, Boys' Clubs, Girl Scouts, Girls Clubs, Camp Fire Girls, Young Men's Christian Associations, Young Women's Christian Association, and 4-H Clubs are dedicated to helping young people develop healthy bodies and well-rounded personalities. Most of these organizations work informally with adolescents or pre-adolescents in small groups over a span of a few years. They offer the young person an excellent opportunity to develop a self-confident personality, including an acceptance of his sexual identity; they also offer him practice in forming intimate, meaningful relationships with others, both of his own and the opposite sex. The sexual aspects of interpersonal relationships become especially important during adolescence when cultural expectation pushes young people toward dating, and their own heightened sex drive urges them toward exploration.

It is not possible to give information without at the same time conveying attitudes, and the attitudes of adults determine the values of the young, which in turn determine their behavior. The values that young people hold are those that have been demonstrated by the persons they respect.

The churches, of course, are specifically concerned with the values in our society and more than any other institution except the home are expected to take responsibility for the development of attitudes in keeping with their religious and moral precepts. However, such value positions are only meaningful to young people if they are clearly enunciated and are demonstrated as useful in today's society.

Perhaps the most consistent informers about adult attitudes and builders of young people's ideals today are not the traditional institutions that purposefully outline and pursue programs or policies of education but rather the mass media of communication: the television that the child watches from the time he is too small to respond to much more than the movement and the sound to the time he is able to sit for several hours absorbed in its entertainment programs and its advertisements that use sexual appeal to sell products; the magazine illustrations, the comic strips, the paperback book covers, the films that make the sparsely clad body a common sight and the seductive female or male an appealing personality. The child exists so constantly in the midst of these stimuli that as his own understanding grows they become increasingly meaningful to him. This is sex education in the context of commercialism, of entertainment, and the message it conveys, while often indirect, is powerful.

All these agencies of society—the home, the school, the community agency, the church, the mass media—bring their messages to the child in one way or another almost from infancy. Some of the messages are direct, some are subtle; they are seen, heard, felt. Some of them are quiet, some loud; some are conspicuous chiefly because of their absence. Some are true; some, half-true; some, false. Altogether they are very inconsistent. As a result our children come to adolescence confused, curious, and often determined to find out on their own.

If the adults who touch the lives of children could determine what their own values are, if they could know beyond question why they hold these values, and if they could demonstrate them in their daily living, children would get their message. If adults themselves could put sexual matters into the normal context of living, young people would be better able to do the same. The ultimate problem for adults is not so much how to educate children and adolescents as how to work out their own problems and how to convey their attitudes to the young people whose lives they influence. That adults who are significant for them do not readily have all the solutions will not distress the children nearly so much as people seem to think. Children will not feel confused about seeking many of their own answers to the problems of interpersonal, intersexual relations if they realize that adults too are honestly seeking solutions. . . .

Who it is that is responsible for sex education becomes clearer when we recognize that sex education is a segment of an individual's total preparation for living in a complex world of interrelatedness, and that information and attitudes specifically regarding sex are normal parts of knowledge and of a social value structure. Every adult who deals with children or adolescents in any way is likely at some time or another, in some way, to influence significantly the attitudes that help determine how a child will use himself—sexually as well as in other ways—in relation to other people.

Because most adults today have not had

the advantage of growing up in a society in which the kind of sex education advocated here was available, many adults find it difficult to deal with their own attitudes and to communicate them in an open way to children and adolescents. Some adults, however, are able to do this better than others, and those who *can*, must! The opportunity that adults have to do so will largely be determined by their role in relation to the young. The parent has the longest and most intense relationship with the child and so the greatest opportunity; the teacher, the school nurse, the school counselor, and the principal each has significant opportunities from time to time, as does the youth leader, the clergyman, and the religious educator. So, too, does the advertising man, the sales manager, the editor, the journalist, the filmmaker, the television or radio director. . . .

Helping children grow into sexual maturity is not easy for a generation of adults who have grown up in a society frightened of sex. It can only be done by breaking through the silence and half-truths that have obscured their own knowledge and feeling and by establishing a broader objective than mere "sex education." This means striving for the development of the whole personality, for producing a man or woman able to feel genuine concern for the welfare of others, eager and able to establish intimate relationships with others, desirous of parenthood, and capable of assuming the responsibility of his own freedom.

Part Three

The Turnabout Years:
Ages Ten
to Seventeen

Eleven-year-olds are generally quite concerned about their sexual identity and about family-life problems, and typically ask such questions as why there are so many sperm cells and just one egg, if people have sex just to make babies, what contraception is, how a person knows if she can have babies when she grows up, why parents get divorced, at what age it is all right to get married, and how a person knows he or she is in love. It is clear that by the age of ten or eleven children know enough to ask intelligent questions about reproduction, parenthood, marriage, love, and sexuality. Their curiosity about their bodies and about each other is the forerunner of the heightened interest that accompanies the onset of puberty and adolescent development.

The years that begin when a child reaches ten are significant ones in relation to the continued growth and understanding of his or her sexual identity. With puberty comes increasing biological and environmental stress accompanied by emotional changes and role shifts. The young person finds that, although his or her biological sex is only one part of total personality, society uses this index to influence what is expected in the way of behavior, education, friends, dress, and emotional expression. Because of society's demands, a person's sexual identity may be the single most important factor in influencing his or her life-style.

In an attempt to understand the development of sexual identity, the reader is encouraged to reflect on the years in his or her own life labeled the "turnabout" years, which mark the time when a person is making the transition from childhood to adulthood. The turnabout years are marked by physiological changes and by a degree of uncertainty about what behavior is expected. During this period, the individual searches for ways to integrate his or her new sexual maturity into a unique life-style so as not significantly to disrupt continuity of identity. Their attempt to retain identity while incorporating the new elements of sexuality into the system is one reason why adolescents form strong peer attachments during this period. In order to resolve the conflicts of values that arise, they seek comfort from friends and from "conforming" to other adolescents. "Puppy love," as the relationship between teenagers is labeled by many, may not be the sexually oriented relationship so many parents fear, but instead is often an exaggerated identification with another young person who gives intimacy and an opportunity to try on the new sexual self-image. Hence, it may be more social and psychological than sexual. To be sure, the change in sexual identity prompts the need for a close relationship, but such a need is more complex than one determined solely by sexual urges.

The first three readings in Part Three explore the effects of the anatomical, physiological, and emotional changes—and the individual's adjustments to them—in terms of their implications for setting patterns for sex-role identification during this period as well as later. In the first selection, Morton Eisenberg points out the fact that the turnabout years mark the end of childhood, thus producing special problems for the adolescent, who is moving into a period of his or her life which will not be as familiar and as well supported by parents. Furthermore, the so-called generation gap makes communication and understanding more difficult between children and their parents, and the support which parents previously gave to the child now may seem irrelevant in its content to the young person. The adolescent feels more alone than he or she has ever felt and turns rather automatically to the peer group for support. Since the search for identity continues, the kinds of influences peers exert on each other during these years are of paramount importance to the values that are formed and in the development of the total personality. The kind of adult man or woman, sex partner, husband or wife, and parent each person ultimately becomes has strong roots in the impact of the social and biological forces at work in these years. According to Eisenberg, most young people will achieve a stable sense of adult identity. Nevertheless, the inability of

many people to adjust to adult roles can often be directly traced to faulty coping in the turnabout years.

The second and third selections focus on the physical changes of the young person and the psychological implications of such changes. Ellen Rothchild concentrates on the girl's feminine identity and discusses the problems involved in adjusting to pubertal changes. Bodily changes are obvious signs that childhood is in the past and that a new emotional identity is developing to accompany the new physical identity. Donald Weatherley reports on research on early and late maturing males and emphasizes that pubertal onset is a crucial turning point for personality functioning. Both articles emphasize the importance of a young person's body image to his or her conception of how he or she appears to others and to his or her behavior toward others. The body image is closely tied to the individual's feelings of self-worth, to his or her goals in life, and to the ability to relate easily to peers. It is perhaps true that the way persons view themselves is more important in determining behavior than is the way they actually look.

Adults often find it hard to understand the way adolescents regard themselves physically. Teen-agers often complain about their size, weight, facial features, bone structure, and coloring. Some are even disturbed if they are too attractive, and a girl may be self-conscious about an unusually well-developed bosom which attracts more attention than she can comfortably cope with. Part of the reason for the adolescent's self-consciousness about appearance is that, since sexual development accompanies the physical growth, he or she has difficulty separating these changes. Similarly, sexual development becomes completely associated with the concept of being male or female for most young people, and sexual urges are linked to personality and self-worth. Consequently, self-consciousness is common, as the young person becomes acutely and sometimes painfully aware of his or her emerging identity.

The fourth article, by Gertrude Couch,

explores some of the questions that young people are concerned about as a result of the developmental changes they are undergoing. She reports the results of a conference in which young people and adults discussed questions of growth and development relating to sexual maturation and sex behavior. The questions reflect the social and cultural pressures young people feel and the search—that is so much a part of this age—for a meaningful way to integrate sexual maturing into larger value systems.

In the fifth article, on the shift in boy-girl relationships, Carlfred Broderick and Jean Weaver show that the male-female relationship itself increasingly becomes the focus of heterosexual social contacts during the adolescent years. Romanticism begins to be a central theme in communication between the sexes and, as this happens, social confidence seems to suffer. The authors de-emphasize the Freudian concept of a latency period which suddenly gives way to a full-blown new interest in the opposite sex; instead they feel that there is simply a change in the kind of interest which boys and girls feel for each other. Younger children have romantic fantasies, but the boy-girl relationship itself is not the focus of such fantasies, as it is in adolescent years. Hostile, exploitative, and noninteractional responses gradually decrease during adolescence, as the individual turns instead to interest in romantic relationships. Gradually, the child who has been cared for by parents becomes the young adult who can care for a member of the opposite sex. The emotional maturity to give and receive this kind of love indicates the beginning of over-all maturity. The young person who has successfully passed through the turnabout years is now ready to search for his or her adult identity and to achieve intimacy, love, and eventually marriage and responsibility for the next generation. Of course, not all individuals are well prepared by their adolescence for adulthood; also, many young people go immediately into marriage and child rearing without having successfully completed adolescence. No doubt, the reason that many teen-age marriages end in divorce is that the individuals hurried the steps to maturity.

The last article in this section, by Evelyn Duvall, explores adolescent love relationships in terms of the often acute adolescent need for closeness. Although some early love affairs result in enduring marriages, a great number of such affairs seem to be premature involvements that result in immature marriages. Duvall suggests that only when the individual has begun to have a strong and well-formed sense of identity can he or she cope with intimacy and love. One who is not yet sure of his or her own identity is not developmentally ready for an enduring, unselfish close relationship; such an individual may instead demand more from his or her partner than he or she is willing to give in return.

9

SEXUALITY AND ITS IMPLICATIONS FOR PERSONAL IDENTITY AND FULFILLMENT

Morton S. Eisenberg

The life situations in which a young person can experiment toward becoming an adult, as well as the totality of childhood experiences that shape his destiny, differ widely from individual to individual, and from one part of our society to another. All these factors will influence adolescence in the form of its expression. Nevertheless, the broad interaction between the biological, the psychological, and the social aspects of adolescence—for that is my frame of reference—has general application.

I shall not attempt to establish an ethic of sexual behavior. Psychology and sociology can only study morality; they cannot decide what society ought to consider as "good" or "bad" behavior. Although investigation of morality does influence such decisions, it does not arbitrate them. The fact that sexual morality can be a subject for discussion in such an open public forum as this, is in itself indicative of the change that has occurred in our attitude toward sexuality. When many of us were adolescents such a discussion as this would have been inconceivable, or at least shocking. It would be no less absurd to label this event antimoral than it would be to assume that adolescent sexual behavior and the changing social code of the youth of our society is anti-moral—but I will have more to say about this shortly.

We are hindered in our efforts to gain some perspective on this subject because it is overcast with an intensity of emotion and confusion that is the usual consequence of the collision between the older generation and the younger generation. It is a collision that has its roots in the complex changes that take place when our children reach this stage of transition between childhood and adulthood.

In primitive societies, with the onset of puberty, young boys or girls were conducted with elaborate "rites of passage" into adulthood. Their predetermined roles of wife, mother, husband, hunter, warrior, worker, were assumed with little delay. In different historical eras, e.g., before the industrial revolution and even through the first part of our own century, when the speed of change was slower, young people gradually assumed commitment to the responsibilities of adulthood—work, marirage, and children, within the supportive confines of a larger family unit wherein the experience of the several generations was similar.

Today it is even impossible for parents to help their children with third grade arithmetic. Under these earlier conditions, the uncertainties, conflicts, and fears preliminary to an adolescent's development of an adult sense of personal identity, were seldom present.

On the other hand, in our rapidly changing society where occupational choice requires lengthy preparation, where social role is uncertain, and commitment to a sexual mate is deferred, the young boy and girl must set forth from the familiar and relatively comfortable shores of their childhood into a land that is new and strange. The contours of this strange land are constantly in flux—beset by forces acting upon it from many directions. The most decisive of these forces is the result of advancing biological maturity. The awakening of the endocrine system, an event predetermined by an innate genetic timetable, will within a few years transform the body of the young boy and girl into that of a sexually mature man and woman.

These biological changes bring in their wake profound psychological consequences. Above all there is a vast increase in the intensity of the sexual drives, bringing with them a dramatic end to the quiescence of the latency period, and a disruption of the personality organization of childhood.

Psychoanalysis has shown that adult sexuality is a force that has its archaic expression in the dim history of one's life. In the course of development from infancy to adulthood, the pleasure-seeking activities motivated by this force change according to an inborn biological schedule, culminating in the mature sexual needs existing between a man and a woman.

However, unlike other genetically determined maturational events, the evolution of sexuality is highly influenced by the growing child's relationships with its parents. The course of development of sexuality and morality is very much rooted in the lengthy dependency of the human infant on his parents, and especially in the early months of life, on his mother. She is the ultimate source of his frustration, his pleasure, and his survival.

There is a great deal we do not understand about the nature of the communication between a mother and her baby in these early months. Nevertheless, we do know that the child's total experiences of frustration and pleasure within the matrix of this uniquely human tie form a bridge to another human being and to the world outside of himself. It is within this bond that the core of his sense of himself as a separate entity, and the foundation of his ability to love, first take shape. We also know that because of this intense tie between a mother and her baby, her attitudes will enhance or discourage certain kinds of responses. This is true not only in the immediate sense, but also in the sense in which she transmits the cultural expectations of her society.

Throughout childhood the young boy or girl takes into his expanding self traits, qualities, values, ideals—positive and negative—after the model of his parents, or rather his perception of them. This internal model is a crucial factor in the identity system of childhood. Around the third or fourth year of his life, this process of identity formation is catalyzed further by the maturing of his sexuality. As the sexual drive becomes centered in his genital organs, he makes a startling and disconcerting discovery about his body: He discovers his sexual identity.

The child receives support for the establishment of his sexual identity from the emphasis that his parents place on various masculine and feminine characteristics. More important than this, however, is the degree to which the parents themselves truly accept this masculinity and femininity.

The moral component of the child's identity is also highly influenced by his developing sexuality. Immanuel Kant felt that the moral imperative is innate in man. While it is true that rudimentary precursors of a conscience may exist at birth, any parent knows that "good behavior" is neither bestowed by God nor genetic evolution, but must be learned anew in each generation. The child's ideas of good and bad are at first dependent on his desire to please his parents and the fear of their disapproval. His morality, in other words, is not autonomous or transcendental, but is essentially a morality of restraint, of parental control.

The beginnings of an autonomous conscience arise around the fifth year. This development is spurred by the continuing biological maturation of the sexual drive which now becomes more firmly localized in the genital organs and gives rise to a powerful daydream. To state it in a highly oversimplified way, the core of this daydream is the young child's sexual and possessive interest in the parent of the opposite sex with corresponding rivalrous feelings toward the parent of the same sex.

Psychoanalysis has called the various components of this daydream the Oedipus Complex, after Sophocles' tragedy "Oedipus Rex." Under ordinary circumstances, however, this connotation of relentless punishment and inexorable tragedy is only in the child's imagination. Out of the ashes of this tragedy a great advance in the child's sexual and moral development will occur. He renounces the daydream along with the sexual impulses connected with it. During the period of latency it is gradually relegated to the storehouse of forgotten memories. The energies feeding these urges are freed for use in learning, in play, and mastery of the environment. In its stead there occurs a decisive identification with the parents. The taking in of the qualities of the parents, and especially the parent of the same sex, provides the child with an important stabilizer for his future masculine and feminine mature identity. It establishes as well the foundation for an autonomous moral law within himself.

At the onset of puberty, under the impact of the resurgent sexual drives, the personality integration of latency is disrupted. This reawakening of sexuality in turn threatens to revive the whole gamut of the young persons' emotional interest in their parents, including old and forgotten feelings of dependency and longing. Although the full force of these archaic desires are usually not experienced on a conscious level, the adolescent reacts with various defenses to keep them in check.

Primarily, both the boy and girl attempt to disengage themselves from their parents and to direct these needs to their peers—a direction that is consistent with the demands of healthy development. The urgent necessity for emotional separation from the parents in the direction of greater independence has its long-range rewards, but for the time being it is accompanied by a sense of loss that is reflected in moodiness and a feeling of depression.

This sense of loss that attends the farewell to childhood is similar to that experienced at the end of each decade of one's life: at one's thirtieth, fortieth, fiftieth birthdays, and especially when our children marry and leave our homes, only now—for the young boy and girl—it strikes much deeper, for there is the inner realization that childhood is over and life will never really be the same again. Needless to say, parents, too, find it difficult to separate from their children and to permit them to struggle into a future that leaves their own lives more empty.

The adolescent is caught, in a sense, between the danger of the sexualized and dependent tie to his parents, and the fear of independence and sense of loss that pulls him back to them. In order to give up this supportive relationship of childhood, he must step into the new world of his peers, a world that is devoid of established and secure roles. He must begin to test his abilities, his strength, his fears of the opposite sex, his ideals, and his sense of himself. In

doing so he must risk failure and injury to his self-esteem. Thus, rebellion against parents coexists and alternates with childlike dependency in bewildering succession.

On the one hand the adolescent bristles at the most well-intentioned parental help; on the other hand he will make the most outlandish demands to be catered to and waited on. He will accuse you of nagging when you have to wake him up three times in order to be ready for school. If you wake him only once he will accuse you of not caring whether or not he gets an education. The stronger the dependent need the more violent will be the rebelliousness and anger as a defense against it. I am sure you may be familiar with the experience of parents whose touchy teen-age son is leaving for a date. "Have a good time!" they tell him as he is leaving the house. He answers instantly: "Don't tell me what to do!"

Severe mother-daughter conflicts are not unusual at this stage. They are probably more frequent between mothers and daughters than between sons and either parent. Dependency on mother presents an even greater threat to the girl than to the boy, for it carries with it a threat to the girl's feminine development by intensifying her tie to a woman at a time when she is struggling to achieve a firm sense of her feminine sexuality. For both boy and girl, however, the urgent necessity to relinquish the emotional dependence also means a temporary disengagement from the internalized, psychic model of the parents that has been the foundation of their identity. The rupture of the internalized model results in a fragmentation of the sense of personal identity, which may be experienced as a sense of unreality, a confusion about "who I really am," and a groping for a philosophy of life or an ideology upon which to anchor for the time being a stable feeling of self.

The dissolution of the internalized model of the parents includes as well a partial negation of the values and standards of the parents that have been appropriate to childhood and have served well prior to this time. The temporary negation and realignment of these values is a necessary concomitant to growing up, and to the achievement of an independent and autonomous value system of one's own. Eventually and ideally there will be a remodeling within the personality of a morality based not only on the past, but also on the exercise of judgment and discrimination as applied to the realities and responsibilities of living as an adult in his own generation.

Adolescent sexual attitudes and behavior at first have little similarity to those of a mature relationship between a man and a woman. Sexual feelings as well as the newly-won physical maturity are often felt as alien, and not as integrated components of the self. Frequently the sexual drive is used as an instrument to relieve some of the conflicts of adolescence, for example, as an assertion of masculinity or femininity. With boys there is a great deal of exaggerated boasting with peers about sexual experience. This usually is at considerable variance from the actual facts. For girls it may provide an outlet for defiant self-assertion and hostility to her parents. The adolescent's feelings of loneliness and depression may be temporarily relieved by the illusion of love, created by the physical closeness to another human being. Intimacy with the opposite sex may be avoided altogether because of intense feelings of fear and guilt. Sometimes the negation of the moral code of the parents results in even more rigid self-imposed standards. I am thinking of a young man who, rewarded with a goodnight kiss after a pleasant evening, proceeded to give the girl a lecture about her unladylike behavior!

The sexual behavior of adolescents, as a statement of independence from the parents, is sometimes so extremely specious that only the young people themselves fail to discern it. For example, I would like to cite one young couple, nineteen and twenty-one. During the course of an intense attachment to each other, an illegitimate pregnancy occurred, followed in a few months by a marriage they both wanted. The spurious motive of this sexual independence was betrayed by the fact that both of them proceeded successfully to perpetrate an elaborate hoax on their parents, in which the out-of-wedlock pregnancy was concealed—including the birth of the baby and its placement for adoption

—so terrified were they of parental alienation and censure as punishment for the forbidden sexual relationship.

In many instances the guilt over the sexual relationship necessitates idealizing it as love, which may in turn result in marriage. This effects a closure of the adolescent process; a pseudo-resolution that once and for all terminates the search for identity around a premature commitment to a permanent sexual relationship. For an adolescent, it is putting on the cloak of adulthood while carrying into the relationship the unresolved conflicts of the past, and an identity that remains dependent on the childhood image of the parents. Obviously, it is wrong to assume that adolescent sexual behavior and attitudes can be explained only on the basis of a desire for physical pleasure.

Although sexuality can be exploited in the service of more infantile needs, it already has in it the seed of what will become an expression of a deep and intimate bond between a man and a woman. Gradually, near the end of adolescence, these attitudes give way to sexual interest and the need to express it within the framework of a deep emotional bond to a sexual partner. This marks the integration of sexuality into the personality structure, and is an important element in the realization of adult identity.

The harmonious integration of sexuality and morality is influenced not only by the interrelationship of the forces within the personality, but is also dependent upon the social and cultural setting in which these biological and psychological events unfold and reciprocate. At every phase of his life cycle the growing individual meets in his social environment patterned expectations, restrictions, opportunities, and an image of himself determined by his society and the particular subculture in which he matures. This social environment can be either positive or negative in meeting the requirements for growth. If it does not meet these requirements, the particular phase of development will run an abortive or deviant course—imposing lasting deformities on the personality. . . .

The acceleration of historical change has

produced a wide and ever-increasing gap between the older generation and the younger generation. Within the time-span of a single generation, the march of history has produced unprecedented social, political, and technological changes. These phenomena are reflected in such terms as population explosion, sexual revolution, information explosion, and mass communication. There is little doubt that the standard-setting function of tradition has been weakened. In the area of relationship between the sexes, this is certainly true. The morality of authoritative restraint, enforced by parental control, religious dictum, and the economic dependency of women has given way. In the absence of these traditional restraints, the adolescent attempts to resolve his code for sexual behavior within the relationship of his peers. It is possible to assume that the coercive power of these external controls are integrated into the personality in such a way that they then function as autonomous moral directives. While this is true and appropriate in childhood, in adulthood such external controls encourage dependency and inhibit the formation of independent internalized values.

Therefore, if a youth borrows automatically the outward form of another authority, the peer group, little has been gained in moral growth. This fact is behind the fear of the older generation that external standards of sexual license will replace standards of restraint.

The few sociological studies that have been done so far *do* support the existence of a change in the direction of greater sexual freedom among college students. The studies of this rather narrow segment of youth *do not*, however, support the thesis that this change is a revolution in favor of amorality, occasional sensational news articles notwithstanding. They do suggest that the change is in the direction of a more autonomous regulation of sexual behavior which sanctions premarital sexual intercourse within the confines of a serious and exclusive relationship. In only a very small percentage of these studies can the women's sexual behavior be typified as casual or promiscuous. It is highly probable that in these few instances we are

observing deviant development wherein pseudo-sexuality is the expression of a serious emotional disturbance, and represents a failure to resolve internal psychic conflicts of adolescence.

Observations from another source seem, at first glance, to substantiate an increasing disregard for established social mores. I am referring to the great increase in the number of out-of-wedlock pregnancies; actually an increase of from 10 to 22 per 100 unmarried women over a 15-year period. However, these statistics do not represent a sudden crisis, but a very gradual long-term trend that can be traced back at least thirty years. Interestingly enough, the startling increase is in the age group from twenty to thirty years, not in the teen-age group. The proportion of teen-age unmarried mothers is even slightly lower than in earlier years —in terms of percentages.

Perhaps those who interpret these figures to indicate the breakdown of previous standards and restraints along with the diffusion of a "fun morality" are right. But the evidence is not convincing. Undoubtedly, sociological and cultural changes must be taken into account. From my own frame of reference as a consultant to social agencies working with these young women, the internal psychological causes of the out-of-wedlock pregnancy were striking. For some of them out-of-wedlock pregnancy represented a quasi-solution to an insoluble internal conflict. For others it was an inevitable crisis on the path to adulthood.

The establishment, then, of a firm sense of identity is dependent on the interaction of the various segments of the personality with each other and with the traditions, opportunities, and style of life that the adolescent meets in the world around him. The force of maturing sexuality itself is responsible for the dissolution of the ties to the parents and the shaking up of the whole fabric of the personality configuration of childhood.

In more primitive cultures and more distant historical times, adolescence was curtailed. Under those conditions, the childhood structure of the parent changed very little. The personal identity of the adult was more irrevocably tied to the childhood relationship with the parents, and accordingly, to the traditions, values, and standards of the past.

A youth of our society has to weather a more prolonged period of uncertainty and turmoil than any other generation preceding him. He must enter into a new kind of relationship with his peers, where he must embark on a period of experimentation in which he tests his interests and capabilities, his ideals and values, and his emerging sexual identity. Gradually, he will organize into a cohesive whole, with a stable sense of himself that is founded on his unique personal attributes. In this process he is evolving a new kind of sexual morality—a morality no longer dependent for its enforcement on the power of external restraints.

There are the prophets of doom who warn of the disintegration of tradition and morality, and who picture an unsolvable dilemma for the youth of our time. There are the optimists who anticipate that the weakening of the authoritative controls of the past will lead to the evolution of a sexual morality free from irrational fear and guilt, based on independent judgment, reason, and an understanding of adult responsibilities to oneself and to other human beings.

Perhaps it is too soon to tell. I take my stand, however, with the optimists.

10

"ANATOMY IS DESTINY": PSYCHOLOGICAL IMPLICATIONS OF ADOLESCENT PHYSICAL CHANGES IN GIRLS

Ellen Rothchild

By referring to her developing breasts as "just baby fat," a tomboyish 12-year-old indicated her hopeful anticipation that they might disappear. The paraphrase from Napoleon, that anatomy is destiny, was too painful for her to acknowledge. Yet never more acutely than at puberty, when physical change is so rapid, does a girl's anatomy influence her feelings about herself, her identity, her relationships to others, and her role in life. . . .

Adolescence is not the first period during which a girl's anatomy is important to her. As early as 2 or 3 years, children become aware of sexual differences, and girls commonly appear less pleased with the discovery than boys. Often one observes a little girl attempting to urinate standing up, stuffing a toy under a skirt to represent a penis, or preferring pants to dresses. Investigations into comparative anatomy are rife among both sexes; children make endless comparisons between themselves and other children, between themselves and adults. These comparisons are not always openly apparent, and games such as "playing doctor" provide a vehicle for covert investigation. . . . The early years, during which little change is apparent in bodily sexual characteristics, serve the girl as a period during which she can begin to accept her anatomy. . . .

The vicissitudes of previous development and experience contribute to individual variations in the pubertal girl's acceptance of her anatomy. Feelings about her newly changing body vary from one adolescent to the next, as well as being mixed—both positive and negative—within the same individual. The attitudes of others affect her satisfaction with herself. . . .

Few girls can report directly and accurately how they feel about their pubertal changes. Regarding menstruation, Anne Frank confided in her diary:

I think what is happening to me is so wonderful and not only what can be seen on my body, but all that is taking place inside. I never discuss myself or any of these things with anybody; that is why I have to talk to myself about them.

Each time I have a period—and that has only been three times—I have a feeling that in spite of all the pain, unpleasantness, and nastiness, I have a sweet secret, and that is why, although it is nothing but a nuisance to me in a way, I always long for the time that I shall feel that secret within me again.[1]

Ordinarily, on asking a girl of 14 or 15 for retrospective information regarding her menarche, one receives a brief, ultra-casual outline of how she knew all about what to expect beforehand and how unremarkable everything was. To learn more one must be present at the time or else read between the lines. And, in contrast to the incisive quality of menarche, the more gradual development of secondary sex characters evokes reactions which are likely to be remembered and reported with even less accuracy. . . .

If one observes junior high school girls as a group, one is struck with the importance physical growth assumes; how well a girl is "stacked" becomes a factor in her status among her peers. By seventh or eighth grade, some girls are well advanced in physical development while others are nowhere near so; discrepancies vitally affect self-concepts.[2] Researches into bodily comparisons, frequent in preschool years, are revived again in the junior high school girl

who may be well aware of and deeply interested in how she compares with her peers. Many girls can list for one both qualitatively and quantitatively the degrees to which each individual in the class has developed, right down to what bra size each wears. Locker room comparisons may be sufficiently embarrassing or exciting so that a number of girls try to avoid gym altogether, and the request to the pediatrician for a medical exam on some flimsy grounds is common.

As individuals, apart from the group, girls can feel self-conscious anywhere.

A 15-year-old girl described feeling certain that, as she walked down the street, every male eye was appraising and mentally undressing her. While one part of her was proud, another part wanted to take cover and hide. She reported, "I don't really know how I should be feeling."

Other individual concerns relate to leaving childhood and becoming an adult, sexual woman:

Such was the dilemma of the girl who passed off her breast development as "baby fat." A similar anxiety sometimes underlies the shaving of pubic hair.

Some girls appear to welcome breast development with exaggerated delight as if it were something to flaunt and show off. Among these there are a number for whom breast development does not represent a feminine attribute as much as it does an acquisition now finally comparable to what boys have which the girl feels she has so far lacked.

The genital sexual implications of developing a "shape" were clearly expressed by a 12-year-old who made up rhymes about "shape" and "rape." She explained that the dangers of having a "shape" could be avoided by behaving like a "rack."

Ordinarily the conscious feelings about external bodily changes are most often mixed ones of pride, self-consciousness, misgivings, and pleasure. Many of these feelings are reflected in the tremendous investment girls make in their physical appearance; hours can be spent in narcissistic preoccupation with dieting, skin care, hair styles, and fashion. Displacements away from the body may be represented by more sublimated "styles"—a girl's adoption of a particular personal manner of speech or gesture which she calls her own, her own individual tastes, interests, beliefs, and choice of friends. . . .

Reactions to menstruation are at least as varied as those to external physical changes. Age-old cultural attitudes of awe and dread of the menstruating female no doubt contribute, in some measure, to the individual girl's reactions. In many primitive societies taboos are placed against the menstruating woman touching or associating with others for fear she might bring about disease, injury, emasculation, or even death. Pliny's *Natural History*, written in the first century A.D., recorded that menstruating women turn wine to vinegar, kill bees and seedlings with their touch, turn milk sour, and cripple horses. And, though there is no medical basis, similar superstitions and taboos persist in present day beliefs that during her menses a woman should not shower, wash her hair, have intercourse, ride horseback, or eat certain foods.

Prior to present educational trends, unrealistic attitudes were blamed on lack of enlightenment. Havelock Ellis cited a now-classic report from the French press in which a girl of 15 threw herself into the Seine River: "She was rescued and on being brought before the police commissioner, said that she had been attacked by an 'unknown disease' which had driven her to despair. Discreet inquiry revealed that the mysterious malady was one common to all women and the girl was restored to her insufficiently punished parents."[3]

In this day of fifth grade hygiene movies, when, if her mother, her sisters, or her friends have not enlightened her, the school will, girls know much more about the whole reproductive process and their role in it than they did a generation ago. Yet, though girls are prepared in the schools for the biologic changes, they are seldom prepared for the changes in feeling. Side by side with a conscious awareness of medical facts, even the most enlightened adolescent may entertain her own private sentiments. Though not necessarily conscious, certain feelings and ideas commonly exist which are at variance with all our attempts at rational explanation and preparation.

One set of ideas is that this monthly discharge of waste material signifies that the girl has nothing but a dirty, disgusting hole; since there is no sphincter, the girl cannot even control what emerges.

A prepubertal girl believed that menstruating would be akin to wetting the bed. She was quite sure that boys never wet for they can so much better control where they urinate.

A post-menarcheal girl connected the darker color of menstrual blood with dirt, sin, and disease.

Some girls handle the feelings of shame and disgust by refusing to wear sanitary napkins, hiding their soiled underclothes, and telling no one of their periods.

Another idea is that to bleed must mean that the girl has been injured, damaged, or not made right.

Immediately after attending her school hygiene movies on menstruation, a 12-year-old girl regaled me with "sick jokes" (i.e., "No, of course you can't go swimming. You know your hooks will get rusty"). She told a ghost story about a girl whose feet were "bloody stumps," and she complained of having broken several things that day— her glasses, her transistor radio. Further discussion confirmed that the movie had roused ideas of damage and mutilation.

For all their previous enlightenment, on their first bleeding some girls must return in horrified disbelief to check the toilet seat for the nail or piece of glass which must have cut them.

When the idea exists that genital bleeding represents an injury, a girl may feel somehow responsible by virtue of something she has done, such as masturbate.

In an effort to deny any connection, when asked what she understood about menses, a 13-year-old girl replied suavely, "Oh yes,

I know all about that. Girls menstruate and boys masturbate."

Such ideation may impel a girl at menarche to relinquish old habits which she views as dirty and uncontrollable, such as masturbation, thumb-sucking, or enuresis.

An 11-year-old girl was unable to fall asleep at night without simultaneously sucking her thumb and stroking a pair of her brother's underpants. Though ashamed of the habit she was unable to give it up. Returning from a summer vacation, she reported proudly that she no longer sucked her thumb. When I asked how she had accomplished this feat, she described accompanying her father on a trip to New York City where she had gotten dressed up, dined at Trader Vic's, and attended a Broadway play. She explained that she had felt so grownup and, reflecting that it was too babyish to continue sucking her thumb, she had forthwith given it up. To me this seemed an insufficient stimulus to renounce such a tenacious habit. Subsequently her mother told me that on the night the girl went to the theater she had had her first period.

This is not to suggest, however, that adolescence is the long-awaited remedy for habit disorders.

The commoner conscious attitudes usually parallel those described by Anne Frank. Girls seem generally to regard their periods as something of a nuisance but well worth exploiting as an excuse from gym, as a prestige item among their peers—having "joined the club"—and as a source of pride and pleasure in becoming a woman and now being able to bear children. Since little has actually changed in the girl's status, there is also the disappointment that she does not suddenly have the right to all the privileges of a grown woman. . . .

Differences in the psychological significance of the first dramatic pubertal physical experiences—the boy's first ejaculations and the girl's menarche—lend truth to the statement of the girl who differentiated the sexes by masturbation and menstruation. The boy's first emissions, usually orgastic

and frequently leading to masturbation, contrast strikingly with the menstruating girl's avoidance of touching her bleeding genitals. Thus, boys are likely to experience more conscious guilt than girls because of the accompanying erotic activity. Though proud of the other visible manifestations of their new-found virility, boys usually take exaggerated precautions to hide the evidences of wet dreams, perhaps only secretly discussing or demonstrating ejaculations among their fellows. Girls, freed from such conscious guilt, are more openly proud of their menarche and may advertise it not only to friends but even to adults. On a less conscious level, the pain associated with menstruation further assuages the girl's guilty feelings; if she has engaged in the forbidden, then the painful aspect of her menses can seem a penance for wrong-doing and helps to wipe the slate clean.[4]

If her periods are fairly regular a girl has some psychologic advantage over a boy in that this bodily phenomenon is stable and predictable in contrast to the unpredictability and uncontrollability of the pubertal boy's spontaneous erections and nocturnal emissions. The pain which accompanies menstruation can be localized to a specific part of the body which the girl could not previously feel, aiding the girl's orientation to her physical boundaries at a time when they seem to change so rapidly. When a girl is fortunate enough to settle rapidly into regular cycles, then this predictable event with its localizeable sensation can serve the girl as an organizer, a nidus around which she can build some of her developing sense of physical and psychological self.[5]. . .

At least as far-ranging in effect, for both sexes, is the influence of sexual maturation on shifting family relationships. While the girl is developing into a shapely young woman, her mother may in the meantime have become a little greyer, perhaps a little dumpier. The girl is now in a far better position to compete with her mother for a man than she was, say, at 3 when she was told she must wait for a seeming eternity before gaining her mother's mature feminine endowments. While agreeable in some ways, the more equal sexual footing of mother and daughter also enhances conflict for the girl. Pleased on the one hand, a girl can also feel guilty that she now has the potential for outdoing her mother in the popularity contest. Such feelings of conflict may underlie some of the familiar teen-age behavior of dressing like a slob or being as unlike the mother as possible in other ways, eschewing parental mores or picking fights with a parent who "doesn't understand." If she dresses like a beatnik, then how could she possibly be attractive? And, if she can invite punishment, then her guilt may be assuaged. The well-known obnoxiousness of this period, the slammed bedroom doors and hostile silences are accompanied by a general move out of the home in favor of more engrossing relationships with peers. While this is trying to parents, it is vital that the adolescent make this move to independence. If she is not to remain tied forever to home and parents, if she is to grow and develop a separate, distinct identity, the adolescent must remove herself to the world of her peers where she will ultimately live, work, and love. . . .

There is a danger of our meeting the girl with the expectations accorded either a child or a grown woman when the teenage girl is simultaneously both and neither. For the unstable internal physiologic equilibrium of adolescence is paralleled by a remarkable, if transitory, emotional instability, which is manifested in wide swings of mood and mercurial fluctuations of interests, attitudes, and relationships. The task of becoming used to a new, changing body and personality is accompanied by a temporary lessening of the adolescent's sureness of herself, of her ability to anticipate and control her reactions. . . .

Although physical and psychologic adolescence places many stresses on the course of growth, most girls traverse their adolescence quite successfully and it is the parents who emerge bruised from the experience. Judicious hand-holding, explanation and anticipation that this too will pass, offered to parents, can frequently carry a girl farther than some of our frantic efforts to deal directly with phenomena which appear initially so disturbing yet are often so ephemeral in the course of normal adolescence. . . .

Though of fundamental biologic importance, the anatomic sexual changes of adolescence are also decisive for psychic growth. These changes are welcomed with a variety of emotional reactions and serve, psychologically, to consolidate a girl's feminine identity and support her eventual growth toward individuality and independence.

REFERENCES

1. Frank, A. *The Diary of a Young Girl.* New York: Doubleday and Co., 1952, p. 143.

2. Schonfeld, W. A. "Body-Image in Adolescents: A Psychiatric Concept for the Pediatrician." *Pediatrics,* 31:845, 1963.

3. Ellis, H. *Studies in the Psychology of Sex.* Vol. 2. New York: Random House, 1942, Part 3, p. 66.

4. Jacobson, E. *The Self and the Object World.* New York: International Universities Press, 1964, pp. 162–164.

5. Kestenberg, J. "Menarche." In Lorand, S., and Schneer, H. I., eds. *Adolescents: Psychoanalytic Approach to Problems and Therapy.* New York: Hoeber, 1961, p. 19.

11

SELF-PERCEIVED RATE OF PHYSICAL MATURATION AND PERSONALITY IN LATE ADOLESCENCE

Donald Weatherley

It has long been recognized that the timing of puberty and of the marked physical changes which herald its onset is subject to wide individual differences. It is relatively recently, however, that attention has been drawn to the differential impact on personal and social adjustment of these individual differences in the rate of physical maturation. This issue has been brought into sharp focus by a recent series of reports stemming from the California Adolescent Growth Study, a project which involved the intensive observation and testing of a group of approximately 180 boys and girls over a seven-year period.[1] These reports were based on comparisons made with a variety of behavioral and personality measures of groups of extremely early and extremely late maturers (the upper and lower 20 percent of the total Growth Study sample).

Clear-cut results were found for boys. Both trained adult observers and peers described the late-maturing boys' behavior in less favorable terms than that of the early maturers. For example, at age 16 the late maturers were rated by adults as significantly less attractive in physique, less well groomed, less moderate in their behavior, more affected, more tense appearing, and more eager. Peers described the late maturers as more restless, less reserved, less grown-up, and more bossy.[2] In brief, the tense, active, attention-seeking behavior of the late maturers contrasted sharply with the self-assured, well modulated, socially appropriate behavior manifested by the group of early maturers. Moreover, the late maturers were chosen much less frequently than early maturers for positions of leadership in their school and were much less prominent in extracurricular activities.[3]

An analysis of TAT protocols obtained when the boys were 17 years old revealed personality differences consistent with the behavior differences found between early and late maturers. These data indicated that accompanying the late maturers' less adaptive social behaviors were heightened feelings of inadequacy, negative self-conceptions, feelings of rejection and domination, and persistent dependency needs paradoxically coupled with a rebellious quest for autonomy and freedom from restraint.[4]

Finally, a follow-up study[5] provided evidence that the personality differences between the early- and the late-maturing boys persisted into adulthood long after physical differences between the groups had disappeared. The male subjects of the Adolescent Growth Study were administered two objective tests of personality (the California Psychological Inventory and the Edwards Personal Preference Schedule) when they had reached an average age of 33. The test results indicated that as adults the late maturers were less capable of conveying a good impression, less self-controlled, less responsible, less dominant, and more inclined to turn to others for help than were the early maturers—a pattern of personality differences quite similar to the pattern that had emerged when the groups were compared in adolescence.

The results of this series of studies on males add up to a consistent picture which makes good theoretical sense. A large, strong stature is a central aspect of the ideal masculine model in our society. Thus, it is reasonable to assume that the early attainment of the physical attributes associated with maturity serves as a social stimulus which evokes from both peers and adults a reaction of respect, acceptance, and the expectation that the individual concerned will be capable of relatively mature social behavior. Such a reaction from others serves to support and reinforce adaptive, "grownup" actions and contributes to feelings of confidence and security in the early-maturing boys. On the other hand, the late maturer must cope with the developmental demands of the junior high and high school period with the liability of a relatively small, immature appearing physical stature. His appearance is likely to call out in others at least mild reactions of derogation and the expectation that he is capable of only ineffectual, immature behavior. Such reactions constitute a kind of social environment which is conducive to feelings of inadequacy, insecurity, and defensive, "small-boy" behavior. Such behavior once initiated may well be self-sustaining, since it is likely to only intensify the negative environmental reactions which gave rise to it in the first place. This interpretation, fully consistent with the evidence produced by the investigations of the Growth Study workers, implies that the late-maturing boy is likely to be involved in a circular psychosocial process in which reactions of others and his own reactions interact with unhappy consequences for his personal and social adjustment. . . .

Although the California workers' findings for boys were generally clear-cut and consistent, the conclusions they generated rested, in one sense at least, on a quite narrow empirical base. . . . All the studies reviewed earlier involved the same small group of Ss, all of whom lived in the Berkeley, California, area. Furthermore, despite the fact that these reports have appeared relatively recently in the literature, all but the one concerning the follow-up study were based on data gathered more than two decades ago; the Growth Study Ss were, at the time the present study was undertaken, close to 40 years old—literally old enough to be the parents of today's adolescents.

It should be noted, however, that the present study was by no means a contemporary replication of earlier research; it differed in several important respects from the California investigations. The Ss in this study were on the average about two years older than were the Ss at the completion of the Adolescent Growth Study. A number of objective personality measures were used in the present study, only one of which (the Edwards Personal Preference Schedule) was used in the California research and then only in the follow-up study.[6] The most noteworthy distinction between the study reported here and the previous research in this area had to do with the nature of the measure of rate of physical maturation. The California studies used an objective skeletal-age index of physical maturation as a basis for identifying early and late maturers. In the present study a simple self-report measure of relative maturational rate was used. Its use involved the assumption that adolescents have a fairly accurate idea of the relative timing of their physical maturation and can reliably report this information.

Obviously, any one or more of the factors mentioned above could be responsible for differences found between results of the present study and the findings of the California series of investigations; such differences might not be easy to interpret. On the other hand, it was felt that if the present study yielded findings with implications convergent with those generated by previous research, especially that dealing with males where prior evidence was most definitive, the generality of the conclusions reached would be strongly supported. . . .

The Ss were 234 male and 202 female college students enrolled in the elementary psychology course at the University of Colorado. The mean age of the girls was 19.4 ($SD = 2.6$), the mean age of the boys, 19.9 ($SD = 1.9$).

Early in the semester the MMPI K scale[7] and the Taylor Manifest Anxiety Scale (TMAS)[8] were administered to the Ss in large group sessions. Approximately five weeks later 96 of the boys and 92 of the girls took the Edwards Personal Preference Schedule (EPPS).[9]

In order to obtain measures reflecting degree of identification with parents and peers, the Ss were asked in the initial testing sessions to give self-ratings of the degree to which they saw themselves as similar to each of the following individuals: their mother, father, same-sex best friend, and opposite-sex best friend. These self-ratings of perceived similarity were obtained for each of the following dimensions:

overall personality, intelligence, warmth, orderliness, political views, and religious views. Seven-point rating scales were used, yielding scores which ranged from one (indicating the lowest degree of perceived similarity) to seven (indicating the highest degree of perceived similarity).

Rate of physical maturation was assessed by responses to the following multiple-choice question presented to the Ss during the initial testing sessions: "With regard to your physical maturation, you would say that you matured: (a) quite early, (b) somewhat early, (c) average, (d) somewhat late, (e) quite late." These alternatives were assigned weights from one (quite early) to five (quite late) so that the choice made by each S could be represented as a numerical score. In addition, each S was categorized into one of three groups on the basis of his response to the physical maturation question. Individuals who had chosen either the alternative "quite early" or "somewhat early" were considered early maturers. Those who had chosen the alternative "average," were considered average maturers. Those who had chosen the alternatives "somewhat late" or "quite late" were categorized as late maturers. . . .

A final word is in order regarding the measure of physical maturation used in the present study. An assumption involved in the use of this measure was that individuals are both aware of the relative rate of their physical maturation and are willing to report it with reasonable accuracy. The generally high degree of congruence between the results based on the simple self-report measure used in the present study and previous findings based on an objective skeletal-age measure of physical maturation is evidence bolstering this assumption. The veridicality of such self-ratings cannot be firmly established, of course, without directly comparing the ratings with an objective measure of physical growth. Nevertheless, the present results constitute sufficient indirect evidence of the validity of the self-report measure of physical maturation to encourage the use of a measure of this sort in situations where it is impractical to obtain objective indices of maturational rate.

The present study and those done earlier have clearly established the importance of rate of physical maturation as a variable influencing personality development at least in boys; this variable deserves further study. Especially interesting would be research bearing upon the interaction of the maturation variable and variables such as social class membership, parental child-rearing practices, or peer-group social structure. . . .

In the case of boys, the findings of the present study are clear-cut. They indicate that the late-maturing boy of college age is less likely than his earlier-maturing peers to have satisfactorily resolved the conflicts normally attending the transition from childhood to adulthood. He is more inclined to seek attention and affection from others and less inclined to assume a position of dominance and leadership over others. Yet he is not ready to accept the dictates of authority gracefully; he is inclined, rather, to defy authority and assert unconventional behavior in a rebellious vein. In view of the evidence of these potentially competing forces at work within him, it is not surprising that the late maturer also tends to acknowledge a heightened level of subjective tension and readiness to indulge in guilt-implying self-abasement. Nor is it surprising that he tends to see himself as being different from his peers and parents.

The foregoing portrait of the late-maturing boy is, of course, misleading in that it ignores the obviously large overlap among the groups studied and the obviously appreciable individual differences within the group of late maturers. It does, however, serve to bring into focus a central conclusion to be drawn from the results of the present study: late maturation is associated with less mature appearing, less "healthy" appearing personality characteristics. The high degree of congruence between the results of this study and the results of previous studies which involved quite different procedures, measures, and subjects, underscores the generality and importance of rate of physical maturation as a variable influencing personality development in boys.

A second conclusion which can be drawn

from the results of the present study, a conclusion which involves a more precise description of the nature of the relation between rate of maturation and personality in boys, has no precedent in the earlier work done as part of the California Adolescent Growth Study. These earlier investigations used an extreme-groups design in which individuals who were extremely late in maturing were compared with individuals extremely early in maturation; no comparisons were made between either of these groups and a group of individuals whose rate of maturation was average. The inclusion in the present study of the group of average maturers made possible an inference concerning the relative impact upon personality characteristics of early versus late maturation when each extreme group was compared to an average group. . . . Many fewer significant differences were found when the group of early-maturing boys was compared with the group of average maturers (of a total of 41 comparisons only 1 reached significance at the .05 level or less) than when late maturers were compared with the average maturers (9 of the 41 comparisons made were significant at the .05 level or less). The early- and average-maturing groups were quite similar to one another in the personality attributes they manifested, while the late maturers were set apart from both of these groups. Thus it is clear that the relations found between rate of physical maturation and the personality characteristics measured were not in general linear ones. The implication is that while late maturation is apparently a handicap to the personality development of boys, early maturation may not be an asset; it appears rather to have an effect on personality development no different from the effect of an average rate of physical maturation.

NOTES

[1] H. E. Jones, "The California Adolescent Growth Study," *J. Educ. Res.*, XXXI (1938), 561–567.

[2] M. C. Jones and N. Bayley, "Physical Maturing Among Boys as Related to Behavior," *J. Educ. Psych.*, XLI (1950), 129–148.

[3] M. C. Jones, "A Study of Socialization Patterns at the High School Level," *J. Genet. Psychol.*, XCIII (1958), 87–111.

[4] P. H. Mussen and M. C. Jones, "Self-Conceptions, Motivations, and Interpersonal Attitudes of Late- and Early-Maturing Boys," *Child Developm.*, XXVIII (1957), 243–256.

[5] M. C. Jones, "The Later Careers of Boys Who Were Early- or Late-Maturing," *Child Developm.*, XXVIII (1957), 113–128.

[6] Ibid.

[7] J. C. McKinley, S. R. Hathaway, and P. E. Meehl, "The Minnesota Multiphasic Personality Inventory: VI. The K Scale," *J. Consult. Psychol.*, XII (1948), 20–31.

[8] J. A. Taylor, "A Personality Scale of Manifest Anxiety," *J. Abnorm. Soc. Psychol.*, XLVIII (1953), 285–290.

[9] A. L. Edwards, *Manual for the Edwards Personal Preference Schedule* (Psychological Corp., 1959).

12

YOUTH LOOKS AT SEX

Gertrude B. Couch

"Why not *consult* boys and girls about what they think?" So asked the subcommittee of the Detroit Commission on Children and Youth last spring when planning a city-wide Youth Health Conference to consider pertinent issues related to sex education for youth today. This unusual approach brought together a representative group of high school-age young people, not to "tell them" what they should know in this complex aspect of growth and development relating to sexual maturation and sex behavior, but rather to "inquire" from them what they felt were the unmet needs of youth. The purposes of the meeting were to explore: (1) what it is they felt young people need to know in order to cope with social situations with which they are confronted; (2) when they thought this information and guidance should be given; (3) by whom they felt it could best be handled; and (4) exactly what kind of help they considered most essential and presently most lacking in their environment.

On October 19, 1966, a one-day Youth Health Conference was held on the campus of Wayne State University sponsored by the Detroit Commission on Children and Youth, jointly with the Michigan School Health Association and the Division of Health and Physical Education of Wayne State University. This was the fourth annual health conference which has been conducted by the Youth Commission for high school students in Detroit, each meeting focused upon some timely and significant health problem. Due to the marked increase in social problems associated with sexual behavior among teen-agers in recent years, this topic was selected for major consideration in 1966.

A planning committee composed of leading health educators in the city schools and local universities, representatives of Merrill-Palmer Institute, pediatricians, social workers, and psychiatrists associated with juvenile courts, and religious education leaders of the Catholic, Jewish, and Protestant faiths met periodically through the late spring and summer months to establish clear-cut objectives and to work out the necessary details of the conference. The predominant idea which continued to emerge through many hours of conference planning was, "Let's do it differently this time. Let's not structure the conference in terms of adult values and adult perceptions of problems. Let's see what young people themselves think. Maybe they have some insights and viewpoints which we need to know more about, if we truly want to do a more effective job of sex education."

It was decided that every public and parochial senior high school principal in the City of Detroit should be asked to select one boy and one girl in the 11th or 12th grades to serve as delegates to the conference. Young people who spoke easily before others and who were considered to have good rapport with their peers were particularly sought. In addition, the school administrator was asked to invite one faculty representative who had particular responsibility and/or interest in the area of sex education and guidance, and a parent or community representative who was actively involved in school-community programs for youth. From the 22 public and 55 parochial secondary schools in Detroit, a total of 110 high school boys and girls participated in the conference, along with about 60 to 80 interested adults.

The conference started with an informal luncheon during which delegates from the various schools were able to become acquainted with each other. The key speaker at the opening session was Dr. Aaron Rutledge, well-known lecturer, writer, and clinician in the field of marriage counselling, a member of the board of directors of SIECUS, and a member of the faculty of the Merrill-Palmer Institute. He stressed the great need for helping young people get not just some, but *all* the pertinent information available in the area of sex. He emphasized the need for opportunities to talk about attitudes and feelings about interpersonal relationships, as well as for education based on scientific facts. He recommended a full understanding of the negative aspects of sex as well as the positive, not because of fear, but in order to be able to make wise decisions and to learn to live responsibly. Dr. Rutledge concluded by pointing out to the young people at this conference that there were truly many adults, both in schools and in churches today, sincerely concerned about boys and girls in their problems, willing to admit their ineptness in meeting these needs, and seriously seeking help in order to do a better job. He urged that the delegates at this conference try to reflect the opinions of their friends and classmates, as well as themselves, and share their ideas of how to cope with this subject.

The participants were then divided into separate groups for informal discussion. All adult delegates met in one large room where a question and answer period was conducted under the combined leadership of Dr. Rutledge and Monsignor Clifford Sawher, director of the Family Life Bureau for the Catholic Archdiocese of Detroit. Both men stressed the "total" approach to sex education, with instruction throughout a child's life from home, church, and school. Dr. Rutledge reiterated that "factual enlightenment not associated with a value system that includes sexuality is of little consequence." Audience questions ranged from: "How should the venereal disease problem be handled?" to "What about state laws that prohibit instruction in certain aspects of sex education, such as birth control?" and "What is the historical relationship between celibacy and creativity?" At the end of this session, the evaluation forms returned by the adult participants showed a 100 percent favorable reaction to this type of conference.

Meanwhile, the teen-age delegates had been regrouped into eleven small discussion groups of approximately 10 to 12 persons each, under the skilled direction of carefully selected leaders, most of whom had professional backgrounds in guidance or counselling. College students, chosen from health education classes in two local universities in Detroit, served as recorders for each group. The methodological approach agreed upon in these groups was to structure the discussion as little as possible, to emphasize a permissive environment for expression of ideas, and to encourage maximum participation from every young person in attendance. It was hoped that in each group a broad approach to the topic might be developed rather than to pursue any particular aspect in depth.

Analysis of the verbatim reports from these eleven discussion groups indicates that topics covered generally fell into one of the following categories:

Category   I: Meanings and values attached to sexuality

Category   II: *Who* should teach about sex, *what* should be taught, and *when*

Category III: Parents as sex educators

Category   IV: Sex education in the schools

Category   V: Role of peers in sex education

Category   VI: Other community influences upon understandings or attitudes about sex

Category VII: Special problems related to sex

Category I. Questions brought up for discussion in this area, either by group leaders or students, included such topics as: "Why is adequate sex education considered necessary? What is its purpose? What is the relation between love and intercourse? What is the meaning of sexual expression? Why is sex bad?"

The young people recognized the long-range values inherent in sex education by such remarks as that they felt its purpose was to "prepare them for marriage," "for relationships," and in order to help them teach their own children better some day. As to the meaning of sexual expression, answers varied widely—some persons indicating that they felt the meaning was different for men than for women, or different before and after marriage. They expressed the opinion that if sex was considered bad, it was a reflection of adult attitudes toward sex. One young person observed that it was "supposed to be bad right up until marriage and then it wasn't"—a difficult transition to make.

Category II. Many boys and girls expressed strong concern for the poor timing of their sex education. Speaking of their own age group, they said that attitudes had long since been formed, conclusions, either false or sound, had already been drawn, and that sex education at this time of life was "too little and too late." The majority agreed to the great importance of schools' emphasizing this topic during junior high school years, sometime between sixth and ninth grades. Some felt this depended on the emotional maturity and readiness of the individual child. However, they all agreed readily to the idea that this subject is not a new one to most sixth graders, who have already been exposed to "dirty words" and to many kinds of ideas about sex.

Therefore, young people attending this conference highly favored a simple and direct approach to some of the scientific facts about sex and reproduction as early as 8 or 9 years of age, as soon as children "were able to understand them." This would prepare them better for more pertinent discussions about boy-girl relationships by the time they had reached junior high school and had started to date.

Almost universally, however, the youth of today, as reflected by opinions expressed at this meeting, look to parents first and foremost for the foundation for understanding and early attitudes about sex. The most frequently expressed opinion was that whenever a young person asks a sincere question, he deserves to be answered honestly, no matter what his age. One youth remarked sagely that "that very first question" is often a turning point in a child's life and that if the parent laughs, derides him, or lets him down at this point, it may be permanently damaging. Reflecting the emotional impact of this topic, a number of boys and girls expressed the desire for a parent (or

at least someone "very close," like an older brother or sister) to be the first to answer a child's questions, followed by the school which can supplement home instructions more fully.

In answer to an often-asked question: "What kind of a person do you think can give you the best help in sex education?" there was a wide variety of responses. Many persons felt a doctor would be the best choice, some specified a teacher, particularly the science teacher, a health education teacher, or the coach; others chose parents, and more specifically, the father or the mother, while several students in parochial schools designated "a lay person." The composite qualities desired in a sex educator were that he or she be a young person, open-minded, warm, empathetic, with a flexible personality, skill in teaching, experienced, and specially educated for this rather complex subject.

Those they especially did *not* want to to teach them were the parents "who think your mind is dirty if you even ask a question," the parent who is himself a poor marital example, the parent who is shy and embarrassed when the subject of sex is brought up, the teacher who cannot hold the respect of a class and control "giggling," the football coach "who could put a fellow off the team for getting in trouble with a girl," nuns who "skip over it all lightly," and priests or ministers whose answers "always come out the same."

Topics suggested most frequently for inclusion in sex instruction were:

1. specifics about sexual intercourse;
2. "all the facts";
3. venereal disease information;
4. contraceptives, especially "the pill."

Many items were mentioned by at least some conference delegates, such as:

1. how *not* to get a girl pregnant;
2. how *not* to have a child;
3. more about the emotional side of sex, about one's feelings;
4. ideal marriage relations;
5. preliminaries to sexual intercourse, i.e., necking and petting;

6. love and sex;
7. family relations;
8. physiological processes and changes as men and women mature;
9. the beauty of sex, not always the bad side;
10. homosexuality, especially among boys "who need to know how to protect themselves from older men, when hitch-hiking, etc."

Students showed little interest in discussion from the moralistic viewpoints, or on why one should or should not do something, apparently preferring to make those decisions for themselves. Biological facts were considered to be not only fundamentals to be acquired early in life, but essential stepping-stones to better self-understanding sought by adolescents about themselves and their needs.

Category III was related specifically to parents as sex educators. As has been stated before, parents were identified often for the first choice, if not the major source of sex guidance in early years, for various reasons, such as that the parent "really knows the child" or because "it's their responsibility to help us form the right attitudes early." But an almost universal complaint was that parents were not able to or did not do an adequate job. They were judged in some cases to be uninformed themselves, to be suspicious of their children, to imply condemnation of a youth's behavior if information were sought, to act ashamed of the topic, to appear shy and embarrassed, evasive or uncomfortable, and apparently to be unable to cope with the reality that their children were really growing up. Many young people expressed the wish that parents themselves might be given some instruction through the schools or some community agency in order to help them fulfill their parental responsibility more adequately.

Category IV related to sex education in the schools. This source of help has been as disappointing to most youth as that which they sought in the homes. Students reported that "very little" was taught in most schools, that when the topic came up, many teachers "beat around the bush," and that what instruction there was lacked

depth and came too late. One youth described it as "just scientific facts, nothing on how we really feel" and summarized by saying "we need more *real* knowledge." One young delegate hazarded the opinion that: "The school is probably afraid that if they talk too freely in a coeducational classroom, it might produce a general moral breakdown!" In some schools, the students had observed their teachers themselves to be embarrassed, "blushing a lot." One teacher was reported to have admitted that she was not legally permitted to teach about birth control and other related topics raised by some pupils; the girl relating this incident ended pleadingly, "Where *can* we find out things? *No one* really tells us." The comment by one boy that in his school the only help received was from the football coach, who gave his regular "sex talk" drew many understanding chuckles from other boys in the group. Some girls brought out the fact that their teachers had merely emphasized a lot of vaguely understood "don'ts"—"don't let a boy sit too close to you"; "don't let him breathe on you," leaving the pupils themselves to interpret these dire warnings.

Many felt that books on the subject were either out-dated, inadequate, or inaccessible. They resented the fact that too often such books were kept behind the library desk, were available only upon special request to the librarian, and often only at the cost of some awkwardness and embarrassment.

They most frequently associated teaching about sex with biology classes, although in these situations it was limited to mere learning of scientific facts. A few students described instructions received in a family-living class, which apparently led into discussions of dating and courtship, but to only a limited degree with, as one young person remarked, "lots left out." A very few mentioned this topic being included in a sociology class or in health education or hygiene. None felt satisfied with the depth of instruction, the most common complaint being that they were given no help in understanding their own or each other's feelings, and how to cope with them. The most frequently expressed opinion was the need for small discussion groups, conducted in an unhampered and open manner, by a person who could really be trusted. Although not expressed in professional terms, they seemed to be seeking a group counselling approach as a preferred method of instruction.

A few were hesitant about having mixed classes exclusively, suggesting that earliest sex education classes might be better in single-sex groups—but that if boys and girls were taught separately, they might invite each other in for joint discussions of certain topics. However, the majority of students strongly favored mixed classes, expressing the opinion that "you learn more that way," "you soon get used to it and don't even think about it." They felt it was most important for boys and girls to share their opinions. Several suggested the pertinent advantages of having boys taught by women teachers and girls by men teachers.

It was suggested that one teacher in a school be specially prepared to deal with this subject, or as one young person described it: "He should have to go to a sex education school first." They agreed that the skill and personality of the teacher was a key factor, whoever he might be.

In *Category V* are grouped the opinions expressed about sex education as obtained from or shared with one's peers. On the positive side are the teen-agers' reports that often when parents have failed them in this subject, they have turned to older siblings or to older friends for further information. In some instances there exists a greater feeling of trust and confidence between close friends than between a child and his parents since, as expressed by one student, "We all face the same kind of problems." Some would even turn first of all to a close friend (presumably of the same sex) if faced with any major crisis in this area.

Facts about venereal disease, masturbation, and use of contraceptives were among those topics shared by young people with each other, as well as close, more intimate discussions of how to deal with personal situations. On the negative side, the opinion was expressed that the kind of information passed along in group contacts with one's peers is considerably less valuable. They had little respect for what was "picked

up on the streets," expressed the opinion that "locker room talk" often cheapened the subject which was discussed in the form of dirty jokes, or at best was merely a passing along of "grape-vine talk."

As for talking intimately about this topic with the opposite sex, such as on a date, the boys and girls had reservations. Some felt a date was primarily a social situation for fun and not for sex. Although one young person brought up the fact that going steady often "leads to situations which can get out of control," another (a boy) immediately countered with the opinion that "if a boy really likes a girl, it seems to me he'd respect her wishes." Talking about sex was considered "too intimate a topic" to be broached on dates by some and "too dangerous" or suggestive a topic by others. Those who favored discussion of this subject qualified it by stating that it "depends on the relationship between the two," and also that it is much easier to talk about sex after a class discussion in school.

Category VI includes the impact on sex understanding of other individuals or groups besides parents, friends, and the school. Since a high proportion of youths participating in this conference attended parochial schools, many naturally expressed very definite opinions as to the role of the church. Some were quite outspoken in criticism of the way sex education has been handled. Their perception was of clergy who were both inexperienced and basically uninterested in matters of sex and who thus could be of little help to young people in learning to cope with their personal problems in this area. Their major complaint was that the church stressed "all the don'ts," and moralized to youth, although never really explaining why they shouldn't do things. Both boys and girls from parochial schools indicated a marked preference for a "lay teacher" who, as they said, would be better able to give them "practical advice." One young seminarian, however, rose to the defense of the church, saying that his guidance counsellor had been very frank and outspoken because "if you're going to be a priest, you need to have all the facts in order to help others."

On the other hand, when one group of

students was asked where they would go for help if any of them had a serious sex problem (i.e., had perhaps contracted a venereal disease), several promptly named their confessor. One young boy replied, "I'd never want to tell my parents or anyone! Guess I'd just pray and die quietly." Consistent with other related opinions expressed, many boys and girls felt the need for the home, the school, and the church to work together more closely and to encourage open and frank discussions.

In several groups, the students brought up the subject of the general influence upon their life of sex as depicted in television commercials, ads, movies, and daily life experiences. They felt it was represented to them as glamorous and desirable, yet adults didn't help them to understand the other sides of it. Consequently, young people got all the blame when they "got into trouble."

Category VII. In several groups specific problems were posed for consideration, such as "should a girl who is obviously pregnant be allowed to continue school?" "Should a pregnant teacher still work in a school?" "Is nude swimming a problem for many boys?" "What would you do if you thought you had a venereal disease?" or "if you faced a serious sex problem?"

To the first question the answers were definitely in the affirmative, as to permitting a pregnant pupil or teacher to continue in school if she chose to be there. Anything less, one person explained was "hiding sex —which is what we're trying to overcome." In the same vein, boys were not in agreement with parental anxieties over nude swimming, although they admitted that differences of opinion might be found. The latter questions pertaining to sources of available help offered the most difficulty. Some felt there "just wasn't anyone in the school one could go to"; others said "a close friend," "a minister," "a doctor," or "my parents, since they'd find out anyway." Many felt completely at a loss, saying that the only thing they were sure of is that their parents would be the *last* ones they'd tell because they felt parents "trusted them and they'd hate to let them down."

In summary, the following generalizations may be drawn from the many frank opinions of boys and girls expressed in their eleven discussion groups:

1. practically no one felt adequately prepared to cope with the sex problems of adolescence;
2. concern seemed to be focused mainly on premarital sex relations in high school years.
3. much less thought was given to the total role of sexuality in life situations, or to other related aspects of family-life education;
4. ideas about parents were rather ambivalent, i.e., some expressed open hostility or antagonism towards parents for having failed them in an important area of guidance, while others spoke wistfully of help for parents themselves so that when children needed their help, a better job could be done;
5. although many young persons wanted children to get guidance in sex matters very early (ranging anywhere from 4 to 5 years of age when first questions were asked to the lower elementary grades), most agreed that the greatest emphasis should be placed on sex education in the junior high school years;
6. rather than exactly *who* could teach them about sex, discussion focused on the *kind* of a person. Young people felt they had sought, too often unsuccessfully, for someone they could trust, regardless of age, sex, or functional role.

CONCLUSIONS

What youth are asking for today, if this conference is any indication, runs the gamut from condoning of free sex relations, information on how to avoid social consequences of the sex act, and no moralizing or criticism, to faith, trust, and understanding, and an earlier and greater emphasis on instruction about values and attitudes toward sex.

It was felt by those who attended this one-day conference that the outcomes were indeed significant. They presented a serious challenge to adult members of society on every front—home, school, church, and informed youth groups—to face up honestly to the charge of ineptness in the field of sex education.

PTA groups have a responsibility to offer constructive assistance to parents everywhere. Teachers should find short-term institutes, workshops, and graduate courses increasingly available in the community to aid them in developing not only the essential understandings but the skills needed for more effective communication with youth. Church leaders of all faiths must dare to face themselves critically and reevaluate the methods by which they seek to offer guidance and help to our young generation.

Law makers may well need to scrutinize any restrictions on sex education which might in fact defeat the larger goals of enlightened sex behavior generally sought. The educational leaders in Detroit have already accepted this challenge and are even now engaged in deepening and extending their professional programs to reach more youth and to teach them what they need and want to know in a more meaningful way.

It is too early to evaluate the total results of this conference. It can only be hoped that rather than serving as an end in itself, this worthwhile endeavor has served as a springboard to much needed action.

13

THE PERCEPTUAL CONTEXT OF BOY-GIRL COMMUNICATION

Carlfred B. Broderick and Jean Weaver

A great deal has been written about the significance of various aspects of communication in courtship and marriage. For this reason those interested in children's social development have often stressed the importance of establishing ways of relating to the opposite sex as a major task of adolescent development. And yet nothing is known about the typical development of boy-girl communication over the formative years. Earlier reports of the present study have traced the steps by which children move gradually from the romantic fantasies of secret crushes in preadolescence to the establishment of a heterosexual social world in later adolescence,[1] but even these shed little light on the communication aspect of the development.

The present report attempts to contribute to the understanding of this important subject through an analysis of the way young people construe situations which provide the opportunity for communication. The assumption is that the way a heterosexual situation is interpreted largely determines the type of message which is likely to be sent and the type of reception it is likely to get. Data will be presented relative to whether boys and girls typically perceived the same situational stimulus in similar ways or differently, whether these perceptions change with age, and, if so, whether they converge or diverge. Several related questions will also be explored. It is hoped that these data may provide the foundation for hypotheses about the content and consequences of various types of heterosexual communication at these ages.

MEASURES

The subjects, gathered in groups, were presented with a questionnaire which was constructed as follows: On the front and back of the first page were instructions and standard background questions plus a place to list the names of one's closest friends. Following this was a warm-up cartoon, showing two children of their own sex walking together. In connection with this picture (and with each of the following two pictures) they were instructed to tell what was happening in the picture, why, and what each person was thinking. The purpose of the first cartoon was to give an opportunity to practice responding to this type of stimulus and also to deemphasize the heterosexual nature of the other pictures. This practice picture was then followed by two "conversational" settings pictured on facing pages. (See Figure 1.) The first picture showed a front view of a boy and girl

standing side by side staring out of the picture. The second showed a boy and girl sitting side by side on a bench. (See Figure 1.)

These were followed by cartoons depicting two action situations, also on facing pages. (See Figure 2.) In one (picture 3), a boy running after a girl is depicted. In the other (picture 4) a girl running after a boy is presented. For these pictures the instructions were to tell: What is happening now? Why? What will happen next? How will the girl feel then? How will the boy feel then?

Fifth- through eighth-grade subjects were given a set of pictures with body proportions which were basically prepubescent, while ninth to twelfth graders were given pictures with adolescent proportions. This was found to be necessary by pretests which showed that older subjects tended to see the younger pictures as "children" and not to identify with them. As a control on the differential impact of the stimuli, one eighth-grade class was given the adolescent set of pictures. Their responses did not differ noticeably (or significantly) from those of eighth graders who received the preadolescent set.

Following the pictures came a series of questions on various social heterosexual activities. This material has been reported elsewhere. . . .

FIGURE 1. CONVERSATIONAL SETTINGS: STIMULUS PICTURES 1 AND 2. PRE-ADOLESCENT FORMS (ADOLESCENT FORMS IN INSET).

FIGURE 2. ACTION SETTINGS: STIMULUS PICTURES 3 AND 4. PREADOLESCENT
FORMS (ADOLESCENT FORMS IN INSET).

SUBJECTS

The data were collected in the spring of
1962, in central Pennsylvania. The sample
consists of 3,551 boys and girls distributed
by age and sex as shown in Table 1. It included all of the fifth through twelfth graders attending the ten elementary and four
junior-senior high schools selected for the
study. The schools were chosen to include
rural, urban, and suburban areas, with the
full range of social classes. All of the rural
and suburban children were white, but
about one-quarter of the urban children
were Negro. For purposes of the present
analysis, ten- and eleven-year-olds were grouped
together, as were 12- and 13-year-olds, 14-
and 15-year-olds, and 16- and 17-year-olds.
Students 18 years old or older were dropped
from the sample.

ANALYSIS OF DATA

Responses to Conversational Settings (Pictures 1 and 2)

The responses of the children to the two
conversational settings were divisible into
four main categories. . . . The majority of
both sexes defined both the standing and
sitting situations as having romantic potential; that is, there was clear evidence of
a positive heterosexual (as opposed to
merely social) interest on the part of the
boy or the girl in the picture (or most often,
on the part of both). For example, here are
three responses typical of this "romantic"
definition of the situation:

*A boy is walking a girl home from the movie.
. . . because they're in love. [The girl is
thinking] Why doesn't he kiss me. [The boy
is thinking] I'd like to hold her hand. [Boy
age 11, picture 1.]*
    *A boy and girl is going on a date. Be-
cause they are very close boy friend and
girl friend [The girl is thinking about] getting an education. [The boy is thinking
about] getting married. [Girl age 13, picture 1.]*
    *There is a boy and girl sitting beside
each other. And the boy looks like he is try-*

TABLE 1. TOTAL NUMBER IN
EACH AGE-SEX GROUP

	Ages				
	10–11	*12–13*	*14–15*	*16–17*	*Total*
Boys	299	442	580	408	1,729
Girls	298	478	623	423	1,822
Total	597	920	1,203	831	3,551

ing to take her hand, because he likes her alot. She is probably thinking weather to take his hand or not. He is probably thinking weather she is going to take his hand or not. [Girl age 14, picture 2.]

The second most frequent type of response (roughly one-quarter of the entire group) also focused upon the interpersonal aspects of the situation, but gave no clear evidence of any romantic implications.

It looks like they were fussing about something . . . over something someone said. [The girl is thinking] Why would someone say what they did? [The boy is thinking] I don't think anyone said it, I think she made it up. [Girl age 12, picture 1.]

A boy and a girl are sitting together because they might like each other. She is probably thinking what will happen next or who will they meet. He is thinking what can he do to have fun, like go for a horseback ride, etc. [Girl age 12, picture 2.]

The third most frequent type of response (about 15 percent) defined the situation as focused upon some circumstance, such as a game or waiting for a bus, which had no important interpersonal focus.

Boy and girl walking, because they want to get someplace. [The girl is thinking] where she is going. [The boy is thinking] where he is going. [Boy age 17, picture 1.]

They are standing watching for the parade to come. They want to see the different things in the parade and someone in the band they know. She's thinking about her best girlfriend being in the parade. He's thinking about the rocket that is supposed to come through. [Girl age 14, picture 1.]

The least common type of response (only one or two percent) were those indicating that the situation was viewed as social in the negative sense; i.e., the theme was hostile or sexually exploitative rather than friendly or "romantic" as described above.

A boy and girl sitting on an old bench at a square dance, because he can't sit anywhere else. She is thinking how to get away

from him. He is thinking why doesn't she move. [Boy age 11, picture 2.]

A boy and girl are sitting on a bench. The boy wants to make out with the girl. The girl is thinking about the boy. The boy is trying to think of some way to ask the girl. [Boy age 17, picture 2.]

. . . The boys more often than the girls did show a tendency to perceive the couple as romantically involved. On their part the girls tended to impute mere friendship to the relationships more often than the boys did. This may be nothing more than coyness on the part of the girls, of course, but of such stuff are communication difficulties sometimes spun. . . .

The older the respondents, the more likely they were to view the boy-girl situation in the light of its potential for romantic interaction. The boys responded this way more than the girls at every age. The tendency to view boy-girl situations as noninterpersonal in their focus decreased with age for both sexes. So also did hostile and exploitative foci.

The previously noted tendency for girls to use the "just friends" category more than boys is most pronounced at ages 12–13 and 14–15. This is consistent with the notion that a "cool" approach to boy-girl relations is a more prominent strategy for girls during these difficult inbetween years. Further on in the analysis it becomes clear that boys too, at these middle ages, are more likely to resort to indirect courtship strategies (such as teasing).

Romantic subthemes. A further analysis of the responses of those who perceived the couple in a romantic context showed that there were at least three quite different types of communication settings grouped under this general heading. The most common interpretation was what might be called the *developing romance.* In it one or both parties were viewed as trying to get a romantic relationship initiated, or, if already initiated, as trying to move it along toward a more established status:

A boy is walking with a girl because he likes or loves her. She is thinking whether to go to the school dance with him or an-

other boy. He is trying to think of a way to ask her to the dance. [Boy age 11, picture 1.]

The boy is trying to become acquainted with the girl and is gradually moving closer to her. The girl seems to be in a position to talk to strangers, and the boy seems to be a little uneasy and probably uncomfortable. The girl is telling herself to act as calm as possible and to try not to show her anxiety over the fact that the boy considers her pretty enough to talk to. The boy definitely is very nervous and is hoping that he can make a good impression with the girl. He is probably concerned over the fact that she might not consider him handsome and won't want to talk to him. [Boy age 17, picture 2.]

. . . Boys—and especially younger boys—are more likely to conceptualize the romantic situation in these terms than girls their own age. Girls are increasingly likely to employ this interpretation as they grow older, so that by 16–17 there is virtually no difference between the sexes.

A second context for communication that shows some tendency to increase with age and also is more commonly found in boys' responses than in girls' is the *complicated romance*. This is a situation in which either there is some frustration in the initial stages of a relationship (such as lack of reciprocity) that keeps it from ever getting off the ground or there is a quarrel or misunderstanding that threatens an already established relationship.

The boy and girl have just met each other. They both want to make a good impression with the other but they feel wound up inside so they are too afraid to—because instantly they were attracted to each other. But if you like the person you are many times frightened to say anything so you keep your mouth SHUT! Probably she is desperately thinking of something witty and cute to say to the boy she has just met. She probably feels funny in her stomach and wishing she knew him better. He is thinking something very masculine to say that will impress the girl quite highly. If one of them said something, no matter how dumb, they would probably feel more at ease. But they

are too much afraid since they think it will ruin their chances for further advancement. [Girl age 16, picture 2.]

This couple have just arrived at the girl's home. They have had a fight. They are going steady and maybe they are seeing too much of each other. They find that they are being mean and trying to make the other jealous more and more as time passes. The girl is sorry that they are not getting along but she has too much pride to say that she is sorry, so she just sits there and waits for him to speak first. The boy is also sorry and wants to tell the girl, but he is afraid that she is mad at him and won't speak to him. He wonders why they quarrel like this all the time. [Girl age 16, picture 2.]

A third context for heterosexual communication as described by these boys and girls was the uncomplicated, *established romance*.

My girl and I are going to the dance. It is a Saturday night and the moon is full and it is very warm out. We think a lot of each other and we both enjoy dancing. [Boy age 16, picture 1.]

The girl and boy are sitting on a bench because the boy wants her too. She is thinking about a baby. He is thinking about the same thing. [Girl age 12, picture 2.]

This type of interpretation is more likely to be made by girls than boys, and it decreases with age.

The large majority of romantic interpretations of these boy-girl situations can be assigned to one of these three major categories. There are, however, a residual group that do not fit any of these categories. This group does not exceed 16 percent for any age-sex group and averages about ten percent overall.

Degree of social adequacy. One other dimension of these subjects' perception of boy-girl relations was abstracted from these responses, namely, the degree of social adequacy projected onto the boy and the girl in the pictures, irrespective of the definition of the setting.

These data are too complex to present fully here since they involve boys' perceptions of boys, boys' perceptions of girls, girls' perceptions of boys, and girls' perceptions of girls for each stimulus picture and for each age group, but a summary of the main findings may be useful. Only a minority of stories provided sufficient information on this point.[2] Those that did were coded as revealing a sense of social adequacy and security or as revealing mild, moderate, or severe degrees of social inadequacy and discomfort. It was expected that one's sense of adequacy might increase with age and experience, but the opposite was true. The girls told stories in which the couple[3] felt socially adequate and secure in about 20 percent of the codable cases at ages ten to 11, and the frequency of this perception steadily decreased to less than ten percent at 16–17. For the boys, the drop was from about 15 percent to less than five percent over the same age span.

The most common category, especially at the young age levels, was mild social inadequacy (that is, being unsure of how to act or what to say or wondering what the other person thought of one). This tended to be more characteristic of boys' than of girls' stories.[4] Feelings of moderate social inadequacy (shyness, fear, embarrassment, inability to express feelings) were quite rare at the ten to 11-year age but became very common in responses at later ages.[5] Very few (under five percent) at any age told stories, in response to these first two pictures, which showed a feeling of severe social inadequacy (feeling stupid, terrible, awful, that one "goofed," etc.). Thus, the very large majority of subjects who told stories that gave evidence of the level of social adequacy projected feelings of mild to moderate social inadequacy in these boy-girl situations, and their feelings of inadequacy increased rather than decreased with age.

Responses to the Action Settings (Pictures 3 and 4)

It has been noted above that the stimulus values of the first two pictures were identical; that is, each evoked almost exactly the same types of response. The same cannot be said for pictures 3 and 4. Both pictures show a boy and girl running, but in picture 3 the boy is behind and in picture 4 the girl is behind. (See Figure 2.) The difference in responses does not show up in the distribution according to major foci, however; that is, either picture is as likely as the other to be viewed as romantic, friendly, hostile, or nonrelationship centered. . . .

Although these more active situations were interpreted as nonrelationship-oriented or hostile more often than the conversational settings, yet the same general age and sex patterns are in evidence that were noted in the responses to the first two stimulus pictures. The proportion of romantic and social interpretations increased steadily with age while the proportion of nonrelationship-oriented interpretations decreased. The hostile and sexually exploitative responses showed some slight tendency to drop also, especially for boys. Boys again showed a greater tendency at each age to impute romantic overtones to the situation than girls. The girls were more likely to interpret the whole scene as a game or race or as fleeing from some common enemy or running toward some common goal (trying to catch a school bus, for example)—in short, as a situation without an important relational element in it. Again it is not clear why there is this difference of perception between the sexes, but one may speculate that girls often fail to perceive the relational significance which boys attach to joint activities of this type. It may be that gross activities such as running are a more familiar idiom of interaction for boys than for girls and that communication in this idiom may miss the target a good part of the time.

Romantic subthemes. It was in the romantic subthemes that the most dramatic differences between the responses to the two "running" pictures were revealed. Whereas it would appear to make little difference whether the boy or the girl was running behind in most games or in social situations where the heterosexual element was not focal, it obviously makes a difference when the situation is defined as romantic.

Before turning to the differences between a boy chasing a girl and a girl chasing a boy, however, one should note that these two pictures evoked a wider range of types of romantic situations than the conversational pictures did. The categories of "developing relationships" and "established romances" seemed to serve adequately to describe many of the responses, but the category "complicated romance" needed to be further divided into those situations with an optimistic and those with a pessimistic cast; that is, those where the problem is being resolved and those where it remains unresolved.

For example:

[*Optimistic*]
The girl is probably teasing her boyfriend. He got angry and she ran. Because he was mad she ran with him after her. He will probably stop her, and they will both start laughing. [The girl will feel] sorry she teased him too much. [The boy will feel] sorry he got mad because she was teasing him. [Girl age 16, picture 3.]

He has finally got on her nerves and she is chasing him away. Just out of spite because she is tired of his stammering around. She will probably get over it and they will stop and try to start anew. [The girl will feel] better because she will have calmed down and start to think. [The boy will feel] more confident in himself. [Boy age 18, picture 4.]

[*Pessimistic*]
The boy is chasing the girl. He loves her. She will turn around and slap him. [The girl will feel] happy. [The boy will feel] very mad. [Boy age 12, picture 3.]

The girl is chasing the boy. He gave her a ring and she doesn't want it. She will scream at him. She will feel awful. [The boy will feel] awful. [Girl age 11, picture 4.]

Two additional classes of responses were also discriminated out of the residual category. One was labeled *Pre-Romantic Teasing*. These stories involve some act that, on the face of it, is hostile (such as pulling a girl's hair or taking a boy's pencil) but which pleased, rather than offended, the other party because it was interpreted as a social approach:

A boy is chasing a girl. Because she kicked him for fun. The boy will catch the girl and they will kid around about it. She will feel O.K. He will feel happy. [Boy age 11, picture 3.]

The boy is chasing after the girl. She is afraid that he will catch her. The girl teased the boy, and then started running so that the boy would catch her. The boy will catch up to the girl. She will be glad that he caught her. (He will feel) like he has succeeded in doing something that boys should be able to do. [Girl age 14, picture 3.]

A girl is chasing a boy. Because he was kidding her about something like a boyfriend or something like that. The girl will not catch him now, but she will get him later when he is not expecting it. She will feel good. He will feel O.K. [Boy age 11, picture 4.]

The other new category is *Erotic Pursuit*. Examples of this category are the following:

The boy got up enough nerve to put his arm around his girl and he frightened her so she started to run from him. She wasn't expecting it. He will catch her and maybe kiss her. [She will feel] flipped. [The boy will feel] like a heel. [Boy age 18, picture 3.]

The girl is running after the boy and the girl is running faster than the boy, because the girl has stronger legs. The boy will fall. [The girl will feel] strong arms. [The boy will feel] warm lips. [Girl age 15, picture 4.]

The boy and girl tried something; because they are in love. The girl will get in trouble. She has done something wrong and she will not be able to face people. [The boy will feel] sorry for what he did. [Girl age 12, picture 3.]

The significance of differential sex roles in the interpretation of these romantically cast situations shows up . . . in two ways. First, a boy chasing a girl is significantly more likely to be interpreted (1) as an attempt to establish a new relationship, (2) as an attempt to mend a problem in the relationship, and (3) as an attempt to kiss or "make out" with the girl than if the sex roles were reversed. When the girl is doing the chasing, the relationship is more likely to be written off as unsalvageable. In the latter case she is often seen as chasing him in anger for some hurt or affront, or else she is chasing him to make up and is judged to be stupid for thinking that this approach will work.

Boys and girls also showed some significant differences in the ways they interpreted the two pictures. Girls, more often than boys, were willing to interpret these pictures as depicting the innocent, exuberant romp of an established pair. They were also somewhat more likely to interpret both pictures as erotic pursuits although, again, they were quite condemnatory of the girl who used such crude methods to get a kiss.

Boys, on the other hand, were more likely than girls to view the two situations as scenes in a lovers' quarrel with the boy as initially remorseful and then successful when he ran after the girl to make up and the girl as either angry or inept when she ran after the boy. To put it differently, they were more generous in the motives assigned to the boys and less generous in their interpretation of the girls' role, while the girls' interpretations were more generous to their own sex.

One other finding . . . is worth noting, and that is the incidence of what we have called pre-romantic teasing at the various ages. The projection of this phenomenon reaches its peak among the 12- and 13-year-olds, particularly among the girls. It appears that this type of behavior is transitional in nature, bridging the low levels of heterosexual interaction at ten to 11 and the more sophisticated approaches of adolescence.

The data on social adequacy also reflect the lack of symmetry in the two pictured situations. Whereas the responses to the two "inactive" pictures interpreted the boy and girl as sharing the same feelings of adequacy or inadequacy in over 90 percent of the responses, with the two running pictures the case was quite otherwise.

In these pictures it is useful to separate the feelings of social adequacy into feelings of active achievement and success and feelings of passive happiness or security. (These categories were used in the coding of the first two pictures also, but were collapsed for purposes of presentation.) The most common interpretation of the boy-chasing-girl situation is that the boy is successful and the girl is happy. Boys are significantly more likely to give this interpretation than girls. The next most common combination is a simple, balanced boy-happy, girl-happy or carefree romp. One minor theme, more often used by girls than by boys, found the boy blundering and inept initially, but finally running after the girl to apologize and successfully restoring feelings of adequacy and happiness to both. In a variation, also more commonly seen by girls, both the boy and the girl show ineptness and both end up miserable. The only other theme that warrants mention occurs primarily among the older boys and girls and sees both the boy and the girl as feeling that their efforts have been successful. In other words, the role of the girl in initiating the boy's pursuit is recognized.

The girl-chasing-boy picture tended to be interpreted, especially by boys, as either girl successful-boy happy in a symmetrical role reversal or as the boy-happy-girl-happy romp in which sex role was not an important factor. Another fairly common interpretation reflected the role discrepancy directly and judgmentally. In these stories the girl was chasing the boy, hoping to make him like her, but was seen by the boy (and by the respondent) as failing because her tactic was stupid and inept. Less common patterns (all fewer than ten percent) included stories in which both parties were successful in their strategies and stories in which both fail through ineptness and bungling.

CONCLUSIONS

From these data it can be reasoned that there is a natural history of communication between young people of the opposite sex. Between the ages of ten to 17 (which is to say between the fifth and twelfth grades), there is a clear shift toward the boy-girl relationship itself as the focus of heterosexual social situations. As reflected in the stories elicited in this study, communication between the sexes came to have less and less to do with matters external to the pair, and more and more to do with the establishment, maintenance, or repair of what we have called romantic relationships. It is worth noting also that hostile themes which are supposed to be so big a part of the cross-sex relationship in preadolescence, and exploitation which is supposed to play such a part in adolescence, are quite rare even in the pictures which readily lend themselves to a hostile interpretation. Rather, the tone of communication at all ages is predominantly uncertain and stressful and becomes more so with increasing age as gambits such as pre-romantic teasing are dropped in favor of more serious approaches to the opposite sex. The one optimistic note is that with increasing age boys are viewed as being increasingly able to initiate successfully the patching of difficulties. On the other hand, girls see themselves less and less successful in employing these same tactics. Presumably more traditionally subtle tactics are learned.

There were small but systematic differences in the perceptions of the sexes such that the boys at each age perceived the romantic potential of each situation more clearly than the female. It was suggested that this might be interpreted as mere coyness on the part of the female in the conversational setting, since she chose to define the situations as "liking" or social while avoiding reference to the heterosexual aspects. Another possible interpretation is that she simply viewed the heterosexual potential as implicit, to be taken for granted in such social situations and, therefore, failed to spell it out in such a way as to meet the coding criteria for "romantic." In the action situations, however, a different interpretation is suggested, since in this case it was not the "social" but the "nonrelationships" category which accounted for the surplus of females at each age. It would seem that in this instance it is a matter of girls being less perceptive of the interpersonal significance of action situations, presumably because of their traditional focus on the verbal rather than the action medium of conversation.

Of course, one should not lose sight of the fact that the differences between the sexes were not large in absolute terms and that the most accurate generalization from these data would be that boys and girls perceive the heterosexual world in a basically similar way at each age.

It remains for future research to determine the consequences of perceptual differences within a given relationship.

NOTES

[1] Carlfred B. Broderick, "Socio-Sexual Development in a Suburban Community," *Journal of Sex Research*, 2 (April 1966): 1–24. See also Carlfred B. Broderick and George Rowe, "A Scale of Preadolescent Heterosexual Development," *Journal of Marriage and the Family*, 30:1 (February 1968): 97–101.

[2] The proportion whose responses could be coded for projected social adequacy rose for about 15 percent at ages ten to 11 to about 50 percent at ages 16–17.

[3] For these two pictures the level of projected social adequacy was the same for the boy and girl in the picture in over 90 percent of the codable stories.

[4] The percentage of couples characterized in the codable stories by feelings of mild social inadequacy ranged from 55 to 65 percent at the various ages when the girls were telling the story and from 65 to 80 percent when the boys were telling it.

[5] The percentage of couples characterized in the codable stories by feelings of moderate social inadequacy rose from only five percent among the boys' stories at ages ten to 11 to about 25 percent at all later ages and from only 12 percent at ages ten to 11 to 25 percent at 12–13 and 14–15, and 30 percent at ages 16–17 among girls' stories.

14

ADOLESCENT LOVE AS A REFLECTION OF TEEN-AGERS' SEARCH FOR IDENTITY

Evelyn Millis Duvall

Some adults take adolescent love affairs lightly, regarding them as temporary and inconsequential. Others express their amusement at the callow quality of teen-agers' affection, as Booth Tarkington did so well in *Seventeen*. Some parents and teachers view adolescent love with dismay and fear its consequences in premarital sexual precocity or impulsive premature marriage. Still other adults may agree that puppy love often leads to a dog's life, but they feel that teen-agers have a right to make their own mistakes in affairs of the heart, for these affairs, after all, cannot be controlled.

Recognizing these different attitudes toward early love relationships, we can still realize that adolescent love may reflect the life situation of a given teen-ager in ways which make it possible to understand and deal with it in perspective. Granted that America's romantic culture "sells" love on every hand, there must be some reason why some high school students fall in love so early, while others remain fairly cool-headed until they have finished their schooling and are ready to settle down in marriage. Reviewing relevant research leads to three hypotheses.

1. *Teen-agers who feel that they are in love tend to be actively repudiating their parents in one or more ways.* This is suggested by Nye's findings[1] that some adolescents reject their parents more than do others and that teen-agers' behavior is more closely related to the attitude of the child toward the parent than of the parent toward the child.[2] Feeling estranged from his parents, the adolescent may attach himself affectionally to a member of the opposite sex, both to satisfy his emotional hunger and to show his parents that they are not so emotionally important anymore. Conversely, the high school student who has a fairly good relationship with his parents

may be expected to be less involved emotionally in adolescent love affairs.

2. *Those high school students who start early in those involvements which lead to marriage may be expected to plan to marry sooner than those who have not fallen in love and gone steady from an early age.* Some researchers have found a straight-line relationship between adolescents' being in love, going steady, and early marriage. Comparing girls who had married before their high school graduation with matched samples of high school girls who had not married, Burchinal found that married girls had started dating and going steady earlier, had more steady boy friends, felt that they were in love more frequently, and dated more seriously at all ages.[3] Similarly, Moss and Gingles' study revealed that girls who marry young had begun dating earlier and had more serious dating relationships than did high school girls who had not married.[4]

3. *Adolescents with low aspiration levels and inadequate self-concepts may be expected to fall in love and have strong drives toward marriage as an escape from an unpromising life situation.* Recent longitudinal studies of adolescents growing up in a midwestern city found that girls who marry early tend to be socially maladjusted and to be doing poor school work or to be girls who prefer marriage to either college or a career. They also show that "Most of the boys who marry at 18 or before are dropouts, whose school record was poor and whose social adjustment in school was poor."[5] On the other hand, those teen-agers who have a satisfying sense of self and who are anticipating open doors to future education and vocational placement would be expected to be less likely to fall in love and get married until they have realized their other life dreams.

To test these three hypotheses, a sentence-completion, open-end questionnaire was given to all students in attendance on a certain day in both junior and senior high schools in selected communities across the United States. Along with other basic data, the form included a section on which the student checked "Yes," "No," or "Not sure" on such items as:

"Are you in love with some special person right now?"

"Do you have 'an understanding' or are you going steady?"

"Do you plan to marry before you are 21?"

"Do you expect to go to college for four or more years?"

"Would you like your marriage to be like your parents'?"

Some 3,499 usable questionnaires were collected from 1,001 students in grades 8 and 9, and 2,498 were received from students in grades 10, 11, and 12. The schools were located in white collar and blue collar suburban communities, in a large industrial city, and in a homogeneous mountain area. A few more girls than boys were in the schools on the day the form was administered. The total sample was composed of 1,856 girls and 1,643 boys.

Sizable percentages of all students at all grade levels and in all the schools replied "Yes" to the question, "Are you in love with some special person right now?" As might be expected, more girls (36 percent) than boys (25 percent) felt that they were in love. Especially noteworthy is the finding that the percentages of boys and girls who said that they were in love differed greatly both by grade levels and by communities. . . .

The percentage of students who feel they are in love increases from the 8th grade through the 12th grade in the blue collar suburbs, suggesting a gradual emotional involvement as the boy and girl mature. But it is not as simple as that. In the industrial city, the highest percentage of girls (51 percent) who feel they are in love is at the 9th grade level, this percentage being significantly[6] higher than that found in these same schools among 11th grade girls (30 percent). The highest percentages of students in the mountain Mormon schools

who feel that they are in love are found among the junior high school boys, with 40 percent of the 8th grade boys and 35 percent of the 9th grade boys saying that they are in love. These percentages are significantly higher than are found among senior high school boys in the same schools.

Such differences by grade and community in percentages of students of both sexes who feel that they are in love cannot be explained by physiological or emotional maturity alone. Other factors and forces must be operating at any given time and place.

Exploring the over-all thesis that adolescent love is a reflection of the teen-ager's total life situation, the hypotheses are borne out by the data, as follows:

1. A significant relationship exists between *not* wanting a marriage like one's parents and being in love with some special person right now. Those teen-agers who are in the process of repudiating their parents' patterns of marriage are more inclined to be forming close emotional attachments with members of the other sex in their own generation than are those students who want to reproduce their family patterns and who presumably are more closely identified with their parents.

2. A significant relationship exists between going steady and being in love with some special person right now. Couples who see a great deal of one another in mutual exclusiveness, as young people who go steady do, may be expected to become emotionally attached to each other and to feel that they are in love. Some may feel that they go steady because they are more fond of each other than of any one else available at the time. Still others may be responding to the social pressure to feel attached to the person with whom their name is linked as a steady dating partner.

3. A significant relationship exists between *not* expecting to go through college and being in love with some special person while in high school. Conversely, there is a significant relationship between expecting to go to college for four years and *not* being in love while in junior or senior high school. Those who are uncertain about going to college tend to be those who are

not sure that they are in love right now. The trend is clear—those high school students with plans which they fully expect will be realized, as measured by their expectations of going through college, are teen-agers who are much less likely to be in love while in school.

4. A significant relationship exists between planning to marry before 21 and *not* planning to go through college. Teen-agers who plan to marry relatively young tend to be those who do not expect to go through college. Those who expect to marry in their teens tend to be those who are already in love and going steady. Conversely, those who do not plan to marry before they reach 21 tend to be those who expect to go through college. College-bound teen-agers are less often in love while in high school and tend to do less going steady than do students who are not college-bound.

Being in love as a teen-ager appears, in some cases, to be an escape hatch for those who feel that other doors to the future are closed. The boy or girl who does not expect to go through college is far more likely to plan to get married instead. This is especially true of girls who see marriage as a socially approved way of establishing themselves as women. It is more true of young people growing up in industrial areas, where their parents are employed in factories in the service trades, than it is of young people whose parents are themselves college-oriented.

Teen-agers who aspire to contract marriages like those of their parents tend to be less often in love while in school, are less frequently going steady, and are less apt to plan on being married before they are 21. These young people can be seen as finding a satisfying sense of identity in their own families when they are relatively comfortable about continuing their families' way of life. Thus they are less urgent about cutting loose from their parents and developing adolescent love affairs.

Teen-agers who expect to go through college get a sense of identity and purpose through their educational aspirations and so are less inclined to seek it in a love relationship. They may be socially active as members of the younger generation, but

they do not have to balloon their feelings of warmth for others to fill a need in their own lives. These are the teen-agers who get through school, go on to college, and, as their educational plans near completion, find a suitable partner and make a good marriage.

Teachers and parents who are concerned about youth avoiding premature involvements, impulsive love attachments, and immature marriages are wise to provide wider opportunities for teen-agers to find themselves in today's world. Varied educational offerings that enable youth to develop individual talents and special abilities are relevant. A variety of apprentice-like openings in which teen-age boys and girls can get some first-hand experience in a field of work before they become completely committed are helpful. The youth-outreach programs which some communities are inaugurating can go far to help a given teen-ager find models to emulate and to gain experiences which will prevent too early closure of his personality. These programs enlarge the horizons of the younger generation through planned exposure to different cultures and to personalities who have made a place for themselves in such fields as science, arts, and sports.

Erikson[7] points out that only as a young person begins to feel secure in his own identity is he able to establish the kind of mature intimacy with others that augurs well for his full development as a person. Growing up in a society that exaggerates both love and sex, many an adolescent regards falling in love and getting married as the way to adulthood. This is especially true of girls, who all too often have been so impressed with the wife role that it becomes difficult for them to think of themselves as human beings with talents and interests which go beyond those involved in homemaking. Less privileged youth of both sexes are similarly handicapped in finding other satisfying ways of life. In their urge to become, they turn too quickly to becoming husbands and wives as an easy answer to their query, "Who am I?"

Today's teen-agers, who are thrown together with great freedom and little supervision from early ages, need more than ever the kind of guidance that will help them to appraise their own love feelings throughout the second decade of life. Some of the most urgent questions that come from both boys and girls in junior and senior high school have to do with whether or not they are in love, how they can tell when they are really in love, and what are appropriate ways of expressing their love feelings for a person of the other sex.[8] These are the very topics that many parents find difficult to discuss with their teen-age sons and daughters.[9] Only occasionally are these questions included in church and community programs for youth.

Schools that include as major emphases basic education in personality growth, the nature of social and emotional development, and ways in which individuals can move toward establishing their own identity may be contributing greatly to the strength of the younger generation and the solidarity of the homes of tomorrow.

NOTES

[1] F. Ivan Nye, *Family Relationships and Delinquent Behavior* (New York: John Wiley, 1958), pp. 69–78.

[2] Ibid., p. 76.

[3] Lee G. Burchinal, "Adolescent Role Deprivation and High School Marriage," *Marriage and Family Living*, 21 (November 1959): 378–384.

[4] Joel J. Moss and Ruby Gingles, "The Relationship of Personality to the Incidence of Early Marriage," *Marriage and Family Living*, 21 (November 1949): 373–377.

[5] Robert J. Havighurst et al., *Growing up in River City* (New York: John Wiley, 1962), p. 129.

[6] All references to significant differences or relationships are statistically determined and were significant at the .01 level or better in each case.

[7] Erik H. Erikson, "Youth and the Life Cycle," *Children*, March-April 1960.

[8] E. M. Duvall, *Love and the Facts of Life* (New York: Association Press, 1963).

[9] Marvin C. Dubbé, "What Young People Can't Talk Over with Their Parents," *National Parent-Teacher*, 52 (October 1957): 18–20.

Part Four

Searching for Self-Identity as a Young Adult

A major developmental task in the young-adult years is to strike a balance between the newly found freedom to make decisions and the accompanying responsibilities that must be met. Following adolescence, the individual continues to search for self-understanding, but during this period he or she must make some of the most crucial decisions of a lifetime. Life-style is set by decisions about education, occupation, and a marriage partner. The young adult, who is in essense asking "Who am I and how does my identity fit into the scheme of things?" is aware that he or she has made the break with the parental home and must accept responsibility for his or her own life. The individual gradually becomes able to take the necessary steps to move into his or her place in the world and to develop into a functioning adult. The young adult now begins to consolidate the choices made in childhood and adolescence and the influences that have made themselves felt during these years. Each person growing up in our (or any) society has a unique set of assets and handicaps resulting from experiences of adjusting to and participating in the environment—be that environment a harsh or a friendly one. This individuality is cherished by most people and becomes the center of the young adult's maturing personality. While maintaining this individuality, however, one must also respond to other individuals and integrate the demands of others into his or her private world. To be at peace with oneself and at the same time to be able to live in harmony with others is one of the most difficult tasks of maturity; and it is unusually difficult for those handicapped by severe environmental problems, such as poverty.

The developmental stage covered in this section—that of finding one's self-identity —is of immediate interest to the college-aged reader, for it is the stage in which he or she presently is. In no way, however, is the search for self-identity limited to the young adult; it is a life-long pursuit. Nevertheless, its placement following the discussion of adolescence and prior to the chapters on dating, love, and premarital sex reflects its increased importance in the young-adult years.

Discussions of personality and the quest for self-identity almost always begin with a reference to role theory. Role theory, which is based on the necessity for individuals to define themselves within the framework of the social environment in which they live, equates a healthy and mature personality with playing one's various roles to the satisfaction of society. Certainly the roles one plays during a lifetime help determine one's identity; and if they are not played within the range of what is considered normal by society, both the individual and society suffer. However, to explain the self in terms of role-playing alone is insufficient. We often find that some of the roles we play do not seem to be consistent with others and/or with our "total personality." Indeed, it sometimes seems that our "real self" is temporarily subordinated as the role behavior takes over. Hence, it is not uncommon to hear a young man or woman complain that it is not possible "to be myself" at work, or possibly at home.

Occasionally, a person may be so caught up in playing various roles that he or she is not sure who his or her real self is. This has been called *self-alienation* by Karen Horney, Erich Fromm, and other researchers who have attempted to come to grips with the self-identity problem. They have hypothesized that a person who is self-alienated, while possibly a very kind, pleasant, and socially acceptable person, is not capable of the depth of feeling needed to love because he or she does not know his or her own inner depths. Such an individual is incapable of the kind of intimacy upon which solid male-female relationships are built, since such intimacy calls for sufficient knowledge of oneself to be able to give and receive love.

Part Four explores the identity search of the young adult, with an emphasis on both the search for self and the roles assigned to men and women in our society. The part begins with Margaret Mead's article on the kinds of unique self-searching that accompany being a man in our society, as opposed to the self-searching done by women. The biological differences between the two sexes determine, in a basic way, the kind of learning that takes place in a lifetime; one's sex identity is the core part of one's self-identity. As Mead points out, biological differences play an important part in laying the foundations of each person's way of life, as they set the tone for the relationship between the sexes during childhood, courtship, marriage, and family years. But she also points out that each person is a human being first and a sexual being second. In other words, it is not likely that any young person would want to retain his or her masculinity or femininity at the price of humanness. A man would find it less threatening to become a human female than to become a male lion. To keep one's humanity is of paramount importance; only through being a whole human being can a man or woman realize sex membership fully. Clearly, a sense of identity comes not only from inner values and a knowledge of oneself, but also from standards and values picked up through socialization. It is essential to understand one's socially learned sexual identity to know one's total self.

In the second article in this part, Theodore Lidz discusses the tasks involved in achieving self-identity and the ability to develop an intimate relationship with another person. Many writers have described the identification struggle as an adolescent phenomenon, which it is in part. But with the prolongation of adolescence because of the extension of formal schooling, young people often form much of their adult identity much later than they did a few generations ago. Lidz examines the basic questions concerning life work, life-style, and the choice of a marriage partner—which are usually made during the young-adult years—in light of the progress made in the discovery of one's own identity. These years are decisive ones and set the stage for each individual's one and only life. His or her next fifty or sixty years will be affected by the choices made during this particular period; thus, decisions must be made with as much self-knowledge as possible.

The next two articles describe the questions young men and young women are currently asking about changing sex roles in our society. Past training and past experiences as well as interests and abilities which seem unique to each sex need to be woven into a pattern which incorporates both biological and social factors that determine behavior as a male or as a female. Since the socialization processes have had a profound impact on the kind of young adult one turns out to be, each person finds that he or she is a part of the whole. But as an individual's awareness of the total environment and his or her place in it increases, so does his or her knowledge of identity.

The first of the two selections, by Myron Brenton, describes some of the questions currently facing the young man in our society as he seeks to understand and adapt to contemporary pressures pushing for new models of masculinity. The traditional roles for men and women are being seen by many as nonfunctional in today's world, where a sharp task division is no longer necessary the way it was a few generations ago. *Role-blurring* or *unisex*—the terms used to describe the freedom men and women have to break out of the narrow roles—has caused confusion for many. The author explores this confusion and de-

scribes some possible solutions for a young man seeking his male identity. In the second of the articles on changing sex roles, Caroline Bird writes of the new roles for women in our society and traces a little of the history of what is today called the women's liberation movement. She sees the changing identity of women as a complex reality caused by multiple factors of an economic, philosophical, and sociological nature.

Since the articles by Brenton and Bird address themselves more to the white, middle-class identity, it is necessary to get a more complete picture by including information on other important segments of society. For instance, young black men and women in today's world are often faced with quite a different set of problems in achieving adult identity. In the fifth article, Barbara Rhodes discusses the changing roles of black women and black men and the implications of these roles for the next generation. Rhodes feels that if these changes are passed on to the next generation, a real knowledge of self may develop, upon which a strong self-caring and pride can be based. Unity between men and women of minority groups seems to be an overriding theme, for such groups often feel they must fight for their very existence against the majority, and thus cannot afford to challenge each other on the basis of sex discrimination.

15

TO BOTH THEIR OWN

Margaret Mead

We have seen how children of each sex learn, from their own bodies and the way in which others respond to their bodies, that they are male and female. And we have seen that each sex position can be stated as the surer one, with the other sex a pallid or compensatory or imperfect version of the other. We have seen that the girl may feel herself an incomplete person and spend her life trying to imitate male achievements, and that equally the boy may feel himself incomplete and spend his life in symbolic and far-fetched imitations of the girl's maternity. Each sex may be distorted by the presence of the other sex, or it may be given a fuller sense of sex membership. Either solution is possible, neither is inevitable. If parents define one child as less complete, less potentially gifted, with less right to be free, less claim to love and protection, or less a source of pride to themselves than the other, the child of that sex will, in many cases, feel envy. If society defines each sex as having inalienable and valuable qualities of its own but does not relate those qualities to the reproductive differences between the sexes, then each sex may be proud and strong, but some of the values that come from sex contrast will be lacking. If women are defined without reference to their maternity, men may find that their own masculinity seems inadequate, because its continuance into paternity will also lose definition. And if men are defined in terms of paternity rather than as lovers, women will find that their own capacities of wifehood have been muted in favor of their capacities for motherhood.

Externally at some given period of history and in some set of social arrangements it may often look as if one sex gained and the other lost, but such gains and losses must in the end be temporary. To the extent that women are denied the right to use their minds, their sons suffer as well as their daughters. An over-emphasis on the importance of virility will in the end make the lives of men as instrumental as an over-emphasis on their merely reproductive functions makes the lives of women. If our analysis is deep enough and our time-perspective long enough, if we hold in mind all the various possibilities that other cultures hint at or fully embody, it is possible to say that to the extent that either sex is disadvantaged, the whole culture is poorer, and the sex that, superficially, inherits the earth, inherits only a very partial legacy. The more whole the culture, the more whole each member, each man, each woman, each child will be. Each sex is shaped from birth by the presence and the behavior of both sexes, and each sex is dependent upon both. The myths that conjure up islands of women who live all alone without men always contain, and rightly, some flaw in the picture. A one-sex world would be an imperfect world, for it would be a world without a future. Only a denial of life itself makes it possible to deny the interdependence of the sexes. Once that interdependence is recognized and traced in minute detail to the infant's first experience of the contrast between the extra roughness of a shaven cheek and a deeper voice and his mother's softer skin and higher voice, any program which claims that the wholeness of one sex can be advanced without considering the other is automatically disallowed. Isolated consideration of the position of women becomes as essentially one-sided as the isolated consideration of the position of men. We must think instead of how to live in a two-sex world so that each sex will benefit at every point from each expression of the presence of two sexes.

To insist on building a world in which both sexes benefit does not mean that we gloss over or deny the differential vulnerability of either sex, the learnings that are harder for boys, the learnings that are harder for girls, the periods of greater physical vulnerability for one sex than the other. This does not mean that we deny that when both sexes are cared for more by the mother than by the father, the learnings will be different as the boy accepts a first-beloved person who is unlike himself and the girl one who is like herself, as each lives out its first warm contacts with the world with eager little mouths that for one will remain a prototype of adult relationships, but for the other will be reversed. Nor does it mean that we fail to recognize the period when the little girl's sex membership is so much less explicit than the little boy's that while he is proudly, exhibitionistically sure of his masculinity, she has to ignore what seems like a deficiency in herself in favor of a promised future maternity. It means recognizing that training to control elimination, to plan, to respond, to inhibit, appropriately, in terms of time and place, has a different impact on the boy and on the girl. It does mean that we also recognize that as both children seize on the behavior of grown men and women to give them clues as to what their future roles will be, the conspicuousness of pregnancy to which the girl can look forward overshadows the paternal role that is so much harder for a small boy's imagination to follow through. As the girl is left vulnerable to any cultural arrangements that seem to deny her some freedom—the right to use her mind or her body in some way that is permitted to a boy—so the boy is left vulnerable to cultural arrangements that spur him on to efforts that may be beyond his strength, if achievement is defined as necessary to validate an otherwise imperfect maleness.

Giving each sex its due, a full recognition of its special vulnerabilities and needs for protection means looking beyond the superficial resemblances during the period of later childhood when both boys and girls, each having laid many of the problems of sex adjustment aside, seem so eager to learn, and so able to learn the same things. Paced too closely together, with a school system that closes its eyes to the speed with which the girls are outdistancing the boys in height, and the greater ease that girls have in learning certain kinds of lessons, both boys and girls may be injured during this period, the boy given a fear of the superiority of the girl, the girl given a fear of being superior to the boy. Each fear is deeply detrimental to the full development of each sex later, but it operates differently, making the boy angry and grudging about achievement in women, making the girl frightened and deprecatory about her own gifts. At puberty, there is again a difference. The girl's attainment of puberty is definite and clear. Only cultural arrangements which insist that chronological age is more important than maturity, or which fail to recognize that late maturation is as normal as early, can make the girl as doubtful of herself and of her full sex membership as is the boy as he responds to the less sure, less definite signs of his own puberty.

As young adults ready for a full sex relationship, both boy and girl are limited by the irrevocability of a full sex experience for a woman as compared with that of a man. This irrevocability of the severed hymen often stays the man's spontaneity as greatly as it does the girl's. Then in the full sex relationship there is again a shift. The man may live over again phantasies of reentering his mother's body, but the woman must accept her obligation to herself, the willingness to become a body in which new life is sheltered. However, once she has borne a child, her full sex membership, her ability to conceive and carry and bear another human being, is assured and can never be taken away from her. The male who has impregnated a female is given no such full assurance; his paternity remains to the end inferential, his full sex membership has to be referred again and again to continual potency rather than to past paternity. And with advancing years, the woman faces a moment when giving up her productive maternity will occur as irrevocably and unmistakably as the beginning was once signalled at menarche. But the male's loss of his potential paternity, like the diminution of his potency, is gradual, indefinite, reversible. It has neither the quality of a single devastating event, which is the way women often experience the menopause, nor the possibility of a peaceful acceptance of a consummated step in life, which is also possible to women. He keeps the rewards and the psychological hazards that go with a less punctuated aging process.

Our tendency at present is to minimize all these differences in learning, in rhythm, in type and timing of rewards, and at most to try to obliterate particular differences that are seen as handicaps on one sex. If boys are harder to train, train them harder; if girls grow faster than boys, separate them, so the boys won't be damaged; if women have a little less strength than men, invent machines so that they can still do the same work. But every adjustment that minimizes a difference, a vulnerability, in one sex, a differential strength in the other, diminishes their possibility of complementing each other, and corresponds—symbolically—to sealing off the constructive receptivity of the female and the vigorous outgoing constructive activity of the male, muting them both in the end to a duller version of human life, in which each is denied the fullness of humanity that each might have had. Guard each sex in its vulnerable moments we must, protect and cherish them through the crises that at some times are so much harder for one sex than for the other. But as we guard, we may also keep the differences. Simply compensating for differences is in the end a form of denial.

But if each sex is to realize sex membership fully, each boy and each girl must also feel as a whole human being. We are human beings first, and while sex membership very quickly overrides race feeling, so that boys of a race that assumes itself superior will express themselves as more willing to be males of the "inferior" race than to be females in their own, people do not similarly choose not to be human. The most boldly swaggering male would be staggered by the choice of keeping his masculinity at the price of becoming a lion or a stag, the most deeply maternal female would not elect to be turned into a ewe or a doe rather than lose her femininity. Humanity at any price, but please God, a human being of my own sex, fully, sums up the approach that men and women make in every culture in the world. We may bring them up to wish they had been born a member of the other sex, and so impair forever their full and happy functioning, but even so they would not barter away their humanity. Yet we have seen how damaging to full sex membership can be some of the conventions by which each society has differentiated the sexes. Every known society creates and maintains artificial occupational divisions and personality expectations for each sex that limit the humanity of the other sex. One form that these distinctions take is to deny the range of difference among the members of one sex, and so insist that all men should be taller than all women, so that any man who is shorter than any woman is less a man. This is the simplest form of a damaging conventionalization. But there are a thousand others, rooted in our failure to recognize the great variety of human beings who are now mingled and mated in one great mélange that includes temperamental contrasts as great as if the rabbit mated with the lion and sheep with leopards. Characteristic after characteristic in which the differences within a sex are so great that there is enormous overlapping are artificially assigned as masculine or feminine. Hairiness may be repudiated by both sexes and men forced to shave their beards and women to shave their legs and armpits; hairiness may be a proof of maleness, so that women shave their heads and men wear false curls. Shaving takes time, the male who has no beard feels unmanned, the woman who has three hairs between her breasts may be taken for a witch, and even so adjustment to such stereotypes does relatively much less harm than when personality differences are assigned in the same way. If initiative is limited to one sex, especially in sex relationships themselves, a great number of marriages will be distorted and often destroyed, to the extent that the one to whose sex initiative is forbidden is the one of that particular pair who is able to initiate, and so either refrains from the relationship or conceals and manipulates and falsifies it.

As with initiative, so with responsiveness. Each sex is capable of taking certain kinds and certain types of initiative, and some individuals in each sex in relation to some individuals of the other sex, at certain times, in certain places, should, if they are to act as whole individuals, be initiating regardless of their sex, or be responsive regardless of their sex. If the stereotypes forbid this, it is hazardous for each to do so. We may go up the scale from simple physical differences through complementary definitions that overstress the role of sex difference and extend it inappropriately to other aspects of life, to stereotypes of such complex activities as those involved in the formal use of the intellect, in the arts, in government, and in religion.

In all these complex achievements of civilization, those activities which are mankind's glory, and upon which depends our hope of survival in this world that we have built, there has been this tendency to make artificial distinctions that limit an activity to one sex, and by denying the actual potentialities of human beings limit not only both men and women, but also equally the development of the activity itself. Singing may be taken as a very simple example. There are societies in which nobody sings in anything but a flat, rhythmic, dull chant. Significantly enough, Manus, which is built on the duller similarities of men and women, is such a society. There are societies in which women sing, and men sing falsetto. There have probably been societies in which men sang and only women who could sing alto were allowed to sing. There are societies that wished to achieve the full beauty of a chorus which spanned the possibilities of the human voice, but in linking religion and music together also wished to ban women, as unsuited for an active role in the church, from the choir. Boys' voices provide an apparently good substitute. So also do eunuchs, and so in the end we may have music modelled on a perfect orchestration of men and women's voices, but at the price of the exclusion of women and the castration of men.

Throughout history, the more complex activities have been defined and redefined, now as male, now as female, now as neither, sometimes as drawing equally on the gifts of both sexes, sometimes as drawing differentially on both sexes. When an activity to which each could have contributed—and probably all complex activities belong in this class—is limited to one sex, a rich differentiated quality is lost from the activity itself. Once a complex activity is defined as belonging to one sex, the entrance of the other sex into it is made difficult and compromising. There is no heavy taboo in Bali against a woman if she wishes, or a man if he wishes, practicing the special arts of the other sex. But painting in Bali has been a male art. When a gifted little adolescent girl in the village of Batoean, where there were already some sixty young men experimenting with the modern innovation of painting on paper, tried a new way of painting—by setting down what she saw rather than painting conventional stylized representations of the world —the boy artists derided and discouraged her until she gave up and made poor imitations of their style. The very difference in sex that made it possible for her to see a little differently, and so make an innovation, also made her so vulnerable that her innovation could be destroyed. Conversely, the entrance of one sex into the activities of the other if the other has less prestige may be simply destructive. In ancient Samoa, the women made lovely bark-cloth, pressing out the fluctuating, beautifully soft lines against mats on which the pattern was sewed in coconut-leaf riblets. When iron tools were introduced, the men, because men were defined as the carvers, learned to carve wooden pattern-boards that were stronger and easier to work with than the old fragile mats. But the designs, made for an art for which they had no feeling, suffered, became stiff and dull, and even the women's attempt to get some freedom back into the designs by painting imitations rather than using the boards failed.

In religion we find the same gamut. Religious experience and religious leadership may be permitted to one sex alone, and the periodic outbreak of vision in the wrong sex may be penalized. A woman may be branded as a witch, a man as an invert. The whole picture may become so confused between real gift and social definition of sex role that we get the final institutionalized patterns that confuse sex inversion, transvestitism, and religious functions, as among some Siberian tribes. It is always possible for society to deny to one sex that which both sexes are able to do; no human gift is strong enough to flower fully in a person who is threatened with loss of sex membership. The insistence on limiting a two-sex potentiality to one sex results in the terrible tragedies of wrong definition of one's own sex in the man who becomes a homosexual because of the way in which society defines his desire to paint or to dance, or in the woman who becomes a homosexual because she likes to ride horses, or use a slide-rule. If the interest the other sex takes in a one-sex activity is strong enough, then the intruders may win, as men have been largely driven from teaching in the schools of the United States. Or even more peculiar things may happen. In some particular place and time a developing medical practice may include obstetrics within the proper sphere of the doctor. Those male physicians who have had the strongest interest in the reproductive capacities of women may gravitate initially towards obstetrics and pediatrics. So also may females whose interest in medicine has been defined as male. There may come to be a group of practitioners that includes males who have been very strongly influenced by their conceptions of what a female role is, and females who are strongly repelled by their conceptions of the limitations of the female role. Together they may shape medical practice into strange forms in which the women who might make a contribution from a first-hand knowledge of femininity are silent, and the men are left freer to follow their phantasies than they would have been had there been no women among them. Such a development may sometimes finally include a determination to indoctrinate women in "natural child-birth," in fact to return to them the simple power of bearing their own children, which in the course of a most devoted but one-sided development of medicine has practically been taken away from them.

I have elaborated this particular example in some detail, because no matter with what goodwill we may embark on a program of actually rearing both men and women to make their full and special contributions in all the complex processes of civilization—medicine and law, education and religion, the arts and sciences—the task will be very difficult. Where an occupation or an art is defined as feminine, the males who are attracted to it are either already in some way injured or may be injured if they try to practice it. If simple social definition does not set them to doubting their manhood, the very feminine rules and procedures of the occupation itself may so befuddle and exasperate them that they inevitably do not do different and good work, but similar and worse work, than the women who are already there. When an occupation is defined as masculine, the women who first enter it will be similarly handicapped. They may have entered it out of a simple drive to act like a male, to compete with males, to prove that they are as good as males. Such a drive, compensatory and derivative rather than primary, will blur their vision and make clumsy fingers that should be deft as they try to act out the behavior of the other sex, deemed so desirable. Or if they enter the occupation not out of any desire to compete with men, but out of simple primary motivations, of curiosity or a desire to create or to participate in some activity that is fascinating in itself, they too, like the men who enter occupations in which women have set the style, will find themselves handicapped at every turn by a style that has been completely set by the other sex. As the member of another culture fumbles and stumbles in a different land, with hand stretched out for a door-knob that is not there, a foot raised for a step that is missing, an appetite that rises insistently at an hour when there is no food, and an ear trained to wake to sounds that are never heard in these strange streets, so the immigrant coming into an occupation that has been the sole preserve of the other sex will stumble and fumble and do less than is in him or her to do. How can such an immigrant compete with those whose upbringing fits them to find their way, effortlessly, gracefully, with never a false step or a wasted motion? Whether it be the arts or the sciences, the whole pattern of thought, the whole symbolic system within which the novice must work, facilitates every step taken by the expected sex, obstructs every step taken by the unexpected sex. These same one-sex patterns also restrict the sex that practices them the longer they are practiced by one sex alone, and not made new by the interwoven imaginations of both. It may even be that one of the explanations which lie behind the decline of great periods of civilized activity, when philosophies fail, arts decline, and religions lose their vigor, may be found to be a too rigid adherence to the insights and the gifts of one sex. The higher the development of some faculty of creativeness that has been defined as rigidly male or rigidly female, the more the personality of the practitioner is split, and the deeper the danger that the personal life of mating and parenthood, which must be keyed to the presence of the other sex, may be divorced from the creative life of thought and action. This may in turn result in a secondary solution, such as the split in Greek society between the uneducated wife and the sophisticated mistress; it may push a large part of society towards celibacy or homosexuality, simply because a heterosexual relationship involves unbearable complications. The deeper the commitment to a creative activity becomes, be it government or science, industry or the arts, religion or exploration, the more the participating individuals will seek wholeness in it, and the more they will be vulnerable if the activity itself is one that only partially expresses our full two-sexed humanity.

There is likewise the very simple consideration that when we have no indication that intelligence is limited to one sex, any occupational restriction that prevents gifted women from exercising their gifts leaves them, and also the world that is sorely in need of every gift, the poorer. I have not put this consideration first, because there is still the possibility that the world might lose more by sacrificing sex differentiation than it would lose by limiting the exercise of that intelligence to certain ways of life. It is of very doubtful value to enlist the

gifts of women if bringing women into fields that have been defined as male frightens the men, unsexes the women, muffles and distorts the contribution the women could make, either because their presence excludes men from the occupation or because it changes the quality of the men who enter it. There is slight gain if the struggle the intruders have to go through limits any primary feminine contribution they could make. It can be cogently argued that the profession of education—which should be by both sexes for both sexes—has lost as much if not more than it has gained as men departed not only from the primary grades, where the special gifts of women were badly needed, but from the higher grades, where boys have suffered because taught only by women. Men teachers took refuge in the universities, where they jealously guard their departments against the entrance of any woman into fields where women's insights are needed. Such sequence can well make one pause, and suggest that the cure is often worse than the disease.

This is more likely to be so whenever women's abilities are seen quantitatively in relation to men's. The phrasing is then that there are many women who are as bright or brighter, as strong or stronger, as good or better organizers, than men. Crusades based on the rights of women to enter any field are likely to recoil upon themselves. The entrance of women is defined as competitive, and this is dangerous, whether the competition be expressed in the Soviet woman railroad engineer's plaint that women are allowed to run only engines on freight trains, or in the devastating antagonisms that are likely to occur in America, where it is so hard to forgive any person who wins in the same race, although so easy to acclaim success in races one has not entered. Almost every excursion of American women into fields that women had never, or at least not for many epochs, entered has been phrased in just these competitive terms. How dangerous it is can be measured in many ways: by the big poster advertisements on the Pacific coast in the spring of 1948, which advertised bread with a girl wielding the bat and the boy behind her holding the catcher's mit; by the "Here's How" in the New York subway, in which a text that describes the wedding-ring as a sign of subjection is illustrated by a *male* in evening-dress putting a ring on his *own* third finger. It is folly to ignore the signs which warn us that the present terms on which women are lured by their own curiosities and drives developed under the same educational system as boys, or forced by social conditions that deny homes and children to many women—a fourth of American women reach the menopause having borne no children—are bad for both men and women. We have to count very carefully what gains there are, what possibilities there are of drawing rapidly enough upon the sensitivities of both men and women to right the balance and still go on.

There will be very great temptations in America to right the balance rudely, to tighten the lines against the continued entrance of women into these new fields, rather than to change the nature of that entrance. To the extent that we do go backwards we lose an opportunity to make the social inventions that will make it possible for women to contribute as much to civilization as they now contribute to the continuance of the race. As matters now stand and have stood through history, we have drawn on the gifts of men in both ways, and on the gifts of women almost entirely in one way. From each sex, society has asked that they so live that others may be born, that they cherish their masculinity and femininity, discipline it to the demands of parenthood, and leave new lives behind them when they die. This has meant that men had to be willing to choose, win, and keep women as lovers, protect and provide for them as husbands, and protect and provide for their children as fathers. It has meant that women have had to be willing to accept men as lovers, live with them as wives, and conceive, bear, feed, and cherish their children. Any society disappears which fails to make these demands on its members and to receive this much from them.

But from men, society has also asked and received something more than this. For thousands of generations men have been asked to do something more than be good lovers and husbands and fathers, even with all that that involved of husbandry and organization and protection against attack. They have been asked to develop and elaborate, each in terms of his own ability, the structure within which the children are reared, to build higher towers, or wider roads, to dream new dreams and see new visions, to penetrate ever farther into the secrets of nature, to learn new ways of making life more human and more rewarding. And within the whole adventure there has been a silent subtle division of labor, which had its roots perhaps in a period of history when the creativeness of bearing children outweighted in splendor every act that men performed, however they danced and pantomimed their pretence that the novices were really their children after all. In this division of labor, there was the assumption that bearing children is enough for the women, and in the rest of the task all the elaborations belong to men. This assumption becomes the less tenable the more men succeed in those elaborations which they have taken on themselves. As a civilization becomes complex, human life is defined in individual terms as well as in the service of the race, and the great structures of law and government, religion and art and science, become something highly valued for themselves. Practiced by men, they become indicators of masculine humanity, and men take great pride in these achievements. To the extent that women are barred from them, women become less human. An illiterate woman is no less human than an illiterate man. As long as few men write and most men cannot, a woman may suffer no loss in her sense of herself. But when writing becomes almost universal—access to books, increased precision of thought, possibilities of communication—then if women cannot learn to write because they are women, they lose in stature, and the whole subtle process begins by which the wholeness of both sexes is undermined. When the women's sense of loss of participation is compensated for by other forms of power, by the iron will of the mother-in-law who has been the docile, home-bound wife—as in China and Japan—then the equilibrating pattern may take the form of covert distortions of human relationships that may persist over centuries. When women's sense of impaired participation in society is expressed directly, in rebellion against the restrictions that it has placed on her, we may find instead the sort of freedom for women that occurred just before the breakdown of the Roman Empire, or in the goals of the women's movement of the last century. But whatever the compensatory adjustment within the society, women's belief in their own power to contribute directly to human culture will be subtly and deeply impaired, and men's isolation, either covertly threatened or openly attacked, in a world that they have built alone will increase.

If we once accept the premise that we can build a better world by using the different gifts of each sex, we shall have two kinds of freedom, freedom to use untapped gifts of each sex, and freedom to admit freely and cultivate in each sex their special superiorities. We may well find that there are certain fields, such as the physical sciences, mathematics, and instrumental music, in which men by virtue of their sex, as well as by virtue of their qualities as specially gifted human beings, will always have that razor-edge of extra gift which makes all the difference, and that while women may easily follow where men lead, men will always make the new discoveries. We may equally well find that women, through the learning involved in maternity, which once experienced can be taught more easily to all women, even childless women, than to men, have a special superiority in those human sciences which involve that type of understanding which until it is analyzed is called intuition. If intuition is based, as it seems to be, upon an ability to recognize difference from the self rather than upon one to project the self in building a construct or a hypothesis, it may well be that the greatest intuitive gifts will be found among women. Just as for endless ages men's mathematical gifts were neglected and people counted one, two, two and one, and a dog, or were limited to counting on the fingers of their hands, so women's intuitive gifts have lain fallow, uncultivated, uncivilized.

Once it is possible to say it is as important to take women's gifts and make them available to both men and women, in transmittable form, as it was to take men's gifts and make the civilization built upon them available to both men and women, we shall have enriched our society. And we shall be ready to synthesize both kinds of gifts in the sciences, which are now sadly lopsided with their far greater knowledge of how to destroy than of how to construct, far better equipped to analyze the world of matter into which man can project his intelligence than the world of human relations, which requires the socialized use of intuition. The mother who must learn that the infant who was but an hour ago a part of her body is now a different individual, with its own hungers and its own needs, and that if she listens to her own body to interpret the child, the child will die, is schooled in an irreplaceable school. As she learns to attend to that different individual, she develops a special way of thinking and feeling about human beings. We can leave these special learnings at the present level, or convert them into a more elaborate part of our civilization. Already the men and women who are working together in the human sciences are finding the greatly increased understanding that comes from the way in which their insights complement each other. We are learning that we pay different prices for our insights: for instance, to understand the way a culture socializes children a man must return in imagination to childhood, but a woman has also another and different path, to learn to understand the mothers of these children. Yet both are necessary, and the skill of one sex gives only a partial answer. We can build a whole society only by using both the gifts special to each sex and those shared by both sexes—by using the gifts of the whole of humanity.

Every step away from a tangled situation, in which moves and countermoves have been made over centuries, is a painful step, itself inevitably imperfect. Here is a vicious circle to which it is not possible to assign either a beginning or an end, in which men's overestimation of women's roles, or women's overestimation of men's roles, leads one sex or the other to arrogate, to neglect, or even to relinquish part of our so dearly won humanity. Those who would break the circle are themselves a product of it, express some of its defects in their every gesture, may be only strong enough to challenge it, not able actually to break it. Yet once identified, once analyzed, it should be possible to create a climate of opinion in which others, a little less the product of the dark past because they have been reared with a light in their hand that can

shine backwards as well as forwards, may in turn take the next step. Only by recognizing that each change in human society must be made by those who carry in every cell of their bodies the very reason why the change is necessary can we school our hearts to the patience to build truly and well, recognizing that it is not only the price, but also the glory, of our humanity that civilization must be built by human beings.

16

THE YOUNG ADULT

Theodore Lidz

The lengthy developmental process as a dependent apprentice in living draws to a close as the individual attains an identity and the ability to live intimately with a member of the opposite sex, and contemplates forming a family of his own. He has attained adult status with the completion of physical maturation, and hopefully he has become sufficiently well integrated and emotionally mature to utilize the opportunities and accept the responsibilities that accompany it. He has reached a decisive point on his journey. He has dropped the pilot and now starts sailing on his own—but he has been taught to navigate and he has been provided with charts, albeit they are charts that can be only approximately correct for the currents and reefs change constantly. He has practiced under more or less competent supervision, taken trips in sheltered waters, and now he assumes responsibility and must accept the consequences of his decisions. Usually he asks another to share the journey, and soon

others join them, bidden and unbidden, and their welfare depends upon his skills and stability.

The young adult's energies and interests can now be directed beyond his own growth and development. His independence from his natal family requires that he achieve an interdependence with others and find his place in the social system. Through vocation and marriage he is united to networks of persons, finds tasks that demand involvement, and gains roles into which he fits and is fitted which help define his identity. He is virtually forced to become less self-centered through the very pursuit of his own interests.

The time when adult life starts is not set chronologically, for a person may have entered upon his vocation and selected a spouse some time in adolescence: but if he is still uncommitted, he must make an occupational choice early in adulthood, as must virtually all men. Most individuals will also give up their much sought independence to share with another in marriage. Then the life cycle rounds to the point at which the young adult is again confronted by the start of life, but now as a member of the parental generation, and he often undergoes a profound personality reorientation as he becomes involved in the unfolding of a child's life. The period ends at a somewhat indefinite time, approximately when children's needs no longer form a major focus of attention, and usually around the age of forty when he has attained a stable position in society or, at least, when he realizes that he must come to terms with what he will be able to make out of his one and only life.

The young adult is at the height of his physical and mental vigor as he launches upon making his way and establishing his place in the world; and his energies are usually expended more effectively than they were during adolescence. The expansiveness of adolescence had usually given way to efforts at consolidation in late adolescence, but the young adult must focus his energies and interests even more definitively as he commits himself to a specific way of life and usually to marriage with its libidinal investment in a single significant person. Now, more than ever, alternative ways of life must be renounced to permit the singleness of purpose required for success and to consolidate his identity; and his intimacy becomes reserved for a single person to make possible meaningful sharing with a spouse. Although commitment to another person entails the danger of being carried along in the other's inadequacies or misfortunes, its avoidance carries the penalty of lack of opportunity to be meaningful to others and have others become meaningful to the self.

Vocational choice and marital choice are two of the most significant decisions of a lifetime. Although they are sometimes made easily and even seemingly casually, they are both extremely complex matters that are resultants of the individual's entire personality development. They are two cardinal resultants of the lengthy process of achieving adulthood that we have been tracing; and now these decisions will become major determinants of the course of the individual's further personality development, of

the satisfactions that will be gained from life, and of the trials and problems that will ensue and strain the integration of the personality and perhaps even warp it. The individual's own capacities and integration markedly influence his choices of occupation and spouse, and then influence how he can cope with and gain fulfillment from both—and subsequently from being a parent. . . .

What does the young man or woman require within the self to make these essential decisions and have a reasonable chance of gaining strength and finding satisfaction from them? Fortunately, perhaps, the psychiatrist is not required to sit in judgment and only very few persons seek his opinion and permission. We have followed the phasic preparation since birth for the assumption of adult status, and we shall not attempt to summarize here the steps by which a person integrates, achieves an ego identity and a capacity for true intimacy. We shall but attempt to state briefly some of the essential and some of the desirable aspects of a person's integration at this stage of life. . . . Although it is simple to illustrate how deficiencies in achieving such capacities can lead a person into serious difficulties, we hesitate to call them requisites rather than desiderata, for few, if any, persons have all of these attributes, and the attainment of any of them always remains a matter of "more or less." We are considering an ideal, so to speak, to convey how a mature young adult might be integrated.

The young man or woman has . . . become reasonably independent of his parents. He has established fairly clear boundaries between himself and his parents; properly, he has not been burned in the process and become wary of ever relating intimately again, but he recognizes that his own and his parents' paths now diverge because they are moving toward different goals. If his early development went well, the revolt through which he gained his own identity has subsided and he can appreciate his parents on a fairly realistic basis. He no longer needs them as essential objects who support and direct him, for they have been internalized and are thus a salient part of his identity; and now he will continue to take into himself their characteristics as spouses and parents as he becomes a spouse and a parent himself. His identity also includes derivatives from other significant figures, including those he has sought to reject. When his early family environment had been unfortunate, later relationships with teachers, friends, or friends' parents may have furnished stabilizing forces, more suitable objects for identification, and more hopeful objectives. He does not confuse new significant persons in his life with his parents or siblings to the extent of repetitively reenacting old intrafamilial problems. He does not, for example, awaken at night uncertain whether he is sleeping with his wife or mother, as did the son of a highly seductive woman; or repeat with his son and his wife an old rivalry with his brother for the mother's affection and esteem.

As a result of the reorganization accomplished during adolescence, those components of the superego derived from internalization of the parents and their directives are less important. The individual may still follow his parents' dictates, but because they have been incorporated into his own ethical system rather than because of fear of displeasing the parents. Indeed, . . . much of what had been reasonable and useful in the superego now becomes part of the ego, and becomes more and more fully incorporated into the core of the ego—that is to say, into the basic orientation upon which decisions are made. The directives which help the individual to decide what is acceptable and unacceptable behavior now concern social and cultural norms and ideologic standards that are superordinate to parental dictates. The parents are no longer seen from the perspective of the child and, concomitantly, the superego permits latitude for sexual outlets which, in turn, can help diminish the urgency of id impulsions. Although certain impulses, desires, and behavior arouse guilt, shame, or anxiety, these emotions are more likely to become signals to alter behavior or attitudes rather than leading to self-punitive depressions.

The ego tends to have greater control, considering one's ultimate well-being be-

fore giving in to immediate gratifications. A mass of data garnered from personal experience as well as from the person's cultural heritage can be utilized in reaching decisions. It can be manipulated imaginatively in an effort to try out alternative courses and their probable consequences, and also for fantasied gratifications; but the person distinguishes between pure fantasy and what it might be possible for him to realize. Magic and wishful thinking have given way before the need to turn fantasy into action so as to be able to gain the realization of wishes. The young adult now knows enough about himself and the world to decide whether the realization of a wish or a fantasy is a possibility worth pursuing.

A major aspect of the ego's ability to carry out adaptive behavior concerns the capacities to tolerate tensions and the inevitable anxieties of life and still adhere to objectives and work through difficulties. The ability to adhere to commitments is usually taken as an index of "character," for it permits consistency and the avoidance of distraction by each attractive opportunity —whether it is an opportunity at work extraneous to one's own goals or a sexual distraction. The adult cannot be like Harpo Marx and whirl away from what he is doing to follow each pair of shapely legs that pass. Whereas at some periods in adolescence each fork in a road seems to require a decision, as the course of a life may be changed by following one path rather than the other, now that commitments have been made, the objectives determine the ultimate direction and it matters little if one route or the other is followed for a stretch in progressing toward the goal.

Tensions and frustrations create anxiety and depressive spells but do not lead too often to a search for regressive solace in sensuality, in sleep, or in loss of self-awareness through the use of alcohol or narcotics. Frustrations are recognized as a part of life and, although avoided, they are accepted when necessary without mobilizing undue hostility and aggression—and such aggression as is aroused is directed toward overcoming the frustration rather than in vengeance or in hurting the self or those whom one needs. Various mechanisms of defense help control anxiety, but they are not called into play to an extent that markedly distorts the perception of the world or blinds one to realistic difficulties which must be faced and managed.

Now that problems of dependency and symbiotic strivings have been worked through, the boundaries of the self are secure enough for the young adult no longer unconsciously to fear losing his identity when he seeks after intimacy. He does not fear that a needed person will devour, engulf, or annihilate him; or that the loss of the self in orgasm will lead to obliteration; nor will he confuse the self with a child, as does a mother who feeds her child when she is hungry. The individual is also now secure enough in his or her gender identity not to need to prove his masculinity or her femininity to the self and others by repetitive compulsive sexual activity, or in undue masculine aggressivity or feminine seductiveness. . . .

The developmental achievements that we have been considering as necessary for proper behavior in early adult life have been presented in black and white terms. In actuality no one outgrows childhood needs and dependency strivings so fully; no one progresses to adulthood unscarred by emotional traumata and more or less injurious relationships; no one manages to avoid being caught up in trying to solve some old problems; everyone continues to be somewhat motivated to gratify residual pregenital strivings; and we all utilize defenses of our ego that are no longer really necessary, and transfer characteristics of parents onto other significant persons. These are the things that color personalities and provide a distinctiveness and human frailty to all.

Still, such deficiencies, to sum up, should not lead a person to invest too much energy and effort in repetitively seeking after solutions to old problems poured ever again into new bottles, and should not prevent him from seeking completion in the present and the future rather than through the impossible task of remaking the past. The adult, too, should be capable of accepting the realization that many of the ways and rules of society are arbitrary, but that people need such regulations in order to live together—and he does not feel deceived and cheated by the arbitrariness of the rules; and he finds his place in the social system, accepting it while hoping to improve it. Nor is he so readily disillusioned by other individuals, for faced by the difficulties in living he has become more tolerant of the failures and even deceptions of others.

Whatever his preparation, the time has come for the young adult to make his own way in the world; he can delay and linger in the protection of his home, or in the halls of his alma mater where the storms of the world are filtered and refined, but he cannot tarry too long without commitment and the direction it provides. The choice of an occupation and the choice of a mate are the decisions that start him on his way. While both of these choices are often made as a rather natural progression in the path that a life has been taking, they are both highly *overdetermined*, tending to be resultants of the total developmental process together with the realistic opportunities available at the critical time of life. Although a single factor may clearly predominate in leading to a decision, a variety of factors virtually always enters consideration; and the conscious motives are often only rationalizations of unconscious forces that are exerting an indirect and disguised but powerful influence. The decisions may be no less useful and no less wise because of such unconscious influences, for unconscious motives may direct a person to significant and essential needs that are neglected or denied consciously, and because unconscious decisions can include repressed memories and intangible and nebulous perceptions and associations that may have considerable importance.

17

THE AMERICAN MALE

Myron Brenton

"He may have been a big hero in high school —president of the student body or a star athlete, that sort of thing. But then he gets out into the world, and he becomes a cog in the organization, and he comes home feeling defeated." Psychotherapist Jeanne Knakal, during a conversation with the author.

This is . . . about the plight of the contemporary American male. It's about the increasingly difficult choices he is having to make, about the multiplicity of demands he is having to meet, and, most of all, about the invisible straitjacket that still keeps him bound to antiquated patriarchal notions of what he must do or be in order to prove himself a man.

To be sure, the great outpouring of words about the contemporary American woman these past few years has made it seem as though the male either had no problems or didn't count enough to have them aired. An avalanche of books, magazine articles, television documentaries, radio talk shows, and socio-psychological symposiums has been concerned with her troubles. Her psyche—anguished, unfulfilled—has been laid bare for all of us to see. Her basic problem—how to integrate her traditional roles of wife and mother with the wider opportunities now open to her—is being discussed almost without end.

These observations aren't meant to disparage or to deny the reality of the American woman's problems. But when the plight of woman is given such intense scrutiny, a curiously distorting effect tends to be created. Suddenly the world is seen only through the feminist prism. Suddenly the woman stands sharply removed from society as a whole, as though her difficulties could really be isolated from the roilings and seethings of societal change that affect both

sexes. To the extent that the plight of men is ignored, that of women tends to seem less real. . . .

This is not to suggest that the American male . . . is unmindful of what he has. He knows he's in the midst of material plenty —at the very least, plenty more than his father and grandfather had. He knows that his relationship with his wife and kids is more relaxed and easygoing and multifaceted than he recalls his father's or grandfather's being. So, when discontent is expressed, it's often expressed ambiguously —with both puzzlement and regret that this physical and psychical plentitude should create its own problems, exact its own toll. There's a hint of guilt, too, almost as though internally an accusing voice were saying, "You *know* how well off you are, you ungrateful son of a bitch. Why don't you *act* like it?"

Even if the restless, discontented feeling is no more than a faint emotional pinprick most of the time, easy to live with under the palliative effects of the daily routine, there are brief abrupt moments of painful clarity. I remember many men who confessed, when I interviewed them, that their military-service experience was—in retrospect—the time that they felt most "manly," or "rugged, the way a man ought to feel," or "the best time of my life someways, but don't tell my wife." I remember the magazine editor, a hidden corner of his mind illuminated by a couple of drinks, who swept his arms to encompass the concrete-and-glass-faced pillars of civilization that line both sides of Madison Avenue and shouted, "Every so often I feel like making it all disappear—start fresh. Hey, man, wouldn't you have liked to be a pioneer?" I remember the insurance underwriter who, while talking quietly to me, suddenly slapped his desk sharply with the flat of his hand and burst out, "There are times when I want to chuck it all and take a raft down the Amazon!" A week later he called to say that he was starting to take karate lessons. . . .

Actually, the impulse that drove him to learn karate typifies a common masculine dilemma these days. It's really two dilemmas, interconnected by their relationship to the ancient images of maleness. They are:

1. *How to reconcile the sedentary, over-refined present, which is marked by an extreme lack of physical challenges, with the age-old image of the male as hunter, builder, hewer of wood, and drawer of water—a male who, in short, establishes a primitive contact between himself and his surroundings.*

2. *How to reconcile the supposedly democratic present, with its emphasis on equal rights for women, with the age-old image of the male as provider, protector, and possessor—a male who, in short, is given unquestioned sanction to exercise his patriarchal duties and prerogatives.* . . .

Many of the enormous new demands being made on the American male—demands he'd just as soon forget by losing himself in his job, on the golf course, in the home workshop, or elsewhere—find their wellspring in the female's more direct assumption of power and greater expectation of having her own needs gratified. Then too, women are proving their competency in all the intellectual and occupational fields that were formerly tagged "For Men Only." While they still have a long way to go before they can claim equal pay for equal work, women are able to maintain themselves quite nicely without male financial support, although in most states alimony laws are still based on the unfair and unrealistic assumption that women are close to helpless. The old-fashioned diaphragm and the new-fashioned pill allow women to have more freedom of decision in regard to their sexual relations. Add to this the fact that an increasing number of women are entering recreational and social domains heretofore exclusively reserved for men. What it adds up to is that masculinity is no longer assured solely by virtue of female dependency. For a significant number of men this is still an overwhelming fact. It

renders them hostile and resentful toward women. Needless to say, hostile and resentful men create women similarly disposed toward them. The result is increased competition—not cooperation—between the sexes. . . .

Within the family itself the dislocations caused by the equalitarian trend have been considerably aggravated by another overwhelming change in family patterns over the past 100 years or so. Yesteryear's family was sizable. It included—in addition to parents and children—uncles, aunts, grandparents, siblings, and other members of the extended family. By contrast, today's family constellation has shrunk. It has largely become what the sociologists call nuclear, meaning that it consists only of father, mother, and offspring living together under one roof. This may seem an academic fact, something primarily of interest to social scientists. Actually, it's of tremendous importance to the male who is a husband and father. He's put in a position quite distinct from that of family men in earlier times.

This is so because . . . he's the single source of both male affection and male authority within this modern family. In times past, if a man was harsh or if he couldn't show affection, his wife would turn to other men in her family—her father, grandfather, brothers, or uncles—for succor, for nurture. They were right there, living in the same house or fairly close by. Now she must rely almost exclusively on her husband. If he doesn't live up to this added dimension of responsibility, she may channel all her affections toward her children or may plunge into extramarital affairs. Overmothered children are a common phenomenon in the United States, and infidelity on the part of wives is growing.

The same set of circumstances applies to the male's role as father. If in the past he failed to meet his paternal responsibilities, there were always other male family members around to act as surrogate fathers. Today it's all up to the father alone. If he ducks out on these responsibilities, the entire child-rearing job falls on his wife. This, again, may cause her to do more smothering than mothering. To be sure, working—that is, earning a living—is one aspect of fathering. It's one means that the father has of extending protection to his family. But it's *just* one. If he concentrates on this to the exclusion of other aspects, it becomes not a form of fathering, but an escape. . . .

[Earlier] I posed the question of how the male can reconcile the overrefined, sedentary present with the images of the male as he was in the past. There are two answers to this question. The first is that he can't do it. The second is that he doesn't really want to, not at the price he would have to pay. To return to a kind of romantic physical primitivism would mean laying to waste the gains of civilization and starting fresh. This is impossible. That man isn't static is his beauty and genius and uniqueness. He grows, and he builds. He develops, and he evolves. The process is as ceaseless as the rhythms of nature. It's often remarked how far mankind is moving away from the earth, the soil, the elemental facets of life. This is true, and it's an inevitable process. Therein lies one of the dilemmas of modern man. He has a need to build and a longing for what is basic: the green of trees; the brown of earth; the blue of open skies. Yet the more he builds, the more difficult it becomes to realize the other longing. It's the reason that throughways out of cities like New York are thronged on warm-weather weekends, the reason that a freshly caught bass broiled on the bank of a river tastes incomparably better than in any restaurant.

Many of the men I talked to, business and professional men, as well as men who worked in factories, conveyed the idea that they felt something was missing, something that—although they didn't define it quite so precisely—could be summed up as a lack of primitive contact with life, with themselves. These modern American men, leading their soft and affluent American lives, felt out of touch with their bodies, felt a physical distancing between their bodies and their minds.

Some men try to overcome this feeling by keeping up their muscle tone; they go in for exercise. For others, it's weekend sports or summertime treks in wilderness spots. Nothing seems more anomalous than the well-dressed, carefully groomed business-man who, for eleven months of the year, rides to work in his power-steering, power-brake, automatic-drive car; has the elevator whisk him up to his air-conditioned office; pushes buttons to summon secretaries; barks instructions into the phone beside him; dictates letters into a transcriber; and lunches in plush restaurants—and who, on weekends, tosses a handball around, wearing a dirty sweatshirt, or carries his lunch in a simple paper bag when he goes fishing. Yet nothing could be more understandable. It's a way of replenishing himself, of reestablishing that primitive contact.

While it helps, it's only a partial solution. It doesn't go far enough, deep enough. Such activities aren't really integrated into the modern man's life. They're a thing apart. This is one reason that most men take the less demanding path of spectator sports and that physical fitness becomes a national problem. Many American males, even some who actively disliked the experience, look back on their military service as the one time in their adult lives when they felt in peak shape physically. There's a good reason for this, and it goes beyond the fact that the military places much emphasis on physical activity. More important, this activity is integrated into the totality of military life. This was also the case in civilian life—generations ago. When man was hunter, fisherman, hewer of wood—when he had to use his wits *and* his body to meet the challenges of survival—there was an integration of the physical and mental. As Margaret Mead observed when we discussed the subject, males have to learn again to trust their own bodies. She suggested that there should be ways for young boys in our culture to test their bodies as youngsters once did with bows and arrows in hunting. . . .

If the American male is not to become a neurotic weakling, as anthropologist H. R. Hays already accuses him of being, he has no recourse but to exercise his responsibility for choice on every level. The old roads are swiftly being closed to him, one by one. He can no longer surely and definitely confirm his masculinity in terms of unidimensional and sexually differentiated roles. He can no longer do so on the basis of female inferiority in the practical affairs of the world. Whether or not he knows how to fix the faucet, whether or not he takes to mowing the lawn, such matters are quite beside the point. So is physical configuration. It's remarkable how two men with the same physical conformation, even when they conform precisely to the stereotypes—tall, handsome, broad-shouldered—can project such a different air. One conveys a feeling of confidence and ease, of a person who knows who he is; the other seems weak and easily led. It's largely in the way he handles his choices—indeed, whether he has the autonomy to make them at all—that is at the crux of his manly stance. In this sense there's a merging of masculinity and individuality; in fact, they must be considered together. This also holds true, of course, for femininity. The person of either sex who has a sense of his own worth as an individual and who does not long to assume the mantle of the opposite sex doesn't worry about his sexual identity. It's there automatically, with or without reference to elaborate stereotypes.

Admittedly, the times are not conducive to this sense of self-worth. They're not conducive to the easy acceptance of one's sex, to individualism (except in a narrow, insular sense). As long as men feel that the equality of women will emasculate them, it is exactly what will happen. As long as men identify themselves so narrowly with the breadwinning role, with the competitive demands of their consumer society, with narrow and noncreative work, their psychic equilibrium will be shaky.

The question of identity in the larger sense, of individuality, has been viewed in many contexts and written about from many different points of view. David Riesman's *The Lonely Crowd* saw the American character changing from an inner-directed one to one in which Everyman *is* Everyman, whose outer-directed character is formed chiefly by the example of peers and contemporaries. William H. Whyte's *The Organization Man* saw the individual submerging himself wholly in the needs of the organization—be it corporate, governmental, or whatever—and leading the bureaucratized life in which adjustment becomes the greater good. Erich Fromm, in *The Sane Society*, wrote about the variety of conformist pressures on the individual who, in a democracy, supposedly has convictions and a will:

The facts, however, are that the modern, alienated individual has opinions and prejudices, likes and dislikes, are manipulated in likes, but no will. His opinions and prejudices, likes and dislikes, are manipulated in the same way as his taste is, by powerful propaganda machines—which might not be effective were he not already conditioned to such influences by advertising and by his whole alienated way of life.[1]

Implicit in each statement is the view that the technological society which man has created is taking over, is crushing man's ability to make his choices with any degree of autonomy. That is, he cannot stand back. He cannot weigh. He cannot pick and choose, cannot see the whole because of the economic and other pressures which manipulate him to see only the parts. Such books and the studies they reflect are immensely valuable in the perspective they give of the changing American society—a society whose greatness lies in the emphasis it has historically placed on the worth of the individual. But without in the least meaning to, they carry a built-in danger, as this book may well do, too. They seem to make the forces at work on the individual appear so powerful that an air of inevitability is somehow conveyed, that short of superhuman effort, short of really drastic economic or political change, the future will be like the present, only more so.

But is the individual really doomed to be a cipher—well fed, with creature comforts readily at hand—but a cipher all the same? The advertisers advertise, the manipulators manipulate, sex is single-mindedly extolled, a high degree of competitiveness fuels the individual and collective life of the nation, and man comes to see himself primarily as economic man; *yet although the scope and potential for autonomous choice have been drastically reduced, they have not disappeared.* Some people *are* making their choices in life on an individual, not mass, basis. Societal pressures can't be minimized and should be spotlighted, but at the same time individual responsibility must not be totally ignored. This may seem a naive view. Let me be naive. Ever since the popularization of psychiatry began, it has been fashionable—and easy—to blame one's own neurotic behavior on an unhappy childhood. As the popularization of sociology proceeds apace, it's becoming fashionable to blame all manner of social and personal aberration on society. Too often forgotten is the fact that each individual, whether by direct action or by default, also bears responsibility for the patterns of his society.

Parents who themselves are disturbed personalities make it extremely difficult for their offspring not to turn into neurotics, and society does bear heavy responsibility for the mental health—or lack of it—of its members. The Calvinistic notion—or, if you will, that of Joseph P. Kennedy—is that the individual can, all by himself, cope with almost anything in life. If that were ever possible, it would be ridiculous to insist that it is possible today. Today it's impossible for the individual to cope with the world all by himself. Today he cannot be totally independent. He need not be totally dependent, but he must be interdependent. Robert L. Heilbroner has pointed out:

Whereas man made his peace with nature very largely as an individual—as a farmer, a hunter, a fisherman, a sailor—he makes his peace with technology through social organization. The technology itself demands organization in order to function, and the environment it creates in turn calls forth organization in order for men to function within it.[2]

It's not in the cards for individualism in the mid-1960's to be what it was in the nineteenth or eighteenth century, nor is it irretrievably lost. Man has to pay a price for his wonderful medicines that prolong life, his extraordinary gadgets of comfort, but need he turn over *all* his money? Must we say that the individual—as individual—is totally helpless? That he has no alternative but to submit passively to the forces that shape him and that he in turn has helped shape? That there's no point at which he can be expected to take some initiative because the societal pressures are simply too great? . . .

There is a new way to masculinity, a new concept of what it means to be a man. It has little to do with how strong the male is physically, how adept he is at ordering people around, how expensive his cars are, how versatile he is with a set of tools, or how closely he identifies with all the other stereotyped attitudes and acts. It has everything to do with the way he manages his life— the way he conducts himself as a human being in terms of his wife, his children, his business associates, his friends, his neighbors, and his compatriots in the community —and with his ability to make decisions, with his courage to say no, as well as yes, with his perception into the consequences of his actions and decisions. This isn't the easy way. It could hardly be called the path of least resistance. But there's no turning back the clock. With the equality of women an inexorable trend, with the traditional male patterns increasingly losing their significance for a variety of reasons, it is— at bottom—the only alternative to what may well become psychic castration.

What I am saying is that no matter how much American males may yearn for the simpler, more clearly defined times gone by, their yearnings are futile. They have the choice of remaining what collectively they are—a sex at bay—or of redefining themselves in the light of the changing culture. Historically, in the relationship between men and women and between men and men, this is a new approach. And it is the ultimate masculine challenge. It's the ultimate challenge because it does away with stereotypes, guidelines, and life plans. It simply requires a man to be more fully human, more fully responsive, and more fully functioning than he has ever before allowed himself to be. This is the freedom that equality of the sexes offers him.

If he's afraid to take this freedom, the American male will wind up enslaving himself all the more. If he grasps it, he may at last come to see that he's not really as fragile as his patriarchal concepts have made him out to be.

NOTES

1 Erich Fromm, *The Sane Society* (New York: Holt, Rinehart, and Winston, 1955), p. 339.

2 Robert L. Heilbroner, *The Future as History* (New York: Harper & Row, 1959), p. 74.

18

THE NEW WOMAN

Caroline Bird

Just four years ago, the successful women I interviewed were spending a lot of energy proving that their husbands and children were not neglected, demonstrating their "femininity" by tottering around in frilly clothes, and insisting that they liked men better than women. They could say that they envied this or that privilege of men if they smiled or shrugged when they said it. But not many dared to say that they wished they were male, that they preferred to be single or childless, or that they liked the company of women better than that of men.

Today, a surprising number of women all over the country are daring to say precisely those things. These four years, in fact, have ushered in—almost incredibly—an entirely new era for American women. Consider what has been happening:

New York State has stopped inquiring into a woman's reasons for wanting an abortion and California into her reasons for wanting a divorce. Some colleges have abandoned all responsibility for the private lives of women students. Many newspapers have given up the attempt to classify job ads by sex. Women are admitted to scores of clubs, restaurants, colleges, and jobs formerly closed to them, and every Ivy League college has women students on some basis or other. Congress has removed the legal barrier to women generals and admirals. The venerable Protestant Episcopal Church has abolished its women's division and is presently considering the elevation of women to the priesthood.

Women are also gaining at work. Favorable court decisions are striking down the state labor laws which had "protected" factory women from the hours and duties which led to promotion and competition from union men. The proportion of women in graduate school is rising, and the gap between the starting salaries of men and women college graduates is narrowing.

Quite clearly, too, women are more assertive of their rights. They are filing charges of discrimination on the basis of sex with the Equal Employment Opportunity Commission and Government agencies charged with eliminating discrimination from the civil service. The Equal Rights Amendment forbidding legal distinction of any kind between male and female citizens has attracted support from women who just a little while ago had judged it "too far out" to be worth political effort. When Senator Birch Bayh announced hearings on the amendment, 100 witnesses asked to testify, mostly for it. Virtually everybody in the woman's rights movement has moved to new, more radical ground.

But the most startling innovation since 1966 has been the appearance of a new kind of woman, more alien to American tradition than the flapper of the 1920s, the mansuited, career spinster of the 1930s, or the Rosie who riveted the bombers during World War ii. Virtually nonexistent in 1966, the new, liberated woman can today be found on every college campus and in every sizable American city.

The American woman she most resembles is a character successful women had patronized as necessary, perhaps, in her time, but thankfully needed no more: the politically alert, fiercely autonomous, and sometimes man-hating suffragette who won the vote for women at the end of World War i by militant hunger strikes and street demonstrations. Well-educated, privileged, the new liberated woman is often attractive and almost always young—seldom over 25. She is, in addition, idealistic, intense but soft-spoken. And she is furious. Men can't believe her even when they see her. In their book, she's an impossibility: a beautiful or potentially beautiful woman who is deliberately throwing away the advantages of her sex.

She is not fighting to liberate herself from sex repressions. In her privileged circles, her mother and sometimes her grandmother accomplished that. Nor is she out to broaden her horizons to include man's world. The new women scorn requesting, politely or otherwise, that men please move over and give them a piece of the action (the middle-of-the-road New Feminism of the National Organization for Women). They want to remake the world men have created, from top to bottom.

All the new women don't see eye to eye. Still, a majority could probably be mustered for the following platform.

Love is the most important human relationship and is available to any two or more individuals of any sex who care deeply for each other and are committed to contributing to each other's personal growth. Love may or may not include sexual relationships and should not be confused with *romantic love,* a put-up job they think is utilized to trap women into giving up their own identities.

Home and family (including the cooking, cleaning, and shopping) must be an egalitarian institution to which all contribute equally. It can comprise any combination of adults and children, whether related by blood or sexual ties, who find it rewarding to live together. New forms of home and family must be developed by personal experimentation.

Children must be a fully optional responsibility for both men and women. Women must have the right to terminate any pregnancy for any reason, and no loss of prestige should attach to any person who chooses not to reproduce. The rearing of children shall be the equal responsibility of mother and father and shall not be considered a full-time job for anyone, or the source of any woman's identity.

Divorce must be available to either partner without fault.

Alimony degrades a wife by assuming that she has been supported in return for sexual favors and is entitled to severance pay when she is jilted.

Jobs must be available to both sexes on the basis of individually determined capacity, without presumption that the required capacity is more likely to occur in a member of one sex than the other.

Consumer goods shall not be promoted as contributors to masculinity or femininity or by exploiting the sexual attraction of women employees or images.

Media shall not brainwash women and girls into accepting a limited, domestic role.

Schools—ditto.

Sex differences in ability and responses which can be proven by objective testing must be ascribed to the way boys and girls are brought up, until they can be specifically attributed to anatomical differences.

Sex roles based on a division of labor between men and women are not inevitable in the world of the future just because they have been universal in the past.

Psychoanalysis has crippled women by attempting to "adjust" them to a feminine role unacceptable to free human beings.

Freud made the mistake of assuming that Victorian marriage and family arrangements which subordinated women to men were inevitable and desirable.

Marx saw that the bourgeois family enslaved women by making them the private property of their men.

None of these thoughts is really new. What *is* new is that they have been welded together into a coherent philosophy on the basis of which women can make personal decisions on husbands, jobs, schools, birth control methods, alimony, child-rearing, and politics. The Women's Liberation Movement (WLM), more familiarly known as Women's Lib, is, if anything, overorganized. At the Second Congress to Unite Women held in New York this past May [1970], 600 women represented scores of the shifting new groups which were turning up with names like Bread and Roses, The Feminists, the Media Women, Redstockings, OWL (Older Women's Liberation), SALT (Sisters All Learning Together), as well as WITCH (Women's International Terrorist Conspiracy from Hell).

The movement began with bright, white girls from privileged homes who were free to join the student movement for Negro rights in college because they weren't pushed to marry well or earn money. When they went South for the movement, they found themselves identifying with the blacks more easily than the white boys. They knew how it felt to shut up; take a back seat; accept segregation, exclusion from clubs, restaurants, and meetings; lower their sights to work which was "realistically" open to them; cope with imputations of natural inferiority; and see themselves portrayed in print and picture as stereotypes rather than individuals.

In 1967 it began to dawn on the girls who had gone into the radical movement fulltime after graduation that they were toting coffee and typing, like office girls in business establishments. Those who had joined the movement to escape suburban domesticity found themselves making beds and washing dishes like their legally married mothers. Not taken seriously, refused an opportunity for more substantial participation, these movement women who were "feminists" concluded in 1968 that they couldn't really be liberated unless they did it all by themselves, and while most hoped to rejoin men after their liberation, most excluded men. (The Feminists of New York actually limit to one-third the number of members who may be formally or informally married.)

Women's Liberation made its national debut in September 1968 by halting—if only for a few seconds—the television crowning of Miss America at Atlantic City. They picketed the contest with signs "Let's Judge Ourselves as People." They brought "freedom trash baskets" into which they proposed to dump hair curlers, false eyelashes, girdles, bras, and other devices for making themselves over into the standard sex object. They crowned a live sheep. They threw a stink bomb. They chanted, "We Shall Not Be Used." And some of them got arrested.

Women saw the point, even when they violently, and somewhat defensively, denied that they felt "used." The pageant had long made women feel uneasy, but few had verbalized or even admitted the discomfort they experienced at the spectacle of women parading in a competition to determine which one was most attractive to men. It was hard to say anything against a beauty contest without sounding envious or hostile. The rhetoric of revolution removes this embarrassment by making the notion that women are against each other a myth perpetrated by men to keep women from joining together against their "oppression.". . .

The Miss America protest was a model of what the Communists used to call "agit-prop," or the art of making revolutionary capital out of a current event. It was also the proving ground for what they thought was a brilliant new rationale for dealing with a hostile press. The protesting women made the media carry the message by laying down their own ground rules for press coverage. They refused to talk to male reporters. They refused to identify a leader. And they insisted on speaking as an anonymous group. Radicals have sometimes refused to identify their leaders in order to protect them from arrest, but Women's Lib did so in part to refute the notion that women are unable to cooperate. In the revolutionary vocabulary, group action is a "zap."

Zap, used still, is maddening to the media.

So too is the attitude of Women's Lib. No group or individual in living memory has ever treated the press so disparagingly. But it has worked. Caught off guard, intrigued, or merely stunned, the print media [have] given Women's Lib more space than the brassiest press agent could possibly hold out to the most gullible potential client.

Even more innovative is the solution Women's Lib has developed to the gut problems of any social action; how to recruit new members. The technique is "consciousness raising." A consciousness-raising session is informal, intimate. Ideally, a dozen or more women get together to talk about their experiences *as women,* to call to mind the little slights, frustrations, and hangups they have put out of mind as inevitable.

There is, say the feminists, a well of anger hidden somewhere inside the gentlest women. Consciousness raising lets the genie out of the bottle. Once a woman admits to herself how she has been victimized, she can never go back to the Garden of Eden. She gets angrier and angrier and she infects the women around her. Every woman who admits she is a victim makes it that much harder for the next woman to pretend she isn't a victim. The anger feeds on itself, and it is contagious. That's what Women's Lib is all about. It is less a movement than a revolutionary state of mind. But is it, really, a revolution?

According to the article on Revolution in the *New Encyclopedia of Social Science,* revolutions are most likely to occur when the old order is breaking down, the despots are reforming themselves, the condition of the oppressed is improving, widening education has created a "revolution of expectations," and a war complicates the work of the ruling class. Read "men" for the powers that be, "women" for the oppressed, and paragraphs of the essay take on new and striking sense.

The old order, the patriarchal system, *is* breaking down: more women are single or divorced, more wives are self-supporting, more children are born out of wedlock, more sex is extramarital. The despots *are* reforming themselves: more men, particularly younger men, treat women as companions rather than sex objects. The condition of women *is* improving, but perhaps not as fast as widening education is raising expectations. Finally, a war *is* distracting attention from domestic reforms that would improve the status of women, not the least of which is the establishment of publicly-supported child care centers. . . .

The analogies go even further, to the characteristics of the movement itself. Like political revolutions, Women's Lib is afflicted with schisms, exhausting ideological debate, suspicion of charismatic leaders and experts or professionals who have earned their credentials under the established system. Many of the younger groups are not particularly eager, for instance, to be lectured by authors like Betty Friedan or Caroline Bird. They want and need to speak for themselves, in their own idiom. And like other revolutionaries, they are almost pathologically afraid—as well they might be—that in a general upheaval, some sister (comrade, brother) might feather her own nest. This fear, plus the need for solidarity among the oppressed, explains to some degree why they need consensus decisions.

For all the similarities to classical revolutions, there is one great divide: women can't revolt against society in quite the same way that workers or blacks can revolt. Sex lines cut across class lines. As a bitter feminist has put it, women are the only oppressed class that lives with the master race. They cannot, like the black separatists, really secede from society. For the most part, men are part of the daily lives of even the most fire-breathing feminists.

What is actually happening, I think, is something that carries a wider meaning even than the status of women, trying as that status may be to those concerned about it. The notion of women as an oppressed group has surfaced in every revolution of modern history. The "demands" of the Congress to Unite Women would not have surprised Mary Wollstonecraft, who wrote *A Vindication of the Rights of Women* in 1792, the year they deposed Louis XVI. They would have delighted Elizabeth Cady Stanton, whose Seneca Falls "Declaration of Principles" demanded the vote for women at a time when the issue of slavery threatened the survival of the United States.

Women's Liberation is spreading because American society is in a comparable state of revolution. It reflects not only the revolt of the black separatists, whose rhetoric it follows so closely, but the general loss of credibility in all constituted authority—political, educational, intellectual, religious, even military.

Where will women come out? If previous revolutionary periods are any guide, the answer is: "Better—at least so far as their status as women is concerned." Beyond that, and just as importantly, the answer has to be: "No better than the society as a whole comes out."

19

THE CHANGING ROLE OF THE BLACK WOMAN

Barbara Rhodes

In Nkhrumah's *Handbook of Revolutionary Warfare for Freedom Fighters in Africa*, he says, "The degree of a country's revolutionary awareness is measured by the political maturity of its women." This statement should provoke serious thought in America because of the Black people's intense struggle for liberation and the growing revolutionary spirit. Several years ago the prevalent philosophy toward Black women expressed by a militant Black organization was that the only position of the Black woman in the revolution was prone. That Black people have developed in terms of their revolutionary consciousness is evidenced by the fact that they have now reached the point of concern with the position of the Black woman in a revolution.

We are not now involved in a revolution. We are, however, involved in the building of a revolutionary consciousness. As a Black woman living in the United States today, I strongly feel that the necessity for a political maturity of Black women must be recognized. It must be recognized by Black men, and most importantly, by Black women themselves. Black women must examine the role that has been de-

fined for them by this white society, a role that society has systematically used to elevate them above their Black men. The white society calls it the "matriarchy." That role shows the Black woman's adaptability to conditions imposed upon her Black man and upon her in this country. But when the white society defines the role of the Black woman as a matriarch, it is done in a negative way. It is not that a matriarch is to be criticized; many societies function very effectively under a matriarchal system. However, American society is traditionally patriarchal, and so the women's assumption of head of the household becomes a point from which to attack the male, who is not fulfilling his function in terms of this society's expectations.

The Black woman has often allowed herself to be confused because of the role which white society says she should play as a woman and the role they force her to play as a Black woman. In this confusion, Black women have attempted to act like white women. This is neither possible nor desirable. The white reality is not the Black reality. The role the white woman plays in this white world the Black woman cannot play. And she must not try. The Black woman must be involved in the struggle for the liberation of her people.

How is the Black woman to be involved? Many Black women in their newfound Black consciousness feel that they must look to the Black man to define their role, as they once accepted the role defined for women by the white man. But this is not necessary. There is no role for the Black woman that can be outlined and handed to her by someone else. Defining roles is expedient, but it is not always effective. Take the role historically assigned to Black women as a matriarch. This role defining allows for value judgments, judgments that elevate the Black woman at the expense of the Black man. The Black man cannot perform in the role assigned to man by white society because it is a role defined for white men. But the white man, he who stops the Black man from assuming this role, attacks the Black man on the basis of his not functioning in this role. Because the role is defined, if one does not carry out its definition, one can be attacked. This is expediency. An effective relationship in terms of the functions of Black men and women would be that distribution of functions which best relates to their Black reality. This is not expedient. But it is functional, and we as Black people are concerned with survival. It is the white man who is concerned with expediency. When it comes to Blacks, the white man's expediency keeps him on top.

The Black woman must act from a base of political awareness. This is the guiding principle in terms of her functioning. Then, as a mother, teacher, neighbor, or organization member, she is functioning in the building of the revolutionary consciousness of Black people.

How does a Black woman become politically aware? First, she must discard the myth of femininity that would effectively halt her progress. By femininity, I do not mean such superficial feminine traits as tone of voice and language. I am talking about the femininity that would prevent the Black woman from dealing seriously with ideas. The Black woman must free her mind from these restraints. She must open her mind to the ideologies of the Black struggle and allow it to consider total involvement in the effort to liberate Black people.

Black women must open their minds to all ideas that involve their survival. This is the education they must pass on to their Black children. They must continue to be effective counterparts of their Black men. The relationship between man and woman and the relationship between mother and child are extremely important for Black people. Black children must not be allowed to be conditioned by a white society, unaware of their Black reality. They must be conditioned by a Black mother, to the realities of this society and the realities of involvement in a Black liberation struggle.

No more will Black men submit to the emasculation inherent in the calling of their Black women matriarchs. They are determined to claim the total dignity of manhood at whatever cost. The role of the Black woman as it relates to that will be crucial. What is this role? Black women must supply the answers for themselves. Only they can determine how they will relate to these changing times. The suggestions that follow reflect the thoughts of one Black woman. . . .

When the Black woman is faced with the multiple problems of raising a Black child in a white society, is it enough for her to say to the child, "Listen, my child, Black is beautiful"? Does the child understand what the mother is saying? Does this enable him to deal with the white environment as a proud, assured Black person? I say a resounding no! A child can understand when he is told, "You are beautiful." A child cannot understand when he is told, "Black is beautiful; you are Black and you are beautiful." The child does not understand the suffering and pain that has given significance to the phrase "Black is beautiful." The child does not understand the depths of darkness from which Black people have ascended, proudly lifting the darkness with them, glorifying in this darkness that is their Black selves, and proclaiming its beauty as innate and proud that it is manifest without. How can the child know all this? To the child, this phrase is empty rhetoric. As surely as he knows that darkness follows light in the passing of the days, he will come to know this. When he comes to this knowledge of his Blackness, he will willingly embrace it if he has been truly made to believe in his beauty as a person. "Child, you are beautiful. You are truly beautiful." This is what Black mothers must tell their children. In word and in deed, the Black mother must affirm all those qualities that make a person a total and beautiful person. She must affirm them from a conviction that she is beautiful. She must have no questions, no doubts. "Listen, my child, this fact let no one question; from it flows the strength of your existence. You are a beautiful person."

Not only must the Black mother affirm the beauty of her child, she must nurture it. It lies in the child like the seed of an oak tree with potential to develop into strength and endurance. But it must be nurtured. It must be cultivated carefully, for a seed has not yet taken root and lies vulnerable. Cultivate it; let its roots sink into the soil that is the child's very being, and it cannot be destroyed.

The child must be taught that there are those who would rob him of his beauty, that there are those who would deny its existence. The child must be taught that those who would so approach him are his enemies. He must be taught to identify his enemies. He must be taught to defend the beauty that is the wellspring of his being. This belief in his beauty is the foundation of his belief in all other things that make him a total person. From its flows the confidence that nurtures growth of intellect. From it flows the faith in self that nurtures courage to act. It is the very foundation from which springs courage to act. It is the very foundation from which springs the child's power to assert self. Love of self is a powerful weapon. It is man's best weapon in the war of survival. Black mothers must arm their every child with this weapon. When man loves self, he would rather be destroyed attempting to save self than let another destroy him. He will take whatever means necessary to assure the survival of the self he loves. Whatever means necessary. . . .

How is the Black mother to teach her child to identify his enemies? Who are those who would deny the beauty of the Black child, and why do they proceed systematically to do so? The answer to these questions is contained in the history of America. It is contained in a history based in large part on the denial of the beauty of the Black man and woman. This denial has robbed the Black man of one of his most essential weapons in the war of survival, love of self. By so robbing the Black man in America, this country has been able to keep him subjugated, to heap its frustrations upon him, and to use him to sustain the myth of white superiority.

The Black mother must open her mind to the facts of history, for these facts attest to the creation of the myth of white superiority largely at the expense of Black human beings. In its most recent pages, history attests to outrage after outrage being perpetrated on Black people because of the necessity of sustaining this myth. The outrage of little girls being bombed in a church in Alabama in 1964, of Black leaders being assassinated, Evers in Mississippi and King in Tennessee. Incident after incident of physical atrocities have been enacted against Black people. As many atrocities are being committed today as 150 years ago.

However, the Black mother must look further than a review of the physical inhumanity of white America to the Black man. She must look closely at the psychological atrocities perpetrated against Black human beings. These psychological atrocities had their birth during slavery and have survived to this very day, attaining, as they age, a higher degree of sophistication. It is these psychological atrocities that must be combatted because they work to destroy the Black man's love of self. These psychological atrocities have no compassion for the child, for it is the child that offers the most fertile ground. How should the Black mother begin in this effort to unveil the psychological networks devised to destroy her children? She must first begin with the knowledge that she has been a victim of this design. She must first begin with a real knowledge of self, no matter how painful this knowledge may be.

Part Five

Dating Behavior

In much of the world, dating behavior begins early in the individual's developmental cycle and is a part of his or her life before adult identity is established. Early heterosexual relationships are an important part of the search for self-identity. But dating is not confined to young people; it is also experienced (or reexperienced) by a growing number of divorced and widowed adults. Statistics indicate that six out of seven persons who divorce eventually remarry—hence, many individuals discover a need to date when they are older.

On Saturday nights in towns and cities all over the United States single adolescents and single adults participate in the recreation of dating. They may work or study all week; the weekends bring a different, although not necessarily more relaxed, kind of action. Weekends are a time when single men and women seek each other's company, and a time when they bring their pleasant and satisfying—or perhaps painful and frustrating—relationships into focus. Nowhere is this pattern more apparent than in college communities, although specific dating behavior varies in different regions of the country and from campus to campus. So ubiquitous is college dating that many novelists have portrayed feelings of dating men and women; and characters in many of the novels, such as Faulkner's *Sanctuary*, Durrell's *Clea*, and Siegel's *Love Story*, have similar attitudes in relating to the opposite sex. And these attitudes are not new; Ovid wrote of the ways of seeking out a suitable companion in the remarkable and sophisticated guidebook for single women and men, *The Art of Love:*

The hunter knows well the appropriate valley in which to spread his nets for deer, and he knows where the wild boars roam. The fowler is familiar with the forests where he can catch his birds. The fisherman is well aware of the waters that abound with fish and knows where to cast his hook. You, too, who seek subjects for lasting love affairs, must first learn of the places where they gather. Your own city has as many for you as there are stars in the sky. They will not come floating down to you out of thin air; your eyes must search for the right one.[1]

Things have not changed much in two thousand years, despite almost constant reference to today's "new" codes of conduct relating to the behavior of men and women.

But if ideas have not changed much in terms of the search for the opposite sex, there have nevertheless been changes in the patterns of male-female relationships once the search is over. In the twentieth-century United States, as we saw in Part One, there has developed a unique and most interesting set of such patterns, in which the emphasis has increasingly been on allowing men and women relative freedom to choose heterosexual partners from the moment of the first date to the commitment of marriage. Mate selection is the end result of such dating and courtship for approximately 95 percent of the men and women in this country.

Dating is generally thought of as the relationship between a male and a female who are not ready to make a commitment of a serious nature and are seeking companionship and perfecting their skills with the opposite sex. Similarly, the older person who is dating may be relearning these skills after years of marriage and may find that the patterns have changed considerably in the interim. Patterns of dating have changed rather drastically in only a few years, in fact. For example, only a generation or so ago, it was considered improper for a young woman to call her male friends on the telephone or to initiate a date except under unusual circumstances clearly understood by all. Today, it is rare for a woman to feel inhibitions about telephoning or tendering invitations to men friends. Only a short time ago, a man was expected to give an invitation several days in advance, and many women would refuse a last minute invitation, even if it meant staying home instead. It was a matter of reputation and pride to be given advance notice. Today, most young people take a more casual approach. Rarely are the formalities of a prearranged date necessary; often young people just congregate at parties or movies and pair off for the evening. This casual approach is often uncomfortable for the parents, who are used to the prearranged date in which the male comes up to the door and meets the parents before taking their daughter out. In some instances, the parents' "cultural lag" has caused serious misunderstanding with their children over what is proper dating behavior.

This modern, uncommitted kind of dating serves as a type of "screening" process and may lead to a preference for one partner to date—to "going steady." The couple may be planning to get married, or they may regard the relationship as a deep and comfortable, but not permanent, one. Going steady with an eye to eventual marriage has often been termed "engaged to be engaged" and will be covered in Part Eight.

The readings in this section explore casual dating and the kind of steady dating that does not involve a permanent commitment. The first article, by James Skipper and Gilbert Nass, proposes a framework which can be used to analyze dating behavior and to understand types of interaction in the dating process. Their framework is based on studies of the various dating patterns of many groups; and they conclude that the individual's degree of motivation for dating is directly related to the amount of emotional involvement. Further, they found that the partner who has the most emotional involvement is the one who has the least control over the dating situation.

In the next article, Jack Balswick and James Anderson discuss dating in terms of role theory and focus on sexual expectations which arise in a dating situation. A certain amount of misunderstanding about sexual behavior seems to be a part of the early dating process and may lead, as the authors hypothesize, to liberalized sexual standards.

Morton Hunt has written extensively about the older person who has experienced marriage and who finds a changed world waiting when dating resumes after the end of a marriage. His article contrasts dating among young people with the dating of the formerly married and explores the adjustments made by persons who have been divorced or widowed. It is probable that divorced persons face a special set of circumstances in their feelings about the opposite sex that a person deprived of a spouse by death would not face. However, there are also similarities, since both the divorced and widowed presumably have not been involved in dating for a number of months or years.

While men and women in the United States today probably have as free a choice as any in the world of whom to date and eventually to marry, there are still restricting factors—such as social class, economic level, educational level, and parental influence—which keep the choice from being a totally free one. Certainly, race, ethnic background, and religion are currently limiting factors in the dating picture in the United States. The article by Frank Petroni is a thoughtful look at current aspects of interracial dating, primarily between blacks and whites. The multiple pressures to which young people are subjected in their attempts to date a partner from another race are discussed. It is pointed out in this article—and substantiated by other research —that there is considerable opposition to dating between black women and white men, and that this pattern occurs much less frequently than does black male-white female dating. This is probably due in large measure to the historical relationships that white men have had with black women and to the meaning attached to sex by the black male. There are studies to indicate that black women generally do not date white men because of objections made by black men, even though black men may date white women.

In the last article, Larry Barnett discusses interfaith dating and marriage, which is more common than interracial dating and marriage in the United States today. In the past, an overwhelming number of young people stayed very close to their religious convictions when they picked a partner to date. Today, this seems to be changing in some denominations and in some geographical areas. However, it appears that, even with fewer young people participating in organized religion and with the growing tolerance of various denominations toward interfaith dating, the majority of young people still marry within their own faith. So while dating patterns have relaxed considerably, marriage patterns have moved much more slowly. Endogamy and homogamy still seem to be the guiding principles in dating and mate selection, although in more casual relationships, which seem to make up much of early dating, there are opportunities to explore other life-styles and value patterns.

NOTES

[1] Ovid, *The Art of Love,* trans. Jack Shapiro (Hollywood: Laurida Books, 1967), pp. 12–13.

20

DATING BEHAVIOR:
A FRAMEWORK FOR ANALYSIS AND AN ILLUSTRATION

James K. Skipper, Jr., and Gilbert Nass

Dating is a form of behavior which most people in the United States experience during adolescence and early adulthood. Usually dating is stereotyped as a romantic, exciting, interesting, and valuable experience in and of itself. Moreover, it is felt that it makes a salient contribution to the individual's socialization into the adult roles of the society, eventual marriage, and establishment of home and family. Although it is recognized that dating may sometimes be problematic and filled with frustrations, the eventual rewards are thought to greatly outweigh momentary uncertainty.

Because the general American view of dating is positive and optimistic, one often fails to appreciate some of the important problems inherent in different types of dating situations. This sometimes prevents a systematic examination of dating and an analysis of how it affects and is affected by other social structures and processes.

This paper presents a framework for studying dating situations which was derived from the analysis of a particular type of dating encounter, that involving the young Caucasian female, age 18 to 21, from working-class or middle-class background, away from home, pursuing a specialized education in a large, urban, hospital school of nursing. This analysis is used to illustrate the usefulness of the framework, but in no way does it *test* the hypotheses which the authors suggest. The data and general impressions presented here were gathered informally and do not constitute a systematic nor complete study of the topic. They are based on the authors' observations and interviews with 120 student nurses, 25 male medical students, interns, and residents, and on questionnaire material collected from 50 college males.

FRAMEWORK FOR ANALYSIS

A number of writers have discussed the various functions of dating. In summary, their work indicates that dating probably serves at least four main functions for the individual.

1. Dating may be a form of recreation. It provides entertainment for the individuals involved and is a source of immediate enjoyment.

2. Dating may be a form of socialization. It provides an opportunity for individuals of opposite sex to get to know each other, learn to adjust to each other, and to develop appropriate techniques of interaction.

3. Dating may be a means of status grading and status achievement. By dating and being seen with persons who are rated "highly desirable" by one's peer group, an individual may raise his status and prestige within his group.

4. Dating may be a form of courtship. It provides an opportunity for unmarried individuals to associate with each other for the purpose of selecting a mate whom they may eventually marry.

We suggest that in most cases the functions of dating are manifest, not latent. In other words, individuals' most common motivations in dating correspond roughly to the most common functions of dating, even though all possible motivations would not so correspond.[1] Although individuals may have several motivations for dating each other, we suggest that each has one motivation which is probably more important (primary) than the others. However, individuals' primary motivations in dating each other may or may not be the same.

For example, a girl may date a wealthy boy who drives an expensive sports car just in order to be seen with him (status seeking). The boy on the other hand may be dating the girl in order to learn something about women (socialization). In another case a boy may date an attractive girl because he desires a sexual experience with her (recreation). The girl may be dating the boy because she views him as a potential husband (courtship).

For purposes of analysis, in any dating relationship the individuals' primary motivations in dating may be placed on a continuum ranging from completely expressive (dating as an end in itself) to completely instrumental (dating as a means to some larger goal). The individuals' emotional involvement in the dating relationship may also be placed on a continuum ranging from no emotional involvement to complete emotional involvement. Although it may be possible empirically for individuals to fall anywhere on the two continua, theoretically it seems logical that there would be a positive correlation between the degree of instrumentality implicit in an individual's motivation for dating and his degree of emotional involvement. The authors suggest that:

1. An individual whose primary motivation in dating is mate selection is likely to have a strong instrumental orientation and a strong emotional involvement.
2. An individual whose primary motivation in dating is either socialization or status seeking is likely to have a low instrumental orientation and a low emotional involvement.
3. An individual whose primary motivation in dating is recreation is likely to have a strong expressive orientation (low instrumental) and a low emotional involvement.

Whenever an individual (A) has much to gain from maintaining a social relationship with another individual (B), (A) is likely to become distressed if it appears the relationship is going to discontinue before he has a chance to derive his full satisfaction from it. If (B) has less to gain from maintaining the relationship with (A), than (A) does with (B), then (B) is in a better position to control the relationship than (A). (B) has the better bargaining position. He can attempt to win concessions from (A) by threatening to discontinue the relationship. To the extent to which (A) is willing to meet (B's) demands, (B) controls the relationship.

In reference to dating relationships it is suggested:

1. The greater the emotional involvement of individuals dating each other, the greater will be their desire to continue their relationship.
2. The greater the instrumental orientation of individuals dating each other, the greater will be their desire to continue their dating relationship.
3. The greater the disparity between the emotional involvement and/or the instrumental orientation between individuals dating each other, the greater the likelihood that conflict and distress will occur in their dating relationship.
4. In the disparate dating situation, the individual with the greater emotional involvement and/or instrumental orientation will suffer the greater distress.
5. In the disparate dating situation, the individual with the greater emotional involvement and/or instrumental orientation will have the least control over the relationship.

With this framework in mind, in the remainder of this paper the authors will be concerned with analyzing a dating situation where the males' primary motivation is recreation and the females' primary motivation is courtship. Particular attention will be paid to the question of why the parties have the motivations they do in dating each other, the consequences of these motivations for their dating, and how their interaction is affected by other social structures and processes.

AN ILLUSTRATIVE DATING SITUATION

Considerable evidence suggests that many post-high school females attending institutions of higher learning are vitally concerned with their dating experience and their marital prospects. A great deal of their expressed concern centers around what they regard as "the limited quantity and quality" of available and eligible prospective mates. Often their distress leads them to compulsive and blind involvement with "anyone who shows the slightest interest." These involvements are usually disappointing from the female point of view. They seldom lead to either rewarding or lasting relationships, let alone permanent ones.

For the young girl attending nursing school, this problem appears to be escalated. Both Davis and Mauksch, among other expert observers, have noted the great number of nursing students who have expressed concern about their difficulties in establishing meaningful relationships with young men. These were difficulties they evidently did not have before entering nursing school. We also observed such behavior at an urban nursing school. This type of problem was encountered frequently. Typically, it was expressed as follows:

I never had these kinds of problems before I came here. I was never what you call shy and I always thought I was kind of attractive and had a good personality. I never had any difficulty in getting dates with the right type of boys in high school. But then it was not so important. Now it is, and all I do is keep getting mixed up with the wrong kinds of guys and I don't even know it. It is making me miserable and I can hardly think of anything else. I used to think I knew what was right to do and what was wrong. Now I am not sure. I just don't know. Maybe that's my problem. Anyway, I have got to latch on to someone pretty soon. After all, I am almost twenty-one years old. Most of my friends are married already, or at least engaged.

Well of course I have been looking for a man, for about two years now. I have met some nice ones. But it is gosh darn hard to get them to think about marriage. They are just happy fooling around with you.

An intriguing question is, why should this problem exist at all? Why should these young girls be so anxious about dating, their relationships with men, and their prospects for marriage? Objectively, it would seem reasonable to assume that the pursuit of higher education and a career in nursing would provide them with a feeling of security for the future, increase their confidence and ability to establish relationships with men, and generally enhance their marketability and potential for marriage.[2] But in many cases this did not seem to happen. The authors' investigation uncovered a number of potential hypotheses which may aid in understanding and explaining this phenomenon.

Examination of social class behavior suggests that the working class adheres strongly to defining the adult role of women in terms of homemaker-mother. The range of vocational alternatives is often limited by such factors as opportunity, motivation, and money. Given this focus of commitment to the homemaker-mother role, role behaviors avoiding appropriate socialization are discouraged. An excellent example of this is the oft-stated idea that college is not necessary for girls who desire to get married and raise a family. Rather, working class girls are directly trained to seek as their paramount societal position that of homemaker-mother. The security of this position is seldom questioned. High school and immediate post-high school dating are directed toward landing a "good young fellow," establishing a home, and having children.[3]

The middle-class female in late high school and immediately after high school is also trained for the homemaker-mother position.[4] However, the parameters of her training are far more extensive. She can consider higher education as a legitimate right resulting from her socioeconomic status. She can consider a career-oriented rather than job-oriented occupational position. She can consider learning skills which qualify her for assuming a companionship position in her marriage and/or becoming an active community member. Nevertheless, these other activities are not evaluated so much as alternatives to the homemaker-mother role as they are activities likely to enrich it and be supportive and complementary to it. In other words, they are viewed more as means toward the goal of establishing a more successful homemaker-mother position than as alternatives to it. Thus, in spite of a number of differences in social background and socialization, the main goal in life of many working-class and middle-class girls is exactly the same: marriage, home, and family.[5]

Since most student nurses come from working-class or middle-class homes, it is understandable and predictable, although perhaps contrary to some popular beliefs, that these young women are not primarily interested in a career in nursing. A commitment to a professional career had little to do with their recruitment to the field.[6] The overriding goal of nursing students is marriage, home, and family and the roles of wife, homemaker, and mother. So strong is this orientation to the traditional female role that in one study it was discovered that even in a school placing strong emphasis on the development of career and leadership orientation in its students, over 87 percent at both admission and graduation ranked "home and family" as *the* adult female role which they stressed the most.[7] Crowin and Taves summarized the crucial importance of the marriage goals to the prospective nurse when they wrote:

The prospect of marriage and children permeates every aspect of nursing; no aspect of the profession can be completely understood apart from the influence of marriage plans and their frustration.[8]

Given this focus of commitment, it is understandable why nursing students may place such great emphasis on the courtship function of dating. However, this only partially explains their unusual anxiety over their dating and their subjectively perceived failure to make adequate progress toward the marriage goal. Several other variables must be considered if one is to understand the true nature of the nursing student's difficulties.

The dating dilemma begins with the eco-

logical setting. Most nursing schools are set in urban environments. This fact has far-reaching consequences. The school which is the primary basis of this report was located in a metropolitan complex of several million inhabitants. It was situated approximately two miles from the central business district in an area of light industry populated by lower income classes of various ethnic groups. It was part of a large medical center consisting of several hospitals, medical school, and a number of auxiliary institutions. Due to the type of schooling, the extent of on-the-job training, and the restrictive curfews on leaving the dormitory during free night hours, the nursing students were virtually imprisoned within the confines of the medical center for the greater part of each week. The physical boundaries directed and dictated the types of dating contacts available for them. These contacts may be classified into four main categories:

I. High school acquaintances from the home town area.
II. Local lower-class working boys.
III. College boys from schools located some distance from the medical center but within the greater metropolitan area.
IV. Medical men; students, interns, residents, and occasionally attending physicians working in the medical center.

For each of these categories of male contacts there were built-in deterrents to sequential courtship for the nursing student. Although objectively these obstacles were not necessarily inherent in the situation and without solution, from the student's point of view they often seemed to be and were a constant source of worry, strain, and anxiety. Various major problems were involved with each category of male contacts.

Time and space were the major difficulties involved in continuing relationships with former high school acquaintances. The vast majority of the girls' homes were not situated in the local metropolitan area but in the surrounding hinterland. Thus, the simple fact of physical distance was a barrier. Combined with limited free time during the work week and vacations which were few and far between, dating of "home town" boys with any regularity was possible only in rare cases. Although relationships firmly established before the girl left for school were often maintained by mail, those which were not so established very often ended in frustration. Many of the girls perceived this time-distance problem at an early stage in their student career and consequently directed their energies and attentions to other, more accessible categories of males. Nevertheless, those girls who did manage to maintain successful dating interactions "back home," culminating in formal engagement with the symbolic ring, received high esteem and were much admired and envied.[9]

On occasion the students would come in casual contact with boys living in the area contiguous to the medical center. These young men were of low social class origin and either unemployed or holding unskilled or semi-skilled jobs. Few had been graduated from high school. The girls maintained a high degree of social distance between themselves and this category of boys and rarely dated them. In fact, they were usually shunned and avoided at all costs. To put it very bluntly, the girls did not consider these boys to be "good enough" for them.

In contrast to the boys back home and those in the immediate area, college boys from various metropolitan schools afforded a dating opportunity which continually appealed to the girls. They were quite optimistic about college boys as dates. In a few instances, from the girls' definition of the situation, a highly romantic, rewarding, and successful (engagement) dating experience evolved from these contacts. From these few successful courtships a myth developed among the "less fortunate" girls that college boys offered unlimited opportunities for normal dating. This was far from the reality of the situation. There existed a barrier to successful dating interaction with college boys that almost none of the girls perceived immediately, and which the vast majority of the girls persisted in refusing to

recognize. The barrier concerned the college boys' definition of what "kind of girl" a nurse or nursing student is. By training and practice, the nurse becomes a manipulator of human bodies. This manipulation involves intimate knowledge, contact, and actual handling of all parts of the human body including the "private parts" of both males and females. This knowledgeability marks the student nurse. The content of her work role overlaps into her social relationships, especially dating situations. She is defined by college boys as "someone who knows the score," "an easy mark," "a goodtime girl," "a chick who likes it," etc. This common, stereotyped image is frequently portrayed in widely circulated magazines.

For example, the following passage concerning the off-duty nurse appeared in an article titled "The Private World of Nurses":

Under this prophylactic white uniform beats a black lace heart. Ripe and shining peach-slice legs where the ghostly Supp-hose was. Fat pink moons of flesh backing out of sling back pumps, gone the Hi-Treads of day. Perfume. Ruby cashmere. Color, color, color, then back to the hospital floor, on any old pretense.

Only a skirt and sweater, but it is the metamorphosis that hits them. Real hair, naked heels, and ruby cashmere shoulders contrast sharply with the great white vestal virgin pyre of the nurses' station. Miss Rachik and the wilder of her uniformed sisters learn that fast. Any excuse, but drop back to your floor dressed like real people. Maybe one night Dr. Brown will. . . .[10]

A quotation from another article, "Is it True What They Say About Nurses?" is even more to the point.

The girl who chooses a career in nursing almost automatically acquires a "reputation" —in the old-fashioned sense of the word— whether or not she wants or deserves it. For somehow the out-of-the-sickroom connotation of the word "nurse" implies a promiscuity that's unmatched by any other female profession except the oldest.

This libidinous public image stems in part from popular writers, who seem to de-

light in ascribing chameleon-like charms to the nurse; she's cool, starched, and impersonal by day, unstarched to the point of nymphomania by night. Indeed, if one is to accept as believable the sexual goings-on in doctors-and-nurses novels, movies, and TV shows, one can only conclude that nurses swing on the job as much as off.[11]

At one of the universities in the area, a sample of 50 college boys (sophomores, juniors, and seniors) were asked to rate their expectations of college girls, working girls, and student nurses regarding permissiveness in sexual intimacies during casual dating. . . . The data indicate that, in the college boys' expectations, student nurses were "faster" in sexual permissiveness than either working girls or college girls.

This stereotype of the basic nature of the kind of girl who would become a nurse plays an important part in defining the dating situation. Many college boys define the student nurse in terms of her "glamour-girl-fun value" and only later, if at all, her potential as a wife and homemaker. As one of the young men put it:

When one of the guys starts dating one of those student nurses, you know damn well he is just out "to get a little." Oh, he may try to "con" her a bit. But that's the story, Dad.

This stereotype is the basis for college boys' defining the dating of student nurses in terms of recreation (sex) and not courtship. Not only is the student nurse defined as "knowing the score," particularly about sexual matters, but in addition the "knowing" is transformed into "she likes it!" From the typical college boy's definition of the situation, these are girls to have fun with but not the type one takes home to mother. In this respect the student nurse and the divorcee may have comparable problems which tend to obstruct the attainment of a courtship relation.

The student nurse is placed in a precarious position. If she is not cooperative and does not meet the college boys' expectations of sexual permissiveness, she is likely to be dropped immediately and have no further dates. If she is cooperative, she easily builds a reputation and becomes fair game for her current dating partner and later his friends and fraternity brothers. The authors suspect that more girls than not choose to solve the dilemma by being more permissive than they normally would, just in order to keep dating. As one young lady commented:

Whether you like it or not, you have to go along with them, at least some of the time. Otherwise, you get left out and sitting in the dorm all the time.

This type of behavior, of course, is evidence that there is an element of truth in the stereotype. Further evidence is provided by 12 of the college boys included in the survey, . . . who claimed to have dated all three classes of girls; student nurses, working girls, and college girls. . . . The reported experiences of these boys roughly substantiates the stereotype. Only one of the 12 boys placed either college girls or working girls in the very permissive category, compared to five who placed student nurses in that category.

Strangely enough, few of the nursing students were able to forecast the difficulties involved in these dating encounters in advance or to recognize them realistically when they did occur.

I always think things are going along fine. We seem to be getting along fine and then "bam" it's all over. I guess it must be me.

It is hard for me to believe what you are suggesting. I am not like that at all. Where do the boys get that idea about nurses? They are wrong about us. I am sure of that.

The girls seemed incapable of taking the college boys' definition of the situation, even after they had been hurt several times. Characteristically, they failed to see any patterns evolving in these situations. Usually they tended to place the blame entirely on themselves and/or the boy or the unique circumstances of the particular dating encounter. Perhaps one of the major factors involved in partially explaining why the girls did not become more aware of these patterns in their dating was that the great majority of them attempted to deal with the problem alone. Very seldom did they share these confidences with each other.

I would like to talk about my problems in dating some of these guys, but I don't want to be the only one. You know what I mean? You look pretty foolish when you tell all and nobody else does.

Although the problems of boys and dating were popular topics of group sessions, the discussions were almost always on the superficial level. Very rarely did the girls come to grips with the real issues that were bothering them. If they had, they might have discovered that their own individual problems were far from unique, being commonly shared with many other girls. This might have allowed them to take a more rational approach to their own individual difficulties and saved them a great deal of mental anguish.

Ecological restrictions tended to expose student nurses to males involved in the medical profession more frequently than to any other of the three categories. Medical students, interns, and residents formed the bulk of the men with whom the girls came in constant contact. Almost all the difficulties in dating which the girls experienced with college boys were equally true of their encounters with males attached to the medical profession. However, the magnitude of the problem was exaggerated by several additional variables.

First, most of the nursing students' potential dating partners in the cultural milieu of the medical center were "occupational transients." They were spending only a few short interim years in the community before leaving to establish roots and practice elsewhere. Many of these men were not ready to get serious and establish a sequential courtship pattern with any girl. Similar to the patterns of other types of transients, it was often difficult for them to develop a sense of commitment within the community setting and especially in their interactions with student nurses. Also, these men were subject to long hours of work and study, usually under great pressure.

They had limited free time for fun and amusement. When they did, they often wanted to take advantage of every minute. One intern commented in an informal interview:

When I get a chance, I want to cut loose and really live a little. I need an immediate and complete release from all the stress and pressure.

Another explained:

We don't have much time to fool around. So when we do, we want to date a girl who is pretty lively and ready to go; I mean a real swinger. Do you understand?

Similar to the college boys, the medical men had an entirely expressive orientation in dating student nurses. Their motivation was strictly recreation with as little emotional involvement as possible. However, this orientation was not always clear to the girls they were dating. In fact the medical men sometimes went out of their way to convince the girls that their motivation and emotional involvement were much stronger than they actually were.

In their interaction with college boys, the student nurses were approximately of equal age and experience as their potential dating partners. This was not the case with medical functionaries, where a definite age differential existed favoring the male. Expose the female to males four to ten years her senior, and in this type of situation the weight of differential experience becomes a crucial factor. The opportunity for controlling the relationship rides overwhelmingly with the male. It is he who possesses the superior power, experience, and interactional skills in the dating relationship.

Another variable impinging upon the dating relationship was the occupational prestige structure. The medical doctor possesses great status, prestige, respect, and authority in his formal work relationships with patients, nurses, and other hospital personnel. He is perfectly aware of his dominant position as are all other parties with whom he interacts. The assumption of one's own charisma[12] can be a powerful, positive psychological mechanism for any male medical student, intern, resident, etc. Not unlike the student nurse, the medical man's work role also overlaps into the dating situation, not so much in terms of the actual content of the role, but more in terms of rank and authority in the occupational prestige structure. In the dating sequence, the medical man does not set aside lightly the legitimate authority claims of his professional work role. The medical trainee—be he student, intern, or resident—is an heir apparent to the highest authority position in the hospital, and he quickly and easily incorporates a self-conception compatible with his evolving elite status. This attitude pervades the medical trainee's social contacts with subordinate nurses. He tends to expect them to follow and obey his wishes as they are required to do in the work relationship. Moreover, he often uses his power and authority to gain his way. When the student nurse believes the physician is to be admired and venerated and also to be trusted and obeyed, then in a dating relationship she is placed in a vulnerable and compromising situation.

The possibility of exploitation is very high. For example, one nursing student reported she became acquainted with an intern, started seeing him in a group dating situation, became sexually intimate and eventually very serious about him, only to discover he was already married; the whole charade was carried out with the knowledgeable aid of the intern's friends and cohorts.

The student nurse's dilemma in dating medical men appeared to be even more distressful than in her dating college boys. If the girl was not sexually permissive in dating, she faced not only the threat of never being asked for future dates but also the possibility of some petty reprisal in the work relationship. If she was permissive, she had to live with the feeling (very often warranted) that many of the males with whom she came in contact during working hours in the hospital would be well-informed about her off-duty activities, and, if her degree of sexual permissiveness went against her own norms, she was also likely to suffer severe distress and guilt.

SUMMARY AND CONCLUSIONS

The preceding paragraphs have presented an illustration of a dating situation in which the males' primary motivation in dating is recreation and the females' primary motivation is courtship. The authors have attempted to analyze some of the reasons behind the motivations, the consequences of the motivations for interaction, and some of the social factors affecting both the motivations and the interaction. However, it must be understood that this illustration was not presented as an example of *all* dating situations involving student nurses, for it is not. Based on the authors' experience at one urban nursing school, they estimate that the type of dating problems described in this paper resulted in severe distress for only about one out of every four girls. Whether this is a representative pattern for student nurses or not is a problem for further, more extensive, and much more systematic research.

The real concern of this paper is not with this particular dating situation per se, but with the dating problems it illustrates, some important sociological variables which affect dating interaction, and the usefulness of the theoretical framework presented earlier for analyzing dating situations. Individuals' motivations in dating are affected by social variables, as are their choices of actual dating partners and the course of their dating relationship. In the authors' example the girls' primary motivation in dating was courtship, which was directly related to their desire to get married and their definition of the ideal adult role of women as homemaker-mother. Ecological restrictions forced the girls into contact with two types of dating partners, college boys and medical men, both of which tended to date student nurses for recreation, not courtship. In the case of college boys, this was directly related to their belief in the stereotype of a nurse as a sexually permissive woman. In addition to the stereotype, the medical men were influenced by their occupational transiency, their need but little time for recreation, and the ecological availability of the student nurses.

The authors suggest that if one is able to

learn individuals' primary motivations in dating, their degree of instrumental orientation, and their degree of emotional involvement, one will be able to predict something about the conflict which is likely to take place in the relationship, which partner is likely to control the relationship, and which partner is likely to experience the most distress.

The student nurses' courtship motivation involved a higher degree of instrumental orientation and emotional involvement than the males' recreation motivation. These differences produced conflict in the dating encounters. The male controlled the relationship in large part because he had less to lose if it was discontinued. He was not emotionally involved with *the* student nurse and could easily find another for purposes of recreation. The student nurse on the other hand had to keep the relationship "going" if she was to achieve the goal of eventual marriage. Under the circumstances her emotional involvement with a particular boy was bound to be greater than his to her. Therefore, the student nurse was in a poor bargaining position and forced to make concessions (in this case being more sexually permissive than she would normally) in order to maintain the relationship. This situation caused the girls much distress.

The variables which the authors isolated in the dating of student nurses may be of equal importance in other settings. For example what part do ecological barriers play in determining dating partners in rural as opposed to urban areas, small schools vs. large schools, all-male or -female institutions compared to those which are coed? Is courtship the main motivation in dating of most college and working girls? Are there other groups besides nurses who have acquired social stereotypes which may influence the motivation of their dating partners? Are athletes and beauty queens dated primarily by those seeking status?

The type of framework presented here may be used to analyze any dating situation. To test the authors' hypotheses, procedures must first be instituted to ascertain dating partners' motivations in dating each other, their degree of instrumental orientation, and their emotional involvement. From an analysis of these data, one should be able to test whether the degree of instrumental orientation and the degree of emotional involvement are in fact associated with individuals' motivations in dating. One would also be able to discover from these data the relative frequencies of the motivations between the sexes, whether individuals have other motivations than those cited, and if individuals have more than one primary motivation in dating. A wide range of dating situations must be examined varying the individuals' primary motivations. Assuming just four primary motivations, there are ten separate combinations to be analyzed: courtship-courtship, courtship-recreation, courtship-status seeking, courtship-socialization, recreation-recreation, recreation-status seeking, recreation-socialization, status seeking-status seeking, status seeking-socialization, and socialization-socialization. Finally, the degree to which motivations may vary in importance or perhaps even change completely during the course of dating should be considered.

NOTES

1 There may be a number of other motives for dating which are not directly related to the functions listed. For instance, a girl may date a boy simply to make another boy jealous or to take the boy away from another girl. If spy novels and films are any criteria, individuals sometimes date with the sole motivation of gaining information. However, the authors assume (subject to empirical check) that these are relatively uncommon motivations for dating.

2 J. Richard Udry, *The Social Context of Marriage*, Philadelphia: J. B. Lippincott Company, 1966, pp. 212–213.

3 Ruth Caven, *The American Family*, New York: Corwell, 1963, pp. 149–152; Lee Burchinal, "Trends and Prospects for Young Marriages in the United States," *Journal of Marriage and the Family*, 27 (1965): 249; William Goode, *World Revolution and Family Patterns*, New York: Free Press of Glencoe, 1963, pp. 10–18, 65–66, 371, 373.

[4] Caven, op. cit., pp. 121–124.

[5] Udry, op. cit., p. 57; Lamar Empey, "Role Expectations of Young Women Regarding Marriage and a Career," *Marriage and Family Living*, 20 (1958): 152–156.

[6] Fred Katz and Harry Martin, "Career Choice Processes," *Social Forces*, 41 (1962): 149–154.

[7] Fred Davis and Virginia Olsen, "The Career Outlook of Professionally Educated Women," *Psychiatry*, 28 (1965): 334–345.

[8] Ronald Corwin and Martin Taves, "Nursing and Other Health Professions," in *Handbook of Medical Sociology*, ed. by Howard Freeman, Sol Levine, and Leo Reeder, Englewood Cliffs, New Jersey: Prentice-Hall, 1963, pp. 200–201.

[9] The "engagement success" of these girls was a source of anxiety to the other students who were having dating problems. It served as a constant reminder of their own difficulties and perceived failure.

[10] Gail Sheely, "The Private World of Nurses," *Cosmopolitan*, May (1966), p. 54.

[11] Colette Hoppmann, "Is It True What They Say About Nurses?" *Pageant*, 21:9 (March 1966): 33–34.

[12] Harvey Smith, "The Hospital's Dual Status System," in *Social Organization and Behavior*, ed. by R. L. Simpson and I. H. Simpson, New York: Wiley, 1964, pp. 303–308.

21

ROLE DEFINITION IN THE UNARRANGED DATE

Jack O. Balswick and James A. Anderson

This paper is concerned with the accuracy of role definition on the part of individuals in dating situations. The dyadic dating situation can be characterized as a situation where behavior of the partners is mutually determined. Thus a successful "date" depends upon the accuracy of an individual's perception of his or her partner's expectations. This accuracy would be especially important where the dating partners are new to each other and may be unsure as to what would be defined as proper behavior.

The consideration of this study will center upon the degree of similarity between (1) the male's prescription of the female's role and the female's perception of the male's prescription of the female role, and (2) the female's prescription of the male role and the male's perception of the female's prescription of the male role. The primary determinant of male behavior is not the female's prescription of his role, but rather what he *thinks* her prescription of his role is. Likewise, the primary determinant of female behavior is not the male's prescription of her role, but rather what she *thinks* his prescription of her role is. Essentially then this study is concerned with testing an individual's ability to use a dating partner as a "looking-glass self."[1]

METHODOLOGY

Questionnaires were distributed to 600 students enrolled in a midwestern university. These questionnaires were distributed on a class basis with the classes chosen to represent the sex and rank in class ratio exhibited by the entire university population. A return of 417 (70 percent) questionnaires was obtained. All data are based upon a male N of 187 and a female N of 230. In the relevant section of this questionnaire, subjects were asked questions concerning their behavior on an unarranged date. An unarranged date was defined as a date not arranged prior to the time of the date, which was considered to begin when a girl accepts the offer to pair off. The more common term for the unarranged date would be the "pickup date." A prearranged date was defined as a date arranged at least one day in advance. Reference to a "bar" in certain questions was taken to mean either a "21-year-old bar" or "18-year-old" beer bar, which happened to be the main place where unarranged dates were formulated in this university setting.

FEMALE ACCURACY IN ROLE DEFINITION

Five questions were asked concerning expected female sexual behavior. Males were asked to answer as males, and females were asked to answer as if they were a male. All questions were to be answered with either "yes" or "no" responses. Table 1 gives the questions as well as a summary of the results.

In her responses to all the questions, the female perceives the male's prescription of her role as being more permissive than is the case. The female is fairly accurate in judging the male's expectation of her sexual behavior relative to the type of date, but in response to three of the four remaining questions, the female's overjudgment of the male's view of her permissiveness is statistically significant.

This breakdown in accuracy suggests a breakdown in communication. First if it is assumed that dating is often an exploitative relationship, then the male may be setting up demands. The male may act as if he expects a date to be freer sexually after drinking, to give a goodnight kiss on the first date, or to "make out" on an unarranged date. This acting may simply be an attempt to influence the girl and may not be expected to be entirely successful. The male may reason that he must give the impression of expecting high permissiveness in order to influence the girl to be a little more permis-

TABLE 1. PERCENT OF AFFIRMATIVE ANSWERS FOR MALES AND FEMALES FOR QUESTIONS CONCERNING MALE EXPECTATIONS OF FEMALE BEHAVIOR

Questions	The Male's Prescription of the Female Role	The Female's Perception of the Male's Prescription of the Female Role
1. Do you expect a girl to be freer sexually on an unarranged date than on a prearranged date?	43.5	46.5
2. Do you expect a girl who has been drinking to be freer sexually?	88.1	97.0*
3. Do you expect a girl always to give you a goodnight kiss after a date of any kind?	56.0	68.3*
4. If a girl accepts a ride home from a bar with you alone, do you expect her to "make out" for a while?	43.0	57.4*
5. If a girl agrees to walk home from a bar with you alone, do you expect her to "make out" with you?	42.0	45.2

* A Chi-square test shows this difference to be significant at the .01 level of confidence.

sive than she intended. This interpretation is similar to what is presented by Gorer in his discussion of the male "line."[2] Gorer suggests that the use of the "line" is in large part a friendly deception played on the casual date to obtain favors from one's partner. In this interpretation, then, we assume that the female is accurate in defining the role prescribed by the male's expressed expectations. She is, however, unable to distinguish between the assumed expectations of the male's line and the actual expectations of his social code.

MALE ACCURACY IN ROLE DEFINITION

Five questions were asked concerning expected male sexual behavior. Females were asked to answer as females, and males were asked to answer as if they were a female. Table 2 gives the questions as well as a summary of the results.

In all instances the male perceives the female's prescription of his role as being more aggressive than is actually the case. However, the male only slightly misjudges the female's expectations of his sexual behavior relative to the type of date and is quite accurate in judging the female's expectation of his sexual aggressiveness after he has been drinking. But for the remaining questions the male's accuracy breaks down and appears to be substantially less accurate than the female's. Males greatly overestimate the female's expectation that "a boy will always try to kiss her goodnight after a date of any kind." In regard to the question "If a boy offers you a ride home from a bar, do you expect to 'make out' for a while?" over twice as many males as females predict that a girl would respond in the affirmative. For question 5, "If a boy offers to walk you home from a bar do you expect to 'make out'?" almost three times as many males as females feel that a girl would respond in the affirmative.

When it comes to sexual behavior on a pickup date, it appears as if the male is far from accurate in reading his partner's expectations of himself. Males think that females expect them to be far more aggressive than females actually expect. Here again the interpretation of this result can be based on communication patterns. As Gorer notes, the success of the male depends on

TABLE 2. PERCENT OF AFFIRMATIVE ANSWERS FOR MALES AND FEMALES FOR QUESTIONS CONCERNING FEMALE EXPECTATIONS OF MALE BEHAVIOR

Questions	The Female's Prescription of the Male Role	The Male's Perception of the Female's Prescription of the Male Role
1. Do you expect a boy to be more aggressive sexually on an unarranged date than on a prearranged date?	55.7	63.5
2. Do you expect a boy who has been drinking to "try" more sexually?	87.0	88.6
3. Do you expect a boy always to try to kiss you goodnight after a date of any kind?	52.6	71.9*
4. If a boy offers you a ride home alone from a bar, do you expect to "make out" a while?	23.0	52.3*
5. If a boy offers to walk you home alone from a bar, do you expect to "make out"?	15.2	44.0*

* A Chi-square test shows this difference to be significant at the .01 level of confidence.

the success of his line; the success of the female depends on how she successfully parries this line. In effect she develops a line of her own which may give the impression that she expects the male to be aggressive. She parodies the male line by saying, "He thinks he is the big, manly, aggressive type, so I will play along with his game." She may also mislead the male by causing him to feel that she is more permissive than she actually is for purposes of sustaining the social contact. The male in turn reads this potential permissiveness as a demand for aggressive behavior which escalates his perception of her expectations.

IMPLICATIONS FOR SOCIAL BEHAVIOR RELEVANT TO THE DATING FUNCTION

If the male's line is an impediment to the female's understanding of the social situation, it is also true that the male is impeded in his understanding by the female's line. In fact, our data suggest that the male is victimized to a greater extent than the female by the deceptions practiced. In either case, however, the result is that both male and female perceive the other as demanding more of them than is the case. Presumably the lines are discarded by both sexes as the couple progresses toward more serious dating stages and improved role definition results. However, this improvement may not occur—a fact which may be the source of the occlusion of communication channels characteristic of many marriages.

IMPLICATIONS FOR SEXUAL STANDARDS

In our culture where unstructured social interaction takes place, such as in the unarranged date, a great amount of "looking-glass selfism" must take place. In such situations it is very easy for role-taking to be inaccurate. It appears that this is the case in the unstructured date on a college campus. The inaccuracy of role expectation can be in two directions: (1) to perceive *less* prescribed sexual behavior than is actually prescribed; or (2) to perceive *more* prescribed sexual behavior than is actually prescribed. It is possible to contend that the direction of perceptive inaccuracy is a reflection of the trend in sexual standards.

To perceive more prescribed sexual behavior than is actually prescribed will result in a redefinition of one's own personal standard towards the liberal direction. The looking-glass self process does not end with an idea of what one thinks another thinks of him but rather with a resulting self-feeling. This self-feeling reflects the degree of conformity to or deviance from the perceived expectations of others. The person is under psychological pressure to change in direct relation to the extent that his personal role is felt to be deviant. Individuals will adjust their own personal standards according to how much they value the expectations of members of the opposite sex. The individual comes to see himself as he thinks others see him. The result of the found inaccuracy in perceived role prescription is the likelihood that sexual standards will be liberalized.

SUMMARY

It has been found that both males and females misread the sexual expectations of members of the opposite sex, and both always do so in the direction of increased permissiveness. Both males and females think that the opposite sexes' role prescriptions are more permissive than they actually are. This paper has suggested that the common use of a "line" by both male and female can be blamed for the inaccuracy in perceived role prescription.

Implications of these findings for the dating function and sexual behavior standards were drawn.

NOTES

[1] Cooley coined the term "looking-glass self" in explaining the development of the social self. The operations in the looking-glass self process include: (1) how we imagine that we appear to another person (note that this may not be objectively accurate); (2) how we imagine that another person judges what we think he sees; and (3) some sort of resulting self-feeling. See Charles Horton Cooley, *Human Nature and the Social Order* (New York: Schocken Books, 1964), pp. 168–210.

[2] Geoffrey Gorer, *The American People: A Study in National Character* (New York: W. W. Norton & Company, Inc., 1948), pp. 114–117.

22

THE WORLD OF THE FORMERLY MARRIED

Morton Hunt

Every society has its own way of matching up its unmarried people. During nearly all of Western history, parents and other elders performed this function, judging for themselves the compatibility of the prospective mates, and using such business acumen as they had to get the best possible terms. Paying only minor heed to the wishes of their children, they shuffled and sorted them, sometimes used go-betweens and marriage brokers to locate prospects, bargained and dickered with each other over money and property, and managed one way or another to pair off most of their young.

This system worked well enough for many centuries. But the new mobility and democracy of American life began to affect it: after the colonial period, most young men and women began to have a good deal to say about the matter, and could refuse someone urged on them by their parents or even choose someone their parents disapproved of. By fifty years ago, parental control was rapidly declining, society was becoming too vast and fluid for families to know all about each other, and love was supplanting practical motives as the reason for marrying; under these conditions, the old method of mate selection finally collapsed altogether, and a new one—dating —spontaneously appeared, in which the unmarried young took over the job of finding partners for themselves. Their marketplace was the school, the party, and the neighborhood, where they could freely test out different partners, meet unchaperoned and without commitment or change of status, and make their final choice largely on the basis of emotional needs. Despite all its faults, dating was well-adapted to modern society and, for all anyone can prove to the contrary, has performed its function as effectively as the older methods did in their time.

But while the unmarried young always have been a concern of society, the Formerly Married never have: in the past there were almost no FMs, or so few that little pressure existed for the invention of a social mechanism to bring them together. They have appeared in large quantities only in very recent times; then, because the marketplace of the unmarried young was inappropriate or unavailable to most of them, a marketplace for the Formerly Married began to develop which is still being enlarged and modified every year.

By and large, most newly separated people are unaware of the many opportunities and methods this marketplace now offers for meeting potential partners. Some feel quite hopeless about their prospects at first, and say things such as: "I can't seem to meet any women who are right for me." "How on earth do you get back into circulation after nine years of marriage?" "Where are all those divorced men I used to hear about?" "How do I start? Where should I go? What should I do?" "Where *is* everybody?"

Even if the novice has begun to make a few sorties—to a cocktail party, a country-club dance, an evening at a church social—he or she may still feel powerless to find the right kind of unattached partners to start dating. Before he does, he may know many aimless evenings and interminable weekends filled with bitter envy of couples walking hand in hand, and a feeling of isolation and helplessness. This is true for at least half the men and three-quarters of the women—and, surprisingly, almost as true for the attractive as the plain, the city-dweller as the suburbanite.

But this is before they have begun to discover the many possibilities that exist nowadays for meeting people of their own kind and finding suitable dating partners. Many of these possibilities strike the novice as distasteful, improper, or even degrading; but to judge from the amount of dating activity among the Formerly Married and their high remarriage rate, the marketplace as it now exists is serving its purpose surprisingly well. . . .

Most recently separated people, when they first feel ready to date, are aware only of the conventional and conservative ways of meeting potential partners. Of these the most familiar and nearest to hand is the introduction or meeting arranged by friends or, less frequently, by relatives. The FM has been seeing or talking to these people already, they know his or her degree of distress, loneliness, and hunger for new companionship, and it takes only a hint or suggestion to send them thumbing through their address books for a name to suggest. After this first effort, some of them continue for years to ply him or her with names of people they come across from time to time. Professor Goode's survey (the basis of his book, *After Divorce*), and a survey by August Hollingshead, a professor of sociology at Yale, give similar figures: friends are a principal source of new contacts for over a third of the FMs queried, and relatives for about one-sixth.

Unfortunately, a very high proportion of the people met in this fashion are singularly unsuitable—especially when they have been suggested by married friends rather than single ones. Dispensers of advice to the separated and divorced often say that married friends are the best means of meeting potential dates, but many experienced FMs say that married friends have an uncanny knack of choosing the wrong people. . . .

Nevertheless, introductions by married friends do satisfy at least a minority of FMs, occasionally produce a hit, and are a preeminently "safe" avenue of meeting, since the intermediary friends know each person and are able to vouch for good behavior. This method also avoids the risk—always greater for women than for men—of being thought too loose or too eager; the introduction through friends has the sanction of custom, and fits the mores of the married world. . . .

Unmarried friends or other formerly married people are less demanding and less inhibiting. They are freer of distortions of judgment when they select someone to suggest to the new FM, and more understanding and uncritical if the meeting is not a success. Thanks to their own experiences, and the mores of the world they inhabit, such friends usually avoid setting up an evening in which the man and woman are formally paired off with each other. Veteran FMs know that the important thing is to save face and to guard against unduly trying social situations; the smaller the degree of commitment the better, since it puts less strain on the people being introduced, should they not be attracted to each other. Single people and FMs therefore may tell a man and a woman about each other privately, invite each one to drop by some evening when there are a few people coming over, and leave each one free to pretend that the other is not his or her reason for being there.

Even freer of surveillance and structure is the method in which the go-between friend tells each one about the other, and then lets them make contact by telephone. Almost always, of course, the initiative rests with the man. Such telephone calls are not easy for him to make at first. The man who has been married for years may feel as nervous and awkward when he starts that first conversation as he did when he was a gawky adolescent; the woman receiving her first call may find herself straining for talk to fill up the long pauses. The novice has forgotten the skills he or she once had long ago. But since usually only one of the two people is the novice, the more experienced one soon puts the other at ease, not so much by any specific remarks as by a manner which indicates that such phone calls are perfectly normal and expected among FMs and that two people in similar circumstances need feel no awkwardness with each other. . . .

But . . . the method is a gamble far more often lost than won. For self-introduction on the telephone, if it goes well, leads to a blind date, a species of appointment with profound drawbacks. For one thing, the blind date is somewhat embarrassing, being reminiscent of adolescence and the overeagerness to date for the mere sake of dating. But more importantly, the telephone conceals as much as it reveals; one may read into a voice, during a ten-minute conversation, all those traits he or she is hoping to find, but when the door opens on the appointed night someone else is there instead—the same person but not the hoped-for person. . . .

The conventional methods are, in sum, of limited value; the Formerly Married need exposure to a much wider array of human beings than these can provide. At fifteen, one could view almost any passable-looking boy or girl as a suitable date; even at nineteen or twenty, one was still unformed and flexible enough to make a go of

it, for a while, with nearly anyone who met the minimum requirements. But the formerly married man or woman has a wealth of personal history, and an accumulation of cherished tastes and dear experiences; to find some other human being who can fit into one's elaborate matrix of identity, and into whose own matrix one can fit correspondingly, is exceedingly difficult and requires a far wider search than it did in youth. Although a substantial minority of the Formerly Married, either because of inhibitions or the force of local custom, rely entirely on conservative methods of meeting new partners, a majority soon become willing to go beyond them and to try less conventional alternatives that promise better to satisfy their needs. . . .

The resumption of dating is as difficult and filled with anxiety for the FM as the first shaky steps a patient takes after serious illness and prolonged confinement to bed. Yet such is the recuperative power of the normal psyche that three out of four FMs, despite any practical difficulties they may experience in finding suitable partners, do begin dating within the first year, and over nine out of ten do so before the end of the second. . . .

Many of the Formerly Married find that dating never-married or widowed people is far less satisfactory than dating other FMs. Among the people I queried, fellow-FMs were preferred as dates about two to one over the other two categories of unattached people combined; this preference was particularly marked among people in their upper thirties and above.

The formerly married man suspects that the never-married girl of thirty or more has deep emotional problems—fear of men, fear of sex, and so on. Even if this is not the case, or if she is younger, he finds that many of his most significant recent experiences are not particularly meaningful or interesting to her; he may talk about his children, or about married life, or about the strangeness of returning to single ways, but instead of responding with complete understanding as a formerly married woman would, she listens and replies with obvious effort, as though he were speaking in a foreign tongue she had studied but was not fluent in. She does, of course, have the great advantage of being a more convenient date—there are no baby-sitting or scheduling problems, and she can easily go places with him, stay out late, even remain at his place without advance planning; yet even these advantages are outweighed by the sense of fellowship and understanding he finds in women who have been married before. And FM women, in their turn, have equally strong suspicions and reservations about unmarried men in their thirties or older. Most of these men, even if attractive, agreeable, and well-off, seem incomplete or unreachable to FM women who date them. . . .

Widows and widowers, though they have been married, seem to most FMs even less satisfactory as dates than do the never-married. The formerly married man going on a date with a widow is aware in a matter of minutes that it is a distinctly different experience from dating a formerly married woman. The widow may be friendly and talkative on the surface, but there is an almost tangible barrier between her and the man; she is insulated, and no current of feeling flows between them. . . .

Undoubtedly there are a number of widows and widowers who do not act like this, and it is true that the Formerly Married and the widowed do mingle, date, and enter into affairs with each other. But the fact remains that by and large they are somewhat antagonistic toward each other, and prefer to date their own kind. The preference is neither temporary nor superficial; much later on, the Formerly Married and the widowed will show the same inclinations when they come to select partners for remarriage.

The Formerly Married, in their initial dating experiences, gain new skills, a sense of identity, and a comforting familiarity with the mores of the world they now live in. But even more important than these is the aid and stimulus they get in their task of revaluing themselves and repairing their egos. In a collapsing marriage, a man or woman may feel worthless, unsexed, prematurely old; out of that marriage and beginning to date, the same person may perceive himself or herself as valuable, sexual,

and youthful. Most FMs, at this phase of adjustment, have a heady and exciting sense of self-esteem. . . .

This regained respect and liking for one's self, though it may seem somewhat superficial and vain, is a prerequisite for more profound experiences that are to follow, and a significant advance toward the recapture of emotional health. Dating, though it may sometimes look like an adolescent and contrived form of heterosexual interaction, is an effective way for the FM to reappraise and reconstruct himself, even while exploring and testing the qualities he needs in a potential love-partner. It is a psychotherapeutic experience, invaluable as far as it goes, though it goes only a part of the way. If it is time-consuming, chancy, and often expensive, it shares these characteristics with other forms of psychotherapeutic experience—but at least it is fun some of the time, which one can rarely say of the others. . . .

Postmarital dating differs in various respects from premarital dating, and nowhere more sharply than in the area of the sexual overture—the male "pass" or the female "come-on." (Since the pass is common and the come-on rare, and since moreover it is the pass that is often regarded as the problem, I will concentrate on the former.) The main differences lie in the far greater speed and frankness with which such overtures are made, and in their permissibility very early in the acquaintance of the dating couple. "Permissibility" does not mean that the woman routinely acquiesces, but that in the World of the Formerly Married it is within the bounds of convention for the man to try.

Most middle-class FMs dated when they were of college age, anywhere from ten to thirty years ago. The mores of that stratum of American society, though they varied somewhat in the different parts of the country, generally allowed the boy to be a mild sexual aggressor and the girl to be defensive but not entirely unyielding. His advances were slow and relatively tactful, her concessions were gradual and based on the development of feeling between them. Usually she held the line at necking for a number of dates, until he and she began to be somewhat emotionally involved; then she might allow him to advance as far as light petting, and still later as far as heavy petting, where she would hold the line much longer; he neither insisted on intercourse nor had much chance of achieving it until they considered themselves to be deeply in love or were actually married.

Today the young are often said by the middle-aged to be uninhibited and virtually promiscuous, but it is an old complaint; adults, throughout the ages, have always thought the young to be on the brink of ruin. Actually, the young are doing much what their parents did, the major difference being that they arrive at each stage of sexual behavior a few years earlier, and so have more experience; by and large, they are not promiscuous or libertine about sex, but still expect and seek it chiefly within steady and emotionally meaningful relationships. Hence, even young FMs who were dating only a few years ago at first find the general behavior of formerly married men and women startling; older FMs, of course, are even more likely to be shocked. . . .

Formerly married men and women are often plagued by contradictory sets of feelings, and by behavior that belies or frustrates their stated aims: they are creatures of paradox; in psychological terms, they are ambivalent. This was true of their feelings about their spouses during the disintegrating phase of marriage, and their feelings about the freedom of the early weeks of separation or divorce. It is similarly true of their feelings about the purpose of dating, for although its ultimate goal is to find a potential replacement for the missing spouse, many formerly married men and women use dating chiefly for other goals—including even the avoidance of mate-selection.

At first, this may be useful. The majority of newly separated or divorced people face a long period of emotional reconstruction, and the premature effort to choose and to love may result in a poor choice and an impermanent love—the well-known "rebound" effect, rightfully decried by folk wisdom. It is therefore all to the good that dating has so few built-in demands, and can be used to try out emotional relationships on a very shallow level, without any requirement to love or even to care. . . .

If everyone went directly from a dissolving marriage into a new love that eventually became a new marriage, none of the ambivalence and the problems involved in dating would exist. But although a few people do this, the great majority do not, nor can they. For they must first go through a long process of healing and rehabilitation, during which they are unable to love either wisely or well. Dating, for all its hazards, helps them get ready to do just that. Tissue and bones, after a serious injury, must knit together before the limb can be used again, but then the limb must be exercised in order to regain its strength and mobility. So it is with the feelings: when we have been damaged in our ability to love ourselves and others, we need to knit up and regrow those abilities, then exercise them, so that at last we may use them in a normal and complete fashion.

23

TEEN-AGE INTERRACIAL DATING

Frank A. Petroni

Early in the still unfolding story of school desegregation, many observers were saying that what white opponents of integration were most afraid of was interracial sex. People who had been comforting themselves with such abstractions as "Negroes are OK, but I wouldn't want my daughter to marry one," now, with desegregation, had suddenly to cope (they thought) with a real possibility, not a farfetched hypothesis.

Be this as it may, I doubt there are many Americans who have not, at one time or another, had to cope with the question of interracial sex, either in imagination—"what would happen if . . ."—or in fact. Interracial dating and interracial marriage are social realities, however much white racists and black nationalists may deplore it.

A few years ago, while I was with the Menninger Foundation in Topeka, Kansas, my wife and I had an opportunity to study the extent of, and students' feelings about, interracial dating at a desegregated high school. Our procedure was rather unorthodox. Instead of trying to gather a 5 percent random sample of the 3,000-member student body, we began slowly by letting our initial student contacts tell us what they considered to be the principal "types" of student in the school. They distinguished 12 such types: middle-class whites, hippies, peaceniks, white trash, "sedits" (upper-class blacks), elites, conservatives, racists, niggers, militants, athletes, and hoods. Then, and again through our initial contacts, we brought in other students and roughly classified them according to "type." In this way, I believe we got a representative cross section of the social world of this high school. We interviewed the boys and girls in groups of three or four, and in time 25 groups came to our house for these conversations. We had two refusals: a black girl canceled her appointment after Martin Luther King

was killed, and a boy told us he wouldn't talk to white people.

Few topics demonstrate the multiple pressures students are subject to better than interracial dating. These pressures come from parents, teachers, counselors, school administrators, and peers. However, mixed dating is emphatically not a barometer of the amount of "integration" in a desegregated school; that is not the reason we chose to study it.

Needless to say, the students did not all share the same point of view on interracial dating. Yet, most of them—independent of race—did feel that it was none of the school's business: if students wanted to date interracially, the school had no right to stop them.

WHITE BOYS AND BLACK GIRLS

Not one student knew of a case of interracial dating involving a white boy and a black girl. There was considerable speculation about why. A conservative white girl said that white boys are too proud to date blacks. The two white boys with her disagreed: both said that it's because black girls aren't as pretty as white girls. One of the two also suggested that blacks and whites have little in common and so he would not consider dating a black. Note the popular stereotypes in this answer:

Well, there are cultural differences, and their attitudes are different. I think that's what makes the difference. They're easygoing. They like to have a lot of fun. They don't think about the future, about things that are important like getting a job, or supporting a family. They don't try for grades. They're just out to have a good time.

Even when black girls met an individual's standard of physical attractiveness, however, white boys spoke of other obstacles: where to go, how to ignore community disapproval and what to do about family and friends who disapprove. These conflicts are cogently summarized in the response of a white boy who considered dating a black:

I think if you dated a Negro, you would lose a lot of so-called friends. But you would probably gain some Negro friends. I contemplated asking this Negro girl for a date, but I chickened out. I thought, where would I take her? The only place where people wouldn't stare at me would be a drive-in movie, and I don't have a car. If you went to a restaurant, you would get dirty looks from people. I couldn't take her home and introduce her to my mom; she'd probably kill me.

Social obstacles apart, there is some doubt in my mind whether a black girl, in the school we studied, would go out with a white boy even if asked. Each black girl we interviewed was asked, "Suppose a white boy asked you out, how easy would it be for you to accept?" One girl answered: "Any white boy who asked me out, I would know what he wants. For a Negro boy to have a white girl is some sort of status symbol, but if a white boy asked me out, it would be a step down for him. I would think he wants something I'm not about to give him."

Other black girls spoke of the double standard between boys and girls, and how girls were less free to date interracially because their reputations would be ruined. Fear for one's reputation was also a factor among white girls. The students associated interracial dating with sex; and girls, be they black or white, stood to lose the most. Yet sex was not always associated with dating. There was no reference to sex when respondents talked about dating within one's race. Sometimes the reference to sex in interracial dating was subtle, but nonetheless it was present. A white girl's comment demonstrates this: "When you think

of mixed dating, you always think of a colored boy with a white girl. And you always think it is the white girl who is low. If it was a white boy with a colored girl, then it would be the white boy who was low."

When asked for the meaning of low, another white girl said: "Well, generally the public thinks that the girl has low standards and low morals, if she's willing to go out with a Negro."

Particularly among "elite" blacks, parental disapproval of interracial dating also stood between black young women and dates with white boys. Most of the black students in this strata stated that their parents would not tolerate interracial dating. The parents expected their children to compete with white students academically, for school offices, and in extracurricular activities; socially, however, they expected them to stay with blacks.

Still other respondents saw the white boys' reluctance to date blacks as essentially a matter of status considerations. If the belief that *all* whites are better than *all* blacks is general in this society (and it showed up among some of the blacks in our sample as well), then the response of an 18-year-old black girl, who was given the highest academic award the school has to offer, makes sense:

White boys would be scared to ask us out anyway. The Negro boys will ask white girls out, but white boys will never ask Negro girls out. For a Negro boy, going out with a white girl is an accomplishment; it raises his status, even if the white girl is lower-class. All white kids are supposed to be better than Negro kids. If a white boy dated a Negro, even if the white boy was one of the "trashy" kind, and the girl was, say me, his status would drop. They would ask him if he was hard-up or something. White boys would be stepping down if they asked Negro girls for dates.

Aside from the black girl's fear of parental disapproval and loss of her reputation, we were told that few blacks would accept a date from a white boy because of pressures from black young men, who would object if black girls dated whites. However, this pressure doesn't appear to count for much with the elite, college-bound black girl; it was the athletic girl who gave us this answer. Unlike her elite counterpart, the athletic black girl was not preoccupied with achieving what the white man prized for whites: academic achievement, social popularity, and a svelte figure. The reference group for these girls was the black community. A star on the girl's track team said:

No Negro girls that I know of have ever been dated by a white guy. There are some that wish they could. In fact, I know some white guys, myself, I wouldn't mind going out with, but the Negro girls are mostly afraid. Even if a white guy asked them out, they wouldn't go out with them. Negro boys don't like for Negro girls to date white guys. Sometimes I see white guys who look nice, and I stop and talk to them. The Negro boys get upset. They are real screwy. They can date white girls, but we can't date white guys.

THE REACTION OF BLACK MALES

The black young men in our sample at times disagreed on how they would react to dating between white boys and black girls, but in general their answers fell into one of the categories predicted by the black girls. A boy, who has dated white girls, admitted to the double standard alleged by the girl athlete. He told us:

You know, I think that Negro boys would detest having a Negro girl go out with a white boy. They don't want Negro girls to date white boys. They don't like it. I feel like that, and I think I'm a hypocrite. I've been out with white girls, but I don't like it if a Negro girl goes out with a white boy. If I see a colored girl with a white boy, I think, why didn't she date me, or another Negro? What's he got that I ain't got?

Not all blacks who date whites felt this way. The young man whom we just quoted identified positively with the black com-

munity. But another young man, with a steady white girl friend, and who prized white over black, had this to say: "I don't think most of the white boys would ask Negro girls out. Maybe I shouldn't say this, but I think any Negro girl would consider it a privilege to have a white boy ask her out. I feel if a colored girl is good enough to get a white boy, they should go out together."

It was easier for most of the students, white or black, to talk about interracial dating in which the girl is white. This is the kind of dating most of them have seen. Some students, however, had seen black girls with white boys at the state university and in larger communities. One black spoke frankly of his reactions when he first saw a white man with a black woman:

You see this at the colleges [white boys with Negro girls]. You know, it's a funny thing now that you mention it, you never see Negro girls with white boys here. I was in New York once. It was kind of funny; I saw this Negro girl with a white guy. I was shocked. You know, I looked, and it seemed kind of funny to me. I mean you see white girls with Negro boys, but you never see a Negro girl with a white guy; it kind of shocks you at first.

BLACK MALES AND WHITE GIRLS

The pressures from parents, teachers, counselors, peers, and the community are also brought to bear on the black boy and white girl who cross the barrier against interracial dating. As one student poignantly put it, "For those who violate this convention, the tuition is high." Just how high is exemplified by the white girl in the most talked about relationship involving an interracial couple.

Around Christmas time, I got to know this colored guy real well and wanted to date him. There was a big mix-up; my parents didn't like it. My parents put a lot of pressure on me not to go out with him. They are the type people, like Dad, who says he's not prejudiced. He even has them *working in his office, but he wants them to stay in their place. At school there was a lot of talking behind my back and snickering when I walked down the hallway. I tried to tell myself it didn't matter what people thought, but it still hurt. It hurt an awful lot. My parents made me feel so guilty. They made me feel so cheap. They were worried about what people would say. They made me feel like two pieces of dirt. You know, I never thought interracial dating was a good idea, but when I met this colored guy, it changed me. I never went with anyone I really liked before. I think this changes your outlook. It gives you hope, when you find someone you really like.*

SEX AND DATING

That sexual intercourse is associated with interracial dating is indicated by the fact that one reaction to such dating is to question the girl's moral standards. We heard this frequently from both white girls and boys, but particularly the latter. Prior to dating a black, however, the girl's personal conduct is rarely mentioned. It seems as if the disbelief among the white community that a white girl would date a black is softened by the rationalization that she "must be immoral." One white girl found it hard to accept this student reaction: "I got kind of sick of the kids throwing her to the dogs. There were times when you had to take a stand. You either turned the other cheek, or you fought back for her. They thought she was cheap, and they said nasty things about her. Even the guy I'm dating, he's that way, too."

However, a white girl doesn't have to date a black to have others question her morality. Just talking to a black student can result in the same labeling process. A liberal white girl, identified as a hippie, told us: "One day we were talking to some black power students in front of school. Some adults going by in cars made some filthy remarks. You can imagine what they think of white women, hanging around talking to Negroes. They shot it right out as they

drove by. These are the good, white middle-class people."

A very articulate black youth described a similar incident in which he was talking to a white girl: "One time I was walking down the stairs outside school. I was standing with this white girl, and we were talking. About six white kids drove by and yelled, 'White trash, you're nothing but white trash.' I guess because she was white and I'm black, and we were talking, she was white trash."

Other blacks, aware of the white community's reaction to white girls who date or talk in public with blacks, were prevented from asking white girls out because they did not want to ruin the girls' reputations. The son of a prominent black professional, who was a football letterman, in the student government, and extremely popular, refused to date a white girl for this reason.

In general, I would say that just the fact that I was taking out a white girl, the imaginations would go wild. They think the moral standards are lower in interracial dating. There's this one white girl I goofed around with a lot. It's gone beyond the friendship stage, but we never dated. If I did go out with a white girl, it would be hard to take her anyplace. I would have to think about it for a while before I took out a white girl, because I feel she would be downgraded. I wouldn't want to ruin her reputation.

White girls who date across the color line find themselves unacceptable to white boys. Most of the students agreed that to date interracially limited a girl's field of potential dates. For many white girls, knowledge of this reaction on the part of white boys served as a deterrent to interracial dating. Nevertheless, a number of white girls told us they were attracted to certain black young men. One of the girls who did defy her society reported this also. She said, "When I was dating him, I was surprised at how many girls wanted to date colored guys. They would come up to me and ask me things. They really wanted to date colored guys, but they were afraid."

WHITE "BOYCOTT"

We found, too, that the white boycott (as it were) persisted after the interracial couple no longer dated, albeit only among white boys still in school. Girls who broke off their relationship with blacks were dated by older whites in the community. But to regain admission as an acceptable date among the high school boys, a girl would have to move to a new community to lose the pejorative label, which is part of the price for dating interracially.

The black male who dates a white girl does not escape criticism from his own race, particularly the black girls. Part of their disapproval is motivated, again, by the lack of reciprocity: black girls were not dated by whites. When a high status black, generally an athlete, dated a white girl, he was replaced by neither a high status nor low status white. The black girls' resentment is summarized in the answer of one of our respondents, identified as a "militant."

Well, in junior high, the Negro girls resented the fact that I went out with a white girl, and they really got onto me. They feel inferior. The white girls get all the guys. Some hostility between the Negro girls and white girls comes from this. The Negro girls kind of feel left out. She doesn't have white guys to date, and she doesn't have Negro guys to date. She says, "Hey, gal, you dating that Negro, and I can't get a date with him." This kind of builds up a resentment in her.

Pressure on the black male comes in two forms. First, his racial identification may be questioned. Often he is accused of thinking he is white. Second, retaliation by black girls can be more direct and swift. There were reports of boys physically beaten for dating a white girl. However, this response was the exception; it was more common for girls to spread the rumor that a boy is an "Uncle Tom."

PARENTAL PRESSURES

The double threat of losing one's reputation and losing favor among the white boys pre-vented many white girls from dating blacks. Yet the pressures do not end there. Interracial dating is a test of the white liberal's commitment to civil rights—a test that few have passed. A number of white students spoke of their disappointment in their parents who gave lipservice to "liberalism" but in the final analysis were prejudiced. White girls reported this more often than white boys. However, white girls *tested* their parents more often. A white girl who sensed this in one of her parents said:

This Negro friend of mine gets along beautifully with my mother, but not my father. He senses this, too. After meeting my father, he said my father didn't like him. This is something new for me because my father and mother have always been liberal. Now that he has been over to my house a couple of times, my father is acting strange. I guess I'm learning something about him I didn't know before.

Sometimes the parental reaction isn't as subtle as the feeling that one's father doesn't approve of interracial dating. A rather tough black girl, who admitted that at one time she was a hood, told us what happened to a white girl, who used to date her ex-boy friend:

For many Negro boys, dating white girls is their way of showing their superiority, their way of trying to hurt the white man. This boy I used to date went with a white girl once. She went through hell with her parents and everyone else to go out with him. But he didn't really care. He was just showing off. Her father even spit in her face. Her parents attacked her; they beat her and called her a slut.

Parental disapproval of interracial dating is not restricted to whites. The blacks reported a generation gap between themselves, their parents, and their grandparents on this issue. In general, they reported that the intensity of the disapproval varied directly with age. Thus, grandparents showed more disapproval than parents. By and large, however, the black students agreed that the mixed couple that chooses to go out together should have that choice without interference from members of the adult community, be they parents, teachers, counselors, school administrators, or anonymous members of the community.

The sample included few Mexican-Americans; those interviewed, however, reported the same phenomenon: Mexican parents, like white and black parents, objected to interracial dating. An outspoken Mexican-American girl related the Mexican parents' position. Her answer reveals the confusion parental inconsistencies can create for a young person.

Mom always said have your fun as long as you're young, and as long as you marry a Mexican. I don't feel that way. If I fall in love with a Negro, I'll marry him. If I fall in love with a white, I'll marry a white. My parents would frown on us dating a Negro, even if he has higher standards than the Mexicans we date now: even if the Negro's father was a lawyer or a doctor, and he was a better person than many of the lower-class Mexicans we date now. I don't understand it. They would rather see us go out with white people, who aren't as good, just because of skin color. They say they want the best for us; if the best meant going out with a Negro, they would say no!

THE SCHOOL

As if the pressures of peers, parents, and community were not enough, those who try to break down the barrier against interracial dating, or who ignore it, must also cope with teachers, counselors, and school administrators, who, by and large, are united on this issue. In a word, boy-girl relationships should be white-white, or black-black, but not black-white.

It became apparent to us that when we discussed the school's position on interracial dating, the students' objections to interference became more emotionally charged. This suggested to us that the students perceived the school and its functionaries as having less legitimacy than either parents or peers in attempting to control and dictate norms for their social life.

The hostility was increased by the fact that both black and white students perceived a selective interference by the school. The teachers, counselors, and school administrators did not interfere with interracial dating per se. Their interference increased in direct proportion to the white girl's social status. A black girl described this selective process to us.

I think it's their business, not the school's. She was crazy about him, and he was crazy about her. They went to school to get an education, and that's what the school should be concerned with: giving them an education. Instead, they threatened him, they said he wouldn't get an athletic scholarship. I felt this was entirely wrong for the school to interfere. It's not the school's affair to concern itself with whether or not the students have companionship. It's their business to teach. These kids aren't the only couple at school. But she was somebody. With some of the other couples, the girls aren't important. In fact, one of the other girls is just white "trash." They don't say too much to these others; it's the important ones they want to save.

Another girl left little doubt of the painful slur implicit in this attitude of the school functionaries: "If you're a low white person, the administration could care less, but if you're a higher white person, they're worried that you might be dragged down by a Negro."

Although we cannot be certain, there is a possibility that the school's policy in these matters is dictated by the reality of the situation. There was little that the school could do to low status students who dated across the color line; the school did not have an effective lever to stop them from continuing except to inform the parents, and most parents already knew. The only other course open to them was to expel the students for the slightest infraction of the rules. Among high status students, however, the school could threaten removal from the very positions the students worked to achieve. Black athletes were called in and ordered to desist or forfeit their chances for an athletic scholarship; others were threatened with removal from the team. And white girls were told they could not run for a school office, they were not eligible to become cheerleaders, and they would receive no assistance in obtaining a scholarship.

SUMMARY AND CONCLUSIONS

Interracial dating was one of the most emotionally charged subjects in our discussions with these young people. Although we have not cited all our respondents in this brief presentation, all of them had opinions on the issue. There was complete agreement on the type of interracial dating that occurred. In no case was the male white and the female black. Generally the black male, who dated a white girl, was a high status athlete; however, by high status we are not referring to his father's socioeconomic position in the community. This may, or may not, have been high; in most cases it was not.

The fact that black students with prestige took up with white girls was a source of tension between black and white girls. More than her male counterpart, the black girl preached black separatism. Some students felt that this was because the girls did not share a sports experience such as that shared by black and white boys. On the surface, that may appear to be right. However, since there was little camaraderie between black and white athletes off the field or court, direct competition for high status blacks in the dating-mating complex seems to be a more plausible explanation for the friction between white and black girls.

While interracial dating was not commonplace, it did exist, and those who did it paid a heavy price. Payment was exacted from peers, parents, the community, teachers, counselors, and other school administrators. In short, the entire social world of these teen-agers was united against them. There was no citadel to protect them. When school and peers were allied against them, there was no comfort from their parents. The couple had each other, and a small enclave of "friends," but even among the latter, the attrition rate was high.

Join this to the implication that their moral standards were lower if they dated interracially, and it is small wonder that few felt strong enough to weather all these assaults.

24

RESEARCH IN INTERRELIGIOUS DATING AND MARRIAGE

Larry D. Barnett

Interfaith dating and marriage appear to have increased during the present century (2, 27), and the consensus of authorities in the marriage and family life field is that the United States will continue to experience an increase in the number of interreligious dates and marriages. This increase and the trend toward earlier dating and marriage—today, the typical female is married about two years, and the typical male about four years, after leaving high school—make it important for family life teachers to be aware of facts pertaining to such intergroup associations, for they will increasingly have to deal with them.

This article, by presenting a summary of recent research on the subject of interreligious dating and marriage, will provide information on the following questions: What has caused the increase in interfaith associations? What conditions are found to accompany it? What special problems are encountered by persons crossing religious lines to find a mate? And how do couples resolve these problems?

Let us first turn to the causes of the increase in cross-faith dating and marriage—causes which may, in fact, apply to all forms of mixed dating and marriage. Studies (1, 2, 9, 12, 22, 27) indicate that the following interacting factors foster mixed associations:

1) *Existence of the group as a minority.* In a community in which a group is a minority, its rate of intermarriage will be higher than in a setting in which the group is a majority.

2) *Unbalanced sex ratio.* In a community in which one sex outnumbers the other, traditional barriers are crossed with increased frequency as members of the more numerous sex seek mates.

3) *Development of cultural similarities.* As groups with different backgrounds come into contact, similarities in values and attitudes are developed. This encourages intermarriage, since people tend to marry those who are culturally similar to themselves.

4) *Disturbing psychological factors.* Rebellion against and feelings of rejection toward one's own group lead to an identification with and marriage into an out-group.

5) *Acceptance of certain cultural values.* The democratic ideal, the romantic complex, and the belief in the right of youth to choose their own mates without interference by family and community facilitate the crossing of group lines in dating and in marriage.

6) *Weakening of institutional controls over marriage.* The various religions, for example, are finding their members to be increasingly unwilling to accept church control over the selection of spouses.

The writer suggests that these factors are part and parcel of the broader phenomenon of social and cultural change. As change occurs, these factors obtain, and intermarriages follow. In turn, these factors and intermarriages foster further changes in the social system. Therefore, a society like ours, which is characterized not only by a great deal of change but also by values holding change itself as desirable, will have cross-group dates and marriages to a much greater extent than a cohesive, stable society. Moreover, since change is cumulative, there will be an increasing amount of intermarriage.

In discussing the conditions related to interfaith dating and marrying, we are not saying that the relationship is a cause-and-effect one. Some third factor may produce both the condition and the mixed religious association.

The conditions associated with interreligious dates and marriages are as follows:

1) Apparently more Catholics intermarry than Protestants and more Protestants than Jews (10, 17, 23, 26), although two studies (11, 14) have shown that the Protestants have the highest frequency of mixed marriages and Catholics the next highest.

2) Those who are religiously less devout intermarry to a greater extent than the religiously more devout (3, 8, 13, 17, 23).

An interesting point arises in connection with these first two conditions. According to the first, Jews have the lowest rate of intermarriage; according to the second, the religiously more devout also have a lower frequency of mixed religious marriages. Thus, it would logically follow that Jews are more religious than either Protestants or Catholics. However, this does not seem to be the case, for studies (6, 7, 18) have demonstrated that Jews are the least religious (in terms of religious participation and acceptance of church doctrine) of the three groups.

Can this contradiction be explained? The writer suggests that, in the case of the Jew, it is not adherence to the religion which causes the higher rate of same-group marriage but rather social pressures deriving from the cohesiveness of the Jewish community. That this might be the answer is supported by a study (25) of Jewish-Gentile marriages which found that the family of the Gentile partner is more accepting of the couple than is the family of the Jewish part-
.ner.

3) In Jewish-Gentile marriages, it is the Jewish male who marries the Gentile female in the vast majority of cases (14, 17, 19, 24), but research to date is not consistent in its findings of a relationship between sex and mixed Catholic-Protestant marriages: three studies (3, 15, 27) found that it is the Protestant male who marries the Catholic female—that is, Protestant males and Catholic females intermarry more frequently than Protestant females and Catholic males—and one study (2) found just the reverse, while the data from two studies (14, 17) showed no trend.

4) When a Protestant enters an interfaith marriage, the spouse is more likely to be a Catholic than a Jew (2, 4); and when a Catholic enters an interfaith marriage, the mate is more likely to be a Protestant than a Jew. Jews who marry across the lines of religion choose Catholics and Protestants as mates with equal frequency (4).

5) In the case of a cross-religious marriage, Catholics appear to be least inclined to change to their spouse's faith, and Protestants appear most willing to do so, with Jews standing between the two in their willingness to change religions (6, 17, 23).

6) An interreligious marriage is more likely to be a first marriage than a remarriage (2, 5).

7) Persons marrying someone of a different religion are very often partially or completely rejected by parents and in-laws; for example, Slotkin (25) found in his sample of Jewish-Gentile marriages that 43 percent of the young adults met with at least some rejection by both families. (However, the fact that over half of the couples —57 percent—were partly or wholly accepted by their families should also be emphasized.)

8) Those who had, as youth, weak ties to their parents, whose parental families have been characterized by disorganization and stress, are more likely to engage in interfaith dates and marriages than those who lived in a cohesive family (8, 9, 13, 15, 20).

9) Apparently, those who engage in mixed religious associations are of a higher socioeconomic status as measured by income (20), education (24), and housing (27) than those who do not, although one study (3) reports an inverse correlation between status level and favorable attitudes toward religious intermarriage.

10) Interfaith dating appears to be more characteristic of those who date more frequently than the average (8), and young adults appear to be more willing to cross religious lines when dating than when marrying (23).

11) Interfaith dates and marriages are more frequently found in cities of 5,000 to 100,000 population than in cities having fewer than 5,000 or more than 100,000 persons (27).

12) In terms of divorce, interfaith marriages have a greater failure rate than intrafaith marriages; still, the majority of such marriages are successful (5, 16, 19, 28).

This leads to the third question: What special problems are encountered by those who date and marry persons of another religion? At this point, we must leave research behind. In spite of the significance of the problem, there apparently has been no thorough investigation of it, pointing to a gap in our knowledge which needs attention.

Mace (21), however, out of his long and extensive experience in marriage counseling, believes that there are five problems:

1) *Different religions create attitudes which are basically different.* These attitudinal differences (e.g., on sex) may result in the failure of the marital partners to attain spiritual unity.

2) *Different religions create different action patterns and values.* Religion, as one form of culture, results in patterns of action (e.g., dietary laws) and personal values (e.g., as to the meaning of life) which vary between the different religions, thus providing areas of conflict.

3) *Conflict in ties to church and family*

is possible. If both spouses retain their original faith, ties to their church and to the family they have established may often clash.

4) *Tensions with relatives may be serious.*

5) *Religious training of the children may present problems.* If the couple decides to rear their children in one or the other of their original faiths, competition and jealousy may arise over which of the children are to be raised in each religion. Thus the family will be divided.

Notwithstanding the additional problems created by a marriage of persons of different faiths, the fact that the majority of such marriages are successful—if divorce is an adequate criterion of marital success and failure—must be kept in mind. Therefore, the special problems of interfaith marriages are coped with. It appears that there are three major ways in which this is done (2, 19):

1) One or both of the marital partners completely drops his church membership;

2) The two continue in their original faith; or

3) One spouse joins the church of the other.

One study (2) found that the third solution is the one most commonly employed, while another study (19) showed that the first solution is used most often. In any case, Mace (21) suggests the third—where one spouse completely and wholeheartedly changes to the religion of the other—as the best course of action for solving the problems created by a cross-religious marriage.

In summary, we have looked at four aspects of interfaith dates and marriages: (1) their causes, (2) the conditions associated with them, (3) the special problems found in this type of marriage, and (4) the ways in which couples resolve these problems.

REFERENCES

1. Barron, Milton L., "Research on Intermarriage: A Survey of Accomplishments and Prospects," *American Journal of Sociology*, 57 (November 1951): 249–55.

2. Bossard, James, and Harold C. Letts, "Mixed Marriages Involving Lutherans—A Research Report," *Marriage and Family Living*, 18 (November 1956): 308–10.

3. Burchinal, Lee G., "Membership Groups and Attitudes Toward Cross-Religious Dating and Marriage," *Marriage and Family Living*, 22 (August 1960): 248–53.

4. Cantril, Hadley, ed. *Public Opinion, 1935–1946*, Princeton, Princeton University Press, 1951, p. 431.

5. Chancellor, Loren E., and Thomas P. Monahan, "Religious Preference and Interreligious Mixtures in Marriages and Divorces in Iowa," *American Journal of Sociology*, 61 (November 1955): 233–39.

6. Christopherson, Victor A., and James Walters, "Responses of Protestants, Catholics, and Jews Concerning Marriage and Family Life," *Sociology and Social Research*, 43 (September-October 1958): 16–22.

7. Cox, Christine, "A Study of the Religious Practices, Values, and Attitudes in a Selected Group of Families," *Dissertation Abstracts*, 17 (November 1957): 2703–04.

8. Freeman, Howard E., and Gene G. Kassebaum, "Exogamous Dating in a Southern City," *Jewish Social Studies*, 18 (January 1956): 55–60.

9. Freeman, Linton, "Homogamy in Interethnic Mate Selection," *Sociology and Social Research*, 39 (July-August 1955): 369–77.

10. Glick, Paul C., "Intermarriage and Fertility Patterns Among Persons in Major Religious Groups," *Marriage and Family Living*, 22 (August 1960): 281–82.

11. Golden, Joseph, "Characteristics of the Negro-White Intermarried in Philadelphia," *American Sociological Review*, 18 (April 1953): 177–83.

12. Golden, Joseph, "Facilitating Factors in Negro-White Intermarriage," *Phylon*, 20 (Fall 1959): 273–84.

13. Heiss, Jerold S., "Premarital Characteristics of the Religiously Intermarried in an Urban Area," *American Sociological Review*, 25 (February 1960): 47–55.

14. Hollingshead, August B., "Cultural Factors in the Selection of Marriage Mates," in *Selected Studies in Marriage and the Family*, Robert F. Winch and Robert McGinnis, ed., New York, Henry Holt and Company, 1953, pp. 399–412.

15. Hunt, Chester L., and Richard W. Collier, "Intermarriage and Cultural Change: A Study of Philippine-American Marriages," *Social Forces*, 35 (March 1957): 223–30.

16. Landis, Judson T., "Marriages of Mixed and Non-Mixed Religious Faiths," *American Sociological Review*, 14 (June 1949): 401–07.

17. Landis, Judson T., "Religiousness, Family Relationships, and Family Values in Protestant, Catholic, and Jewish Families," *Marriage and Family Living*, 22 (November 1960): 341–47.

18. Lantz, Herman, "Religious Participation and Social Orientation of 1,000 University Students," *Sociology and Social Research*, 33 (March-April 1949): 285–90.

19. Leiffer, Murray H., "Mixed Marriages and Church Loyalty," *The Christian Century*, 66 (January 19, 1949): 78–80.

20. Locke, Harvey, George Sabagh, and Mary M. Thomes, "Interfaith Marriages," *Social Problems*, 4 (April 1957): 329–33.

21. Mace, David R., "The Truth About Mixed Marriages," *Woman's Home Companion*, 78 (July 1951): 36–37, 43–44.

22. Panunzio, Constantine, "Intermarriage in Los Angeles," *American Journal of Sociology*, 47 (March 1942): 690–701.

23. Prince, Alfred J., "Attitudes of College Students Toward Inter-Faith Marriage," *Coordinator*, 5 (September 1956): 11–23.

24. Shanks, Hershel, "Jewish-Gentile Intermarriage: Facts and Trends," *Commentary*, 16 (October 1953): 370–75.

25. Slotkin, J. S., "Adjustment in Jewish-Gentile Intermarriages," *Social Forces*, 21 (December 1942): 226–30.

26. Sontheimer, Morton, "Would You Approve Your Child's Marrying a Protestant, a Catholic, a Jew?" *Woman's Home Companion*, 80 (March 1953): 30–31, 100.

27. Thomas, John L., "The Factor of Religion in the Selection of Marriage Mates," *American Sociological Review*, 16 (August 1951): 487–91.

28. Weeks, H. A., "Differential Divorce Rates by Occupation," *Social Forces*, 21 (March 1943): 334–37.

Part Six

Intimacy and Love

Dating one person for a protracted period of time usually leads to a closeness and familiarity based on shared experiences and an exploration that is often called "getting to know you." Obviously, there are various degrees of closeness and familiarity, for every individual has a different amount of willingness to be open and to be receptive to the other's openness. If two people truly share each other's feelings and a mutuality of caring and closeness emerge, the experience of intimacy may occur. A bond is strengthened between the pair, and a trust grows upon the knowledge that each in a way becomes responsible to the other and agrees not to violate the integrity of the other. Without this kind of trust, true intimacy would be risky, which may account for the rarity of its existence in the early years of adult life. There are, of course, degrees of intimacy also; and many have questioned whether complete intimacy ever occurs between two people. People often delude themselves into believing they are having an intimate relationship with another because they spend a great deal of time together or are engaged in physical acts of closeness. It has been suggested that such "plastic" intimacy may be an attempt to ward off the real thing by people who are frightened by closeness, responsibility, and commitment as a result of their lack of a secure self-identity. Real intimacy may well require maturity and could be the key to understanding the difference between infatuation and love.

It is generally believed that there is a vast difference between infatuation, or "romantic love," and mature love. And yet, in the United States, it is probable that infatuation is usually the beginning of mature love. Not every case of romantic love, by any means, grows into an intimate, mature, loving relationship; but almost all of the latter begin with infatuation. Many couples do not stop to examine an infatuation and may assume it is strong and stable enough to be the basis of a lifetime commitment. That this is not always the case is indicated by some research showing that a person who feels "in love" tends to believe the other times were infatuation and that the current feeling is "real love." Because no objective criteria have been devised to measure the elusive quality of love, resarch has not given a great deal of help to those trying to distinguish infatuation from mature love. The question of how to tell "true love" may never be answered to the satisfaction of everyone concerned, but the readings in this section present some of the current views on this controversial subject.

The first article, by George Bach and Ronald Deutsch, deals with the topic of intimacy and the deeper qualities which lead to the development of mature love. It is emphasized that a person must have a sense of self-identity and honesty in order to identify with and be concerned with the welfare of another individual. The immature person cannot relate in the total giving, as well as total receiving, fashion which Bach and Deutsch deem necessary to experience true intimacy.

In the second reading, William Goode explores the universality of love. Individual love relationships seem to occur everywhere, but a distinction must be made between true, mature love and the romantic love complex. Goode points out that very few cultures have possessed the latter —the United States, Northwest Europe, Polynesia, and the eleventh and twelfth century European nobility are among the few that have. The "sweetest story ever told" is not universal: some may find it;

others may consider it a delightful fairy tale; and others may see it as an unreachable ideal, as have many of the world's poets, writers, composers, and artists.

Ira Reiss provides a sociological interpretation of love in the third selection. Marriage and family textbooks have treated the topic extensively and have defined love in many different ways. Reiss discusses these and other basic findings of sociological literature and proposes a new approach to the analysis of love, in which the major types of love relationships are distinguished.

An interesting study by William Kephart is the fourth selection. Kephart explores the romantic inclinations and experiences of male and female college students. Some readers may be surprised to note that the male-female difference in romantic orientation is substantial, with the female having a greater measure of rational control over her romantic inclinations than the male.

The final reading, by Ernest Van Den Haag, discusses the relationship between love and the possibility of marriage. Van Den Haag draws a clear distinction between three types of love: romantic love, physical attraction leading to sexual desire, and love as "the psychic gratification which only the loved one can give." This article becomes a note upon which to begin the discussion in Part Seven of sexual attraction and premarital sex.

25

INTIMACY

George R. Bach and Ronald M. Deutsch

By the millions, men and women yearn for intimate love and cannot find it—not knowing how easily intimacy can be experienced, how effectively the emptiness can be filled.

Some are truly alone. And night after night, day after day, they stalk one another, at once both the hunters and the hunted. They prowl the singles bars and clubs and hotels and cruises and weekend trips. They haunt church socials and civic meetings, office water coolers and public tennis courts, the ski slopes and the beaches and the charter flights to Europe.

Robed and groomed and scented for the ritual, the brasher ones reach out, and the quiet ones watch and dream and wait. Then, with rare exceptions, everyone goes home, if not empty-handed at least empty-hearted, feeling a little more lonely, a little more hopeless—chilled in contrast with the warmth of communion they sought and did not find.

Others have lives that are filled, even overcrowded with people, or perhaps devoted to one important person they see regularly, sleep or live with. Yet most of them, too, have an inner sense of isolation. They feel a nagging, frustrated hunger for authentic intimacy that no amount of romance or infatuation, not even the engagement notice in the newspaper, may really satisfy. Why, they wonder, do they feel alone? Why does the old restlessness persist?

For both these groups the disappointment of the intimate longing is genuinely tragic. It leaves the disappointed empty, bitter, full of self-doubt. Some crowd the consulting rooms of psychotherapy. Most of them end by dismissing the longing as a naive, adolescent dream. But it is adult, it is real, and it is necessary.

This yearning is well documented by the clinical research of the senior author of this book, in his work as consulting psychol-

ogist, with well over two thousand single men and women of all ages and from all walks of life. It is confirmed by his efforts with thousands more whose love had led to marriage but, as is the usual case, not intimacy. . . .

Why does today's psychologist see intimate love as so important? Because what men and women seek from love today is no longer a romantic luxury; it is an essential of emotional survival. Less and less it is a hunt for the excitement of infatuation, or for the doubtful security of the marriage nest. More and more it is the hope of finding in intimate love something of personal validity, personal relevance, a confirmation of one's existence.

For in today's world, when men and women are made to feel as faceless as numbers on a list, they want intimate love to provide the feelings of worth and identity that preserve sanity and meaning. They hunger for one pair of eyes to give them true recognition and acceptance, for one heart that understands and can be understood. Only genuine intimacy satisfies these hungers.

When the quest for intimacy fails, personality is endangered. Those who fail tend to blame themselves, and to doubt their adequacy as men and women. They develop self-images of being cold, unfeeling, selfish, perhaps incapable of mature love and so doomed to inner isolation.

Since isolation is a prime cause of neurosis, they experience true neurotic symptoms—anxiety, anger, and depression. These feelings build the isolating walls still higher around them, shutting out the intimacy they seek, closing tightly the lonely ring.

Yet the walls and the ring can be broken. We have learned in clinical research that the great majority of men and women, contrary to their secret fears, are perfectly capable of the intimacy for which they long. They can quickly assimilate a new attitude, understanding, and style of loving. When they do, they learn how to see through the misguiding conventions and taboos, through the exploitation and anxiety that block them from genuinely intimate relationships.

In a surprisingly short time, they are able to *create* such relationships—rapidly, and with any of almost innumerable others. They can assess the potentials of such loves, realize them, sustain them, and if need be, end the associations with a minimum of pain for both partners.

In some respects, the purposes of the intimacy that is created vary as widely as the people from whose problems our pairing system came—people who were studied and counseled on college campuses and in youth groups, in work with divorce lawyers and conciliation courts, in group and individual psychotherapy with mature singles who felt isolated, in regular contacts with such divorce organizations as "Parents Without Partners." Their wishes ranged from companionship to better sexual expression, from loving friendship to eventual marriage.

On the other hand, some wishes are common to nearly all singles. Most want to meet new people and identify those with the best potential for true intimacy; to reduce their fears of rejection by others; to protect themselves from manipulation and exploitation; to guard against repeatedly choosing unrewarding partners. When they find a potential intimate, they want to get insight rapidly into what sort of partner he or she will make, and how to convey something of their genuine selves to him or her at once. In other words, they want to know how to make intimate love begin with a stranger.

When love does begin, they want to know how to make it grow, and how to keep one partner or the other from feeling either engulfed or held at too chilly a distance. They want to prevent being deceived by a well-meaning but over-accommodating partner, and to know how to compromise and cooperate without so smothering their own real wishes and feelings that they become inwardly resentful. . . .

Certainly, enormous numbers of today's men and women, driven by their intimate longing, are impatient with the old non-intimate ways of loving—with the old etiquette, traditions, myths, and pseudo-science. They are experimenting with new styles and new ethics. A new and aware generation has sensed that the old ways—which we call the *courting system*—cheat them of intimacy. They are rebelling against that system and have begun an intimate revolution, to overthrow the romantic establishment.

The signs of the revolution are everywhere, as the rebels attack the institutions and forms of courting love. But despite their honest effort most of the rebels manage to cultivate only the outward semblances of the intimacy they seek. The closeness, the authenticity, the transparency, the freedom of expression of intimate love elude them.

Instead, they manage only an ersatz intimacy—with emphasis on public nudity, free-and-easy copulation, partner-swapping, and an occasional orgy. Their "candor" is only a shadow—of four-letter words, self-pitying confessions, amateur psychoanalysis and encounter, and blunt attacks on others in the name of honesty.

When the sexes get together, the rebels end with only a shallow "togetherness" proximity. When they do away with stereotyped sex roles, they are left with the impotence and confused identity of "unisex."

The intimate revolution has so far produced only tantalizing glimpses of true intimate warmth, and the price has been high. Underneath, the old non-intimate system continues to operate. The roles and the rigid etiquette look changed, sometimes radically. But they function as before, masking reality and denying intimacy.

Plainly, though the intimate revolution has a bright banner and a powerful drive, it is doomed until it finds a method, and one that is not confining but free, self-expressive, and genuine. Such a method, proven and workable, is *pairing*. . . .

Pairing is a new way of making love begin. To understand the system and how it leads to intimacy, it helps to understand the courting system—the old style and attitudes of loving with which today's adults have grown up.

Dictionaries define courting as seeking affection, trying to win applause or favor, holding out inducements. So when one courts, one puts on one's best face, inflates strengths, conceals weaknesses, and generally seeks to manipulate the other person. The courter neither presents the reality of his own self, nor explores the reality of his partner. The object is to create a sunshine smoothness without conflict, to capture by pleasing. Whatever might cause roughness or dissonance in the relationship is hidden behind illusions; it is avoided by as much giving-in (accommodation) as one can bear, and by the emotional tip-toeing required by "etiquette."

The courter begins by creating a façade that he thinks will attract. Having attracted a partner in this way, he may be saddled more or less permanently with the chore of playing the role that he has assigned to himself. He dares not step out of character for fear of perhaps losing some of his partner's love.

To be real, in the courting style of love, is to be endangered. And here trouble begins. For roles are by definition rigid. They become confining, stultifying. Beneath the sunshine surface, resentment grows.

Small wonder that courting partners are as much strangers when they love as when they meet, that they are likely to remain strangers in an affair or marriage. Small wonder that, for them, intimacy becomes impossible.

The divorced and more mature single people are especially dissatisfied with such surface love. They have traveled the road. They know it leads nowhere. Yet they cannot find an alternative. They are frustrated by what seems to them an inescapable trap of superficiality. They go through every intimate motion; they fall in love, they talk into the small hours, they live together. Yet intimacy seems to evade them. They are impatient with the time it takes to form and assess a relationship. They are bored and embittered by the secrecy that hides real feelings, by the adolescent maneuverings, the little seduction games, the good-time, fixed-smile dating routine.

Time and life, they feel, are wasting. And they sense that something is wrong at a deeper level. That something, traditional psychology holds, is probably neurosis. In the early history of the individual, something went wrong as the child developed his style of relating to others. In adulthood, then, some fear or anger blocks the fulfillment of the intimate longing. Most therapists believe that if the neurosis is resolved, intimate relationships are sure to form.

It is reasonable sounding theory. In practice, it does not work well. Since failure to reach intimate love can cause neurosis, which came first, the neurosis or the failure of love? Also, if the traditional theory is correct, then perhaps ninety percent or more of men and women are in need of psychological therapy. For only a handful of couples seem to achieve anything like intimate love. There are not enough therapists to listen even to a tiny fraction of these couples, and, besides, the therapy is not too successful. Popular impression to the contrary, when therapists, such as marriage counselors, hold meetings, one primary topic almost invariably is: why *is* their therapy effective in only a minority of cases?

The story of Jan, a divorcee who attended one of our pairing classes, illustrates the failure of traditional psychology in dealing with many intimate relationships. In her first session, she was asked why she had come to the class.

"I went right from a very sheltered school life into marriage," she said. "I never felt adequate for my husband in any way. I mean, I couldn't really talk to him about a lot of personal things, and I was frigid. After three years, we were divorced, and I went into analysis.

"After a year of that, I understood a lot about myself. I had been angry with men, and I wasn't any more. For example, I could come. I felt free, and I started having a lot of company and going to bed a lot."

"But why are you here?" one of the other girls asked. "You still haven't said."

"Because—" Jan answered, and her eyes

were moist. "Because with all the men, I still feel alone. I can't really reach them. I'm not free. *I'm just an easy lay.*"

Neither Jan's freedom from old conventions, won by the intimate revolution, nor her inner freedom from the angers of her childhood, secured through psychoanalysis, had allowed her to create intimate bonding in love. The problem is an extremely common one.

The ideal of the courting system might be expressed as the formula: *one plus one equals one.* Two people are to become one flesh, one heart, a new entity known as "We," and the individuals supposedly recede or disappear. The proposition is as difficult emotionally as it is in mathematics. It means that each partner's answer to any important question ought to match the other partner's. Many experiences have been reported in our pairing classes to show the hamstringing absurdity of this idea.

Julie is asking Nick, a fellow college student, about a test-yourself quiz she is reading in a magazine:

Julie: Do we like to use four-letter words during sex?

Nick: (Looks up warily, uncertain about what to say.) Well, we have used them sometimes, I guess. I mean, what kind of four-letter words?

Julie: Well, I suppose words like—(she becomes uneasy and watches him.) Like for —doing things, and body parts, I guess. I don't know. Do you think we like to?

Nick: (He does sometimes like to be blunt. But he is being asked what "we" like, so he maneuvers to please.) You've used them sometimes, haven't you?

Julie: Yes. But I think only after you do.

Nick: Hmm.

Such "we" conversations become fencing matches, testing grounds for courting roles. Nick and Julie hesitate to commit themselves, for fear of what the other will think, so both become cautious and self-conscious about using any coarse language during intercourse. Each thinks that the other one thinks such language is indelicate. In point of fact, both are turned on by explicit words during sex. But their courting style

has now cut them off from a small but mutually satisfying expression.

Today's intimate revolutionaries usually ignore the "we" concept. Unable to reach intimacy, they often try to convince themselves that they do not want *any* interdependence. Their cult is autonomy—independence carried to the extreme.

"You do your thing," their philosophy goes, "and I'll do mine. No questions or promises. If by some lucky coincidence we happen to get together now and then, groovy. Beautiful." It is not really beautiful. It is lonely. It is as fruitful as insisting that *one plus one equals one plus one.* One is not changed by the other.

Traditional psychology often produces a similar effect by counseling: "One cannot really make another happy or unhappy, and one cannot take responsibility for another's emotions. So one simply plays out one's own hand. The partner does not have to stay if he does not want to. He is responsible for what happens to him. One must work out conflicts within oneself and then learn to accept whatever results in one's relationships."

We often compare this to the building of a fire. Conventional psychology sees two logs; the better the logs, the better the fire. So it aims to perfect the logs, on the assumption that the fire will take care of itself.

We have found this approach to have limited effectiveness. Our philosophy and understanding of intimate relationships may be expressed by the formula: *one plus one equals three.* The three elements are: the man, the woman, and their relationship.

To us, the crucial element is the fire between the logs, the dynamics between the pair. While our students might take years to understand themselves, they can be taught to see and understand their relationships very quickly. And when they are mobilized toward good relationships, the buried fears and angers within the individual tend to be resolved. Psychoanalysis proves to be unnecessary for most of those who can achieve intimate love by pairing. And most can.

Obviously the old courting system persists because it serves some real emotional needs. What are they? Studying courting behavior, we were struck by the endless role-playing, the complex web of illusions that the partners spun, the careful collusions with which the partners maintained these illusions. Plainly, the role-playing and illusions of courting hide the reality of the individuals and their relationship. When reality is denied, it is because it is frightening. So the courting system must persist because it deals with some important fear.

What fear? We found that courting illusions had much the same theme: "We are *right* for each other, so we automatically please and fulfill one another. Real conflict must be kept hidden at any price because it would signify that we are not predestined lovers, after all."

So the fear from which the courting system protects people is a deep and powerful one, the fear of rejection, of separation from love. Except for fear about survival, there is probably no more potent emotion in the human heart.

Rejection fears appear very early in any relationship. As soon as affections are engaged, the courting lover begins to feel a subtle tension and discomfort. Poets call these feelings lovesickness and, ironically, often celebrate them as *proof* of love.

The lovesick partner feels something like this: "I am tense and uneasy, because I am trying hard to guess what you want me to be, so that you will love me. Once I psych out what you find lovable, I will bend myself out of shape to conform to your idea of lovability for fear you may stop loving me. I dare not show you my real self, because I feel inadequate, since I know inwardly that I do not exactly fit your notion of lovability. And I am afraid to take a real look at you, too, because you might not fit into my idea of what is lovable."

This feeling is destructive. It is usually perceived only as vaguely weakened identity and sense of worth, as a kind of wistful loneliness. Underneath, usually hidden even from himself, the lover is resentful and feels trapped because he cannot express what he authentically is.

The pairing system deals with the same fears, not by concealing them, but by confronting and resolving them. Once these fears are dealt with, the bars to intimate love are down. If one can handle the fears, one need not hide from them or from the realities that produce them. If one can then be genuine, so, usually, can one's partner. For genuineness creates trust and confidence.

The pairing partner has no need to manipulate and exploit to get what he wants of another. He can ask, without guilt, and what he gets is given freely, without prices or strings. Pairing also helps with sex problems because those that are emotionally caused result from hidden fear or hostility.

When a woman withholds her orgasm, or when a man ejaculates prematurely, for example, hostility is often the reason. Such partners are saying to one another: "I will not allow you the fulfillment of feeling like a complete man or woman."

Since pairing permits and demands open expression and resolution of fear and anger, these emotions need not be expressed covertly, in or out of bed. Pairing also eliminates the common fears that to love is to submit to control and become engulfed. These fears often mar sex by blocking a surrender to the experience. Pairing reduces these fears by reinforcing the sense of worth and identity.

When intimate love is created by pairing, the lover feels: "I am more myself because I know that you see me as myself. I know that the authentic me is the person you love. So I can be that person fully and proudly and with delight."

Love expressed through pairing, intimate love, never causes lovesickness. It brings a sense of joy and well-being. The pairer does not feel static, but free to change and grow. His horizons become enlarged by love, not narrowed.

An old adage of love is that men and women ought not to try and change one another. The courter, of course, does not dare to change; he would produce deep anxiety in himself and his partner. The pairer can respond to reasonable, specific requests for change in his behavior. He can take the risk because he feels loved in reality, and so his risk is small.

26

THE THEORETICAL IMPORTANCE OF LOVE

William J. Goode

Because love often determines the intensity of an attraction toward or away from an intimate relationship with another person, it can become one element in a decision or action. Nevertheless, serious sociological attention has only infrequently been given to love. Moreover, analyses of love generally have been confined to mate choice in the Western World, while the structural importance of love has been for the most part ignored. The present paper views love in a broad perspective, focusing on the structural patterns by which societies keep in check the potentially disruptive effect of love relationships on mate choice and stratification systems.

TYPES OF LITERATURE ON LOVE

For obvious reasons, the printed material on love is immense. For our present purposes, it may be classified as follows:

1. Poetic, humanistic, literary, erotic, pornographic: By far the largest body of all literature on love views it as a sweeping experience. The poet arouses our sympathy and empathy. The essayist enjoys, and asks the reader to enjoy, the interplay of people in love. The storyteller—Bocaccio, Chaucer, Dante—pulls back the curtain of human souls and lets the reader watch the intimate lives of others caught in an emotion we all know. Others—Vatsyayana, Ovid, William IX Count of Poitiers and Duke of Aquitaine, Marie de France, Andreas Capellanus—have written how-to-do-it books, that is, how to conduct oneself in love relations, to persuade others to succumb to one's love wishes, or to excite and satisfy one's sex partner.[1]

2. Marital counseling: Many modern sociologists have commented on the importance of romantic love in America and its lesser importance in other societies, and have disparaged it as a poor basis for marriage, or as immaturity. Perhaps the best known of these arguments are those of Ernest R. Mowrer, Ernest W. Burgess, Mabel A. Elliott, Andrew G. Truxal, Francis E. Merrill, and Ernest R. Groves.[2] The antithesis of romantic love, in such analyses, is "conjugal" love; the love between a settled, domestic couple.

A few sociologists, remaining within this same evaluative context, have instead claimed that love also has salutary effects in our society. Thus, for example, William L. Kolb[3] has tried to demonstrate that the marital counselors who attack romantic love are really attacking some fundamental values of our larger society, such as individualism, freedom, and personality growth. Beigel[4] has argued that if the female is sexually repressed, only the psychotherapist or love can help her overcome her inhibitions. He claims further that one influence of love in our society is that it extenuates illicit sexual relations; he goes on to assert: "Seen in proper perspective, [love] has not only done no harm as a prerequisite to marriage, but it has mitigated the impact that a too-fast-moving and unorganized conversion to new socioeconomic constellations has had upon our whole culture and it has saved monogamous marriage from complete disorganization."

In addition, there is widespread comment among marriage analysts, that in a rootless society, with few common bases for companionship, romantic love holds a couple together long enough to allow them to begin marriage. That is, it functions to attract people powerfully together, and to hold them through the difficult first months of the marriage, when their different backgrounds would otherwise make an adjustment troublesome.

3. Although the writers cited above concede the structural importance of love im-

plicitly, since they are arguing that it is either harmful or helpful to various values and goals of our society, a third group has given explicit if unsystematic attention to its structural importance. Here, most of the available propositions point to the functions of love, but a few deal with the conditions under which love relationships occur. They include:

(1) An implicit or assumed descriptive proposition is that love as a common prelude to and basis of marriage is rare, perhaps to be found as a pattern only in the United States.

(2) Most explanations of the conditions which create love are psychological, stemming from Freud's notion that love is "aim-inhibited sex."[5] This idea is expressed, for example, by Waller who says that love is an idealized passion which develops from the frustration of sex.[6] This proposition, although rather crudely stated and incorrect as a general explanation, is widely accepted.

(3) Of course, a predisposition to love is created by the socialization experience. Thus some textbooks on the family devote extended discussion to the ways in which our society socializes for love. The child, for example, is told that he or she will grow up to fall in love with some one, and early attempts are made to pair the child with children of the opposite sex. There is much joshing of children about falling in love; myths and stories about love and courtship are heard by children; and so on.

(4) A further proposition (the source of which I have not been able to locate) is that, in a society in which a very close attachment between parent and child prevails, a love complex is necessary in order to motivate the child to free him from his attachment to his parents.

(5) Love is also described as one final or crystallizing element in the decision to marry, which is otherwise structured by factors such as class, ethnic origin, religion, education, and residence.

(6) Parsons has suggested three factors which "underlie the prominence of the romantic context in our culture": (a) the youth culture frees the individual from family attachments, thus permitting him to fall in love; (b) love is a substitute for the interlocking of kinship roles found in other societies, and thus motivates the individual to conform to proper marital role behavior; and (c) the structural isolation of the family so frees the married partners' affective inclinations that they are able to love one another.[7]

(7) Robert F. Winch has developed a theory of "complementary needs" which essentially states that the underlying dynamic in the process of falling in love is an interaction between (a) the perceived psychological attributes of one individual and (b) the complementary psychological attributes of the person falling in love, such that the needs of the latter are felt to be met by the perceived attributes of the former and *vice versa*. These needs are derived from Murray's list of personality characteristics. Winch thus does not attempt to solve the problem of why our society has a love complex, but how it is that specific individuals fall in love with each other rather than with someone else.[8]

(8) Winch and others have also analyzed the effect of love upon various institutions or social patterns: Love themes are prominently displayed in the media of entertainment and communication, in consumption patterns, and so on.[9]

4. Finally, there is the cross-cultural work of anthropologists, who in the main have ignored love as a factor of importance in kinship patterns. The implicit understanding seems to be that love as a pattern is found only in the United States, although of course individual cases of love are sometimes recorded. The term "love" is practically never found in indexes of anthropological monographs on specific societies or in general anthropology textbooks. It is perhaps not an exaggeration to say that

Lowie's comment of a generation ago would still be accepted by a substantial number of anthropologists:

But of love among savages? . . . Passion, of course, is taken for granted; affection, which many travelers vouch for, might be conceded; but Love? Well, the romantic sentiment occurs in simpler conditions, as with us—in fiction. . . . So Love exists for the savage as it does for ourselves—in adolescence, in fiction, among the poetically minded.[10]

A still more skeptical opinion is Linton's scathing sneer:

All societies recognize that there are occasional violent, emotional attachments between persons of opposite sex, but our present American culture is practically the only one which has attempted to capitalize these, and make them the basis for marriage. . . . The hero of the modern American movie is always a romantic lover, just as the hero of the old Arab epic is always an epileptic. A cynic may suspect that in any ordinary population the percentage of individuals with a capacity for romantic love of the Hollywood type was about as large as that of persons able to throw genuine epileptic fits.[11]

In Murdock's book on kinship and marriage, there is almost no mention, if any, of love.[12] Should we therefore conclude that, cross-culturally, love is not important, and thus cannot be of great importance structurally? If there is only one significant case, perhaps it is safe to view love as generally unimportant in social structure and to concentrate rather on the nature and functions of romantic love within the Western societies in which love is obviously prevalent. As brought out below, however, many anthropologists have in fact described love *patterns*. And one of them, Max Gluckman,[13] has recently subsumed a wide range of observations under the broad principle that love relationships between husband and wife estrange the couple from their kin, who therefore try in various ways to undermine that love. This principle is applicable to many more societies (for example, China

and India) than Gluckman himself discusses.

THE PROBLEM AND ITS CONCEPTUAL CLARIFICATION

The preceding propositions (except those denying that love is distributed widely) can be grouped under two main questions: What are the consequences of romantic love in the United States? How is the emotion of love aroused or created in our society? The present paper deals with the first question. For theoretical purposes both questions must be reformulated, however, since they implicitly refer only to our peculiar system of romantic love. Thus: (1) In what ways do various love patterns fit into the social structure, especially into the systems of mate choice and stratification? (2) What are the structural conditions under which a range of love patterns occurs in various societies? These are overlapping questions, but their starting point and assumptions are different. The first assumes that love relationships are a universal psychosocial possibility, and that different social systems make different adjustments to their potential disruptiveness. The second does not take love for granted, and supposes rather that such relationships will be rare unless certain structural factors are present. Since in both cases the analysis need not depend upon the correctness of the assumption, the problem may be chosen arbitrarily. Let us begin with the first.

We face at once the problem of defining "love." Here, love is defined as a strong emotional attachment, a cathexis, between adolescents or adults of opposite sexes, with at least the components of sex desire and tenderness. Verbal definitions of this emotional relationship are notoriously open to attack; this one is no more likely to satisfy critics than others. Agreement is made difficult by value judgments: one critic would exclude anything but "true" love, another casts out "infatuation," another objects to "puppy love," while others would separate sex desire from love because sex presumably is degrading. Nevertheless, most of us have had the experience of love, just as we have been greedy, or melancholy, or moved by hate (defining "true" hate seems not to be a problem). The experience can be referred to without great ambiguity, and a refined measure of various degrees of intensity or purity of love is unnecessary for the aims of the present analysis.

Since love may be related in diverse ways to the social structure, it is necessary to forego the dichotomy of "romantic love—no romantic love" in favor of a continuum or range between polar types. At one pole, a strong love attraction is socially viewed as a laughable or tragic aberration; at the other, it is mildly shameful to marry without being in love with one's intended spouse. This is a gradation from negative sanction to positive approval, ranging at the same time from low or almost nonexistent institutionalization of love to high institutionalization.

The urban middle classes of contemporary Western society, especially in the United States, are found toward the latter pole. Japan and China, in spite of the important movement toward European patterns, fall toward the pole of low institutionalization. Village and urban India is farther toward the center, for there the ideal relationship has been one which at least generated love after marriage, and sometimes after betrothal, in contrast with the mere respect owed between Japanese and Chinese spouses. Greece after Alexander, Rome of the Empire, and perhaps the later period of the Roman Republic as well, are near the center, but somewhat toward the pole of institutionalization, for love matches appear to have increased in frequency—a trend denounced by moralists.[14]

This conceptual continuum helps to clarify our problem and to interpret the propositions reviewed above. Thus it may be noted, first, that individual love relationships may occur even in societies in which love is viewed as irrelevant to mate choice and excluded from the decision to marry. As Linton conceded, some violent love attachments may be found in any society. In our own, the Song of Solomon, Jacob's love of Rachel, and Michal's love for David are classic tales. The Mahabharata, the great Indian epic, includes love themes. Romantic love appears early in Japanese literature,

and the use of Mt. Fuji as a locale for the suicide of star crossed lovers is not a myth invented by editors of tabloids. There is the familiar tragic Chinese story to be found on the traditional "willowplate," with its lovers transformed into doves. And so it goes—individual love relationships seem to occur everywhere. But this fact does not change the position of a society on the continuum.

Second, reading both Linton's and Lowie's comments in this new conceptual context reduces their theoretical importance, for they are both merely saying that people do not *live by* the romantic complex, here or anywhere else. Some few couples in love will brave social pressures, physical dangers, or the gods themselves, but nowhere is this usual. Violent, self-sufficient love is not common anywhere. In this respect, of course, the U.S. is not set apart from other systems.

Third, we can separate a *love pattern* from the romantic love *complex*. Under the former, love is a permissible, expected prelude to marriage, and a usual element of courtship—thus, at about the center of the continuum, but toward the pole of institutionalization. The romantic love complex (one pole of the continuum) includes, in addition, an ideological prescription that falling in love is a highly desirable basis of courtship and marriage; love is strongly institutionalized. In contemporary United States, many individuals would even claim that entering marriage without being in love requires some such rationalization as asserting that one is too old for such romances or that one must "think of practical matters like money." To be sure, both anthropologists and sociologists often exaggerate the American commitment to romance; nevertheless, a behavioral and value complex of this type is found here.

But this complex is rare. Perhaps only the following cultures possess the romantic love value complex: modern urban United States, Northwestern Europe, Polynesia, and the European nobility of the eleventh and twelfth centuries. Certainly, it is to be found in no other major civilization. On the other hand, the *love pattern*, which views love as a basis for the final decision to marry, may be relatively common.

WHY LOVE MUST BE CONTROLLED

Since strong love attachments apparently can occur in any society and since (as we shall show) love is frequently a basis for and prelude to marriage, it must be controlled or channeled in some way. More specifically, the stratification and lineage patterns would be weakened greatly if love's potentially disruptive effects were not kept in check. The importance of this situation may be seen most clearly by considering one of the major functions of the family, status placement, which in every society links the structures of stratification, kinship lines, and mate choice. (To show how the very similar comments which have been made about sex are not quite correct would take us too far afield; in any event, to the extent that they are correct, the succeeding analysis applies equally to the control of sex.)

Both the child's placement in the social structure and choice of mates are socially important because both placement and choice link two kinship lines together. Courtship or mate choice, therefore, cannot be ignored by either family or society. To permit random mating would mean radical change in the existing social structure. If the family as a unit of society is important, then mate choice is too.

Kinfolk or immediate family can disregard the question of who marries whom, only if a marriage is not seen as a link between kin lines, only if no property, power, lineage honor, totemic relationships, and the like are believed to flow from the kin lines through the spouses to their offspring. Universally, however, these are believed to follow kin lines. Mate choice thus has consequences for the social structure. But love may affect mate choice. Both mate choice and love, therefore, are too important to be left to children.

THE CONTROL OF LOVE

Since considerable energy and resources may be required to push youngsters who are in love into proper role behavior, love must be controlled *before* it appears. Love relationships must either be kept to a small number or they must be so directed that they do not run counter to the approved kinship linkages. There are only a few institutional patterns by which this control is achieved.

1. Certainly the simplest, and perhaps the most widely used, structural pattern for coping with this problem is child marriage. If the child is betrothed, married, or both before he has had any opportunity to interact intimately as an adolescent with other children, then he has no resources with which to oppose the marriage. He cannot earn a living, he is physically weak, and is socially dominated by his elders. Moreover, strong love attachments occur only rarely before puberty. An example of this pattern was to be found in India, where the young bride went to live with her husband in a marriage which was not physically consummated until much later, within his father's household.[15]

2. Often, child marriage is linked with a second structural pattern, in which the kinship rules define rather closely a class of eligible future spouses. The marriage is determined by birth within narrow limits. Here, the major decision, which is made by elders, is *when* the marriage is to occur. Thus, among the Murngin, *galle*, the father's sister's child, is scheduled to marry *due*, the mother's brother's child.[16] In the case of the "four-class" double-descent system, each individual is a member of *both* a matri-moiety and a patri-moiety and must marry someone who belongs to neither; the four-classes are (1) ego's own class, (2) those whose matri-moiety is the same as ego's but whose patri-moiety is different, (3) those who are in ego's patri-moiety but not in his matri-moiety, and (4) those who are in neither of ego's moieties, that is, who are in the cell diagonally from his own.[17] Problems arise at times under these systems if the appropriate kinship cell—for example, parallel cousin or cross-cousin—is empty. But nowhere, apparently, is the definition so rigid as to exclude some choice and, therefore, some dickering, wrangling, and haggling between the elders of the two families.

3. A society can prevent widespread development of adolescent love relationships by socially isolating young people from potential mates, whether eligible or ineligible as spouses. Under such a pattern, elders can arrange the marriages of either children or adolescents with little likelihood that their plans will be disrupted by love attachments. Obviously, this arrangement cannot operate effectively in most primitive societies, where youngsters see one another rather frequently.

Not only is this pattern more common in civilizations than in primitive societies, but is found more frequently in the upper social strata. *Social* segregation is difficult unless it is supported by physical segregation—the harem of Islam, the zenana of India—or by a large household system with individuals whose duty it is to supervise nubile girls. Social segregation is thus expensive. Perhaps the best known example of simple social segregation was found in China, where youthful marriages took place between young people who had not previously met because they lived in different villages; they could not marry fellow-villagers since ideally almost all inhabitants belonged to the same *tsu*.

It should be emphasized that the primary function of physical or social isolation in these cases is to minimize informal or intimate social interaction. Limited social contacts of a highly ritualized or formal type in the presence of elders, as in Japan, have a similar, if less extreme, result.

4. A fourth type of pattern seems to exist, although it is not clear cut; and specific cases shade off toward types three and five. Here, there is close supervision by duennas or close relatives, but not actual social segregation. A high value is placed on female chastity (which perhaps is the case in every major civilization until its "decadence") viewed either as the product of self-restraint, as among the 17th Century Puritans, or as a marketable commodity. Thus love as play is not developed; marriage is supposed to be considered by the young as a duty and a possible family alliance. This pattern falls between types three and five because love is permitted before marriage, but only between eligibles.

Ideally, it occurs only between a betrothed couple, and, except as marital love, there is no encouragement for it to appear at all. Family elders largely make the specific choice of mate, whether or not intermediaries carry out the arrangements. In the preliminary stages youngsters engage in courtship under supervision, with the understanding that this will permit the development of affection prior to marriage.

I do not believe that the empirical data show where this pattern is prevalent, outside of Western Civilization. The West is a special case, because of its peculiar relationship to Christianity, in which from its earliest days in Rome there has been a complex tension between asceticism and love. This type of limited love marked French, English, and Italian upper class family life from the 11th to the 14th Centuries, as well as 17th Century Puritanism in England and New England.

5. The fifth type of pattern permits or actually encourages love relationships, and love is a commonly expected element in mate choice. Choice in this system is *formally* free. In their teens youngsters begin their love play, with or without consummating sexual intercourse, within a group of peers. They may at times choose love partners whom they and others do not consider suitable spouses. Gradually, however, their range of choice is narrowed and eventually their affections center on one individual. This person is likely to be more eligible as a mate according to general social norms, and as judged by peers and parents, than the average individual with whom the youngster formerly indulged in love play.

For reasons that are not yet clear, this pattern is nearly always associated with a strong development of an adolescent peer group system, although the latter may occur without the love pattern. One source of social control, then, is the individual's own teen-age companions, who persistently rate the present and probable future accomplishments of each individual.

Another source of control lies with the parents of both boy and girl. In our society, parents threaten, cajole, wheedle, bribe, and persuade their children to "go with the right people," during both the early love play and later courtship phases.[18] Primarily, they seek to control love relationships by influencing the informal social contacts of their children: moving to appropriate neighborhoods and schools, giving parties and helping to make out invitation lists, by making their children aware that certain individuals have ineligibility traits (race, religion, manners, tastes, clothing, and so on). Since youngsters fall in love with those with whom they associate, control over informal relationships also controls substantially the focus of affection. The results of such control are well known and are documented in the more than one hundred studies of homogamy in this country: most marriages take place between couples in the same class, religious, racial, and educational levels.

As Robert Wikman has shown in a generally unfamiliar (in the United States) but superb investigation, this pattern was found among 18th Century Swedish farmer adolescents, was widely distributed in other Germanic areas, and extends in time from the 19th Century back to almost certainly the late Middle Ages. In these cases, sexual intercourse was taken for granted, social contact was closely supervised by the peer group, and final consent to marriage was withheld or granted by the parents who owned the land.

Such cases are not confined to Western society. Polynesia exhibits a similar pattern, with some variation from society to society, the best known examples of which are perhaps Mead's Manu'ans and Firth's Tikopia. Probably the most familiar Melanesian cases are the Trobriands and Dobu, where the systems resemble those of the Kiwai Papuans of the Trans-Fly and the Siuai Papuans of the Solomon Islands. Linton found this pattern among the Tanala. Although Radcliffe-Brown holds that the pattern is not common in Africa, it is clearly found among the Nuer, the Kgatla (Tswana-speaking), and the Bavenda (here, without sanctioned sexual intercourse).

A more complete classification, making use of the distinctions suggested in this paper, would show, I believe, that a large minority of known societies exhibit this pattern. I would suggest, moreover, that such a study would reveal that the degree to which love as a usual, expected prelude to marriage is correlated with (1) the degree of free choice of mate permitted in the society and (2) the degree to which husband-wife solidarity is the strategic solidarity of the kinship structure.

LOVE CONTROL AND CLASS

These sociostructural explanations of how love is controlled lead to a subsidiary but important hypothesis: From one society to another, and from one *class* to another within the same society, the sociostructural importance of maintaining kinship lines according to rule will be rated differently by the families within them. Consequently, the degree to which control over mate choice, and therefore over the prevalence of a love pattern among adolescents, will also vary. Since, within any stratified society, this concern with the maintenance of intact and acceptable kin lines will be greater in the upper strata, it follows that noble or upper strata will maintain stricter control over love and courtship behavior than lower strata. The two correlations suggested in the preceding paragraph also apply: husband-wife solidarity is less strategic relative to clan solidarity in the upper than in the lower strata, and there is less free choice of mate.

Thus it is that, although in Polynesia generally most youngsters indulged in considerable love play, princesses were supervised strictly. Similarly, in China lower class youngsters often met their spouses before marriage. In our own society, the "upper upper" class maintains much greater control than the lower strata over the informal social contacts of their nubile young. Even among the Dobu, where there are few controls and little stratification, differences in control exist at the extremes: a child betrothal may be arranged between outstanding gardening families, who try to prevent their youngsters from being entangled with wastrel families. In answer to my query about this pattern among the Nuer, Evans-Pritchard writes:

You are probably right that a wealthy man has more control over his son's affairs than a poor man. A man with several wives has a more authoritarian position in his home. Also, a man with many cattle is in a position to permit or refuse a son to marry, whereas a lad whose father is poor may have to depend on the support of kinsmen. In general, I would say that a Nuer father is not interested in the personal side of things. His son is free to marry any girl he likes and the father does not consider the selection to be his affair until the point is reached when cattle have to be discussed.[19]

The upper strata have much more at stake in the maintenance of the social structure and thus are more strongly motivated to control the courtship and marriage decisions of their young. Correspondingly, their young have much more to lose than lower strata youth, so that upper strata elders *can* wield more power.

CONCLUSION

In this analysis I have attempted to show the integration of love with various types of social structures. As against considerable contemporary opinion among both sociologists and anthropologists, I suggest that love is a universal psychological potential, which is controlled by a range of five structural patterns, all of which are attempts to see to it that youngsters do not make entirely free choices of their future spouses. Only if kin lines are unimportant, and this condition is found in no society as a whole, will entirely free choice be permitted. Some structural arrangements seek to prevent entirely the outbreak of love, while others harness it. Since the kin lines of the upper strata are of greater social importance to them than those of lower strata are to the lower strata members, the former exercise a more effective control over this choice. Even where there is almost a formally free choice of mate—and I have suggested that this pattern is widespread, to be found among a substantial segment of the earth's societies—this choice is guided by peer group and parents toward a mate who will be acceptable to the kin and friend groupings. The theoretical importance of love is thus to be seen in the sociostructural patterns which are developed to keep it from disrupting existing social arrangements.

NOTES

[1] Vatsyayana, *The Kama Sutra*, Delhi: Rajkamal, 1948; Ovid, "The Loves," and "Remedies of Love," in *The Art of Love*, Cambridge, Mass.: Harvard University Press, 1939; Andreas Capellanus, *The Art of Courtly Love*, translated by John J. Parry, New York: Columbia University Press, 1941; Paul Tuffrau, editor, *Marie de France: Les Lais de Marie de France*, Paris L'edition d'art, 1925; see also Julian Harris, *Marie de France*, New York: Institute of French Studies, 1930, esp. Chapter 3. All authors but the first *also* had the goal of writing literature.

[2] Ernest R. Mowrer, *Family Disorganization*, Chicago: The University of Chicago Press, 1927, pp. 158–165; Ernest W. Burgess and Harvey J. Locke, *The Family*, New York: American Book, 1953, pp. 436–437; Mabel A. Elliott and Francis E. Merrill, *Social Disorganization*, New York: Harper, 1950, pp. 366–384; Andrew G. Truxal and Francis E. Merrill, *The Family in American Culture*, New York: Prentice-Hall, 1947, pp. 120–124, 507–509; Ernest R. Groves and Gladys Hoagland Groves, *The Contemporary American Family*, New York: Lippincott, 1947, pp. 321–324.

[3] William L. Kolb, "Sociologically Established Norms and Democratic Values," *Social Forces*, 26 (May 1948): 451–456.

[4] Hugo G. Beigel, "Romantic Love," *American Sociological Review*, 16 (June 1951): 326–334.

[5] Sigmund Freud, *Group Psychology and the Analysis of the Ego*, London: Hogarth, 1922, p. 72.

[6] Willard Waller, *The Family*, New York: Dryden, 1938, pp. 189–192.

7 Talcott Parsons, *Essays in Sociological Theory*, Glencoe, Ill.: Free Press, 1949, pp. 187–189.

8 Robert F. Winch, *Mate Selection*, New York: Harper, 1958.

9 See, e.g., Robert F. Winch, *The Modern Family*, New York: Holt, 1952, Chapter 14.

10 Robert H. Lowie, "Sex and Marriage," in John F. McDermott, editor, *The Sex Problem in Modern Society*, New York: Modern Library, 1931, p. 146.

11 Ralph Linton, *The Study of Man*, New York: Appleton-Century, 1936, p. 175.

12 George Peter Murdock, *Social Structure*, New York: Macmillan, 1949.

13 Max Gluckman, *Custom and Conflict in Africa*, Oxford: Basil Blackwell, 1955, Chapter 3.

14 See Ludwig Friedländer, *Roman Life and Manners under the Early Empire* (Seventh Edition), translated by A. Magnus, New York: Dutton, 1908, Vol. 1, Chapter 5, "The Position of Women."

15 Frieda M. Das, *Purdah*, New York: Vanguard, 1932; Kingsley Davis, *The Population of India and Pakistan*, Princeton: Princeton University Press, 1951, p. 112. There was a widespread custom of taking one's bride from a village other than one's own.

16 W. Lloyd Warner, *Black Civilization*, New York: Harper, 1937, pp. 82–84. They may also become "sweethearts" at puberty; see pp. 86–89.

17 See Murdock, op. cit., pp. 53 ff. et passim for discussions of double-descent.

18 Marvin B. Sussman, "Parental Participation in Mate Selection and Its Effect upon Family Continuity," *Social Forces*, 32 (October 1953): 76–81.

19 Personal letter, dated January 9, 1958. . . .

27

TOWARD A SOCIOLOGY
OF THE HETEROSEXUAL LOVE RELATIONSHIP

Ira L. Reiss

The heterosexual love relationship is one of the most vital and one of the most neglected aspects of courtship behavior. Recently the author examined the sociological literature, in particular the marriage and family textbooks, to discern the type of analysis present. In addition preliminary research was conducted on a new approach toward analyzing the love relationship. The purpose of this article is to put forth the basic findings of the above studies and, thereby, to propose a new direction for the sociological study of the heterosexual love relationship.

TEXTBOOK TREATMENT
OF THE LOVE RELATIONSHIP

An examination of twenty-six textbooks in marriage and the family revealed that twenty of these books took a rather limited or restricted approach to the heterosexual love relationship—that is, they most often focused on one type of love, which was usually described as the "best," "real," or "true" type.[1] Other types, besides the preferred type, would commonly be viewed as not real forms of love or as inferior in quality to the true type of love. The following are several quotations from these marriage and the family textbooks which illustrate this restricted approach:

Although one may fall precipitously into a condition of violent infatuation, it takes time for real love to develop. . . . Genuine love is centered on one person only.[2]

Love at first sight is actually impossible, because love between two individuals is always a product of intimate and complex interaction, which depends upon varied types of experiences.[3]

. . . love never makes the individual less effective, less fully functioning; rather it promotes growth and increases awareness of meanings, needs, and opportunities in the world about one.[4]

We can admit that young couples may be, and usually are, "terribly infatuated" or "awfully thrilled" with each other, but we hesitate to apply the word "love" to such untested relationships [untested by many years of marriage.][5]

Genuine love is possible only when couples know each other well. . . . Is it actually possible to "fall in love at first sight"? The answer is "no.". . . If a person has serious doubts as to whether or not he is in love, obviously he is not.[6]

These textbook authors appear to have accepted one of our cultural beliefs; namely, that a "marriage type love" is the real form of love, and that such love is to be preferred over other emotional states such as romantic love or "infatuation."[7] Although this restriction of analysis by a preferred type of love may afford insight into this preferred type, it does limit the objective investigation of other cultural forms of love in American society. In short, to the extent that this more restricted approach is emphasized, a more comprehensive sociological approach is minimized.[8]. . . .

A SOCIOLOGICAL THEORY OF LOVE

The above examination of the literature gives one the impression that what is needed in our approach to love is a frame of reference which is more fully on the sociological level. As a step toward this goal, a general theoretical approach to the heterosexual love relationship has been formulated which, it is believed, takes account of the psychological level but brings into central focus the social and cultural levels. As will be shown, this formulation is in accord with the research evidence in this area, and interviews of numerous students also seem to support this conceptualization.[9] The following theory is put forth only as a first attempt to formulate the broad outlines of a sociological theory of the heterosexual love relationship.

First, it is important to describe the processes through which it is proposed all of our major cultural types of love develop. In American society young people meet under a variety of informal conditions such as at a party, a dance, or in school. After meeting, these two people become aware of the presence or lack of a feeling of rapport.[10] That is, they may feel quite at ease and relaxed and be willing and desirous to talk about themselves and learn more about the other person, or they may feel quite ill at ease and watch the clock until the evening ends. To the sociologist the vital question is *not* just whether a couple feels rapport because they complement each other or are similar to each other in their personality needs. Such information certainly can be valuable, as Winch has shown; but the crucial sociological question is: What are the social and cultural background factors which make this type of couple capable of feeling rapport—what social and cultural variables are related to particular personality needs? Certainly, if cultural backgrounds differ too sharply the people involved would be unable to communicate at all. However, if cultural backgrounds differ in some particular ways they may still be compatible; while the same amount of difference in other directions makes compatibility most unlikely.

Thus, it is one of the sociologist's tasks to discern what role cultural background plays in heterosexual love relationships. This can be done on a more precise level than just seeing if the two people are of the same religion or education group. The latter has been done for us by Burgess and Wallin—but one must also see what cultural factors made these two particular people, who are of the same religious and education group, feel rapport for each other. The specific way each views and defines his social roles may be a fruitful area to examine.[11] For example, within the same religious, educational, and income group there are divisions regarding how equalitarian the female role should be, and those people whose definitions of the female role are alike may well be more apt to feel rapport for each other. As a preliminary testing of this approach, seventy-four students were asked to select from ten personality needs which ones they felt to be the most important in their best love relationship. Table I shows some of the results of this pilot study.

These results are surely not conclusive but they are suggestive. In need number 9, for example, only 22 percent of the boys stated that they felt it most important in their love relationship to have "someone to look up to." Seventy percent of the girls checked this response. This large difference seems to reflect the double standard in our society which brings girls up with more of an orientation to want to love someone they can "look up to."[12] A girl who felt this need

would, it seems, blend well with a boy who did *not* feel this need, and both of these attitudes are traceable to our double-standard culture. This is one way in which we may connect personality needs with cultural background. Other needs in Table I suggest cultural variables, e.g., the higher percentage of men who need their ambition stimulated and the higher percentage of girls who need help in decisions.[13]

It should be emphasized that this is but a pilot study and much further work is needed to refine this method of analysis and test some of the above interpretations. The effort here is merely aimed at showing that one can analyze the rapport aspect of a relationship in terms of the cultural background which makes such rapport possible.[14]

The feeling of rapport seems to be the first step in the development of heterosexual love relationships. Concomitant with such rapport is a second process which may be labeled "self-revelation." When one feels at ease in a social relationship he is more likely to reveal intimate aspects of his existence. He is, under such conditions, more likely to tell of his hopes, desires, fears, and ambitions. He is also more likely to engage in sexual activities, according to recent studies on college students.[15] Here, too, the

TABLE I. PERSONALITY NEEDS WHICH COLLEGE STUDENTS CONSIDER TO BE MOST IMPORTANT IN THEIR BEST LOVE RELATIONSHIP*

Personality Needs for Someone:	*Boys (Percentage)*	*Girls (Percentage)*
1. Who loves me	87	95
2. To confide in	60	65
3. Who shows me a lot of affection	40	53
4. Who respects my ideals	50	74
5. Who appreciates what I want to achieve	32	28
6. Who understands my moods	36	23
7. Who helps me in making important decisions	16	28
8. To stimulate my ambition	16	7
9. I can look up to very much	22	70
10. Who gives me self-confidence in my relations with people	32	19

* Each student was allowed to check as many of the ten as he thought were "most important." These ten needs are the same as Anselm Strauss used; see "Personality Needs and Marital Choice," *Social Forces*, 25 (March 1947): 332–335. The questionnaire was administered by R. Wayne Kernodle and the author in 1958 to 74 of our "marriage" students (43 girls, 31 boys). A more rigorous testing is planned for the future.

sociologist need not focus on the psychological aspects—he can, instead, look at the cultural backgrounds of the participants. The cultural background of each person should help determine what he feels is proper to reveal, i.e., whether petting is acceptable, whether talking about one's personal ambitions is proper, or whether discussing religion is right. The person's cultural background will define what and how much one should reveal when a certain amount of rapport is present.

The above process of self-revelation is vital to the development of love, and it is through this that a third process occurs; namely, the development of mutual dependencies, or, more technically put, of interdependent habit systems. One becomes dependent on the other person to fulfill one's own habits: e.g., one needs the other person to tell one's ideas or feelings; one needs the other person to joke with; one needs the other person to fulfill one's sexual desires. When such habitual expectations are not fulfilled, loneliness and frustration are experienced. Thus, such habits tend to perpetuate a relationship. The type of habits which are established are culturally determined, in large measure, for these habits are outgrowths of the revelations, and the type of revelation is culturally regulated.

Finally, a fourth process is involved, and that is personality need fulfillment. The needs referred to here are needs such as the basic needs in Table I, which were examined in relation to feelings of rapport. As has been shown, these needs seem to vary with cultural background. These four processes are in a sense really one process, for when one feels rapport, he reveals himself and becomes dependent, thereby fulfilling his personality needs. The circularity is most clearly seen in that the needs being fulfilled were the original reason for feeling rapport. In summary, then, the cultural background produces certain types of personality needs in particular groups of people, and when these people meet other groups which have similar or complementary backgrounds they feel rapport, reveal themselves, become dependent, and thereby fulfill these personality needs.

Since these four processes turn one into the other and are constantly occurring, the above formulation concerning the development of love will be called the "Wheel Theory." This is, of course, merely a label for the above four processes—one which was chosen because the term has explanatory value and helps emphasize the circularity and unity of these four processes. As has been mentioned, the key interest for the sociologist would be in the cultural and social factors underlying these four processes as they occur between various types of young people. [Figure 1] is a graphic representation of this theory.

FIGURE 1. GRAPHIC PRESENTATION OF THE WHEEL THEORY OF THE DEVELOPMENT OF LOVE.

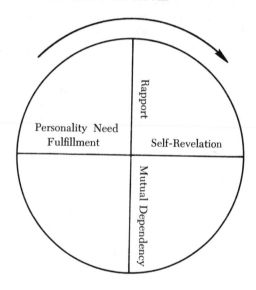

Of course, the "wheel" can turn in a negative direction and "unwind"; that is, the relationship can weaken when an argument or competing interest, or such, occur. Such an event can lessen rapport and that, in turn, decreases self-revelation, mutual dependency, and need fulfillment. This decrease further lessens rapport and can thus continue to "unwind" the relationship. The wheel can also continue to turn indefinitely in a positive direction as long as the four processes continue to be activated. In this fashion the rapport, revelation, dependency, and fulfillment processes can continue to "turn" for as long and as intensely as the cultural backgrounds of the people involved will allow.

Upon inspection it can be seen that the four spokes of the wheel are processes which universally occur in any primary relationship, i.e., the general description would apply to the development of a friendship relationship or a parent-child relationship. The four wheel processes would be involved in a primary relationship in Samoa as well as in New York. Thus, heterosexual love in America is the cultural development and elaboration of *one* type of primary relationship.

We give a specific meaning and content to this type of heterosexual love relation that distinguishes it from all other types of primary relations. For the last thousand years the Western world has singled out the heterosexual type of primary relationship for special attention.[16] Some other cultures have people who fall in love, but usually they do not use such love feelings as the basis for marriage. Such feelings most often develop after marriage and they lack the "romantic" aura ours possess. Goode has recently put forth evidence on the relative potentiality and actuality of love relationships in other cultures.[17]

Love in America is culturally defined regarding how intense the feelings should be before one calls it "love," and how one should behave when he believes he is in love. Although such cultural definitions are widely shared there still are some people who will apply the label "love" to a relationship quite freely, and some others who require so much that they may never believe a relationship is intense enough to be love. There may possibly be variation by social classes as to what is required before using the term "love" to describe a heterosexual primary relationship.

The symptoms which go along with love vary from the Hollywood variety of walking into doors and losing one's appetite to the more "rational" type of symptoms which involve knowing the person thoroughly and wanting to be with him. These symptoms are learned in much the same way we learn other cultural forms. The kind of symptoms one displays depends in large measure on the type of love one accepts. The author's studies of college love affairs indicate that love in American culture may be hypothetically classified into several types, which have varying degrees of support in our society: (1) ultra romantic love at first sight, (2) sexual love where the sexual factor is dominant, (3) rational love where the intellectual appraisal of the affair is important, and (4) probably several other mixed varieties. Much more research is needed to verify and extend this typology.

All of these types of love can be explained theoretically as developing via the wheel processes of rapport, revelation, dependency, and fulfillment. The romantic variety just goes through these processes in rapid order and one feels he knows the person fully—he feels the rapport, reveals himself, becomes dependent, and feels fulfilled, all sometimes in the course of one evening! The sexual type of love merely emphasizes one way around the wheel—one way of revealing oneself.[18] The rational type of love emphasizes the need to know each other under a variety of circumstances and to evaluate the relationship before allowing oneself to become too involved. This type of love seems to be increasingly popular among college students.[19] It involves a larger number of rapport, revelation, dependency, and fulfillment factors than do the other love types.

FINAL COMMENTS

With the Wheel Theory, one can distinguish and describe the development and maintenance of the major types of love relationships. Love, thus, can be viewed as a type of primary relationship which our culture has singled out for special attention. The problem becomes to discern what cultural forms have been given to this primary relationship and what cultural backgrounds tend to promote the possibility of this type of primary relationship. In this fashion one can avoid the more restricted approaches referred to above. Instead one can analyze the characteristics and consequences of each type of love in various segments of our culture and society. Goode's recent analysis suggests that love attitudes may differ considerably by social class.[20] The Wheel Theory thus affords a broad over-all conception which can encompass all the heterosexual love relationships.

Furthermore, the Wheel Theory does not depend on the truth or falsity of the complementary needs or homogamy conceptions. Rather, if one desires he may incorporate Winch's notion of complementary mating as well as the homogamy and personality-need views of Burgess and Wallin and Strauss.[21] Such explanations are compatible with the Wheel Theory and future research can resolve any competing conceptions which exist among these explanations.

In addition the Wheel Theory seems to be capable of accounting for and integrating much of the available specific field research evidence on love relationships. For example, some of the key findings in this area by Strauss show that 100 percent personality need fulfillment is had by only a minority of the couples in his sample (18 percent); Burgess and Wallin in their study of 1000 engaged couples showed how very common doubt and conflict were in engaged love relationships; Ellis in his study of 500 college girls points out that about a quarter of them had experienced simultaneous loves.[22] These are representative findings and they all are explainable by the Wheel Theory: e.g., if love does develop through the culturally directed processes of a primary relationship involving rapport, revelation, dependency, and need fulfillment, then one would expect that there would be wide differences in the amount of needs which were fulfilled in any one relationship; that the very common failure to fully satisfy one's needs might well make one have some doubts and conflicts concerning the value of the relationship; and it also follows that although one has fulfilled some of his needs in one love relationship, he may fall simultaneously in love with another person who is capable of fulfilling different combinations of needs.

NOTES

[1] The 26 books examined represent the author's total collection over the years from teaching in this field. They comprise almost all of the widely used books in this area. The following 20 books of the 26 examined were found to have a "restricted" approach. Specific page numbers indicate the most relevant portions. Ray B. Baber, *Marriage and the Family*, New York: McGraw-Hill, 1953, p. 137; Howard Becker and Reuben Hill, eds. *Family Marriage and Parenthood*, selection by J. K. Folsom, Boston: D. C. Heath, 1955, pp. 212, 221; Henry A. Bowman, *Marriage for Moderns*, New York: Crowell, 1953, p. 403; Ruth S. Cavan, *The American Family*, New York: Crowell, 1953, p. 403; Evelyn M. Duvall, *Family Development*, New York: Lippincott, 1957, p. 355; Evelyn M. Duvall and Reuben Hill, *When You Marry*, New York: D. C. Heath, 1953, p. 32; Morris Fishbein, M.D., and Ruby Jo Reeves Kennedy, eds. *Modern Marriage and Family Living*, selection by H. Bowman, New York: Oxford, 1957, pp. 135, 139; Norman E. Himes and Donald L. Taylor, *Your Marriage*, New York: Rinehart, 1955, pp. 22–23; J. L. Hirning and Alma L. Hirning, *Marriage Adjustment*, New York: American, 1956, pp. 122, 123, 125; John J. Kane, *Marriage and the Family*, New York: Dryden, 1954, pp. 79–81; Earl Lomon Koos, *Marriage*, New York: Holt, 1957, pp. 106, 109, 110; Judson T. Landis and Mary G. Landis, *Building a Successful Marriage*, New Jersey: Prentice-Hall, 1958, pp. 166–169; Paul H. Landis, *Making the Most of Marriage*, New York: Appleton-Century Crofts, 1955, p. 105; E. E. LeMasters, *Modern Courtship and Marriage*, New York: Macmillan, 1957, p. 61; Alexander F. Magoun, *Love and Marriage*, New York: Harper, 1956, p. 7; Meyer F. Nimkoff, *Marriage and the Family*, New York: Houghton Mifflin, 1947, p. 376; James A. Peterson, *Education for Marriage*, New York: Scribner's, 1956, p. 15; Rex A. Skidmore and Anthron S. Cannon, *Building Your Marriage*, New York: Harper, 1951, pp. 57–61; Willard Waller and Reuben Hill, *The Family*, New York: Dryden, 1951, pp. 114, 128; Robert F. Winch and Robert McGinnis, eds. *Marriage and the Family*, selection by J. K. Folsom, New York: Holt, 1953, p. 359. The following six books did not spend much

time on love, and others took a more comprehensive approach: Ernest W. Burgess and Harvey J. Lock, *The Family*, New York: American, 1953; Robert Geib Foster, *Marriage and Family Relationships*, New York: Macmillan, 1950; Clifford Kirkpatrick, *The Family*, New York: Ronald, 1955; Judson T. Landis and Mary G. Landis, eds. *Readings in Marriage and the Family*, New York: Prentice-Hall, 1952; Arthur R. Olsen, Emily H. Mudd, and Hugo Bourdeau, eds. *Marriage and Family Relations*, Harrisburg: Stackpole, 1953; Andrew Truxal and Francis E. Merrill, *Marriage and the Family in American Culture*, New York: Prentice-Hall, 1953.

[2] Bowman, op. cit., pp. 32–37.

[3] Hirning and Hirning, op. cit., p. 125.

[4] Landis and Landis, op. cit., p. 169.

[5] LeMasters, op. cit., p. 61.

[6] Skidmore and Cannon, op. cit., pp. 57–61.

[7] Much of the doubt individuals display concerning their love affairs is not about whether they are experiencing *some* kind of love relationship but rather about whether they are experiencing a *particular* type of love, one capable of being the basis for marriage. The textbooks emphasize this type of love as the only type and make many people anxious and confused. These people do not see love as existing on a continuum but rather as an all-or-none state most difficult to discover and constantly subject to doubts.

[8] Whenever a controversial or highly emotional issue such as love or sex is involved, the danger of provincial approaches increases. One tends not to recognize as valid cultural forms, those beliefs which one feels to be in error. This seems to be the case concerning forms of love beliefs such as romantic love. For a criticism of some of the marriage and family textbooks for their restricted treatment of premarital coitus see Ira L. Reiss, "The Treatment of Pre-Marital Coitus in 'Marriage and the Family' Texts," *Social Problems* 4 (April 1957): 334–338.

[9] The author has interviewed dozens of individuals over the past several years concerning the development of their love relationships. However, these interviews can only be suggestive and not conclusive evidence for the theory of love to be presented here. Other, more systematic research is referred to elsewhere.

[10] There are articles relevant to the study of dyadic rapport, such as Howard Becker and Ruth H. Useem, "Sociological Analysis of the Dyad," *American Sociological Review*, 7 (February 1942): 13–26; Leonard S. Cottrell, Jr., and Rosalind F. Dymond, "The Empathic Responses," *Psychiatry*, 12 (November 1949): 355–359.

[11] Burgess and Wallin do include role conceptions in their analysis of homogamy. However, they do so in the sense of showing correlations and not fully in the sense of showing what, if any, causal relations underlie such correlations.

[12] For an analysis of the double standard see: Ira L. Reiss, "The Double Standard in Premarital Sexual Intercourse: A Neglected Concept," *Social Forces*, 34 (March 1956): 224–230.

[13] Another interesting point was that most of the girls who checked need No. 4 (someone who respects my ideals), also checked need No. 9 (someone I can look up to very much), showing that although the double standard may be modified to the point where girls want to have their ideals respected, the same girls want a boy whom they can "look up to." This relationship between No. 4 and No. 9 did not hold for the boys.

[14] The oft asked question "Why did this particular person fall in love with this other particular person?" can be answered by sociologists in terms of our approach. From our point of view, the love object could have been a number of people with similar sociocultural characteristics. Chance factors led to it being this particular person. Thus, even here an "individualistic" explanation is not needed.

[15] Winston Ehrmann's study of students at the University of Florida is the source of this statement. Ehrmann found that coitus was three times as likely to occur when love was involved. Winston Ehrmann, *Premarital Dating Behavior*, New York: Henry Holt, 1959.

[16] For a brief discussion of the development of romantic love see Hugo Beigel, "Romantic Love," *American Sociological Review*, 16 (June 1951): 326–334. Dr. Beigel is planning to publish a book on romantic love later this year. See also Dennis De Rougemont, *Love in the Western World*, New York: Harcourt Brace, 1940.

[17] William J. Goode, "The Theoretical Importance of Love," *American Sociological Re-*

view, 24 (February 1959): 37–48. Our explanation of love as a type of primary relationship fits in with Goode's findings that heterosexual love is more common than once thought and that many cultures set up specific controls to prevent its occurrence. For if heterosexual love develops as do other primary relationships, then it is more of an ever-present possibility, and one would expect to find it more widespread or to find specific controls set up against it. This is precisely what Goode found.

[18] One important area of love is its relation to sexual standards and behavior. This relation is developed at length in a book by the author: *Premarital Sexual Standards* (to be published by The Free Press in the Spring of 1960).

[19] Burgess and Wallin, op. cit., p. 170. Over two-thirds of the engaged couples in this study refused to call their relationship "head-over-heels in love" because that phrase smacked too much of ultra romantic love notions. The author's interviews with college students also tend to support this popularity of a "rational" type love. However, there are quite strong emotional attachments to some of the older romantic love notions, even among those who are intellectually "liberated."

[20] Goode, op. cit., p. 46.

[21] Burgess and Wallin do not speak of homogamy alone—they emphasize personality need fulfillment as vital in love. Even though they do not stress the necessity for getting behind personality needs to their social and cultural correlates, their approach is still quite compatible with the Wheel Theory. See Burgess and Wallin, op. cit., pp. 202–204, 212.

[22] Strauss, op. cit., p. 333. Burgess and Wallin, op. cit., pp. 179–182, 247; Albert Ellis, "A Study of Human Love Relationships," *The Journal of Genetic Psychology*, 75 (September 1949): 61–71.

28

SOME CORRELATES OF ROMANTIC LOVE

William M. Kephart

It is strange, in a society in which romantic love presumably serves as the basis for marriage, that love itself has been largely rejected as a topic for serious study. The mate selection process has been widely investigated, and a number of promising theories (homogamy, heterogamy, complementarity, values, role theory, etc.) have been developed. The focus of these selection theories, however, is not on the romantic element per se except insofar as the latter is held to derive from the theoretical factor—or set of factors—under consideration.

We know next to nothing, for instance, about the frequency or intensity of love among the various population elements. We do not know whether there are significant age and sex differences or whether there is correlativity between love and such variables as personality type, I.Q., social class, marital status, and other components of behavior routinely studied by students of the family. More than anything else, the present study is an attempt to focus attention on a meaningful research area. . . .

The figures reported herein are based on questionnaires filled out by 1,079 white college students from five colleges in the

Philadelphia metropolitan area. It was felt advisable for all respondents to have at least one year of college experience; hence, freshmen were excluded from the study. The questionnaire was pretested and revised several times before the final form was administered. Administration of the questionnaire and related instruments was done by the author in classes selected by course-heads.

The sample comprised 576 females and 503 males, with an age-range from 18 to 24. . . .

In view of the nonrandom nature of the sample, substantive findings should be viewed merely as suggestive. The findings are probably representative of Northeast metropolitan (white) college students, but whether they are or not—or whether findings from college populations in other parts of the country will differ from those reported here—only subsequent research can determine. . . .

When the study was first undertaken, some difficulty was expected with regard to terms such as infatuation and love. The difficulty did not materialize. During the pretests it was evident that college students were no strangers to love; in fact, on the final form of the questionnaire, only three percent of the respondents reported that they felt sure "they did not know what love was." It may be true, as popular writers have alleged, that love means different things to different people, but the present study suggests that, to most people, love means the same thing. Furthermore, romantic experience seems to be gratifying rather than, as is sometimes claimed, traumatic. Less than five percent of the respondents felt that their "total infatuation and love experience had made them unhappier."

The difference between love and infatuation may be an arbitrary one. In a literal sense, "infatuate" means "to make fatuous" or "to affect with romantic folly." Young people, however, are more likely to use the term infatuation to describe a romantic experience which has simply "faded out" in relatively quick fashion and in which the emotional commitment was—ret-

rospectively at least—unsustainable. The key word here may be "retrospectively," since respondents invariably described their current experience as love rather than infatuation, the latter term usually being used in the past tense. It is understandable, therefore, that most respondents reported few love experiences as compared to the number of infatuations. Correlation analysis in the present study includes both categories. . . .

Although it is commonly believed that females fall in love more often than males, the answer is anything but a simple statistic. Girls mature earlier than boys, and they also marry at an earlier age. In any premarital sample, therefore, the two sexes are on a different time span with respect to romantic experience. In the present study, both males and females started dating at about the same age (median age, 13). However, the reported median age at first infatuation was 13.0 for females, 13.6 for males. For first love experience, the corresponding ages were 17.1 and 17.7, respectively.

The significance of this differential time span is readily apparent from an examination of the "closeness-to-marriage" status of college students. . . . Predictably, most of the girls were in love at the time of the survey, most of the boys were not.

For the entire sample, the median number of times infatuated was 5.6 for females, 4.5 for males. The corresponding figures for falling in love were 1.3 for females, 1.2 for males. In terms of a college profile, it is apparent that the romantic experience (infatuation and love) of females is somewhat more extensive than that of the males, the respective medians being 7.0 and 5.7.

When age is held constant, however, a curious time pattern emerges. . . .

Age for age, the romantic experience (RE) figure for females is greater than that for males, although by age 23–24 the difference virtually disappears. But how does one explain the fact that for males the cumulative number of RE's predictably increases with age, while for females this number—after age 20—*tends to decrease?* The latter phenomenon is, by definition, impossible. Theoretically, of course, the female-reporting anomaly could be due either to the disparate age groups involved or to sampling variability. However, similar results occur in a half-dozen other areas of the study; e.g., even the "number of different boys dated" reportedly decreases with age! In all of these areas, cumulative female experience is reported to decline with age, while male experience shows the expected increase. . . .

It is the writer's belief that in the reporting of female RE's a displacement factor is operating. New experiences tend to "crowd out" previous ones. In retrospect, love affairs are relegated to infatuations, and some of the latter either fade out altogether or are remembered merely as passing fancies. Why this so-called romantic displacement operates for females and not for males is an interesting sociological phenomenon.

Although both sexes in our society are conditioned to uphold the monogamistic form of marriage, it is the female who is more likely to fill the role of marital custodian. Perhaps because marriage is more central to her life, it is she who is the acknowledged protagonist of the one-man-one-woman matrimonial ideal. In a normative sense, it is more or less expected that the wife will be a "one-man woman," an expectation which has premarital adumbrations; e.g., the girl who is engaged does not as a rule evidence much interest in anyone but her fiancé. Even her general dating experience, while certainly not lacking in romantic identification, is more consciously "matrimonial" than in the case of the male. The point is this: the high-school-and-college-age female may have more romantic experiences than her male counterpart, but, as she passes from the teens to the twenties and nears the matrimonial state, previous RE's tend to be rejected inasmuch as they impinge on the monogamistic ideal.

If this analysis is correct, the previously mentioned romantic displacement is a function not simply of the female's age, but of her closeness to marriage. By the same token, a decrement of this kind would not be expected for the male. . . .

The trend is as expected: cumulative RE's for females reportedly decrease with closeness to marriage, while the opposite is true for males. In the present college sample, no one was over age 24. However, during a talk with a Philadelphia-area chapter of the American Association of University Women, the writer was able to collect written responses concerning the number of premarital romantic experiences. The median number of reported RE's for this group of 81 married women, age range 28–47, was 5.4, a figure substantially smaller than that reported by the married females in the college sample. (Neither the writer nor anyone else has collected data relative to the number of *postmarital* RE's, but on the basis of the above findings, it would be rather surprising if the figure for husbands were not found to be larger than that for wives.)

Implicit in the above analysis is the suggestion that the female's romantic conation is more adaptive and directive than that of the male. Apparently she is able to exercise a greater measure of control over her romantic inclinations, adapting them to the exigencies of marital selection. Available research would seem to support this view. It has been shown, for example, that when social class lines are crossed, men are far more likely to "marry down" than women.[1] Also, women are less likely to be influenced by physical appearance than men. In the present study, the percentage of those who reported that they were "very easily attracted" to the opposite sex was nearly twice as high for males as for females, similar findings having been reported by Burgess and Wallin[2] and by Prince.[3]

Another possible example of the directedness of female romanticism is the fact that in the present study only 31.4 percent of the females reported that they had ever been infatuated or in love with a younger boy, whereas 61.4 percent of the males reported that they had been infatuated or in love with an older girl. Furthermore, those females who had been romantically involved with a younger boy showed some evidence of maladjustment, i.e., they had relatively poor college grades and made comparatively poor scores on the Bell Personality Inventory. . . .

Males who reported that they had been infatuated or in love with an older female did not differ in college grades . . . or in personality test scores . . . from the others.

Also included in the present study was the question, "If a boy (girl) had all the other qualities you desired, would you marry this person if you were not in love with him (her)?". . .

Whereas almost two-thirds of the males unequivocally answered "no," less than one-quarter of the females did so. This contrast again illustrates the male-female difference in romantic orientation. As one girl remarked on the questionnaire: "I'm undecided. It's rather hard to give a 'yes' or 'no' answer to this question. If a boy had all the other qualities I desired, and I was not in love with him—well, I think I could talk myself into falling in love!". . .

The question, then, as to which sex falls in love more often may be the wrong question. At the high-school and college ages, females do seem to have somewhat more extensive romantic experience than do males. By the early twenties the RE differential between the sexes is apparently reduced. For students of the family, however, a more important question suggests itself: in what way—or ways—does the romantic orientation of females differ from that of males, and what is the significance of this differential with respect to the theoretics of mate selection?

Findings from the present study suggest that, contrary to rather strong popular impression, the female is not pushed hither and yon by her romantic compulsions. On the contrary, she seems to have a greater measure of rational control over her romantic inclinations than the male. This control manifests itself in a kind of matrimonial directedness, and as the female passes from the teens to the twenties and nears the "monogamistic ideal" she tends to forget or reject some of the romantic experiences she has already had. The male does not evidence a similar rejection pattern. (Other contrasts between the male and female romantic orientation, particularly in terms of personality-test-score correlates, have also been found, but these results will be discussed in a later paper.)

This male-female differential may explain, at least in part, why mate selection theories based on personality configurations of homogamy, heterogamy, or complementarity are still being debated. According to these prototypes, the mate selection process involves a reciprocative personality relationship of some kind. It can be hypothesized, for example, that persons with high dominance scores will (a) tend to choose mates with high dominance scores (homogamy) or (b) tend to choose mates with high deference scores (complementarity). In either case, the relationship would be reciprocative. . . .

But if, to a certain degree, the female tends to select on the basis of some independent, non-reciprocative factor—such as partner's family background—the theory of personality homogamy or complementarity would be delimited by a statistical intrusion of unknown magnitude. Residual variations in mate selection which fall outside the perimeters of homogamy/complementarity would not invalidate the general theoretical proposition; in fact, the latter might be strengthened in terms of a reduced—hence, more realistic—statistical expectancy. Applicability of the theory, however, ·would depend in good part on the identification of the residual factors. The male-female difference in romantic orientation would seem to be one of the generic factors worthy of further research attention.

NOTES

[1] August Hollingshead, "Cultural Factors in the Selection of Marriage Mates," *American Sociological Review*, 15 (October 1950):625; also, A. Philip and Thomas McCormick, "Age at Marriage and Mate Selection: Madison, Wisconsin," *American Sociological Review*, 16 (February 1951): 46.

[2] Ernest Burgess and Paul Wallin, *Engagement and Marriage,* Philadelphia: J. B. Lippincott, 1953, p. 160.

[3] Alfred J. Prince, "Factors in Mate Selection," *Family Life Coordinator,* 10 (July 1961): 58.

29

LOVE OR MARRIAGE?

Ernest Van Den Haag

If someone asks, "Why do people marry?" he meets indignation or astonishment. The question seems absurd if not immoral: the desirability of marriage is regarded as unquestionable. Divorce, on the other hand, strikes us as a problem worthy of serious and therapeutic attention. Yet marriage precedes divorce as a rule, and frequently causes it.

What explains marriage? People divorce often but they marry still more often. Lately they also marry—and divorce, of course—younger than they used to, particularly in the middle classes (most statistics understate the change by averaging all classes). And the young have a disproportionate share of divorces. However, their hasty exertions to get out of wedlock puzzle me less than their eagerness to rush into it in the first place.

A hundred years ago there was every reason to marry young—though middle-class people seldom did. The unmarried state had heavy disadvantages for both sexes. Custom did not permit girls to be educated, to work, or to have social, let alone sexual, freedom. Men were free but since women were not, they had only prostitutes for partners. (When enforced, the double standard is certainly self-defeating.) And, though less restricted than girls shackled to their families, single men often led a grim and uncomfortable life. A wife was nearly indispensable, if only to darn socks, sew, cook, clean, take care of her man. Altogether, both sexes needed marriage far more than now—no TV, cars, dates, drip-dry shirts, cleaners, canned foods—and not much hospital care, insurance, or social security. The family was all-important.

Marriage is no longer quite so indispensable a convenience; yet we find people marrying more than ever, and earlier. To be sure, prosperity makes marriage more possible. But why are the young exploiting the possibility so sedulously? Has the yearning for love become more urgent and widespread?

What has happened is that the physical conveniences which reduced the material usefulness of marriage have also loosened the bonds of family life. Many other bonds that sustained us psychologically were weakened as they were extended: beliefs became vague; associations impersonal, discontinuous, and casual. Our contacts are many, our relationships few: our lives, externally crowded, often are internally isolated; we remain but tenuously linked to each other and our ties come easily undone. One feels lonely surrounded by crowds and machines in an unbounded, abstract world that has become morally unintelligible; and we have so much time now to feel lonely in.

Thus one longs, perhaps more acutely than in the past, for somebody to be tangibly, individually, and definitely one's own, body and soul.

This is the promise of marriage. Movies, songs, TV, romance magazines, all intensify the belief that love alone makes life worthwhile, is perpetual, conquers the world's evils, and is fulfilled and certified by marriage. "Science" hastens to confirm as much. Doesn't popular psychology, brandishing the banner of Freud with more enthusiasm than knowledge, tell us, in effect, that any male who stays single is selfish or homosexual or mother-dominated and generally neurotic? and any unmarried female frustrated (or worse, not frustrated) and neurotic? A "normal" person, we are told, must love and thereupon marry. Thus love and marriage are identified with each other and with normality, three thousand years of experience notwithstanding. The yearning for love, attended by anxiety to prove oneself well-adjusted and normal, turns into eagerness to get married.

The young may justly say that they merely practice what their parents preached. For, indeed, the idea that "love and marriage go together like a horse and carriage" has been drummed into their heads, so much that it finally has come to seem entirely natural. Yet, nothing could be less so. Love has long delighted and distressed mankind, and marriage has comforted us steadily and well. Both, however, are denatured—paradoxically enough, by their stanchest supporters—when they are expected to "go together." For love is a very unruly horse, far more apt to run away and overturn the carriage than to draw it. That is why, in the past, people seldom thought of harnessing marriage to love. They felt that each has its own motive power: one primed for a lifelong journey; the other for an ardent improvisation, a voyage of discovery. . . .

Though by no means weaker, the marital bond is quite different from the bond of love. If you like, it is a different bond of love—less taut, perhaps, and more durable. By confusing these two related but in many ways dissimilar bonds, we stand to lose the virtues and gain the vices of both: the spontaneous passion of love and the deliberate permanence of marriage are equally endangered as we try to live up to an ideal which bogs down one and unhinges the other.

Marriage is an immemorial institution which, in some form, exists everywhere. Its main purpose always was to unite and to continue the families of bride and groom and to further their economic and social position. The families, therefore, were the main interested parties. Often marriages were arranged (and sometimes they took place) before the future husbands or wives were old enough to talk. Even when they were grown up, they felt, as did their parents, that the major purpose of marriage was to continue the family, to produce children. Certainly women hoped for kind and vigorous providers and men for faithful mothers and good housekeepers; both undoubtedly hoped for affection, too; but love did not strike either of them as indispensable and certainly not as sufficient for marriage.

Unlike marriage, love has only recently come to be generally accepted as something more than a frenzied state of pleasure and pain. It is a welcome innovation—but easily ruined by marriage; which in turn has a hard time surviving confusion with love. Marriage counselors usually recognize this last point, but people in love seldom consult them. Perhaps their limited clientele colors the views of too many marriage counselors: instead of acknowledging that love and marriage are different but equally genuine relationships, they depict love as a kind of dependable wheel horse that can be harnessed to the carriage of married life. For them, any other kind of love must be an "immature" or "neurotic" fantasy, something to be condemned as Hollywood-inspired, "unrealistic" romanticism. It is as though a man opposed to horse racing—for good reasons perhaps—were to argue that race horses are not real, that all real horses are draft horses. Thus marriage counselors often insist that the only "real" and "true" love is "mature"—it is the comfortable workaday relation Mommy and Daddy have. The children find it hard to believe that there is nothing more to it.

They are quite right. And they have on their side the great literature of the world, and philosophers from Plato to Santayana. What is wrong with Hollywood romance surely is not that it is romantic, but that its romances are shoddy clichés. And since Hollywood shuns the true dimensions of conflict, love in the movies is usually confirmed by marriage and marriage by love, in accordance with wishful fantasy, though not with truth.

Was the love Tristan bore Isolde "mature" or "neurotic"? They loved each other before and after Isolde was married—to King Mark. It never occurred to them to marry each other; they even cut short an extramarital idyll together in the forest. (And Tristan too, while protesting love for Isolde, got married to some other girl.) Dante saw, but never actually met, Beatrice until he reached the nether world, which is the place for permanent romance. Of course, he was a married man.

It is foolish to pretend that the passionate romantic longing doesn't exist or is "neurotic," i.e., shouldn't exist; it is as foolish to pretend that romantic love can be made part of a cozy domesticity. The truth is simple enough, though it can make life awfully complicated: there are two things, love and affection (or marital love), not one; they do not usually pull together as a team; they tend to draw us in different directions, if they are present at the same time. God nowhere promised to make this a simple world.

In the West, love came to be socially approved around the twelfth century. It became a fashionable subject of discussion then, and even of disputation, in formal "courts of love" convoked to argue its merits and to elaborate its true characteristics. Poets and singers created the models and images of love. They still do—though mass production has perhaps affected the quality; what else makes the teen-age crooners idols to their followers and what else do they croon about? In medieval times, as now, manuals were written, codifying the behavior recommended to lovers. With a difference though. Today's manuals are produced not by men of letters, but by doctors and therapists, as though love, sex, and marriage were diseases or therapeutic problems—which they promptly become if one reads too many of these guidebooks (any one is one too many). Today's manuals bear titles like "Married Love" (unmarried lovers can manage without help, I guess); but regardless of title, they concentrate on sex. In handbooks on dating they tell how to avoid it; in handbooks on marriage, how to go about it. . . .

The troubadours usually took sex and marriage for granted and dealt with love—the newest and still the most surprising and fascinating of all relationships. And also the most unstable. They conceived love as a longing, a tension between desire and fulfillment. This feeling, of course, had been known before they celebrated it. Plato described love as a desire for something one does not have, implying that it is a longing, not a fulfillment. But in ancient Greece, love was regarded diffidently, as rather undesirable, an intoxication, a bewitchment, a divine punishment—usually for neglecting sex. The troubadours thought differently, although, unlike many moderns, they did not deny that love is a passion, something one suffers.[1] But they thought it a sweet suffering to be cultivated, and they celebrated it in song and story.

The troubadours clearly distinguished love and sex. Love was to them a yearning for a psychic gratification which the lover feels only the beloved can give; sex, an impersonal desire anybody possessing certain fairly common characteristics can gratify by physical actions. Unlike love, sex can thrive without an intense personal relationship and may erode it if it exists. Indeed, the Romans sometimes wondered if love would not blunt and tame their sexual pleasures, whereas the troubadours fretted lest sex abate the fervor of love's longing. They never fully resolved the contest between love and sex; nor has anyone else. (To define it away is, of course, not to solve it.)

We try to cope with this contest by fusing love and sex. (Every high-school student is taught that the two go together.) This, as Freud pointed out, does not always succeed and may moderate both, but, as he also implied, it is the best we can hope for. In the words of William Butler Yeats, "Desire dies because every touch consumes the myth and yet, a myth that cannot be consumed becomes a specter. . . ."

Romantics, who want love's desiring to be conclusive, though endless, often link it to death: if nothing further can happen and rival its significance, if one dies before it does, love indeed is the end. But this is ending the game as much as winning it—certainly an ambiguous move. The religious too perpetuate longing by placing the beloved altogether out of physical reach. The "bride of Christ" who retires to a convent longs for her Redeemer—and she will continue to yearn, as long as she lives, for union with a God at once human and divine, incarnating life and love everlasting. In its highest sense, love is a reaching for divine perfection, an act of creation. And always, it is a longing.

Since love is longing, experts in the Middle Ages held that one could not love someone who could not be longed for—for instance, one's wife. Hence, the Comtesse de Champagne told her court in 1174: "Love cannot extend its rights over two married persons." If one were to marry one's love, one would exchange the sweet torment of desire, the yearning, for that which fulfills it. Thus the tension of hope would be replaced by the comfort of certainty. He who longs to long, who wants the tension of desire, surely should not marry. In former times, of course, he married—the better to love someone else's wife.

When sexual objects are easily and guiltlessly accessible, in a society that does not object to promiscuity, romantic love seldom prospers. For example, in imperial Rome it was rare and in Tahiti unknown. And love is unlikely to arouse the heart of someone brought up in a harem, where the idea of uniqueness has a hard time. Love flowers best in a monogamous environment morally opposed to unrestrained sex, and interested in cultivating individual experience. In such an environment, longing may be valued for itself. Thus, love as we know it is a Christian legacy, though Christianity in the main repudiates romantic love where the object is worldly, and accepts passion only when transcendent, when God is the object—or when muted into affection: marital love. . . .

Let me hazard a Freudian guess about the genesis of the longing we call love. It continues and reproduces the child's first feeling for his parent—the original source of unconditioned and unconditional love. But what is recreated is the child's image, the idealized mother or father, young and uniquely beautiful, and not the empirical parent others see. The unconsummated love for this ideal parent (and it could be someone else important in the child's experience) remains as an intense longing. Yet any fulfillment now must also become a disappointment—a substitute, cheating the longing that wants to long. Nonetheless most of us marry and replace the ideal with an imperfect reality. We repudiate our longing or we keep it but shift its object. If we don't, we may resent our partners for helping us "consume the myth," and leaving us shorn of longing—which is what Don Giovanni found so intolerable, and what saddens many a faithful husband.

Sexual gratification, of course, diminishes sexual desire for the time being. But it does more. It changes love. The longing may become gratitude; the desire tenderness; love may become affectionate companionship—"After such knowledge, what forgiveness?" Depending on character and circumstance, love may also be replaced by indifference or hostility.

One thing is certain though: if the relationship is stabilized, love is replaced by other emotions. (Marriage thus has often been recommended as the cure for love. But it does not always work.) The only way to keep love is to try to keep up—or reestablish—the distance between lovers that was inevitably shortened by intimacy and possession, and thus, possibly, regain desire and longing. Lovers sometimes do so by quarreling. And some personalities are remote enough, or inexhaustible enough, to be longed for even when possessed. But this has disadvantages as well. And the deliberate and artificial devices counseled by romance magazines and marriage manuals ("surprise your husband . . .")—even when they do not originate with the love of pretense—are unlikely to yield more than the pretense of love.

The sexual act itself may serve as a vehicle for numberless feelings: lust, vanity, and self-assertion, doubt and curiosity, possessiveness, anxiety, hostility, anger, or indifferent release from boredom. Yet, though seldom the only motive, and often absent altogether, love nowadays is given as the one natural and moral reason which authorizes and even ordains sexual relations. What we have done is draw a moral conclusion from a rule of popular psychology: that "it is gratifying, and therefore healthy and natural, to make love when you love, and frustrating, and therefore unhealthy and unnatural, not to; we must follow nature; but sex without love is unnatural and therefore immoral."

Now, as a psychological rule, this is surely wrong; it can be as healthy to frustrate as it is to gratify one's desires. Sometimes gratification is very unhealthy; sometimes frustration is. Nor can psychological health be accepted as morally decisive. Sanity, sanitation, and morality are all desirable, but they are not identical; our wanting all of them is the problem, not the solution. It may be quite "healthy" to run away with your neighbor's wife, but not, therefore, right. And there is nothing unhealthy about wishing to kill someone who has injured you—but this does not morally justify doing so. Finally, to say "we must follow nature" is always specious: we follow nature in whatever we do—we can't ever do what nature does not let us do. Why then identify nature only with the nonintellectual, the sensual, or the emotional possibilities? On this view, it would be unnatural to read: literacy is a gift of nature only if we include the intellect and training in nature's realm. If we do, it makes no sense to call a rule unnatural merely because it restrains an urge: the urge is no more natural than the restraint.

The combination of love and sex is no more natural than the separation. Thus, what one decides about restraining or indulging an emotion, or a sexual urge, rests on religious, social, or personal values, none of which can claim to be more natural than any other.

Not that some indulgences and some inhibitions may not be healthier than others. But one cannot flatly say which are good or bad for every man. It depends on their origins and effects in the personalities involved. Without knowing these, more cannot be said—except, perhaps, that we should try not to use others, or even ourselves, merely as a means—at least not habitually and in personal relations. Sex, unalloyed, sometimes leads to this original sin which our moral tradition condemns. Psychologically, too, the continued use of persons merely as instruments ultimately frustrates both the user and the used. This caution, though it justifies no positive action, may help perceive problems; it does not solve them; no general rule can. . . .

What about marriage? In our society, couples usually invite the families to their weddings, although the decision to marry is made exclusively by bride and groom. However, a license must be obtained and the marriage registered; and it can be dissolved only by a court of law. Religious ceremonies state the meaning of marriage clearly. The couple are asked to promise "forsaking all others, [to] keep thee only unto her [him], so long as ye both shall live." The vow does not say, "as long as ye both shall want to," because marriage is a promise to continue even when one no longer wishes to. If marriage were to end when love does, it would be redundant: why solemnly ask two people to promise to be with each other for as long as they want to be with each other?

Marriage was to cement the family by tying people together "till death do us part" in the face of the fickleness of their emotions. The authority of state and church was to see to it that they kept a promise voluntarily made, but binding, and that could not be unmade. Whether it sprang from love did not matter. Marriage differed from a love affair inasmuch as it continued regardless of love. Cupid shoots his arrows without rhyme or reason. But marriage is a deliberate rational act, a public institution making the family independent of Cupid's whims. Once enlisted, the volunteers couldn't quit, even when they didn't like it any longer. That was the point.

The idea that marriage must be synchronous with love or even affection nullifies it altogether. (That affection should coincide with marriage is, of course, desirable, though it does not always happen.) We would have to reword the marriage vow. Instead of saying, "till death do us part," we might say, "till we get bored with each other"; and, instead of "forsaking all others," "till someone better comes along." Clearly, if the couple intend to stay "married" only as long as they want to, they only pretend to be married: they are having an affair with legal trimmings. To marry is to vow fidelity regardless of any future feeling, to vow the most earnest attempt to avoid contrary feelings altogether, but, at any rate, not to give in to them.

Perhaps this sounds grim. But it needn't be if one marries for affection more than for love. For affection, marital love may grow with knowledge and intimacy and shared experience. Thus marriage itself, when accepted as something other than a love affair, may foster affection. Affection differs from love as fulfillment differs from desire. Further, love longs for what desire and imagination make uniquely and per-fectly lovable. Possession erodes it. Affection, however,—which is love of a different, of a perhaps more moral and less aesthetic kind—cares deeply also for what is unlovable without transforming it into beauty. It cares for the unvarnished person, not the splendid image. Time can strengthen it. But the husband who wants to remain a splendid image must provide a swan to draw him away, or find a wife who can restrain her curiosity about his real person—something that Lohengrin did not succeed in doing. Whereas love stresses the unique form perfection takes in the lover's mind, affection stresses the uniqueness of the actual person.

One may grow from the other. But not when this other is expected to remain unchanged. And affection probably grows more easily if not preceded by enchantment. For the disenchantment which often follows may turn husband and wife against each other, and send them looking elsewhere for reenchantment—which distance lends so easily. Indeed, nothing else does.

NOTES

1 . . . *I am in love*
And that is my shame.
What hurts the soul
My soul adores,
No better than a beast
Upon all fours.

So says W. B. Yeats. About eight centuries earlier, Chrestien de Troyes expressed the same sentiment.

Part Seven

Sex Outside of Marriage

Premarital sex may occur at any time in the sequence of events prior to marriage or between marriages. The range of sexual behavior involved in this pattern is wide; it is possible that masturbation, petting, and homosexual behavior, as well as heterosexual coitus, should be included in a discussion of sex outside of marriage. In general, however, premarital sex usually means the experience of sexual intercourse between a male and a female.

It was pointed out in Part Six that physical attraction and its resulting behavior are not always accompanied by love, nor even by romanticism; nor are sex and intimacy companions in every case. In fact, some types of sexual encounters may actually be aimed at avoiding intimacy. The "Don Juans" who go from partner to partner rarely stay long enough for closeness to grow; often, they really do not like women at all and use them to bolster a sagging sexual ego and to impress other men with their records. The woman who "collects" men almost as trophies exhibits the same characteristics, although she may only become involved sexually when she feels that she must do so to capture the current target.

For those people who never marry (currently 5 to 6 percent in the United States), premarital sex is the only kind ever experienced. The never-married man or woman of middle-age, for instance, who engages in sexual relations presents a particular type of premarital sex that is not usually the subject of research analysis nor of popular media treatment. Since there appears to be growing number of persons who are choosing not to marry—or, at least, to postpone such a commitment for many years—sex for the never-married deserves more attention from those who chronicle patterns of male-female behavior.

We are covering premarital sex after the discussions of dating, intimacy, and love because there seems to be a consensus that a great part of sex outside marriage takes place between men and women who have known each other for a considerable period of time, have achieved a relative closeness, and may even be contemplating or actually planning marriage. There is even evidence that sexual intimacy frequently leads to marriage and the establishment of a family. Those who view sexual attraction as a basic instinct for the purpose of insuring the survival of the human species thus see premarital sex as a phenomenon that naturally moves partners in the direction of a permanent union. Others point to society's standards concerning sexual behavior as the main factor behind the strong ties between premarital sexual intimacy and eventual marriage. Whatever the explanation, it is not difficult to find research to link the two; and while there may be speculation about what the future holds in store, at present it is safe to say that sex before marriage moves men and women toward marriage in a large number of cases.

Sex before marriage, or in between marriages, is nothing new historically, although the increased number of women involved and the openness with which it is discussed today has led many to believe that a sexual revolution has occurred. In fact, there are those who believe that the United States has been in a kind of continuous sexual revolution since the revolution of the colonies against England. A glance at history shows clearly, however, that the sexual standards of today that alarm so many are not all that revolutionary compared to times past. There appear to be morality cycles of irregular duration, which are related to a large number of social and economic factors that cause relaxation of sexual restriction—or, conversely, that cause very strict standards. Historians of sexual behavior say that the current cycle began shortly before the turn of this century. Hence, it is not a revolution, as was the War for Independence, but instead appears to be a slowly growing trend which is related to, among other things, industrialization, urbanization, and technological advances, which are making anonymity and freedom from certain restraints a way of life. As we mentioned above, more unmarried women are involved than in the recent past, but the number of unmarried men has stayed about the same. The data seem to indicate that couples who have known each other for some time are more apt to engage in premarital sex, which accounts in part for the rise in the number of women in-

volved. As behavior has been slowly changing, so have attitudes concerning the behavior, until today attitudes toward sex outside of marriage have probably changed more than the actual behavior has. Many people who are grandparents today may have been involved in premarital sex, but they certainly didn't talk about it. Openness in discussing sexual behavior has led to the widely held notion that "everybody is doing it," but research studies indicate that this conclusion does not follow, at least not yet.

The first article in this part, a discussion of sexual attraction, offers a cross-cultural and historical view of the ideas and standards which men and women use to determine who is sexually appealing. Just what constitutes sex appeal has long been debated, but almost everyone agrees that it does exist. There are cultural as well as individual differences in what appeals to men about women and to women about men. Sexual attractiveness is almost always a part of mate selection in the United States as well as in most of the rest of the world. Psychologically, it is triggered by clues which are meaningful to each person as a result of his or her whole life experience and constitutes a kind of image of the ideal person of the opposite sex.

Next, a careful look at sex before marriage is offered by Eleanore Luckey and Gilbert Nass, whose article also reports on beliefs of college-aged young people in the United States, Canada, Germany, England, and Norway. The comparative study deals with differences in sex-role behavior, independence from parents, attitudes toward marriage and sex behavior, and sexual experience. In each of the countries studied, the men were less conservative in their views than the women, which points to a widespread cultural difference between men and women in matters pertaining to sex.

The next three articles, two from *Life* and one from *Time*, explore the life of the singles, both in college and after graduation. The articles deal with the growing phenomenon of a more casual approach to sex; the ones from *Life* concentrate on the arrangements for couples to live together without marrying and to share coeducational dormitories with unlimited visitation privileges. Such living arrangements provide a great deal more than mere sexual gratification for the men and women who choose this pattern. In fact, there is some evidence that sexual activity is lower in frequency among students who share living accomodations than on campuses where coeducational dorms and off-campus living arrangements are not allowed.

Unwanted pregnancy is frequently mentioned as a consequence of sex—even in this day of enlightenment on contraception —and sex outside of marriage may often result in just such a pregnancy. Although an increasing number of young women are keeping the children they bear outside of marriage, there has been an increase in legal abortions to end pregnancies. Garrett Hardin's article takes a look at the abortion controversy and discusses the problems involved in an unwanted pregnancy.

Sex researchers are beginning to find that homosexual activities are more and more prominent in the lives of the unmarried and also constitute part of sex outside mar-

riage, even for those who are married. Since homosexual marriages are not considered legal in any of the fifty states, it is not uncommon for homosexuals to be married legally to a person of the opposite sex but to have sexual affairs of a homosexual nature. The taboos in our society concerning homosexuality seem to be lessening; and it is possible that, as more and more young people are free to "come out," the number of *known* male and female homosexuals will increase and that society may someday recognize the homosexual marriage.

In his article, Robert Sherwin discusses the legal aspects of sex, to try to put both law and the new behavior patterns into perspective. The author points to the lag of forty to sixty years which has historically seemed to exist between the adoption of behavior by a society and the legal codification of that behavior. At present, in nearly every state, there are many laws which, if enforced, could bring fines and prison sentences to consenting adults who are engaging in sexual behavior they consider to be normal and not a matter for criminal action.

30

UNDERSTANDING SEXUAL ATTRACTION

From *Story of Life*

From more than a mile away some male moths can sense the presence of a female of their species and fly unerringly towards her. There is no doubt that the female moth has sex appeal. For human beings, the subject is more complicated. Human beings, alone among living creatures, worry about whether they are sexually attractive or not. Some try to exert more sex appeal

than they feel they have naturally (and to do so may borrow the furry skins of wild beasts, the scented substances from flowers and animal glands). And some try to exert less sex appeal, wrapped in the somber colors of religious communities.

Sex appeal, among humans, is *not* a "thing" that one possesses in the way one either has or does not have a pair of shoes.

The girl with shining hair, warm smile, and curving figure obviously "has" sex appeal in that men's heads turn, with something like the enthusiasm of the male moth, when she passes. Breasts, legs, eyes, and hair are triggers to sexual response. And most people have spent time before a mirror wondering about themselves and their ability to attract a partner. But really to find out about our own powers to attract or be attractive sexually is more than a matter of adding up vital statistics and buying aids to beauty. We have to know something about the deepest instincts and emotions of humanity in general, ourselves in particular.

First, it is fortunate for the survival of the human species that men and women are attracted by, and attractive to, each other. For sexual attraction is the first step towards love, marriage, home-making, and child-bearing. It is a natural and basic instinct shared in its essentials with the animal world, but immensely complex in its expression in human society.

This basic interest in the opposite sex has its roots in infancy. It can be seen developing in young children of pre-school age. A little girl, for example, usually shows by the time she is three a marked response to her father. She will behave coquettishly in his presence and may act in a similar fashion with any male friends of the family who call at the house. Men obviously intrigue her in a way which women do not. At one time or another most little girls have said, "When I grow up I'm going to marry my Daddy."

A little boy for his part usually remains emotionally tied to his mother throughout infancy. Though fond and admiring of his father, it is mother who holds a special place in his affection. He may be very possessive of her and show this by jealousy of the father's privileged position in relationship to her.

Sigmund Freud, the founder of psychoanalysis, studying young children, coined the term "Oedipus complex," to explain his view that, in normal development, the young child passes through a period of being strongly attracted to the parent of the opposite sex.

Pre-school children, then, accept the idea of an intimate bond between a man and a woman, and their games will usually include playing at "weddings" and "mothers and fathers." They show great interest in the physical differences between the sexes and they want to know about sexual development and the mechanics of conception. This inquisitiveness is natural, but underlying it is a preoccupation with the attraction which one sex exercises over the other.

In adolescence the longing to be loved and to find someone to love is extended by maturing sexuality with its profound physical and emotional changes, and a new awareness of the part played by each sex in intimate relationships.

But the love-experiences of childhood are not completely left behind. Psychologists find that most adolescents have, over the years of childhood, built up some kind of "image" of the person they would like to love and be loved by. This image is probably a compound picture of the men or women who have been important to the child earlier on. A boy, for example, may have a clear idea of the kind of girl who would appeal to him—blonde, slim, with trim ankles. It is probable that this mental image includes elements of the idealized mother or sister or, perhaps, a teacher.

In a parallel fashion a girl may have a mental image of the kind of man she would like to be loved by—though research shows that girls tend to emphasize qualities in the character of a desired male, rather than merely his appearance. He may, for example, be thought of as gentle, good with children, honest, and courageous.

As well as having an image of the type of girl who attracts him, the adolescent boy is very conscious at this time that he must put to the test his *own* powers of attraction. For the adolescent stands on the threshold of manhood and is aware that this implies new experiences, new powers, new responsibilities. If he can attract a girl he is reassured because his adult male status is recognized and sponsored by a member of the opposite sex.

To make quite sure that girls notice him and feel admiration for his emergent masculinity, the boy's behavior is likely to be exhibitionistic and ostentatious. And the girl will experiment with clothes, make-up, hair styles, and flirtatious mannerisms, testing out different ways to attract male attention.

This concern over the ability to attract a member of the opposite sex continues to a certain extent throughout the individual's life. And it leads to much speculation about what exactly constitutes sex appeal. It obviously does not rest on physical beauty alone for many men and women who cannot be called beautiful or handsome succeed in attracting members of the opposite sex.

So many other elements and qualities contribute to a woman's appeal—tenderness, kindness, gaiety, charm—that fashionable features and a perfect figure cannot even be considered the main ingredients. It was Cleopatra's vitality as much as her beauty that captivated Antony.

Similarly, many men who appear at first sight to lack physical appeal succeed in establishing warm relationships with women. The reason is that women admire qualities, like courage, forcefulness, ambition, protectiveness, aggression, and self-confidence in a man just as much as physical prowess or bearing. Rasputin was unkempt and (reputedly) smelly; Napoleon was small in stature; Byron had a club foot—but all of them exerted a fascination over women.

It is also the case, occasionally, that a woman is attracted to a man *because* he is *not* masculine, but gives the appearance of needing a woman to look after him. In this he unconsciously appeals primarily to her maternal feeling and only secondarily to her sexual needs as a woman.

Sex appeal is normally a natural endowment in the sense that the child who has been brought up in a reasonably normal and loving home will be attracted by and will wish to be attractive to, women. He will, therefore, behave in a relaxed and friendly way with the other sex. He will seek feminine company and respond in a warm and affectionate manner to any sign of interest in a woman who appeals to him. But there are, however, some people who, for one reason or another, are unable to respond in this fashion: they will appear excruciatingly shy, diffident, defensive, and

"distant" and as a result, even though physically attractive, their behavior hinders the development of relationships, friendly or erotic, with the opposite sex.

But physical beauty is obviously an asset to anybody, and as a convenient starting-off point most young adults seek to make themselves as personally attractive as possible.

Throughout history men and women have used cosmetics and other aids to increase their impact on the opposite sex. The ancient Assyrians wore their hair in a profusion of curls: Ovid reminds his male reader that to attract the ladies he must pay attention to bodily cleanliness and avoid scruffy hair and garments: during the eighteenth century European men and women both decked themselves in high, powdered wigs and squeezed themselves into corsets. All this effort was directed towards improving what nature had provided in the way of sex-appeal.

But, of course, ideas and standards of beauty and desirability are subject to fashion. Fashions in anatomical architecture, for instance, vary enormously. During the 1960's, the kind of feminine ideal in the West was the slim, narrow-hipped girl. Towards the close of the last century, the preferred sexually attractive figure was the bosomy girl with a wasp waist and wide pelvis who wore a bustle to add further emphasis to the hour-glass shape. Compare this with the medieval ideal of the slender, tiny-breasted Venus with a softly rounded stomach. And again—if the paintings of Rubens can be taken as a representation of a contemporary ideal—girls who today would be regarded as somewhat plump were thought to be enticing and seductive.

Clothes, too, have followed shapes and the cultural climate of the times. And in many periods, men have not hesitated to dress as showily as their womenfolk. In the Middle Ages, young men of the upper classes, reflecting the age of the troubadors and the concept of lively chivalry, wore extravagant costume and bright colors. The Elizabethan dandy, adventurous and confident, was as gaily decorated, jewelled, and perfumed as his lady. With the advent of puritanism, however, came a complete change in fashion. Clothes became sober in style and somber in color—while the woman who used cosmetics was considered "loose."

To the religious extremist, sex and sin were scarcely differentiated. Sexual intercourse was permissible only within marriage and with conception intended. It was considered sinful for a woman to dress in gay colors in order to attract a man's attentions: rather, she must conceal her body in enveloping garments to avoid stirring male desire at all. The strictest of all the Puritan sects even required their womenfolk to hide their hair under close-fitting hats.

In the Victorian age, a certain amount of decoration in women's clothes was acceptable (though the dress of the men was very restrained), but a form of puritanism pervaded upper and middle class society. It was expected that the sole aim of a "virtuous" woman was to marry an "upright" man and bear his children: no "respectable" woman was supposed to take pleasure in sexual intercourse: if she did enjoy love-making it was a source of secret shame. Thus the attitude to sex-appeal, as such, was colored by a certain amount of hypocrisy. However, beginning with the work of Freud, there has been a far-reaching reaction. Freud was able to show that, no matter how earnestly he may deny it, every individual possesses a sexual drive, and that emotional health depends to a large extent upon the degree to which sexuality and love are interwoven in experience.

Not unnaturally, the concept of sexual attraction varies not only between different historical periods but between one culture and another. Few Western men would be attracted by the deeply-scarred face of the women in certain African tribes, nor would they consider as sexually stimulating the minute feet crippled by binding of the Chinese women of fifty years ago. Equally well, no Western woman would find the face of a Papuan native, with a bone thrust through his nose, a sexually exciting image. What one culture finds sexually desirable is closely related to the local ideas of manhood or womanhood.

Ideas of what is alluring in costume vary widely, too: the concealment of the Japanese kimono and the Indian sari contrast markedly with the figure-revealing mini-skirt and tight sweater of the Western girl, but within the respective cultures the different outfits perform the same functions of emphasizing prevailing concepts of femininity. Which *part* of the female body must be concealed by costume is also a matter of local, usually religious custom.

Sex appeal cannot be viewed as a static thing. It is always *there* in the sense that men will always be aware of women as desirable, exciting, and potentially lovable creatures. And women cannot ignore the existence of men as strong, protective, and stimulating companions. Great variations, however, take place in the ways in which both men and women choose to emphasize their essential masculinity or femininity, in the hope that sexual attractiveness will lead on to mature love and mutual belonging.

31

A COMPARISON OF SEXUAL ATTITUDES AND BEHAVIOR IN AN INTERNATIONAL SAMPLE

Eleanore B. Luckey and Gilbert D. Nass

Sexual attitudes and practices of college and university youth have recently been surveyed and reported by numerous investigators. The present study includes data from the United States, Canada, England, Norway, and Germany. It should be stressed at the outset that this research was not designed to pinpoint such facts as how many men and women were having sexual outlets and how many times per week and what kind of outlets these were. The investigation purports rather to be a comparative study that suggests existing sexual attitudes and behaviors and reports similarities and differences which seem to exist between the sampled national populations. . . .

Unmarried, undergraduate university students from five countries were included in the sample. The United States was represented by 21 colleges and universities. These were selected with the aim of geographical distribution that would insure adequate representation of the entire country. Seven were in eastern states: a New England men's college, a private university in New York City, an Ivy League university, a state university in New England, a state college in New England, a private women's college in the northeast, and a private women's college known to have liberal parietal rules. Five were in middlewestern states: a state university, a Catholic university in a metropolitan area, a Protestant university in a nonmetropolitan area, a private coed university in a metropolitan area, and one in a nonmetropolitan area. Three were in southern states: a state university, a state university in the upper south, and a private university in a metropolitan area. Finally, six were in western states: a state university in the Rocky Mountain area, a state university in the southwest and one in the northwest, a state university in California and a private

one there, and a state college in the southwest.

Contained in the American sample were two all-male colleges and two all-female colleges; two were specifically church-related. Public and private, metropolitan and nonmetropolitan, secular and nonsecular, coeducational and sexually segregated schools were included. The varied sample was chosen to provide data suggestive of a national picture. In each school 100 students were contacted; in schools that were coeducational the population was half male and half female.

A major university was selected from each of the other countries. An equal number of men and women were chosen from each population. From the German University information was solicited from 450 individuals; each of the other foreign populations was 300. The 150 additional subjects in the German sample were included in order to compensate for using a mailed questionnaire rather than one personally handed to the subjects; it was assumed that the response rate would be lower. Choosing one university that is "typical" of any country's student population is difficult if not impossible—this being especially true in England because of the variety of university types. However, in each country the choice of a large university was made because of its diversified population both geographically and demographically.

The number of respondents was gratifying; out of a total of 3,450 solicitations there were 2,230 subjects (64.6 percent) who responded, representing a 66.8 percent return from the United States sample and a 61.6 percent from the foreign universities. The return was considered generally higher than can be expected from a study of this kind and implies an adequate sample from which to generalize. It is interesting that in the North American samples more women responded than men, but in all the European samples the reverse was true. This suggests that European women may be more reluctant to discuss sexual matters than the American and that American men are more reticent than European.

In the United States only third- and fourth-year students were included in the study, but because foreign universities are not structurally comparable with American universities, the subjects were selected according to age; those between 20 and 22 were included. In all samples the ages were *very* similar; the mean for men being 21.1 years and for women, 20.9 years. . . .

An inventory composed of 42 questions was designed so that answers could be solicited by checking or circling appropriate responses. In some instances explanatory or further comments were invited. The questionnaire was headed simply "College Checklist" and included questions on social sex roles including career roles for women, attitudes toward marriage especially with regard to sexual behavior, general views on affectional and sexual relationships, affectional and sexual experience of the respondent, and age.

The questionnaire along with a cover letter of explanation was distributed on each of the campuses, except the German, by student distributors who were supervised by a reliable assistant. Confidentiality and anonymity were assured, and stamped, addressed envelopes provided for direct return to the investigators. The German questionnaire which is the only one translated from English to the native language was *mailed* to a random sample of students. In all cases a randomly selected sample was attempted; although in schools where a goodly number of students were known to fit into a special category (for example, students living in their own apartments off campus), a special attempt was made to include some of these subjects.

There were some minor differences in questionnaires in order to keep them appropriate to the population with which they were being used. The German translation modified some of the questions, and there-

fore the data are not comparable; this will account for lack of German data in some categories. . . .

When asked if they thought individuals and society functioned best if male and female roles in life were different though equal, Canadian students provided the strongest approval; Norwegian students were by a considerable margin the least enthusiastic.

Coeducational living arrangements—with men and women occupying separate rooms but in the same dormitories, on the same floors, and in the same wings—were looked on with much more favor in the European schools than in those in Canada and the United States. In all cases men were more disposed to these living arrangements than were women.

At all universities there was little support for separating the sexes in the classroom. Fifteen percent of the males and 10 percent of the females in the United States sample indicated that they believed such separation "would produce a better environment for study." The Canadian and English response was similar, but only five percent of the Norway students held such a belief.

The subjects were asked, "Is a four-year college education generally as essential for the personal fulfillment and life satisfaction of girls as it is for men of comparable intelligence?" As might be expected, there were decidedly more women than men who replied affirmatively. In Norway 91.8 percent of the women and 81 percent of the men replied affirmatively. Only two-thirds of the American men were sure. European men and women were much closer in their agreement than were the North American, and more were sure that there should be equal education. The widest discrepancy between male and female subjects was found in the United States.

Female subjects were asked if they had seriously in mind an occupational career that they would like to pursue most of the next 20 years. Many more of the English and Norwegian women had such careers in mind than those of other countries. Half or fewer of the Canadian, German, and American women planned careers, but more than three-fourths of English and Norwegian. The dilemma posed by career-marriage decisions for women was seen to exist to a considerable degree in all countries. When they were asked if they believed a good many bright girls consciously downgraded their ambitions for a career because of fear that it might hurt their chances of marriage, 71 percent of the Canadians agreed as compared to 57 percent of those in the United States; although about 60 percent of the men in each of the two countries held this position. In all countries except the United States, more women than men believed this to be true. There was a marked difference between opinions of European men, of whom only about a third thought women had to play down their ambitions in contrast with those in North America. Although the percentage of assenting women ranged from 71 to 38, the greatest difference existed between American and Canadian women. There is no ready explanation of this difference, which is inconsistent with practically all the other findings indicating the United States and Canadian populations hold similar views.

Sex role differences were generally emphasized to a greater extent in the North American countries than in the English and Scandinavian sample where men and women expect more equalization and less differentiation. European students, to a greater extent than American students, preferred both mixed-sex dormitory arrangements and classrooms. The European women planned to have careers, saw it as not interfering with marital roles, and recognized [the] need for education. Their men agreed. Americans and Canadians tended more to see the woman's place in the home. . . .

Interesting ambiguities with regard to notions of parental independence were presented by the variation in opinions as to whether or not a strong society would be produced if social arrangements could be made that would enable all young people to be financially independent of their parents by the age of 21 regardless of whether they pursued higher education or not. England and Norway gave this idea the greatest support with about half of them agreeing to it. Germany gave it the least.

Men generally favored the idea to a greater extent than women.

A related dimension, that of the parentally financed undergraduate marriage, was supported by two-fifths of the English students, both men and women. About a fourth of the Canadian and United States students supported the position; less than a fifth of Norwegian men did.

The view that young people under 21 desire more guidelines and limits received the greatest support from Canadian and United States students (men 36 percent, women 54 percent). Only about 20 percent of the English supported the position, and in all countries women indicated a greater desire for guidelines than men.

Each national sample provided a different pattern in picking the category of people who should set male-female intimacy guidelines. Among persons who felt there was a need for more clearly defined standards, Canadian and American students most frequently designated "parents" and "adults" should be those to set the standards. English students favored "youthful peers" and "adults," and Norwegian students cited "parents" and "schools." "Churches" were virtually ignored by all males and were not much more frequently cited by the females.

Although no clear-cut or well-defined pattern emerged from these findings, it can be generally concluded that the English and Scandinavian youth favored greater financial and moral independence from the parental generation than the North American. However, the majority of young people in all countries rejected social arrangements which would make them financially independent of parents by age 21. They also rejected parentally financed education-marriage. Decidedly more North American than European students, and women more than men, felt guidelines and limits were needed for sexual standards, and only in England were "youthful peers" favored over adults for determining such standards. . . .

Marriage was given a strong vote of confidence by all the samples, as the majority responded negatively to the question, "Can you visualize a happy, satisfying life for yourself that might not include marriage?"

About 20 percent more Canadian and American youth responded "no" than European. Ten percent more of the Norwegian men than women replied negatively; this is the only response where the male percentage was higher than the female. Some of the subjects were not sure; English men more frequently indicated the "uncertain" response (31.6 percent) than any other group. Canadian females (15.7 percent) were less often in doubt than any other group. Twenty-nine percent of the Norwegian females and 26.2 percent of English females responded that they *could* be happy though unmarried, but only about 15 percent of Canadian and American women replied in the affirmative. About a fourth of the male subjects in the United States, Norway, and England believed they could live happily though unmarried. Few Canadian subjects—either men or women—indicated they fancied an unmarried life. Again it is the European samples that have indicated a greater break with the traditional pattern.

The ideal age for marriage was fairly uniform among the universities. Males at all schools indicated about 25 as the modal choice. American women most frequently indicated an age between 21 and 23; all other national groups indicated a year or two older. In general, both men and women in all samples indicated a preference for the man to be slightly older than the woman.

The idea that a couple who marry should have their first full sexual experience together found the greatest support among Canadian and Norwegian females. The least support was by English females. The range of difference was greater between female samples. The greatest congruence between the sexes was found in the United States sample, where about one-half thought this true.

An additional specification that the sexual experience should be "only after marriage" was preferred by all female subjects when compared to male and was marked by subjects of both sexes more frequently in American universities. English men and women, and then Norwegian, marked this qualification least frequently.

In an attempt to appraise attitudes toward the double standard sex code, the question was asked:

Do you think it is reasonable for a male who has experienced coitus elsewhere to expect that the girl he hopes to marry be chaste at the time of marriage?

A "yes" response was interpreted as potential support for the double standard. Virtually no support was given the idea by Norwegian students. American and Canadian females most strongly supported the double standard position with approximately a third of them agreeing; a fifth of the men from these same two countries held this view.

The German questionnaire was modified to read:

One often hears the opinion that it is better for a marriage if the girl is still a virgin before marriage but the man has had sexual experience beforehand. Other people say a man with sexual experience cannot expect to marry a virgin girl. With which opinion do you agree most?

Only 13.2 percent of the men and 18.9 percent of the women supported the double standard position. About a fourth of the women and a fifth of the men believed neither partner should have experience before marriage; two-thirds of the men and slightly more than half the women believed that both partners should have premarital experience. In all samples subjects rejected the double standard—European students more than North American. Interestingly, in all countries except England, women more frequently than men *supported* the double standard.

Also related to attitudes held toward the double standard was the inquiry:

Would it trouble you to marry a person who had experienced premarital coitus with someone else before becoming seriously involved with you?

The percentage of women answering "No" was highest in the United States and lowest in Canada; the greatest percentage of men was in Norway and the lowest, in Canada. Twice as many women as men in the

United States answered "No," and this represented by far the greatest discrepancy between the sexes in any one sample. As was expected, in all cases men indicated more concern than women about the chastity of their marital partner. This suggests that some male students, also primarily American and Canadian, encourage the double standard.

In all the samples both men and women subjects were approximately equally divided between those who held the opinion that an individual might have had numerous sexual affairs before marriage and still bring a deep and enduring commitment to the person he marries and those who either did not think so or were uncertain about it. Certainly it can be said that numerous premarriage sexual partners were not seen as a serious deterrent to the marriage relationship by the majority of students in each of the samples. Sexual activity prior to marriage was viewed negatively by more females than males, and Norwegian women were the most skeptical. Except for the American sample, the difference between countries was not so great as between the two sexes of specific countries. In the United States men and women showed remarkable agreement. It's interesting that in the United States and Canada, where there is considerably less premarital coitus, there are almost as many students who believe numerous sexual affairs would not interfere with marriage as in those countries where there is more premarital coitus. This would indicate that it is not fear that the experience would destroy some quality in the marriage that acts as a deterrent to premarital intercourse.

When asked the following question, "Yes" responses were high in the English and Norwegian samples; low in the American and German:

Regardless of age (after 16) or the stage of formal commitment, do you feel that full intimacy is appropriate if both persons desire it and they have a sense of trust, loyalty, protectiveness, and love?

In general, women subjects consistently were more reluctant to sanction such in-

timacy. The category receiving the greatest number of responses from all subjects in all countries was "Only if mature."

The following question was answered most frequently by all students in all countries by "Only if married" for ages prior to 18. However, generally marriage is seen as less important as the age of the individual increases.

What kind of relationship should prevail before a male and female should consider coitus as personally and socially reasonable?

Both English men and women, more than any other nationality, indicated that "going steady" and being "casually attracted" between ages 14–17 were appropriate conditions for intercourse; English women checked the response indicating coitus was appropriate *only* in marriage substantially less frequently than did women of any other country in all age categories from 14 to 24 and over.

The widest gap between categories for both men and women, in all age groups, and among all nationalities was between "going steady" and "good friends." In many instances but without a discernible pattern, more male subjects considered it appropriate to have coitus with one to whom he was casually attracted than with a good friend. Women seemed to favor slightly the friend over the casual attraction. These findings undoubtedly reflect the romantic concept that being in love and being physically attracted to a sexual partner is more appropriate than is a basis of friendship.

The English were generally more acceptant than other nationalities of premarital intercourse under a variety of conditions and at younger ages. Females in all samples generally expressed considerably greater support than did the males for consideration of coitus "only if married." Canadian females, the most conservative group, gave no support for coitus outside the married or engaged relationship for ages 14–17, but 27 percent approved when the age was 24 or over. Chronological age, which probably was judged to reflect personal maturity, was held by all subjects as an important factor in determining under what conditions coitus was appropriate.

When questioned about the opinion that a good lovemaking relationship was "almost always consummated by" mutual, simultaneous orgasm, respondents showed no national differences and no differences within the sexes. About half of the men thought it was true, about a third of the women.

By studying the opinions that were expressed toward marriage and sexual behavior, one can generally conclude that although traditional values are held to some extent in all countries, what may be called "liberal views" are also to be found in each of the national samples. European countries are more liberal than those on the North American continent. Men are less invested in marriage and less restricted in sex than women. Marriage is still an overwhelmingly popular way of life, and the age of marriage is ideally the early twenties. Indicative of a swing away from the traditional was the evidence that the double standard of sexual morals is definitely on its way out, and students are not greatly concerned about the first sexual experience being in marriage or being with the partner who eventually becomes the spouse. Even having several sexual partners before marriage was not judged particularly detrimental to the marriage. Age was viewed as a very important factor determining under what conditions coitus was appropriate; the older the individual the more freedom he had.

The English in general were seen to have the least restrictive attitudes toward sexual behavior. Norwegian women, although liberal, tended to be a good deal less liberal than their men. The Canadian sample held somewhat more conservative attitudes than the United States, but in most instances the two samples resembled each other and could be contrasted with the European samples. . . .

When women were asked to classify the men whom they had dated in the past year into those they thought (a) would be frightened by real intimacy; (b) those who seemed content with gestures of intimacy such as a farewell embrace; (c) those who were happy enough if their hands were allowed to wander; and (d) those who were disappointed if they couldn't persuade the girl to go all the way, more American and Canadian girls marked *b* than any other response. English and Norwegian marked *d* and German marked *c*. The contrast between Canadian and American women when compared to English women is particularly noticeable on response *d*. The North American women indicated that men were decidedly less demanding than English women reported men to be.

Canadian and United States men give a very congruent picture of their dates during the past year. Both indicated most of their dates usually went along for fun up to the point of light petting. English male students most frequently suggested the partner resisted real intimacies unless there had been talk of love. German students most frequently indicated their dates were pretty conservative beyond perhaps a goodnight kiss, and Norwegian men most frequently described their dates as "happy to go as far as I want to go, short of coitus."

The description that "They seem to want to go all the way if we have a chance" was marked most frequently by Norwegian students and least frequently by Canadian students. Specific behaviors of dating partners cannot be determined with any reliability by the responses of either women or men subjects or by comparing the two. The multiple responses of male students are especially difficult to interpret; however the composite picture of dating behavior that does appear from the data is one of conservatism in Canada and the United States, where men and women agree that gestures of affection and light petting are modal. In contrast more European women (especially English and Norwegian) reported that men are disappointed if "you don't want to go all the way," and more European men reported that women want to go all the way! The fact that European students do indeed engage in more sexual activity on dates was confirmed when subjects reported on their own sexual behavior.

Subjects were asked to indicate their participation in a spectrum of sexual behaviors from light embracing and holding hands to coitus. Among the males, Canadian students generally indicated the highest frequencies of participation in the casual and light petting behavior categories, and the English students the highest in general petting, nude embrace, and coitus. German men consistently reported the lowest rate of involvement in all categories. The pattern of behaviors reported by American and Canadian men was strikingly similar in all categories, with Canadian men consistently reporting somewhat more conservative behavior.

As would be expected, there is a decided drop in the number of subjects who report petting below the waist of the girl and petting below the waist of *both* the man and the girl. Mutual genital petting behavior is reported only slightly more frequently than coitus by men subjects of all countries and by women in European countries; however, 15 percent more American and Canadian girls report mutual genital petting than report coitus. Apparently a crucial point in determining whether most subjects continue to coitus or not is mutual genital petting. This is *less* true for girls in Canada and the United States than for any other group.

The reported coital participation among males in order of frequency was: England highest, followed by Norway, then the United States and Canada, and lowest Germany. The pattern indicated by German and Norwegian men is that coitus is more frequent than mutual genital petting. All the other samples reported that for some five to eight percent of the men, genital petting does not continue to coitus.

Men who reported involvement in whipping and spanking together with sexual intimacy were most frequently English. The second highest frequency for men was the United States sample which reported less than half the incidence of the English. German men reported the least.

English men reported the greatest patronage of prostitutes; then the German; and lowest were the Norwegian. A little more than four percent of United States and Canadian men reported they had had sex on a pay-as-you-go-basis. It is especially interesting to note that Germany, which had the lowest coital percentage, had the second highest percentage of prostitution, and Norway which has the second highest coital involvement has the lowest prostitution reported. This leads one to conclude

that quite a different set of values operate in the two countries, and that Germany maintains more of the traditional point of view and condones the double standard to a greater extent.

Women subjects in general reported less participation in all categories of sexual behavior than men did. The highest rates for sexual behavior except for light embraces were reported by English women. Canadian, American, and German females showed similar and slightly less participation through the less intimate and the petting behaviors to the nude embrace; in these same categories the Norwegian females consistently reported the least participation. However, with the nude embrace and coitus, the international female pattern changed; a greater proportion of German and Norwegian women reported involvement and a lesser proportion of Canadian and American women. It can be assumed that petting as a prelude to coitus is more frequently the practice with European women, but with American and Canadian women it is either an end in itself or is the cutoff point of sexual activity. The order of coital frequency as indicated by women subjects is: highest, English; then Germany; Norway; and finally the United States and Canada. These data would tend to confirm the male responses which followed the same pattern except for Germany.

A third of the English women reported "one-night stands"; and although more than 20 percent less frequently reported, the Norwegian females ranked second highest. The United States, Canada, and Germany followed in that order. Although the percentages reported by men subjects were considerably higher, the order of frequency was the same.

The one behavior category in which the female subjects reported in both a similar pattern and a similar percentage as the males within their respective sample was that of "whipping and spanking." The generally low percentage may account somewhat for this finding. Both England and Norway, which report a proportionately greater number of students engaged in these sadomasochistic practices, also rank high in coital frequency. The positive correlation of the two factors can be speculated upon, but accounting for the relationship remains for further investigation.

The ages at first petting and first coital experience are given in Table 1. The mean age for males at first petting was lowest (15.6 years) in England and Norway, eight months older in the United States, and a year older for both Canada and Germany. English females began petting earliest at age 15.6; Norwegian females almost a year later; German females at age 17; and finally Canadian and American females still four months later. English students who began petting youngest also had intercourse youngest. German and Norwegian students who were the oldest at first intercourse began petting experiences at approximately the same ages as men in other samples. United States and Canadian men and women report the shortest interval between the age at which they began petting and the age at which it was consummated in intercourse. In all cases men reported first petting at an age younger than women; except for Canadian and English men who reported first coitus at nearly the same age as Canadian and English women, men were also younger at age of first coitus.

It is interesting to note the pattern of delay between first petting and first coitus for each sample. The shortest interval is demonstrated by the Canadian and American girl. This is followed by the American man and the English man and woman. Norwegian and German men and women delay coitus for the longest intervals—all over two years—and Norwegian men wait nearly three years.

Considerable variation exists in the sample in the reported number of coital partners. The greatest promiscuity was reported by English students, with almost three-fourths of the males reporting "several" and "many" partners; and two-thirds of the females reported in these same categories. About 58 percent of the American male students reported "several" and "many" partners; about half the Norwegian males reported "several" and "many" partners; only a third of the German men reported in those categories. As is to be expected, women students in all samples were less promiscuous. Nearly half of the German, American, and Canadian women reported only "one partner," and congruently, fewer of them indicated "many" and "several." Fewer than a fourth of the Canadian and German women marked these combined categories. About a third of the American women and nearly half of the Norwegian women marked these. Nearly two-thirds of the English women marked one or the other of these categories.

Alcohol was not reported as a major factor in first coital experience by many of the

TABLE 1.   MEAN AGES OF MALES AND FEMALES AT AGE OF FIRST PETTING EXPERIENCE AND OF FIRST COITUS

Universities	First Petting Mean Age		First Coitus Mean Age	
	Males	Females	Males	Females
United States (N)	16.3 (608)	17.3 (612)	17.9 (374)	18.7 (297)
Canada	16.6 (85)	17.3 (76)	18.5 (50)	18.4 (29)
England	15.6 (117)	15.8 (81)	17.5 (90)	17.5 (57)
Germany	16.6 (107)	17.0 (90)	19.0 (61)	19.5 (57)
Norway	15.6 (73)	16.5 (50)	18.4 (53)	18.8 (29)

subjects. More English females reported they were under the influence of alcohol when they first had intercourse than any other group in the sample; even so, more than half indicated, "I and my partner had not had anything alcoholic to drink." The English had the highest rate reporting "both under the influence of alcohol"; and the German the lowest except for Norwegian women, none of whom reported the couple had been under the influence of alcohol. More Canadian youth than any other reported *no* involvement with alcohol and first coitus—about three-fourths; 68 percent of the Norwegian men and women reported in that same category and about two-thirds of the American men and women. More English men and women reported alcohol was involved with one or the other or both partners than any other nationality.

Although there are some irregularities and unevenness of pattern, the total picture that one gains from looking at these data is a consistent one presented by the agreement of each sex and by congruent findings in each category of behavior. The English student has more sexual activity, begins younger, has more partners, has more one-night stands, more sadomasochistic experiences, and is more likely to have been influenced by alcohol at the time of the first coital experience.

North American students are less experienced and generally more conservative; the Canadian youth is somewhat less liberal than his counterpart in the United States. The Norwegian student tends to be less the "swinger" than the English. Premarital sexual experience does not start so early and is restricted to fewer partners. Although the picture of German students is not so clear, they generally occupy a place between the liberal English and Norwegian samples and the North American.

SUMMARY AND DISCUSSION

(1) Sex Role Differences

Some interesting consistencies and inconsistencies are presented by the findings with regard to sex role differences when the various countries are compared. Although in the United States and Canada more students agreed that men and women were indeed different though equal, and fewer than half of the Norwegian students took this position, it was the Norwegian students who in the largest percentage indicated that a four-year college education was generally as essential for women as men. English students tended to agree with the Norwegian; and consistent with this both Norwegian and English female students expressed in greater numbers an intent to follow a career over most of the first 20 years of their out-of-college life.

The Canadian and United States students presented a different picture from the European in that more of them stressed "equality but difference," and fewer of them believed a four-year college education is necessary for women. The North American women tended to be less interested in a career. Canadian men and women more than those of any other country believed women consciously downgraded career ambitions in favor of marriage potential. The European students generally felt this was less true.

European schools favored coed living arrangements much more than North American students, but all students favored mixed classes in the classroom.

Making a broad generalization from these statistics, we could say with reliability that the European students—both men and women—indicated a greater acceptance of sexual equality of opportunity, both in the academic world and in the professional. Canadian men and women expressed ideas which to a greater extent indicated that the female's role and her preparation for it was marital rather than professional. They denied, however, that this marital role was not "equal" with the male role.

(2) Parental Independence

English students favored independence from parents and early marriage with financial support from parents to a greater extent than students of any other nation and rejected the idea that more definite guidelines and limits for youth were needed. Both American and Canadian students were less inclined to want either earlier independence or subsidized marriage and were more inclined to think adult guidelines would be a good idea. There was virtually no support given to religious agencies as a crucial molder of guidelines or limits for youth in the realm of sexual intimacy.

One might conclude from these responses that English youth felt more competent to start and manage life on their own, given the freedom to do so.

(3) Attitudes Toward Marriage and Sexual Behavior

That the majority of youth the world around (or at least in this sample) still believe a satisfying life includes marriage is indicated; however, North American students were more sure of this than European. It was surprising to the investigators, however, that nearly a quarter of the samples said marriage was *not* necessary. All samples agreed that men should marry ideally at about age 25 and women at about 23.

Except in England, women more than men favored the idea that the man and woman who marry should have their first sexual experience together. Again the more conservative answers were expressed by the North American students, who preferred coital partners to be marriage partners and were more skeptical of promiscuity and its influence in marriage than were the European students.

Women students in general were more conservative (even in liberal countries) than were men. The women, as much as or more than the men, seem to perpetuate the double standard, and it was perpetuated by North American youth more generally than European. Women are willing to accept lack of chastity on the part of the male more readily than the male accepted the lack of chastity of the female; although Norwegian students did not seem to value premarital chastity, they rejected promiscuity and the double standard of behavior.

English students seem to operate most nearly on the single sex standard, and that standard was described as liberal. Again, United States and Canadian students were more conservative; they were more caught in the traditional double standard.

The majority of students in all samples agree that "maturity" should be a major criteria on which decision and choice of coital partners should be determined; English students, when compared with students from other countries, indicated that this choice can be made at an earlier age.

(4) Sexual Experience and Behavior

Reports by both men and women subjects of their sexual behavior was consistent with their attitudes. More European than North American women reported that men wanted to "go farther on dates"; more European than American men said that women were willing to go farther! Canadian and American men and women were more conservative—content with petting and necking.

North American women, contrary to European women, indicated their dates were generally content with a moderate degree of intimacy instead of disappointment if they would not go all the way. European men, contrary to North American men, indicated women dates seemed to want to go all the way when the opportunity was available.

While the investigators tried to construct patterns of sexual behavior from the responses of men and women students indicating their degree of involvement in activities which range from light embracing to coitus, it became obvious that English men and women more freely participate in a gamut of sexual activities including more genital petting, more frequent coitus, more patronage of prostitution, more sadomasochistic practices, more one-night stands. They start both petting and coitus at a younger age, have more sexual partners, and report alcohol has been a factor in initial coital experience. The general ranking of male student coital rates by countries provides the following descending order: England, Norway, United States, Canada,

Germany. The order for female student coital rates was: England, Germany, Norway, United States, and Canada.

Canadian and American youth report patterns of behavior very similar to each other and are in general to be considered conservative regarding sexual behavior. German students hold the most conservative attitudes and exhibit the most restricted behavior among the European samples; Norwegian students were more liberal, and the English consistently the most liberal. Females, as one would expect, are more conservative in all countries than are the males. English women, however, hold views and behave very similarly to English men.

It can be generally concluded from looking at this mass of data that both attitudes and behavior of North American students are more conservative than those of the European. On the background of other studies done earlier, it is evident that there is an increasingly liberal attitude toward sex and generally more premarital participation.

The study gives a reliable report on sexual attitudes and behaviors held by university students in the participating countries, but it fails in that it gives little clue to the meaning or motivation associated with these. Meaning can perhaps be projected into the statistics, but so much of interpretation lies in the eye of the interpreter, that these investigators prefer to let the statistics speak for themselves as they can. The cross-cultural aspects of these data have provided a sound basis on which a comparative assessment of general trends in university students' sexual attitudes and behavior can be made. The variations that have been found suggest the need for further study to explicate and inquire into the meaning of the differential findings, as well as to continue the incorporation of research controls through cross-cultural analysis.

32

"THE ARRANGEMENT" AT COLLEGE: PART I

William A. McWhirter

On April 16, 1968 the Judicial Council of Barnard College at Columbia University listened gravely as one of its sophomores admitted that for two years she had lived out of wedlock with a Columbia Undergraduate, violated school regulations, and had lied in doing so. But Linda LeClair, who stood and smiled at the council as she read her statement, was unrepentant: the fault, she declared, was Barnard's. "I have disregarded a regulation which I believe to be unjust," said Linda LeClair.

The campus Jewish and Protestant counselors agreed. So did a philosophy professor. And the Judicial Council, which voted to suspend Linda from the Barnard snack bar. "Terrific," said Linda LeClair.

A sexual anthropologist of some future century, analyzing the pill, the drive-in, the works of Harold Robbins, the Tween-Bra, and all the other artifacts of the American Sexual Revolution, may consider the case of Linda LeClair and her boyfriend, Peter Behr, as a moment in which the morality of an era changed. Linda was headlined as "Barnard's Kiss-and-Tell Girl." She got a letter from a Billy Jones, Jr., of "Bronxville

Manor, N.J.": "What kind of material are we going to have to build a better world if WHOREDOM takes over." *No question mark.* And from a "Not So Old-fashioned Parent" with "an old Jewish saying 'From A Sow's Ear You Cannot Make A Silk Purse.'" A Wisconsin undergraduate wrote to ask if he should live with his girl friend (Linda and Peter replied it all depends); as a statistic perhaps, a woman revealed that her parents lived together in 1897; and someone sent a Roy Rogers and Dale Evans prayer leaflet.

Martha Peterson, the president of Barnard, in a letter she wrote to Barnard alumnae around the world, faintly referred to "difficult moments" in a "rather unpleasant two months" involving that affair of "the sophomore in question." "We learned also," said Miss Peterson, "to our regret, that public interest in sex on the college campus is insatiable."

The case of Linda LeClair, to Miss Peterson's further regret, may have stimulated the public interest in what is becoming a new reality on the U.S. campus—the unwed and unlawful union or, more simply put, in 1968, The Arrangement. It had been, it seems, always on the way, like some oncoming meteor or posse, until now only overhead or down the road or somewhere else. Linda, of course, did not usher in a sexual revolution on the campus; she only announced that it has been there for some time.

Few contingency plans ever saved their institutions from the revolutions that overtook them. Still, in the past five years virtually every major campus in the U.S. has tried to reform itself in advance of the new order. Most of the old measures of social conduct—the ones that said a couple must have at least three feet touching the floor at all times, or that when sitting together their heads must be at least six inches apart, or that when visiting a dorm room during the proper hours they must leave the door open at book width—have been scrapped. In most cases, visiting hours for dates in the dorms have been lengthened, room visits extended, overnight leaves from the dormitories allowed, off-campus residency requirements reduced. In areas as conservative as the University of Texas in Austin, coeducational dorms are under construction, and virtually everywhere that legendary Necker Checker, a cross between Mary Worth and Casey the Cop—the Dorm Mother—is on her way out. The universities, for the most part, stop short of distributing the pill to unmarried students, but their reasons have little to do with student conduct. "It's purely a matter of logistics," says Dr. Donald MacKinnon, director of the health service at UCLA. "We don't have space for repeated physical examinations for girls on pills." Still, the new campus freedoms were seldom free enough for the students who, in record numbers, have slipped off campus into everything from bare attics to furnished apartments, splitting the rent and sharing pad, bed, and shopping cart in an all-American-style live-in.

In the past month, *Life* has surveyed one university as it confronts the new morality, has spoken with the professional observers of the phenomenon, and interviewed more than 75 couples on a dozen U.S. campuses. The backgrounds of the couples were too divergent for any generalization; neither family income, political action, age, sexual experience, maturity, nor home life provide any common denominator. The couples do and they do not come on scholarships and from fat-cat ranch-style homes; they do and they do not have hang-ups; they do and they do not resent their fathers, brothers, sisters; they do and they do not keep house well, dress neatly, live happily. All of them do claim, however, that the old strictures *thou shalt not, thou wilt not, thou should not, thou wouldn't dare* have come tumbling down, and in their place nothing much has gone up: "It's a very passive thing with us," explained one couple living together in New York. "We aren't doing it purposely against anything, we just don't see anything wrong with it, and so we go ahead and do it." The Renaissance inquiry *Que sais-je?* ("What do I know?") has more often become "What do I care?" And the arrangement takes just about any form under the sun.

In Santa Barbara, near the University of California campus, couples double and triple up in Isla Vista, a swinging array of stucco flats, sliding picture windows, carports, and porches with charcoal grills.

In New Orleans, Patty fixes supper for Al, then walks with him through the French Quarter to evening mass at St. Louis Cathedral; she kisses him on the cheek and he leaves to catch the bus for night classes at Louisiana State University. Under their arrangement, he or she may or may not be home that night; the rule is "Don't get hung up." At Berkeley, in a modern apartment with Picasso prints, a TV set propped up on concrete blocks, and a dressing table covered with eight bottles of after-shave and cologne, two cans of spray deodorant, hair spray, hand lotion, perfume, and an empty rum bottle, Ed, 22, and Carol, 21, live with two of Ed's roommates, sharing their bedroom with one of them. "He uses ear plugs," Ed says. On the closet door is a poster from Planned Parenthood: "Hallelujah, the Pill."

In California, George and Kathy live in a corner apartment in a roomy old frame house a few doors down from a Presbyterian church in a pleasant, tree-shaded neighborhood. George is a '67 psychology graduate, working at a center for the mentally retarded in a nearby town, and an amateur painter. Kathy was a junior Phi Beta Kappa and was approached to be a *Playboy* playmate; she declined.

In Los Angeles, Jo is a bouncy, jubilant coed at UCLA who says *kinda, gonna, wanna, sorta, groovy;* her guy, Steve, is a man, he says, of few words. They go to the movies. In Florida, Bob and Marie live in a log cabin beside a lake; he writes fiction and poetry. Across the country, Tom and Paget live in a large apartment in a bogus Tudor-style building and own a 40-foot boat.

In such times as these, however, history will often have its little joke. And so it was this spring at Barnard when it found as its symbol of this revolution a champion as staunch, as bold, and as unalluring as Linda LeClair.

Linda is ruddy, good-natured, out-going, woodsy, and overweight. She and Peter both have the slightly rumpled look of campers at least a couple of days past a fresh change of clothing. Pilgrim plain,

Yankee stubborn, she joyfully struts, swaggers, and speaks over the sound of a jackhammer in the street. But at times, Linda appears to sit at a distance and watch, bewildered and amused by what has happened. "Sometimes I find it hard to think of myself as a person any more," she says. "I have ceased to exist. I am Linda LeClair, the issue. The other day Peter and I went to a lecture and listened to a discussion of the LeClair affair. I swear I looked around to see who she was and if she was there."

Peter is, well, mostly just Peter, earnest, well-meaning, and full of plans. He signs his letters "Yours respectfully in peace," and he was most respectful when he wrote an objecting four-page letter to his draft board last fall. "I am trying to make sense of the world around me," he said. "I am trying to understand why poverty, ignorance, violence, hate, and starvation exist when man has it in his power to overcome these forces." They plan to march to Resurrection City and perhaps spend the summer at a Connecticut farm for nonviolence.

Sitting on the lawn in front of the entrance to Barnard, Peter called over to Linda, already up and growing restless.

"Hey, he wants to know if I was your first encounter? Was I?"

"My first real one," Linda said softly. Then she grinned. "Get up, Peter; the revolution's calling."

The revolution does not mean everyone has joined it, so much as that anybody can. And Linda and Peter are, by all indications far more symbols than typical members. The greatest gap, of course, occurred when they went public. Virtually none of the couples in *Life's* survey would consent to the use of their names even when they allowed themselves to be photographed. State laws (some of which do forbid "lewd and lascivious" cohabitation and govern fornication in detail) rarely concerned them so much as the effect on their families. Most had not told their parents of their arrangement and shielded themselves by either paying double rent or switching apartments. ("Everyone," says a Barnard girl, "ends up paying rent somewhere, but hardly ever in the apartment she's living in.")

The parents who know are naturally far

more numerous than the ones who are told. In those cases, their children believe, they would just prefer not to be confronted. They continue calling or sending mail to one at the other's apartment, all the while pretending that at the critical point their children separate and retreat to safe corners.

The ones who do share their children's confidence are usually just resigned to the arrangement. Sometimes they are curious, sometimes helpful. One parent, when told, suggested that the couple should avoid buying expensive furniture which would become an "albatross" when, as he assumed, they broke up. Another offered to pay for a second apartment to maintain appearances.

"I told her she has to live with her own conscience," explained one California mother. "She told me that she felt very comfortable, that her conscience didn't bother her, so that was it. That satisfied me. My husband and I just briefly looked at each other and said we'd accept it."

To judge by the arrangement, the sexual revolution may come to an even duller and more conventional end than did the old standard. The couples endlessly claim its chief benefits to be comfort, security, and happiness. Father Edward Hanrahan, dean of students at Boston College, even hazards a guess that "they have less sex than they did before they started living together."

"We're not hippies," says a coed in New York City. "We're not revolutionaries. We're not even very social." If this is liberation, 20 years of anxiety by their parents seems to have been in vain.

The couples are not prepared to have children outside marriage. "I don't care for my kids being illegitimate particularly," says a UCLA coed. A physical education major in Ohio says gallantly: "If she became pregnant, I would marry her right away. I don't have the right to force a child to start life as an outcast." Linda LeClair in her freshman year knew of six pregnancies in her dormitory; five ended in abortions and the sixth in adoption, after which the mother tried to commit suicide.

Free and sprung, the couples are self-admittedly on the square side. They see a small circle of friends, study, drive each other out for pizzas, and even save some money. But nearly all of them picture their situations as ideal. In fact, when the parent of a college undergraduate finds his child cheerful, clear-eyed, and relaxed, his checkbook balanced, his grades going up, and wanting to strike up a conversation, perhaps he should begin to suspect something. The couples' philosophy seems less indebted to *Playboy* than *Peanuts*, in which sex is not so much a pleasure as a warm puppy. "Besides being my lover," says Meredith, a California girl, "Bob is my best friend in all the world."

"I'm much more serene," says another student. "I don't seek crowds or artificial entertainment. It gives one a great deal of comfort and peace of mind."

"Living together," says Laura in San Francisco, "is nice on Sunday mornings when you have nothing to do. It's a warm-blankety thing for me emotionally."

A few, however, care enough to preach the advantages of the relationship. "It's not exactly the new morality that everyone used to talk about a few years ago," a Harvard senior says. "It's a fundamental new consciousness that is much bigger than morality."

And then there is Wayne of Berkeley: "We started expressing ourselves and it was accurate because we could feel it. Through our conversations we really got to like each other [several months after they were already living together]. It was not a physical thing at first at all. I sat down and I just watched her. And I had lots of really very good thoughts as I watched her. I could see the integrity of her independence. So I said to myself, maybe this is a very good thing."

"We're not just eating and sleeping together," says a Detroit student, "we're protesting the war together."

The couples claim they are united for reasons of health, politics, economy, truth, beauty, or, as a Michigan State student says, "because living together helps studies." Anything, in fact, but sex. Or, forbid it, love. "We think it's kind of corny to say it, although I am usually the one to broach it," explains Millie at Berkeley. "I say it, that I love Ned, because I feel I have to because I want him to know, but then I want to slap myself; it sounds too Dick-and-Jane-in-the-spring." The couples even sound a bit stiff-backed when they refer to sex; more than a few of them used the neo-Biblical refrain, "to have sex."

At Berkeley, however, one undergraduate became virtually the sole exponent to suggest that there might be something more to living together than just the discovery of a meaning to life. "We like what we are doing," he says. "We're quite happy the way we are. Living together we can screw all the time."

One advantage of the arrangement, of course, is that it is so easily entered into—no blood tests, no papers, no waiting. In fact, there is often so little to be said about so unset and undetermined an undertaking that, most often, nothing is said at all. "People fall into it," says Linda LeClair. "It's a nonverbal thing."

Take DeeDee and Mike at Columbia. "We began studying together," she says. "Then I made his dinner before we studied. Then we came back and I made him coffee. At first, I let him out. Then he let himself out, then he stayed and I made him coffee in the morning. Then he went shopping for groceries and in a week he was here all the time."

"Do you consider yourselves engaged or going steady or . . . ?" a couple at Florida State University in Tallahassee was asked. "We don't consider ourselves anything," the nonmate said. "We've never tried to pin it down." In Iowa City, Iowa, a girl says, "I guess he came and never left." At L.S.U.,

Dale says brightly that her arrangement with Tom "is the first time I've gone steady."

Presumably the end of the arrangement should be just as casual as its beginning. But it rarely works that way and most of the students say they are ready to accept that. There is no joint account to close out, no property to divide, no family, no ties. Still, the nonmarriage works most often to bind. "Sometimes I think of moving back to the sorority house," says Marilyn, "but I can't leave for more than a few minutes without turning around and coming right back." The couples also say the break would be equally painful and traumatic if they had been having an affair or dating steadily. Much of what began nonverbally remains that way; the students do not see too clearly through their rationalizations—and probably understand the wisdom of not trying too hard to. Perhaps half the couples will marry after school. The figure, the *Life* reporters estimate, would be considerably higher if the girls had their way. But then it is hard to ask only one revolution to change all things.

Many of the couples seem to have embarked on an experiment happily and exuberantly on all levels, gaining a variety and depth from a single relationship that once was considered too much a burden for the young.

Only one parent felt that her son had been set back somewhat by his arrangement. Her son, a track star in Los Angeles, just wasn't jumping as high as he used to.

33

"THE ARRANGEMENT" AT COLLEGE: PART II

Albert Rosenfeld

How real, how revolutionary is the "sexual revolution" on the campus? Though no one has yet carried out any truly definitive research in this area, a number of scientists and statisticians have done significant studies that provide tentative answers. The most ambitious of these is an in-depth survey of 1,200 students at 12 colleges by Drs. William Simon and John Gagnon of Indiana University's Institute for Sex Research (formerly headed by Kinsey). Similar studies have been made by Dr. Ira L. Reiss of the University of Iowa as well as by Dr. Joseph Katz of Stanford's Institute for the Study of Human Problems.

The findings of all three are in substantial agreement—and are confirmed by the observations of Dr. William H. Masters and Mrs. Virginia E. Johnson, the pioneer sex researchers who wrote *Human Sexual Response*. Their travels over the past few years have given them ample opportunity to gain insight into students' sexual values and attitudes, through long and free-wheeling bull sessions on campuses all over the country.

The consensus is that (1) the sexual revolution is real, but (2) its extent is highly exaggerated. Measured in terms of promiscuity, of students hopping into bed with anyone who happens to strike their fancy, it is simply a myth. Promiscuity does exist, of course, and has its visible and highly vocal supporters. But promiscuity was not invented by the current college generation, and the evidence indicates that it is no more common than it ever was.

The more important changes in student sexuality are seen in attitude rather than behavior. "If behavior has not altered in the last century as much as we might think," says Dr. Reiss, "attitudes *have*—and attitudes and behavior seem closer today than for many generations." Sex is thought of less in terms of the mere sex act itself and more as just one ingredient of a total relationship. "Sexual intimacy, where it occurs," says Dr. Katz, "takes place in the context of a relationship that is serious rather than casual." And in that context it grows less furtive and more open—and certainly more openly discussed. It is not that students do not feel guilty about sex, especially as they begin a new phase, whether it is kissing, petting, or actual intercourse. But Dr. Reiss finds that "guilt feelings do not generally inhibit their sexual behavior." Once they begin, they tend to continue. The result is not remorse, but a gradual diminution of guilt. The fact that students are more open about sex does not mean they think they have it all figured out. Beneath the "cool" façade they still experience a great deal of anxiety.

The shift in view is much more evident among females than among males. Though precise figures are not yet available, it is evident from current studies that the proportion of coeds who participate in premarital sex has gone up phenomenally in the last 10 to 20 years, while the percentage of males who do so has remained just about the same. By their senior year in college, a high percentage of the females and an even higher percentage of the males have had sexual intercourse, although a sizable number of both sexes still maintain their virginity throughout their college years. It is also true that a good many students of both sexes never even date, so the "revolution" cannot be considered universal by any means.

While the average coed has shed some of her inhibitions about premarital sex, she has certainly not abandoned a moral outlook. What we are seeing, Dr. Katz points out, is "not so much a decline in moral codes as a change in their contents." A girl may not consider it immoral to sleep with a man she is in love with or wants to marry; but the same girl may consider it quite immoral to engage in indiscriminate sex—even if only necking or petting in the back seat of a car—with casual dates for whom she has no real feeling or attachment. In this sense, actions that were once acceptable no longer are.

Some of these revised standards have begun to brush off on the males. For one thing, now that it is no longer unthinkable for a "nice girl" to engage in sex, it is rarely necessary for a college man to undergo his sexual initiation in the company of a prostitute. Strangely enough, the greater willingness of the female has made the male less rather than more promiscuous. He too tends to seek longer-lasting relationships in which he feels relatively comfortable and secure.

"The double standard on the campus is dead," says Dr. Masters flatly. But this is not borne out by the recent studies. Males still have sex more frequently and more promiscuously than females. Many still do tend to regard girls as sex objects, while girls seldom take such a limited view of males. But the disparity in both attitude and behavior is much less than it used to be. And the double standard might indeed vanish were it not for an unexpected obstacle: the females don't *want* it to vanish. This contradicts the popular stereotyped version of the situation, where the woman demands sexual equality while the man protests mightily. The surprising fact is that males are much readier to extend equal sexual privileges than the females are willing to accept them.

Nor do most of the young women who practice premarital intercourse consider themselves to be in revolt against their parents' moral codes. Many of these have parents who, as their daughters see it, hold fairly liberal views about sex. Among students, the most permissive in terms of either practicing premarital sex themselves or condoning it in others is the only child. The least permissive is the oldest child who feels responsible for his younger brothers and sisters. Among parents, the degree of permissiveness in regard to premarital sex tends to decline as their own children move into the vulnerable age ranges.

There has been much speculation that the pill has accelerated the willingness to engage in sex. The studies all refute this. As long as any effective means of contraception is at hand, those who want to have sex do; and the arrival of a more effective or simpler contraceptive does not appreciably change the situation. For that matter, the high number of premarital pregnancies indicates that the absence of contraception is not necessarily a deterrent. "The presence of the pill does not make people decide to have sex," says Dr. Gagnon. "It is after they decide to have sex that they go get the pill."

As a rule it is largely in the junior and senior years that coeds, by this time considerably influenced by open talk as well as by the example of others, reach the point where they feel it is all right to have sex in a relationship where love—and the hope (though not the assurance) of marriage—resides. "These relationships," says Dr. Simon, "are not experimental sexual unions. In fact, the erotic component is surprisingly small. I have had couples protest indignantly the idea that sex was the major factor that brought them together. One young man insisted, 'We are not sleeping together, we are *living* together.' These couples tend to be quite conventionally monogamous, with no swapping around of partners. They are very much like old married folks, who would rather play bridge than make love. Sometimes the only consideration that keeps them from actually getting married is economic—they don't want the old man to stop sending his checks. Those who look to the campus scene for sexual titillation are bound to be disappointed."

Dr. Reiss predicts "a period of greater permissiveness, and even greater frankness" ahead, and a continuing trend toward equalization of sexual behavior. Like Dr. Masters, he foresees the steady erosion of the double standard. "With the decline of the double standard and the growth of healthier, more open sexual attitudes," says Dr. Masters, "we will see less promiscuity than ever, and stronger rather than weaker relationships." Drs. Simon and Gagnon see sex playing a much less important role in human relationships as it takes on a different perspective.

But they warn that no one can really foresee how things will go in the future. Young people have clearly been adopting independent sexual standards and values. "Even though the revolution so far has been much less radical than some people have believed," says Dr. Simon, "the current generation *has* made an open break with tradition. The major result so far is a much greater freedom to *talk* about sex. How far the next generation may go toward translating the talk into action is an open question."

34

THE PLEASURES AND PAIN OF THE SINGLE LIFE

Time Essay

There is a new, privileged, spotlighted, envied group in the U.S. It is composed of "the singles"—the young unmarried whose label connotes, as in tennis, an endeavor more vigorous, more skilled, and more fun than mere doubles. Proportionately, there are [more] singles in the population [under 35] than there were 20 years ago, because young Americans are tending to marry at a [later] age. . . . They are the focus of a major part of advertising and salesmanship, the direct target of new approaches in housing and entertainment, the considerable despair of some established institutions, and the apostolate of a freer code of mores for the young. In some quarters, they are called—or like to call themselves—the "swingles."

Not every single, nor perhaps even a majority, participates fully in the subculture. To enjoy it to a considerable degree, a single must be relatively young, relatively well-to-do, and live in a big city. Participation begins with graduation from college, which represents both in symbol and reality an end of dependence on family. The new graduate takes off for the big city, looking for a job and an apartment of his or her own. And he begins determinedly to swing. In the ultimate, this means buying the highest of hi-fis, the deepest of modern sofas, the heppest of pop artifacts, the most seductive of lounging pajamas or sports jackets. If sooner or later a prospective mate moves in, the big city does not mind. Few landlords would dream of objecting, and sophisticated married friends ask coupled singles for a weekend with no thought of separate rooms. . . .

The new freedom is the more radical for the single girl. Because of her increased economic competence and society's· more permissive moral standards, today's swinging single is free in a myriad of ways her mother never dreamed of—freer morally from the restraints of home and the strictures of religion, freer economically from dependence on family allowance, freer geographically from the confines of the home town, and freer sexually through her increased security against unwanted pregnancy. Today's maiden is often assumed to be less concerned with being chaste than being chased—and caught, perhaps often— before she marries.

For the male, the impact is more obvious

if less real. In magazines devoted to his interests, the happily unmarried man is seen as surrounded by elaborate hi-fi speakers (which he may never be able to afford), appealed to by makers of Great Books and good booze (which he may never read or drink), praised by haberdashers and hairdressers for his swinging singularity (which he earnestly aspires to), and pursued by indefatigably seductive girls. Once a docile follower of the style of his elders, the new bachelor finds himself the mold of fashion, with his mating plumage studied and envied by beaten-down husbands who, in comparison, begin to feel as tired and scruffy as a suburban lawn in a dry summer. The late John F. Kennedy, himself a swinging bachelor until 36, neatly framed both the stimulating and debilitating aspects of bachelorhood in a wry note that he wrote to Paul Fay in 1953: "I gave everything a good deal of thought—so am getting married this fall. This means the end of a promising political career as it has been based up to now almost completely on the old sex appeal."

Sex appeal aside, market analysts agree that the singles have more "discriminatory buying power" than any other group. "They are not tied down by mortgage payments and insurance policies," points out Advertising Executive Kenneth Corman. Thus they offer a rich bonanza for sellers of sports cars and flowered vests, stretch pants and elaborate lingerie, costume jewelry and queenly cosmetics, ski weekends and Florida vacations, and other amenities that, without being absolutely essential, contribute to the joy of living. The statisticians, in their computerized wisdom, figure the singles as a $60 billion market. To those who object that the young marrieds after all buy more of the solid things of life, from houses to dishwashers, the merchandisers briskly point out that the young marrieds are an ephemeral market, image-wise. As soon as they conceive a child, they become conservative and budget-minded, and "disposable income" suddenly evokes not vacation trips but diaper service. While the young wife is still working and before the baby is born, they are, in effect, "singles together." While the image to sell is singledom, the

real focus is on youth and glamour. This idea was classically exploited by Ford's highly successful sales strategy for the Mustang—aiming at the single as a way of bagging many a married. "Youth is the key to the market," says Grey Advertising's Murray W. Gross. "Everything is on a youth trend—even products for the man or woman of 65." Dean Acheson, . . . former U.S. Secretary of State, touched neatly on another side of this point recently when he said that "today only the blunt" refer to the middle 60s as "old age.". . .

Along with their freedom, the singles have discovered that their habitat—the big city—is an assembly of strangers. As strangers, they need a place to meet, some social mechanism that is the equivalent of the high school dance or the corner soda fountain or the church young people's group, where boys and girls can meet, measure, consider, examine, sample, negotiate. Across the nation, entrepreneurs have found a demand for housing complexes catering specifically to the singles, with organized cocktail parties, dances, fun, and games. Chicago's Sandburg Village comprises six high-rise buildings, offers a single-minded supermarket of activities: bridge and ski clubs, touch football, excursions, painting classes, and parties on the sun deck. The Los Angeles area's South Bay Club apartments, which started with $1,000 capital three years ago and is now capitalized at $11 million, has 933 apartments jammed with singles and a waiting list, will add 1,500 apartment units next year. Atlanta's Peachtree Apartments puts out a *Towne Crier* that advertises the merry events in the life of "PTA" dwellers, reports marriages among the clientele, and invites newcomers to parties where, says the *Crier* archly, "prizes are awarded to the drunkest" and "we never call the police."

In some cities, Friday's newspapers are studded with ads offering the single a pub, a pad, or party, or anyway a place to meet. Many of these offers mean simply that the promoter has hired a hall. But even with admission charges at the customary $2 or $3 each, the singles flock there in desperate numbers and with such dependable persistence that a promoter can count on as much as $2,000 for one night's work. Some operations remain sleezy reruns of the '30s dance joints, where lonely out-of-town girls gather in groups of twos and threes while guys on the prowl case the merchandise. But most have evolved from the primeval sludge of the lonely-hearts club, and owners now consider themselves a smooth amalgam of mogul and psychiatrist.

The Young College Graduates Club, which meets every Friday, usually in the Moderne Ballroom of Manhattan's Belmont Plaza Hotel, requires all applicants to show proof of college attendance—even though this proof may be as questionable as a college ring that fits. House Party, a New York organization that provides "warm, cozy," homelike places for singles to meet, is so austere that it serves no liquor and thoroughly examines the credentials of its primarily professional clientele. "We strive," claims President Ronald Garretson, "to create an atmosphere for people who don't care to sit on a bar stool or get tapped on the shoulder at a dance." The atmosphere seems to be irresistible. Fourteen thousand members pay $10 a year to belong, another 6,000 pay up to $3 apiece to drop in on weekends, and House Party ("If you are looking for a date or a lifetime mate House Party is for you") soon hopes to have franchises in Philadelphia and Chicago. The comparable Never on Friday Club (never a date, that is) of Los Angeles has gone from 7,000 members in 1964 to 64,000 [in 1967].

Computer services, which were once treated as a joke, have turned into a solid business. Typical is the Compute-A-Date division of the American Compute-A-Service Co., Inc., of Chicago, which started only a year ago but already has some 6,000 names. Vice President John Damijanic, 28, says that a girl applicant can expect an average of one dinner from each of her five computer-chosen dates; at an entrance fee of $6, she is ahead almost as soon as she fills out the little card specifying preferences (white, Negro, Oriental, Indian, Arab, Protestant, Catholic, Jewish, nonreligious, other, divorced) and gets a match with her own card of self-analysis—which includes such questions as whether she believes sexual activity is healthful. Most popular answer: "In some ways yes, other ways no."

In city after city, run of the gin-mill bars have been turned into "dating bars." What converts an ordinary bar into a dating bar is a weekend admission fee (usually $1), a large welcome for single girls, and a good neighborhood. In Manhattan, the neighborhood is along First Avenue in the 50s and 60s, an area well populated by airline stewardesses and young career women, converted brownstones with quaint apartments that attract upwardly mobile young executives. Nearly every night, there are lines of singles, male and female, waiting to get in to Mr. Laffs, Maxwell's Plum, and Friday's. In Chicago it is The Store, in San Francisco it is Paoli's. In Dallas, it is the TGIF (Thank God It's Friday).

The travel and resort business puts on special promotions for the singles. There is the beach or travel party club—a solution to traveling alone—such as the Club Méditerranée, which has built a 500,000-member clientele in Europe and is successfully offering equal opportunities to Americans. The Méditerranée's basic gimmick for togetherness is that you always sit at a table for eight—but you can change tables for any meal. This spring Hilton Hotels launched a special tour to Puerto Rico aimed at the singles market: "What can you expect for $133 on your Hilton Swingles Week in San Juan?" A welcoming cocktail and plenty of action, "fashion shows, cinema, horse racing, free feature motion pictures, and a souvenir photograph of you and your new friends . . . Sound like your line of fun?" In the first four months, Hilton reported happily, it had 1,200 applicants—even if it was the off season. . . .

So coddled and cosseted, the single in America, it would seem, might be the happiest of men or women. But on closer examination, despite the frivolity and freedom, the swingers' velocity is not quite as rapid as it at first appears.

In fact, the unmarried in America are in many respects at a clear disadvantage. The single male who goes to the hospital stays there an average nine days longer than the married man—presumably because there is no one at home to take care of him during convalescence. The married man gets more out of life—in years, that is—because the single man tends to die earlier. A study at the Mental Research Institute at Berkeley, Calif., of men and women, nearly all of whom were 23 years old or more, found that the single male ranks highest in severe neurotic symptoms. Whether he is neurotic because he is single, or single because he is neurotic, is not clear. The study did find that the least unhappy person is the married man.

For business careers, singlehood has its liabilities. As Vance Packard reports in *The Pyramid Climbers:* "In general the bachelor is viewed with circumspection, especially if he is not well known to the people appraising him." If he is still in his 20s, the personnel manager worries whether he is too busy with his love life to devote full attention to his job. "The worst status of all is that of a bachelor beyond the age of 36. The investigators wonder why he isn't married. Is it because he isn't virile? Is he old-maidish? Can't he get along with people?" Maybe he can't. "Failure to marry in either sex is the consequence of a fear of it," says Psychiatrist Irving Bieber. "There is increasing recognition that bachelorhood is symptomatic of psychopathology and that even though women may yearn for a husband, home, and family they withdraw from fulfilling their wishes because the anxiety they associate with marrying is more powerful than their desire for it.". . .

As for the sex revolution, it is not all that it is gossiped to be. For one thing, only a relatively small proportion of the total single population participates. John H. Gagnon of Indiana University's Institute for Sex Research points out that 50 percent of all brides are still virgins, and another 25 percent have slept with only their prospective mate. Says Gagnon: "The bulk of intercourse continues to be oriented toward marriage. We haven't passed any sexual watershed." For every modern swinger, there is an untold number of the merely forlorn. The ratio is as old as mankind, unrecorded and unrecordable, but it is roughly the ratio of glamor girls to plain Janes. Today's plain Janes have opportunities their spinster aunts never did —trips to Europe, a Peace Corps assignment in Asia, interesting jobs in research or government. And in all of these places, they have a chance to display a mettle that may attract a man who might otherwise have been addled by a momentary attraction to a dumb blonde. But many of them end up living lives of quiet desperation, punctuated by pathetic sorties to dating clubs or organized dances or singles weekends. Despite the frenetically gay ads, these are often exercises of last resort. An ad for a weekend at the Concord Hotel in the Catskills offers an insight into the dark side of the single life. Promising a phantasmagoria of pleasures, the ad saves its ultimate weapon for the end. "This," it says, "may be your last 'singles party.'"

The side that this approach appeals to is well analyzed in quite familiar terms by Judy McKeown, at 23 a TV personality in Chicago and still single: "You can go out every night with a different guy, but after a while you're bound to get tired of it, because all the running around you're doing is in a circle. Really, you don't get anything. You don't get to learn anything about people. You'll find six months of it is a very long time. After that, you're asking yourself, 'What's going on? What's it all about?'" The more lasting relationships that the singles develop are based on their own standards, even if they contrast sharply with those upheld by, say, the late Dorothy Dix, who told a young girl asking for advice: "Why should he marry you after six months if he can get what he wants now? Do you really believe he will marry you after he's had you for a while?" The modern single's answer is yes, and if he does not, there is something wrong with the relationship and it is just as well that he doesn't.

The greatest pressure on the singles is the classic one—loneliness. In prosaic terms, this is coming back to an apartment where the breakfast dishes are still unwashed, the morning paper exactly where it was dropped, where nothing has moved. Mayo Mohs, a freelance journalist still single at 33, puts the unmarried's problem in a frame of reference that is more romantic and more telling: "The lack a single person feels most acutely is when he leaves his group to go off somewhere on a trip, one of those trips that his single status lets him enjoy. It can occur in front of a castle, on the quiet deck of a boat going up the Rhine, or on any overlook anywhere, looking at a sunset. Faced with such a sight, the natural tendency is to want to turn to someone to say, 'Isn't that beautiful!' and to enjoy it together. And when you turn, there isn't anyone there."

Most singles know that a single man cannot be a thing of beauty and a boy forever and that a single girl is like a single letter in the alphabet, waiting to mean something to someone. Even the most swinging single, who has been insisting "Not yet," inevitably crosses a watershed when the question becomes a panicky "Is it too late?" Ultimately, the singles devoutly wish that they weren't.

35

ABORTION—OR COMPULSORY PREGNANCY?

Garrett Hardin

The year 1967 produced the first fissures in the dam that had prevented all change in the abortion-prohibition laws of the United States for three-quarters of a century. Two states adopted laws that allowed abortion in the "hardship cases" of rape, incest, and probability of a deformed child. A third approved the first two "indications," but not the last. All three took some note of the mental health of the pregnant woman, in varying language; how this language will be translated into practice remains to be seen. In almost two dozen other states, attempts to modify the laws were made but foundered at various stages in the legislative process. It is quite evident that the issue will continue to be a live one for many years to come.

The legislative turmoil was preceded and accompanied by a fast-growing popular literature. The word "abortion" has ceased to be a dirty word—which is a cultural advance. However, the *word* was so long under taboo that the ability to think about the *fact* seems to have suffered a sort of logical atrophy from disuse. Popular articles, regardless of their conclusions, tend to be over-emotional and to take a moralistic rather than an operational view of the matter. Nits are picked, hairs split. It is quite clear that many of the authors are not at all clear what question they are attacking.

It is axiomatic in science that progress hinges on asking the right question. Surprisingly, once the right question is asked the answer seems almost to tumble forth. That is a retrospective view; in prospect, it takes genuine (and mysterious) insight to see correctly into the brambles created by previous, ill-chosen verbalizations.

The abortion problem is, I think, a particularly neat example of a problem in which most of the difficulties are actually created by asking the wrong question. I submit further that once the right question is asked the whole untidy mess miraculously dissolves, leaving in its place a very simple public policy recommendation. . . .

The wrong question, the one almost invariably asked, is this: "How can we justify an abortion?" This assumes that there are weightly public reasons for encouraging pregnancies, or that abortions, per se, somehow threaten public peace. A direct examination of the legitimacy of these assumptions will be made later. For the present, let us pursue the question as asked and see what a morass it leads to.

Almost all the present legislative attempts take as their model a bill proposed by the American Law Institute which emphasizes three justifications for legal abortion: rape, incest, and the probability of a defective child. Whatever else may be said about this bill, it is clear that it affects only the periphery of the social problem. The Arden House Conference Committee[1] estimated the number of illegal abortions in the United States to be between 200,000 and 1,200,000 per year. A California legislator, Anthony C. Beilenson,[2] has estimated that the American Law Institute bill (which he favors) would legalize not more than four percent of the presently illegal abortions. Obviously, the "problem" of illegal abortion will be scarcely affected by the passage of the laws so far proposed in the United States.

I have calculated[3] that the number of rape-induced pregnancies in the United States is about 800 per year. The number is not large, but for the woman raped the total number is irrelevant. What matters to her is that she be relieved of her unwanted burden. But a law which puts the burden of proof on her compels her to risk a second harrowing experience. How can she *prove* to the district attorney that she was raped? He could really know whether or not she gave consent only if he could get inside her mind; this he cannot do. Here is the philosopher's "egocentric predicament" that none of us can escape. In an effort to help the district attorney sustain the illusion that he can escape this predicament, a talented woman may put on a dramatic performance, with copious tears and other signs of anguish. But what if the raped woman is not an actress? What if her temperament is stoic? In its operation, the law will act against the interests of calm, undramatic women. Is that what we want? It is safe to say also that district attorneys will hear less favorably the pleas of poor women, the general assumption of middle-class agents being that the poor are less responsible in sex anyway.[4] Is it to the interest of society that the poor bear more children, whether rape-engendered or not?

A wryly amusing difficulty has been raised with respect to rape. Suppose the woman is married and having regular intercourse with her husband. Suppose that following a rape by an unknown intruder she finds herself pregnant. Is she legally entitled to an abortion? How does she know whose child she is carrying anyway? If it is her husband's child, abortion is illegal. If she carries it to term, and if blood tests then exclude the husband as the father, as they would in a fraction of the cases, is the woman then entitled to a *delayed* abortion? But this is ridiculous: this is infanticide, which no one is proposing. Such is the bramble bush into which we are led by a *reluctant* consent for abortion in cases of rape. . . .

The majority of the public support abortion in cases of a suspected deformity of the child[5] just as they do in cases of rape. Again, however, if the burden of proof rests on the one who requests the operation, we encounter difficulties in administration. Between 80,000 and 160,000 defective children are born every year in the United States. The number stated depends on two important issues: (a) how severe a defect must be before it is counted as such and (b) whether or not one counts as birth defects those defects that are not *detected* until later. (Deafness and various other defects produced by fetal rubella may not be detected until a year or so after birth.) However many defective infants there may be, what is the prospect of detecting them before birth?

The sad answer is: the prospects are poor. A small percentage can be picked up by microscopic examination of tissues of the fetus. But "amniocentesis"—the form of biopsy required to procure such tissues—is itself somewhat dangerous to both the mother and fetus; most abnormalities will not be detectable by a microscopic examination of the fetal cells; and 96 to 98 percent of all fetuses are normal anyway. All these considerations are a contraindication of routine amniocentesis.

When experience indicates that the probability of a deformed fetus is above the "background level" of 2 to 4 percent, is abortion justified? At what level? 10 percent? 50? 80? Or only at 100 percent? Suppose a particular medical history indicates a probability of 20 percent that the baby will be defective. If we routinely abort such cases, it is undeniable that four normal fetuses will be destroyed for every one abnormal. Those who assume that a fetus is an object of high value are appalled at this "wastage." Not uncommonly they ask, "Why not wait until the baby is born and then suffocate those that are deformed?" Such a question is unquestionably rhetoric and sardonic; if serious, it implies that infanticide has no more emotional meaning to a woman than abortion, an assumption that is surely contrary to fact. . . .

Men who are willing to see abortion-prohibition laws relaxed somewhat, but not completely, frequently raise a question about the "rights" of the father. Should we allow a woman to make a unilateral decision for an abortion? Should not her husband have a say in the matter? (After all, he contributed just as many chromosomes to the fetus as she.)

I do not know what weight to give this objection. I have encountered it repeatedly in the discussion section following a public meeting. It is clear that some men are disturbed at finding themselves powerless in such a situation and want the law to give them some power of decision.

Yet powerless men are—and it is nature that has made them so. If we give the father a right of veto in abortion decisions, the wife has a very simple reply to her husband: "I'm sorry, dear, I wasn't going to tell you this, but you've forced my hand. This is not your child." With such a statement she could always deny her husband's right to decide.

Why husbands should demand power in such matters is a fit subject for depth analysis. In the absence of such, perhaps the best thing we can say to men who are "hung up" on this issue is this: "Do you really want to live for another eight months with a woman whom you are compelling to be pregnant against her will?"

Or, in terms of public policy, do we want to pass laws which give men the right to compel their wives to be pregnant? Psychologically, such compulsion is akin to

rape. Is it in the public interest to encourage rape? . . .

The question "How can we justify an abortion?" proves least efficient in solving the real problems of this world when we try to evaluate what are usually called "socioeconomic indications." The hardship cases—rape, incest, probability of a deformed child—have been amply publicized, and as a result the majority of the public accepts them as valid indicators; but hardship cases constitute only a few percent of the need. By contrast, if a woman has more children than she feels she can handle, or if her children are coming too close together, there is little public sympathy for her plight. A poll[5] conducted by the National Opinion Research Center in December, 1965, showed that only 15 percent of the respondents replied "Yes" to this question: "Please tell me whether or not you think it should be possible for a pregnant woman to obtain a legal abortion if she is married and does not want any more children." Yet this indication, which received the lowest rate of approval, accounts for the vast majority of instances in which women want—and illegally get—relief from unwanted pregnancy.

There is a marked discrepancy between the magnitude of the need and the degree of public sympathy. Part of the reason for this discrepancy is attributable to the emotional impact of the words used to describe the need. "Rape," "incest," "deformed child"—these words are rich in emotional connotations. "Socioeconomic indications" is a pale bit of jargon, suggesting at best that the abortion is wanted because the woman lives by culpably materialistic standards. "Socioeconomic indications" tugs at no one's heartstrings; the hyphenated abomination hides the human reality to which it obliquely refers. To show the sort of human problem to which this label may be attached, let me quote a letter I received from one woman. (The story is unique, but it is one of a large class of similar true stories.)

I had an illegal abortion 2½ years ago. I left my church because of the guilt I felt. I had six children when my husband left me to live with another woman. We weren't divorced and I went to work to help support them. When he would come to visit the children he would sometimes stay after they were asleep. I became pregnant. When I told my husband, and asked him to please come back, he informed me that the woman he was living with was five months pregnant and ill, and that he couldn't leave her —not at that time anyway.

I got the name of a doctor in San Francisco from a Dr. friend who was visiting here from there. This Dr. (Ob. and Gyn.) had a good legitimate practice in the main part of the city and was a kindly, compassionate man who believes as you do, that it is better for everyone not to bring an unwanted child into the world.

It was over before I knew it. I thought I was just having an examination at the time. He even tried to make me not feel guilty by telling me that the long automobile trip had already started a spontaneous abortion. He charged me $25. That was on Fri. and on Mon. I was back at work. I never suffered any ill from it.

The other woman's child died shortly after birth and six months later my husband asked if he could come back. We don't have a perfect marriage but my children have a father. My being able to work has helped us out of a deep financial debt. I shall always remember the sympathy I received from that Dr. and wish there were more like him with the courage to do what they believe is right.

Her operation was illegal, and would be illegal under most of the "reform" legislation now being proposed, if interpreted strictly. Fortunately some physicians are willing to indulge in more liberal interpretations, but they make these interpretations not on medical grounds, in the strict sense, but on social and economic grounds. Understandably, many physicians are unwilling to venture so far from the secure base of pure physical medicine. As one Catholic physician put it:

Can the patient afford to have another child? Will the older children have sufficient educational opportunities if their parents have another child? Aren't two, three, or four children enough? I am afraid such statements are frequently made in the discussion of a proposed therapeutic abortion. [But] we should be doctors of medicine, not socioeconomic prophets.[6]

To this a non-Catholic physician added: "I sometimes wish I were an obstetrician in a Catholic hospital so that I would not have to make any of these decisions. The only position to take in which I would have no misgivings is to do no interruptions at all."[7] . . .

The question "How can we justify an abortion?" plainly leads to great difficulties. It is operationally unmanageable: it leads to inconsistencies in practice and inequities by any moral standard. All these can be completely avoided if we ask the right question, namely: *"How can we justify compulsory pregnancy?"*

By casting the problem in this form, we call attention to its relationship to the slavery issue. Somewhat more than a century ago men in the Western world asked the question: "How can we justify compulsory servitude?" and came up with the answer: *"By no means whatever."* Is the answer any different to the related question: "How can we justify compulsory pregnancy?" Certainly pregnancy is a form of servitude; if continued to term it results in parenthood, which is also a kind of servitude, to be continued for the best years of a woman's life. It is difficult to see how it can be argued that this kind of servitude will be more productive of social good if it is compulsory rather than voluntary. A study[8] made of Swedish children born when their mothers were refused the abortions they had requested showed that unwanted children, as compared with their controls, as they grew up were more often picked up for drunkenness, or antisocial or criminal behavior; they received less education; they received more psychiatric care; and they were more often exempted from military service by reason of defect. Moreover, the females in the group married earlier and had children earlier, thus no doubt tending to create a vicious circle of poorly tended children who in their turn would produce more poorly tended children. How then does society gain by increasing the number of unwanted children? No one has volunteered an answer to this question.

Of course if there were a shortage of children, then society might say that it needs all the children it can get—unwanted or not. But I am unaware of any recent rumors of a shortage of children. . . .

The end result of an abortion—the elimination of an unwanted fetus—is surely good. But is the act itself somehow damaging? For several generations it was widely believed that abortion was intrinsically dangerous, either physically or psychologically. It is now very clear that the widespread belief is quite unjustified. The evidence for this statement is found in a bulky literature which has been summarized in Lawrence Lader's *Abortion*[9] and the collection of essays brought together by Alan Guttmacher.[10]

In tackling questions of this sort, it is imperative that we identify correctly the alternatives facing us. (All moral and practical problems involve a comparison of alternative actions.) Many of the arguments of the prohibitionists implicitly assume that the alternatives facing the woman are these:

abortion———no abortion

This is false. A person can never do nothing. The pregnant woman is going to do something, whether she wishes to or not. (She cannot roll time backward and live her life over.)

People often ask: "Isn't contraception better than abortion?" Implied by this question are these alternatives:

abortion———contraception

But these are not the alternatives that face the woman who asks to be aborted. She *is* pregnant. She cannot roll time backward and use contraception more successfully than she did before. Contraceptives are never foolproof anyway. It is commonly accepted that the failure rate of our best contraceptive, the "pill," is around one per cent, i.e., one failure per hundred woman-years of use. I have earlier shown[11] that this failure rate produces about a quarter of a million of unwanted pregnancies a year in the United States. Abortion is not

so much an alternative to contraception as it is a subsidiary method of birth control, to be used when the primary method fails —as it often does.

The woman *is* pregnant: this is the base level at which moral decision begins. If she is pregnant against her will, does it matter to society whether or not she was careless or unskillful in her use of contraception? In any case, she is threatening society with an unwanted child, for which society will pay dearly. The real alternatives facing the woman (and society) are clearly these:

abortion———compulsory pregnancy

When we recognize that these are the real, operational alternatives, the false problems created by pseudo-alternatives vanish. . . .

Only one weighty objection to abortion remains to be discussed, and this is the question of "loss." When a fetus is destroyed, has something valuable been destroyed? The fetus has the potentiality of becoming a human being. A human being is valuable. Therefore is not the fetus of equal value? This question must be answered.

It can be answered, but not briefly. What does the embryo receive from its parents that might be of value? There are only three possibilities: substance, energy, and information. As for the substance in the fertilized egg, it is not remarkable: merely the sort of thing one might find in any piece of meat, human or animal, and there is very little of it—only one and a half micrograms, which is about a half of a billionth of an ounce. The energy content of this tiny amount of material is likewise negligible. As the zygote develops into an embryo, both its substance and its energy content increase (at the expense of the mother); but this is not a very important matter— even an adult, viewed from this standpoint, is only a hundred and fifty pounds of meat!

Clearly, the humanly significant thing that is contributed to the zygote by the parents is the information that "tells" the fertilized egg how to develop into a human being. This information is in the form of a chemical tape called "DNA," a double set of two chemical supermolecules each of which has about three billion "spots" that can be coded with any one of four different possibilities, symbolized by *A*, *T*, *G*, and *C*. (For comparison, the Morse code offers three possibilities in coding: dot, dash, and space.) It is the particular sequence of these four chemical possibilities in the DNA that directs the zygote in its development into a human being. The DNA constitutes the information needed to produce a valuable human being. The question is: is this information precious? I have argued elsewhere[12] that it is not:

Consider the case of a man who is about to begin to build a $50,000 house. As he stands on the site looking at the blueprints a practical joker comes along and sets fire to the blueprints. The question is: can the owner go to the law and collect $50,000 for his lost blueprints? The answer is obvious: since another set of blueprints can be produced for the cost of only a few dollars, that is all they are worth. (A court might award a bit more for the loss of the owner's time, but that is a minor matter.) The moral: a nonunique copy of information that specifies a valuable structure is itself almost valueless.

This principle is precisely applicable to the moral problem of abortion. The zygote, which contains the complete specification of a valuable human being, is not a human being, and is almost valueless. . . . The early stages of an individual fetus have had very little human effort invested in them; they are of very little worth. The loss occasioned by an abortion is independent of whether the abortion is spontaneous or induced. (Just as the loss incurred by the burning of a set of blueprints is independent of whether the causal agent was lightning or an arsonist.)

A set of blueprints is not a house; the DNA of a zygote is not a human being. The analogy is singularly exact, though there are two respects in which it is deficient. These respects are interesting rather than important. First, we have the remarkable fact that the blueprints of the zygote are constantly replicated and incorporated in every cell of the human body. This is interesting, but it has no moral significance. There is no moral obligation to conserve DNA—if there were, no man would be al- *lowed to brush his teeth and gums, for in this brutal operation hundreds of sets of DNA are destroyed daily.*

The other anomaly of the human information problem is connected with the fact that the information that is destroyed in an aborted embryo is unique (unlike the house blueprints). But it is unique in a way that is without moral significance. A favorite argument of abortion-prohibitionists is this: "What if Beethoven's mother had had an abortion?" The question moves us; but when we think it over we realize we can just as relevantly ask: "What if Hitler's mother had had an abortion?" Each conceptus is unique, but not in any way that has a moral consequence. The expected potential value of each aborted child is exactly that of the average child born. It is meaningless to say that humanity loses when a particular *child is not born, or is not conceived. A human female, at birth, has about 30,000 eggs in her ovaries. If she bears only 3 children in her lifetime, is there any meaningful sense in which we can say that mankind has suffered a loss in those other 29,997 fruitless eggs? (Yet one of them might have been a super-Beethoven!)*

People who worry about the moral danger of abortion do so because they think of the fetus as a human being, hence equate feticide with murder. Whether the fetus is or is not a human being is a matter of definition, not fact; and we can define any way we wish. In terms of the human problem involved, it would be unwise to define the fetus as human (hence tactically unwise ever to refer to the fetus as an "unborn child"). Analysis based on the deepest insights of molecular biology indicates the wisdom of sharply distinguishing the information for a valuable structure from the completed structure itself. It is interesting, and gratifying, to note that this modern insight is completely congruent with common law governing the disposal of dead fetuses. Abortion-prohibitionists generally insist that abortion is murder, and that an embryo is a person; but no state or nation, so far as I know, requires the dead fetus to be treated like a dead person. Although all of the states in the United States severely limit what can be done with a dead human body, no cognizance is taken of dead fetuses up to about five months' prenatal life. The early fetus may, with impunity, be flushed down the toilet or thrown out with the garbage—which shows that we never have regarded it as a human being. Scientific analysis confirms what we have always known. . . .

What is the the future of compulsory pregnancy? The immediate future is not hopeful. Far too many medical people misconceive the real problem. One physician has written:

Might not a practical, workable solution to this most difficult problem by found by setting up, in every hospital, an abortion committee comprising a specialist in obstetrics and gynecology, a psychiatrist, and a clergyman or priest? The patient and her husband—if any—would meet with these men who would do all in their power to persuade the woman not to undergo the abortion. (I have found that the promise of a postpartum sterilization will frequently enable even married women with all the children they can care for to accept this one more, final pregnancy.) If, however, the committee members fail to change the woman's mind, they can make it very clear that they disapprove of the abortion, but prefer that it be safely done in a hospital rather than bungled in a basement somewhere.[13]

What this author has in mind is plainly not a system of legalizing abortion but a system of managing compulsory pregnancy. It is this philosophy which governs pregnancies in the Scandinavian countries,[14] where the experience of a full generation of

women has shown that women do not want their pregnancies to be managed by the state. Illegal abortions have remained at a high level in these countries, and recent years have seen the development of a considerable female tourist trade to Poland, where abortions are easy to obtain. Unfortunately, American legislatures are now proposing to follow the provably unworkable system of Scandinavia.

The drift down this erroneous path is not wholly innocent. Abortion-prohibitionists are showing signs of recognizing "legalization" along Scandinavian lines as one more roadblock that can be thrown in the way of the abolition of compulsory pregnancy. To cite an example: on February 9, 1966, the *Courier,* a publication of the Winona, Minnesota, Diocese, urged that Catholics support a reform law based on the American Law Institute model, because the passage of such a law would "take a lot of steam out of the abortion advocate's argument" and would "defeat a creeping abortionism of disastrous importance."[15]

Wherever a Scandinavian or American Law Institute type of bill is passed, it is probable that cautious legislators will then urge a moratorium for several years while the results of the new law are being assessed (though they are easily predictable from the Scandinavian experience). As Lord Morley once said: "Small reforms are the worst enemies of great reforms." Because of the backwardness of education in these matters, caused by the long taboo under which the subject of abortion labored, it seems highly likely that our present system of compulsory pregnancy will continue substantially without change until the true nature of the alternatives facing us is more widely recognized.

NOTES

[1] Mary Steichen Calderone (ed.), *Abortion in the United States* (New York: Hoeber-Harper, 1958), p. 178.

[2] Anthony C. Beilenson, "Abortion and Common Sense," *Per/Se,* 1 (1966): 24.

[3] Garrett Hardin, "Semantic Aspects of Abortion," *ETC.,* 24 (1967): 263.

⁴ Lee Rainwater, *And the Poor Get Children* (Chicago: Quadrangle Books, 1960), p. ix and chap. 1.

⁵ Alice S. Rossi, "Abortion Laws and Their Victims," *Trans-action*, 3 (September-October 1966): 7.

⁶ Calderone (ed.), op. cit., p. 103.

⁷ Ibid., p. 123.

⁸ Hans Forssman and Inga Thuwe, "One Hundred and Twenty Children Born after Application for Therapeutic Abortion Refused," *Acta Psychiatrica Scandinavica*, 42 (1966): 71.

⁹ Lawrence Lader, *Abortion* (Indianapolis: Bobbs-Merrill, 1966).

¹⁰ Alan F. Guttmacher (ed.), *The Case for Legalized Abortion* (Berkeley, California: Diablo Press, 1967).

¹¹ Garrett Hardin, "A Scientist's Case for Abortion," *Redbook* (May 1967): 62.

¹² Garrett Hardin, "Blueprints, DNA, and Abortion: A Scientific and Ethical Analysis," *Medical Opinion and Review*, 3:2 (1967): 74.

¹³ H. Curtis Wood, Jr., "Letter to the Editor," *Medical Opinion and Review*, 3:11 (1967): 19.

¹⁴ David T. Smith (ed.), *Abortion and the Law* (Cleveland: Western Reserve University, 1967), p. 179.

¹⁵ Anonymous, *Association for the Study of Abortion Newsletter*, 2:3 (1967): 6.

36

THE LAW AND SEXUAL RELATIONSHIPS

Robert Veit Sherwin

It is most embarrassing to any lawyer, who is proud of being a member of the legal profession, to write an analysis of the law as it pertains to sex, especially when this analysis must be part of a group of articles written by representatives of other disciplines, such as psychiatry and sociology. The greater availability and the greater depth of professionalism in research materials in the field of psychology, psychiatry, and sociology make most evident the lack of comparable data concerning law and sex.

There are many reasons for this. In the first place, the laws concerning sex are much like public highways that surround large cities. By the time a much needed public highway gets built, it is often already outmoded on the very day that it is opened.

In the same way, the laws concerning sex, which are actually codifications of attitudes and customs already long in existence, may very quickly be inappropriate very shortly after the enactment of said laws.

Secondly, unlike outmoded highways, sex laws can be ignored as if they did not exist, which can and does aggravate the situation instead of improving it. It must be remembered that the problem of sex administration straddles two houses, the courthouse and the church, and each tends to blame the other for the violation of sexual mores.

Thirdly, there are certain elements present in the legal administration of sexual mores that are absent in other phases of the law which cause many of the difficulties to be outlined in this article. For one thing, lawyers depend upon the decisions written by the judges concerning the judicial interpretation of the law. Very few cases involving the violation of sex laws get beyond the Police Court or the Magistrate's Court level, and are thus not recorded in official books available to the legal profession. It is only when the occasional case is appealed to an Appellate Court that a record is made of that case for purposes of study and analysis. Because of the embarrassment to the accused's family, lack of funds, etc., appeals are seldom taken by convicted defendants. . . .

Two major arguments are raised by those in the field who feel that the laws concerning sex, as they presently exist, are outmoded and ineffective. The first point concerns sex laws that attempt to control behavior that should be controlled by the church, the school, or the home. In this category would be many forms of sexual expression to be discussed, which Justice Learned Hand deemed to be "questions of taste" rather than an act to be punished by law. Various forms of sexual expression when performed by consenting adults in the privacy of the home would be in this category. The second point raised is that there are certain acts [that], although criminal in a minor sense, are impossible to enforce with any degree of effectiveness and, therefore, should be deleted from the Criminal Code to improve the effectiveness of the Criminal Code in the preventive sense. An illustration of this point would be the act of adultery. In New York State alone, there have been something less than five convictions of the act of adultery in 66 years, despite the fact that thousands of divorces are granted by the New York Courts every year on the grounds that an adulterous act has been committed.

It is, therefore, the purpose of this article to dissect the law in action, as it is applied to sexual behavior under the current pressures that affect the sexual mores of the community at large. . . .

The emphasis, for better or worse, during the last fifty years concerning the sexual emancipation of the female has been to change the position of the female from that of a mere receptacle for the male penis, in return for her support and maintenance, to that of an equal sex partner fully entitled to all the various forms of sexual satisfaction, in accordance with her own needs. In view of the complexity of female anatomy and, more specifically, in view of the emergence of the clitoris as one of the more important means of achievement of sexual satisfaction for the female, serious results have been created when the attempt is made to apply a law which is appropriate only if one pretends that there is no such thing as a clitoris.[1] Since the function of sexual administration was originally in the hands of the church, sexual intercourse (in the penis-vagina sense of the word) was considered strictly as a means of propagation; questions of pleasure and emotional fulfillment were uncontemplated. The omission of pleasure was reenforced so as to avoid sexual satisfaction at the expense of failure to propagate. Hence a typical statute reads:

Every person who shall carnally know, or shall have sexual intercourse in any manner with any animal or bird, or shall carnally know any male or female by the anus (rectum) or with the mouth or tongue; or shall attempt intercourse with a dead body is guilty of Sodomy.[2]

This type of statute, with many variations in as many jurisdictions, represents a typical example of a law which is usually entitled "Crime Against Nature," "Lewd and Lascivious Behavior," or "Sodomy." Some jurisdictions even include the specific act of mutual masturbation in the category of crimes against nature. The fact that all such statutes do not differentiate between people who are married to one another and those who are not (such as is done in adultery statutes) results in categorizing as a crime any of the various forms of sexual expression generally recommended to aid and induce the female orgasm even though the man and woman are married to each other.

As if the above were not patently disturbing enough, such illegal acts in most jurisdictions are classed as felonies and bring, in many instances, imprisonment of sixty years to life and, in one jurisdiction, a minimum sentence of life at hard labor. It is interesting to note in passing, that in this same jurisdiction the penalty for having intercourse with a cow brings only five years of imprisonment.

As an illustration, the following case within the author's own experience should be noted. In a Midwestern town, a young couple, the groom being twenty-two years and his bride nineteen, were experiencing sexual difficulties: premature ejaculation and difficulties in the wife's achieving an orgasm. Through their own experimentation they finally solved the problem by means of sexual intercourse plus the use of cunnilinctus to help her achieve her orgasm. Some months thereafter, the husband brought home the news to his young wife that the act of cunnilinctus was a crime in their state, punishable by sixty years in prison or more. They actually arrived at a point of hysteria, which caused them to have themselves arrested by the police authorities. Family contacts averted any court decision on the case.

Comment should also be made about the legal dilemma faced by the psychiatrist (or psychologist, marriage counsellor, etc.). Assuming that a wife is seeking to become a more satisfactory sexual partner both for the sake of her husband and herself, she may well seek professional help. Under the law of most jurisdictions, to advise the commission of a criminal act is, in and of itself, a criminal act. Thus when a psychiatrist advises precoital techniques[3] to a patient, he is committing a crime by so advising. Because of the period of hostile patient attitudes toward the psychiatrist which often happens in the natural progress of therapy, many psychiatrists, psychologists, and marriage counsellors hesitate to prescribe forms of sexual expression that violate the state law. This may be due to the psychiatrist's own concern for the jeopardy in which he would be placed if a patient publicly accused him of advocating the commission of criminal acts. In other cases, the psychiatrist may feel that to advocate behavior which the patient knows is listed as a crime might help the patient sexually, but that such behavior might do harm to the patient, therapeutically speaking, if the patient were to accept it as being illegal.

One need only mention in passing the effect of these laws on the planning of any high school or college course, . . . such as family relations. Any detailed discourse on sexual relationships would necessarily jeopardize the instructor for the same reasons which affect the psychologist and psychiatrist. . . .

In the two-headed problem (paternity suits and abortion) of the unwed mother, almost insurmountable problems face the social worker, the physician, and the attorney in trying to arrive at a logical and appropriate solution that is in keeping with the latest knowledge of the various scientific disciplines involved. Paternity suits, popularly considered a hopeless trap for the innocent male, are in the author's opinion devastatingly rigged, against the female. The requirements in most jurisdictions are barbaric in terms of consideration for human dignity. For example, in a paternity trial, the female must describe, in open Court in very explicit terms how, when, and where the male defendant's penis entered her vagina and the Court record must show that she used those terms. The entire procedure implicitly indicates that the Court regards her as a whore, and that the only reason the Court listens to her at all is for the sake of the taxpayer, in that support for the child (not for her) should be obtained from the father rather than from welfare. The ultimate is reached in at least one state, where, if the girl wishes to give up her baby for adoption, she must somehow persuade the alleged father to sign permission for the adoption, or must publicly state on the record in Court that she has no idea who the father is or what his name may be, thus publicly confessing that she is promiscuous. This situation is especially unfair since it is generally conceded that the lady of commercial virtue avoids pregnancy with a high degree of efficiency, as does the girl who is habitually active sexually. More often than not, however, the unwed mother cannot be classed as promiscuous.

As to the problem of abortion, the law is fraught with lack of appropriateness and what most would agree is out-and-out cruelty. In jurisdictions where the law permits a therapeutic abortion when the life of the mother is in danger either for physical or for psychiatric reasons, physicians and psychiatrists, as well as various "abortion boards" of hospitals, are fearful enough that permission is granted to only a very small percentage of those cases which fit into the narrow definitions described by law. Very little success has thus far been achieved in changing the law to more liberal proportions; the reasons for this will be discussed in more detail. Suffice it to say at the moment that the fear of opening the door to multitudes of pregnancies among the unwed and the immoral seems to force the retention of the punitive and irrational aspect of the abortion laws. There are many cases on record where permission to abort had actually been granted by a hospital board because of serious danger to the life of the mother, only to be withdrawn when the members of the board discovered that the mother in question was unmarried. By some odd method of reasoning, the members of each of these boards felt that it was within their province to sentence the mother to possible death because of her lack of marital status.

In the area of homosexuality, even though most statutes are sufficiently general in terms to include both men and women, there have been few, if any, recorded convictions of females for such activity. As a matter of curious fact, in a recent article in a publication (entitled *The Ladder*—1965) published by The Daughters of Belitis, a group consisting of lesbians and those interested in lesbian problems, the author actually complained about this. Even in matters of crime, the author felt, the woman is listed as second rate in our society, in that she is not considered important enough to be prosecuted for engaging in homosexual acts. A very well-known, now deceased, gynecologist of the author's acquaintance quite seriously advocated a homosexual experience for women prior to marriage, on the theory that no one can teach a woman about her sexual sensitivities better than another woman. It may well be that the good doctor was simply finding another way to cry out against the ignorance concerning sex and the lack of education and preparation for mature sexual activities in our so-

ciety. Many among the doctor's female patients wrote him letters of gratitude, stating how much the homosexual experience had helped in developing and promoting a better heterosexual relationship with their husbands. Regardless of the actual value of such advice, it is mentioned in passing as an indication of incredible lack of education and understanding in what should be an objective approach to the administration of sex.

Yet another form of discrimination against the female is in the preponderance of laws concerning prostitution. Minutely detailed statutes are devoted to punishing cab drivers who direct a passenger to a prostitute, to depriving employment agencies of their licenses if they send an employee to clean a house or home used as the scene of prostitution, and to the punishing of a person who lives off the proceeds of a prostitute or who merely consorts or is seen in public with a known prostitute. All these and more make more blatant the fact that what allows the crime of prostitution to survive as one of our leading industries (in terms of blackmail, bribery of public officials, and tax deductible expense accounts of big business) is the absence of the one law that is most appropriate—namely, the law that punishes the customer who uses the prostitute. In all but a very few jurisdictions, the use of a prostitute is not a felony or a misdemeanor. This simple fact encourages the prostitute to assume the calculated risk to earn large sums of money, and to use occasional periods of imprisonment for purposes of a well needed rest. If the customer were in similar jeopardy of imprisonment, the payment of large sums of money to the prostitute would be discouraged for the customer would then stand to lose with little or no chance to gain. Because of the structure of sex administration in the area of prostitution, the real problems involved in the relevant fields of psychiatry, sexology, and sociology affecting both the customer and the prostitute are almost completely ignored, and the world of prostitution remains deeply buried in the atmosphere of judicial impotency. . . .

There are, of course, legal problems involved in the male's sexual expression similar to those described above concerning females. Except for the State of Illinois, whose new code of laws will be described later, all states hold that almost any form of sexual expression not involving the connection of the male penis with the female vagina is illegal; this is either so stated specifically, or is implied by virtue of the vagueness of the statutes. The male problem of premature ejaculation is professionally dealt with, in part, by advising the man to cause the female orgasm prior to the connection of the penis with the vagina, here again the problem of being advised to commit crimes arises. Also, there are other problems concerning the male which would necessitate that professional advice be given to the female concerning precoital techniques she might perform for her husband, thus again violating the criminal code. But there are several further problems created that are uniquely problems of the male. . . .

[A] topic too vast for more than passing mention is the problem of pornography and the law. Although the placing of this problem in this section is not meant to indicate that the female has no use for, and is not aroused by pornography, the chief purchaser and user of pornography appears to be the male. Confusion caused by the collision between the concepts of freedom of the press, censorship, license, and the right of the state to police in the name of law and order is just as great today as it was fifty years ago. The problem of defining terms such as "literary art," "obscenity," and "hardcore pornography" practically insure an incredibly large traffic in so-called illegal pornography for many years to come. Despite the fact that progress (to be described below) has been made in certain other areas of sex administration, very little progress, if any at all, can be demonstrated in the area of pornography.

Although the original concept of statutory rape may have been more than justified (protection of the female in spite of herself), the method of carrying out this concept has proved a dismal failure and one most harmful to the legal safety of the male.

In the first place, in the light of today's knowledge of the discrepancy between the actual emotional maturity of a person and that person's chronological age, and the oversimplified device of specifying the exact age of consent of the female entirely defeats the well-intentioned purpose of the statute. It has resulted, for instance, in the conviction of a boy fifteen years of age for having sexual intercourse with a girl seventeen and one-half years of age, for the sole and insufficient reason that the girl was under eighteen. In some states even though the statute's wording was changed to avoid the situation just described, the original concept behind the statute was recommended without a single protest. To illustrate, New York State amended the statutory rape law by stating that no male under twenty-one years of age could be indicted or convicted for statutory rape. Nevertheless, to single out one particular case, five boys were indicted and convicted as youthful offenders, even though the girl in question was a known prostitute, was older than all of the boys involved, and but three weeks short of her eighteenth birthday at the time of the crime. One might add in passing that in spite of the admission on the part of the girl that she had received monies from all five boys, no legal action of any kind was taken against her. No one would suggest that the young female be left unprotected, but the time is long overdue for a reappraisal of this particular statute (which is of comparatively recent origin, compared to other biblically oriented sex statutes) by rewriting the statutory rape law, incorporating psychiatric, psychological, and social materials at our disposal.

Just as the cruelty of the law towards females is most intense in its treatment of unwed mothers, the equivalent of such inquisition is present in the legal treatment of the male homosexual. The entrapment of homosexuals by police officers in plain-clothes has been too often described for repetition here. Suffice it to say that the masochistic aspect of the desire of the homosexual to subconsciously trap himself, and thus alleviate his guilt through the punitive atmosphere of the average criminal court is evidence of the complete ineptness of the present laws concerning the homosexual. One could say that the law must have been designed to specifically aggravate the condition of homosexuality, rather than to protect society and the individual homosexual, as all criminal codes are supposed to do. So great is the hostility of society-at-large that as of this writing, the Section that would have made homosexual acts between consenting adults in private legal has been eliminated from the Proposed Revised Criminal Code of the State of New York by an overwhelming vote. As a further example, although the entrapment of a person by law enforcement officers is unconstitutional both in the Federal Constitution and in most State Constitutions, no lawyer, to the author's knowledge, would dare use entrapment as a defense for his client when the charge concerns homosexuality, because even the most blatant set of facts indicating obvious entrapment would be categorically denied by most Courts as constituting entrapment.

The subjects of transvestism and transsexualism in re the legal treatment available indicate to a greater degree the discrepancy between psychiatry and law. No specific statutes exist, as yet, that actually deal with the two subjects mentioned. When necessary, completely inappropriate statutes are used regardless of the results obtained. Statutes such as disturbing the peace, disorderly conduct, and mayhem have all been used even though the deeper aspects concerning the individual and society are completely ignored and, if anything, both the individual and society are left in far greater danger than if nothing had been done at all. . . .

It would be fair to say that to be alive is to have a sexual problem. This statement is not meant to be facetious, but rather it indicates the magnitude of the task of making society come face to face with deep-seated feelings of conflict concerning sex. The expressions "Let George do it," and "There ought to be a law" are in this instance synonymous; the reason for the perpetuation of laws concerning sex for interminable periods of time lies in the individual's "Let George do it" feeling that all you have to do to solve such "evil," "dirty," and "ungodly" problems is to make a law which prohibits them. The individual's false security is further enhanced by the law's provision for severe penalties for violations. The impossibility of enforcement of such laws,

and their devastating results, are seldom, if ever, understood by the community. The need to create appropriate laws is constantly branded with the desire to create lawlessness. Many commissions have been formed to study and recommended revisions and, except in one State, all such recommendations have been "swept under the rug."

Only in the State of Illinois was a revised code actually passed, becoming effective January 1, 1962. This code reflects great credit on those who wrote the code, and on the Illinois Legislature. The code can be briefly summarized as follows: All laws prohibiting sexual acts between consenting adults in privacy were eliminated from the criminal code. Those laws which remain concern themselves with sexual crimes performed (a) in public, (b) against children, and (c) with force. It is interesting to note that even though a crime of adultery remains in the Illinois Code as a misdemeanor, it must be proven that the behavior of the offenders was "open and notorious, . . ."[4] It should also be noted that no change was made concerning the crime of abortion and "lawful abortion," such abortion being lawful only if performed by a licensed physician, in a licensed hospital or other licensed facilities, and necessary for the preservation of the woman's life.

The habit of ignoring problems rather than making a law appropriate is so ingrained that it would seem, at the moment, that there is little hope for wide-spread changes in the various State Codes in the United States. It is too early to properly evaluate the success or failure of the Illinois Code. The method of change was a quiet one, so that a general "hue and cry" may yet be forthcoming in Illinois, depending on the skill of the law enforcement agencies, the type of cases which may arise and be reported in the daily papers, and the resulting public demand for "backward" revision of the criminal statutes.

In general, permitting of archaic laws—archaic since they no longer serve their purpose because of changes in public mores, and increased knowledge in the social sciences—to remain as part of the criminal code means they will remain unenforced for the most part, despite the fact that they are violated openly every hour of the day. To fail to enforce any law is to automatically affect the enforceability of all law.

The Illinois Code, therefore, has caused a long step to be taken toward improving the efficiency of law enforcement, by restricting those acts of a sexual nature to be called a crime to those which do not depend on the invasion of personal privacy for their discovery and allow for the most part freedom of will between consenting adults. It is already difficult to maintain a large enough police force to enforce the law in public places, to protect the individual from violence, and the child from harm without the additional thousands that would be needed to police the internal areas of one's home. As the late Justice Learned Hand consistently maintained years ago, all sex practices (except those involving force, public view, or the participation of children) are matters of taste, and should not be administered or regulated within the provisions of the law, but rather through the school, the church, and the home. The Illinois Code is designed around this concept. . . .

Reference should be made to a distinction existing in the legal administration of sex between unenforce*able* and unenfor*ced* laws. A clear recognition and understanding of this distinction would be a very real step forward in achieving fairness and efficiency in the structure of laws concerning sex. In the category of unenforceable laws, one finds statutes which are concerned with prohibiting various forms of sexual expression between consenting adults (such as oral-genital contacts, etc.). By eliminating (as the Illinois Code does) those statutes which are obviously unenforceable, the problem of dealing with the remainder becomes clarified and, therefore, much simpler.

As to the category of the unenforced statute, the causes of such unenforcement are largely twofold. First, there are those cases in which the prescribed penalties for the crime committed are so outlandishly inappropriate that a judge simply refuses to inflict cruelty on a . . . defendant and indulges in the fiction that the facts of the case really indicate some lesser crime (such as the crime of rape being reduced to the crime of simple assault), and thus imposes a lesser punishment. Second, in many cases the facts really do not fit into any of the statutes presently "on the books," so that the judge is forced to select some statute at random, whether it is appropriate or not, so as to satisfy public opinion in the community over which he presides.

As to the immediate future, there is no question that there is evidence of a sexual renaissance, but such evidence would seem to be least observable in the area of legal administration of sexual expression. There are glimmers of important changes in the near future. The normal forty to sixty year lag which has always existed between the creation of mores and codification of such mores into statute seems about up, so that one has hope that the dawn of appropriate legal administration of human sexual behavior is closer at hand than would appear on the surface.

NOTES

[1] Illustrations are numerous; one need only contemplate the effect on a woman patient with a conservative background, religious training, etc., when she is told that she has committed a felony while making love to her husband by permitting an oral-genital contact to help her achieve orgasm. It is important to note that the term "Sodomy," or the titles "Crime Against Nature" and "Lewd-Lascivious Behavior" contain acts within them that include, either by specific mention or vague reference, the acts of fellatio, cunnilinctus, and mutual masturbation.

[2] This example is a composite statute based on the average "Crime Against Nature" type of statute that appears in most states. It is important to note that all states have some form

of this statute, with the exception of Illinois. In some states such as New York, the statute has been expanded to include first degree, second degree, and third degree gradations of crimes. Note too that no distinction is made as to whether or not the participants are married or single.

[3] If a psychiatrist advises a female patient that certain precoital acts described in Footnote (1) would aid her in her physical fulfillment and in her marriage, he is advising her to commit the crimes of Sodomy, etc. If the act is a felony in the state in which the psychiatrist practices, his act of so advising becomes a felony.

[4] *Illinois Crim. Code:* Sec. 11–7.

Part Eight

The Decision to Marry

Ultimately, nearly everyone marries; as we mentioned earlier, the figure is presently at about 95 percent. Recently, the age at first marriage seems to be going up; and in 1971, the largest number of persons under thirty-five years of age remained single since the turn of the century. The reason for this increase has to do with attitude changes and social and economic changes. An important factor in the choice to delay marriage is, of course, that many no longer see marriage as the only way to engage in sex. There is no telling how many young people married in the past in order to make a sexual relationship—whether already in progress or just acutely desired—a legitimate one in the eyes of the partners and society. Further, with contraceptive knowledge and increased opportunity for abortion, people no longer have to worry as much about an unwanted pregnancy; shotgun weddings are almost a thing of the past. Other factors involved in delaying marriage or perhaps causing a decision not to marry at all are the women's liberation movement, which has shown that marriage is not the only socially approved and satisfying life for women; the economic recession, which has made unemployment higher than in recent years; the shift in population, which has temporarily created an abundance of women of marriageable age following the "baby boom" of the 1950s; and, to a smaller extent, the Gay Liberation Movement, which is encouraging homosexuals to "come out" openly and, therefore, resist a heterosexual marriage for the sake of appearances. All of these variables working together may cause fewer persons to marry over the years, but it is not expected that the overall figure will drop enough to change the fact that nearly everyone marries at least once in a lifetime.

In the United States, the choice of a mate is a relatively free one made by the individual partners based on their being in love with each other. Of course, no choice can be considered truly free, since families and friends usually have some influence, as do the advertising media and other social-learning aspects of a person's life that lead to sex stereotyping. However, the couple do choose each other—or "happen" to each other—and they do make the decision to marry for whatever reasons they may have. Usually, the principle reason given is that of being in love and, for many, this seems to be enough. There is a romantic notion that if one is in love, everything else will work out. No doubt, this accounts in large measure for the high divorce rate a few years later when the partners recognize that love is not a panacea for all problems, or even that what they thought was love was something else.

The question of what causes two people to pick each other has interested researchers for a long time and is probably the most thoroughly studied of all topics in the field of marriage and the family. Obviously, propinquity is a necessary factor—after all, it is vital that the couple get together in the first place for the process to begin. Occasionally, we hear about a couple who "fall in love" by correspondence, set a wedding date, and plan to live happily ever after; but while it makes a good story, it is rare and risky. Research tells us that two people are more likely to marry when they live, work, or go to school in the same neighborhood, and this is especially important for a young person who is not geographically mobile. Even in this day of rapid and relatively inexpensive travel, there are a great many people who never leave their home towns and who could thus only marry a local person or, in some cases, a visitor to the community. Since young people of marriageable age go away to work or to school at the peak time for choosing a partner, offices and college campuses often replace the neighborhood as centers for mate selection. In fact, the college admissions director and the corporate personnel director may be modern-day marriage brokers without even knowing it.

While propinquity is necessary, it is not sufficient to explain mate selection—obviously, not everyone who meets marries. Several other theories have been advanced to explain mate attraction. One popular idea that has been rather well substantiated is that persons who are similar to each other in socioeconomic background and who share interests, values, and ways of behaving will be drawn to each other. It is a rather well-accepted theory of human behavior that we seek out persons who validate us as human beings and who approve of our life-styles. Furthermore, it is easier to live with someone who agrees on core values and whose behavior makes us feel comfortable. Consequently, mixed marriages introduce conflicts and take more compromise and effort to work out than do homogamous relationships.

The first article in this section, by Eloise Snyder, is a rather unique study of similarity of attitudes of couples who marry. Snyder reports attitudes of the couples while they were still in high school and not dating each other, and then matches them at a later date when forty of them did marry a class member. The interesting suggestion put forth in this article is that the couple does not necessarily start out with similar attitudes, but that they mold each other's attitudes during later interaction. While this study in no way denies the theory of homogamy, it does point to the fact that similarity between couples probably grows as they work out successful relationships.

Another favorite explanation for why two people decide on each other is that we seek out persons who complement us—who have qualities we lack and are seeking. Thus, a quiet, socially introverted individual might be attracted to an outgoing, fun-loving mate who could open social doors he or she could not manage alone. There is a certain amount of evidence to indicate that complementary-need selection frequently takes place, although it is not thought to operate at as conscious a level as homogamy and probably is not among the first factors at work, as is similarity. A part of the problem with the theory of complementary needs is that romantic love seems to put blinders on couples; they usually are not the best judges of each other's personalities because of their subjective involvement with each other. A certain amount of idealization takes place, and what each thinks he or she is getting in a mate may be colored by what each wants to perceive. In the second article, Bruce Eckland examines biological, social, and, particularly, personality factors in mate selection and points out the problems and strengths of each. Eckland indicates rather clearly the complexity of mate choice, and demonstrates that it is a process begun in childhood with the development of the needs, wants, and expectations of each person.

Many studies have indicated that prior to marriage both men and women have given some thought to what they want in a mate. Some persons have a very definite idea; others admit to only a general notion based on what they have learned about what makes a good marriage. Movies, television, and periodicals, as well as models from family and friends, probably play a part in setting up an image of the ideal mate. Hearing a young person describe what is desired, and then seeing what he or she picks as representative of that desire, leads to the conclusion that a great deal of idealization of that choice must have taken place to produce the looks of satisfaction on the faces of the bride and groom. A few years later, when the idealization often begins to tarnish, couples wonder how they could have been so misled and often complain that their mates have changed. In a successful marriage, of course, the couple would be likely to continue to believe that each had gotten what he or she bargained for; and indeed they may have, or they would have adjusted to reality and gone about recuperating from the shattering of their idealism. Actually, the important factor in mate selection is probably not the notion of what one wants in an ideal mate, but instead the idealization of the chosen mate—after the decision has been made to be in love.

In his article, Bernard Murstein discusses the ideal image and shows how the choice of a marriage partner is influenced by the needs one mate has and his or her self-perception. Since most "common sense" literature has assumed that personality factors loom large in mate selection, the fact that idealization throws up a smoke screen in the selection process may be somewhat unsettling to some.

Once the decision is made to marry, the traditional next step has been to make a public announcement, which implies an engagement. In actuality, many couples today bypass a formal engagement and may substitute living together as a way of getting to know each other. Jewelers are not going out of business and the society pages are not empty of pictures and announcements of engagements, but the trend toward a more informal treatment of the decision to marry is clear-cut. Sometimes a tentative decision to marry has preceded the final one by many months, and tokens such as class rings, pins, and lavaliers are given to signify such a state; but perhaps no engagement ring is given—only a wedding ring at the time of the ceremony. All of the tradition surrounding engagement, such as the bridal showers, seem to center around the woman. The women's liberation movement has challenged this as sexist, claiming that the woman is the object of publicity and festivity because it is thought that she has finally "caught a man" and so has fulfilled her destiny!

The period between the decision to marry and the wedding—whether a formal, traditional engagement, a month of wedding plans, or a year of living together—is usually used to explore facets of married life and to make certain decisions and plans for the wedding and the couple's future together. When this serious talk and negotiation begins, many couples take back their decision to marry or, at least, deeply question whether or not to proceed. Various studies have indicated that engagement is an effective mechanism for screening out problem relationships and that every broken engagement is probably a cause for rejoicing. However, the other conclusion sometimes drawn—that successful engagements spell successful marriages—does not hold true, for the future cannot be predicted this surely; unforeseen problems will arise and individuals will change. In the fourth selection, by Rhona Rapoport, the relationship of the adjustments made during the engagement period to the quality of young married life is discussed. It becomes apparent that the nature of the marriage relationship is being formed prior to the wedding by the way the couple relate to and how much they get to know about each other.

There have always been couples who have lived together before or instead of marrying; but in the United States within the last ten years, growing numbers of couples are deciding to live together as a test of whether or not they want to marry. The question is frequently raised about whether or not this is a valid test; a good point can be made that one certainly should get to know another better by living with him or her. However, the success of a marriage depends on more than simply getting to know each other; as was pointed out earlier, knowing a person well at the time of marriage does not mean that the future changes each will make and the problems that will occur can be predicted and prepared for.

The value of a trial marriage also seems to depend on the reasons for the couple's living together in the first place. A large number of couples start living together long before they think seriously about marriage, and many first begin to live together out of convenience and perhaps to avoid legal marriage. Obviously, these are quite different circumstances from the couple who wants to marry but decides to try living together first. The former may drift into marriage ultimately because they have become dependent upon each other or because it will end pressures from families and society in general. Neither of these is a good reason to marry and probably will not make for future enduring relationships. In her article on trial marriages, Miriam Berger traces the concept both historically and cross-culturally and recommends that research be conducted to determine the effectiveness of living together as a preparation for successful marriage.

In spite of widespread knowledge and availability of contraceptives, many marriages take place each year because a child has been conceived. Usually, these are young couples, and, in the past, it was estimated that as high as 70 to 80 percent of teen-age marriages involved a pregnancy. The divorce rate is astoundingly high for such marriages, not only because of the pregnancy and forced nature of the marriage, but also because youth lacks experience, education, financial resources, and, often, family support. Fortunately, many adults now recognize that pregnancy, in and of itself, is not a good reason to get married; despite this, many parents still seem to push young people into marriage when a pregnancy is discovered because it is "the only decent thing to do."

Some experts who have studied premarital pregnancy believe that the young woman many times romanticizes the pregnancy and feels that marriage to the father will provide her with the emotional security she desires. There is evidence that the problem of child neglect and abuse is closely related to overburdened, inexperienced, immature parents, and further research has indicated that a child so treated often grows up to play out an inadequate parenting role, so that a cycle is started which is difficult to stop.

In the last article, Dean Hepworth deals with the implications of a forced marriage and considers ways of helping couples involved in them. Perhaps such young couples can receive counseling in which they are shown viable alternatives to marriage, or those who decide to marry might be given aid so that they will not feel so alone with their problems.

37

ATTITUDES:
A STUDY OF HOMOGAMY AND MARITAL SELECTIVITY

Eloise C. Snyder

The fact that in American society one man and one woman select each other as husband and wife from a population of potential mates has attracted much attention from both sociologists and psychologists. In fact, the interest has been so great that a specific area referred to as assortative mating studies has evolved. The express purpose of these studies is to determine who marries whom. In this area, there are two hypotheses. The first is homogamy, which postulates that likes marry likes; the second is heterogamy, which postulates that opposites marry each other.

Among the many items with which assortative mating studies have been concerned are intelligence, religion, education, social class, ethnic origin, residential propinquity, race, attitudes, physical characteristics, psychological characteristics, and social characteristics. For the most part, couples were found to be homogamous in regard to these items, with certain exceptions in regard to physical and psychological characteristics.

However, a review of assortative mating literature seems to point up two important problems. The first pertains to the phase of the man-woman relationship (i.e., pre-dating, dating, engagement, or marriage) in which the couples studied were involved. The second problem concerns the paucity of studies in which persons who selected each other for marriage are compared with those whom they did not select. This latter problem raises the following question: Granting that A and B, who married each other, share certain similarities (and dissimilarities), would they also share these similarities (and dissimilarities) with C, D, and E, whom they did not marry?

The purpose of this paper is to report on a study which attempts to deal with these two problems. In so doing, the item selected

for study is that of attitudes, and the population studied consists of sophomore students from 13 rural high schools located throughout Pennsylvania. A total of 561 students were studied, 40 of whom subsequently married a member of their class. The largest class contained 112 students, and the smallest contained 17 students. . . .

In many assortative mating studies, the couples were tested after they had already married. The findings of these studies, insofar as they pertain to items which do not change (e.g., race) or which can be objectively obtained through recall (e.g., age at time of marriage), are not affected by this procedure. However, the findings which pertain to items which can change or which cannot be obtained through recall (e.g., attitudes and the like) are affected.

Thus items which may be altered by the adjustive interaction of the couple cannot be measured during marriage and the results of these measurements be said to apply to a period prior to the marriage. Many researchers, recognizing this flaw, attempted to minimize its effect by obtaining data for their studies prior to the couples' marriages. They studied only engaged couples. Although this modified procedure served to reduce the effect which each couple's interaction may have had upon the data, inasmuch as engagement is generally recognized as the period during which many, if not most, of the personal adjustments are made, the influence of interaction was by no means eliminated.

Therefore, the present study was undertaken in an attempt to test the attitudes of couples who subsequently married each other, not after they had become engaged or married but just prior to their dating each other. Some of the couples may have been acquainted with each other at the time of testing, but their interaction was extremely limited and is not believed to have had an appreciable effect upon rendering their attitudes more similar (or dissimilar).

Attitudes were chosen as the test item because, although attitudes have been repeatedly referred to in the literature as being homogamous, the studies tested couples after they had had extensive interaction with each other and, as noted previously, the similarity of attitudes thus may have been a result of this interaction and may not have been present initially.

The first section of the instrument used to measure attitudes is concerned with the individual's responses (approve, undecided, or disapprove) to 14 areas of behavior: Church Attendance, Attending Dances, Loafing Uptown, Dating, Divorce, Social Drinking, Use of Tobacco, Card Playing, Staying Out Late, Attending Sunday Movies, Sabbath Labor, Failing in School, Use of Spending Money, Use of Make-up.

The second section of the attitude instrument is concerned with the individual's attitudes toward his peers, family, and community. The method of assessing the individual's attitudes toward these groups is based upon how he felt that they acted in regard to the 14 areas of behavior noted previously. For example, how did he think each of these groups acted in regard to church attendance, dances, loafing, dating, drinking, divorce, etc.? Were they too critical, satisfactory, or not critical enough with respect to these behaviors?

In analyzing the results of the attitudes, it was fairly easy to ascertain the similarity or dissimilarity involved. For example, if both marital partners approved of social drinking, it was said that they were similar in their attitude toward social drinking. If, however, one partner approved and the other either disapproved or was undecided, it was said that they were dissimilar in their attitude toward social drinking. The same procedure was followed for the section pertaining to the couples' attitudes toward their peers, their families, and their communities. . . .

The degree of attitude similarity shared by the partners within each of the 20 couples studied was not very high. The partners in each relationship were similar to one another in only 55 percent of their attitudes relating to the areas of behavior, in only 54 percent of those pertaining to their peers, and in only 51 percent of those concerning their families, and they were, indeed, more dissimilar than similar in their attitudes toward their communities—60 percent and 40 percent respectively. This degree of attitude similarity within each relationship is lower than would have been expected in view of previous research. This is probably due to the fact that in the previous studies, the couples were either engaged or married at the time of testing, which gave them an opportunity for a greater degree of personal interaction. This personal interaction may have had the tendency to make their attitudes more similar than they were prior to such interaction. However, since the data of the present study were collected prior to the engagement or marriage of the couples, they had had less opportunity for such personal interaction, which may explain the lesser degree of attitude similarity found by this study.

It may be that if each of these couples were tested now (after marriage), the degree of attitude similarity would show a marked increase. An attempt to retest these couples proved futile, however, because in eight cases the partners were not living together (in two cases the husbands were employed away from the area and returned to their wives only on weekends, while in six cases the husbands were in the armed services and the wives remained at home). Since it was felt that this separation would have affected the attitudinal adjustments of these couples, the retest was not continued. . . .

The second problem which one confronts in attempting to gain some understanding of marriage selection is the limited attention given in assortative mating research to comparing those persons who select each other as marriage partners with those whom they do not select. In the most recent studies, some attention is given to the "field of eligibles." A comparison of the person whom one marries with those whom he does not marry (the field of eligibles) has important bearing on the entire area of assortative mating. In the present paper, however, this point will be considered only as it relates to homogamy and will concern only one item, attitudes.

Exactly how significant is it when, upon reaching into a barrel, one comes out with two oranges? Obviously, the significance of such an act would depend, among other things, upon what else was in the barrel. Likewise, one can question exactly how important it is to discover that A and B, who married each other, are similar. If each could have shared this similarity with C, D, and E whom he did not marry, then the significance of the similarity would seem to be fairly minimal. If, on the other hand, the similarity shared by A and B were unique to them, that is, if neither could have shared this with anyone else, then the significance of similarity is maximal.

This suggests that the significance of finding homogamy (or heterogamy, for that matter) is dependent upon the number and variety of choices which people had in selecting their mates. Undoubtedly, those who have done research in this area are aware of this "principle of significance" and its importance; in spite of this, however, most research is concerned only with the couples who marry each other and makes no attempt to compare these data with data concerning the other choices which each person had but did not choose as a marriage partner.

In this regard, it might be argued that, in a very general way, assortative mating research does consider the choices which people have in selecting a mate. Reference is made here to the assumption that for each person, every other person of the opposite sex is a potential marriage partner. Thus, it would seem that there are an infinite number and variety of marital choices for each person, making any similarity in marriage selection seem exceedingly significant. It must be recognized, however, that the usefulness of such an assumption is extremely doubtful. It is known, for instance, that in American society, people tend to marry persons with whom they have interacted. It is also known that, due to social norms and social circumstances, there is a greater tendency to interact within one's own groups than there is to interact outside of these groups. Therefore, an assumption

which does not take into account the considerable effects which culture has upon the choice of a mate, both in terms of social distance and physical distance, is open to considerable criticism.

In the study being reported in this paper, an attempt is made to determine whether those similar attitudes which were shared by the couples are unique to them or whether, instead, the same similarity would have resulted if each partner had chosen to marry someone else. Determining the boundaries of this field of choices is not a simple task. It is possible, for example, that the choices should have included only those persons whom each of the partners had dated; it is also possible that the choices should have been broader, including all of the students attending the high school which the partners attended. The boundaries decided upon in this study, that is, the field of choices for each person, was considered to consist of all members of the sophomore class in which the couples were members. Although the decision regarding this field of choices is not flawless, it is hoped that it nevertheless is sufficiently exacting to render some preliminary insights. . . .

The attitudes found to be homogamous (the same for both members of the relationship) were measured against the attitudes of the remaining members of the class in order to determine whether the similarity of the couple was fairly unique to them or if it might merely have been a result of a greater incidence in the field. If A resembled B, whom he married, did he also resemble C, D, and E, whom he did not marry?

The crucial concept in the analysis of this part of the study is that of "selectivity." Selectivity has the following three characteristics:

1. It is reciprocal; that is, it is a result of interaction between the pair, since neither partner is a passive agent.
2. It is discriminating; that is, one chooses a person as a marital partner to the exclusion of all other marital probabilities.
3. It is unique; that is, the marital partners share traits which are not common to the field and which are there-

fore not merely the result of a function of the greater incidence of these traits in the field.

Therefore, selectivity does not exist when the similar (or dissimilar) characteristics are common to all other marital probabilities; it does exist when the similar (or dissimilar) characteristics are more or less unique to the marital couple and not common to their field. It is obvious that the concept of selectivity has broader application than the use to which it is put in this paper. It can be employed meaningfully with respect to any of the items studied in assortative mating research. For present purposes, however, its application will be limited to the study of attitudes. The procedure used in determining selectivity with respect to attitudes follows.

1. The homogamous attitudes of the marital couples were tabulated.
2. The attitudes of each member of the class (by sex) in which the couple held membership were also tabulated in order to determine the exact percentage of the class whose attitudes were the same as those of the marital pair.
3. The percentage of the class which fell outside of the attitude range of the marital couple was regarded as the "percentage of selectivity." These percentages of selectivity were assigned the following values:

Percentages of Selective Homogamy

100–81	very selective homogamy
80–61	rather selective homogamy
60–41	chance selectivity
40–21	rather nonselective homogamy
20–0	very nonselective homogamy

. . . Of all the homogamous attitudes, 38 percent reflected chance selectivity, while selective homogamy ("very" and "rather") and nonselective homogamy ("very" and "rather") were somewhat equal, showing 32 percent and 30 percent respectively. This suggests that, while a little over one-third of the homogamous attitudes were due to chance selectivity, a little less than one-third were found to be unique to the couples, and a little less than one-third were found to be the result of the greater incidence in the field. These findings might cast some doubt upon the assumption that similarity of attitudes among married couples is somehow unique to them and was in some way an important factor in determining the choice of a marriage partner.

With respect to the specific categories of attitudes, it appears that homogamous attitudes pertaining to the family show the least selectivity and that those pertaining to the community show the most selectivity. This latter point is interesting, because it will be remembered that it was precisely in this category (attitudes toward the community) that the couples were least homogamous—only 40 percent. This implies that, although the couples did not show a high degree of similarity in their attitudes toward the community, the attitudes that they did share were quite unique to them. . . .

The present study attempted to answer two questions: "How homogamous were the attitudes of married couples prior to the time that they dated each other?" And, "How unique to the couple were the homogamous attitudes which they did share?" The answer to both questions was, "Not very."

This suggests that if attitude similarity among married pairs exists, as research seems to show, this similarity must be the result of the adjustive interaction shared by the couple and not necessarily an affinity present at the outset of the relationship. The same explanation may also pertain to any uniqueness of attitudes which may be shared by the marital couple.

It must be noted, however, that these findings were obtained from a primarily rural population, were based on a relatively small number of cases, and are concerned with only certain attitudes. As such, they should be regarded as being merely suggestive. It is thought, however, that in spite of these limitations, this study does point up the need for more assortative mating research conducted prior to the couples' marriages, engagements, or even serious pre-engagement involvements, if possible.

38

THEORIES OF MATE SELECTION

Bruce K. Eckland

This paper is devoted to a review and clarification of questions which both social and biological scientists might regard as crucial to an understanding of nonrandom mate selection. Owing to the numerous facets of the topic, the diverse nature of the criteria by which selection occurs, and the sharp differences in the scientific orientations of students who have directed their attention to the problem, it does not seem possible at this time to shape the apparent chaos into perfect, or even near-perfect, order and, out of this, develop a generalized theory of mate selection. Nevertheless, it is one of our objectives to systematize some of our thinking on the topic and consider certain gaps and weaknesses in our present theories and research.

Before embarking on this task, it would be proper to ask why the problem is worth investigating. . . . If the social and biological scientists had a better understanding of mate selection, what would happen to other parts of our knowledge or practice as a result? Despite the fact that our questions arise from quite different perspectives, there is at least one obvious point at which they cut across the various fields. This point is our common interest in the evolution of human societies, and assortative mating in this context is one of the important links between the physical and cultural components of man's evolution.

Looking first from the geneticists' side, at the core of the problem lies the whole issue of natural selection. Any divergence from perfect panmixia, i.e., random mating, splits the genetic composition of the human population into complex systems of subordinate populations. These may range from geographically isolated "races" to socially isolated caste, ethnic, or economic groups. Regardless of the nature of the boundaries, each group is viewed as a biological entity, differing statistically from other groups with respect to certain genes. To the extent that different mating groups produce more or fewer children, "natural" selection takes place.

In the absence of differential fertility, assortative mating alone does not alter the gene frequencies of the total population. Nevertheless, it *does* change the distribution and population variance of genes and this, itself, is of considerable importance. Hirsch (1967), for example, has stated:

As the social, ethnic, and economic barriers to education are removed throughout the world, and as the quality of education approaches a more uniformly high level of effectiveness, heredity may be expected to make an ever larger contribution to individual differences in intellectual functioning and consequently to success in our increasingly complex civilization. Universally compulsory education, improved methods of ability assessment and career counseling, and prolongation of the years of schooling further into the reproductive period of life can only increase the degree of positive assortative mating in our population. From a geneticist's point of view our attempt to create the great society might prove to be the greatest selective breeding experiment ever undertaken. (p. 128)

. . . Also from the biological point of view, it is probable that assortative mating is becoming an increasingly important factor relative to others affecting the character of the gene pool. Infant mortality, for instance, does not appear to exert the same kind of selection pressure on the populations of Western societies today that it did a hundred, or even fifty, years ago. Likewise, accompanying the rise of mass education and spread of birth control information, fertility differentials appear to have narrowed markedly, especially in this country. For example, the spread is not nearly as great as it once was between the number of children in lower and upper socioeconomic families. It is not altogether clear, of course, just how the relaxation of selection pressures of this kind would, in the long run, affect future generations. Yet, assuming, as some have suggested, that these trends will continue, then a broader understanding of the nature and causes of mate selection may eventually become one of the outstanding objectives of population geneticists. One reason is that the more the assortative mating, the greater the rate of genetic selection. If nearly all members of a society produce and most reproduce about the same number of children, and these in turn live to reproduce, it might then be just as important to know who mates with whom as to know who reproduces and how much.

The interest of social scientists in mate selection has been more uneven and much more diffuse. Some anthropologists undoubtedly come closest to sharing the evolutionary perspective of geneticists, as indicated by their work in a variety of overlapping areas which deal in one way or another with mating, e.g., genetic drift, hybridization, and kinship systems. In contrast, sociologists have been less sensitive to genetic theories. We share with others an evolutionary approach, but one that rests almost wholly on social and cultural rather than physical processes. Nonetheless, mate selection lies at the core of a number of sociological problems. These range, for example from studies of the manner in which class endogamy is perpetuated from one generation to the next to studies in which endogamy is conceived as a function of marital stability. While sociologists have helped to ascertain many facts as well as having developed a few quasi-theories about assortative mating, it is rather difficult when reviewing our literature on the subject to distinguish between that which is scientifically consequential and that which is scientifically trivial. The general orientation of social scientists, in any case, is far from trivial and can be used instructively

in the region of mate selection and in ways heretofore neglected by population geneticists. Some of their "theories" will be reviewed later in this paper. . . .

Mate selection is *not* simply a matter of preference or choice. Despite the increased freedom and opportunities that young people have to select what they believe is the "ideal" mate, there are a host of factors, many *well* beyond the control of the individual, which severely limit the number of eligible persons from which to choose. As unpalatable as this proposition may be, it rests on a rather large volume of data, which suggests that the regulatory system of society enforces in predictable ways a variety of norms and sometimes specific rules about who may marry whom. Perhaps the most important point I will have to make in this paper is that geneticists must begin to recast their assumptions about the nature of culture and society, just as sociologists must recast their thinking about genetics.

Assuming that both geneticists and sociologists do reconsider their positions and assuming, too, that each discipline has a hold on some part of the truth, there still remains the unfilled gap in the kinds of knowledge needed to develop a set of interlocking theories between the social and biological sciences with regard to mate selection. I do not question that organic and cultural evolution can and, in many ways, must be studied as separate phenomena. The point is, however, that they do interact and this, too, should be studied; and to do so will require a much broader historical perspective than most geneticists and social scientists have exhibited up to now.   .

An interaction model of organic and cultural evolution must specify the precise nature of the relationships between the hereditary factors and environmental influences. Although certainly a very old idea, the notion of *interaction* has lain relatively dormant until recent years, probably largely due to the nature-nurture controversy and the racist arguments that covered most of the first half of the twentieth century. . . . As before, we are dealing with the processes by which generational replacement and change occur. However, in addition to the duplication of most genes and most cultural traits in each succeeding generation, new patterns invariably emerge through the interaction of heredity and environment. Briefly, and with no intent on my part to intimate either purpose or consciousness, (a) genes restrict the possible range of man's development and (b) within these limits he alters his environment or cultural arrangements in such ways as to change the frequencies or distribution of genes in the next generation which (c) enables him to carry out further changes.

It is important to note here that the interaction of heredity and environment does not occur within the duration of a single generation, a point that social scientists, in particular, need to recognize. Holding for inspection a very short segment of the life span of a single cohort, as so often we do, it is not possible to observe, even to logically think about, heredity and environment in interaction. Within the span of one generation, the relationship appears only as a one-way process, with the genetic makeup of individuals determining the norms of reaction to the environment. The path from environment *back* to genetics which actually allows us to speak in terms of *inter*action appears only *between* generations. . . . The cultural environment, of course, may have an immediate and direct effect upon an individual's endocrine system, as well as other physiological and morphological structures, but it cannot, as far as we know, alter his genes. Environment can only alter their phenotypic expression and, owing to selective mating, the genes of one's progeny in the next generation.

We have now moved into a position whereby we might raise two rather crucial questions regarding the search for significant variables in mate selection, that is, significant in the context of an interaction model. The first is: What genotypes have social definitions attached to their behavioral manifestations or, conversely, what physical, personality, and social traits depend on our genes? The answer requires determining how much, if any, of the variance of a particular trait is due to heredity (and how much to environment). For example, taking the operational definition of intelligence we now employ, if none of the variance can be attributed to genetic sources, then no matter how intense assortative mating is for intelligence, we most certainly would exclude it from any further consideration in our model. . . . Every character is determined during the lifetime of that individual, with genotypes determining part of the course of development and not the other way around. . . .

The second question is: What criteria for mate selection are *functionally* relevant within a particular population at a particular time? This question, of course, raises some long-standing issues in genetics regarding the "adaptive" quality of characteristics which are genetically variable. It appears, for example, that some traits like the O, A, B, and AB blood types for the most part are adaptively neutral or, at least, it is not known how they affect the biological or social fitness of their possessors in any significant way. Likewise, there are traits like eye color which apparently have no clear functional value and yet seem to be involved in the sorting which unites one mate with another. . . . Any delimiting, therefore, of the class of mate selection variables we eventually must take into account should deal, on the one hand, with traits which are understood in terms of genetic processes and partly in terms of social and other environmental processes and, on the other hand, with traits whose survival or social value is at least partly understood. . . .

The disappearance of unilineal kinship systems in Western societies has led to a decline of kinship control over mate selection. The resulting freedom which young people now enjoy has brought about an enormously complex system. No doubt, the selection process actually begins long before the adolescent's first "date." Moreover, under conditions of serial monogamy where it is possible to have many wives but only one at a time, the process for some probably never ends. Determining the "choice" are a myriad of emotional experiences and it is these experiences, along with a variety of subconscious drives and needs, upon which most psychological and other "individualistic" theories are based. . . .

Some of the earliest and perhaps most radical theories of mate selection suggested that what guides a man to choose a woman (it was seldom thought to be the other way around) is instinct. Scholars believed that there must be for each particular man a particular woman who, for reasons involving the survival of the species, corresponded most perfectly with him. A modern rendition of the same idea is Carl Jung's belief that falling in love is being caught by one's "anima." That is, every man inherits an anima which is an "archetypal form" expressing a particular female image he carries within his genes. When the right woman comes along, the one who corresponds to the archetype, he instantly is "seized." However, no one, as far as we know, has actually discovered any pure biologically determined tendencies to assortative mating. . . .

A psychoanalytic view, based on the Oedipus configuration, has been that in terms of temperament and physical appearance one's ideal mate is a parent substitute. The boy, thus, seeks someone like his mother and the girl seeks someone like her father. While it admittedly would seem reasonable to expect parent images to either encourage or discourage a person marrying someone like his parent, no clear evidence has been produced to support the hypothesis. Sometimes striking resemblances between a man's wife and his mother, or a woman's husband and her father, have been noted. Apparently, however, these are only "accidents," occurring hardly more frequently than expected by chance. . . .

Another generally unproven assumption, at least with respect to any well-known personality traits, involves the notion that "likes attract." Cattell and Nesselroade (1967) recently found significant correlations between husband and wife on a number of personality traits among both stably and unstably married couples. The correlations, moreover, were substantially higher (and more often in the predicted direction) among the "normal" than among the unstably married couples. As the authors admit, however, it was not possible to determine whether the tendency of these couples to resemble each other was the basis for their initial attraction ("birds of a feather flock together") or whether the correlations were simply an outgrowth of the marital experience. Although the ordering of the variables is not clear, the evidence does tend to suggest that the stability of marriage and, thus the number of progeny of any particular set of parents, may depend to some extent on degrees of likeness. . . .

Probably as old as any other is the notion that "opposites attract"; for example, little men love big women, or a masochistic male desiring punishment seeks out a sadistic female who hungers to give it. Only in the past 20 years has a definitive theory along these lines been formulated and put to empirical test. This is Winch's theory of complementary needs which hypothesizes that each individual seeks that person who will provide him with maximum need gratification. The specific need pattern and personality of each partner will be "complementary" (Winch, 1958). Accordingly, dominant women, for example, would tend to choose submissive men as mates rather than similarly dominant or aggressive ones. The results of a dozen or so investigations, however, are inconclusive, at best. More often than not, researchers have been unable to find a pattern of complementary differences. No less significant than other difficulties inherent in the problem is the discouraging fact that the correlation between what an individual thinks is the personality of his mate and the actual personality of his mate is quite small (Udry, 1966). Nevertheless, the theory that either mate selection or marital stability involves an exchange of interdependent behaviors resulting from complementary rather than similar needs and personalities is a compelling idea and perhaps deserves more attention.

No firm conclusions can yet be reached about the reasons for similarity (or complementariness) of personality and physical traits in assortative mating. (Even the degree of association or disassociation on most personality characteristics is largely unknown.) To state that "like attracts like" or "opposites attract," we know are oversimplifications. Moreover, few attempts to provide the kinds of explanations we seek have thus far stood up to empirical tests. . . .

In a very general way, social homogamy is a critical point in the integration or continuity of the family and other social institutions. It is a mechanism which serves to maintain the status quo and conserve traditional values and beliefs. And, because marriage itself is such a vital institution, it is not too difficult to understand why so many of the social characteristics which are important variables generally in society, such as race, religion, or class, are also the important variables in mate selection. Thus, most studies in the United States report a very high rate, over 99 percent, for racial endogamy, an overall rate perhaps as high as 90 percent for religious homogamy, and moderately high rates, 50 percent to 80 percent for class homogamy, the exact figures depending on the nature of the index used and the methods employed to calculate the rate.

One possible way of illustrating the conserving or maintenance function of social homogamy in mate selection is to try to visualize momentarily how a contemporary society would operate under conditions of *random* mating. Considering their proportions in the population, Negroes actually would be more likely to marry whites than other Negroes, Catholics more often than not would marry Protestants, and a college graduate would be more apt to marry a high school dropout than to marry another college graduate. In a like manner, about as often as not, dull would marry bright, old would marry young, Democrats would marry Republicans, and teetotalers would marry drinkers. What would be the end result of this kind of social heterogamy? A new melting pot, or chaos?

It seems that, in the absence of "arranged marriages," a variety of controls governs mate selection and, in the process, substantially reduces the availability of certain individuals as potential mates. Many structures in society undoubtedly carry out these functions, sometimes in quite indirect ways, such as the subtle manner in which the promotion of an "organization man" may be based, in part, on how well his mate's characteristics meet the qualifications of a "company wife." Thus, despite the "liberation" of mate selection and the romantic ideals of lovers who are convinced that social differences must not be allowed to stand in their way, probably one of the most important functions of both the elaborate "rating and dating" complex and the ceremonial "engagement" is to allow a society to make apparent who may "marry upward" and under what conditions exogamy is permitted. We are referring here, then, not merely to society's control over the orderly replacement of personnel, but to its integration and the transmission of culture as well.

Rather than reviewing any very well-formulated theories (since there may be none) in the remaining discussion, I have attempted to touch upon a fairly broad range of conditions under which homogamy, as a social fact, relates to other aspects of contemporary societies. . . .

Whether we are speaking about place of residence, school, work, or such abstruse features of human ecology as the bus or streetcar routes along which people travel, propinquity obviously plays a major part in mate selection since, in nearly all cases, it is a precondition for engaging in interaction. (The mail-order bride, for instance, is one of several exceptions.) A person usually "selects" a mate from the group of people he knows. Findings which illustrate the function of distance have been duplicated in dozens of studies. In Columbus, Ohio, it was once found that more than half of the adults who had been married in that city had actually lived within 16 blocks of one another at the time of their first date (Clarke, 1952). Cherished notions about romantic love notwithstanding, the chances are about 50–50 that the "one and only" lives within walking distance.

As many authors have pointed out, people are not distributed through space in a random fashion. In fact, where people live, or work and play, corresponds so closely with one's social class (and race) that it is not quite clear whether propinquity, as a factor in mate selection, is simply a function of class endogamy or, the other way around, class endogamy is a function of propinquity. Ramsøy's (1966) recent attempt to resolve this issue, I want to note, misses the mark almost completely. Investigating over 5000 couples living in Oslo, Norway, she concludes that propinquity and social homogamy are "totally independent of one another" and, therefore, rejects the long-standing argument that "residential segregation of socioeconomic and cultural groups in cities represents a kind of structural underpinning both to propinquity in mate selection and to homogamy." More specifically, the author shows that "couples who lived very near one another before marriage were no more likely to be of the same occupational status than couples who lived at opposite sides of the city." This is astonishing, but misleading. The author equated the social status of the bride and, implicitly, her social class origin with *her* occupation at the time of marriage. No socioeconomic index other than the bride's occupation unfortunately was known to the investigator and, thus, it was a convenient although poorly considered jump to make. To most sociologists, it should be a great surprise to find in any Western society, including Norway, that the occupations young women hold before marriage give a very clear indication of their social status, relative either to the occupational status of men they marry or to their own places of residence. . . .

An explanation often cited in the literature on mate selection, as well as in that on the more general topic of interpersonal attraction, deals in one form or another with the principle of exchange. A Marxian view, marriage is an exchange involving both the assets and liabilities which each partner brings to the relationship. Thus, a college-educated woman seldom brings any special earning power to the marriage, but rather she typically enters into contract with a male college graduate for whom her diploma is a social asset which may benefit his own career and possibly those of his children. In exchange, he offers her, with a fair degree of confidence, middle-class respectability. Norms of reciprocity might also help to explain the finding that most borderline mentally retarded women successfully marry and even, in some cases, marry upward, if they are physically attractive. This particular theory, however, has not been well-developed in regard to mate selection, despite its repeated usage. Also, it may be a more appropriate explanation of deviations from assortative mating or instances of negative mate selection than of positive selection. . . .

In contrast to the inconclusive evidence regarding assortative mating in terms of personality characteristics, numerous studies do indicate that married couples (and engaged couples) show far more consensus on various matters than do randomly matched couples. Even on some rather generalized values, as in the area of aesthetics or economics, social homogamy occurs. Apparently, our perception that other persons share with us the same or similar value orientations and beliefs facilitates considerably our attraction to them (Burgess and Wallin, 1943).

The importance of norms and values in mate selection, part of the social fabric of every society, also can be illustrated in a more direct way by looking at some of the specific sanctions that we pass along from generation to generation. Without really asking why, children quite routinely are brought up to believe that gentlemen prefer blondes (which may be only a myth perpetuated by the cosmetic industry), that girls should marry someone older rather than younger than themselves (which leaves most of them widows later on), and that a man should be at least a little taller than the woman whom he marries (which places the conspicuously tall girl at an enormous disadvantage). Simple folkways as such beliefs presently are, they nevertheless influence in predictable ways the "choice" of many individuals. . . .

We have already noted that the field of eligible mates is largely confined to the same social stratum to which an individual's family of orientation belongs. Social-class endogamy not only plays a significant part in the process of mate selection, it may also help to explain other forms of assortative mating. For example, part of the reason why marriage partners or engaged couples share many of the same values and beliefs no doubt is because they come from the same social backgrounds.

There are at least five explanations which can be offered for the persistence of class endogamy, each of which sounds reasonable enough and probably has a hold on some part of the truth.

First, simply to turn the next to last statement around, persons from the same class tend to marry *because* they share the same values (which reflect class differences) and not because they are otherwise aware or especially concerned about each other's background.

Second, during the period of dating and courtship most young people reside at the home of their parents. (Excluded here, of course, are the large minority in residential colleges and those who have left both school and home to take an apartment near their place of work.) The location of parental homes reflects the socioeconomic status of the family and is the general basis for residential segregation. With respect to both within and between communities, the pattern of segregation places potential mates with different backgrounds at greater distances than those with similar backgrounds. Thus, to the extent that the function of distance (or propinquity) limits the field of eligibles, it also encourages class endogamy by restricting class exogamy.

Third, class endogamy in some cases is simply a function of the interlocking nature of class and ethnicity. A middle-class Negro, for example, probably is prevented from an exogamous marriage with a member of the upper-class not so much because class barriers block it but because he (or she) is a Negro. The majority of the eligible mates in the class above are whites and, in this instance, what appears to be class endogamy is really racial endogamy.

Fourth, ascriptive norms of the family exert a great deal of pressure on persons, especially in the higher strata, to marry someone of their "own kind," meaning the same social level. The pressures that parents exert in this regard sometimes are thought to have more than anything else to do with the process and certainly are visible at nearly every point at which young people come into meaningful contact with one another. Norms of kinship regarding the future status of a child may be involved, for example, in the parent's move to the right community, sending a child to a prep school, or seeing that he gets into the proper college.

Fifth, and an increasingly convincing argument, even as the structure of opportunities for social mobility open through direct competition within the educational system, class endogamy persists owing to the educational advantages (or disadvantages) accrued from one's family of orientation. Most colleges, whether commuter or residential, are matrimonial agencies. As suggested earlier, despite whatever else a woman may gain from her (or, more often, her parents') investment in higher education, the most important thing she can get out of college is the proper husband or at least the credentials that would increase her bargaining power in an exchange later on. Given the fact that men generally confer their status (whether achieved or ascribed) upon women and not the other way around (female proclamations to the contrary notwithstanding), marriage as a product of higher education has far more functional value for women than vocational or other more intrinsic rewards.

To carry this argument a bit further, access to college depends in large measure on the academic aptitude (or intelligence) of the applicants. Moreover, the hierarchical ordering of colleges which is based on this selectivity has led to a system of higher education which, in many ways, replicates the essential elements of the class structure. Differentiating those who go to college from those who do not, as well as where one goes to college, are *both* aptitude and social class. These two variables correspond so closely that despite the most stringent policies at some universities where academic aptitude and performance are the central criteria for admissions and where economic aid is no longer a major factor, students still come predominantly from the higher socioeconomic classes. For whatever the reason, genetic and environmental, this correspondence facilitates the intermarriage of individuals with similar social backgrounds, especially on American campuses where the sex ratio has been declining. It is interesting to note in this context that

Warren's recent study of a representative sample of adults showed that roughly half of the similarity in class backgrounds of mates was due to assortative mating by education (Warren, 1966). . . .

While intermarriage is both a cause and consequence in the assimilation of the descendants of different ethnic origin, various writers claim that the American "melting pot" has failed to materialize. Religious and racial lines in particular are far from being obliterated. In fact, the very low frequency of exogamous marriages across these lines itself underscores the strength of the cleavages. Most authors also agree that nationality is not as binding as either race or religion as a factor in mate selection. Nation-type solidarities are still found among some urban groups (Italians and Poles) and rural groups (Swedes and Finns), but our public school system and open class structure have softened considerably what were once rather rigid boundaries. There is some evidence, too, that religious cleavages have been softening somewhat, and perhaps are continuing to soften as the functions of this institution become increasingly secular and social-problem oriented. On the other hand, racial boundaries, from the view of mate selection, appear to be as binding today as at any previous point in history; at least I have found no evidence to the contrary. The gains that Negroes have made in the schools and at the polls during the past ten years apparently have not softened the color line with respect to intermarriage.

Explanations of racial endogamy in America, some of which would take us back several centuries in time, are too varied to discuss here. It might be well to point out, however, that cultural and even legal prohibitions probably have relatively little to do with the present low rate of interracial marriage. As one author has stated, "the whole structure of social relationships between white and Negroes in the United States has been organized in such a way as to prevent whites and Negroes from meeting, especially under circumstances which would lead to identifying each other as eligible partners. . . . Under these circumstances, the few interracial marriages which do occur are the ones

which need explaining" (Udry, 1966).

For the population geneticist, too, it would seem that the deviant cases are the ones which require attention. Elsewhere I have suggested, for example, that genes associated with intelligence may simply drift across the white and Negro populations since it appears that only certain morphological features, like skin color, actually operate to maintain the color line. In other words, if the skin of an individual with Negro ancestry is sufficiently light, he may "pass" (with no strings attached) into the white population. Even just a lighter-than-average complexion "for a Negro" probably enhances his chances of consummating what we socially define as an "interracial" marriage. In neither the first or second case, however, is intelligence necessarily involved.

If intelligence *were* associated in any predictable way with racial exogamy, the drift would not be random and we would then have a number of interesting questions to raise. For instance, do only the lighter *and* brighter pass, and, if so, what effect, if any, would this be likely to have on the character of the Negro gene pool? What, too, is the character of the inflow of genes from the white population? We do know that the great majority of legally consummated interracial marriages involve Negro men and white women. Does this information provide any clues? And, what about the illegitimate progeny of white males and Negro prostitutes? How often are they placed for adoption in white households and with what consequences? Before taking any of these questions too seriously, we would want to have many more facts. For obvious reasons, our knowledge is extremely meager. . . .

In conclusion, five brief comments may be made upon the present state of research and theories of mate selection as revealed in the foregoing discussion.

First, there is a great deal of evidence of homogamous or assortative mating but relatively few theories to explain it and no satisfactory way of classifying its many forms.

Second, nearly all facts and theories regarding mate selection deal with engaged or married couples and hardly any attention has been given to illegitimacy (including adultery) and its relationship to assortative mating. It may be, such as in the case of miscegenation, that some of the most important aspects of mate selection occur outside the bonds of matrimony.

Third, our heavy emphasis upon courtship and marriage has obscured the fact that people often separate, divorce, and remarry. Mate selection may be a more or less continuous process for some individuals, affecting the character of the progeny of each new set of partners.

Fourth, the relationships between fertility and assortative mating still must be specified. Are there, for example, any patterns of assortative mating on certain traits, like education, which affect the number of children a couple will have?

Fifth, most of the factors in mate selec-

tion appear to covary. We discussed some of the more obvious problems in this regard, such as the relationship between residential segregation (propinquity) and class endogamy. It would appear that much more work of this sort will need to be done.

In regard to the last point, it would also appear that it is precisely here that social scientists, and sociologists in particular, may best serve the needs of population geneticists. Through the application of causal (chain) models and multivariate techniques, it may eventually be possible to sort out the relevant from the irrelevant and to specify in fairly precise terms not only the distribution of assortative mating in the social structure with regard to any particular trait, but also the ordering of variables and processes which restrict the field of eligibles.

REFERENCES

Burgess, Ernest W., and Paul Wallin. "Homogamy in Social Characteristics." *American Journal of Sociology,* 49 (1943): 109–124.

Cattell, Raymond B., and John R. Nesselroade. "'Likeness' and 'Completeness' Theories Examined by 16 Personality Factor Measures on Stably and Unstably Married Couples." (Advanced Publication No. 7.) The Laboratory of Personality and Group Analysis, University of Illinois, 1967.

Clarke, Alfred C. "An Examination of the Operation of Residential Propinquity as a Factor in Mate Selection." *American Sociological Review,* 17 (1952): 17–22.

Hirsch, Jerry. "Behavior-Genetic, or 'Experimental,' Analysis: The Challenge of Science Versus the Lure of Technology." *American Psychology,* 22 (1967): 118–130.

Ramsøy, Natalie Rogoff, "Assortative Mating and the Structure of Cities." *American Sociological Review,* 51 (1966): 773–786.

Udry, J. Richard. *The Social Context of Marriage.* Philadelphia: J. P. Lippincott, 1966.

Warren, Bruce L. "A Multiple Variable Approach to the Assortative Mating Phenomenon." *Eugenics Quarterly,* 13 (1966): 285–290.

Winch, Robert. *Mate Selection.* New York: Harper and Row, 1958.

39

SELF–IDEAL-SELF DISCREPANCY AND THE CHOICE OF MARITAL PARTNER

Bernard I. Murstein

The choice of marital partner is a problem faced by more than 90 percent of the American population at least once during their lives. Considering the importance of choice, it is regrettable that so little information on the process is available. What knowledge we possess is largely restricted to the area of sociology. With respect to such variables as age, religion, values, education, and socioeconomic standing, the evidence indicates that homogamy is associated with marital choice. When we inquire into the effect of psychological determinants, however, we run into a great diversity of theories and little confirming evidence. . . .

It appears that no one theory has gained any extensive support in the literature. This failure may be attributed to the lack of sufficient attention to three critical factors which may influence the problem of marital choice.

First, the impression is often given in the literature that individuals seek someone with personality characteristics similar or different from the ones they possess according to whether the "homogamy" or opposites-attract theory is being hypothesized. Actually, it seems more reasonable to assume that an individual seeks a partner whom he believes will most enhance his self-esteem and will herself reflect the qualities which he desires to achieve in himself. We should expect, therefore, that an individual's perceptions of his ideal self, ideal spouse, and fiancé(e) should be highly intercorrelated.

Returning now to the question of whether the individual will seek to choose someone similar or opposite to himself, it seems logical to assume that if he is highly satisfied with himself as determined by a high self–ideal-self correlation, and if it is true, as I have suggested, that the perception of the ideal spouse and fiancée are highly correlated with his ideal self, then it follows that he will attempt to marry someone whom he perceives as highly similar to himself. If, on the other hand, he is quite dissatisfied with himself (low self–ideal-self correlation), he will still want to marry someone whom he perceives as close to both his ideal spouse and ideal self. If he succeeds in this goal, however, it follows that he will be marrying someone whom he perceives as dissimilar to himself, since he perceives his self as being distant from his ideal self. . . .

A study by Goodman (1964) bears on this problem somewhat. Working with newly married couples, he administered the Bills Index of Adjustment and Values as a measure of self-esteem and also gave his Ss the Edwards Personal Preference Schedule. He found that couples with high self-esteem tended to manifest positive correlations for various needs in their self-concepts, whereas those with low self-esteem showed negative correlations, a finding quite consistent with the views expressed here. However, Goodman used married couples; therefore, he had to assume that his couples had actually chosen each other on the basis of self-esteem. Also, he did not specifically measure the relationship of self-esteem to the perception of similarity in the partner. His findings, therefore, do not directly bear on the question of perceived similarity and marital choice. In sum, it is proposed that individuals seek to marry those who possess ideally desirable qualities and that the perceived similarity or difference between the partner and the self is a derivative of the extent of distance between the self and the trinity of desiderata: the ideal spouse, fiancé(e), and ideal self.

The second factor which has received insufficient attention has been the failure to recognize that "to seek" is not necessarily equivalent to "finding." An individual may desire certain qualities in a spouse, but his success in achieving his goal will depend on his own assets in the marital mart. These may include such "external" considerations as the sociological variables mentioned earlier as well as physical attraction. Also crucially important in our culture is the individual's general social adequacy and his ability to meet the interactional needs of his partner.

In an earlier report (Murstein, 1967), it was shown that college Ss tend to become engaged to persons of greater than chance similarity in neurotic status. Further, couples who broke up prior to marriage were shown to have been negatively correlated with respect to an index of neuroticism, whereas couples making good courtship progress showed a positive correlation. In considering marital choice in a normal college population, the self–ideal-self discrepancy should be an even more appropriate index to use, since there is less curtailment of range for this variable than for neuroticism in such a population.

It seems plausible that persons with high self–ideal-self congruence exude a certain self-confidence that is considered a desirable characteristic in a marital partner. Not everyone, however, can produce comparable assets of their own to win such a person no matter how much they may desire to do so; consequently, persons with low self–ideal-self congruence are more likely to fail to attract high congruence persons than are high self–ideal-self congruence persons. The result is that there should be a positive correlation between the self–ideal-self congruence of couples planning to marry.

The third factor causing difficulty is that the treatment of marital choice in the literature often confounds the analytical process by which the researcher measures the personality characteristics of Ss with the decision processes operating in the act of marital choice. "A" may be shown to want a certain behavior from "B," and B may want to express that behavior. This factor may serve to suggest a convenient fiction: that A and B discuss and catalogue the strength of each need in each other and thereby decide whether or not to marry.

In reality, most engaged couples do not discuss specific need patterns. Moreover, the courting pattern is one that does not generally permit a full and complete understanding of the other individual's perceptions. Certainly, it is evident that most couples find after marrying and living together for some time that there was much they did not know about their spouse before marriage.

It seems more fruitful, therefore, to acknowledge that the decision to marry really involves two separate decisions, one on the part of each member. In the absence, relatively speaking, of extensive interaction between the members of the couple, intraperceptual congruence (perceptions wholly within a given person) should have considerably more weight than interperceptual congruence, which involves two different persons. . . .

The arguments put forth regarding the choice of a marital partner lead to the following hypotheses: (*a*) Persons tend to become engaged to individuals of a similar level of self–ideal-self acceptance, (*b*) the perception of the partner as similar or different is a function of the level of self-acceptance, (*c*) persons who are low in self-acceptance are forced to settle for potential marriage partners who do not approximate their concept of ideal spouse as closely as is the case for persons of high self-acceptance, and (*d*) perceived role fit between perception of fiancé and ideal spouse will be significantly higher for intraperceptions (perceived role fit) than for interperceptions (actual role fit involving perceptions from both partners).

METHOD

The sample consisted of 99 couples who were "going steady" or were engaged, and who had volunteered to participate in the study for which they were paid $20 per couple. The sample was largely drawn from three Connecticut colleges or universities, only 13 of the 198 Ss indicating that they were neither students nor college graduates. The average age of the men and women was 21.1 and 19.8, respectively. Background questionnaires revealed that the sample was a relatively homogeneous upper middle class one.

To test the hypotheses, a modified version of the Edwards Personal Preference Schedule was employed. The standard test consists of paired sentences representing different needs roughly equated for social desirability with the intention that S be forced to express his personal choice rather than the more socially acceptable one. . . .

The Ss were tested on any one of several testing dates and took the revised form as part of a larger battery of tests and questionnaires. The tests were coded to assure anonymity, and the couples sat apart and were not allowed to communicate with anyone except the administrator. Each S took the test four times from four different points of view: self, ideal self, fiancé(e), and ideal spouse (the order of the tests being balanced to avoid order effects). . . .

DISCUSSION

Taken as a totality, the findings strongly support the presence of psychological factors in marital selection and reject the notion expressed by Reiss that psychological factors are unimportant and are essentially derivatives of sociological factors. Considering the selectivity of the present population with respect to age, socioeconomic class, and schooling, it would be difficult to view the results as dependent on these variables.

The importance of self–ideal-self congruence in selection of a marital partner apparently rests strongly on the concept of the self, since the ideal selves of our high and low groups show no significant differences which could not be attributed to chance. The perception of the partner as similar or different for men is also clearly a function of differences in the self-concept. For women, it apparently depends on the difference between high and low Ss both on the self-concept and on the perception of the fiancé. The fact that high women were lower than low women on exhibition, heterosexuality, and aggression suggests that the

former are not assertive and that high self-acceptance in women may be associated with an adherence to more traditional nonassertive roles. The data were not intended to investigate this question, however, and only future research can determine the veridicality of this speculation.

The data are consistent with the belief that self-acceptance is a negotiable asset in marital choice. It may be argued, nevertheless, that the fact that high men and women are more satisfied with their partner with respect to their ideal-spouse expectations than are low men and women is due to another factor than marital negotiation. Are low persons, who are presumably critical of themselves, also apt to be equally critical of their partner (low boyfriend or girlfriend, ideal-spouse correlation) without this fact indicating that they actually settle for less desirable partners? This question is assuredly extremely difficult to answer directly because rationalization processes might make it unlikely that an individual would admit to himself that he was settling for a second-rate partner. However, there is research evidence that strongly indicates that low self-esteem persons are less demanding in their relationship with the opposite sex.

Walster (1965) showed that female Ss whose self-esteem had been experimentally lowered were more attracted to an attractive young man than female Ss whose self-esteem had been raised. Further, Kiesler and Baral (1967) showed that low self-esteem men were less likely to attempt to date a physically attractive woman than were high self-esteem men; consequently, it seems reasonable to conclude that the lower boyfriend (girlfriend), ideal-spouse correlation for low Ss is a result of less satisfactory choices rather than of a more critical perception of their partners.

Finally, the large difference between the correlations representing satisfaction with the spouse via the perceptions stemming from a single S (intraperceptions) as compared to the evaluation of partner satisfaction when the perceptions of both partners are considered (interperceptions) merits some discussion. It is somewhat surprising to discover that when the self-concept of one member of a couple is compared with the ideal spouse desired by the other member, the result is zero-order correlation. Thus, even though this group was largely committed to marriage, the self-concept of one member of the couple bore no relationship to the ideal spouse desired by the other. In the eyes of both partners considered individually, however, their partner was quite close to their ideal spouse.

Based on the revised Personal Preference Schedule, the satisfaction with the partner is largely a projected wish that is uncorrected because of the narrow range of behavior each partner exhibits to the other prior to marriage. With a wider sample of behavior after marriage, one might expect that the magnitude of the interperception correlations would increase and that of the intraperception correlations would decrease. Thus, the self-concept should move closer to the ideal desired by the partner as the individual changed to meet the aspirations of the partner and as the partner lowered his standards for the other to a more realistic level. The passage of time, however,

should also bring a clearer realization that many of the attributes assigned to the spouse were not actually possessed by him; hence, a certain disappointment with marriage must be the inevitable lot of most persons the longer they are married. This finding has been well documented by Pineo (1961), Blood and Wolfe (1965), and numerous others.

It must be added concerning the present findings that the size of the correlations is certainly a function of the nature of the test used. The Personal Preference Schedule contains no items specifically related to marriage, and it might be expected that the size of the interperception correlations would rise with specific marriage-oriented questions. However, the size of the difference between the intraperception and interperception correlations suggests that methodological and content factors could not alone account for this difference. In sum, while self-acceptance operated selectively in the choice of partner, self-deception seemed to be a nondiscriminating factor operating on all of the Ss.

REFERENCES

Blood, R. O., Jr., & Wolfe, D. M. *Husbands and Wives*. New York: Free Press, 1965.

Goodman, M. "Expressed Self-Acceptance and Interspousal Needs: A Basis for Mate Selection." *Journal of Counseling Psychology*, 11 (1964): 129–135.

Kiesler, S. B., & Baral, R. L. "The Search for a Romantic Partner: The Effects of Self-Esteem and Physical Attractiveness on Romantic Behavior." Unpublished paper, Connecticut College, 1967.

Murstein, B. I. "The Relationship of Mental Health to Marital Choice and Courtship Progress." *Journal of Marriage and the Family*, 29 (1967): 447–451.

Pineo, P. "Disenchantment in the Later Years of Marriage." *Marriage and Family Living*, 23 (1961): 3–11.

Reiss, I. L. "Toward a Sociology of the Heterosexual Love Relationship." *Marriage and Family Living*, 22 (1960): 139–145.

Walster, E. "The Effect of Self-Esteem on Romantic Liking." *Journal of Experimental Social Psychology*, 1 (1965): 184–197.

40

THE TRANSITION FROM ENGAGEMENT TO MARRIAGE

Rhona Rapoport

Marriage is a complex social-psychological phenomenon. From a sociological point of view, the decision to get married involves an undertaking to form a new familial unit in society; this undertaking usually involves two already formed families (of orientation) as well as various groups with which each individual articulates. Getting married also involves participating in a major role transition in society. Whether it is successfully traversed or not will determine whether the particular new social unit is formed or not. From a societal point of view then, it is important that this transition be traversed successfully for the social institution of marriage to continue in some form. From the point of view of the individuals concerned, there are also major psychological determinants and consequences. Marriage can be seen both as providing an opportunity for growth and maturation of personality and as reinvoking a return to and repetition of certain preoccupations of childhood. The return to an exclusive two-person relationship, perhaps for the first time since early childhood, stimulates the reemergence of both the good and bad experiences of earlier periods of development. "This makes the marriage relationship especially open to a richness of emotional experience and, by the same token, renders it particularly vulnerable to emotional disturbances."[1]. . .

Given the fact that getting married involves a transition of vital importance to one's person, to the ones with whom one was intimately involved before the marriage, and to one's subsequent family of procreation, then it seems important to consider the processes that are involved for individuals making the transition. There are indications from the marriage and family field and from other fields of social-psychological enquiry that the manner in which the transition is made has major effects on subsequent events. For instance, if we view the engagement as a vital part of the getting married process, we have to consider the effects of a broken engagement and the evidence that there are important stresses present in courtship and engagement.

The importance and problematic character of the transition from the unmarried to married status is indicated by the variety of rituals associated with it. The rituals associated with marriage are rich in examples of *rites de passage* of which there are so many in simpler societies. In our modern Western society, marriage is still usually treated as a ritual (rooted in the cultural logics and practices relating to the supernatural) and has a variety of ceremonial customs associated with it, such as the engagement ring, the bridal costume, the honeymoon, and so on.

What follows derives from a research program underway in the Harvard School of Public Health's Community Mental Health Program. The research is committed to a study of the developmental phases in the life cycles of families and to the mental illness and mental health effects on individuals traversing the developmental phases. Getting married is viewed as one of many "normal" but significant *critical transitions* from one social status to another in the life cycle of the individual in his family and work contexts. In the family developmental cycle, major status transitions include the changes involved in having a child, children leaving home, and one's spouse dying. . . . In more traditional societies these normal transitions tended to be emphatically marked by ceremonial elaboration of ritual activity. These rituals seemed to function to ease the transitions for the individuals concerned (and for society) by dealing with the psychic and social implications of the changes entailed. Given the relative diversity of cultural norms, the secularization and rapidity of social changes in modern urban life, each significant role transition involves some degree of uncertainty, for the handling of which the traditionally prescribed rituals and resolutions tend to be inadequate. Major social role transitions are seen as inherently disrupting events providing for individuals new social environmental contexts within which they relate to one another. As an individual's social role changes, his image of himself is affected, the way in which others expect him to behave changes, and his legitimate expectations for the behavior of others alter. As all this goes on, the *individual may grow and develop under* the impact of the new stimuli or he may find them so burdensome and distressing that he is impaired in his functioning, in extreme cases *developing symptoms of emotional disturbance*. . . . Unlike adolescence which, for example, involves role changes partly as a consequence of biological growth processes, getting married involves changes by virtue of a decision on the part of the individuals to take a step that is marked by an explicit legal transition point. This step sets in motion forces which may lead to deep and enduring consequences, positive as well as negative.

We conceive of the getting married transition then as characterized by a change in the state of both the personal systems and social systems of the individuals concerned. Before the new steady state is achieved, role-relational patterns are fluid and there may be more or less sense of personal disorganization. Once having been traversed, the critical role transition is a point of no return. In getting married, individuals undergo a change of role relationships from those that held for them when single, never-married individuals. Constituting a new family of procreation in our society usually involves new living arrangements on a neo-local basis. While similar transitions may occur later, the notion of critical role transition implies important consequences for subsequent events entailed in the new state established consequent to the crisis. The state following the crisis can be favorable or unfavorable, depending on how the crisis itself is dealt with. The restoration of the new steady state in the various personality and social systems involved, is the work of

coming through the critical transition. *This work is conceptualized as a series of tasks, specific to each of the many critical role transitions* that punctuate the flow of life. The fact that an individual performs the tasks of one role transition satisfactorily does not necessarily imply that he can accomplish *all* role transitional tasks with comparable ease or effectiveness. Each transition has tasks specific to it. The accomplishment of these tasks affects outcome for the particular role transition. In general, one would expect favorable outcome to early life crises to enhance the chances for favorable outcomes to later crises in the life cycle.

Our major immediate research aim is to be able to predict from patterns of task accomplishment during the critical transition to patterns of outcome some time after the transition. More specifically, we attempt to measure task accomplishment by the end of the engagement period and relate this to outcome one year after marriage. . . .

The critical role transition of "getting married" is seen as having 3 subphases: the *engagement period* which ends with the *rite de passage* of the wedding, the *honeymoon*, and the *early marriage period* which is taken to end two-three months after the wedding. As the result of an initial exploratory study and perusal of the literature, a series of tasks were postulated as inherent for each subphase. It is essential to our approach that the tasks delineated are phase-specific. While much of the task work, both behavioral and intrapsychic, may have been done before the subphase in which it presumably becomes crucial to accomplish the tasks, it is postulated that failure to come to grips with them by the end of the period for which they are specific, will lead to deleterious consequences for the individuals and/or social systems concerned.

The phase-specific tasks that have been postulated for the engagement period have been divided into two major groups:—personal (including intrapsychic) and interpersonal.

The three tasks considered salient in the area of intrapersonal preparation for marriage are: (I) making oneself ready to take over the role of husband/wife; (II) disengaging (or altering the form of engagement) of oneself from especially close relationships that compete or interfere with commitment to the new marital relationship; (III) accommodating patterns of gratifications of premarital life to patterns of the newly formed couple (marital) relationship.

For the first task our concern is with assessing each person's degree of *readiness to take over the new role of husband/wife by the time of marriage*. This involves the whole prospect of living in close physical relations with another person. It is also concerned with the extent to which particular individuals feel ready to enter into a situation in which they know what the potentialities and limitations are from an economic point of view, and in which they are able to work out an arrangement that deals both with keeping the household financially viable and with their own self-images as worker, breadwinner, supporter, on the one hand, and homemaker, helper, enhancer, on the other, such that the individual's sense of readiness is realistic in the context of the relationship that he is entering.

The second task focuses on the *work to be done by people to disengage themselves from relationships that interfere with commitment to the marital relationship*. In order to assess the degree of accomplishment on this task, we are concerned with the existence of such competing relationships, with whom they are, how it is perceived that such ties will relate to the proposed marital relationship, and how possible conflicts are resolved.

Accommodating the competing gratifications of premarital life to the new couple (marital) relationship is the third task in making oneself personally prepared for marriage. We are concerned here with whether individuals feel that getting married does involve relinquishing gratifications, such as going to frequent dances if one of the couple does not desire this, and the gratifications of romantic courtship behavior.

Our general focus here is on how far there has been a shift from self-orientation to mutuality by the end of the engagement period and the development of a couple identity. As for the couple's interpersonal preparation for marriage, we are concerned

with the work that has to be done to develop an interpersonal adjustment or accommodation that will be satisfactory in the marital relationship.

The set of interpersonal tasks that we are concerned with here relates to and draws on intrapersonal phenomena and extrafamilial (or couple) relationships but focuses on the phenomena in the premarital (engaged) couple's relationship. The concern throughout is on the work necessary to make this relationship a satisfactory and harmonious one. Our key organizing concept is that of *fit*. We wish to assess the couple's *fit* on a number of salient variables. A good fit may be arrived at in various ways. Partners need not be identical in the way they do things or in their personality configuration. Two partners may have a similar orientation to some aspect of life and the result may be conflict or unhappy competition in the relationship. Conversely, discrepant orientations do not necessarily indicate a poor fit. They may complement one another.

We are interested in how far the couple has accomplished the work involved for each of the following tasks:

1. establishing a couple identity;
2. developing a mutually satisfactory sexual adjustment for the engagement period;
3. developing a mutually satisfactory agreement regarding family planning;
4. establishing a mutually satisfactory system of communication between the pair;
5. establishing a mutually satisfactory pattern with regard to relatives;
6. developing a mutually satisfactory pattern with regard to friends;
7. developing a mutually satisfactory pattern with regard to work;
8. developing a mutually satisfactory pattern of decision-making;
9. planning specifically for the wedding, honeymoon, and the early months of marriage that lie ahead. . . .

To date, we have worked with 12 couples traversing the critical role transition of getting married, as part of a research program on phases of the family life cycle. The early exploratory work was with young couples who were either getting married or had just been married or were pregnant for the first time. The interviewing in this exploratory series covered the period prior to marriage (where relevant), immediately after the marriage, and continued for up to eighteen months after the wedding.

In the next stage we pursued more systematically some aspects of our interest in the first phase of family life, namely, engagement and early marriage. This phase ended with the decision to focus our concern on the personal and social resources that couples bring to a marriage; the way they cope with the tasks and challenges presented by this phase in the family life cycle; how much their personal resources alter between engagement and the first few months of marriage; and how coping techniques and task accomplishment relate to outcomes (one year later) measured in various ways and relating to mental health state, the state of the couple relationship, and readiness for the next phase of family life.

We then began a new exploratory series of six couples all of whom were students in their final year at a local college, and all of whom were within six months of their marriage. Our aim with this series was to see how the couples handled the three subphases of the "getting married" phase of family life, viz, the *engagement, honeymoon,* and *early marriage* period (up to three months after marriage); phase-specific tasks were postulated for each of these subphases and it was decided to focus on the relationship of task accomplishment on these tasks and the fit between the couple on task accomplishment, to various measurements of outcome. More systematic ways of interviewing were devised and all interviews supervised for data gaps and for the management of transference-countertransference phenomena. In the summer of 1962, a start was made toward further operationalizing our tasks and refining categories to be used for ratings on task accomplishment. Each task for each subphase has been broken down into a battery of items which are rated on a 7-point scale, both for the individuals and for the couple at the completion of the interviewing program.

Work is proceeding on the development of coding and rating categories for all three subphases of the critical transition. In addition, we are now exploring more focally the outcome side of our set of relationships. At this stage, we are concerned with correlating task accomplishment with outcomes, with the subsequent aim of predicting from task accomplishment to outcomes. To this end, we are doing exploratory work with 30 couples who have already been married six months to a year so as to develop our ideas as to what criteria for outcomes are most useful and, by the use of retrospective data, to obtain some feeling for whether task accomplishment and outcomes are, in fact, related to each other. . . .

We will continue our attempts to relate patterns of task accomplishment to outcomes by working with a larger sample and with contrasting samples of known good and bad outcomes from the mental health point of view; this phase will be followed by a predictive study. It is likely that we shall select our next sample in such a way as to control for occupational phase, e.g., by taking graduating engineering students who are getting married. Apart from this, however, it is hoped that the "getting married" study is only a part of a long-term program on family developmental phases and that work on the second family phase could start even before the prediction study for the getting married phase is completed. Once the latter is well set up, it should be possible to start on the next stage, much of our exploratory work could be done on our existing series as pregnancy follows fairly rapidly for many couples.

SUMMARY OBSERVATIONS ON THE SIX EXPLORATORY CASES

The men in this exploratory series were all students from a university whose courses are given on "cooperative" basis (i.e., alternating work and study periods). The students of the university come from lower-middle and upper-lower class backgrounds, were upwardly mobile and of different religious affiliations.

At this stage we give only a description

of the sort of patterns of task accomplishment manifested by these couples. We shall briefly indicate their premarital characteristics and then, in some detail, their patterns of task-accomplishment.

The boys were 23–26 and the girls 20–23 years old. In all the cases, the boys and girls had known one another fairly well for 3–5 years before their marriage, although their formal engagement period was 6–12 months. In every case, the first meeting between the members of the couples occurred over five years prior to the study, most of them going back to high-school acquaintanceships. While this group is conspicuous for their long period of dating, they are also notable for the absence of premarital sexual intercourse between them. The girls were all virgins at the time of marriage—a conspicuous difference from the highly urbanized cosmopolitan collegiate populations, but not from the overall national student tendency. In four of the couples, the male had had sexual relations with other women. These had ranged from one extreme of many sexual encounters, through a situation in which it had been tried once. The presence of a double standard of sexuality was pronounced among those couples in which the boy but not the girl had had sexual experience. All the couples engaged in necking and petting, often with strain on their decision not to go further before marriage. They usually devised ways of not seeing too much of each other alone, to deal with this conflict.

The couples were different in the degree of formalization of the various stages between first date and getting married. They all went through stages involving public announcement of their engagement, of being given and wearing a diamond ring, of formal church weddings and receptions. They differed in whether they insisted on formalizing stages of "being pinned," going steady, having exclusive dating rights, and so on, as well as in the degree to which their behavior reflected exclusive commitment for spare-time relationships. In one case all the spare time was spent on preparation for the marriage—fixing up the home, planning the furnishings, and so on. In another case, the girl spent many bitter evenings alone while her fiance participated in extracurricular activities in which he was so active —dramatics, athletics, choir, fraternity meetings, etc.—many of which had drawn her to him as an interesting, active person, but which now interfered with their building a closer relationship.

These couples worked at examining their basis for making a joint life together. They sought to find out what their areas of mutual interest were, to accommodate their activities to areas of interest to both members, and to discuss their plans for the future. On the other hand, while these couples showed the general trend toward democratization of the marital relationship, with concern shown for both the female's life plans and needs and the male's, there was a clear subordination of the female's to the male's occupational aspirations. None of the women planned to work beyond what would be necessary for completing their husband's education. The couples' work on their relationship appeared most "prosaic." This is something very difficult to verbalize. It relates to a fairly low level of emotional intensity in the interaction in the couples; at the risk of over-generalization, one might say there is a quality of gliding over life, meeting it at an intellectual level with very little excitement and involvement. The couples do what is considered the right thing in the current age of enlightenment; they discuss their future plans, explore their mutual interests and feelings about things, show consideration for one another's viewpoints and so on. On the other hand, with the exception of two couples, there was little intensity underlying their developing relationship. The boys tended to be impressed with the girls for their attractiveness, or their social capacities. In one couple, however, there was relatively intense soul-searching about how they would fit together and complement one another in their personal development; in another couple this was done on a more intellectual plane, but with similar preoccupation; in the third couple the interaction might best be described as fitting the neurotic interaction pattern of intensity. She often considered him silly and immature; he often considered her difficult, not sufficiently interested in making a good relationship with his parents, not sufficiently committed to their future marital relationship to give up other contacts, etc. On the other hand, he felt that he needed her maturity and support; she felt that he was kind and energetic, making it probable that he would provide her with a good home. They were the only couple that mentioned "falling in love."

With reference to the actual decision to marry and the entry into a formal engagement status, with setting of date for the wedding, etc., the decision was jointly arrived at in all cases, and it cannot be said that either member was entirely the leader in determining the details of the engagement or marriage. Aside from cautionary advice from a priest in the case of the intermarriage, there were few others involved in the decision-making process. In one case, the parents came into the picture as providing social controls against the girl staying with her fiance too long in the house they were preparing while engaged, especially in the evening, because of what the neighbors might say. In other cases, siblings played an indirect role—e.g., in the case where the girl's siblings had the couple over frequently to visit with their families, reinforcing the young man's desire to settle into this kind of family life.

The kinds of factors that entered into the actual setting of the date of marriage were as follows: the man's army service began just following graduation, so they decided to marry somewhat earlier than graduation, rather than waiting. This was reenforced by a felt sexual urgency, as the couple had previously decided to abstain from premarital intercourse and yet became very aroused in their patterns of petting. In another case, the time was shifted to take into account a religious holiday, Lent. The most conspicuous determiner of the date of marriage was the point of graduation of the male from university. Most set their dates to follow this rather closely.

In most cases, the details of the wedding plans were left to the female, though the male usually went over the plans with her, especially the list of invited guests. In most cases, the plans for the honeymoon were left to the male, often without the female

wanting to know too much about it in advance.

With regard to the couples' preparedness to take on the roles of husband and wife, one conspicuous feature of these couples was the lack of domestic role rehearsals to be found among the women. However, they were perfectly competent to earn their livings. In every case the girl planned to continue her work after marriage until pregnancy forced her to stop. It was only in the Protestant couple that birth control was planned in order to allow the secretary wife to support her husband during graduate work.

On the male side, the fact that we chose university students made the sample biased in the direction of studying individuals who were heavily engaged in the preparation to assume an occupational role. However, within the series we found a considerable range of variation in the degree to which the male was happy about his occupational choice, committed to it, and effective in the performance of it. Even the engineers, who had focused commitments to a particular line of professional competence, went through interesting shifts during the engagement period that seemed associated with getting married. In one case, the young man chose a higher paying industrial job rather than a lower paying academic one that he seemed to prefer; in another case, an engineer chose to go on to take a graduate degree in mathematics (while his dental hygienist wife helped to support them) so that he would eventually have a more stable and secure occupation, as he saw it; the third engineer did not do very well in his studies, and did not graduate as scheduled because of having to return to complete a failed course. He tried unsuccessfully to get a job for the period following marriage while he made up his deficiency. Others decided to prolong their studies.

With regard to the task of altering close relationships that might compete with the marital relationship, the couples represented a range of types: in one case the male had no friends, his parents had retired, his relationships with his much older siblings were attenuated, and his relationship with his fiancee had no competition on this level. On the other extreme, the male had a range of extracurricular activities that claimed most of his spare time; he had part-time jobs to increase his earnings, and he even had lingering contacts with an "old flame," though this was dealt with terminally just prior to the formal engagement. Intermediate cases showed one or another of these attachments for the male, but in most cases this was seen as temporary, to be changed following marriage when the new pattern was to be set up. In the case of the women, all showed problems associated with separating from their attachments to their parental families, particularly their mothers. There was one couple in which the girl had an active wish to get away from her familial situation, and this influenced her husband's choice of an industrial job at some distance from home rather than the academic graduate assistantship at home.

In the course of the engagement period, considerable work was done by the males, especially, giving up the patterns of gratification they had been accustomed to prior to this period. The definite impression gained was one of an asymmetry in the work to be done with this task; the women were mainly keyed up to get married, though in some cases they postponed it for various ostensible reasons, and the males wished to marry but tended to have a difficult time giving up all their other activities and gratifications.

The task of achieving a couple identity was one that seemed most uniformly well accomplished by all the couples at a superficial level. All talked in "we" terms, all presented themselves publicly to family and friends as a pair, all subscribed in principle to the joint planning of areas of mutual interest. They differed, of course, in the degree to which and the quality with which they actually felt this sense of "we-ness." On the one hand, some of the couples seemed to feel almost incomplete without one another, with constant eye contact, checking for corroboration when any opinion was expressed, reluctance to be without the other, and so on. And, on the other hand, there was the person who subscribed intellectually to all these ideals, but found

it difficult in practice to include his fiancee in all his activities even going to the point of dissembling on at least one occasion.

We have already mentioned the pattern of sexual experience with which these couples entered the engagement. Though in all cases but one the commitment to getting married was so strong as to make a breaking off of the engagement highly unlikely, there remained in every case a strong compulsion to avoid sexual relations until marriage. Where the individuals felt their sexual feelings arising to the point of threatening this resolve, they erected barriers against their doing anything impulsively. This took the form in one couple of avoiding "petting" following being out together; with another couple it took the form of avoiding being too much together in the house they were decorating for themselves; in a third it took the form of avoiding parking at night, as they felt they might get carried away and lose control. There seem to have been three interlocking sorts of variables involved in the relationships observed during this period: first, individuals varied in terms of the manifest strength of their sexual drives. This led to their noting that one of them was the one that had to be controlled, or to control himself. This was not directly related to a second consideration—though obviously there are possibilities of covert interrelationships—namely, the degree of fear of sexuality expressed. This, where found in manifest form, tended to be a female phenomenon, with the girl expressing fear of the actual physical experience that was impending. Doubtless some of the males felt fears, perhaps on a more diffuse level, which shaded off into the area where both males and females felt anxieties about being able to satisfy their partners. Looking at the overall pattern, it is interesting to note that this anxiety was most manifest among females in the engagement period but during the honeymoon it tended to shift, following the female's sexual "awakening," so that it was the male who felt more anxiety in the ensuing period about being able to satisfy the female. The third factor, found strongly in only one case, had to do with the definition of sexuality generally. While all the couples showed, to some extent, the double standard for virginity, there was only one couple in which this feeling went to such an extreme that we were impressed that their feelings colored sexuality generally. There are indications throughout the professional literature that there are difficulties in traversing the discontinuity where sex is defined as sinful out of marriage but all right in marriage for the girl. Where this reaches the point, as with our one couple, that he felt his prior experience with sexuality had made him feel dirty, and her feelings about sexual relations were so strong that she said that she would break off her engagement if she ever found out that he had had sexual relations, one feels that the transition will be very difficult.

With regard to family planning, all of the Catholic couples save the one that failed to graduate (and had obtained special permission from his parish priest to practice the rhythm method on the grounds of economic hardship) planned to start immediately on having children. (Ironically, they were the first couple to conceive.) The Protestant couple practiced birth control and she intended to keep from becoming pregnant until he had finished his master's degree and taken a good job as a teacher. Even among the rather conservative Catholic couples there were differences between the individuals in terms of how much their own feeling might be strong enough to over-ride their religious convictions on the matter. The main axis of difference among the couples was less in terms of whether or not they desired to use birth control, but in terms of how explicit they made their orientation toward later phases of family life in general.

This leads to the general task of establishing a satisfactory pattern of communications in the relationship. The couples varied much more in terms of their actual communication patterns than in terms of their degree of satisfaction with the pattern. On one extreme is the couple in which each experiences a release in the other's presence. Each is able to say things about how he feels that were not possible alone, and there is not any sense of concealment, but only of opening up with one another. In the

other extreme couple, there was much non-communication and malcommunication, though both said that they could tell one another everything. She would not discuss sex with him, even after they both attended a church (Pre-Cana) conference on marriage. She would not tell him when she had her menstrual period. He did not tell her about his premarital sexual experience, and was very fearful that the knowledge would get to her through the research. He felt that she was too critical of him and not supportive enough; she felt that his way of teasing, which he saw as affectionate, was annoying. In between these extremes, there were various kinds of asymmetries, with a general tendency for the girls to be somewhat more communicative than the boys about what they were doing and how they were feeling about things.

This same asymmetry was seen in the social relationships pattern, with the girl being more oriented, on the whole, toward forming a joint network of relationships than the boy, who tended to feel that he had more to give up during this period. The girls' relationships with their parents seemed, during the engagement period, to be functional in the sense that many of the preparations for the wedding are materially assisted by the cooperation of the girls' families, while the boys' external relationships are less functional, serving only as centrifugal distractions.

We have already discussed some of the prominent elements of their patterns as to work following the marriage, their attempts to find leisure pursuits of mutual interest, and their division of labor for the actual wedding itself. Conspicuous throughout all the phases and aspects of the engagement is the tendency toward jointness in decision-making. Even with the couples that show the most conservative tendencies with regard to division of labor internal to the family, we found they adopted the norm of mutual discussion and decision-making. Their acceptance of the norm of mutual agreement as the basis for decision-making is so strong that they tend not to be able to describe how any particular decisions tend to be made—they "just happen," sometimes with one taking the initiative, sometimes with the other. This does not always work out in practice, of course, and the males showed some of their covert resentment at the degree of female involvement in various indirect ways—like just not taking action on something decided. In the couple with poorest task accomplishment, we noted a striking contrast between the overt norm and the actual pattern. He said that the man should be the boss (the only couple in which this came out so clearly) and that men should decide the big things and women the small things in family life. In fact, he was inordinately dependent on her, considered her superior judgment essential to him, and she said that she could always get him to do what she wanted.

In general, we felt that our couples suffered from the obverse bias to many of the couples studied with similarly intensive methods but drawn from a clinical population. Because they tended to do fairly well in their task accomplishment, and to have been selected on the basis of volunteering in a university context where no therapeutic assistance was offered, they were biased toward normality. While the series gave us a picture of some of the tendencies to be observed among American couples in this social class group nowadays, it is comparatively less useful as a way of getting striking patterns prognostic of mental health difficulties, the use to which clinical cases have always been so effectively put. In our next research stage we hope to obtain a heavier sampling of potentially poor-outcome types to balance this bias and get a better picture of the range of processes to be observed.

NOTES

[1] L. Pincus, ed., *Marriage: Studies in Emotional Conflict and Growth* (London: Methuen, 1960), p. 22.

41

TRIAL MARRIAGE: HARNESSING THE TREND CONSTRUCTIVELY

Miriam E. Berger

Trial marriage has been practiced among the Peruvian Indians of Vicos in the Andes for more than four centuries. Arranged by the parents in the earlier form, the purpose was to test the girl's work abilities and the couple's general compatibility. In modern Vicos there is a free choice of marriage partners with romantic love playing an important role, but men still seek responsible, hardworking girls who have mastered household skills and can help in the fields. Study of couples who entered a trial marriage for the first time indicated that the average duration of such trials was less than fifteen months and that 83 percent of the relationships were finalized with marriage. There was no stigma if the couple had children, but did not marry. Permanent separations after marriage were rare, occurring in two to three percent of the cases. One of the advantages of these trial marriages . . . was the ease of transition from adolescence to adulthood. The couple acquired certain social and sexual advantages of adulthood without assuming full responsibility.

The Trobrianders had a "bachelor's house" in which courting couples slept together and had exclusive sex prior to marriage. In contrast to Western civilization, before marriage Trobriand couples were not permitted to eat together or share any interests, except sex.

In the eighteenth century, Maurice of Saxony, illegitimate son of the Elector Augustus the Strong and Countess Aurora of Konigsmark, sought a solution to the marriage problem. He recommended temporary marriages, contracted for a limited time. If the partners agreed, the contract could be prolonged, but marriage for life was a "betrayal of the self, an unnatural compulsion." (Lewinsohn, 1956)

"Bundling" originated in Europe and was brought to the New World in the eighteenth century. In New England, where it was too cold to sit up late, courting couples were permitted, with parental approval, to get into bed with their clothes on. Some bundling experiences were probably innocent, especially when they included a centerboard for the bed (Marriage Museum), but "certainly many got sexually involved and married when conception occurred." (Scott, 1960; Fielding, 1961)

"Trial nights," an old Teutonic custom, (Marriage Museum) is still practiced today in Staphorst, Holland, an insular, inbred town whose customs have for centuries sealed them off from contemporary life. The swain spends three nights a week with his girl friend, with the knowledge of her parents who hope she will prove fertile. Until she becomes pregnant, there can be no marriage. If she is barren, the community regards her with primitive suspicion and contempt. Once she is pregnant, however, the marriage must take place. . . .

The first American to propose trial marriage as a concept was Judge Ben B. Lindsay. (1927) Bertrand Russell, who was then teaching in New York, approved of Lindsay's Companionate Marriage, but felt it did not go far enough. Russell favored trial marriage for university students and believed that work and sex were more easily combined "in a quasi-permanent relationship, than in the scramble and excitement of parties and drunken orgies" that were prevalent during the Prohibition Era. Russell felt that if a man and woman chose to live together without having children, it was no one's business but their own. He believed it undesirable for a couple to marry for the purpose of raising a family without first having had sexual experience. (Russell, 1929)

Lindsay and Russell were ostracized, and the concept of trial marriage lay dormant until an evolving sexual morality led anthropologist Margaret Mead to revive it. (Mead, 1966) Building on Lindsay's Companionate Marriage, she recommended a two-step marriage: *individual,* in which there would be a simple ceremony, limited economic responsibilities, easy divorce, if desired, and no children; and *parental marriage,* which would be entered into as a second step by couples who were ready to undertake the lifetime obligations of parenthood, would be more difficult to enter into and break off, and would entail mutual continuing responsibility for any children. Her rationale was that sex, now considered a normal need in youth, often drove them into premature and early marriage, frequently leading to unhappiness and divorce. She made the plea that divorce be granted before children are conceived, so that only wanted children of stable marriages are brought into the world. Responses to Dr. Mead's proposal (Mead, 1968), ranged from disapproval for tampering with tradition (instead of helping couples adjust to traditional marriage) to complaints from students for setting up too much structure. A typical student response was: "Why get married? Why can't we live together, with a full sex life, with no pregnancy, until we're ready to get married and have children?"

Margaret Mead's two-step marriage was

elaborated on by Michael Scriven, a philosophy professor, who proposed a three-step plan:

We try to make one institution achieve three aims, which all too often lie in perpendicular dimensions. The aims are sexual satisfaction, social security, and sensible spawning. The solution would be to create three types of marriage arranged so that any combination is possible: preliminary, personal, and parental marriage. The first would simply be legitimized cohabitation, contractually insulated against escalation into "de facto" commitment. It would be a prerequisite for other kinds and would impose a period of a year's trial relationships before the possibility of conversion to personal marriage. . . . (Scriven, 1967)

In *The Sexual Wilderness*, Vance Packard (1968) concluded that the first two years of marriage are the most difficult. He recommended a two-year confirmation period, after which the marriage would become final or would be dissolved. Packard felt that this proposal differed from trial marriage because the couple would marry in earnest and with the hope that the marriage would be permanent. He saw trial marriage as highly tentative and little more than unstructured cohabitation. Packard's concept is based on his conviction that the expectation of permanency contributes to success in that it motivates a couple to work hard to adapting, and is, in fact, a strong stabilizing and reinforcing factor.

In "Marriage as a Statutory Five Year Renewable Contract," Virginia Satir, family therapist, said:

Maybe there needs to be something like an apprentice period . . . in which potential partners have a chance to explore deeply and experiment with their relationship, experience the other and find out whether his fantasy matched the reality. Was it really possible through daily living to have a process in which each was able to enhance the growth of the other, while at the same time enhancing his own? What is it like to have to undertake joint ventures and to be with each other every day? It would seem that in this socially approved context, the chances

of greater realness and authenticity continuing would be increased, and the relationship would deepen, since it started on a reality base. (1967)

Another variation of the renewable contract concept was proposed by Mervyn Cadwallader, a sociology professor, in "Marriage as a Wretched Institution":

Marriage was not designed to bear the burdens now being asked of it by the urban American middle class. It was an institution that evolved over centuries to meet some very specific needs of a nonindustrial society. . . . Marriage was not designed as a mechanism for providing friendship, erotic experience, romantic love, personal fulfillment, continuous lay psychotherapy, or recreation. Its purposes . . . have changed radically, yet we cling desperately to the outmoded structures of the past. . . . The basic structure of Western marriage is never questioned, alternatives are not proposed or discussed. . . . Why not permit a flexible contract, for one or more years, with periodic options to renew? If a couple grew disenchanted with their life together, they would not feel trapped for life. . . . They would not have to go through the destructive agonies of divorce, and carry about the stigma of marital failure, like the mark of Cain on their foreheads. Instead of a declaration of war, they could simply let their contracts lapse and while still friendly, be free to continue their romantic quest. . . . What of the children in a society that is moving inexorably toward consecutive, plural marriages? . . . If the bitter and poisonous denouement of divorce could be avoided by a frank acceptance of short-term marriages, both adults and children would benefit. Any time spouses treat each other decently, generously, and respectfully, their children will benefit. (Cadwallader, 1966)

Today many young people have carried the concept of trial marriage a step further, as Bertrand Russell advocated, by living with a roommate of the opposite sex. Sociologist Robert N. Whitehurst coined a word to describe them, "unmalias," a condensation of unmarried liaisons. (1969) Whitehurst mentions some of the problems encountered by students who have an "experimental semester of living together," such as when a male senior must leave the campus for graduate school, job, or military service. (1969)

The Harrad Experiment (Rimmer, 1966) incorporated some of the above mentioned ideas on trial marriage and added some new dimensions. In Rimmer's novel, college students lived with computer-selected roommates of the opposite sex. Unlike the informal arrangements now made by college students on their own, the Harrad Experiment was controlled and guided by the Tenhausens, a husband-and-wife team of sociologist and marriage counselor. The novel focused on several couples who married after four years of living together. The students attended various neighboring colleges, but roomed at Harrad during the four years, and were required to take a course in human values at Harrad taught by the Tenhausens and to do required reading in the subjects of marriage, love, sex, contraception, moral values, philosophy, etc. Whenever the students were troubled about their relationships, the Tenhausens were available for consultation. There was also considerable peer support through endless discussions of common problems. Rimmer favored a structured, socially approved form of premarital experimentation that would give the male and female an opportunity to realize themselves fully, without guilt, and to adjust to their new marital roles without legal entanglement, recognizing marriage as the commitment a couple makes to society when they decide to have children. (1969) Accused of trying to undermine America's family structure Rimmer asserted that, on the contrary, he believed a strong family, to be a *sine qua non* of social existence and that his proposals would strengthen and preserve that structure.

In an article in *The Humanist* (1970) Rustum and Della Roy discussed alternatives to traditional marriage in view of the increasing divorce rate:

By one simple swish of tradition, we can incorporate all the recent suggestions for trial marriage . . . and cover them all under the decent rug of the "engagement"—engagements with minor differences—that in today's society, they entitle a couple to live together, but not to have children. . . . By no means need this become the universal norm.

. . . A workshop led by the author was conducted at the annual meeting of the National Council on Family Relations in 1969. The participants were primarily college instructors of marriage and family courses, but included a social worker, a clergyman, a sociologist, and a college counselor of students. The following is a summary of the highlights of the workshop:

It was agreed that there ought to be alternative methods of courtship, approved by society, that would serve as a better preparation for marriage than dating. Those opposed to trial marriage as one such alternative felt it was not the same as a real marriage and therefore not a valid preparation for marriage. It was also subject to exploitation and abuse, as was any method of courtship, and was more to the interest of the male than the female, who is likely to be more concerned about security. Opponents also pointed out that it takes a great deal of maturity to make a relationship work, and if a couple are not mature enough to marry, they may not be mature enough to end a relationship when indicated, nor to cope with the attendant rejection, not to mention accidental pregnancy, or a partner who flits from one relationship to another.

Those who favored trial marriage felt it should be morally sanctioned by society as an optional alternative. . . .

Although many clergymen disapprove of trial marriage, there have been some notable exceptions. Typical of the negative opinion is that of Dean John Coburn of the Episcopal Theological School, Massachusetts:

How can two people trust one another on a temporary basis? Marriage is a total commitment, and trial marriage is a contradiction in terms. (Eddy, 1968)

On the other hand, a Unitarian minister, Robert M. Eddy (1968), regarding the casual promiscuity and resulting unwanted children as tragic developments of the new morality, offered the following alternatives:

(1) that parents continue the financial support of their college-attending children who are having companionate marriages

(2) that it be illegal for youngsters under the age of seventeen to conceive; that seventeen to nineteen year olds, after obtaining parental consent, might live together with the privileges and responsibilities of the relationship defined by a contract as detailed or loose as the parents would desire. Such a relationship could be solemnized by a rite similar to the wedding ceremony and could be ended by mutual consent, as long as the couple did not have children. The next type of cohabitation agreement essentially would be identical to the present marriage relationship, but under the new system, would be limited to adults and would be, in effect, a license to raise children.

. . . One critical issue is whether trial marriage is a valid test and preparation for marriage. Some probably know of couples for whom trial marriage culminated in a satisfactory legal marriage. Nevertheless, the following case studies raise questions about the validity of trial marriage as a test:

Sue, age 24, was referred for psychotherapy because of severe anxiety symptoms that had their onset immediately after marriage. She had lived with her husband six months prior to marriage, during which phase she had been relaxed, her real self, and not unduly concerned over the success of the relationship. Exploration revealed that Sue was so anxious for the marriage to succeed that she was repressing all negative feelings, and denying her identity in an effort to fulfill her image of a good wife. Now she was afraid of becoming as aggressive, argumentative, and opinionated as she had been as a teen-ager.

Ada, age 22, came for psychotherapy because of severe obsessional symptoms. Since her marriage two years earlier, she had been frigid. She had lived with her husband weekends for one year prior to marriage, during which phase she had experienced orgasm. The source of conflict revealed in the exploration was that after marriage she felt her husband was too demanding sexually, that he valued her only for sex, which made it demeaning to her, and that she found it difficult to limit him. She had transferred her excessive need to have her parents' approval to having her husband's approval, resolving the conflict by denying her resentment and thereby becoming frigid and obsessional.

Sue's and Ada's trial marriages were not deliberate tests; both had drifted into their living-together experiences. Perhaps, when the trial marriage is deliberate, similar anxieties would occur before, rather than after the permanent marriage. Was it just that trial marriage was not a valid test for these women with neurotic personalities? It is only the troubled who come to the attention of the professional. Study of the marriages of a large sample of couples who first had trial marriages might provide more reliable information upon which to base a conclusion. In planning the research design, it would be necessary: (1) to distinguish between deliberate trials and unstructured cohabitation that happened to result in permanency; and (2) to explore whether motivation to adapt (Packard, 1968; Lederer and Jackson, 1968) differed during the trial and in permanency.

REFERENCES

Cadwallader, Mervyn. "Marriage as a Wretched Institution," *Atlantic Monthly*, 218 (1966): 62–66.

Eddy, Robert M. "Why We Must Allow Sexual Freedom for Teens," *Pageant*, September 1968, 118–129.

Fielding, Wm. J. *Strange Customs of Courtship and Marriage*, London: Souvenir Press, 1961.

Lederer, Wm. J., and Don D. Jackson. *The Mirages of Marriage.* New York: W. W. Norton and Company, 1968, Ch. 21–23.

Lewinsohn, Richard. *The History of Sexual Customs,* New York: Harper Brothers, 1958. Original edition in German, 1956, translated by Alexander Mayce.

Lindsay, Ben B. "The Companionate Marriage," *Redbook,* October 1926, March 1927.

Marriage Museum, formerly located at 1991 Broadway, New York, N.Y.

Mead, Margaret. "Marriage in Two Steps." *Redbook,* 127 (1966): 48–49.

Mead, Margaret. "A Continuing Dialogue on Marriage," *Redbook,* 130 (1968): 44.

Packard, Vance. *The Sexual Wilderness.* New York: David McKay Company, 1968, 466–468.

Rimmer, Robert H. *The Harrad Experiment.* Los Angeles: Sherbourne Press, 1966.

Rimmer, Robert H. *The Harrad Letters.* New York: New American Library, 1969.

Roy, Rustum, and Della Roy. "Is Monogamy Outdated?" *The Humanist,* 30 (1970): 24.

Russell, Bertrand. *Marriage and Morals.* New York: Liveright Publishing Company, 1929.

Satir, Virginia. "Marriage as a Statutory Five Year Renewable Contract." Paper presented at the American Psychological Association 75th Annual Convention, Washington, D.C., September 1, 1967. Copy available from author, P.O. Box 15248, San Francisco, Calif. 94115.

Scott, George Ryley. *Marriage—An Inquiry Relating to all Races and Nations from Antiquity to Present Day.* New York: Key Publishing Company, 1960.

Scriven, Michael. "Putting the Sex Back into Sex Education," *Phi Delta* 49 (1968), based on a paper given at a Notre Dame University Conference on "The Role of Women," Fall, 1967.

Whitehurst, Robert. "The Unmalias on Campus," presented at NCFR Annual Meeting, 1969. Copy available from author, University of Windsor, Windsor, Ontario, Canada.

Whitehurst, Robert. "The Double Standard and Male Dominance in Non-Marital Living Arrangements: A Preliminary Statement," paper presented at the American Orthopsychiatric Association Meeting, New York, 1969. Copy available from author, University of Windsor, Windsor, Ontario, Canada.

42

THE CLINICAL IMPLICATIONS
OF PERCEPTUAL DISTORTIONS IN FORCED MARRIAGES

Dean H. Hepworth

Marriage counseling with couples who have married because of premarital pregnancy frequently poses problems peculiar to, and resulting from, the "forced" nature of these marriages. The paucity of published material on the clinical implications of forced marriage is surprising when we consider the magnitude of the problem as reflected in statistical studies. Although none of the studies has been sufficiently broad in scope to be representative of the United States as a whole, there has been enough consistency in the findings to warrant some generalizations.

During the past three decades, Harold T. Christensen has been the chief contributor to the body of knowledge regarding the incidence and outcome of marriages that follow premarital conception. In longitudinal studies employing the method of record linkage, Christensen's most recent research shows that nearly one fifth of the first-born children in Ohio and one eighth in Utah were conceived before the parents' marriage.[1]

After a comprehensive survey based on his own study in Philadelphia and on the findings of others, Thomas P. Monahan drew the conclusion that ". . . it could very well be that if all the facts were known *conception* takes place before marriage in about one out of five cases in the United States. . . ."[2]

. . . Forced marriages occur under widely varying degrees of pressure. In some instances, marriage has been planned but deferred until certain endeavors regarded by one or both partners as prerequisite to the marriage have been completed. Frequent contacts during a long courtship tend to foster increasing emotional closeness and physical familiarity. Despite the strong intentions of both partners to postpone sexual relations until they are married, sexual intercourse is often the natural consequence of increasing intimacy. Although the couple's future plans may be thwarted by the untimely pregnancy, frustrations may well be transcended by their attachment to each other. Such persons often accept their plight philosophically; they feel that they would have married each other in any event and the pregnancy has merely hastened the inevitable. But even when the pressure is minimal because both partners choose to enter the marriage willingly, there may be a great deal of psychological stress caused by pressure from other sources.

In other cases, pressure may be virtually nonexistent. Monahan has made the following observation: ". . . it should be recognized that some premarital pregnancy in the United States may be merely a form of marriage precontract, or an anticipation of marriage, as it is in some other societies."[3]

At the other extreme, however, is the couple who have been acquainted for only a brief time before sexual intimacy; there are very few emotional bonds between them,

both before and after conception. Marriage to each other, therefore, probably has not been a goal of either partner. When the pregnancy becomes known, it often brings about a relentless bombardment of pressures from many sources. Parents and relatives usually react with shock and dismay. Fear of social ostracism, stemming from cultural taboos toward premarital pregnancy, adds to the exigency of the situation. From within, each partner may be buffeted by an aroused and vindictive superego. The stresses of the couple's dilemma are further augmented by an extremely narrow range of alternatives, none of which is wholly remedial and all of which are fraught with complications, misgivings, anxieties, and guilt. The course of action that will best mitigate these impelling pressures is chosen. The young couple often accedes to the dictates of parents, of other authority figures, and of conscience. As a result, a "shotgun marriage" takes place.

Christensen found that when marriage followed premarital pregnancy, the rate of divorce was substantially higher than the average divorce rate for the areas studied.[4] Moreover, family doctors, who are perhaps closest to the problem, estimate that the rate of failure of these marriages ranges from 50 percent to 100 percent; most doctors suggest about 80 percent.[5] The high rate of marital failure in forced marriages has been ascribed to lack of adequate preparation for marriage, lack of love, disillusionment, resentment about being too quickly tied down with responsibilities, and guilt and blame stemming from the violation of moral codes. . . .

Another factor in forced marriages that often exerts a profound influence on the marriage partners is the loss of freedom of choice when the marriage is forced or hastened by premarital pregnancy. Certainly this factor may seem elementary, but the possible psychological ramifications are far-reaching. The marriage counselor should be alert to the sometimes subtle manifestations of conflict that derive from the psychological meaning of the loss of the freedom of choice. I have subsumed the many possible psychological reactions under the term *the freedom-of-choice complex.*

Traditionally, freedom of choice in the selection of a marital partner has been a precious right of Americans. This right is often asserted, for example, by elopement when there is parental opposition to marriage. Another assertion of this right may be premarital pregnancy, which represents rebellion against parental prohibition of freedom to marry whom one chooses. Though pregnancy may well be the means by which a daughter "arranges" her marriage, this form of assertion, ironically, has a double meaning. Through this assertion of the right to choose, the daughter's marriage becomes forced, and she thus surrenders the very freedom she was seeking. . . .

The psychological impact of the loss of freedom to choose has been evidenced many times by the reaction of the young man to his partner's pregnancy. Devaluation of her is common. His image of her sometimes becomes so altered that the girl who previously had been attractive, appealing, and highly desirable suddenly seems to have lost those qualities. Feelings of love and respect often change to indifference or contempt. Moreover, feelings of loyalty and devotion may well be supplanted by a sense of obligation or, at the other extreme, unconcern.

If feelings toward the partner become overwhelmingly negative, alternatives other than marriage may be chosen. These may include forced abortion, relinquishment of the newborn child for adoption, or retention of the child by the mother even though she is unmarried. Couples who elect one of these alternatives, however, usually do not come to the attention of marriage counselors. Others who marry under great pressure in the absence of strong emotional bonds tend to lack a desire to preserve the marriage and often apply to a divorce court soon after marriage.

Even when reciprocal positive feelings have been predominant at the time of marriage, feelings of devaluation for the partner may emerge later, either under stress or after the newness of the marriage has worn off. This phenomenon is not peculiar to forced marriages, but the dynamics in such marriages often are unique.

The following case example deals with extramarital involvement, a reaction sometimes associated with negative perceptual distortions of the marital partner. I do not suggest that infidelity is a typical or usual occurrence in forced marriages. The perceptual distortions and the underlying dynamics in this case are, however, characteristic of patterns typically observed in these marriages.

Mr. C had been happily married for six years. A promotion at work brought with it a private office and a secretary. The new secretary, an attractive divorcee, was very solicitous, if not seductive. Mr. C was responsive, and increasing familiarity gradually led to expressions of affection between them.

At home Mr. C began to find fault with his wife and became more and more irritable. Mrs. C was hurt and confused by his criticism and his gradual withdrawal of affection. When all her efforts to please him failed, she contacted a marriage counselor. Mr. C half-heartedly agreed to try marriage counseling. After a brief introductory joint interview, the counselor made an arrangement to see them separately.

Mr. C talked about his dissatisfaction with his wife and compared her unfavorably with his secretary. He felt that he and his secretary were ideally matched, and he resented that fact that he was not free to marry her. After several interviews, he began to discuss his feelings of animosity toward his wife and his devaluation of her. He blamed her for having become pregnant during their courtship and his "having to get married."

It was apparent to the counselor after talking with Mr. and Mrs. C that their relationship had been mutually satisfying before Mr. C's involvement with his secretary. It was also evident that Mr. C had not resolved his negative feelings about his forced marriage and that because of his new situation they emerged with sufficient intensity to cause negative distortions in his perceptions of his wife and his marriage. He was also using the circumstances of his marriage to minimize his marital responsibility and to justify his extramarital interest.

Problems associated with extramarital involvement obviously are not confined to forced marriages. In such cases, the counselor is confronted with a different challenge, however, and, at best, the prognosis is often not favorable. The difficulty derives in great part from indifference or from lack of motivation, stemming from the withdrawal by one or both partners from the emotional investment required by marriage. The prognosis is least favorable if the extramarital involvement has been preceded by a gradual deterioration of the marriage relationship (as was not the case with Mr. and Mrs. C), culminating in a search by one or both partners for new sources of gratification for their emotional needs.

It need hardly be said that in forced marriages extramarital involvement cannot be attributed solely to the freedom-of-choice complex. In the case of Mr. C we see behavior resulting from the interplay of many factors. Many individuals, like Mr. C, lack a mature sense of responsibility for their actions, have an inadequately developed superego, and tend to blame others for their difficulties. . . .

Devaluation of the partner is a more common reaction to forced marriage among men than among women. This can be attributed to the fact that the man's traditional role as aggressor in courtship grants him the right to pursue any woman of his choice. It is the male, therefore, who is more inclined to resent surrendering his freedom of choice when the marriage is forced. His partner often becomes the object of his resentment, which he expresses by devaluating her.

The woman, of course, also has freedom of choice in courtship. However, her role is passive, and her choice is limited to would-be suitors. A woman's reaction to a forced marriage is characterized by lowered self-esteem and doubt about her partner's love. These feelings are reinforced by self-recrimination, guilt, and shame over the moral transgression, which is far more devastating to her than to her partner. These psychological stresses often have a drastic effect on the woman's self-image and can be responsible for her self-depreciation as well as her insecurity in the marital relationship.

It should be noted that these stresses are primarily of internal origin and exist irrespective of the partner's attitude, although, to a considerable degree, the latter either aggravates or mitigates the feelings.

The psychological investment in the freedom to be chosen sometimes assumes almost unbelievable proportions. In the case of one forced marriage, the wife, after several happy years of marriage, maneuvered her bewildered husband into a divorce. She "permitted" him to court her for several months and then remarried him. Her husband's devotion to her had never really been questioned except by her. It was apparent that her actions were related not to the reality situation but to her need to be "chosen" by her husband.

Feelings of uncertainty about a partner's love, although more common among women, are by no means limited to them. A case in point is that of a couple who had been married for seventeen years. During counseling, it was learned their marriage had been forced. The two had met as university students and had planned to marry after graduation. The young woman's pregnancy had altered their plans. Both had been in love at the time of their marriage, but they confided to the counselor that they had never since discussed their feelings about the circumstances of their marriage. Each privately wondered whether the other would have chosen him, although each had no doubt he would have chosen the other.

The counselor helped each partner to examine his uncertainties further. The partners themselves then discussed their feelings one night en route to the movies. The result, as reported by the husband, was that they held hands during the movie and "necked like a pair of teen-agers." They felt closer and more secure in their relationship than at any previous time.

Self-devaluation is not only damaging to individual morale but may also undermine marital interaction as well. The spouse who is self-depreciating is easily taken for granted and tends to foster or to reinforce feelings of devaluation on the part of the partner. Furthermore, such insecurity tends to cause hypersensitivity and submissiveness and may stifle assertiveness because of fear of abandonment by the partner.

To compensate for the loss of self-esteem and to win the questioned acceptance and love, it is not uncommon for a spouse to cater excessively to the partner. The results are seldom rewarding and may, in fact, be self-defeating by leading to increased demands and criticism. The self-depreciating and sometimes guilt-ridden spouse thus tends to be masochistic and is highly vulnerable to manipulation and exploitation by the partner. . . .

The problem of forced marriages is alarming in view of the incidence and outcome of these marriages. A factor unique to such marriages, which causes or contributes to marital conflict, is the psychological impact of the loss of freedom of choice when marriage is forced by pregnancy. Perceptual distortions of the partner and/or in the self-image often result. The husband more commonly develops negatively distorted perceptions of his wife, whereas the wife tends to develop negative distortions in her self-image. These distortions have a deleterious effect on marital interaction and, if not recognized and resolved, may undermine a marriage.

REFERENCES

[1] Harold T. Christensen, "Child Spacing Analysis Via Record Linkage: New Data Plus a Summing Up from Earlier Reports," *Marriage and Family Living*, 25 (August 1963): 274.

[2] Thomas P. Monahan, "Premarital Pregnancy in the United States: A Critical Review and Some New Findings," *Eugenics Quarterly*, 7 (September 1960): 145.

[3] Ibid., p. 144.

[4] Christensen, op. cit., p. 276.

[5] *Public Health Concepts in Social Work Education*, Proceedings of a seminar held at Princeton University, Princeton, New Jersey, March 4–9, 1962, Council on Social Work Education, New York, 1962, p. 128.

Part Nine

The Transition
to Being Married

Couples who have lived together before getting married are explicit in saying that some things are just not the same after the wedding takes place. Some report they worked harder at the relationship while they were unwed and that the legality of the relationship somehow caused them to begin to take each other for granted. Still others report that not much changed in their ways of relating to each other on a personal level but that marriage actually brought a change in life-style. Once married, couples are now socially recognized units with certain obligations to family, friends, and community; and their avowed permanence now allows them to become consumers of such nonperishable items as furniture and appliances.

Those who have not lived together prior to their wedding, and this is still the majority, find the changes even greater. For them, marriage means entering a new social world, in which they have new roles to play. If their own parents' marriages provided them with good—and similiar—role models to identify with, they have learned much about general marital interaction. But if the two sets of parents played their roles very differently or had unsuccessful marriages, problems between the newlyweds may arise concerning expectations of behavior. Many couples lack models of a good relationship as well as training in emotional intimacy and the communication of feelings.

A marriage which has been built only upon romance and sexual attraction soon runs into the troubled waters of the realities of living together: fatigue, illness, bills to be paid, and dirty laundry. Since they are neither providing nor receiving a loving friendship and an atmosphere for personal growth, the partners may often feel cheated and begin to question the value of their marriage. Even couples whose marriages are based on mature love must face these same realities, and there are few ways in which the average couple can get help in working out solutions in their lives. It has been suggested that each family have a marriage and family counselor, patterned after the family medical doctor or dentist, to whom they could turn when good advice is needed and for yearly checkups. In view of the isolation of each new family from their families of orientation and the reluctance of parents and grandparents to "interfere," perhaps this is a needed addition to our society.

The independence of the newly married has customarily started with the honeymoon, a tradition in our society and much of western civilization over the years. Ideally, the honeymoon is thought to provide the couple with a period of time, when they are alone and are not distracted by responsibility and problems, in which they can convert from the single to the married state. Also, the honeymoon has traditionally served the purpose of establishing sexual relations, beginning on the night of the wedding. Usually, it has taken the form of a vacation from work in an environment of relaxation; aside from sexual adjustment, the couple uses it to get acquainted and to recuperate from the strains of the days leading up to the wedding and from the ceremony itself. For many couples today, the honeymoon may seem obsolete, since they have already been living together; but for others, it still serves as the time when the form their relationship is to take will emerge and the tone of their life together may be set. It is likely that a vacation together after the wedding, if only for a rest, can be a meaningful way to start married life, although many couples clearly have no financial resources to include a time away from work for these purposes.

The first article in this section reviews the universal custom of marriage as a contract and discusses its ceremonial and financial aspects. While traditions vary from society to society, the rule everywhere is to recognize some form of marriage and to have certain regulations and values attached, so that partners will have a general idea of what is expected of them as married people.

Frank Cox provides insight into the beginning years of marriage in the next reading, "The Honeymoon Is Over." He discusses interesting marital syndromes which demonstrate some general problems found in many new marriages—the reduction of individual freedom, financial adjustments, and the maturation or lack of maturation of the partners. Young marriages seem to be particularly hazardous—the divorce rate grows higher with each decreasing year of age at marriage.

The third article, by Wells Goodrich, Robert Ryder, and Harold Raush, reports a study done by the authors on couples in their fourth month of marriage to determine the experiences of the individual couples and the ways they were reacting. The success of the marriage in these early months is closely related to the life-style and past experiences of each partner. It may be safe to say that a marriage is only as well-adjusted as the two partners are individually adjusted, and that the process starts in childhood.

As a continuation of the discussion of initial adjustment patterns in marriage, in the next reading Beverly Cutler and William Dyer examine husband-wife expectations and the behavior that results when these expectations do not materialize. The couples studied were college students, who present a special picture of new marriage, but the findings are applicable to a broader population. There are variations in the ways couples meet the different problems they encounter, as well as differences between how the husband and wife approach these problems. Couples' responses to problems range from open discussion to doing nothing; and the data indicate that using a variety of adjustment mechanisms works better and is probably preferable to handling all adjustment situations in the same manner.

Decision-making within the marriage has received a great deal of attention by those interested in the family power structure. In the traditional, male-dominated marriage, the decisions were expected to be made by the husband or delegated by him to the wife, who was held accountable to him. In the equalitarian marriage, which is steadily growing in popularity, the power structure is divided; since there are no generally agreed upon guidelines, the way the division is to be set up often causes confusion and conflict. One thing seems certain from the research—that the balance of power is frequently set rather early in the marriage by each partner's acceptance or rejection of the other's way of reacting to situations requiring a decision. The fifth article, by Vivian Cadden, is a popular treatment of the studies in this area and concludes that power may move from one partner to the other, but rests most commonly with the partner who is the least dependent.

Sexual problems are but one of many adjustments newly married couples must make, but they are so frequently mentioned that they deserve a special place in the treatment of the beginning of married life. Couples who have lived together before marrying often report sex problems that did not appear before marriage; such sexual problems are symptoms of other problems and pressures the couple is feeling. Professional marriage counselors commonly believe that a couple's sex life will often give important clues to the overall relationship. William Lederer and Don Jackson deal with the role of sex in marriage and emphasize that there is no set of standards by which each couple can measure their sex life. Instead, the only pertinent "standard" is the mutual pleasure sex affords the partners; and this can only be determined by the couple themselves.

The life-style of the newly married couple begins to develop in the first months of the marriage. A growing number of young couples today are postponing having children, so there are many more months together just as a couple. Most motherless wives work, for the husband generally has a limited income and setting up a home takes money. Traditionally, the ideal was that the wife would work only until the first child arrived and then devote herself to her children and home. Realistically, economic necessity has kept many young mothers in the labor market, either because the husband does not earn enough or possibly because he has lost his job. And today, many wives are college-educated and have careers which are as important to

them as the husband's or as is child rearing. Hence, couples are today faced with a myriad of decisions, some of which must be made in anticipation of the birth of the first child, since the months prior to becoming parents are far different for most couples from life with a baby.

In the final article in this section, Hilda Krech speaks to some of the current dilemmas facing the young wife in particular, as she and her husband decide how the roles of husband/father and wife/mother will be played. Her solution for women is a compromise between homemaking and outside interests, which is probably the most common pattern marriages take today. However, as the author points out, there can be conflict from and even serious drawbacks to such a compromise. For a woman who has the talent, training, and desire for a career, compromise means that her career is interrupted or drastically slowed down and that the resulting losses may never be regained. As a result, many young couples today, realizing the desires of both partners to pursue a career, are opting either not to have children at all or to divide the responsibilities of child-care evenly. The traditional marriage is undergoing great change, as men and women are recognizing the rights of each other to attain fully their self-potential without being cast into rigid sex roles that are defined by others and do not consider their individual needs. We may be reaching the point where there will never again be just one model for marriage, but instead each couple will forge a pattern uniquely suited to them. While some may feel more comfortable with patterns similiar to those of their families and friends, they will have the freedom to experiment and even to create a completely different life-style in a society that will no longer demand that each couple conform to one model of marriage.

43

MAKING A MARRIAGE

From *Story of Life*

Romantic love between a man and a woman is an intensely personal matter, often involving only the two individuals in a world of their own. But marriage is different. A marriage is a contract forged under the eye of society and sanctioned by it: the wedded state brings rules that bind, duties that may be inescapable, and responsibilities, financial and social, that cannot be ignored without risk of penalties. Marriage is endorsed in some form or another by all cultures in all periods of human history for it is an institution that formalizes and symbolizes the importance of the family. And on the stability of the family structure rests the stability of a society.

One of the major functions of marriage is to control and limit sexuality—that unruly element that all societies attempt to curb in some way in the interests of social stability. Marriage limits sexuality by providing the legitimate circumstances in which sexual intercourse may take place: and it defines as legitimate the children of the married couple. In some societies there is formal or informal endorsement of sexual intercourse outside marriage and there are cases where marriage rites are not expected to take place until the woman is pregnant—for example, among the Dyaks of Borneo and in many European villages just before the industrial revolution: in yet other societies, among the Longua Indians of Paraguay, for instance, although marriage rites take place before sexual intercourse, the marriage is not considered complete and binding until a child has been born. Yet, even in these societies marriage still provides the framework for the long-term relationship of man and woman.

The fact that marriage defines what is a legitimate sexual relationship and which children are legitimate in society's eyes is very important and largely explains why marriage is always a civil contract as well as a convenient social custom. Although there are cases where stable sexual unions occur and families are formed outside marriage—for example "common law marriages" in America or "consensual unions" in the Caribbean—these unions seem to carry less than full social approval.

Marriage is also important in that it gives to members of the family certain rights and duties, certain expected and preferred ways of behaving both to each other and to groups in the wider society. Some people think that the function of defining and distributing role and rights to the marriage partners is the crucial defining characteristic of marriage: in Edmund Leach's phrase, marriage is merely "a bundle of rights."

These rights relate to four areas—sexuality; the birth and rearing of children; domestic and economic services; and property. Each of the partners in the marriage has certain rights, and usually some attendant duties, in all these matters.

Rights relating to sexuality include, in some cases, setting limits as to when sexual intercourse may take place. For instance, in some societies there are regulations governing lovemaking during menstruation and after childbirth; where polygamous marriages are the rule a system of rotation is allocated; in some tribal societies, there is a restriction on love-making just before or just after a man has been to battle.

Rights over children—whether they shall be allowed to live, how and where they shall be reared, educated, and trained for an occupation and status in society—are usually distributed between the marriage partners, or between them and their wider kinship networks or other social groups. In modern Western societies, for example, the State has considerable rights concerning the health and education of children. In some tribal societies—among the Trobriand islanders, for example—most of the rights which in modern Western societies would be the father's concern fall to the mother's brother. Among a certain tribe of the Sudan, a woman could be married to the "name" of a man who had died in battle. When she had children by a lover, who would usually be a stable partner, certain crucial rights over their children fell to the kin of the dead husband. These children would inherit property and status from their legal not their biological father.

Rights and duties relating to the domestic and economic division of labor in the family are often spelled out in elaborate detail in marriage customs and contracts. These include not only informal assumptions about what work traditionally goes with the role of husband and wife, but also precise and binding requirements such as for example the legal obligation on the contemporary American and British husband to maintain his wife and children whether he lives with them or not. Then there are the services or payments which prospective spouses often have to make to the intended partner or his or her family—the bride price in some tribal societies, the dowry in medieval Europe, or Jacob's seven years' service to Laban for Rachel which is described in the first book of the Bible, Genesis.

Rights over property are important in all marriage contracts but they vary enormously from one society to another, and often from one stratum of society to another. Many factors affect the allocation of rights over property in marriage: the status of women in the particular society, the system of inheritance, and the relative importance of the conjugal family and wider kinship groups all affect the degree of control over property which is invested in the husband, wife, children, or extended kin. And other aspects of law and custom relating to the family can be greatly affected by the arrangements over property. The heavy moral odium that surrounded the adulterous wife at certain periods of English history, especially among the landed aristocracy—and the ease with which she could be legally cast off—can partly be explained by the fact that the eldest child of the family inherited the property: the great landed families were

eager to get rid of the errant wife in case their inheritance should pass to an undetected bastard.

Because marriage involves society as well as two individuals, there are normally legal and social controls to prevent people entering lightly into the wedded state. Usually, the man and the woman must be single, or of eligible status, and must agree to the marriage, although in some Islamic and Hindu communities the father or grandfather of a young virgin may dispense with the girl's consent in arranging her marriage. Often, but not universally, there are minimum age requirements. Many cultures, however, have practiced child marriage even where consummation is deferred until puberty. In nineteenth-century India, puberty was customarily the maximum rather than the minimum acceptable age for girls to be married. In many societies the partners' kin must approve of the marriage—and indeed it is often normal for the kin group to initiate and arrange the marriage and to fix all the financial settlements on behalf of the contracting parties. This happens, for instance, in Muslim, Shinto, Confucian, and Hindu marriages.

Financial and property settlements are common to marriages the world over. Such settlements ensure that the new family is soundly based. Sometimes the settlement is designed to compensate the family of the new wife or husband for the loss of valuable labor services, or to provide for the more vulnerable party, usually the wife, in the event of a divorce—the dowry in Islam, for instance, tends to be for the wife's benefit, should she be repudiated by her husband. Almost always there are legal or customary rules to ensure publicity for the marriage and to provide a record of the contractual arrangements: the publishing of banns, residential qualifications, and the presence of formal witnesses at the marriage ceremony all fulfill this function.

Since these controls are primarily of social importance, they form part of civil as well as religious marriages. The eligibility of the contracting parties and of the official conducting the ceremony, residential qualifications, the consent of the parties and of their kin if they are below the age of consent, witnesses, registration, and publicity, form a part of all known civil marriage arrangements. Even in places like Gretna Green in Scotland, where historic custom once (but no longer) made marriage easier than elsewhere in Britain, the only substantial relaxation of these requirements was a shorter period of residence.

Marriage ceremonies have many common elements in widely differing cultures. All have at their center either the tacit, or more often the open, acceptance of the married state by the contracting parties. The statement before an official that the man and the woman accept the statutes and duties of husband and wife under the law of the land is almost the only business of the civil marriage ceremony in America, Britain, the British Commonwealth, the U.S.S.R., and other Eastern European states.

But other customs cling even in some civil ceremonies. The marriage feast is a ritual rejoicing found in all cultures. The scattering of symbols of fertility or prosperity is another common custom—for example, confetti or rice in Christian cultures, dates and sweetmeats in some Muslim and Jewish communities. The presence of bridesmaids and groomsmen at the wedding ceremony is another ancient tradition. Some anthropologists have speculated that the original function of the Best Man was to protect the bridal pair: the newlyweds were often regarded in folk societies as particularly vulnerable to evil spirits and black magic. The honeymoon or at least a short period of privacy for the couple, ritual bathing before the ceremony, the use of veils or a marriage canopy, wearing colors considered specially "pure" (red in Islam, white in the Christian West), a bridal procession beneath crossed swords, the ritual smashing of a wine-glass at the end of *kiddushin*, the Jewish betrothal ceremony, carrying the bride over the threshold of her new home—all these provide a few examples of protective customs which are by no means confined to simple societies or to religious weddings.

Whatever the origin of the wedding customs, they always have the function of imaginatively expressing and impressing on the couple the importance of the step they are taking. Indeed, there are strong indications that civil marriages are felt to be inadequate "rites of passage" if they are too completely stripped of ritual elements—as, for example, are the perfunctory formalities of "conveyor belt" civil marriages in some states.

In addition to all these customs many marriages are, of course, also specifically religious acts. Indeed, despite a slow but steady trend towards civil marriage in modern industrial societies most marriages in the West are still religious services. No religion has ever failed to treat marriage as worthy of religious concern, but some religions—in particular Hinduism and Roman Catholicism—regard marriage as a sacrament and the marriage bond as sacred and indissoluble. It is no accident that the religions that express a mistrust of sexuality often insist either on celibacy or on ultimate withdrawal from family life for a spiritual elite. This tends to be part of a theology which regards over-attachment to any of the things of this world as a hindrance to spirituality.

There are other religions, however, in which sexuality and family ties are not so deeply mistrusted. In Islam, Shintoism, Confucianism, Judaism, and Protestant Christianity, marriage is regarded as a contract rather than a sacrament, and while all these religions hold life-long marriage as an ideal they do not wholly condemn divorce and the first three have even encouraged polygamy. It is in some ways paradoxical that marriage is considered indissoluble in those religious traditions which embody the greatest suspicion of sexuality and family ties, while those religions which mingle family and religious duties most intimately—ancestor worship in Shintoism and Confucianism, family-based rituals in Judaism, for example—regard marriage both as less awesome and as a more fundamental part of religious duty.

Different religious attitudes are reflected in marriage ceremonies as well as in religious rules about divorce and remarriage. Religions which treat marriage as a contract tend to place the couple's acceptance of the duties of the contract at the center of the ceremony, although they also include prayers and blessings and normally use an official of the religion to conduct the ceremony. At a Jewish wedding for instance a major feature is the reading of the *Kettubah,* the man's acceptance of the duties of a Jewish husband. A prominent part of a Muslim wedding is the publication and acceptance of the marriage contracts and financial settlements.

On the other hand, in religions where marriage is a sacrament, the ceremony will tend to feature a symbolic expression of the sacredness of marriage—in Hinduism, for example, the couple, hand in hand, circle the sacred fire, and in Orthodox Christianity the couple are ceremonially crowned. All religious marriages include some element which expresses the couple's acceptance of the main customs and beliefs of the religion itself—for example the nuptial mass at a Roman Catholic wedding, or

the Shinto and Confucian bride's first involvement in the ancestor cults of her husband's family.

Because of various social changes there has been an increase in the divorce rates in the West. Yet it is important to emphasize that this increase is by no means a symptom of the decay of marriage and the family. Research suggests that the vast majority of couples who marry intend to stay married for a lifetime—and even those who seek a divorce mostly remarry. In fact, marriage has never been so popular as it is today. The age of marriage in the West is continually declining and the proportion of the population marrying is increasing.

The divorce rate may well continue to increase slightly for a variety of reasons, but there is little doubt that this is no serious threat to the stability of society or to the continued existence of the family. Marriage undoubtedly has a long and flourishing future.

44

THE HONEYMOON IS OVER

Frank D. Cox

A well-known story in American folklore concerns the young couple who find themselves very much in love. He courted her for a year. They were engaged three months. Then they had a storybook wedding and breathlessly looked forward to a happy-ever-after marriage. They discussed major problems, such as choice of living area and number of children and resolved most of their differences on these issues before marriage. The first year of marriage went smoothly but during the second year the couple has begun to make certain negative observations about one another. These negative

reactions have become increasingly serious until they are now causing open conflict between the two. The husband thinks to himself, "She has changed, she is not the girl she was when we first married." The wife silently complains, "But he is so different than he was at first. He used to be so kind and attentive to me. Now he is mad all the time." After one particularly upsetting encounter, one of the partners decides to discuss the problem with an outside third party. Upon meeting this disinterested party, the partner quickly points out what to him is the major problem. Namely, the spouse has changed and is no longer the person he married.

This all too familiar story probably occurs in the majority of American marriages at some time during the early years. Let us call it the "honeymoon is over" period in the modern American marriage.

In order to understand the dynamics of such a relationship it is necessary to know more about typical boy-girl interaction in this country before the marriage. Obviously, there is a great deal of difference between individual dating patterns and the norms. In addition, these patterns evolve and change with time; thus, the reader should be wary of assuming everyone fits the general picture herein described. However, there are certain generalized patterns that emerge upon study, as has been amply demonstrated by such books as *The Natural History of Love*,[1] by Morton Hunt. The couples tending toward an exaggerated "honeymoon is over" period often exhibit certain typical patterns in their premarital dating behavior as well as in the first year or two of marriage.

These patterns are chiefly composed of two strong trends. The first is that these couples tend to be those who went steady much of their dating life. This does not mean to imply that they went steady only with one another, but rather that they did not "play the field" and limited their dating to a few of the opposite sex through the technique of "going steady." When one "goes steady" he essentially dates one person during a given period of time. The tendency to "go steady" has been on the increase since World War II. Horrocks, in his text on adolescence, says:

Today, both in high school and college, there is an increasing tendency to "go steady," a relationship that may be said to be established somewhere between the third and the sixth date. "Going steady" does not necessarily mean that marriage is in view although even among high-schoolers, there is an increasing possibility that both partners have this understanding.[2]

This tendency to "go steady" combined with a slowly declining average age at mar-

riage[3] tends to limit drastically the number of meaningful heterosexual relations available to the young person. A recent study by Schneider indicates that in 75 percent of the cases going steady involves a social commitment not to date others, and an emotional commitment to the extent that they report being "in love." Over half have also agreed to see each other whenever either of them wants to get together. Over 80 percent of the couples have given serious thought to getting married and nearly 40 percent have an informal agreement to marry.[4]

"Going steady" yields certain advantages in the eyes of the insecure adolescent. It means that the necessity to compete is reduced, dates for social events are assured, costs may be less, and above all, there is a certain comfortable security about it since one does not risk the possible rejection that might result from interacting with a new individual.

The young adult who engages in "going steady" will, however, also suffer several disadvantages. For one, his field of experience with the opposite sex is reduced. This means that his frame of reference for judging a future spouse may be based on a limited number (perhaps as few as two or three) of meaningful opposite sex relationships.[5] Secondly, his freedom to grow through having broad experiences with life is now curtailed because of the obligations to his steady. Thus, the period of life that should supply practice in heterosexual relations as well as an invitation to growth through new experience is partially nullified by "going steady." Hunt, in his fine book on the history of love supports this view when he states:

All too soon, they become anxious to "go steady," and tend to do so earlier and more fixedly than used to be the case. Going steady is evidently reassuring in that it signifies they have been accepted by someone; unfortunately it reduces the utility of the dating pattern itself, since it limits the chances for the wider testing of personalities and possible meanings of love.[6]

Even after marriage, the spouse's frame of reference by which to evaluate his marriage partner remains limited and narrow because the American tends to prize and guard his privacy.[7] In a sense, this marriage is analogous to what the psychologist describes as the "loner" individual. This individual operates quite well as long as his narrow frame of reference fits the reality situation. If, however, the reality should change, it is difficult for him to judge the change because of his isolation tendencies. The same holds true for the "loner" marriage. The statistics show that married couples who enjoy many contacts with the society around them; club memberships, church activities, family ties, etc., tend to have more stable marriages. This would imply that the stability of the "loner" marriage is less. When an argument occurs in the "loner" marriage, the spouse tends to react to it in light of his prior limited heterosexual experiences. If these are not appropriate to the new reality, he then has no place to turn to correct this reaction because of the private quality of his marriage (it is no one else's business).

These, then, are the first factors which tend to create the reaction to marital conflict that one's spouse has changed. In short, one has not had enough experience with the opposite sex nor has one a place to turn to understand the reality and judge it in light of the new marriage relationship.

The second trend is the social creation of an over-romanticized and unrealistic image of the marriage relationship. This image stems, in large part, from mass communication media as well as from the failure of the various social institutions, such as school, family, and the church, to present realistically the problems inherent to sexuality and marriage.

Although education professes to be moving forward in this field, much of the forward movement tends to be "lip service." Many studies report that age mates are the major source of sex information. For example, Angelino and Mech report that the highest percentage of source of first sex information is age mates. The following excerpts from the verbatim reports of the subjects used in this study point up not only the status of sex information received, but the very serious need for adequate sex knowledge:

I think that the parents should have the biggest responsibility in informing their children about sex, but many parents do not perform this responsibility. My knowledge of sex increased as I began to read articles and discuss it with my girl friends. Many times we were misinformed. As near as I can remember I had no sex education at all in elementary school. I would suggest that a program of this type on the grade level be worked into the health course that is offered in many smaller schools.

Most of the classes that frankly discuss these subjects were in college. I think this type of education should be inserted into the school curriculum in junior high—and I think it should be required. In this way every child will have accurate information. I had many misconceptions. I don't think anyone ever gave me the wrong ideas, but I was pretty vague on what they didn't tell me. I think there should be more information given to the public. Most people won't buy these books, but if they were put out through the school, it would help. Parents should also be taught how to explain these things to their children.[8]

Obviously, the chances of other adolescents supplying valid information in a clear, understandable manner are small. It is somewhat analogous to the blind leading the blind. Hence, the schools are apparently failing in their efforts to bring sound realistic understanding to the adolescent in the fields of sex and marriage or there would be less necessity for the adolescent to lean so heavily on his peers for this information.

The inability of the parent to communicate this information successfully to his children is so well-known via satirization in cartoons and jokes that it needs no discussion here. The parents and the schools represent two sources that should lead the young adult to realistic attitudes toward sexuality. To the extent that they fail, peers and mass media fill the vacuum.

A cursory examination of mass media's portrayal of modern sex and marriage quickly confirms the unreality of the image projected. Advertising is especially absurd in depicting marital bliss. Basically, the happy marriage, according to advertising, is based on physical charms and material goods. The right deodorant (don't you wish everyone did?), proper mouth wash (why do some honeymoons last year after year?), and correct hair colors (blonds have more fun), appear to epitomize the physical ideal. Not only do the advertisements subtly undermine reality by exaggeration of the often trivial and superficial, but they directly support the importance of denying truth. For example, the facial cream "Ultra Feminine" advertisement in a popular woman's magazine begins with the following question: "A woman faces so many things. . . . Why should looking her age be one of them?"[9] An example of intellectual distortion can easily be seen in another make-up ad in the same magazine. "A look so nearly nude, it could be nothing at all . . . this is the real you, looking natural as the day you were born."[10] The absurdity of such a statement is obvious. If it were the real you, you would not be covered with make-up and, of course, if you are covered with make-up it is not the real you. One might call it the make-up, in reality, a mask hiding the "real you."

The other half of the ideal marriage as depicted by advertising is the material, epitomized by such things as stoves that cook by themselves and play "Tenderly" when the meal is ready; Mr. Clean, which absolves the woman from cleaning chores; the proper car for manly appeal and, of course, the ultimate necessity of the properly colored toilet paper to match the furnishings.[11]

In addition to advertising, the popular heroine or hero of the serial, novel, movie, or television play bears little resemblance to the statistical norm. He is often one of two types: 1. the stylized, idealized sex symbol, a James Bond, or the bunny of Playboy; or 2. he is the sick, weak hero type such as is portrayed in "Lolita," or by the pouting James Dean.

Rose Franzblau makes another interesting and disturbing observation when she writes,

Another implication arises when a permitted source of sexual stimulation and excitement on the mass media comes to be a safer form of pleasure and release than personal participation in any sexual activity. Because it is acted out for him by someone else, it allays his guilt. It is also a form of escape for the individual, within his own home, from the social controls required of him on the outside. . . . This private viewing can become the youngster's total psychosexual life, and keep him from reaching his psychic maturity normally, at the proper age.[12]

Combining the two trends, a narrow frame of reference and an unrealistic picture of marital bliss, into an individual attitude toward love and marriage, results in a general confusion between the internalized ideal image and external reality. In essence, what the individual with such an attitude does is to marry a projection of his own internalized ideal image. That is, he tends to observe his steady girl, his fiancee, or his spouse through a multi-lens filter system which allows only those rays to pass through which illuminate the imaginary ideal. Erich Fromm, author of the widely read book, *The Art of Loving*,[13] in a recent interview printed in *McCall's Magazine*, answers the interviewer's question about the meaning of "falling in love" as follows:

It is an unfortunate phrase—falling is not standing, and if you take our American phrase "he falls" or "she falls" for someone, what a fantastic phrase this is, to fall for someone. It is the abandonment of judgment, of realism, for an illusion. It is a particular kind of idolatry, where you suddenly build a picture of something wonderful. Only when you come to your senses you see this is not so. Then you start talking to lawyers.[14]

Such a system works well through courtship and the early months of marriage. But as the months stretch into years, the routine of daily living and the intimate prolonged contact tend to wear out the filter system and more and more realism creeps through. Finally, when the negative can no longer be suppressed, the spouse comes to the belief that his partner has changed. In most cases, nothing could be further from the truth. The fact is that for the first time the couple has really begun to look at one another, not as the stereotyped projections of their own imagination, but as fellow human beings. The partner has not changed. It is the first time that he has been truly observed. The person has married a dream, not a reality, and all dreams come to an end upon awakening. This period marks the end of the "honeymoon." It also demonstrates the working of an age-old human tendency to admit to awareness only that which fits previous wishes or assumptions. What we think we see may tell more about the viewer than about the real situation or person being viewed.

In cases where awakening is too rude or the idealized image is too strongly held, the individual may cling to his first reaction that the spouse has changed. This gives the person a rationalization for leaving the spouse and taking up the search again. It is clear that such a person is doomed to failure since there is a slim chance of finding a human who will coincide with his idealized image. John Robert Clark has a pithy description of this occurrence.

In learning how to love a plain human being today, as during the romantic movement, what we usually want unconsciously is a fancy human being with no flaws. When the mental picture we have of someone we love is colored by wishes of childhood, we may love the picture rather than the real person behind it. Naturally, we are disappointed in the person we love if he does not conform to our picture. Since this kind of disappointment has no doubt happened to us before, one might suppose we would then tear up the picture and start all over. On the contrary, we keep the picture and tear up the person. Small wonder that divorce courts are full of couples who never gave themselves a chance to know the real persons behind the pictures in their lives.[15]

On the other hand, the individual who holds a strong idealized image may attempt to change his mate in the direction of his image. Attempting to change one's spouse can lead to trouble. It may arouse hostility on the part of the person being asked to change when they feel they do not want to or that there is no reason to change. It may also arouse guilt feelings when the person does indeed change but fails to meet the idealistic expectations imposed by the partner.

For those who can weather this period of marriage a new potential for true growth, both in marriage and as an individual, is possible. John Sisk in his article, "The Dream Girl as Queen of Utopia," mentions:

Lionel Trilling has called attention to a "solution" to the dilemma: the emergence of a low-keyed, open-eyed, realistic kind of "good sexual partnership," the result of a revolution that has "brought the relationship between marriage and passion love to a virtual end." Porphyron and Madeline "learn to see each other without illusion as they are in reality." They "build a life together" in "the mutuality and warmth of their togetherness."[16]

One's romantic ideal can be a wonderful guideline to give direction to a marriage. But the direction can be maintained and the goals achieved only if there is a firm recognition of the reality from which one may be attempting to move. Realities and idealizations march forward together, not inversely. The ideal is realized only when firmly rooted in reality. . . .

THE ALTRUISTIC-WIFE SYNDROME

Upon the conclusion of World War II, many young men returned to work and school. The government provided the GI Bill which helped those veterans who desired to return to school. These young men were naturally older and generally far more mature than the usual college student. Many of them were married or married soon after beginning college. Thus, the married student descended in mass upon the American colleges and universities. Although it was the circumstances of the war that led to the phenomenon of the married college student, it was not long until their influence was felt by the rest of the student body. If young married veteran couples could sustain a marriage and achieve a college education at the same time, why couldn't other young couples do the same? Thus, the old idea that marriage and higher education were incompatible began to fade. The young couples recognized that they could enjoy the pleasures of marriage and at the same time further the husband's education so as to provide a secure future as well as to fulfill his aspirations. Although they might not have the help of the GI Bill, by living frugally on the wife's earnings and postponing children they could manage until the husband finished his education and began to earn. On the surface this appears logical. The wife will sacrifice a few years of her own schooling and forego some of the traditional expectancies of marriage for the longer range goal of vocationally furthering her husband. Since he will be the future main support of the family, this would pay dividends to the entire family. Many were deceived by the reasonableness of this argument and lauded the girl who was willing to be so altruistic.

Unfortunately, the rationality of the theoretical argument was not born out in the practical situation. First of all, the young couples lacked the experience and resulting maturity of the veteran group. Secondly, although the GI Bill school benefits were small (base pay, $110/month), they were reliable and acted as a healthy supplement to the wife's earnings, relieving at least part of the financial strain.

In light of these two differences, the type of life that the newly married young college couple is forced to live for at least four years and in some cases longer often proves to be devastating. The important adjustments of the first few years of marriage are often postponed. The wife, by virtue of her youth, is usually forced to work at a fairly mundane job such as file clerk or salesgirl. She must leave the tiny apartment each day before 8:00 A.M. and does not return until after 6:00 P.M., usually thoroughly fatigued. He is burdened with homework in the evening and she must turn what energies remain to cooking

and other chores. Thus, evening passes with little if any opportunity for interaction. If she is a bright girl, much of her fatigue will be the result of boredom on the job and lack of self-fulfillment and achievement feelings. Meanwhile her husband is being stimulated by his studies. He is forced to grow and move forward by academic pressures. If he doesn't he might be dropped from the program. Increasingly, he grows away from his wife, at least intellectually. Communication between them grows worse as time passes because she neither has the energy nor the time to keep up with what he is doing. He finds her to be less interesting with each passing day. Although this isn't necessarily her fault, it is a fact of life. How stimulating can a person be after eight hours as a file clerk? As the gap widens, she begins to feel wronged. After all, she is making his academic career possible. Soon, certain recriminations and accusations begin to appear during periods of conflict. The severity of such conflicts is increased further by her own feelings of stagnancy and ensuing jealousy of him and perhaps of the girls with whom he associates on campus. Such recriminations cause the husband to become upset with his position in the marriage; i.e., the dependent spouse. This role is in contradiction to the traditional male role he may be accustomed to in the family. In addition, his feelings of freedom are reduced, and he becomes subject to a powerful blackmail weapon if the girl chooses to use her support of him in such a manner.

Upon graduation day, the wife often receives her own diploma, a divorce subpoena. All of the couple's friends rally to the wife who after so many years of self-sacrifice is treated in such a manner by her ungrateful husband. He must be the lowest cad to treat her in such a way. Yet, close and intelligent scrutiny of their past daily life would have indicated long before graduation that all was not well. In essence, the husband, being young and far from fully developed intellectually, simply grew away from his wife who was forced by circumstances to remain relatively stagnant. As time passed, he came to have far more in common with his female chemistry laboratory partner than he did with his wife. Although the disruption of such a marriage is sad and unfair to the wife, it is certainly no surprise under the circumstances.

Much of the underlying tension in this type of marriage has been glossed over by well-meaning but inept researchers who have tried to demonstrate the advantages of such marriages. Most of these studies were made by questionnaires and were directed at uncovering such things as the relationship between marriage and scholastic achievement. By and large, the studies found that grades improved with marriage; the majority of couples reported satisfactory adjustment in their marriage; most reported that they would do it over again if they were to relive the same period. Yet, these results were deceptive. How many young couples in the midst of this situation would admit that they might not undertake such an endeavor again? This would be to admit failure. Does a slight improvement in grade point average indicate a higher level of learning? The young husband, who because of feelings of obligation toward his hard working wife, fails to buy a book for some course is missing out regardless of what his grades may be. When he comes home to his wife rather than attending the bull session after a controversial class lecture he again is missing out. In addition, many of the earlier studies that reported positive findings about college marriages were influenced by the more mature older veteran population. The underlying problems that gradually undermine such youthful marriages simply did not come to the surface in such superficial studies.[17]

Such a discussion of the inherent problems in this type of marriage should not be construed to mean that each such marriage is doomed to failure. Actually, we do not have good data that relate success in marriage to married college attendance or family support by the wife. Those couples who are mature and anticipate the special problems they will face in such a marriage can probably overcome them. However, there is some question as to whether the costs involved will be offset by the future rewards.

By far the largest cost to these young people is the reduction in personal freedom and opportunity to adventure, both physically and intellectually, which they experience. Landis, in his discussion of the college marriage, says:

Certainly the young person coming to college already married, or who marries during the first two years of college, cuts himself off from much of the teen-age social life which is such a vital part of the college experience. His chances for leadership are undoubtedly greatly reduced, as well as his chance for developing social talents such as are demanded in the numerous extracurricular activities of the campus.[18]

Not only will the married student be cut off from such experiences as these but the normal carefree recreation periods that most young adults enjoy will be greatly reduced. As clearly indicated, the time available to the couple is so limited and/or the finances so strained that even the normal recreation periods found in the average marriage are apt to be missing.

One study reported that the married students have a greater sense of security and feel more settled.[19] It is difficult to think of worse feelings to engender in 19 and 20 year old young adults. This is the one period in a person's life when he can adventure, take chances, and exercise his intellectual and physical being to the limit. Yet we find studies that report feelings of security and being settled as advantages. It would seem that young Americans have moved a long distance from the adventurous attitudes that were held by their wagon train forefathers.

Margaret Mead is one of the few outspoken critics of early marriage, especially the college marriage. She feels that the trend toward early marriage works directly against the intellectual development. The necessity of earning a living for the family takes precedence over intellectual achievement. Family responsibilities deny the youth a chance to explore, challenge, and adventure. She feels that we are creating a "settled, security-loving, unadventurous people" through our emphasis on early marriage.[20]

It is interesting to compare the permissive American attitude toward college marriage with that of most Western European societies. In Europe, students are encouraged to put off marriage as long as possible. Few university men would consider marriage before they are finished with their studies (late 20s). For example, in Western Germany, the average age of marriage for men in the general population is between 25 and 27. For the male university student it is even older. The female generally marries between 23 and 24.[21] Although she marries younger, many of the educated girls much prefer a life of travel and adventure before they will contemplate settling down. In fact, for most educated European youth, the thought of security and being settled is reserved for middle age. Young people would much prefer to spend a summer youth hosteling or seeing Africa via Volkswagen bus rather than staying at home because of a girl or boy-friend.

In general, the altruistic-wife syndrome demonstrates most of the problems inherent in the youthful marriage. There is, first, a general lack of maturity in the relationship. Secondly, there is usually a marginal economic level which greatly increases strain on the pair. Lastly, there is a general loss of freedom and willingness to adventure in the direction of self-fulfillment.[22]

THE INDEPENDENT-CHILD MARRIAGE

Recently there has been a growing trend toward parental subsidization of college marriages. In many ways, such a trend serves to reduce the problems that are found in college marriages. However, as with every new trend, some problems are solved while other problems are produced.

Traditionally, marriage has signified the end of economic dependence upon one's parents. It has always been true that parents who could afford it helped their youngsters even after marriage, but this was usually done through the avenue of gifts or loans. In the past, marriage meant assumption of the major responsibility for the new family. This usually meant the end of schooling in order to work at some occupa-

tion. Parents no longer felt obligated to support their child after marriage. Gradually this attitude has changed. Many modern parents in the face of a youthful marriage which they cannot prevent and recognizing the problems inherent in the altruistic-wife marriage have decided to extend their support through college. Since they would have put him through college if he remained single they can see no reason not to continue this support. In light of the general affluence in America today and the increasing importance of advanced schooling this appears to be an intelligent move.

Numerous sociologists, among them Paul Landis, feel it a wise policy to subsidize the marriage of able and socially mature college students. Since young marriage appears to be here to stay and since few young people set on such a marriage can be deterred, it appears wise to help reduce the pressures inherent in such early marriages. Landis suggests that college campuses should do a great deal more to improve the circumstances in which college marriages must operate. Nurseries and childcare centers should be readily available for those students with children. Better medical care programs, housing, and counseling services should be provided. Social activities, in the form of clubs, recreational groups, etc., should be encouraged.[23]

The subsidized marriage in which both partners can continue school certainly eliminates many of the problems we have discussed. The tendency for the pair to grow apart is reduced since the girl participates directly in the campus life of her husband. Further, their time together is greatly increased, they share the same interests, they are both engaged in bettering themselves and can take pride in one another's achievements rather than feel jealous of them. Their freedom is increased by the reduction of economic worries. They, however, still do not enjoy the freedom of their unwed peers since they must give some of their energies to homemaking.

Although subsidy of the marriage serves to solve numerous problems, it also creates some. The major problem created by such subsidy is to force the young pair to assume incongruent roles. The first role is naturally the adult-independent role of the married spouse. However, since economic support continues from its normal childhood source, the dependent-child role must continue to be played at the same time. In the past, assumption of the adult marital role signaled the end of the child role. In the new situation, the child role must be continued alongside the adult role, hence the name "independent-child marriage."

Numerous tensions are created when both roles must be played simultaneously. The young couple does not enjoy the complete freedom from parental and in-law interference that those who are economically independent might. They are loath to accept the interference that often accompanies the support. If the couple thought a bit more deeply about the problem or projected themselves into their parent's position, they would probably agree that at least some parental control is inherent in parental economic support. It is father's money. He is the one who worked for it and it is the family at home who will perhaps have to cut corners to help the student through college. A father has both the legal and ethical right of control over his earnings. There are very few fathers who, while straining to send several hundred dollars a month to help their child through college, would not object if he decided to use it to buy a new car.

Though perhaps ideally the parents should have no say in the children's marriage except in the financial area, there is usually a larger involvement. One area of concern tends to generate other areas.

Resentments often arise on all sides of such a situation. The spouse of the partner receiving the help may not only resent the generous in-laws, but may resent the partner for being manipulated by his or her parents. This will generate conflict between the child and his parents as well as between the parents and the new spouse. In some cases, both sets of parents are contributing to the economic livelihood of the young people and this complicates the relationships even more. It does serve, however, to reduce the burden on each set of parents from what it would be if only one set carried the entire load.

The young man will often feel guilty and uncomfortable about his continuing dependence. This is especially true if he comes from a family that has stressed self-sufficiency and independence. Even though the family might support him without recriminations, he will feel that he is failing to fulfill his duty. He will feel strongly the obligations to his parents and thus be unable to give his full allegiance to his marriage. In some cases, the young couple will feel so uncomfortable accepting parental aid that they will refuse it even when the parents can afford it. On the whole, however, parental support probably solves more problems than it creates when compared to the altruistic-wife marriage.

Such help should be given and accepted with a clear understanding on both sides of the inherent obligations. Parents should reduce the number of conditions tied to such support to the bare minimum while the couple should clearly understand that there are certain obligations that they must meet in order to receive such help.

MARRIAGE AND MILITARY SERVICE[24]

Since World War II the American male has had to contend with obligatory military service. This period in his life usually comes at a time when possible marriage is very much a part of his life (19–23 years old). Thus it is that today almost every young couple must consider potential military service as an important factor in their marital plans.

The major question that normally arises concerns the effects of prolonged separation on the couple's relationship. Folklore contains a pair of contradictory ideas on the subject. "Absence makes the heart grow fonder." "While the cat is away, the mice will play." In any one instance, it will be difficult to predict which of these alternatives will hold true since it will depend on the individuals involved and the particular circumstances. Statistically, the latter idea predominates as the increased divorce rate immediately following World War II demonstrated.

Fear of separation undoubtedly leads some couples into marriage earlier than they had planned. In a sense, this is marrying because of rather than in spite of military service. The real questions that need to be asked are, would we marry at this time regardless of military service? Has our courtship been long enough for us to establish a stable and meaningful relationship? Are we mature enough to enter marriage? Some investigators feel that if such questions are answered in the affirmative then there is no reason why the couple should not marry before military service.

Unfortunately, the problem is not that simple. Military service does indeed place additional stress on a young marriage. For example, there is no way to predict in advance if the young man will be stationed in an area where his family will be allowed to accompany him. It is certainly best if the family can remain with him despite what hardships of travel and living might be involved. In fact, there can be a great deal of fun and companionship in facing adversities together. However, since one can't predict if the family may remain with the service man, separation must be considered as a possibility.

During separation, how does one handle interaction with the opposite sex? Does each swear a vow of no interaction? How realistic is this for young persons during their most active period of life? If your partner remains a hermit for two years of his life, will this make him a better partner? It seems doubtful. In fact, the person playing the hermit role may become resentful and build up hostilities and jealousies toward the other person.

Should then each person be allowed to have contact with the opposite sex? This, of course, increases the probability of one mate being displaced. After all, the partners are young, usually attractive, and lonely. Thus, what starts out to be a platonic friendship with the opposite sex always runs the risk of turning into something more.

Separation also presents the problem of possible change in one or both of the partners. The younger they are the higher will be the chances for genuine change. Thus,

when they are reunited they are apt to be different in some ways and these differences might so change the relationship as to make it unacceptable to one of them. In addition, separation may cause one or both of the parties to idealize the other. When they come back together there will be a feeling of let-down if idealization has occurred, not because the other person has actually changed but because one's image of him has changed.

If there must be a long period of separation in a relationship for any reason, studies[25] have found that successfully married couples do indeed maintain a close and intimate interaction by doing several things. They write frequent letters that are very detailed, thus allowing each to share the activities, thoughts, and feelings of the other. They exchange frequent pictures of each other, their families, and friends. They often exchange gifts and do special things for special occasions such as telephoning or sending a telegram for a birthday or anniversary. Prolonged separation is trying on any relationship but certainly is to be avoided if possible in a new and unstable union between two very young persons.

CONCLUSION

Despite limitation of the discussion to particular types of young marriages found for the most part in the middle class, the general problems referred to are often a part of any young marriage. First, there will always be a reduction in one's freedom with any marriage. In the young marriage, however, this reduction of freedom often comes before the individual has had a chance to explore, adventure, and test himself. It comes before he really knows just who he is because he is still in the midst of psychological and philosophical growth. Often the marriage will serve to cut off further individual development. On the other hand, if the spouse has the strength to continue individual growth, he may find that his young choice of marital partner is inadequate to his more complete and mature being in later years. One spouse may outgrow the other.

Secondly, there will usually be financial hardship which serves to further reduce one's movement toward self-fulfillment. Such financial strain increases greatly the general level of conflict between spouses. Often after years of hardship and struggle, the couple is unable to enjoy financial success when it finally arrives because of deep-seated hostilities that have grown up over the years.

Thirdly, the general maturity level of an individual is related to his chronological age. Thus, the younger one marries, the less his chances of being mature enough in all ways to meet the problems of responsibility, decision, and compromise demanded in the successful marriage.

Lastly, although we have made no mention of children, it should be obvious that the introduction of children into any marriage serves to exaggerate whatever problems already exist. In general, the idea that children serve to cement a marriage together is faulty. Children are wonderful and are obviously the major reason for the existence of the family institution but it should be clearly recognized that they create many additional problems.

The younger the marriage, the less the chances of success. Although the trend in the United States is in the direction of younger marriage,[26] the problems in such a marriage are great, and far from solved. It is the author's conclusion that marriage should be postponed until at least the middle 20s for the male and that marriage before the completion of education should be discouraged. Man must find an identity and in order to do this he must be alone for awhile. The young marriage is often nothing more than changing dependency from parents to spouse.[27]

NOTES

[1] Morton Hunt, *The Natural History of Love* (New York: Grove Press, 1959).

[2] John Horrocks, *The Psychology of Adolescence* (Boston: Houghton Mifflin, 1962), p. 204.

[3] In 1890 the median age of marriage for men was 26, for women, 22. By 1958, the median ages had dropped to 23 for men, and 20 for women. [Editor's note: In 1972, the median age of marriage went up slightly to 23.3 for men and 20.9 for women.]

[4] Carlfred Broderick, "Going Steady: The Beginning of the End," in *Teenage Marriage and Divorce*, Seymour Farber and Roger Wilson, eds. (Berkeley, Calif.: Diablo Press, 1967), pp. 22–23.

[5] Even as long ago as 1946, the number of meaningful heterosexual relations was narrow. A survey of Navy men, including those to twenty-five years of age, found that on the average they had dated only seven different girls. See *Family Life*, Vol. 6, Oct. 1948.

[6] Hunt, op. cit.

[7] This conclusion is supported by such general values in the American culture as the private house and yard, strong reaction against living with others after marriage, dislike of unannounced visits, etc.

[8] H. Angelino and E. Mech, "Some First Sources of Sex Information as Reported by 67 College Women," *Journal of Psychology*, 39 (1955): 321–324.

[9] *McCall's*, October 1965, p. 9.

[10] Ibid., p. 19.

[11] The general erosive quality of modern advertising on man's values and on his ability to understand reality is made one of the cornerstones of Jules Henry's book, *Culture Against Man*. See Jules Henry, *Culture Against Man* (New York: Random House, 1963), p. 48.

[12] Rose Franzblau, "Sex and the Mass Media," in *Sex Education and the Teenager*, Seymour Farber and Roger Wilson, eds. (Berkeley, Calif.: Diablo Press, 1967), p. 38.

[13] Erich Fromm, *The Art of Loving* (New York: Harper and Bros., 1956).

[14] Erich Fromm, "An Interview with Erich Fromm," *McCall's*, October 1965, p. 215.

[15] John Robert Clark, *The Importance of Being Imperfect* (New York: David McKay Co., 1961).

[16] John Sisk, "The Dream Girl as Queen of Utopia," in *Sex in America*, Anatole Grunwald, ed. (New York: Bantam Books, 1964), pp. 277–278.

[17] Paul Landis, *Making the Most of Marriage* (New York: Appleton-Century-Crofts, 1965), pp. 329–332.

[18] Ibid., p. 333.

[19] Judson and Mary Landis, *Readings in Marriage and the Family* (Englewood Cliffs, N.J.: Prentice-Hall, 1952), pp. 114–116.

[20] Margaret Mead, *U.S. News and World Report,* June 6, 1960.

[21] *The Bulletin,* Press and Information Office of the German Federal Government, Bonn, Germany, June 14, 1966.

[22] Ruth Cavan in her book, *Marriage and Family in the Modern World,* makes several good suggestions to the young couple who find themselves married before school is completed. Both should continue their education to counter the possibility of one growing away from the other. This probably necessitates taking a little longer to complete one's education. Postpone children until finished with your education. Children tend to add complications rather than reduce them.

[23] Paul Landis, op. cit., p. 334.

[24] This discussion does not concern itself with the professional military marriage. The professional service man offers to his family a unique and different way of life that must be accepted by both parties if there is to be an enduring relationship.

[25] Reuben Hill, *Families Under Stress* (New York: Harper & Row, 1949).

[26] See editor's note in footnote 3, above.

[27] As a result of the California Judiciary Committee's study of the increasing trend toward ever more youthful marriage and parenthood, the committee recommended that a waiting period be established for applicants under 21 years of age. Testimony indicated that anything which slows down, delays, or postpones the all too often hasty and unconsidered youthful plunge into matrimony would be a positive step. Such a preventive program would emphasize making it more difficult to get married. See Robert Furlong, "Easy Marriage, Easy Divorce," in *Teenage Marriage and Divorce,* Seymour Farber and Roger Wilson, eds. (Berkeley, Calif.: Diablo Press, 1967), pp. 110–111. [Editor's note: California passed a law in 1971 as a result of this recommendation which makes court permission mandatory for anyone under the age of 18 who wishes to marry.]

45

PATTERNS OF NEWLYWED MARRIAGE

Wells Goodrich, Robert G. Ryder, and Harold L. Raush

The general aim of this exploratory investigation is to take one step toward a taxonomy of newlywed marriage. Our interest has been to study a variety of variables which we hope will describe meaningful psychological differences between marriage relationships, differences which may relate to other significant aspects of family structure. While we have invested in the traditional theories—marriage as an expression of social role theory or as a form of communication or as a focus for the expression of personality—we have made an effort to develop new methods of data gathering and of data analysis. This paper reports on the data of the first stage of a longitudinal study of 50 average middle-class marriages. . . .

Others have investigated variables influencing choice of marital partner, the relationship of marital role values to satisfaction in marriage, interspouse power relationships, and patterns of perceptions spouses hold of each other.[1] In our search for coherent and meaningful differences between couples within a narrowly defined developmental stage of marriage, it seemed wise to include assessment of each of these areas as well as of new areas. To sample as many of the potentials of each couple as possible within the 10–12 hours we spent with them, we have included individual and joint interviews, structured and unstructured sections within these interviews, traditional questionnaires like the Locke-Wallace instrument[2] as well as new questionnaires and direct observations of performance in experimental situations. We have not limited our interest to stable measures of variables. We have studied the total profile of scores received by each couple on all variables and have compared each couple's profile with every other couple's[3] profile.

As has been mentioned in previous publications,[4] the event of getting married for the first time can be viewed as a developmental turning point which introduces a new stage of the life cycle. This new stage demands of the couple a variety of adaptive changes, in some ways similar for husband and wife and in some ways sex-specific. From a somewhat abstract point of view, one can hypothesize that, for a population of couples who live under similar circumstances, these stage demands to change in certain directions will be similar. We have referred to the total process between stage and person as the developmental transaction of early marriage. Implied in this term is the notion that, while all couples being studied are experiencing certain common "developmental presses" toward change, the variety of marriage patterns actually observed represent alternative modes of responding to this common life situation.

The results of this study, then, we have interpreted as providing a tentative set of newlywed marriage patterns which represent various adaptive responses to a common psychosocial and developmental situation: this is the situation of being newlyweds in white, middle-class suburbia. . . .

Couples' names were obtained from local marriage-license records. Those who subsequently agreed to participate constituted about 60 to 80 percent of couples who both were approached and fit our screening criteria, which were as follows: Couples had to be white, to live within a reasonable drive from us, and to have completed high school but not to have obtained any postgraduate degree and not to be presently a full-time student. Husbands had to be between the ages of 20 and 27, and wives were between 18 and 25. It was required that wives were not knowingly pregnant as of three months after marriage. Couples were studied during the fourth month after marriage. The general intent of our screening criteria was to reduce the impact on our data of ethnic and socioeconomic differences so that relationships among other variables might be more clearly revealed.

During this newlywed period, procedures used included six interviews of one to two hours in length, about three hours of questionnaires, Goodrich and Boomer's Color Matching Test, and a quasi-role-playing procedure called "Improvisations." Interviews were administered by highly skilled and experienced social workers. There was a specific set of questions to be asked, but interviewers followed up answers as much as necessary to achieve clarity. First there was a joint interview in the couple's home which focused primarily on the general background of the two spouses and their "marital career," i.e., how they came to be married. Second, each spouse was interviewed individually at National Institutes of Health with the content still focusing primarily on the individual's past history, in this case including his or her adolescent sexual experiences. The Color Matching Test was also administered to the couple during this visit. Questionnaires were filled out by one spouse while the other was being interviewed. These questionnaires assessed patterns of husband-and-wife perception of power and participation in each area pertinent to our interests: relationships with friends, with relatives, occupational matters, houskeeping matters, food-related activities, sexual activities, and prospective parenthood. They also assessed the relative investment of each spouse in each area, as well as each spouse's decision-making style when conflict arose in each area. Couples then visited the National Institutes of Health a second time and received one more individual interview each, this time focusing on relationships with relatives, sexual behavior in marriage, current conflicts in marriage, and prospective view of becoming parents. Questionnaires were again administered, and the evening concluded with administration of the "Improvisations" procedure.[5] Finally there was one more joint interview in the couple's home, surveying information not yet obtained as well as inquiring about anxieties stirred up by the research procedures.

Interviewers rated couples on 21 variables encompassing primarily an evaluation of the marriage and of each spouse's style of relating and communicating during the interviews. There were, for example, ratings of spontaneity, of how much each spouse was liked by the interviewer, of supportiveness and need for support, and other variables. . . .

Methods of data analysis have been reported elsewhere.[6]

A separate principal-component analysis was performed with each subset of data: one for the review ratings, another for the interview content-analysis codes, one for the questionnaires, and one for the Color Matching Test. Factor scores were computed for each analysis, and relations among factors for the full set of data were determined. A final factor matrix was then rotated so as to maximize simple structure among couples. Twenty-eight couples emerged from this procedure who scored near the extreme on one and only one factor. . . .

Speaking in a somewhat approximate way, the primary source of variation among couples was in *closeness to their own parents*. Some couples had little to do with their parents. Others visited them once a week or more often, telephoned them daily, still used closet space in the parents' home, used their car, their washing machine, their checkbook, and, occasionally, their maid. Advice was given by parents, often on request. Young men most often seemed to seek advice from their fathers-in-law. One girl participated in regularly scheduled family meetings. One couple spent their honeymoon with the bride's family.

The second most prominent way in which couples were different from each other was in *marital problems or complaints* as reported by the couples or as judged by our interviewers. We would presume that an interviewer's judgment would depend strongly on what couples chose to relate to him and that willingness of couples to report problems or complain about their marriages might depend on many circumstances. Accordingly differences along this dimension should be interpreted with caution.

Finally, couples varied widely in terms

of *marital role orientation*. At one end of this dimension, say the traditional end, husbands reported little interest in household activities, and wives reported little involvement with occupational matters. At the nontraditional end, husbands were more involved in housework and wives were more involved in occupational matters.

To speak precisely, four factors emerged which looked somewhat like: (1) closeness to husband's family, (2) role orientation, (3) reported problems or complaints, and (4) closeness to wife's family. . . .

We have shown systematic connection between these aspects and recall of earlier life difficulties with the family of origin, enjoyment of sexuality, and a rational or affective communication style. Furthermore the conjunction of these variables within the marital patterns suggests differing developmental processes during this life stage for each sex.

The study suggests that wives who report problems with their families in childhood and in adolescence are to be found among those early marriages reporting unhappiness, doubt, and conflict. These early marital difficulties are diffusely present, ranging from such general impressions as that they feel less identified with their marriage to such specific difficulties as trouble getting along with friends, trouble with the husband's family, and having disagreements over housekeeping. The difficulties are not limited to a few role functions within the relationship. Neither spouse is particularly understanding or supportive of the other. Sexual inadequacies are reported for both spouses. This conjunction of wife complaints about the past with present marital conflict follows the oft-observed psychodynamic formulation of marriage as the stage upon which to enact in symptomatic fashion the expression of poorly defended intrapsychic conflict; therefore, from the point of view of ego psychology, this pattern may be considered expectable. The interesting thing is that our husbands do not follow it.

For the husbands who report emotional strain or problems in childhood or in adolescence, a particular stage-specific and sex-specific set of influences appears to be operating to support certain defenses against the overt enactment of conflict. In our data these husbands have tended to marry maternal, home-centered wives and to have invested themselves single-mindedly in matters of occupational ambition. There is a tendency—not fully explicable—for these marriages to be Jewish rather than Protestant or Catholic. This is a pattern of traditional role orientation, with husbands expressing less interest in housework and wives expressing less interest in working outside the home.

Putting these two sets of results together, one may conjecture that, possibly growing out of the economic constraints on the husband or from the occupational opportunities provided to him, husbands during the newlywed stage tend to suppress the overt expression of inner conflict. The developmental presses support the male should he wish to make a special investment in work achievement at this stage. This adaptive pattern is further strengthened by the husband's choice of a home-centered mate. On the other hand, the troubled wife, who may be seen as the emotional center of the family, or at least more confined to the home, expresses her conflicts from the past more openly within the marriage. One may also wonder whether the traditional value of role segregation observed in the marriages of the troubled ambitious husbands does not also serve the defensive function of sanctioning an avoidance of intimacy which might mobilize a marital enactment of the husband's inner conflicts. In another sense, one may also wonder whether a somewhat culturally "outmoded" value system about marital roles, e.g., nonequalitarian values, will tend to be retained under conditions where this more old-fashioned value system supports the intrapsychic and family defenses required by the individual.

To put the theoretical issue in more general form, middle-class suburbanites live in a changing and somewhat mixed psychosocial milieu. With full social sanction, it is possible for young adults to set up a variety of life styles, each based on different values. During courtship many couples explore values with each other and test each other in regard to situations involving choice of values. The values adhered to . . . serve adaptive and defensive functions. In interpreting our data we have concluded that young couples, whether self-consciously or not, work out a life pattern in which choices are made and positions taken about ties with the extended family, overt expression of conflict, investment in occupational or parental roles, and so forth. The values chosen and roles taken may be assumed to reflect deeper intrapsychic requirements deriving from each spouse's ego defenses.

Turning to the patterns indexed by Factors One and Four, one can see the emerging conjunction of an interesting constellation of variables: close involvement with extended family, a nonaffective style of husband-wife communication, and husbands who are relatively unmotivated toward sexual experience but who anticipate fatherhood to an unusual degree. The couple is child-centered and socially active with friends, more than most. One could speculate that such a pattern could defend against latent marital conflict; a more parsimonious assumption would be that these couples value rational ideals and social role satisfactions more than intimate relationships and affective satisfactions. Here one can discern in the marital behavior, and in the implicit values of the family as a whole, an investment in stability and rationalism rather than in spontaneity and in change. As Sussman and Burchinal[7] have pointed out, many American families are not truly isolated nuclear structures but function within a kin family network. Perhaps our Factors One and Four indicate a special subgroup within such family-attached couples.

It is noteworthy that couples with a high degree of affective expression have cut themselves off from their families. They seem to have a greater investment in sexuality and less (at this stage) in the prospects of child care. It well may be that a contrast between affectively expressive marriages and closeness to relatives might not exist at later stages of the life cycle, or, if it should exist, would have a different interpretation. The presence of these adaptive patterns as *developmental alternatives* may mean that many recently married couples in their early twenties, who live in the same community with relatives, tend through these relationships to enact the residues of late adolescent conflicts over autonomy and dependence. . . .

We have reported the results of an exploratory study of the first stage of marriage in middle-class white suburban couples. The data derived from interviews, experimental problem-solving situations, and from questionnaires; the foci for investigation were developed from role theory, communication theory, and from ideas about early adult personality changes.

An extensive factor-analytic treatment of these data has produced eight patterns of marriage. An interpretation of these has suggested that, during this initial stage of marriage, there are different developmental presses as regards adaptation to inner conflict for the male and for the female. The data also suggest that residual problems of autonomy and dependence in these young couples may correspond to styles of relating to relatives and of husband-wife communication. Implicit in these interpretations is the notion that, at each life stage, there is an interaction between intrapsychic and psychosocial elements which together influence a couple's pattern of adaptation.

NOTES

[1] Roland G. Tharp, "Psychological Patterning in Marriage," *Psychological Bulletin*, 60:2 (March 1963): 97.

[2] H. J. Locke and K. M. Wallace, "Short Marital Adjustment Prediction Tests: Their Reliability and Validity," *Marriage and Family Living*, 21:3 (August 1959): 251.

[3] R. G. Ryder, "Profile Factor Analysis and Variable Factor Analysis," *Psychological Reports*, 15:1 (July 1964): 119.

[4] W. Goodrich, "The Developmental Transaction, A Basic Unit for Research on Child

Mental Health," *Proceedings of the Joint Meeting of the Japanese Society of Psychiatry and Neurology and the American Psychiatric Association,* 1963; D. W. Goodrich, "Possibilities for Preventive Intervention During Initial Personality Formation," in *Prevention of Mental Disorders in Children,* G. Caplan, ed. (New York: Basic Books, Inc., 1961), pp. 149–264.

⁵ The method has been reported on film: Paul Blank, Arden Flint, and Wells Goodrich, "Married Couples in Experimentally Induced Situation," 1962, available on request from Child Research Branch, National Institute of Mental Health.

⁶ Locke and Wallace, op. cit.

⁷ Marvin B. Sussman and Lee Burchinal, "Kin Family Network: Unheralded Structure in Current Conceptualizations of Family Functioning," *Marriage and Family Living,* 24:3 (August 1962): 231.

46

INITIAL ADJUSTMENT PROCESSES IN YOUNG MARRIED COUPLES

Beverly R. Cutler and William G. Dyer

The matter of "adjustment" in marriage is an area of discussion in almost every marriage textbook and class. A number of years ago, Kirkpatrick stated, "The investigation of marital adjustment is still almost a virgin field for sociological research. There is a need for checking of previous research, for contributing additional fragments of evidence, and for a piecing together of the results of isolated studies into a meaningful whole."¹ This condition still appears to exist. . . .

In the literature on marital adjustment, two different approaches are often taken and sometimes intermingled indiscriminately. Some writers refer to adjustment as a state of marriage to be achieved, while other writers refer to adjustment primarily as a process of interaction.

Bowerman feels that both conditions are important. He says:

In addition to measures of overall evaluation of the marriage, there would seem to be considerable use, in both research and counseling, for measures of the degree of adjustment *in the various aspects of the relationship, such as adjustment about financial matters, recreation, homemaking duties, etc. In studying the* processes *of adjustment in marriage, it is necessary to take into account the relationship between different kinds of adjustment which must be made, how these types of adjustment are differentially affected by the various forces affecting the marriage, and how each contributes to the evaluation of the marriage as a whole.²*

When seen as a goal, marital adjustment is commonly equated with such conditions as marital success, marital satisfaction, and marital happiness. It would seem that these terms are all referring to the same end condition which is arrived at through some interactive process. Research-wise it is much easier to develop a measure of marital adjustment or success and then relate a series of independent variables to this dependent condition and discover which variables are most highly related to the condition of adjustment, than it is to investigate the processes couples go through to arrive at the end condition. This paper is an attempt to add "an additional fragment of evidence" to the matter of adjustment as a process. Very little research actually shows the process married couples go through to achieve adjustment.

The focus of this research report is centered on the question, "When a young married person finds that his spouse engages in behavior that violates his expectations, what kinds of actions does he engage in to deal with this disturbance in the relationship?" Adjustment, generally speaking, is the process used in successfully reducing disturbance in a relationship. . . .

Adjustment is defined as the bringing into agreement the behavior of one person with the expectation of another accompanied by a feeling of acceptance of the modified behavior by the one making the adjustment.

From the point of view of role behavior, when conflict in marriage occurs because one person has violated the expectations of his spouse the possible adjustments are:

1. The husband (or wife) can change his role performance completely to meet the role expectations of his partner.

2. The husband (or wife) can change his role expectations, completely, to coincide with the role performance of the partner.

3. There can be a mutual adjustment, each partner altering some. The husband (or wife) can alter his role to a degree and the partner alters his role expectations to a similar degree so that role performance and role expectations are compatible. In each of the above cases the end result is an agreement between role performance and role expectations.

4. There is also another type of adjustment possible. In some cases the couple might recognize a disparity between role performance and role expectations or between norms and also acknowledge that change is difficult or impossible and could "agree to disagree." In such cases the one partner recognizes and respects the position of the other without accepting or adjusting to it. This pattern of "agreeing to disagree" is not adjustment in the same sense as the others listed above. The "adjustment" comes

from both partners agreeing that a certain area is "out of bounds" as far as the application of sanctions are concerned. There is no change in behavior but some change in expectations in that each now expects certain areas not to be raised as issues and that no sanctions will be applied over these "out of bound" issues.

This study focuses on the following problems:

1. Are the initial reactions of young married partners to violations of role expectations (in the sense described above) adjustive or non-adjustive?

2. Do husbands and wives differ in their adjustment processes?

3. Do couples use different adjustments in different areas of marriage?

. . . Following an initial pilot study of depth interviews with ten couples, an extensive questionnaire on marital adjustment was administered to a random sample of young married couples at Brigham Young University during the fall and winter of the 1962–63 school year. Couples were selected on the basis of the husband's enrollment in the University. Since the study was aimed at the adjustment in young married couples, only those couples were selected where the husband was under 23 years of age. There were 75 couples in the sample. Fifteen couples were eliminated for various reasons leaving 60 couples in the study. Participants were asked to fill out the questionnaire separately and privately and not consult the marital partner. . . .

Eighty-five percent of the couples had been married less than three years. Fifty-five percent had no children while 35 percent had one child. All of the couples were members of the L.D.S. (Mormon) church. Seventy-four percent of the couples had known each other for more than one year prior to marriage. Only 13 percent of the husbands and 18 percent of the wives were reared in communities over 100,000. While all of the husbands were in college, 30 percent of the wives had not attended college.

The following areas of marriage were examined in the questionnaire:

1. Verbal expressions of affection.
2. Frequency of sexual intimacy.
3. Spending time at home.
4. Sharing ideas.
5. Care of the home.
6. Personal neatness and appearance.
7. Spending family income.

From the pilot study, it was indicated that the above represented the primary areas within which couples were making adjustments to each other. The questionnaire was constructed to determine the following:

1. The expectations of husbands and wives towards each other in the areas listed above.
2. The ways these expectations are violated by husbands and wives.
3. The responses by the marriage partner when the spouse has violated one's expectations.
4. The reaction of the spouse to the initial responses of the marriage partner.
5. The current feelings of the couple about the area of marriage following the initial adjustment responses and reactions.

For each of the seven areas of marriage examined in the study, the following questions were asked concerning responses to the violation of expectations: (1) In what ways has your spouse failed to live up to your expectations? What has he (she) done to violate your expectations you held for him (her) concerning this aspect of your marriage relationship? (2) If your spouse did not meet your expectations, what did you do? (3) When you responded as indicated in the previous question, what did your spouse do in return?

Initial responses and subsequent reactions were judged either adjustive, non-adjustive, or non-action. An adjustive response is one that brings behavior and expectations closer together and reduces the degree of negative sanction. A non-adjustive response is one that either does not reduce the disparity or sanction or may actually intensify the difference. A third type of response was noted in the pilot study, namely non-action. The problem is recognized but

no action is taken in hopes that the problem will resolve itself through the passing of time. One might conclude that non-action is a non-adjustive response, but the non-adjustive response actually represents a behavioral strategy that was being attempted in some type of behavior. There was no behavior strategy being attempted in non-action, only the hopes were that it would be adjustive in the long run, hence, the decision to make this a special category.

In addition to being adjustive or non-adjustive, responses and reactions to responses were categorized in terms of two dimensions: sharing and valence. This gave the following possible responses in the coding guide:

1. *Adjustive Response*

A. shared positive response—This is a response that is shared with the marriage partner and positive in the sense that it appears to be directed toward achieving adjustment.

B. non-shared positive—This is a non-shared response but also adjustively centered.

2. *Non-Adjustive Response*

A. shared negative—This is a shared response but apparently not given with the idea of facilitating adjustment, hence, a negative valence.

B. non-shared negative—A non-shared response not geared toward facilitating adjustment.

3. *Non-Action*—A non-shared response with suspended valence.

Following are examples of the various possible responses: Respondents would check these categories in response to the question "If your spouse did not meet your expectations, what did you do?"

A. Shared positive response: "Talked it over rather openly and calmly."

B. Non-shared positive: "Didn't say anything at all; just accepted the situation as it was—didn't let it bother me."

C. Shared negative: "Got upset and argued, quarreled, pouted, or sulked with spouse."

D. Non-shared negative: "Got upset, worried about it, cried, or felt sorry for myself; but didn't say anything to my spouse."

E. Non-action: "Didn't say anything at first; just waited to see if things would work out."

. . . 1. *Husbands.* . . . The generally most prevalent strategy adopted by husbands when they felt their wives had violated their expectations was a non-action response. The husbands indicated they initially took a "wait and see" stance but these data do not tell us how the wives perceived these same responses.

The next most prevalent response of the husbands, as perceived by themselves, was an open talking about the problem in a calm manner. These shared, adjustive type responses were followed numerically by non-shared adjustive responses. These two adjustive type responses account for 51 percent of all responses made by husbands. Husbands felt that only five percent of their initial responses were of a non-adjustive type.

For each of the areas taken separately, some differences appear. The non-action strategy is most apparent in *Area 2* which is frequency of sexual intimacy. There were more violations of expectations in this area than any of the others, yet this is the one area where no husband checked a non-shared adjustive response—that is, "didn't say anything at all; just accepted the situation as it was—didn't let it bother me." While non-adjustive responses were rarely indicated at all, this area, more than any other, was one where some husbands admitted making some non-adjustive responses.

Area 1—(Verbal Expressions of Affection) appears to be the area most easily accepted by the husbands without talking it over with his wife. Eight out of 19 husbands with non-met expectations in this area indicated that they accepted this situation as it was—didn't let it bother them.

Area 7—(Spending Family Income) appears to be the area most easily talked about openly and calmly. Seven of 11 violations were met in this manner. *Area 3*—(Spending Time at Home) was the area of least violations. Apparently most of these new husbands were satisfied with the amount of time the wife was spending in the home. Such is not the case, however, with the wives.

2. *Wives.* While 44 percent of the husbands' initial reactions were of the non-action variety, only 31 percent of the responses of the wives were in this category. Wives indicated they responded initially with more shared, adjustive type responses than their husbands and also with more non-adjustive type responses than were admitted by their spouses. Again it should be remembered, this is how the wives perceived their initial responses—not how the spouse experienced it.

Rather consistently, the pattern for the wives in most areas was one of more open sharing in contrast to the non-action strategy which characterized many areas for the husbands. This is especially true in the area of frequency of sexual intimacy. Husbands indicated they generally took a "wait and see" approach, while the wives' initial response was to talk about the problem. Interestingly enough this sensitive area resulted in only two admitted non-adjustive type initial responses. Like the husbands, this was one area where no wife adopted a non-shared adjustive response.

As with the husbands, *Area 1*—(Verbal Expressions of Affection) was the area where more wives adjusted internally without talking about this with their spouses.

Areas 1 and *5* had the highest number of violations marked. These are Verbal Expressions of Affection and Care of the Home, respectively. *Area 5* is also the area with more non-adjustive reactions than any other. It should be remembered that this does not indicate which of the areas was the most important to the couple, only which areas showed the most number of violations of expectations. Care of the Home had the most non-adjustive type reactions on the part of the wife. This may indicate not that she felt strongest about this, but that she felt freer to express her negative feelings about this than any other area.

The area with the fewest expressed violations of expectations was number *Area 6*—(Personal Neatness and Appearance). This was followed by *Area 7*–(Spending the Family Income).

As indicated above, the biggest area of disparity in terms of numbers of violations in the areas was in *Area 3*–(Spending Time at Home). Wives checked violations in this area six times as often as did the husbands. The other areas were relatively similar with some noticeable difference occurring in *Area 5*–(Care of the Home), where the wives had more non-met expectations than did the husbands at a ratio of 25 to 16. . . .

Both husbands and wives felt that the majority of their spouse's reactions to them were of an adjustive nature. In the questionnaire subjects were asked, "When you responded as indicated in the previous question, what did your spouse do in return?" Adjustive responses were the following:

1. "Made a real attempt to change and meet my expectations."
2. "We agreed that we differed, but we have tried to accept this difference."
3. "Said he (she) was sorry and would try to do better, but didn't really change."

This last response was considered to be an adjustive type response even though the spouse with the non-met expectations felt the other had not "really changed." The initial part of adjustment had begun—the spouse knew of the violation, and expressed regret for this and indicated a willingness to "do better." Final adjustment does not come until expectation and behavior are in agreement, but this response indicates that perhaps adjustment has started.

Subjects were also asked to list other responses. Considered as adjustive were such responses as: "He is patient with me and tries to be understanding." "Made a genuine effort to change every now and then." "Got professional doctor's help and counseling."

It is interesting to note that while 44 percent of the husbands' responses and 31 percent of the wives' initial responses were of the non-action type, there were very few subsequent non-action responses. One would normally think that a non-action re-

sponse would be followed by non-action. This may indicate that when one's expectations are violated, one really does give off certain cues about his feelings to which the spouse subsequently responds. A non-action response to the initial reaction was: "(Spouse did) Nothing, since he (she) didn't know how I felt."

Thirty-three percent of the wives' subsequent reactions were felt by the husbands to be non-adjustive, while 26 percent of the husband's reactions to the wife were seen by the wife as non-adjustive. Non-adjustive responses were as follows:

1. "Got upset and argued, complained, or grumbled back."
2. "Suggested that I accept him (her) as he (she) was."
3. "I told him (her) but nothing happened—we just dropped it."

Considered as non-adjustive were written in comments such as: "We quarrel occasionally about it." "He thought it was funny and persisted more strongly."

Some interesting patterns are indicated when we examine the non-adjustive responses and the behavior that elicits a non-adjustive pattern. Nearly half of the non-adjustive responses for both husbands and wives came as a result of an initial shared adjustive reaction. This immediately raises the question—why should a shared adjustive initial reaction result in non-adjustive responses? There are at least these possibilities:

1. While the one reacting initially thinks he is reacting in an open, adjustive way, the marriage partner may not experience this in the way the first intended. The partner may see the initial reaction as critical and punitive while the reacting party thinks he is just talking it over "openly and calmly."
2. The initial reaction may be an open, calm sharing of one's feelings about a problem situation but an adjustive response from the mate presumes such conditions as an adequate level of maturity of the mate, proper timing and suitable circumstances for sharing sensitive information, and a

non-threatening method of presenting the information.

3. The shared information may be presented calmly and openly but the information may be a hard blow to the self-image of the partner and the response may be immediately defensive and not adjustive.

4. Sharing sensitive information may be a violation of the expectations of the other partner. He or she may not expect such things to be talked about and when this is done, non-adjustive type responses result.

Seven non-adjustive responses for both husbands and wives came as a result of initial "non-action." This is another apparent contradiction. How can a non-response result in any type of reaction? The problem here may be in the weakness of the questionnaire in carefully sorting out the sequence of reactions. (Or it may be, as indicated above, that cues as to how the person feels are given off even though he feels there was no response made.) There are indications in examining the data that a person filling out the questionnaire coming to the question, "What was your initial response?" marked a non-action category. The next question asked, "What did your spouse do in return?" It appears that a number of subjects jumped the time sequence and checked what may have been a response later in time. Thus, it appears that a non-adjustive reaction followed a non-action response. This same condition may account for non-shared reactions eliciting non-adjustive responses.

Percentage-wise, the biggest number of non-adjustive responses came as a result of initial negative type reactions for both husbands and wives. There were five negative reactions listed by husbands and these resulted in three non-adjustive reactions. In fact, all three shared negative initial reactions resulted in non-adjustive responses.

Wives indicated 22 negative type reactions initially and these resulted in 11 non-adjustive type subsequent responses from the spouse.

One would tend to predict that a negative reaction would result in further negative type reactions. The data from the husbands in this study are too limited in

this area to allow for any support of this generalization. For the wives, it shows from a limited number of responses, that about 50 percent of the time negative responses on their part resulted in non-adjustment on the part of the other. The data here do not tell us how the other partner feels about making an adjustment to a negative reaction by his spouse. It would seem that adjustments that came from shared positive type responses would be made out of a more positive feeling than adjustment that resulted from negative reactions. . . .

This study was designed to investigate the initial adjustment processes in young, married couples attending college. Adjustment was conceptualized in terms of role expectations, response to expectation violations, and the subsequent reaction to the initial response. The data indicate the following trends in these couples:

1. Husbands, more than wives, appear to adopt a "wait and see" strategy when their wives violate their expectations, according to their self-perceptions. Wives say they more often meet a violation of expectation with an open sharing or talking about the situation or reacting negatively.

2. When difficulties occur, the several areas of marriage appear to be handled differently by married couples. Husbands say they talk openly about violations of expectations in the area of finance but not in the area of frequency of sexual intimacy.

3. Wives and husbands differ in the number of expectation violations in certain areas of marriage. In the area of spending time at home, wives checked a violation of expectations in this area six times more frequently than did husbands. Wives also had more non-met expectations in the area of care of the home.

4. While a considerable number of both husbands and wives reacted to an initial violation of expectations with a non-action response—a "wait and see" strategy—subsequent reactions to the spouse's initial response were very infrequently found in this category. Husbands more than wives felt their spouses reactions to them were non-adjustive in nature.

5. The data of this study indicate that

nearly half of the non-adjustive responses for both husbands and wives came as a result of an open sharing of the feelings about the violation of expectations. Contrary to what might be expected, an open talking about the violation of expectations does not always lead to an adjustment.

6. The data, especially for wives, also show that in a large percentage of times, a negative reaction on the part of one partner does result in an adjustive response by the other. Negative reactions are apparently not always followed by reciprocal negative reactions.

NOTES

[1] Clifford Kirkpatrick, "Factors in Marital Adjustment," *American Journal of Sociology,* 43 (November 1957): 270.

[2] Clark Bowerman, "Adjustment in Marriage, Overall and in Specific Areas," *Sociology and Social Research,* 41 (March–April 1957): 257–263.

47

THE POLITICS OF MARRIAGE: A DELICATE BALANCE

Vivian Cadden

When you really stop to think about it, it seems almost incredible that two human beings can live for as long as, say, six months, let alone a lifetime, in the suffocatingly close proximity—emotional and physical—that marriage throws them into.

It seems reasonable to suppose that years and years ago, when marriage was a minuet choreographed to a fare-thee-well, a man and a woman might have mastered the routine. Husband moved three steps to his job, wife moved two steps to her kitchen; mother fed baby, father disciplined boy; husband initiated sex, wife demurred; husband insisted, wife acceded. As long as the partners followed the score that society had composed, remembered their steps, and performed them with good grace, you had a marriage. Not necessarily a "happy marriage," whatever that may mean, but a workable relationship, a structure in which two people could function without stepping on each other's toes too much.

But today, for heaven's sake, a young man and woman must struggle to follow a faint, confused score, and there is no caller to direct their steps: "Husband steps to the right . . . wife will take a bow. . . ." I marvel that any marriage—and I mean *any* marriage—survives. As an avid amateur marriage-watcher I ponder, along with the professionals, the dynamics of this improbable institution. How do a husband and wife today create the dance themselves? By what ploys, what feints—to change the metaphor—by what maneuvering, what negotiation, what diplomacy, what politics, do they shape this happening called marriage?

Understandably, a lot of people have been concerned with this question since the marriage minuet broke down about 50 years ago. In fact, that breakdown was responsible for the blossoming of an entirely new breed of specialist, the "family-life expert." When family-life experts aren't busy picking up the pieces of defective marriages and trying to glue them back together again ("family therapy," that's called), they are very likely poking into this very matter of the politics of the marriage relationship and the way in which tasks and decision-making are distributed within the family (the "family power structure," that's called).

Riffling through the vast literature on the "family power structure," one can't help being struck by all the bristling terminology that abounds—"husband-dominated," "wife-dominated," "controlling" the relationship, and the like. The family-life experts and the Women's Liberation Movement share a vocabulary of power politics. But marriage is not, after all, an adversary relationship —presumably no one wants to "win" or "lose" the encounter. Why, then, this talk of *politics*, with its implications of wheeling and dealing and throwing one's weight around? Why, when two people have just vowed to "love, honor, and cherish" each other, do the experts assess their relationship in terms of *power?*

If one looks at the evolution of a marriage, particularly in its early years, it seems evident that many aspects of the relationship fall into place almost automatically—by preference, by default, by custom, by the superior ability of one or the other at a particular task and, most of all, by the shared expectations of the husband and the wife. (When a National Institute of Mental Health research team asked newly married couples how they happened to work out their particular arrangements about cooking and serving food, many of them looked completely blank. What was there to work out?) Neither power nor politics comes into play if the husband likes to putter with the car and the wife doesn't and if each of them always expected husbands to take care of cars and the society in which they live expects so too.

But suppose he wants and expects to have children and she does not or she wants to go to work and he doesn't want her to. How are such questions settled? In times past there was no doubt that they were settled on the basis of power—the openly acknowledged legal, economic, physical, God-granted power of the husband. It is not surprising, then, that the family-life experts, trying to explain and illuminate modern marriage, turned to a study of alternative sources of power within the family. If the State to some extent and economic power to a lesser extent and brute force altogether and God more or less no longer regulated marriage, then who or what did, they asked?

They're a contentious lot, these family-life experts, with their surveys and their countersurveys; but if there is anything they agree about it is that the equilibrium —or the disequilibrium—of the family (what they call the "balance of power" in a marriage) is determined very soon, perhaps in the first year of marriage.

"Marriages groove pretty early," says John Gagnon, a State University of New York sociologist, and bales of research about the first years of marriage support this view. A marriage shapes up quickly.

John Haley, the director of the Philadelphia Marriage and Family Center, has a perceptive view of the mechanisms by which this happens. In an article written for the professional journal *Psychiatry*, Dr. Haley sets forth his belief that when one person sends a message to another— whether verbally or bodily, by gesture, by inflection, by the context in which he has transmitted the message—what he is doing is maneuvering to define the relationship between them. In the Haley model, a boy walks over to a girl and puts his arm over her shoulder. By doing so he has defined the degree of intimacy in their relationship. The girl has the choice of accepting or rejecting the relationship as it has been offered. She can let the arm—and the message—stand, thereby accepting the boy's definition. Or she can counter with a maneuver that defines their relationship differently. Or she can let the arm be but toss the boy a smile that says "I'm *letting* you do this." Each message acts out a jockeying to determine what kinds of behavior are to take place in the relationship, and who is to control what is to take place in it. Thus the relationship is defined.

Everyone, Haley believes, is constantly involved in delivering such messages and accepting or countering the other person's definitions.

A wife reaches out to her husband in bed, and by doing so says, "I too can be the initiator of love-making." The husband can either accept this definition of their relationship or reject it. He can respond to her gesture or he can kiss her affectionately on the cheek and roll over and go to sleep. Or by still other kinds of responses, bodily or verbally, he can qualify his acceptance or rejection of her message.

A husband tosses his dirty shirt on a bedroom chair. The message is clear enough: "You are in charge of dirty shirts." His wife can put the shirt in the hamper and later in the washing machine or she can let it lie on the bedroom chair. Or handing him a clean shirt the next day she can say, "I did your shirt," suggesting that she is aware that she has been maneuvered into doing it and that she has done it; still she is maintaining the option of *not* doing it.

And so in this view one may look at the beginning years of marriage as a series of definitions and redefinitions of the relationship: a million messages accepted or rejected or accepted and rejected with qualifications, each determining what sort of behavior is to take place in the relationship.

A key question to which family-life experts have been addressing themselves over the past decades is how these moves and countermoves finally come to rest. After all, two people can't bat around indefinitely the matter of who is responsible for dirty shirts. If they do, they're in trouble. As a matter of fact, Dr. Haley's definition of the unstable family is one in which "neither the husband nor the wife is able to deal with the issue of who has the right to determine the nature of their relationship and under what kinds of circumstances." In this kind of family, Haley says, "children, sex, relatives, recreation, and other areas that call for collaboration, or at least cooperation, im-

mediately bring up the question of 'who will decide what,' which leads almost invariably to discord."

Not only does who-decides-what need to be settled, but also it's important to know how and on what basis the settlement was arrived at. If it is true that the *unstable* family is one in which these crucial allocations of responsibility have not been worked out, it may be supposed that the *stable* family is one in which they have been firmly resolved. But a moment's reflection is enough to dismiss this as a whopping *non sequitur*. Who-decides-what can be settled, all right, but what if I hate the settlement? Suppose I do accept a definition of the relationship that puts me in charge of dirty shirts—but suppose I feel ready to scorch every blasted one of them each time I set up the ironing board? Even an amateur marriage-watcher can see that this sort of thing often happens, and that it jolly well doesn't lead to stable marriages —and even if it does, who needs *that* kind of stable marriage?

So we must know not only what the "balance of power" is but also how it got that way. When push comes to shove, who prevails and why, and on what basis?

The most important and influential stab at this problem was a book called *Husbands and Wives*, written a little more than a decade ago (and instantly noted by *Redbook* as a landmark) by Robert O. Blood and Donald M. Wolfe. Blood and Wolfe had suspected, like many others, that American marriages were no longer regulated completely by tradition and that decisions within the family were no longer made on the basis of "rights" that accrued automatically to one sex or the other. They set out to test this hunch, and if it was confirmed, to find out where power did reside.

To this end they studied the decision-making process in 909 white, middle-class Detroit families. They asked whether the "husband alone," the "wife alone," the "husband usually," the "wife usually," or "both" decided: what job the husband should take; what kind of car to buy; whether to take out insurance; where to go on vacation; whether the wife should work or quit work; who the family doctor would be; how much money should be spent on food. On the basis of the answers, Blood and Wolfe characterized a marriage as "husband-dominated," "wife-dominated," or "equalitarian."

Looking more closely into the fabric of these marriages, they found that when husband and wife had more or less equal education and both worked, the relationship tended to be equalitarian. Parenthood, they observed, brought a sudden loss of power to the wife, since she gave up her job and had at the same time an increased need for her husband's support. The most clearly husband-dominated families were those in which the husband had a high-status job. In such families husbands were likely to decide unilaterally that their wives should not work—thereby further decreasing the power of the wife.

From these observations Blood and Wolfe concluded that power in the family "accrues spontaneously to the partner who has the greater resources at his disposal"—resources such as financial ability, education, competence.

Rereading Blood and Wolfe recently, I was struck again by its pioneering quality. *Husbands and Wives* really did open up a new way of looking at marriage. But I also was struck by a kind of fuddy-duddy quality the book had. My Women's Lib hackles kept rising. (I have a few anti Women's Lib hackles too.) I kept wanting to say, "Oh, come on, now! That's not what marriage is like. You must be kidding!"

I wanted to say, "How can you suggest with a straight face that my deciding how much to spend at the supermarket (actually the supermarket decides how much I spend at the supermarket) is a sign of my power in the family? Who decided I was to decide about food? My husband, of course, disguised in something called 'tradition.' All right. Well, thanks a lot! I don't really mind doing the marketing, but don't let's pretend that I was the one who assigned me the job or that my momentous decisions about chicken once a week or chicken twice a week are an index to my power."

And if some interviewer came around and asked me who decides what about vacations, I'd say, "We both decide." (Pollsters in the family-relations trade almost always query only the wife—easier and cheaper to catch her in the home than her husband in the office—and if they do query both, they're likely to get different answers!) What I said about vacations was true—but it's also a lie. We talk about it a lot, but he decides. But then, he decides because I let him decide. So who, if anyone, is more powerful in that ploy? I let him decide because he likes to and because I'm too busy deciding what's for dinner—that particular "power" he has relinquished graciously to me.

And what about the one who influences the decisions? If decision-making is construed as "having the last word" on a given question, its meaning is clear enough: Someone finally has to take pen in hand and sign that lease or mortgage, and there's no doubt who does that. But how could I have a lifetime record of cajoling my husband into real estate he claims he had no intention of buying—or did he plan to buy it all along?

But if decision-making is considerably more complex than Blood and Wolfe made it out to be and if they chose some pretty inconsequential decisions to chart as well as some important ones, it still remains that who-decides-what in the family and who-decides-who-decides-what can be real clues to the power structure of a marriage. And Blood and Wolfe's theory about the resources that each partner brings to the marriage as determinants of power has basic validity even though over the past decade it has been refined and amended.

Many people have pointed out that their list of resources—financial know-how, education, status, competence—doesn't tell the whole story. Physical attractiveness, for example, can be a "resource" in quite the same sense that education can be. Just as the man with higher educational qualifications has "power" over his less well educated and perhaps less competent wife, so the physically attractive woman has some power to offset the resources that her successful but unattractive husband brings to the marriage. Dr. Gagnon has pointed out that under certain circumstances even weakness can operate as a resource. A sick or ailing partner can coerce his spouse. And everyone knows that the real tyrant in the family is the newborn baby, not to mention the mother who uses the baby to clobber her husband.

David M. Heer, a sociologist at the University of California at Berkeley, has carried Blood and Wolfe a step further. His focus is not so much on the relative resources the partners bring to the marriage but on their market value outside the marriage. He believes that husband and wife each conceive—consciously or unconsciously—the possibility of separation, divorce, and remarriage, and that power rests with the one who can more afford to contemplate that possibility. This theory offers a good explanation of the phenomenon noted by all studies: the young mother with preschool children is low woman on the totem pole as far as power in the family is concerned. Coming on a hypothetical remarriage market with preschool children, she might have a pretty rough time of it.

All of which makes Heer think that ultimately the source of power in any marriage today is the greater willingness to dissolve it. The partner with the lesser resources, with the greater need for the marriage—whether financial or psychological or whatever—is, in the last analysis, the less powerful. Dr. Gerald Caplan, professor of psychiatry at Harvard Medical School, has added an important footnote—it is not actually this relative willingness to quit the relationship, but each partner's *perception* of that threat, that governs the marriage.

If the real source of power, then, is the greater power to go away, politics in marriage has to do with suggesting the use of that power. One plays politics in marriage by saying, in effect, "This is how it would be if I were not here." A wife suggests—not, of course, openly, unless the marriage is far, far gone—that there would be no sex, no food, no children, no warmth, no clean clothes, no smiles if she were not there. A husband suggests ever so subtly, that there would be no money, no protection, no sex,

no status in the community, no one to put up the storm windows.

Husband and wife come to know where the particular power—and weakness—of the other resides. In particular situations they use this knowledge as a weapon, a threat. In the classic marital power play a wife who has to beg for money forces her husband to beg for sex.

In a recent issue of *Journal of Marriage and the Family*, Dr. Constantina Safilios-Rothschild, director of the Family Research Center at Wayne State University, has sketched a vivid picture of this kind of withdrawal of "resources" (and notice how she has broadened Blood and Wolfe's own list of resources) in a marriage.

"A wife," she says, "can prepare the husband's favorite dishes or torture him with badly prepared food; can take good care of his clothes or neglect them; keep a neat and attractive house or leave it sloppy and disorganized; be a great companion and host to his guests and colleagues or a miserable one; be a responsive sexual partner or a frigid one, or totally refuse to have sexual relations with him; be sweet, affectionate, understanding, supporting, and loving or sour, cold, distant, critical, demanding, and unfriendly. . . . Of course the husband also has at his disposal a similar range of 'resources.' A husband may share household tasks with his wife or refuse to do anything because of his 'heavy' schedule and spend that time drinking with friends; he may go out often with his wife or hardly at all, always disappearing in long meetings, conferences, and business trips, even when he is by no means obliged to go to these meetings and trips.

"It must be clarified, however," Dr. Safilios-Rothschild continues (and here, alas, she lapses into the professional jargon that, far from clarifying anything, always manages to muck it up), "that the degree to which the above-mentioned 'resources' can be withdrawn without bringing about a serious marital disorganization depends upon the duration of the withdrawal and most importantly, the degree of emotional-affective attachment of the 'other' spouse upon the withdrawing one."

In other words, the deliberately sulky,

frigid, sloppy, critical, distant wife can go on playing this game for just so long, depending upon whether her husband has a greater need for her or she has a greater need for him. If the latter is true, Dr. Safilios-Rothschild says, "she will be forced to lose out in the power struggle in order not to have to face the possibility of total marital dissolution."

Pondering this, one realizes that Dr. Safilios-Rothschild has clarified something after all. For suddenly everything falls into place. It becomes crystal-clear that *every use of power*, whether open or veiled, whether perceptible or imperceptible, is a tiny step or a giant stride toward the dissolution of the marriage and/or the eventual vanquishing of one partner. Power politics turns marriage into a cold war.

To the extent that a marriage is governed by power and decisions are made on the basis of that power, it is characterized by conflict and rift or by the emotional pain of the powerless partner.

In modern marriages, if the balance of power is approximately equal, the continuous use of power tends to lead to conflict and sometimes to divorce. In the frankly authoritarian family, where power could not be challenged, the results were often despair and mental illness.

Where does that leave us? If we go back to Haley's framework—the defining and redefining of the marriage relationship to a point where who-decides-what is settled—and eliminate the destructive element of power as the determining factor, on what possible basis *can* the dance be composed?

In the introduction to a thoughtful, cogent book, *The Psychology of Power*, the British writer Ronald V. Sampson sets forth a view of human relations that is notable both for its simplicity and for the illumination it brings to many problems.

"Every human being," Sampson writes, "may seek to order his life and his relations with others on the basis of love or on the basis of power." To the extent that power is the prevailing force in a relationship—whether between husband and wife or parent and child, between friends or between colleagues—to that extent love is diminished. We can develop our capacity for power, Sampson believes, or we can develop our capacity for love. We cannot do both. Nor can we opt out of making the choice between the use of power and the use of love in our relationships. "For of necessity," Sampson holds, "everyone at all times and in all positions stands on a relationship with other men which will be predominantly of one character or the other."

Sampson develops his thesis with great skill in many areas, but nowhere is it more apropos than in the realm of marriage. When in those early months or years of marriage the dust of Haley's definitions and redefinitions has settled, husband and wife will stand on a relationship with each other that will be predominantly one of power or one of love. If the bountiful research on the power structure of American marriages suggests that more of them rest on power than on love, let no one despair of the institution, especially those who have newly entered into it.

For Sampson's options are clearly there, and the rewards of forsaking power are high. If those family-life experts have done anything in the past decade, it is to show us—inadvertently, sometimes—the futility of power politics in marriage. And if the Women's Liberation Movement has done anything, it is to make vivid the cost in human waste and human suffering involved in a power-ridden relationship.

It's important to note that Sampson's divergent poles of love and power cannot be reconciled by equal power as the governing force within the marriage. The equal distribution of power will guarantee, to be sure, that the same person does not always carry the entire psychic brunt of the relationship, as women were likely to do in the patriarchal family. But if power is still the guiding principle, you are back to Dr. Safilios-Rothschild's balky wife and balky husband, trading their withdrawals of resources but alternately giving in because of their equal, often neurotic, need for each other. What is needed, Sampson would say, is not equal power, but equal loving and honoring and cherishing.

It should be pointed out too that the existence of love between two people who marry is not a sufficient condition for a love-propelled relationship. There is no doubt that many an authoritarian husband dearly loved his wife and children. But love was not usually the driving force in such families. It was not the force that shaped decisions and allocated roles and responsibilities, and because "power corrupts," love was likely to atrophy. So too the successful young executive who ordains that it does not help his career to have his bride continue in her low-status job may be madly in love with her, but that marriage is as power-driven as one in which love is absent; and there exists the real danger that love may indeed become absent.

Sampson's framework makes it possible to understand how two marriages can have exactly the same profile as far as who-does-what and who-decides-what and still be vastly different in content. 'I can do those dirty shirts because I *must*, lest I face retaliation; whereas another woman may do them because she *wishes* to. One man can drop his shirts off at the laundry on his way to work because he doesn't want to face a sulking or snappish wife on Tuesdays; another husband may do the same thing because he feels his wife is overburdened and he wishes to spare her the chore. There is all the difference in the world, even in the trivia of married life, between subtle coercion and selfless giving.

If power politics in marriage consists of applying pressure by withholding something that is needed or desired, the politics of love are exactly the reverse. They consist of taking off pressure and giving as freely as possible of oneself. Possibly no marriage—no relationship of any kind—is entirely free of the politics of coercion. The reason Sampson's thesis holds so much promise is that every cultivation of our capacity to order our lives on the basis of love helps to dry up that crop of power and wither its bitter fruit.

48

SEX IN MARRIAGE

William J. Lederer and Don D. Jackson

What is the role of sex in marriage?

Like every other element in the marital relationship, sex involves behavior between individuals. The response of each partner varies with his mood, his physical state, and the oscillations of the relationship.

Given adequate physiological and anatomical equipment (which Nature rarely fails to provide) and a modicum of knowledge of sexual techniques, the spouses will enjoy sexual union *when both are in a collaborative mood*. The collaborative exists when each is adding something to the sexual act, not just submitting. When the spouses are not in a loving mood, they still may find in sex release from tension and thus derive another type of pleasure from it, especially if they are in agreement about what they expect, but it is likely to be less fulfilling and often may be frustrating, because one partner has contrary needs which are left unmet.

This sex act—a comparably simple matter —has become the most written about, the most talked of, and the most muddled aspect of marriage. There are several reasons why the role of sex in marriage has become excessively emphasized and distorted.

A cultural fear of sex's losing its effective status in the social structure. This fear is as ancient at least as the Old Testament dictum that "a man . . . shall cleave unto his wife." The expectation is that if this pronouncement is violated the species will not fulfill its obligation to procreate in a familial or nurturing setting.

The fear of desertion and abandonment. In our culture, this fear is stronger in women than in men. Women are tied down by the processes of childbearing and childbirth and require assistance physically and emotionally. In response to this fear, and to provide a weapon for fighting it, the belief has developed in our culture that if one is "sexy" enough, one's mate will *not* desert. The result has been an exaggerated consciousness of sexual performance as a ritual to increase personal security in marriage or to induce marriage. Yet if one is "sexy" enough there is the danger of being *too* "sexy" and violating the ancient commandments.

The female's simulation of sexiness. The male requires an erection to enter into the sex act. If he is uninterested in sex, or afraid of it, he will not have an erection. However, a woman does not have any obvious physiological indications of spontaneous readiness. She can fake sexual spontaneity, and the male (at least for a time) may not be aware of the deceit. The female extends this stimulation of sexual interest into parasexual areas by means of hair dyes, falsies, girdles, cosmetics, perfumes, and high heels. These parasexual devices scream, "Look, I'm sexy. I'm desirable." This may or may not be true, but it is probable that women resent their need to advertise and would prefer to be accepted as they really are; men resent the necessity for sexual deception even though they foster it.

The economic forces in our culture sustain and stimulate these hypocritical actions. Any attempt to alter the pattern involves resisting the advertising and other merchandising techniques used by multi-billion-dollar businesses to peddle false female sexuality. The women who attempt to retain a "natural" appearance, with undoctored hair, no makeup, and so forth, are few in number, and they may (because of cultural conditioning) be regarded by both men and women as deviates. Most of the people who might be inclined to rebel against this type of sexual mores are intimidated by cultural pressures and mass value judgments.

Furthermore, the emphasis upon female sexual paraphernalia is an inherited social custom which long has been associated with the elite. In past ages, makeup, breast accentuators, and the like were worn mainly by the ruling classes, and the tendency to show upward social mobility by imitating the elite still exists. Even today, the wealthier the spouses, the more they exaggerate the difference between the sexes. The wife wears elegant gowns, elaborate hairdos, scintillating jewelry, and expensive furs and perfumes. Her husband may favor dark conservative suits, homburgs, and thick-soled, handmade English shoes.

The erroneous belief that unsatisfactory sexual relations are the major cause of bad marriages. The speciousness here is clear. Unsatisfactory sexual relations are a symptom of marital discord, not the cause of it. It is difficult for the victims to see this because of the mass of propaganda about sex that attacks them day and night, on the street, in the home, in the office. We are such an absurd culture that even mouthwashes and Lysol are related to the sexual aspects of marriage.

John Jones, for example, is dissatisfied with his marriage. On his way to work he may look up and see a billboard with a picture of a nearly nude, beautiful woman, advertising a brand of stockings. John is stimulated sexually and says to himself, "Boy, I'd like to have an affair with something like that." He knows this is wishful thinking, and may even recognize that the beautiful model might be incompatible with him. Next he retreats from the daydream and his thoughts turn toward his wife. But the sexual fantasy he has had about the ad colors his reflections about his marriage relationship, and he thinks, "Golly, Mary's legs might look better in that kind of hosiery." What he means is, "If Mary were a better sexpot we'd both have a happier marriage." He is caught in a double error: the appearance of Mary's legs has nothing to do with the couple's sexual satisfaction, *and* he has forgotten his *own* function in achieving a successful union.

Such a process may be repeated frequently during the day, for John is never permitted to escape advertisements which suggest that sexuality is the key to happiness. Yet there is considerable evidence that an individual's *perception* of the sexual relationship is more related to marital satisfaction than the sexual act itself.

In a survey conducted at an Ohio university, interviews of several hundred couples showed that by and large those who reported their marriages as "satisfactory" gave the frequency of their intercourse as twice a week. Those who reported their marriage as "unsatisfactory" also reported a frequency of twice a week, yet among the unhappy couples the husbands said that twice a week was more than their wives wished but satisfactory from their point of view, and the wives said it was less than their husbands wished but just right for them personally. The "happy" husbands and wives said the frequency of twice a week was satisfying to both themselves *and* their spouses. In other words, the problem was in the couples' communication and not in the actual frequency of their sexual relations.

While sexual problems are often blamed for marital difficulties, one is seldom made aware of the other side of the coin: sexual relations may keep some marriages going, providing virtually the only kind of contact which the spouses have. Psychiatrists and other professionals who treat marital problems are aware that some individuals have been able to establish successful sexual relations with each other although they cannot get together in any other context. Many of these couples have the experience of waking at night to discover themselves involved in sex, with neither partner aware of who took the initiative.

The differences between male and female. The physical differences between male and female contribute to the novelty and adventure of sex. Heterosexuality is extrafascinating and carries with it the illusion of intrigue. At the same time, the differences make understanding one another more difficult. Also, the excessive emphasis on sex as the major factor in marriage results in a distorted viewpoint. The natural differences between male and female are made to appear crucial for the success of a marriage. Actually, a woman will not improve her marriage by achieving a voluptuous bust, legs like a model, and an aura of exotic perfume. If her marriage is an unhappy one, her husband may develop a preference for small-breasted women who dress plainly and do not wear perfume.

Having reviewed some reasons for mistaken attitudes toward sexual intercourse, let us now take a look at its actual role in marriage. What is special about sexual intercourse, a highly satisfying male-female symbiosis, is that it requires a higher degree of collaborative communication than any other kind of behavior exchanged between the spouses. Sex is consequently precious, but also perilous. It is the only relationship act which must have mutual spontaneity for mutual satisfaction. It can only be a conjoint union, and it represents a common goal which is clear and understood by both.

The reason people keep asking where sex fits into marriage is that they have been hoodwinked, bamboozled, pressured, conned, and persuaded that the sexual act is compulsory in their lives and *must be performed alike by everyone;* the "standards" are established by advertisers, publicity for sexpot motion-picture stars, literature, movies, plays, television, and so on. But these are standards of fantasy. Therefore people ask silly questions. How often should we have sex? What is the best position? How intense should it be? Should we scratch and bite each other? What time of day should it be done? The questions sound like inquiries about the type of gymnastic procedures to be followed for attaining muscles like Mr. America's or a rear end or bust like Miss America's. Perhaps even worse off are the myriads of couples who don't dare ask questions and just assume they *must* be abnormal because their own practice differs from some so-called standard.

The problem is obvious. In sex, trying to keep up with the Joneses is the road to disaster. To decide where sex fits into their particular marriage, a couple must look inward at the marriage, not outward at the deceptive advice and make-believe standards set by others. There are no standards, and most "advice" from friends or family is misleading, for few people can speak honestly about their own sex life. Rather than admit their own sex problems and misgivings, friends often let one assume that their sex experiences are indeed superior; otherwise, the implication is, they wouldn't be giving advice.

Can women and men live without sex and still stay healthy?

Yes, they can. People cast away on isolated islands have gone for years without sex and have not experienced any physiological or psychological breakdowns or deficiencies as a result. Priests, nuns, and many mystics, such as the great Mahatma Gandhi, have eschewed sexual union and not damaged their health or decreased their longevity.

Sex, of course, is necessary for propagation; nature has provided this instinctual drive so that the species will survive. The drive is effective because of the variety of intense pleasures derived from its fulfillment. But no harm will occur to the normal individual to whom sex is denied.

Almost all adult human beings somehow have the feeling that experiencing sex frequently is a requirement for good physical and mental health, even if intellectually they know better. Both men and women who have enjoyed sex at regular intervals become frustrated, sometimes desperate, when it is withheld for (what seems to them) a long time. The sex aggressions of men at war in foreign lands and of sailors who have been at sea for months are well known. Such behavior stems more from a feeling of deprivation than from pure physical necessity. A person who volun-

tarily renounces or limits sexual intercourse —as priests, nuns, and others do for varied reasons—suffers no ill health or mental anguish as long as the renunciation corresponds to his emotional needs. If, however, a person desires sexual union and has deep, unmet needs for this form of human intimacy, yet is unable for some reason to meet the need, the resulting sense of deprivation and frustration may create emotional problems.

Sometimes unusual sex actions are stimulated by nonsexual deficiencies. For example, male children with a dread of being abandoned by their mother often will masturbate excessively. Men who have repressed homosexual tendencies (frequently the result of having a passive—or dead —father and a dominant mother) often are inclined to act oversexed in order to "prove their manhood."

The *beliefs* (most of them specious) which most individuals have on "what kind" of sex is desirable, and "how much," have several sources:

1. So-called "scientific" information obtained from books, articles, and lectures.
2. Customs, traditions, and advice conveyed by relatives and friends.
3. Customs, traditions, and examples transmitted by literature, radio, television, movies, and advertising.

Tradition molds many beliefs and habits having to do with sex in marriage. For example, consider the barbaric custom of the honeymoon—paticularly in past centuries, when the girl's chastity was treasured and important. In those days the bride and groom, who hardly knew each other, departed to a strange geographical area and into sexual intimacy. Usually the bride possessed only hearsay information on sexual matters and the husband's sexual experience had not necessarily prepared him to understand the needs of a virginal bride. They hurried away from the courtship milieu of jollity, gregariousness, and traditional optimism into a new sexual environment of their own, and were expected to emerge a week or ten days later with all the tenderness, love, and devotion needed to create a successful, happy marriage—whether or not the sexual experience had been traumatic for one or both of them.

A modern version of the same ritual occurs today, with an additional cultural expectation introduced: the newlyweds are expected to achieve *mutual* sexual satisfaction during the honeymoon. The young couple usually is launched with a lavish wedding and a tremendous amount of effort and expense on the part of both their families. The newlyweds are under pressure to "have fun" on their honeymoon and to return looking radiant and serene. Frequently the opposite happens. We estimate that most honeymoons are periods of frustrating sexual disappointment. The honeymoon may be an exciting novelty, but usually it results in confusion even when there has been premarital sexual experience. The situation of the bride who cried all through her honeymoon is a common one. Sex, like anything else, has to be learned; and even if the two have had relations before marriage, the marriage state places them in a new psychological milieu to which they must adjust. Now they are "legitimate," and they believe that their sexual experience will therefore be better. Now they are legally tied; they cannot walk away from each other. They feel the sex act *must* be a success every time; otherwise, the marriage is disintegrating.

This situation is aggravated by the pronouncements of most sex consultants, books, and articles on marriage. They usually indicate that sex is the keystone of marital success. We disagree. Sex is significant; and good sex is satisfying and emotionally nourishing. Sex is highly desirable, but it is not the only vital force in marriage, either during the honeymoon or later.

The situation is muddied further by the conflicting views of "experts" who give "scientific" information on sex. It is important that all "expert" opinions on sex be taken with a grain of skepticism.

Most "scientific" information on sex comes from two sources: psychiatrists and other physicians writing about data obtained from the experiences of their patients, and social scientists generalizing from data obtained in surveys conducted by means of some type of questionnaire.

In point of fact, conclusions based upon the medical data obtained from patients are not necessarily applicable to most people. Patients go to doctors for the treatment of one or more problems. If they have come for psychiatric therapy, they expect to spend many hours discussing sex and exploring the negative aspects of themselves, their spouses, their friends, and so on. Few (if any) will pay twenty-five or thirty dollars an hour and then spend time discussing pleasant and satisfactory experiences. The gynecologist or the family physician who writes a sex book is scientific only in regard to anatomy. The nonanatomical aspects of the text are based upon his own personal sex experiences plus whatever his ailing patients have told him.

Some of the most popular tracts on sex and marriage are written by gynecologists whose practices consist to a great extent of women who *spontaneously and voluntarily* talk freely to the physician in their efforts to describe their personal discords. The fact that a person talks and answers questions in a doctor's office (instead of in a public bar or a living room) does not prove that the individual is accurate or objective, and certainly does not indicate that his conclusions are generally applicable. Almost all patients' views on sex are subjective and weighted, especially since those who feel the need to discuss their sex lives usually have special problems.

The same difficulty causes the flaws in the Kinsey reports (and in most other studies whose data comes from question-and-answer procedures). Although Kinsey made an important study, one that required courage to initiate, we cannot overlook one important fact: he depended primarily on *volunteers* to answer his questions. Can we be sure that the people who volunteer to answer sex questions are representative? Some of the Kinsey interviews talked two or three hours about their experiences—evidently revealing intimacies was fun for some.

Also, there were considerable differences in experience and ability among Kinsey's interviewers. Only recently, the work of the Department of Psychiatry at Harvard has demonstrated that the nature of an interviewing context (including the interviewer's attitude) has a tremendous influence on the interviewee's response. An interviewer who strongly believes that, say, many wives have intercourse with other men when their husbands are on trips, will come up with much more evidence to support this view than will an interviewer who holds the opposite opinion at the start of the investigation.

Nevertheless, the Kinsey material provides the most complete and reliable data we have on the sexual practices of middle- and upper-class Americans. It reveals that increasingly in our culture, sexual intercourse is not confined to married people; and it is certainly not limited to sexual congress between men and women.

The bulk of the Kinsey material and of other surveys (which primarily relate to college students) concerns homosexuality, masturbation, premarital intercourse, perversion, post-divorce sexual activities, the activities of spinsters and bachelors, and adultery. To our knowledge, *no one has studied a sample of normogenic (average) married couples in significant numbers* and scientifically determined what married people think and do in relation to sex. Little is known about socioeconomic class differences, let alone ethnic idiosyncrasies.

Where does sex fit into marriage? It is almost impossible to estimate (except with respect to a specific married couple, after many hours of interviews) because so few studies have been made on the subject, and those which do exist are limited in scope and objectivity.

The answer to this question also depends upon time and circumstances, for sexual needs are fundamentally psychological. Middle-income spouses who have been married for a year and have no children, but want some, may have different sexual needs from the husband and wife without jobs, so poor they can't pay the rent, who therefore are afraid to have children. A couple married for thirty years, with four children in college, may have different sexual needs from a couple married for five years, with only one child. Such differences are not merely due to age. Boredom plays a more significant role in decreasing the frequency of intercourse than do withering sex glands. Also, a couple whose sex experience is beautiful and satisfying may engage in sex less frequently than an unhappy pair frantically experimenting for a solution to their discord.

There is no accurate sex information which gives exact answers for everyone, since there are so many variables. Yet in the United States, the sex ethic has become all important. As we have already stressed, the fallacious concept that sex determines our lives is spread far and wide by those promoting the tremendous sales of products supposed to enhance sexual attractiveness. Also, "authorities" on sex lecture, write, and give sexual advice *for a fee.* Naturally, they exaggerate the importance of sex in marriage. Offering complicated sex techniques is a profitable profession, and the more difficult the techniques, the longer the expensive counseling will last. The most popular sex manual has been through countless revisions and has outsold all other books except the Bible.

The myth that perfect and heavenly sex must be experienced by an individual before he can consider himself normal has become the foundation for a national mania. Sex success is the theme of social instruction and of almost all advertising, even for products not in any way associated with the sex act.

Spouses who are disappointed in sex are profoundly concerned about their difficulty. This is a reasonable reaction, if the disappointment is well founded. Men often wonder about their manhood or suspect that their wives are frigid or malicious. Wives wonder about their frigidity and suspect that perhaps their husbands are having affairs or that they are effeminate or at least inconsiderate or ignorant of satisfying sexual techniques.

Spouses will try anything to bring about a happier union, *one closer to the sex-success image* which is our national demigod. Many a man and wife have spent a small fortune to go to a posh luxury lodge where they hoped they would miraculously achieve a sexual congress they couldn't bring about in their own bedroom. If the weather is nice and the view is good, something may come of the weekend, but it is not apt to result in unusual sexual satisfaction. People frequently buy new houses, hire interior decorators—with the hope that a fresh environment will improve sexual relations.

If the various manifestations of sex were accepted as natural, and if people could abandon the view that there is a single absolute standard to be reached by all who are normal, the unhappiness of many couples would decrease—*and their performance would automatically improve.*

Our concern in this chapter has been with the problem: Is great, *great,* GREAT SEX necessary for a satisfactory marriage, for a workable marriage? If sex is not up to culturally created expectations, is the marriage a failure?

It need not be a failure. It can be a good marriage even if the partners don't find heaven in bed.

Next, is a less-than-heavenly sex performance "normal"?

No one knows the answer, neither clergymen nor doctors. No one knows what normogenic sex performances are in marriage. Scientists have studied pathological marriages, but not normal ones. Small-sample research (such as that by Epstein and Westley at McGill University) supports our contention that sex is not essential; it has been found that some apparently well-adjusted spouses have "given up" sex after a few years of marriage.

In summary, the important thing to remember is that there is no absolute standard against which the success of married sex can be measured as one would clock a hundred-yard dash. Occasionally, there are medical abnormalities (such as disfigured or diseased genitals, impotence, a pathological fear of sex), but assuming that these are not present, there is only one important question: Is sex a source of pleasure—in the spouses' own judgment?

What is a satisfying sex experience for two people may well be undesirable for two others, and vice versa. For example, it is estimated by most physicians that more than half of all women married an average of ten years and having three children have never experienced an orgasm. In a sampling made of such cases most of the women were not aware that they had not had a full sex act. They derived varying degrees of pleasure from the physical intimacy with their husbands. Equally interesting is the fact that the husbands frequently did not know that their wives voluntarily made the same noises and motions which they *had heard or read* were performed by passionate women; the husbands had accepted these as spontaneous and derived satisfaction from them as evidence of the wives' pleasure.

Spouses should not permit their satisfactions to be influenced by authority figures (such as actors and actresses), advertising, art, literature, and social customs and traditions. Personal sex values concern the two people involved. For example, we know a couple in their seventies. Every evening they bathe and dress elegantly for dinner. They treat each other with the dignity and courtesy of a blossoming courtship. At night when they go to bed they hold each other throughout the night, even though they have not exercised their genitalia for years. The elderly gentleman has described their experience as "having a ten-hour orgasm every night." For these two, it is a complete and wonderful sex act, and a very satisfying and nourishing one. Who is to differ with them?

Is sex important in married life? Yes, it is. It is *one* of the cements which hold the bricks of married life together. But the when, the how, the how often, and the quality can only be determined by the people involved.

49

HOUSEWIFE AND WOMAN? THE BEST OF BOTH WORLDS?

Hilda Sidney Krech

Scoldings, dissections, and revolutionary proposals—all about modern woman—have been filling the air for ten or fifteen years. They've also been filling newspaper columns, books, TV programs, learned journals, not-so-learned journals, and symposia from the Vassar campus to the University of California Medical School. Surprisingly, words about modern woman have been flowing and symposia have been gathering at an increasing rather than a decreasing rate. More surprising still, a lot of people seem to be willing (sometimes even eager) to hear about her once again. I find myself challenged to say something new about her before the subject (and the discussers of the subject) are exhausted.

When I considered the concern—the serious, frivolous, scientific, sympathetic, and sometimes furious concern—that's been lavished on modern woman, and most especially modern American woman, I started wondering why she remains bewildered and bewildering, why her dilemma remains unsolved. And I was struck by the fact that we haven't all been talking about the same American woman.

Most of the talk and most of the criticism has been lavished on the more or less privileged, more or less educated, presumably intelligent woman. She is the one who has encouraged the word "discontented" to be linked with the words "American woman." She has been forced to add the feeling of guilt to her feelings of frustration because so many people for so many years have been telling her how lucky she is. And she is. And she knows it. But still—but still what? Her dissatisfaction is about equally divided between what she *does* do and what she *does not* do.

Speaking with women who are quite happily married, one often gets the feeling that housework and child care are both too much and too little for each one of them; too much because they take all her time, energy, and thought during the period when her children need constantly to be fed, clothed in clean clothes, fetched and carried, and tended to in one way or another; too little in that she'd somehow been led to believe that she would be using her time and her talents and her energy quite differently—at least for a portion of each day. All through school and, for many, through college as well, these talents—whether artistic, intellectual, practical, or human—have been respected and encouraged.

Though, deep inside, there is nothing she would rather do than be a mother, she often feels, while her children are young, like a drudge. When they are grown, she is a has-been—sometimes feeling that she's a *has*-been without ever really having *been*. She is no longer needed as a full-time mother, yet no longer able to be whatever it was she set out to be all those long years ago. For, contrary to polite and gallant statements which suggest that simply "being a woman" is a vocation, this is not the case.

To make such a woman's discontent stronger still, the truly lucky woman is married to a man who does interesting, challenging, perhaps useful, and sometimes lucrative work which often gets more challenging and useful as the years go by, while her work gets less challenging, less useful. Growing up, she didn't wish she were a boy. She doesn't wish now that she were a man. Yet something is wrong with this picture of the luckiest woman in the world.

In answer to the countless articles, speeches, and books which have painted just such a picture, *The Saturday Evening Post* recently ran an article defending the American woman, refuting the countless statements which accuse her of being "lonely, bored, lazy, sexually inept, frigid,

superficial, harried, militant, overworked."
The adjectives are those of the authors, Dr.
George Gallup and Evan Hill, who made a
survey and then described what they call
the "typical" American woman.

(Though one-third of the married women
in America are employed outside the home,
and though nearly 15 percent of women
over forty-five are widowed or divorced,
the authors specifically state that these
women are not "typical," and therefore,
they are neither discussed nor included in
the composite picture. Getting ahead of
my story for a moment, I'd like to point
out, also, that Gallup and Hill's typical
American woman is forever young, forever
surrounded by young children.)

The charges against the American woman
are untrue, say Dr. Gallup and Mr. Hill.
She is happy; she is content; she wants
only "the simple pleasures"; her family is
"her whole life." Their typical wife sums
up her situation by saying: "If I don't want
to do the dishes or laundry right now, I can
do them later. My only deadline is when
my husband comes home. I'm much more
free than when I was single and working.
A married woman has it made."

Her house may be cluttered, but her
mind is not. Only half of the women interviewed read books at all; only 13 percent
consider "intelligence as a prerequisite in
husbands." The only reference to the life
of the mind in this article quotes the typical wife as saying: "I spend my spare time
broadening my interests so I won't bore
Jim." So I won't bore Jim! Apparently she
doesn't mind boring herself. She may be
free, she may be content, but if she is indeed typical, I can't help considering the
possibility that modern woman, for all her
modern appliances, isn't modern any more.

The Saturday Evening Post's typical
woman, at any rate, knows neither the nagging worry of poverty nor the nagging pull
to be part of the activity and thought of
a world that extends beyond her eventually
made bed, her eventually cleaned house.
But, of course, *she* is not the woman that
commentators have in mind when they talk
about "frustration" or when they describe
the Radcliffe diploma mildewing over the
kitchen sink.

And when we read the *Report of the
President's Commission on the Status of
Women,* the emphasis is on a still different
woman, a woman who works because she
has to or because she wants to give her
children a better life. She cannot be called
a career woman, for she is likely to do
clerical work or saleswork, service work,
factory work, or agricultural work, and only
a small percentage of the women working
in our country today are in professional or
managerial jobs.

Clearly, it is impossible to speak in the
same breath about all these kinds of women,
at least in any meaningful way. Even
within these groups, of course, there are
enormous differences between individual
women—differences in ability, in intellect,
in preferences, in temperament, in values.
But about these differences remarkably little is ever said. This tendency to speak of
women as though they were interchange-
able units like the parts of a Ford is one
reason why (for all the talk) woman's
dilemma remains unsolved.

A second reason is that while we've been
talking, the picture has been changing.
For women have not turned a deaf ear to
this talk. If anything fascinates them, it's
the topic of themselves—a fact which suggests a close relation to the rest of the human race—and they have tried to follow the
suggestions, heed the warnings. While reflecting the feminine condition, therefore,
some of the commentators have, at the
same time, helped to shape that condition.

"Womanpower"—the word and the commodity—was discovered during World War
II. When the war was over and womanpower was no longer needed in factories
and hospitals and schools (or so they
thought), many voices started urging
women to go home, stay home, and like it.
In 1947 Marnya Farnham and Ferdinand
Lundberg wrote *Modern Woman: The Lost
Sex,* in which they predicted: "Close down
the commercial bakeries and canning factories today and women will start being
happier tomorrow."

They were talking to the young women
of my generation who had started out to
do great things—not only the privileged
and the educated; all kinds of girls were

going to have "careers" in those days. Then, as each girl married (always to her great surprise, for she never dreamed she was going to meet George or Bill or Frederick, or if she did, she kept her dreams to herself), she would "throw over her career," as she liked to put it. Sometimes she did so cheerfully, for she knew there really was no career in the making, sometimes reluctantly because it was nearly impossible to keep on after her first or second child arrived. She became a housewife or, as she tended to put it, "just a housewife."

Dorothy Thompson created a new cliché or, at the very least, gave new life to an old one, when she pointed out in 1949 that a wife and mother should never feel apologetic for being "just a housewife" because that homely word means that she is a professional "business manager, cook, nurse, chauffeur, dressmaker, interior decorator, accountant, caterer, teacher, private secretary" all rolled into one. "I simply refuse to share your self-pity," Miss Thompson told the American housewife in the *Ladies' Home Journal*. "You are one of the most successful women I know."

The following year, in *The Atlantic Monthly*, another woman journalist wrote an even angrier article. Agnes E. Meyer not only tried to reassure those women who spent their entire time being mothers; she fiercely denounced those who made some effort to be something in addition to being mothers. She wrote:

Women must boldly announce "that no job is more exacting, more necessary, or more rewarding than that of housewife and mother. . . . There have never been so many women who are unnecessarily torn between marriage and a career. There have never been so many mothers who neglect their children because they find some trivial job more interesting. . . . The poor child whose mother has to work has some inner security because he knows in his little heart that his mother is sacrificing herself for his well-being. But the neglected child from a well-to-do home, who realizes instinctively that his mother prefers her job to him, often hates her with a passionate intensity."[1]

Each time such a statement was made, and they were made often, it was a shot in the arm for those who had felt aimless and demoralized, who had, to quote one of them, "begun to feel stupid with nothing to contribute to an evening's discussion after a solitary morning of housecleaning and an afternoon of keeping peace between the children." Now they were able to face themselves with more self-respect, for they were doing the most important job of all. What's more, they were able to look with *less* respect at their friends who had outside work or interests.

As for these women, the ones involved outside the home as well as within, many of them were intimidated by the strong voices. It was confusing to them, even frightening, to be told they weren't good mothers, to be accused of preferring their outside activities to their children. Increasingly, therefore, many turned their full attention, their full energies upon their little families and shut the door on the world.

And so, while the canneries and bakeries did not literally close down, the spirit of this advice was taken; and many highly educated or trained women have been making their own bread, putting up endless little jellies. But according to the latest attack on the subject, *The Feminine Mystique* by Betty Friedan, these women aren't happy at all but are slowly going mad and battering their children's heads!

Nobody's happy about them either. The consensus at the Vassar symposium held in the spring of 1962 was that: "If the performance of college women from 1920 through World War II has been somewhat disappointing, the mental attitudes of young women since World War II are alarming."

This kind of criticism came from looking inside woman's head and heart. Looking at her from the outside came another kind of criticism—first, the accusation that having no other interest in her life, she latched fiercely onto her children, ruining them, being a "Mom." More recently, still another kind of criticism has been coming: that she hasn't been pulling her weight. "A Huge Waste: Educated Womanpower" is the title of a typical *New York Times* article, this one published in May, 1961. Two years later, under the heading "Tapping a U.S. National Resource," came another *Times* article concerning itself with "the educated woman."

This past summer Max Lerner wrote an article called "Let's Draft Our Girls," and he meant all kinds of girls. Four years earlier *Harper's* had published an article in which Marion Sanders discussed the possibility of drafting not only girls before they become mothers, but also strong, able women after they have finished their full-time mothering, unless they are already engaged in work that has some value. Though her style is gay, almost frivolous, and I don't think Mrs. Sanders seriously wants a draft for women, she does want us to pull our socks up and is quite serious both about the need for teachers, nurses, and social welfare workers and about her scorn for what she calls Non-Work or Sub-Work or Redundant Housewifery—the pointless tasks with which so many middle-aged women fill their lives.

As an example of women she would *not* exempt, she tells about a hospital ladies' auxiliary in Long Island which "boasted that its 900 Pink Pinafore Volunteers last year spent 51,280 hours reading to sick children, giving patients alcohol rubs, and running a gift shop. This averages out to a little more than an hour a week per volunteer—scarcely time to don and doff the pinafores."

In addition, then, to the great differences between different women (about which too little is said), and in addition to the changes constantly taking place in our attitudes and in our ways of living, there is a third reason we've been progressing so slowly in gaining insight into modern woman—her role, her function, her old dilemma. Many true things have been said, but since they aren't all said at the same time, we get part of the picture in one strong statement, another part in another (seemingly contradictory) statement. We never get a full, accurate picture in one glance, but a blurred and confused impression. And while I can't say everything all at once either (not even the things I do know, let alone the things I don't), I'd like to give an example of what I mean.

One often hears that too much is expected of the American woman. "How can she be wife, lover, confidante, companion, hostess, cook, seamstress, floor scrubber, purchasing agent, teacher, chauffeur, child analyst?" ask her defenders.

But in Mrs. Sanders's "Proposition for Women" she speaks of middle-aged and older women with "time for leisurely jaunts to the lonely housewife's dream world of 'shopping'—so different from 'marketing.'" And she describes clubs with many meetings which "did not contribute to anyone's enlightenment since their programs revealed no coherent purpose. (January: Flower Arrangement. February: The Bright Side of Menopause. March: Whither the UN?)" Women caught up in such activities spend an enormous amount of time telephoning to arrange similar meetings which, in Mrs. Sanders's terms, is "Circular (or self-perpetuating) Puttering, a form of Sub-Work."

Both kinds of descriptions are valid, although it's obvious that both apply more accurately to middle-class and upper-class women. What people *don't* always recognize, however, is that the demanding description applies only to a woman's early years when her children are young and she is in constant demand, that the idleness comes later and, worse, it comes gradually, imperceptibly. Most of us have heard a great deal about this bonus of twenty, thirty, or even forty years women now have because they stop bearing children at an earlier age and they live—with health and vigor—much longer than people have ever lived before. And though we're still floundering, are not yet sure exactly what we want to do with this bonus and how to plan for it, many girls and young women are completely unaware of it. This may be hard to believe; but the one sour note in the otherwise sweet *Saturday Evening Post* article is that Dr. Gallup and Mr. Hill report the women they interviewed could not imagine having their children grown and out of the house, leaving them jobless. They had simply never given a thought to this eventuality.

And so women were scolded for going

out of the home and then, more recently, they've been scolded for staying in. The next logical step is to urge women out of the house and into high-powered careers on a par with men's, thus bringing us full circle, back to the feminist days. I'm afraid this step is coming. Whether advertisements follow public opinion or make it I don't quite know, but I've noticed a small straw blowing in the wind which may be significant, the beginning of a trend. After years of picturing lovely ladies who beam with joy while cleaning their toilet bowls or waltzing around the living room with a roll of Alcoa Wrap, some advertisers are taking a new tack. One blouse manufacturer has announced a new advertising campaign addressed to the 24,584,000 "Wonderful Women Who Work." Going even further, a different shirt company recently ran an ad picturing a girl as a naval architect and running a caption which said: "Man's world? Bah! Women are in everything."

The girl is extremely pretty and looks about eighteen and is totally unconvincing as an architect, naval or otherwise. But when I think of the other kind of ad, I realize it's not the unconvincingness that's new, and I wonder if, after pushing housewifery to the limits, they're now going to push for "a career for every girl." Look out for that swinging pendulum; here we go again.

What really alarms me is the strident voice, the strong note of resentment in Betty Friedan's *The Feminine Mystique* when she asks why women are always supposed to be satisfied with second-string careers and second-level positions. Having said that, I suppose I've put myself on the spot and had better explain why *I'm* satisfied. Am I being wishy-washy? Or have I boldly taken the position of defending "the radical middle"? I'll say what I believe and you can decide.

I believe that only the rare, truly exceptional woman with way-above-average ability, energy, and drive can—while maintaining a home and being a real mother to several children—achieve a full-fledged career. It takes enormous flexibility and ingenuity, for the children *do* come first, and women *do* move when the husbands are transferred

on their jobs, and they don't have their mothers living nearby or maiden aunts or maids to lend a hand when the unpredictable but inevitable complications arise. In our society, husbands carry the main financial burden of supporting the family, whether or not their wives have salaries. And in the same spirit, whether it's a matter of tradition or instinct, wives are usually the ones who carry the main responsibility for keeping things running smoothly at home, for being emotionally supportive to their husbands as well as to their children.

We have to face the fact that for all these same reasons, it is extremely difficult to work out even a half-time job or profession or avocation. Why, then, should anyone bother? And why should I believe this to be a sound and satisfying course for a great many women in our time? If someone has strong, specific interests, proven ability, or a shining talent, it may be worthwhile; but why should other young women go out of their way to seek goals, to seek spheres of interest and activity? Aren't they just looking for trouble? In a sense, yes; it may seem that they're deliberately choosing the hard way and that I'm egging them on.

By not making a deliberate choice, however, by drifting along as so many have been doing, being buffeted by the changing winds of social pressure, present-day women who are in a position to choose haven't found their lives hard, exactly, but too many have found them empty, purposeless. Deliberately making their lives hard by adding all sorts of do-it-yourself chores —from paper hanging and upholstery to weaving and preserving—has been tried by many but has turned out to be the answer for relatively few. Not only is it artificial, but it puts something of a strain on the marriage relationship to ask a woman to live in a homespun, horse-and-buggy age while her husband continues to forge ahead in a Dacron, Acrilan, jet age.

However, since so many traditional functions have gradually been taken away from mothers—not only the weaving, canning, and baking which many of us would cheerfully forego, but even teaching children about sex and sewing and social problems (whatever happened to mother's knee, by the way, and all the things a child used to learn there?)—it's obvious that unless she and her life are to become empty, something must be substituted.

As long ago as 1950, Lynn White, Jr., former president of Mills College, recognized this problem clearly. In his book *Educating Our Daughters*, he said:

If the housewife no longer pumps water from the well, she must be sure that the city water supply is pure. She no longer wrings the necks of barnyard hens for dinner, but an honest meat inspection in the interests of public health affects the health of her family. Her children learn their letters at school rather than at her knee, but in return she must work for the P.T.A.

Mr. White saw the question and he gave us one answer. But I believe that in considering it the *only* answer, we may have lost as much as we gained. By calling "homemaking plus volunteer community work" *the* ideal pattern for modern woman, we are threatened with a new kind of standardization. During the years that girls have been educated much as their brothers and their future husbands, they have come to be appreciated as individuals. Parents and teachers, too, have recognized and have even emphasized individual differences, drumming home the idea that there are all kinds of ways of being a valuable person, that "different" doesn't necessarily mean "better or worse." When a girl marries, is she supposed to forget all this and learn, just as girls learned in the past: *this* is the kind of life a good wife and mother leads; this and no other?

There is a second fallacy in the "homemaking-plus volunteer-community-work" formula—at least when it is recommended as a suitable formula for most women. In the old days each mother had (using Lynn White's own example) to haul each pail of water into the house and had to wring the neck of each chicken. But the way things are now, we don't need *all* mothers working for pure food and drug laws, for fluoridation or antifluoridation, or even for the P.T.A. Women going into these volunteer efforts soon find out that not all of them are needed. It soon becomes clear that the purpose of much of their work is occupational therapy—not for others but for themselves. Wanting to be useful, many flit from one volunteer or creative activity to another—one year marching for diseases, the next year making mosaics out of broken bottles, the next year being crazy about mental health.

Since the family itself has shrunk, it's true that certain community concerns have taken the place of certain family concerns. We might say that today's extended family has, reasonably and legitimately, been extended to include the community. But different women can make different contributions to the community—both because different women are different *and* because all sorts of things are needed and duplication of effort is tremendously wasteful. Nor are all contributions measurable by the same standards. Some, such as pure research or pure art, cannot be evaluated at all by most of us. And I wish we could just accept that, as we do with much of man's work, not making a woman feel guilty about or accountable for any work she does which is not clearly contributing to her family—or her extended family, the community.

Now that I'm nearing the end of my paper, I'll make three more wishes. I would like to see less distinction made between the woman who must work for financial reasons and the one who has decided to work. The borderline is so hazy, so vague that only in cases of extreme poverty or where no husband is present and employed can one say that this woman simply must work in order for her family to survive. Beyond that who can say whether women are working for necessities or luxuries? Is a washing machine a necessity or a luxury? Is a college education for her children a necessity or a luxury? I maintain that this is for each couple to decide.

Making a sharp distinction between women who must work and those who have decided to work leaves out of account the powerful but often ignored phenomenon of "mixed motivation." Certainly, in most cases, the second income is needed or at least warmly welcomed; but there are other satisfactions, too, whether it's a feeling of usefulness, of accomplishment, or simply the human contact to be found in any store or office.

In the eyes of many people, saying that a woman *must* work for financial gain casts a reflection on her husband. The question is raised: "Can't he support her?" Ironically, reflections are also cast on the woman who has chosen to work. The question is raised: "Does she really love her children? Is she a good mother?" For all these reasons, then, I think the question of whether a woman is working through choice or necessity is often meaningless and destructive.

My second wish for women is that a less sharp distinction be made between the paid and the volunteer worker. I would like to see a climate of opinion in which the paid woman worker is neither apologetic about needing the money nor arrogant about being "a professional." Were it taken for granted that everyone works to capacity, the professional would become less defensive and the volunteer would become more professional—that is, she would feel a strong and continuing sense of responsibility toward her work and her colleagues, a sense of commitment which would keep her from quitting whenever the going got rough (or boring).

My third wish, then, is just that: a climate of opinion in which it's taken for granted that women will do something with their training, their abilities, their energy once their children are half-grown and they have free time at their disposal. First of all, there is the obvious waste of "womanpower" which was first noticed during the war, but was then forgotten until relatively recently—perhaps because of the Sputnik and our "educational lag," as the shortage of first-rate teachers was called. People can understand that, just as they understand a shortage of nurses. But, again, we have to appreciate that there are all sorts of less obvious needs, and women can make contributions in various and quite varied ways.

I latch onto the economic and social waste, putting it first, because it's respectable, it's measurable, and lately all sorts of people out there in the real world have been noticing that women haven't been pulling their weight. But long before this happened I used to think about the waste from the point of view of the individual women—not so much in terms of what they could do for society, but what a waste it is for *themselves* and how much they would gain by being participating members of society. If it were taken for granted that once a woman's children were grown and no longer needed her full time, she would find a specific place for herself (whether through a job, volunteer work, or in some other way), she would put to better use the little scraps of time available during her busiest years.

As it is now, the short stretches of time she can find for herself are usually frittered away. It's true that during the peak of her motherhood, before the children go to school, when all of them need her almost every hour of the night and day, she has neither time nor energy to spend. The hour here, the half-hour there are needed simply for "relief"—a stolen nap, a few snatched moments of window-shopping, a story read while wheeling a carriage or stirring a pot. I remember a friend who said it was a treat to go to the dentist because she got to sit down.

But this period passes. It passes so gradually, it's true, that there isn't a precise day when a woman can say she has free time to spend and ask herself how to spend it. And just as expenses rise imperceptibly to meet rising income (Parkinson's second law), so chores and errands and what Marion Sanders calls self-perpetuating puttering, what Veblen called ceremonial futility increase as women grow older and their home duties lighter. If a young mother knew, however, that at some future time she would be allowed, encouraged, and expected to use her time, training, and abilities for some purpose, she would have something specific to do with her scraps of time as soon as they started to become just a little bigger and more dependable. Having a goal, a realistic yet flexible goal, would also add zest to a woman's life while she is still young, with time only for a course here, a volunteered hour there, or an hour in the library now and then.

Of course, while she is completely tied down, it's hard for a girl to believe she'll ever have time on her hands, that her house and her days will be empty, and she herself will be unneeded. Reaching the age of forty is like having triplets or winning the Irish Sweepstakes, the unlikely kind of thing that happens only to other people. Yet word could get through to her, somehow, that this might just possibly happen to her.

Another thing that's likely to happen—and this is something that has not been generally recognized—is that a lot of girls who now foresee only marriage and motherhood for themselves will, at some period in their lives, be looking for jobs. The Women's Bureau estimates that of the girls now in high school 8 out of 10—whether because of widowhood, divorce, economic need, emotional need, or psychological need—will at some period be employed. If girls and women could accept this while young, they'd have motivation to keep their skills from rusting, their minds from shrinking, and their work habits from deteriorating.

Perhaps a representative of the Women's Bureau should be invited to confront girls in high school and in college (the majority of whom want and see only motherhood ahead) and say to them: "I have news for you! You will be looking for a job some day, so give it a thought now, so that you'll be qualified for the best, most interesting kind of work of which you are capable." If someone could say it so that the girls would really believe it, this would be helpful—just as it would have been helpful if someone had brought news to the academic and career-minded girls of my generation that, chances were, we would not be pleading at the bar, saving humanity, or running a corporation in ten or fifteen years; we'd be marketing and cooking meals, raising our children and cleaning our houses.

As it is now, even the brightest young girl takes any old job that has a salary attached because it is frankly a stopgap until her future husband comes along or (for the lucky, the truly "in" girls) until her present husband finishes college or professional school. After that, she thinks, she'll never have to see the inside of an office or store again.

Worse than that, it seems to me, is what happens to the women who have followed the prescribed course of devoting themselves fulltime to being wives, homemakers, and mothers and then find themselves—for one reason or another—looking for a job at the age of forty or fifty. They have to start at the bottom of the ladder. If they find themselves in the position of having to earn a living, it is wasteful and absurd, as well as unsatisfying, to plug away in a job far below one's capacities. If they don't have to earn money but are looking for worthwhile work, even volunteer organizations will use them in the lowliest assignments if their work habits and self-discipline have atrophied for lack of exercise. This is unsuitable for many and unbearable for some; and so, those who have any choice in the matter soon give up.

If girls could have the foresight to recognize at the beginning of their lives as women that this time will come—not only with hindsight, after a great deal of trial and error, disappointment, and heartbreak —they could try to look ahead, try to plan ahead, try to achieve some sort of balance between their work life and their personal life. My repeated use of the word "try" means I am well aware that one cannot see one's life stretching ahead, clearly and accurately. And as for planning, I realize that it is, in a sense, planning the unplannable. But if Herman Kahn and the Rand Corporation can think about the unthinkable, women should find that they have a lot to gain by planning the unplannable. If they had a general sort of goal, knowing perfectly well that it would be modified and that the road toward it would swerve and curve and, occasionally, backtrack, their journey would still be richer, more interesting, and more meaningful. If, further, they could accept such a life pattern, not as a makeshift, patched-up compromise, but as a complicated, intricate arrangement necessitated by the fact that they have the privilege and responsibility of being *both* mothers at home *and* women who have a place in the world outside the home, they could do the planning, the arranging (*and* the necessary *re*arranging) without resentment.

Last year in Belgium, while I was talking with some women about the problems connected with doing professional work while, at the same time, living a normal family life, one woman said something which I have thought of many times since then. This woman is a scientist, a *docent* at one of the universities, which is equal, approximately, to the rank of associate professor in America. She is the wife of a businessman, the mother of two sons—one at the university and one in medical school.

"When the boys were little," she told me, "my career, which was just beginning, could move along only very slowly since I was home a good deal then and couldn't spend as much time in the laboratory as my men colleagues. Even when my sons were older, but still young boys, and I had a chance to go to congresses and international meetings, for example—well, I just didn't go. I didn't really want to. Probably I didn't do as much research as I would have done had I been a man and concerned chiefly with my career. And so I didn't progress as much as if I'd been a man. I'm a *docent* now; I might perhaps have become a professor." She gave a shrug as if to say: "So what?" And then she spelled it out, quite beautifully I thought, by saying: "But that's all right for a woman because all the time you've had the pleasure of being a mother too."

And so, when I say that I'm content with second-string or second-level positions, I don't mean that women, because they are *women,* should be content with second best. I mean that if a woman is also going to run her home and be a wife to her husband and a mother to her children, it is a rare woman indeed who can hold down a full-time job which is on a par with her husband's, a rarer one still who can have a full-fledged career.

While I am wishing, I would like to get rid of the word "career" entirely. I've always been amused at the way the word

"career" seems to go with the word "woman" whenever this general subject is being discussed. Most men (except for movie stars, boxers, and diplomats) have to be content with jobs. The reason the word "career" is so dangerous, I feel, when used freely, as it is, in connection with women is that many are left feeling that if they can't have a real "career," why bother at all?

Why bother? It isn't easy, I admit: this juggling of time, of energy, of one's very emotions. Sometimes you're frustrated in all your endeavors at once so that it's hard not to feel you've been left with the worst of both worlds. And yet I feel we have no choice. Maurice Chevalier is supposed to have confided to a friend: "Old age isn't so bad—not when you consider the alternative."

In much the same spirit, I seriously propose that the alternative to living a full, perhaps overful life is being half-dead. And things being the way they are, women are more likely to become victims than men. As long ago as the turn of the century Justice Oliver Wendell Holmes' wife remarked that "Washington is full of interesting men; and the women they married when they were young." This remark was sad then, but it is sadder still today, for modern couples expect more of one another in the way of companionship. We do so for a host of reasons, but one of them has to do with sheer numbers. When you look at the picture on the cover of this conference announcement, a photograph of an old-fashioned family, it's hard to tell who's the mother, who's the father, who's the husband, who's the wife. Somewhere in that large and varied group, I can't help feeling, each man and each woman could surely find a congenial soul. Today, with families small and, furthermore, isolated from grandparents, in-laws, uncles, aunts, cousins, and grown brothers and sisters, an extra demand of understanding and companionship is asked of each husband and each wife—a shared growing and deepening far beyond "developing some interests so as not to bore Jim."

Husbands, particularly, are often asked to carry an extra burden when wives expect them to supply, through their work, not only the family's entire financial support but everything that makes life "interesting." Whether they mean friends, colleagues, prestige, or being in the know depends upon each woman and what is important to her, but there are a great many who live vicariously; there are a great many young ones, newly married, who plan and expect to live vicariously, to have their husband's contact with the world make up for the fact that they have none. This, I maintain, is too much to ask of a man. And so, for the sake of the marriage, if for no other reason, each woman should continue to grow with her husband, to enrich their shared life. Mostly, however, for her own sake should she live to the full and savor to the full her "long intense alliance with the world."

NOTES

[1] Agnes E. Meyer, "Women Aren't Men," *The Atlantic Monthly,* 186 (August 1950): 32–36.

Part Ten

Childbearing and Child-Rearing Years

Even though more and more couples are delaying the birth of the first child and are having fewer children, and although many are not planning to have any children at all, the current figures indicate that over 90 percent of women in the United States have at least one child in a lifetime. Most marriages, then, do become families. Since children are no longer an economic asset to the parents and since many studies have indicated that children do not, in fact, make a marriage happier, it becomes interesting to contemplate the motives of couples who decide to have children. At one time in our history, unselfish reasons might have been given—the species must survive and added population was needed. Even today, a population increase is still encouraged by some nations, but much of the world is tuned into the problems of overpopulation, and large families are being discouraged. As a result, couples who choose not to have children at all seem to be meeting with more approval than in the past. However, potential grandparents often put pressure on a childless couple, and more subtle forces may make them feel that they are missing something in life.

For the first time in history, couples today have a choice about whether or not to have children. Part of the reason is the increased availability and wide variety of contraceptives. In the past, sex inevitably resulted in children unless one of the partners, for one or more reasons, was not physiologically capable of parenthood. With the freedom to choose has come the responsibility to make a wise decision; and it is hoped that the widespread use of contraceptives will result in parents who really want the child and who will thus be better parents.

Most of the reasons for having children today appear to be more personal and self-centered than was true in the past. Socialization plays a major part in the desire for children. From the time a woman is born, she is defined as a potential mother and is encouraged to practice the role by playing with dolls and housekeeping. She learns that childbearing is an approved and expected goal for her and often she may be told that she will not be physiologically and psychologically fulfilled if she does not have children. Her husband, too, may want children because he has been socialized to believe that fatherhood is visible proof that he is a mature male and can be responsible for a family. Still other couples speak of giving each other a gift of their love in the form of a child, or of having a child so they can use the child to love and be loved in return. Some parents acknowledge that they are curious about what they can produce; and still others are so certain they will produce fine specimens that they feel they must not deprive the world of such talent and beauty.

In the first article, Betty Rollin takes a critical look at the many myths surrounding parenthood as well as at some of the popular reasons for having children. She challenges the idea that all couples should have children and points to some of the benefits experienced by childless couples.

Although most couples will probably have children, there is a clear trend toward having fewer children among all social classes, races, and ethnic groups in the United States. Family planning is increasingly being accepted; and even certain religious groups, while not officially softening their policy on birth control, have found that a growing number of their members are nevertheless limiting their families. Fewer than 10 percent of Americans report in surveys that they are opposed to contraception, and it is a safe generalization to make that few married couples today do not use some form of birth control at some time in their married lives. The second article, by Alan Guttmacher, discusses current contraceptive devices and explains how to separate recreational sex from procreational sex. The relative effectiveness of contraceptive methods is of major concern to couples desiring to avoid pregnancy, and the much discussed side effects are clearly being thought about—particularly by women.

Vasectomy and tubal ligation are beginning to become popular means of birth control, although these operations are largely reserved for couples who have already had children. It is estimated that nearly a million vasectomies a year are performed in the United States, mostly on men in the middle and upper classes. The operation is said to be reversible in about 25 percent of the cases, but very few men desire a reversal once they have decided on vasectomy. For men who equate their masculinity with their ability to sire children, the idea of vasectomy is often a threat; it also raises problems for some women, who feel their husbands will not be as virile as before. However, the majority of husbands and wives are happy with this reliable method of birth control—reliable, that is, as long as the wife contains her sex-life within her marriage. A woman who has more than one sex partner must rely on contraceptives she controls, such as birth control pills or perhaps a tubal ligation, which is essentially the female version of a vasectomy. It is more difficult to get a tubal ligation than a vasectomy, for the medical profession is more reluctant, for some reason, to allow women to decide to have such an operation. In some parts of the United States, doctors multiply a woman's age by the number of children she has had; if the total is under 120, the woman has no chance for such freedom from pregnancy. A twenty-five-year-old woman with four children would not qualify, nor would a forty-five-year-old woman with two children! ($25 \times 4 = 100$; $45 \times 2 = 90$.)

Some couples, of course, have the opposite problem. No matter what they try, they cannot have children of their own. Usually, this is due to only one partner's being unable to conceive, and once it is determined which one it is, there are two or three avenues open to them. If it is the wife who has the problem, adoption is the only ready answer. But if it is the husband who is at fault, artificial insemination is another possibility. A recent film, *The Babymaker*, added the fanciful alternative of hiring an attractive young partner for the husband of the sterile woman; this young woman would then conceive and bear his child, so that he and his wife could ultimately adopt. It isn't likely that this method will catch on with many sterile wives, but it is worth a passing mention.

Artificial insemination is not as common as adoption, although it is estimated that as many as 10,000 children each year are born by this method. Often, the sperm donor is unknown to the woman; more frequently, however, the sperm is a collection of her husband's, which has been taken—over a period of time—when his sperm count was a little higher than usual, following a lengthy period since his last ejaculation. Some interesting questions can be raised about paternity resulting from artificial insemination in some states; but in other states, such as California, where paternity is tied to being legally married to the mother, such questions do not arise.

The most common method of having a family for the barren couple is adoption. This is becoming increasingly difficult, since fewer babies are unplanned and since more unmarried mothers are keeping their children. There are many more parents who desire to adopt than there are children available, but it is estimated that over 100,000 petitions to adopt are filed each year in the United States. Of these, a growing number are for older children or for children who are difficult to place because they are racially mixed or, perhaps, defective in some way. In addition, one adoption out of every hundred involves a child from another country.

By whatever means the child enters the picture and creates a family, the transition for the couple to parenthood brings very real adjustments. It has been said that married but childless couples more closely resemble unmarried couples than they do married couples who have children. Marriage itself does not make as much of a difference as does adding a child to the unit. Alice Rossi, in her article on the transition to parenthood, indicates that a certain amount of disenchantment with marriage begins for the wife with the arrival of children. She, no doubt, found her pregnancy a period when she and her husband still had time to talk to each other and to work together, but with the birth of a child things change. She most often withdraws from involvement outside the home and begins to carry a heavy load of home responsibility.

The number of children and their spacing seems to have a decided impact on the success of a marriage. It is known, for instance, that as the number of children increases,

the parents become more authoritarian and the father, in particular, more of a power figure. Spacing is important, as well, and the rate at which children are born adds to the adjustments necessary, due to the increasing size of the family. Harold Christensen reports on the impact of children on marital happiness and concludes that marital happiness does not depend so much on how many children a couple has nor the spacing between the children, but on whether or not the parents have controlled the family planning. Parents with ten children spaced closely together may have just what they planned—"the more the merrier" or "cheaper by the dozen"—or, on the other hand, a couple with only one or two children may be unhappy with how the family took shape.

The mother's role in the lives of her children has received a great deal of attention in the literature, and for years one would have thought that the father was not a very important factor as long as he brought home a paycheck. This is not true, of course, but until recently there has been very little research showing the impact of the father. Today we are aware that the father's influence shows up in many ways. One of these ways is in the obvious area of his earning ability. As the children grow older and cost more to support, if the father's income does not go up, he tends to have less influence on his children and perhaps a weaker resultant feeling of commitment to them. Fathers and their children often see each other in economic terms, although there seems to be a trend, particularly in young families today, for the father to take a more varied and more personally involved role with his children. The reading by John Nash is one of the recent reports on the father's role as seen in contemporary society. Nash provides a useful contrast between the roles of the mother and father that gives a new dimension to what is already known about mothers.

An issue often debated in today's society is the impact of the working mother on her children. The results of studies in this area are somewhat conflicting with regard to the effects on the children, but there is general agreement that employed mothers are as well adjusted to their children as those who are not employed. Often they are better adjusted, particularly if they are satisfied with their jobs and prefer to work outside the home. If better adjusted mothers in turn affect their children more positively—and there is evidence that they do—then the effect of working outside the home can well be a positive one. At any rate, whether or not the mother works is not enough to explain the quality of child-care. More important seems to be whether she likes working, her level of education, her husband's attitude toward her employment, and the plans both parents make and carry out for child-care and household duties. The final article explores the question of what happens to children whose mothers work. The authors, Miriam Yarrow, Phyllis Scott, Louise de Leeuw, and Christine Heinig, studied one hundred mothers of intact families and concluded that the fulfillment or frustration the mother feels from working are the crucial variables in child rearing.

50

MOTHERHOOD: WHO NEEDS IT?

Betty Rollin

Motherhood is in trouble, and it ought to be. A rude question is long overdue: Who needs it? The answer used to be (1) society and (2) women. But now, with the impending horrors of overpopulation, society desperately *doesn't* need it. And women don't need it either. Thanks to The Motherhood Myth—the idea that having babies is something that all normal women instinctively want and need and will enjoy doing—they just *think* they do.

The notion that the maternal wish and the activity of mothering are instinctive or biologically predestined is baloney. Try asking most sociologists, psychologists, psychoanalysts, biologists—many of whom are mothers—about motherhood being instinctive; it's like asking department-store presidents if their Santa Clauses are real. "Motherhood—instinctive?" shouts distinguished sociologist/author Dr. Jessie Bernard. "Biological destiny? Forget biology! If it were biology, people would die from not doing it."

"Women don't need to be mothers any more than they need spaghetti," says Dr. Richard Rabkin, a New York psychiatrist. "But if you're in a world where everyone is eating spaghetti, thinking they need it and want it, you will think so too. Romance has really contaminated science. So-called instincts have to do with stimulation. They are not things that well up inside of you."

"When a woman says with feeling that she craved her baby from within, she is putting into biological language what is psychological," says University of Michigan psychoanalyst and motherhood-researcher Dr. Frederick Wyatt. "There are no instincts," says Dr. William Goode, president-elect of the American Sociological Association. "There are reflexes, like eye-blinking, and drives, like sex. There is no innate drive for children. Otherwise, the enormous cultural pressures that there are to reproduce wouldn't exist. There are no cultural pressures to sell you on getting your hand out of the fire."

There are, to be sure, biologists and

others who go on about biological destiny, that is, the innate or instinctive goal of motherhood. (At the turn of the century, even good old capitalism was explained by a theorist as "the *instinct* of acquisitiveness.") And many psychoanalysts still hold the Freudian view that women feel so rotten about not having a penis that they are necessarily propelled into the child-wish to replace the missing organ. Psychoanalysts also make much of the psychological need to repeat what one's parent of the same sex has done. Since every woman has a mother, it is considered normal to wish to imitate one's mother by being a mother.

There is, surely, a wish to pass on love if one has received it, but to insist women must pass it on in the same way is like insisting that every man whose father is a gardener has to be a gardener. One dissenting psychoanalyst says, simply, "There is a wish to comply with one's biology, yes, but we needn't and sometimes we shouldn't." (Interestingly, the woman who has been the greatest contributor to child therapy and who has probably given more to children than anyone alive is Dr. Anna Freud, Freud's magnificent daughter, who is not a mother.)

Anyway, what an expert cast of hundreds is telling us is, simply, that biological *possibility* and desire are not the same as biological *need*. Women have childbearing equipment. To choose not to use the equipment is no more blocking what is instinctive than it is for a man who, muscles or no, chooses not to be a weight lifter.

So much for the wish. What about the "instinctive" *activity* of mothering? One animal study shows that when a young member of a species is put in a cage, say, with an older member of the same species, the latter will act in a protective, "maternal" way. But that goes for both males and females who have been "mothered" themselves. And studies indicate that a human baby will also respond to whoever is around playing mother—even if it's father. Margaret Mead and many others frequently point out that mothering can be a fine occupation; if you want it, for either sex. Another experiment with monkeys who were brought up without mothers found

them lacking in maternal behavior toward their own offspring. A similar study showed that monkeys brought up without other monkeys of the opposite sex had no interest in mating—all of which suggests that both mothering and mating behavior are learned, not instinctual. And, to turn the cart (or the baby carriage) around, baby ducks who lovingly follow their mothers seemed, in the mother's absence, to just as lovingly follow wooden ducks or even vacuum cleaners.

If motherhood isn't instinctive, when and why, then, was The Motherhood Myth born? Until recently, the entire question of maternal motivation was academic. Sex, like it or not, meant babies. Not that there haven't always been a lot of interesting contraceptive tries. But until the creation of the diaphragm in the 1880s, the birth of babies was largely unavoidable. And, generally speaking, nobody really seemed to mind. For one thing, people tend to be sort of good sports about what seems to be inevitable. For another, in the past, the population needed beefing up. Mortality rates were high, and agricultural cultures, particularly, have always needed children to help out. So because it "just happened" and because it was needed, motherhood was assumed to be innate.

Originally, it was the word of God that got the ball rolling with "Be fruitful and multiply," a practical suggestion, since the only people around then were Adam and Eve. But in no time, supermoralists like St. Augustine changed the tone of the message: "Intercourse, even with one's legitimate wife, is unlawful and wicked where the conception of the offspring is prevented," he, we assume, thundered. And the Roman Catholic position was thus cemented. So then and now, procreation took on a curious value among people who viewed (and view) the pleasures of sex as sinful. One could partake in the sinful pleasure, but feel vindicated by the ensuing birth. Motherhood cleaned up sex. Also, it cleaned up women, who have always been considered somewhat evil, because of Eve's transgression (". . . but the woman was deceived and became a transgressor. Yet woman will be saved through bearing children . . . ," I Timothy, 2:14–15), and somewhat dirty because of menstruation.

And so, based on need, inevitability, and pragmatic fantasy—the Myth *worked*, from society's point of view—the Myth grew like corn in Kansas. And society reinforced it with both laws and propaganda—laws that made woman a chattel, denied her education and personal mobility, and madonna propaganda that she was beautiful and wonderful doing it and it was all beautiful and wonderful to do. (One rarely sees a madonna washing dishes.)

In fact, the Myth persisted—breaking some kind of record for long-lasting fallacies—until something like yesterday. For as the truth about the Myth trickled in—as women's rights increased, as women gradually got the message that it was certainly possible for them to do most things that men did, that they live longer, that their brains were not tinier—then, finally, when the really big news rolled in, that they could *choose* whether or not to be mothers —what happened? The Motherhood Myth soared higher than ever. As Betty Friedan made oh-so-clear in *The Feminine Mystique,* the '40s and '50s produced a group of ladies who not only had babies as if they were going out of style (maybe they were) but, as never before, they turned motherhood into a cult. First, they wallowed in the aesthetics of it all—natural childbirth and nursing became maternal musts. Like heavy-bellied ostriches, they grounded their heads in the sands of motherhood, only coming up for air to say how utterly happy and fulfilled they were. But, as Mrs. Friedan says only too plainly, they weren't. The Myth galloped on, moreover, long after making babies had turned from practical asset to liability for both individual parents *and* society. With the average cost of a middle-class child figured conservatively at $30,000 (not including college), any parent knows that the only people who benefit economically from children are manufacturers of consumer goods. Hence all those gooey motherhood commercials. And the Myth gathered momentum long after sheer numbers, while not yet extinguishing us, have made us intensely uncomfortable. Almost all of our societal problems, from minor discomforts like traffic to major ones like hunger, the population people keep reminding us, have to do with there being too many people. And who suffers most? The kids who have been mindlessly brought into the world, that's who. They are the ones who have to cope with all of the difficult and dehumanizing conditions brought on by overpopulation. They are the ones who have to cope with the psychological nausea of feeling unneeded by society. That's not the only reason for drugs, but, surely, it's a leading contender.

Unfortunately, the population curbers are tripped up by a romantic, stubborn, ideological hurdle. How can birth-control programs really be effective as long as the concept of glorious motherhood remains unchanged? (Even poor old Planned Parenthood has to euphemize—why not Planned Unparenthood?) Particularly among the poor, motherhood is one of the few inherently positive institutions that are accessible. As Berkeley demographer Judith Blake points out, "Poverty-oriented birth control programs do not make sense as a welfare measure . . . as long as existing pronatalist policies . . . encourage mating, pregnancy, and the care, support, and rearing of children." Or, she might have added, as long as the less-than-idyllic child-rearing part of motherhood remains "in small print."

Sure, motherhood gets dumped on sometimes: Philip Wylie's Momism got going in the '40s and Philip Roth's *Portnoy's Complaint* did its best to turn rancid the chicken-soup concept of Jewish motherhood. But these are viewed as the sour cries of a black humorist here, a malcontent there. Everyone shudders, laughs, but it's like the mouse and the elephant joke. Still, the Myth persists. Last April, a Brooklyn woman was indicted on charges of manslaughter and negligent homicide—11 children died in a fire in a building she owned and criminally neglected—"But," sputtered her lawyer, "my client, Mrs. Breslow, is a mother, a grandmother, and a great-grandmother!"

Most remarkably, The Motherhood Myth

persists in the face of the most overwhelming maternal unhappiness and incompetence. If reproduction were merely superfluous and expensive, if the experience were as rich and rewarding as the cliché would have us believe, if it were a predominantly joyous trip for everyone riding —mother, father, child—then the going everybody-should-have-two-children plan would suffice. Certainly, there are a lot of joyous mothers, and their children and (sometimes, not necessarily) their husbands reflect their joy. But a lot of evidence suggests that for more women than anyone wants to admit, motherhood can be miserable. ("If it weren't," says one psychiatrist wryly, "the world wouldn't be in the mess it's in.")

There is a remarkable statistical finding from a recent study of Dr. Bernard's, comparing the mental illness and unhappiness of married mothers and single women. The latter group, it turned out, was both markedly less sick and overtly more happy. Of course, it's not easy to measure slippery attitudes like happiness. "Many women have achieved a kind of reconciliation—a conformity," says Dr. Bernard,

that they interpret as happiness. Since feminine happiness is supposed to lie in devoting one's life to one's husband and children, they do that; so ipso facto, they assume they are happy. And for many women, untrained for independence and "processed" for motherhood, they find their state far preferable to the alternatives, which don't really exist.

Also, unhappy mothers are often loath to admit it. For one thing, if in society's view not to be a mother is to be a freak, not to be a *blissful* mother is to be a witch. Besides, unlike a disappointing marriage, disappointing motherhood cannot be terminated by divorce. Of course, none of that stops such a woman from expressing her dissatisfaction in a variety of ways. Again, it is not only she who suffers but her husband and children as well. Enter the harridan housewife, the carping shrew. The realities of motherhood can turn women into terrible people. And, judging from the

50,000 cases of child abuse in the U.S. each year, some are worse than terrible.

In some cases, the unpleasing realities of motherhood begin even before the beginning. In *Her Infinite Variety*, Morton Hunt describes young married women pregnant for the first time as "very likely to be frightened and depressed, masking these feelings in order not to be considered contemptible. The arrival of pregnancy interrupts a pleasant dream of motherhood and awakens them to the realization that they have too little money, or not enough space, or unresolved marital problems. . . ."

The following are random quotes from interviews with some mothers in Ann Arbor, Mich., who described themselves as reasonably happy. They all had positive things to say about their children, although when asked about the best moment of their day, they *all* confessed it was when the children were in bed. Here is the rest:

Suddenly I had to devote myself to the child totally. I was under the illusion that the baby was going to fit into my life, and I found that I had to switch my life and my schedule to fit him. You think, "I'm in love, I'll get married, and we'll have a baby." First there's two, then three, it's simple and romantic. You don't even think about the work. . . .

You never get away from the responsibility. Even when you leave the children with a sitter, you are not out from under the pressure of the responsibility. . . .

I hate ironing their pants and doing their underwear, and they never put their clothes in the laundry basket. . . . As they get older, they make less demands on your time because they're in school, but the demands are greater in forming their values. . . . Best moment of the day is when all the children are in bed. . . . The worst time of day is 4 P.M., when you have to get dinner started, the kids are tired, hungry and crabby—everybody wants to talk to you about their day . . . your day is only half over.

Once a mother, the responsibility and concern for my children became so encom-

passing. . . . It took a great deal of will to keep up other parts of my personality. . . . To me, motherhood gets harder as they get older because you have less control. . . . In an abstract sense, I'd have several. . . . In the nonabstract, I would not have any. . . .

I had anticipated that the baby would sleep and eat, sleep and eat. Instead, the experience was overwhelming. I really had not thought particularly about what motherhood would mean in a realistic sense. I want to do other things, like to become involved in things that are worthwhile—I don't mean women's clubs—but I don't have the physical energy to go out in the evenings. I feel like I'm missing something . . . the experience of being somewhere with people and having them talking about something—something that's going on in the world.

Every grownup person expects to pay a price for his pleasures, but seldom is the price as vast as the one endured "however happily" by most mothers. We have mentioned the literal cost factor. But what does that mean? For middle-class American women, it means a life style with severe and usually unimagined limitations; i.e., life in the suburbs, because who can afford three bedrooms in the city? And what do suburbs mean? For women, suburbs means other women and children and leftover peanut-butter sandwiches and car pools and seldom-seen husbands. Even the Feminine Mystiqueniks—the housewives who finally admitted that their lives behind brooms (OK, electric brooms) were driving them crazy—were loath to trace their predicament to their children. But it is simply a fact that a childless married woman has no child-work and little housework. She can live in a city, or, if she still chooses the suburbs or the country, she can leave on the commuter train with her husband if she wants to. Even the most ardent job-seeking mother will find little in the way of great opportunities in Scarsdale. Besides, by the time she wakes up, she usually lacks both the preparation for the outside world and the self-confidence to get it. You will

say there are plenty of city-dwelling working mothers. But most of those women do additional-funds-for-the-family kind of work, not the interesting career kind that takes plugging during "childbearing years."

Nor is it a bed of petunias for the mother who does make it professionally. Says writer critic Marya Mannes:

If the creative woman has children, she must pay for this indulgence with a long burden of guilt, for her life will be split three ways between them and her husband and her work. . . . No woman with any heart can compose a paragraph when her child is in trouble. . . . The creative woman has no wife to protect her from intrusion. A man at his desk in a room with closed door is a man at work. A woman at a desk in any room is available.

Speaking of jobs, do remember that mothering, salary or not, is a job. Even those who can afford nurses to handle the nitty-gritty still need to put out emotionally. "Well-cared-for" neurotic rich kids are not exactly unknown in our society. One of the more absurd aspects of the Myth is the underlying assumption that, since most women are biologically equipped to bear children, they are psychologically, mentally, emotionally, and technically equipped (or interested) to rear them. Never mind happiness. To assume that such an exacting, consuming, and important task is something almost all women are equipped to do is far more dangerous and ridiculous than assuming that everyone with vocal chords should seek a career in opera.

A major expectation of the Myth is that children make a not-so-hot marriage hotter, or a hot marriage, hotter still. Yet almost every available study indicates that childless marriages are far happier. One of the biggest, of 850 couples, was conducted by Dr. Harold Feldman of Cornell University, who states his findings in no uncertain terms: "Those couples with children had a significantly lower level of marital satisfaction than did those without children." Some of the reasons are obvious. Even the most adorable children make for additional demands, complications, and hardships in the lives of even the most loving parents. If a woman feels disappointed and trapped in her mother role, it is bound to affect her marriage in any number of ways: she may take out her frustrations directly on her husband, or she may count on him too heavily for what she feels she is missing in her daily life.

". . . You begin to grow away from your husband," says one of the Michigan ladies. "He's working on his career and you're working on your family. But you both must gear your lives to the children. You do things the children enjoy, more than things you might enjoy." More subtle and possibly more serious is what motherhood may do to a woman's sexuality. Often when the stork flies in, sexuality flies out. Both in the emotional minds of some women *and* in the minds of their husbands, when a woman becomes a mother, she stops being a woman. It's not only that motherhood may destroy her physical attractiveness, but its madonna concept may destroy her *feelings* of sexuality.

And what of the payoff? Usually, even the most self-sacrificing maternal self-sacrificers expect a little something back. Gratified parents are not unknown to the Western world, but there are probably at least just as many who feel, to put it crudely, shortchanged. The experiment mentioned earlier—where the baby ducks followed vacuum cleaners instead of their mothers—indicates that what passes for love from baby to mother is merely a rudimentary kind of object attachment. Without necessarily feeling like a Hoover, a lot of women become disheartened because babies and children are not only not interesting to talk to (not everyone thrills at the wonders of da-da-ma-ma talk) but they are generally not empathetic, considerate people. Even the nicest children are not capable of empathy, surely a major ingredient of love, until they are much older. Sometimes they're never capable of it. Dr. Wyatt says that often, in later years particularly, when most of the "returns" are in, it is the "good mother" who suffers most of all. It is then she must face a reality: The child—the appendage with her genes—is not an appendage, but a separate person. What's

more, he or she may be a separate person who doesn't even like her—or whom she doesn't really like.

So if the music is lousy, how come everyone's dancing? Because the motherhood minuet is taught freely from birth, and whether or not she has rhythm or likes the music, every woman is expected to do it. Indeed, she *wants* to do it. Little girls start learning to want—and what to be—when they are still in their cribs. Dr. Miriam Keiffer, a young social psychologist at Bensalem, the Experimental College of Fordham University, points to studies showing that

at six months of age, mothers are already treating their baby girls and boys quite differently. For instance, mothers have been found to touch, comfort, and talk to their females more. If these differences can be found at such an early stage, it's not surprising that the end product is as different as it is. What is surprising is that men and women are, in so many ways, similar.

Some people point to the way little girls play with dolls as proof of their "innate motherliness." But remember, little girls are *given* dolls. When Margaret Mead presented some dolls to New Guinea children, it was the boys, not the girls, who wanted to play with them, which they did by crooning lullabies and rocking them in the most maternal fashion.

By the time they reach adolescence, most girls, unconsciously or not, have learned enough about role definition to qualify for a master's degree. In general, the lesson has been that no matter what kind of career thoughts one may entertain, one must, first and foremost, be a wife and mother. A girl's mother is usually her first teacher. As Dr. Goode says, "A woman is not only taught by society to have a child; she is taught to have a child who will have a child." A woman who has hung her life on The Motherhood Myth will almost always reinforce her young married daughter's early training by pushing for grandchildren. Prospective grandmothers are not the only ones. Husbands, too, can be effective sellers. After all, they have The Fatherhood Myth to cope with. A married man is *supposed to* have children. Often, particularly among Latins, children are a sign of potency. They help him assure the world—and himself—that he is the big man he is supposed to be. Plus, children give him both immortality (whatever that means) and possibly the chance to become "more" in his lifetime through the accomplishments of his children, particularly his son. (Sometimes it's important, however, for the son to do better, but not *too* much better.)

Friends, too, can be counted on as myth-pushers. Naturally one wants to do what one's friends do. One study, by the way, found a correlation between a woman's fertility and that of her three closest friends. The negative sell comes into play here, too. We have seen what the concept of non-mother means (cold, selfish, unwomanly, abnormal). In practice, particularly in the suburbs, it can mean, simply, exclusion—both from child-centered activities (that is, most activities) and child-centered conversations (that is, most conversations). It can also mean being the butt of a lot of unfunny jokes. ("Whaddya waiting for? An immaculate conception? Ha ha.") Worst of all, it can mean being an object of pity.

In case she's escaped all those pressures (that is, if she was brought up in a cave), a young married woman often wants a baby just so that she'll (1) have something to do (motherhood is better than clerk/typist, which is often the only kind of job she can get, since little more has been expected of her and, besides, her boss also expects her to leave and be a mother); (2) have something to hug and possess, to be needed by and have power over; and (3) have something to *be*—e.g., a baby's mother. Motherhood affords an instant identity. First, through wifehood, you are somebody's wife; then you are somebody's mother. Both give not only identity and activity, but status and stardom of a kind. During pregnancy, a woman can look forward to the kind of attention and pampering she may not ever have gotten or may never otherwise get. Some women consider birth the biggest accomplishment of their lives, which may be interpreted as saying not much for the rest of their lives. As Dr. Goode says, "It's like the gambler who may know the roulette wheel is crooked, but it's the only game in town." Also, with motherhood, the feeling of accomplishment is immediate. It is really much faster and easier to make a baby than paint a painting, or write a book, or get to the point of accomplishment in a job. It is also easier in a way to shift focus from self-development to child development—particularly since, for women, self-development is considered selfish. Even unwed mothers may achieve a feeling of this kind. (As we have seen, little thought is given to the aftermath.) And, again, since so many women are underdeveloped as people, they feel that, besides children, they have little else to give—to themselves, their husbands, to their world.

You may ask why then, when the realities do start pouring in, does a woman want to have a second, third, even fourth child? OK, (1) just because reality is pouring in doesn't mean she wants to *face* it. A new baby can help bring back some of the old illusions. Says psychoanalyst Dr. Natalie Shainess, "She may view each successive child as a knight in armor that will rescue her from being a 'bad unhappy mother.'" (2) Next on the horror list of having no children, is having one. It suffices to say that only children are not only OK, they even have a high rate of exceptionality. (3) Both parents usually want at least one child of each sex. The husband, for reasons discussed earlier, probably wants a son. (4) The more children one has, the more of an excuse one has not to develop in any other way.

What's the point? A world without children? Of course not. Nothing could be worse or more unlikely. No matter what anyone says in *Look* or anywhere else, motherhood isn't about to go out like a blown bulb, and who says it should? Only the Myth must go out, and now it seems to be dimming.

The younger-generation females who have been reared on the Myth have not rejected it totally, but at least they recognize it can be more loving to children not to have them. And at least they speak of adopting children instead of bearing them. Moreover, since the new nonbreeders are "less hung-up" on ownership, they seem to recognize that if you dig loving children, you don't necessarily have to own one. The end of The Motherhood Myth might make available more loving women (and men!) for those children who already exist.

When motherhood is no longer culturally compulsory, there will, certainly, be less of it. Women are now beginning to think and do more about development of self, of their individual resources. Far from being selfish, such development is probably our only hope. That means more alternatives for women. And more alternatives mean more selective, better, happier, motherhood—and childhood and husbandhood (or manhood) and peoplehood. It is not a question of whether or not children are sweet and marvelous to have and rear; the question is, even if that's so, whether or not one wants to pay the price for it. It doesn't make sense any more to pretend that women need babies, when what they really need is themselves. If God were still speaking to us in a voice we could hear, even He would probably say, "Be fruitful. Don't multiply."

51

HOW TO SUCCEED AT FAMILY PLANNING

Alan F. Guttmacher

Almost all young couples today take it quite for granted that they will plan their families. Thanks to the tremendous improvements in contraceptive methods, husbands and wives can now look forward to having the number of children they want, spaced according to their needs and wishes.

THE PILL

The major change in birth control methods, of course, has come about because of the development of oral contraceptives, which were first introduced to the public in 1960. Because the pill is virtually 100 percent effective in preventing pregnancy when used as directed, and because it is convenient, this method soon became very popular; by 1965 it was the most popular form of birth control among couples in the United States.

The pill works through a precise but roundabout neurochemical mechanism: it contains two hormones (an estrogen and a progestin) ordinarily produced by the ovary. These substances prevent the pituitary gland from obeying a message from the brain to secrete two other chemicals (gonadotrophic hormones) which in turn trigger monthly ovulation. As long as estrogen and progestin are present in sufficient amounts in the blood, ovulation is suppressed—in just the same way the body's chemistry prevents ovulation during pregnancy. So in this way the pill imitates nature.

In addition to preventing ovulation, the birth control pill keeps the mucus in the vagina scant and sticky and thus inhibits the passage of sperm to the uterus and the fallopian tubes (where conception normally takes place).

Birth control pills can be purchased only with a doctor's prescription and should be taken only under a doctor's direction. The standard procedure with most birth control pills is to take one tablet each day, beginning on the fifth day of the menstrual cycle counting the first day of menstruation as day one. One pill a day is then taken for the next twenty days. One to three days after that, menstrual-like bleeding will begin. Five days later, the woman begins to take the pill again, thus beginning a new cycle. This regimen is being simplified—by the woman initiating her pill-taking on the fifth day of any menstrual cycle, then taking the pill for three weeks, stopping for one week and then starting again for three weeks, regardless of when the bleeding started after she finished her three-week pill course. Since the pill prevents ovulation, the bleeding the woman experiences isn't true menstruation, but is what doctors call withdrawal bleeding, brought about by the cessation of the medication. Such a period is usually briefer, scantier, and freer of the discomfort that some women experience with true menses.

Actually, it is not medically necessary to cease taking the pill for several days each month. The pill is prescribed in this fashion to create a bleeding episode every twenty-seven or twenty-eight days, thus reassuring the woman that all is well. Should a woman occasionally wish to take the pill for twenty-seven days consecutively, thus postponing her period for a week, there is no harm in so doing.

A second form of pill, the sequential type, has also been developed. With this kind of oral contraceptive the woman takes a pill containing one hormone for the first fifteen or sixteen days of her menstrual cycle; during the next five days she takes another pill containing progestin and estrogen. The advantage claimed for this method is that undesirable side effects such as a tendency to gain weight, breast swelling, or nausea, sometimes reported by patients using the standard kind of pill, are lessened.

If pregnancy is desired, the woman simply stops taking the pill and fertility is usually promptly restored.

If a mother does not plan to nurse, she may start taking the pill as soon after delivery as she wishes. But since the hormones in the pill may inhibit milk production, if she does plan to nurse, she should not take the pill until the baby is several weeks old and her milk flow has been well established.

Although there is no substantiation for the belief that taking birth control pills will postpone the onset of menopause, a few gynecologists recommend that the pill be continued during and after menopause to help keep the reproductive organs in a youthful state, and thus generally retard some aspects of the aging process. Most gynecologists, however, believe that hormones such as those contained in birth control pills should be administered only in the presence of unpleasant menopausal symptoms. Pill use, according to this view, should continue only as long as fertility does.

What about side effects, such as breast tenderness, nausea, and weight gain? Side effects are experienced by some women during their early months on the pill. However, such symptoms occur less frequently than they did when oral contraceptives contained larger amounts of hormones than they now do. In any case, the side effects usually disappear after a few months. If a woman does have unpleasant symptoms, she should consult her doctor, who may switch her to another brand, prescribe medical treatment to relieve them, or in some cases suggest another method of birth control.

What about more serious complications? Are there real dangers in using oral contraceptives? As early as 1962 it was suggested that oral contraceptives might increase the likelihood of clot formation in blood vessels (thrombosis) and possible transference of clots through the bloodstream to some distant organ (embolism). The most common site for clot formation was said to be the veins of the pelvis and leg, and the most frequent organ to be involved by an embolus was said to be the lungs. This worrisome problem has been thoroughly investigated by three committees of eminent scientists, one in the United States, one in England, and one in Switzerland sponsored by The World Health Organization. These experts agreed independently that there was no scientific proof of any causal connection between taking the pill and thromboembolism. However, each group left the question open and asked for further study.

Since the three committees met, some important statistical studies which may cause reappraisal of the situation have been published in England. These studies suggest that although such clot conditions occur in women not on the pill, they are more common, though not strikingly so, in pill users. It has long been known that clot complications are slightly increased in frequency during pregnancy and after delivery, and perhaps the pill may have a similar effect. The English studies show a lower incidence of clot complications for women on the pill who are under 35 than those over that age.

I do not take this data too seriously; for one thing, the incidence of thromboembolism seems to have a strange geographic variation. Therefore we cannot apply the English findings exactly to the U.S.A. Our government is supporting similar investigations in this country but they will not be completed for a year or two. When these studies are completed, the situation will be clarified. Until then I am prepared to admit that the use of the pill in some women probably entails a slightly increased hazard of blood clot difficulties, perhaps greater in women who are over 35.

Can the birth control pills cause cancer? This is also not an easy question to answer categorically. The pill was introduced in 1960 and since then deaths from cancer of the cervix and uterus have declined appreciably in this country, 17 and 12 percent respectively. I am not intimating this is a result of widespread use of the pill. No doubt the decline is due to earlier diagnosis and improvement in treatment. However, it seems fair to conclude that the pill is not causing deaths from cancer of the cervix or uterus. The death rate from breast cancer has been stationary for the past decade. These data do not permanently

exonerate the pill because we do not know how long an agent such as a hormone has to act before it causes cancer—if it ever does.

Three new American studies have produced suggestive evidence that the use of the pill over a period of four or more years may increase the frequency of precancerous changes in the cervix or mouth of the womb. I want to emphasize the word precancerous. A woman who has a regular annual "pap" test—a simple procedure made by swabbing cells on a slide for microscopic study with a piece of cotton through a vaginal speculum—carries insurance against progression of such changes. A "pap" smear will pick up danger signals in plenty of time to enable a knowledgeable physician to eliminate the trouble. Therefore, even if further studies show some connection between the pill and increased frequency of precancerous, not cancerous, cervical changes, the "pill" woman being checked by an annual "pap" test faces no increased hazard.

To sum up, we can say that for most women the pill is safe to take for at least ten years. It may also be safe for longer periods, but we cannot yet be sure of this since no one has taken the pill for longer than ten years. As president of Planned Parenthood, I approve the use of oral contraceptives by more than a quarter million women. Were I seriously concerned about the safety of the pill, I would have suggested substituting some other form of birth control.

INTRAUTERINE DEVICES

Another excellent means of contraception is the intrauterine device, or I.U.D. Second only to the pill in reliability, this contraceptive device works mechanically; by its presence as a foreign body within the uterus, an I.U.D. acts to prevent conception.

Of the four types of devices which have been developed, the one which has yielded best overall clinical results is the Lippes loop. Made in four sizes, the loop is shaped like a double "S" with a nylon thread tied to its lower end. The protruding thread aids in determining that the device is in the proper position.

The insertion of an I.U.D. is performed by a physician, and in most cases it is a simple, rapid, and painless procedure. However, eight to ten percent of users have unpleasant symptoms—cramps, irregular staining or bleeding, or very profuse menses. In most cases these problems stop by themselves. Otherwise, removal of the I.U.D. works a prompt cure.

The device is least satisfactory for young women who have never borne a child. Insertion, for them, is more difficult, symptoms are more likely to occur, and spontaneous ejection is more common. In general, the older the woman and the more children she has borne, the better an I.U.D. works for her.

There are some interesting studies being carried on to determine how soon after delivery an I.U.D. can be inserted. They show that four out of five I.U.D.s inserted three or four days after a woman has given birth remain in position. When the couple wants another child the intrauterine device is removed and fertility is promptly restored.

Should a pregnancy occur with an I.U.D. in position, it is likely that the pregnancy will not continue. A 36 percent spontaneous abortion rate is reported in contrast to the usual rate of 10 or 11 percent. The 64 percent who continue pregnant have no unusual or excessive complications and the babies are totally unaffected. An I.U.D. is delivered with the afterbirth, adhering to the outer layer.

Infections are rare, and when they do occur they can be treated with antibiotics without removing the device. The uterus is perforated once in 2,000 to 2,500 insertions. This is painless and the patient is unaware of its occurrence.

What about serious complications? Can the I.U.D. cause cancer? Careful study has produced no evidence of either precancerous or cancerous alterations of cells. A check has been kept on thousands of patients for five years and no evidence of cancer has been found, but since five years is not a very long period, the final verdict cannot yet be known.

In brief, the I.U.D. is highly effective and very simple to use, requiring no action by the patient after its initial insertion. It is the least expensive of all effective birth control methods and though uncomfortable side effects are common, they usually clear up after a month or two.

DIAPHRAGM

Many women rely on the diaphragm to prevent conception. Made of soft rubber, in the shape of a shallow cup, the diaphragm works by fitting snugly over the cervix, thus blocking the entrance of sperm into the uterus. Diaphragms come in a variety of sizes and must be fitted to the woman by a doctor, who will also show her how to insert and remove it and instruct her in its use.

When engaged girls ask to be fitted before their wedding, the opening in the hymen frequently must be enlarged to permit the diaphragm to be used. It's advisable to have the size checked again a few months after the wedding, since the vagina may have been enlarged. Similarly, after childbirth, which stretches vaginal tissues, it's important to be refitted for the diaphragm.

To add to its effectiveness, the diaphragm is generally used with a contraceptive cream or jelly.

For women who use it properly and regularly, the diaphragm is a highly reliable method of birth control.

FOAMS, JELLIES, CREAMS

Designed to be used without a diaphragm, the foams are spermicidal creams and jellies which have been compressed into aerosol containers so that they can be released in a foaming state. Careful studies in the United States and Britain have shown the aerosol foams to be considerably more effective than nonfoaming creams and jellies used alone. The foams are also less expensive than the usual creams and jellies and are more acceptable to many women since their use results in less leakage after intercourse than the nonfoaming creams.

Also available without prescription are nonfoaming creams and jellies designed to be used alone. Though they are more powerful than the creams and jellies to be used with a diaphragm, most physicians believe them to be far less effective than foams or creams and jellies used with a diaphragm.

There are also vaginal tablets and suppositories which can be bought without a prescription and are safe to use. However, they offer less protection than creams and jellies used alone and far less protection than the aerosol foams.

CONDOM

The condom, worn by the man, prevents pregnancy simply by keeping the sperm from entering the vaginal canal.

Condoms are usually made of thin, strong latex and can be purchased without a prescription in drugstores and elsewhere. Although they provide a very high degree of protection against pregnancy (they almost never break if they're used properly), some couples find them unappealing and for this reason prefer other methods of birth control.

CERVICAL CAP

Another device designed to cover the entrance to the uterus, the cervical cap is made of metal or plastic and fits securely over the cervix.

Like the diaphragm, a cap must be fitted carefully by a physician. But self-insertion and placement are much more difficult than with a diaphragm. However, for those who can master the technique, this may be an ideal method of birth control because the cap can be worn for days or weeks at a time without being removed.

Available studies indicate that the effectiveness of the cap in preventing conception is very high—as high as the diaphragm or condom.

THE RHYTHM METHOD

This method requires avoiding intercourse during the period just before, during, and after a woman's ovulation each month—the only time when conception can take place. Unfortunately, as yet we have no certain way of knowing when a woman is about to ovulate. Normally, ovulation occurs shortly before the midpoint of a woman's monthly cycle—some time between the twelfth and the seventeenth day after menstruation begins.

However, very few women menstruate with clockwise regularity, and some women are so irregular that they cannot use this method at all. If the method is to be used, a woman should keep a record of her menstrual cycle for a full year, then determine the time of sexual abstinence according to the variations in her cycles. A doctor can show you how to set up a formula to do this. Women using this method should also know that body temperature rises about six-tenths of a degree when ovulation occurs and remains elevated until just before menstruation. A woman relying on the rhythm method should take her temperature each morning on awakening, before getting out of bed. When she notes that the temperature has remained up for three consecutive mornings, she can be relatively certain that ovulation has occurred.

There is hope that simple procedures will be developed to enable a woman to more accurately predict when ovulation will take place or to cause it to occur at a given time. At present, though the rhythm method is unreliable, it is more effective than no contraceptive method at all.

During this decade we have seen a revolution in birth control practices. All couples can now choose the method that pleases them and can look forward to having their children by choice, not by chance.

52

TRANSITION TO PARENTHOOD

Alice S. Rossi

THE PROBLEM

The central concern in this sociological analysis of parenthood will be with two closely related questions. (1) What is involved in the transition to parenthood: what must be learned and what readjustments of other role commitments must take place in order to move smoothly through the transition from a childless married state to parenthood? (2) What is the effect of parenthood on the adult: in what ways do parents, and in particular mothers, change as a result of their parental experiences?

To get a firmer conceptual handle on the problem, I shall first specify the stages in the development of the parental role and then explore several of the most salient features of the parental role by comparing it with the two other major adult social roles—the marital and work role. Throughout the discussion, special attention will be given to the social changes that have taken place during the past few decades which facilitate or complicate the transition to and the experience of parenthood among young American adults. . . .

What is unique about this perspective on parenthood is the focus on the adult parent rather than the child. Until quite recent years, concern in the behavioral sciences with the parent-child relationship has been confined almost exclusively to the child. Whether a psychological study such as Ferreira's on the influence of the pregnant woman's attitude to maternity upon postnatal behavior of the neonate,[1] Sears and Maccoby's survey of child-rearing practices,[2] or Brody's detailed observations of mothering,[3] the long tradition of studies of maternal deprivation[4] and more recently of maternal employment,[5] the child has been the center of attention. The design of such research has assumed that, if enough were known about what parents were like and what they in fact did in rearing their children, much of the variation among children could be accounted for.

The very different order of questions which emerge when the parent replaces the child as the primary focus of analytic attention can best be shown with an illustration. Let us take, as our example, the point Benedek makes that the child's need for mothering is *absolute* while the need of an adult woman to mother is *relative*.[6] From a concern for the child, this discrepancy in need leads to an analysis of the impact on the child of separation from the mother or inadequacy of mothering. Family systems that provide numerous adults to care for the young child can make up for this discrepancy in need between mother and child, which may be why ethnographic accounts give little evidence of postpartum depression following childbirth in simpler societies. Yet our family system of isolated households, increasingly distant from kinswomen to assist in mothering, requires that new mothers shoulder total responsibility for the infant precisely for that stage of the child's life when his need for mothering is far in excess of the mother's need for the child.

From the perspective of the mother, the question has therefore become: what does maternity deprive her of? Are the intrinsic gratifications of maternity sufficient to compensate for shelving or reducing a woman's involvement in nonfamily interests and social roles? The literature on maternal deprivation cannot answer such questions, because the concept, even in the careful specification Yarrow has given it,[7] has never meant anything but the effect on the child of various kinds of insufficient mothering. Yet what has been seen as a failure or inadequacy of individual women may in fact be a failure of the society to provide institutionalized substitutes for the extended kin to assist in the care of infants and young children. It may be that the role requirements of maternity in the American family system extract too high a price of deprivation for young adult women reared with highly diversified interests and social expectations concerning adult life. Here, as at several points in the course of this paper, familiar problems take on a new and suggestive research dimension when the focus is on the parent rather than the child. . . .

A discussion of the impact of parenthood upon the parent will be assisted by two analytic devices. One is to follow a comparative approach, by asking in what basic structural ways the parental role differs from other primary adult roles. The marital and occupational roles will be used for this comparison. A second device is to specify the phases in the development of a social role. If the total life span may be said to have a cycle, each stage with its unique tasks, then by analogy a role may be said to have a cycle and each stage in that role cycle to have its unique tasks and problems of adjustment. Four broad stages of a role cycle may be specified:

1. *Anticipatory Stage.* All major adult roles have a long history of anticipatory training for them, since parental and school socialization of children is dedicated precisely to this task of producing the kind of competent adult valued by the culture. For our present purposes, however, a narrower conception of the anticipatory stage is preferable: the engagement period in the case of the marital role, pregnancy in the case of the parental role, and the last stages of highly vocationally oriented schooling or on-the-job apprenticeship in the case of an occupational role.

2. *Honeymoon Stage.* This is the time period immediately following the full assumption of the adult role. The inception of this stage is more easily defined than its termination. In the case of the marital role, the honeymoon stage extends from the marriage ceremony itself through the literal honeymoon and on through an unspecified and individually varying period of time. Raush[8] has caught this stage of the marital role in his description of the "psychic honeymoon": that extended postmarital period when, through close intimacy and joint activity, the couple can explore each other's capacities and limitations. I shall arbitrarily consider the onset of pregnancy as marking the end of the honeymoon stage of the marital role. This stage of the parental role may involve an equivalent psychic honeymoon, that post-childbirth period during which, through intimacy and prolonged contact, an attachment between parent and child is laid down. There is a crucial difference, however, from the marital role in this stage. A woman knows her husband as a unique real person when she enters the honeymoon stage of marriage. A good deal of preparatory adjustment on a firm reality-base is possible during the engagement period which is not possible in the equivalent pregnancy period. Fantasy is not corrected by the reality of a specific individual child until the birth of the child. The "quickening" is psychologically of special significance to women precisely because it marks the first evidence of a real baby rather than a purely fantasized one. On this basis alone there is greater interpersonal adjustment and learning during the honeymoon stage of the parental role than of the marital role.

3. *Plateau Stage.* This is the protracted middle period of a role cycle during which the role is fully exercised. Depending on the specific problem under analysis, one would obviously subdivide this large plateau stage further. For my present purposes it is not necessary to do so, since my focus is on the earlier anticipatory and honeymoon stages of the parental role and the overall impact of parenthood on adults.

4. *Disengagement-Termination Stage.* This period immediately precedes and includes the actual termination of the role. Marriage ends with the death of the spouse or, just as definitively, with separation and divorce. A unique characteristic of parental role termination is the fact that it is not clearly marked by any specific act but is an attenuated process of termination with little cultural prescription about when the authority and obligations of a parent end. Many parents, however, experience the marriage of the child as a psychological termination of the active parental role.

UNIQUE FEATURES OF PARENTAL ROLE

With this role cycle suggestion as a broader framework, we can narrow our focus to what are the unique and most salient features of the parental role. In doing so, special attention will be given to two further questions: (1) the impact of social changes over the past few decades in facilitating or complicating the transition to and experience of parenthood and (2) the new interpretations or new research suggested by the focus on the parent rather than the child.

1. *Cultural Pressure to Assume the Role.* On the level of cultural values, men have no freedom of choice where work is concerned: They must work to secure their status as adult men. The equivalent for women has been maternity. There is considerable pressure upon the growing girl and young woman to consider maternity necessary for a woman's fulfillment as an individual and to secure her status as an adult.

This is not to say there are no fluctuations over time in the intensity of the cultural pressure to parenthood. During the depression years of the 1930's, there was more widespread awareness of the economic hardships parenthood can entail, and many demographic experts believe there was a great increase in illegal abortions during those years. Bird has discussed the dread with which a suspected pregnancy was viewed by many American women in the 1930's.[9] Quite a different set of pressures were at work during the 1950's, when the general societal tendency was toward withdrawal from active engagement with the issues of the larger society and a turning in to the gratifications of the private sphere of home and family life. Important in the background were the general affluence of the period and the expanded room and ease of child rearing that go with suburban living. For the past five years, there has been a drop in the birth rate in general, fourth and higher-order births in particular. During this same period there has been increased concern and debate about women's participation in politics and work, with more women now returning to work rather than conceiving the third or fourth child.[10]

2. *Inception of the Parental Role.* The decision to marry and the choice of a mate are voluntary acts of individuals in our family system. Engagements are therefore consciously considered, freely entered, and freely terminated if increased familiarity decreases, rather than increases, intimacy and commitment to the choice. The inception of a pregnancy, unlike the engagement, is not always a voluntary decision, for it may be the unintended consequence of a sexual act that was recreative in intent rather than procreative. Secondly, and again unlike the engagement, the termination of a pregnancy is not socially sanctioned, as shown by current resistance to abortion-law reform.

The implication of this difference is a much higher probability of unwanted pregnancies than of unwanted marriages in our family system. Coupled with the ample clinical evidence of parental rejection and sometimes cruelty to children, it is all the more surprising that there has not been more consistent research attention to the problem of *parental satisfaction,* as there has for long been on *marital satisfaction* or *work satisfaction.* Only the extreme iceberg tip of the parental satisfaction continuum is clearly demarcated and researched, as in the growing concern with "battered babies." Cultural and psychological resistance to the image of a nonnurturant woman may afflict social scientists as well as the American public.

The timing of a first pregnancy is critical to the manner in which parental responsibilities are joined to the marital relationship. The single most important change over the past few decades is extensive and efficient contraceptive usage, since this has meant for a growing proportion of new marriages, the possibility of and increasing preference for some postponement of childbearing after marriage. When pregnancy was likely to follow shortly after marriage, the major transition point in a woman's life was marriage itself. *This transition point is increasingly the first pregnancy rather than marriage.* It is accepted and increasingly expected that women will work after marriage, while household furnishings are acquired and spouses complete their advanced training or gain a foothold in their work.[11] This provides an early marriage period in which the fact of a wife's employment presses for a greater egalitarian relationship between husband and wife in decision-making, commonality of experience, and sharing of household responsibilities.

The balance between individual autonomy and couple mutuality that develops during the honeymoon stage of such a marriage may be important in establishing a pattern that will later affect the quality of the parent-child relationship and the extent of sex-role segregation of duties between the parents. It is only in the context of a growing egalitarian base to the marital relationship that one could find, as Gavron has,[12] a tendency for parents to establish some barriers between themselves and their children, a marital defense against the institution of parenthood as she describes it. This may eventually replace the typical coalition in more traditional families of mother and children against husband-father. Parenthood will continue for some time to impose a degree of temporary segregation of primary responsibilities between husband and wife, but, when this takes place in the context of a previously established egalitarian relationship between the husband and wife, such role segregation may become blurred, with greater recognition of the wife's need for autonomy and the husband's role in the routines of home and child rearing.[13]

There is one further significant social change that has important implications for the changed relationship between husband and wife: the increasing departure from an old pattern of role-inception phasing in which the young person first completed his schooling, then established himself in the world of work, then married and began his family. Marriage and parenthood are increasingly taking place *before* the schooling of the husband, and often of the wife, has been completed.[14] An important reason for this trend lies in the fact that, during the same decades in which the average age of physical-sexual maturation has dropped, the average amount of education which young people obtain has been on the increase. Particularly for the college and graduate or professional school population, family roles are often assumed before the degrees needed to enter careers have been obtained.

Just how long it now takes young people to complete their higher education has been investigated only recently in several longitudinal studies of college-graduate cohorts.[15] College is far less uniformly a four-year period than high school is. A full third of the college freshmen in one study had been out of high school a year or more before entering college.[16] In a large sample of college graduates in 1961, one in five were over 25 years of age at graduation.[17] Thus, financial difficulties, military service, change of career plans, and marriage itself all tend to create interruptions in the college attendance of a significant proportion of college graduates. At the graduate and professional school level, this is even more marked: the mean age of men receiving the doctorate, for example, is 32, and of women, 36.[18] It is the exception rather than the rule for men and women who seek graduate degrees to go directly from college to graduate school and remain there until they secure their degrees.[19]

The major implication of this change is that more men and women are achieving full adult status in family roles while they are still less than fully adult in status terms in the occupational system. Graduate students are, increasingly, men and women with full family responsibilities. Within the family many more husbands and fathers are still students, often quite dependent on the earnings of their wives to see them through their advanced training.[20] No matter what the couple's desires and preferences are, this fact alone presses for more egalitarian relations between husband and wife, just as the adult family status of graduate students presses for more egalitarian relations between students and faculty.

3. *Irrevocability.* If marriages do not work out, there is now widespread acceptance of divorce and remarriage as a solution. The same point applies to the work world: we are free to leave an unsatisfac-

tory job and seek another. But once a pregnancy occurs, there is little possibility of undoing the commitment to parenthood implicit in conception except in the rare instance of placing children for adoption. We can have ex-spouses and ex-jobs but not ex-children. This being so, it is scarcely surprising to find marked differences between the relationship of a parent and one child and the relationship of the same parent with another child. If the culture does not permit pregnancy termination, the equivalent to giving up a child is psychological withdrawal on the part of the parent.

This taps an important area in which a focus on the parent rather than the child may contribute a new interpretive dimension to an old problem: the long history of interest, in the social sciences, in differences among children associated with their sex-birth-order position in their sibling set. Research has largely been based on data gathered about and/or from the children, and interpretations make inferences back to the "probable" quality of the child's relation to a parent and how a parent might differ in relating to a first-born compared to a last-born child. The relevant research, directed at the parents (mothers in particular), remains to be done, but at least a few examples can be suggested of the different order of interpretation that flows from a focus on the parent.

Some birth-order research stresses the influence of sibs upon other sibs, as in Koch's finding that second-born boys with an older sister are more feminine than second-born boys with an older brother.[21] A similar sib-influence interpretation is offered in the major common finding of birth-order correlates, that sociability is greater among last-borns[22] and achievement among first-borns.[23] It has been suggested that last-borns use social skills to increase acceptance by their older sibs or are more peer-oriented because they receive less adult stimulation from parents. The tendency of first-borns to greater achievement has been interpreted in a corollary way, as a reflection of early assumption of responsibility for younger sibs, greater adult stimulation during the time the oldest was the only child

in the family,[24] and the greater significance of the first-born for the larger kinship network of the family.[25]

Sociologists have shown increasing interest in structural family variables in recent years, a primary variable being family size. . . . To find that children in small families differ from children in large families is not simply due to the impact of group size upon individual members but to the very different involvement of the parent with the children and to relations between the parents themselves in small versus large families.

An important clue to a new interpretation can be gained by examining family size from the perspective of parental motivation toward having children. A small family is small for one of two primary reasons: either the parents wanted a small family and achieved their desired size, or they wanted a large family but were not able to attain it. In either case, there is a low probability of unwanted children. Indeed, in the latter eventuality they may take particularly great interest in the children they do have. Small families are therefore most likely to contain parents with a strong and positive orientation to each of the children they have. A large family, by contrast, is large either because the parents achieved the size they desired or because they have more children than they in fact wanted. Large families therefore have a higher probability than small families of including unwanted and unloved children. Consistent with this are Nye's finding that adolescents in small families have better relations with their parents than those in large families[26] and Sears and Maccoby's finding that mothers of large families are more restrictive toward their children than mothers of small families.[27]

This also means that last-born children are more likely to be unwanted than first- or middle-born children, particularly in large families. This is consistent with what is known of abortion patterns among married women, who typically resort to abortion only when they have achieved the number of children they want or feel they can afford to have. Only a small proportion of women faced with such unwanted pregnancies actually resort to abortion. *This suggests the possibility that the last-born child's reliance on social skills may be his device for securing the attention and loving involvement of a parent less positively predisposed to him than to his older siblings.*

In developing this interpretation, rather extreme cases have been stressed. Closer to the normal range, of families in which even the last-born child was desired and planned for, there is still another element which may contribute to the greater sociability of the last-born child. Most parents are themselves aware of the greater ease with which they face the care of a third fragile newborn than the first; clearly, parental skills and confidence are greater with last-born children than with first-born children. But this does not mean that the attitude of the parent is more positive toward the care of the third child than the first. There is no necessary correlation between skills in an area and enjoyment of that area. Searls[28] found that older homemakers are *more* skillful in domestic tasks but experience *less* enjoyment of them than younger homemakers, pointing to a declining euphoria for a particular role with the passage of time. In the same way, older people rate their marriages as "very happy" less often than younger people do.[29] It is perhaps culturally and psychologically more difficult to face the possibility that women may find less enjoyment of the maternal role with the passage of time, though women themselves know the difference between the romantic expectation concerning child care and the incorporation of the first baby into the household and the more realistic expectation and sharper assessment of their own abilities to do an adequate job of mothering as they face a third confinement. Last-born children may experience not only less verbal stimulation from their parents than first-born children but also less prompt and enthusiastic response to their demands —from feeding and diaper-change as infants to requests for stories read at three or a college education at eighteen—simply because the parents experience less intense gratification from the parent role with the third child than they did with the first.

The child's response to this might well be to cultivate winning, pleasing manners in early childhood that blossom as charm and sociability in later life, showing both a greater need to be loved and greater pressure to seek approval.

One last point may be appropriately developed at this juncture. Mention was made earlier that for many women the personal outcome of experience in the parent role is not a higher level of maturation but the negative outcome of a depressed sense of self-worth, if not actual personality deterioration. There is considerable evidence that this is more prevalent than we recognize. On a qualitative level, a close reading of the portrait of the working-class wife in Rainwater,[30] Newsom,[31] Komarovsky,[32] Gavron,[33] or Zweig[34] gives little suggestion that maternity has provided these women with opportunities for personal growth and development. So too, Cohen[35] notes with some surprise that in her sample of middle-class educated couples, as in Pavenstadt's study of lower-income women in Boston, there were more emotional difficulty and lower levels of maturation among multiparous women than primiparous women. On a more extensive sample basis, in Gurin's survey of Americans viewing their mental health,[36] as in Bradburn's reports on happiness,[37] single men are less happy and less active than single women, but among the married respondents the women are unhappier, have more problems, feel inadequate as parents, have a more negative and passive outlook on life, and show a more negative self-image. All of these characteristics increase with age among married women but show no relationship to age among men. While it may be true, as Gurin argues, that women are more introspective and hence more attuned to the psychological facets of experience than men are, this point does not account for the fact that the things which the women report are all on the negative side; few are on the positive side, indicative of euphoric sensitivity and pleasure. The possibility must be faced, and at some point researched, that women lose ground in personal development and self-esteem during the early and middle years of adulthood, whereas men gain ground in these respects during the same years. The retention of a high level of self-esteem may depend upon the adequacy of earlier preparation for major adult roles: men's training adequately prepares them for their primary adult roles in the occupational system, as it does for those women who opt to participate significantly in the work world. Training in the qualities and skills needed for family roles in contemporary society may be inadequate for both sexes, but the lowering of self-esteem occurs only among women because their primary adult roles are within the family system.

4. *Preparation for Parenthood.* Four factors may be given special attention on the question of what preparation American couples bring to parenthood.

a) *Paucity of preparation.* Our educational system is dedicated to the cognitive development of the young, and our primary teaching approach is the pragmatic one of learning by doing. How much one knows and how well he can apply what he knows are the standards by which the child is judged in school, as the employee is judged at work. The child can learn by doing in such subjects as science, mathematics, art work, or shop, but not in the subjects most relevant to successful family life: sex, home maintenance, child care, interpersonal competence, and empathy. If the home is deficient in training in these areas, the child is left with no preparation for a major segment of his adult life. A doctor facing his first patient in private practice has treated numerous patients under close supervision during his internship, but probably a majority of American mothers approach maternity with no previous child-care experience beyond sporadic baby-sitting, perhaps a course in child psychology, or occasional care of younger siblings.

b) *Limited learning during pregnancy.* A second important point makes adjustment to parenthood potentially more stressful than marital adjustment. This is the lack of any realistic training for parenthood during the anticipatory stage of pregnancy. By contrast, during the engagement period preceding marriage, an individual has opportunities to develop the skills and make the adjustments which ease the transition

to marriage. Through discussions of values and life goals, through sexual experimentation, shared social experiences as an engaged couple with friends and relatives, and planning and furnishing an apartment, the engaged couple can make considerable progress in developing mutuality in advance of the marriage itself.[38] No such headstart is possible in the case of pregnancy. What preparation exists is confined to reading, consultation with friends and parents, discussions between husband and wife, and a minor nesting phase in which a place and the equipment for a baby are prepared in the household.[39]

c) *Abruptness of transition.* Thirdly, the birth of a child is not followed by any gradual taking on of responsibility, as in the case of a professional work role. It is as if the woman shifted from a graduate student to a full professor with little intervening apprenticeship experience of slowly increasing responsibility. The new mother starts out immediately on 24-hour duty, with responsibility for a fragile and mysterious infant totally dependent on her care.

If marital adjustment is more difficult for very young brides than more mature ones,[40] adjustment to motherhood may be even more difficult. A woman can adapt a passive dependence on a husband and still have a successful marriage, but a young mother with strong dependency needs is in for difficulty in maternal adjustment, because the role precludes such dependency. This situation was well described in Cohen's study[41] in a case of a young wife with a background of co-ed popularity and a passive dependent relationship to her admired and admiring husband, who collapsed into restricted incapacity when faced with the responsibilities of maintaining a home and caring for a child.

d) *Lack of guidelines to successful parenthood.* If the central task of parenthood is the rearing of children to become the kind of competent adults valued by the society, then an important question facing any parent is what he or she specifically can do to create such a competent adult. This is where the parent is left with few or no guidelines from the expert. Parents can readily inform themselves concerning the young infant's nutritional, clothing, and medical needs and follow the general prescription that a child needs loving physical contact and emotional support. Such advice may be sufficient to produce a healthy, happy, and well-adjusted preschooler, but adult competency is quite another matter.

In fact, the adults who do "succeed" in American society show a complex of characteristics as children that current experts in child-care would evaluate as "poor" to "bad." Biographies of leading authors and artists, as well as the more rigorous research inquiries of creativity among architects[42] or scientists,[43] do not portray childhoods with characteristics currently endorsed by mental health and child-care authorities. Indeed, there is often a predominance of tension in childhood family relations and traumatic loss rather than loving parental support, intense channeling of energy in one area of interest rather than an all-round profile of diverse interests, and social withdrawal and preference for loner activities rather than gregarious sociability. Thus, the stress in current child-rearing advice on a high level of loving support but a low level of discipline or restriction on the behavior of the child—the "developmental" family type as Duvall calls it[44]—is a profile consistent with the focus on mental health, sociability, and adjustment. Yet the combination of both high support and high authority on the part of parents is most strongly related to the child's sense of responsibility, leadership quality, and achievement level, as found in Bronfenbrenner's studies[45] and that of Mussen and Distler.[46]

Brim points out[47] that we are a long way from being able to say just what parent role prescriptions have what effect on the adult characteristics of the child. We know even less about how such parental prescriptions should be changed to adapt to changed conceptions of competency in adulthood. In such an ambiguous context, the great interest parents take in school reports on their children or the pediatrician's assessment of the child's developmental progress should be seen as among the few indices parents have of how well *they* are doing as parents.

NOTES

[1] Antonio J. Ferreira, "The Pregnant Woman's Emotional Attitude and Its Reflection on the Newborn," *American Journal of Orthopsychiatry*, 30 (1960): 553–561.

[2] Robert Sears, E. Maccoby, and H. Levin, *Patterns of Child-Rearing*, Evanston, Illinois: Row, Peterson, 1957.

[3] Sylvia Brody, *Patterns of Mothering: Maternal Influences During Infancy*, New York: International Universities Press, 1956.

[4] Leon J. Yarrow, "Maternal Deprivation: Toward an Empirical and Conceptual Reevaluation," *Psychological Bulletin*, 58:6 (1961): 459–490.

[5] F. Ivan Nye and L. W. Hoffman, *The Employed Mother in America*, Chicago: Rand McNally, 1963; Alice S. Rossi, "Equality Between the Sexes: An Immodest Proposal," *Daedalus*, 93:2 (1964): 607–652.

[6] Therese Benedek, "Parenthood as a Developmental Phase," *Journal of American Psychoanalytic Association*, 7:8 (1959): 389–417.

[7] Yarrow, op. cit.

[8] Harold L. Raush, W. Goodrich, and J. D. Campbell, "Adaptation to the First Years of Marriage," *Psychiatry*, 26:4 (1963): 368–380.

[9] Caroline Bird, *The Invisible Scar*, New York: David McKay Company, 1966.

[10] When it is realized that a mean family size of 3.5 would double the population in 40 years, while a mean of 2.5 would yield a stable population in the same period, the social importance of withholding praise for procreative prowess is clear. At the same time, a drop in the birth rate may reduce the number of unwanted babies born, for such a drop would mean more efficient contraceptive usage and a closer correspondence between desired and attained family size.

11 James A. Davis, *Stipends and Spouses: The Finances of American Arts and Sciences Graduate Students*, Chicago: University of Chicago Press, 1962.

12 Hannah Gavron, *The Captive Wife*, London: Routledge & Kegan Paul, 1966.

13 The recent increase in natural childbirth, prenatal courses for expectant fathers, and greater participation of men during childbirth and postnatal care of the infant may therefore be a *consequence* of greater sharing between husband and wife when both work and jointly maintain their new households during the early months of marriage. Indeed, natural childbirth builds directly on this shifted base to the marital relationship. Goshen-Gottstein has found in an Israeli sample that women with a "traditional" orientation to marriage far exceed women with a "modern" orientation to marriage in menstrual difficulty, dislike of sexual intercourse, and pregnancy disorders and complaints such as vomiting. She argues that traditional women demand and expect little from their husbands and become demanding and narcissistic by means of their children, as shown in pregnancy by an over-exaggeration of symptoms and attention-seeking. Esther R. Goshen-Gottstein, *Marriage and First Pregnancy: Cultural Influences on Attitudes of Israeli Women*, London: Tavistock Publications, 1966. A prolonged psychic honeymoon uncomplicated by an early pregnancy, and with the new acceptance of married women's employment, may help to cement the egalitarian relationship in the marriage and reduce both the tendency to pregnancy difficulties and the need for a narcissistic focus on the children. Such a background is fruitful ground for sympathy toward and acceptance of the natural childbirth ideology.

14 James A. Davis, *Stipends and Spouses: The Finances of American Arts and Sciences Graduate Students*, op. cit.; James A. Davis, *Great Aspirations*, Chicago: Aldine Publishing Company, 1964; Eli Ginsberg, *Life Styles of Educated Women*, New York: Columbia University Press, 1966; Ginsberg, *Educated American Women: Self Portraits*, New York: Columbia University Press, 1967; National Science Foundation, *Two Years After the College Degree —Work and Further Study Patterns*, Washington, D.C.: Government Printing Office, NSF 63–26, 1963.

15 Davis, *Great Aspirations*, op. cit.; Laure Sharp, "Graduate Study and Its Relation to Careers: The Experience of a Recent Cohort of College Graduates," *Journal of Human Resources*, 1:2 (1966): 41–58.

16 James D. Cowhig and C. Nam, "Educational Status, College Plans and Occupational Status of Farm and Nonfarm Youths," U.S. Bureau of the Census Series ERS (P-27). No. 30, 1961.

17 Davis, *Great Aspirations*, op. cit.

18 Lindsey R. Harmon, *Profiles of Ph.D.'s in the Sciences: Summary Report on Follow-up of Doctorate Cohorts, 1935–1960*, Washington, D.C.: National Research Council, Publication 1293, 1965.

19 Sharp, op. cit.

20 Davis, *Stipends and Spouses, The Finances of American Arts and Sciences Graduate Students*, op. cit.

21 Orville G. Brim, "Family Structure and Sex-Role Learning by Children," *Sociometry*, 21 (1958): 1–16; H. L. Koch, "Sissiness and Tomboyishness in Relation to Sibling Characteristics," *Journal of Genetic Psychology*, 88 (1956): 231–244.

22 Charles MacArthur, "Personalities of First and Second Children," *Psychiatry*, 19 (1956): 47–54; S. Schachter, "Birth Order and Sociometric Choice," *Journal of Abnormal and Social Psychology*, 68 (1964): 453–456.

23 Irving Harris, *The Promised Seed*, New York: The Free Press, a division of the Macmillan Co., 1964; Bernard Rosen, "Family Structure and Achievement Motivation," *American Sociological Review*, 26 (1961): 574–585; Alice S. Rossi, "Naming Children in Middle-Class Families," *American Sociological Review*, 30:4 (1965): 499–513; Stanley Schachter, "Birth Order, Eminence and Higher Education," *American Sociological Review*, 28 (1963): 757–768.

24 Harris, op. cit.

25 Rossi, "Naming Children in Middle-Class Families," op. cit.

26 Ivan Nye, "Adolescent-Parent Adjustment: Age, Sex, Sibling, Number, Broken Homes, and Employed Mothers as Variables," *Marriage and Family Living*, 14 (1952): 327–332.

27 Sears et al., op. cit.

28 Laura G. Searls, "Leisure Role Emphasis of College Graduate Homemakers," *Journal of Marriage and the Family*, 28:1 (1966): 77–82.

[29] Norman Bradburn and D. Caplovitz, *Reports on Happiness,* Chicago: Aldine Publishing, 1965.

[30] Lee Rainwater, R. Coleman, and G. Handel, *Workingman's Wife,* New York: Oceana Publications, 1959.

[31] John Newsom and E. Newsom, *Infant Care in an Urban Community,* New York: International Universities Press, 1963.

[32] Mirra Komarovsky, *Blue Collar Marriage,* New York: Random House, 1962.

[33] Gavron, op. cit.

[34] Ferdinand Zweig, *Woman's Life and Labor,* London: Camelot Press, 1952.

[35] Mabel Blake Cohen, "Personal Identity and Sexual Identity," *Psychiatry,* 29:1 (1966): 1–14.

[36] Gerald Gurin, J. Veroff, and S. Feld, *Americans View Their Mental Health,* New York: Basic Books, Monograph Series No. 4, Joint Commission on Mental Illness and Health, 1960.

[37] Bradburn and Caplovitz, op. cit.

[38] Rhona Rapoport, "The Transition from Engagement to Marriage," *Acta Sociologica,* 8:1–2 (1964): 36–65; Raush et al., op. cit.

[39] During the period when marriage was the critical transition in the adult woman's life rather than pregnancy, a good deal of anticipatory "nesting" behavior took place from the time of conception. Now more women work through a considerable portion of the first pregnancy, and such nesting behavior as exists may be confined to a few shopping expeditions or baby showers, thus adding to the abruptness of the transition and the difficulty of adjustment following the birth of a first child.

[40] Lee B. Burchinal, "Adolescent Role Deprivation and High School Marriage," *Marriage and Family Living,* 21 (1959); 378–384; Floyd M. Martinson, "Ego Deficiency as a Factor in Marriage," *American Sociological Review,* 22 (1955): 161–164; J. Joel Moss and Ruby Gingles, "The Relationship of Personality to the Incidence of Early Marriage," *Marriage and Family Living,* 21 (1959): 373–377.

[41] Cohen, op. cit.

[42] Donald W. MacKinnon, "Ceativity and Images of the Self," in *The Study of Lives,* ed. by Robert W. White, New York: Atherton Press, 1963.

[43] Anne Roe, *A Psychological Study of Eminent Biologists, Psychological Monographs,* 65:14 (1951): 68 pages; Anne Roe, "A Psychological Study of Physical Scientists," *Genetic Psychology Monographs,* 43 (1951): 121–239; Anne Roe, "Crucial Life Experiences in the Development of Scientists," in *Talent and Education,* ed. by E. P. Torrance, Minneapolis: University of Minnesota Press, 1960.

[44] Evelyn M. Duvall, "Conceptions of Parenthood," *American Journal of Sociology,* 52 (1946): 193–203.

[45] Urie Bronfenbrenner, "Some Familial Antecedents of Responsibility and Leadership in Adolescents," in *Studies in Leadership,* ed. by L. Petrullo and B. Bass, New York: Holt, Rinehart, and Winston, 1960.

[46] Paul Mussen and L. Distler, "Masculinity, Identification and Father-Son Relationships," *Journal of Abnormal and Social Psychology,* 59 (1959): 350–356.

[47] Orville G. Brim, "The Parent-Child Relation as a Social System: I. Parent and Child Roles," *Child Development,* 28:3 (1957): 343–364.

53

CHILDREN IN THE FAMILY: RELATIONSHIP OF NUMBER AND SPACING TO MARITAL SUCCESS

Harold T. Christensen

This paper is to stress quantitative aspects of parenthood in contrast to the qualitative —though with the realization that the two are interrelated, and with a deliberate attempt to demonstrate how such quantitative patterns as number and spacing of children in the family affect certain qualitative conditions, particularly the stability of the marital relationship. . . .

Demographers and sociologists have long been concerned with questions of fertility measurement and family size. Their pursuit of these concerns has resulted in a descriptive picture something like this: a long-range decline in birthrates, spurred by an expanding cost of childbearing and an increasing knowledge and acceptance of contraception; the existence of wide differentials in fertility, with the higher rates being in the less developed countries and in the lower social strata of a given society; and a pattern within contemporary United States of approximately three children per married woman.

Much more research has taken place on number of births than on the various spacing patterns which separate these events from marriage and from each other. Yet, in recent years there has been an upswing of interest in this latter, and today it is generally recognized that the childbearing phenomenon cannot be completely viewed without the timing (as well as the number) of births being taken into account. The overall child-spacing picture for the United States is about as follows: first birth coming approximately one and one-half years after the wedding; subsequent births coming after intervals that grow progressively longer with each birth; and the existence of a negative correlation between average interval separating births and total number of births. This last-mentioned fact demon-strates how number and spacing are inter-related, which can make possible the prediction of eventual family size once the early spacing intervals are known.

Our present task is more than just picturing these number and spacing patterns within the phenomenon of parenthood. Any science worthy of its name tries to go beyond mere description; it seeks to discover relationships and to generalize as to possible cause and effect sequences. How, then, do number and spacing of children *affect* other things and how they are affected *by* other conditions and events? Number and spacing patterns can be studied as either independent or dependent variables, as either *acting* agents or conditions being *acted upon*.

The theme of the 1967 Groves Conference pretty well dictates the direction that the remainder of this paper is to take: "The Effect of Parenthood Upon Marriage." Thus, we are to treat number and spacing of children as *independent* variables and to study their effects upon marriage, considered as the dependent variable. In other words, we will not be attempting to see what causes parents to space their children or to limit their families as they do, but rather how the number of spacing patterns they end up with cause and effect something else; and the "something else" in this case is the marriage. Furthermore, it would be possible to discuss the effects of number and spacing upon the child's personality or upon something relevant to society at large, such as economic level of living or the prospects of war and peace. But, though each of these alternative designs is extremely important, in its own right, neither fits the structuring of the conference.

Finally, the titling of the particular session of the conference within which this paper was read adds an additional delimiting factor: "Children, Who Needs Them?" The implication of this question is that some parents want or need children more than do others and, most importantly, that the values parents place on children determine to some extent how these children affect the parents. Elsewhere we have labeled this intervention of values into the picture "The Principle of Value Relevance" —meaning that the values people hold are relevant to their behavior and to the consequences of this behavior. Applied to the problem at hand, it means that sheer number and spacing patterns within the family are less determining of marital success than are the degrees of convergence between actual and desired patterns. Values are an important part of the equation; they are intervening variables and, as such, must be taken into account. At least this is the hypothesis. Now let us examine the evidence. . . .

In many societies—particularly those of the historical past and of the non-Western world today—blood bonds are stronger than marital bonds, and hence the parent-child relationship is considered more important than the husband-wife relationship. Not so in the contemporary Western family system, however, and particularly "not so" within the United States today. Here, the consanguine or extended family, which cuts across several generations, has given ground to the nuclear family of husband, wife, and immediate children; kinship ties have been greatly weakened, and children have come to be regarded almost as an appendage to, rather than the reason for, the marriage. In other times and places, asking how parenthood affects the marriage would likely be considered inappropriate. Here and now the question is quite relevant.

It is popularly assumed that children and marital happiness go together and are causally related. This notion is part of our folklore, and at first glance it seems to be given support by the fact that over half of all divorces involve childless couples, suggesting that children hold a marriage together. But these statistics are deceptive, since most divorces occur in the early years

of marriage before many couples would normally start their childbearing and, furthermore, since the association of divorce with childlessness does not prove that these are causally related, only, perhaps, that they are "concomitant results of more fundamental factors in the marital relationship."[1] At any rate, the widely held belief that children serve to bring husband and wife closer together needs to be carefully reexamined. Perhaps they do in some cases, while in other instances children may be destructive to the marital relationship. And, if this latter is *ever* the case, we need to know what it is that makes the difference.

There can be little question but that parenthood in some ways affects the quality of marital interaction. Both LeMasters[2] and Dyer[3] have demonstrated that the birth of the first child constitutes a crisis for parents: by turning the twosome into a threesome and by adding extra chores, especially demanding of the mother, which reduce the time and energy that husband and wife have for each other. Before the advent of parenthood there is only one relationship, husband and wife. With the first child the number is increased to four: husband and wife, father and child, mother and child, and the interacting triad composed of all three. Furthermore, with each additional child, relationship combinations within the family increase in this same exponential fashion, making for greater and greater complexity and fundamentally changing the interactional pattern of the original married pair.

Though the ways in which family size may affect marital interaction need to be further researched, some generalizations can be at least tentatively identified. As number of children to the couple increases, husband and wife experience more interference with their sexual relationship; find less time for shared activities; and move toward greater role specialization, often including a shift in power from an equalitarian toward an authoritarian, or even patriarchal, base. If this latter is true, that is, that the husband's influence goes up with size of family, as some research suggests, this may be because the mother of many children has less bargaining power, since, because of her children, she is in greater need of a husband and in a poorer position to remarry or to find work.[4]

There have been more than a dozen studies testing the possibility of a relationship between family size and marital adjustment—with contradictory results. Several of these studies have reported no relationship, some a relationship in the positive direction, others a relationship in the negative direction, and still others have ended up with irregular and/or ambiguous generalization.[5] Why is there such a confused picture, since, in most cases, the scholars are reputable? Undoubtedly part of the explanation lies in the variety of samples used and the differing research designs employed. But surely if there is a general relationship between these variables it would have shown up more consistently, even granting divergent samples and designs. Perhaps the key to our question is to be found in the conclusion of Lewis M. Terman: he reported, for his sample, no correlation between presence of children and happiness in marriage, but suggested that this may be because opposing influences tend to balance each other out in a large sample and that the presence of children may actually affect any given marriage either way.[6]

After reviewing the literature and noting the contradictory results, Udry said, "there is no reliable relationship between presence or absence of children and marital adjustment"[7]; and Burgess and Wallin concluded:

The research evidence presented in this chapter establishes with considerable if not complete conclusiveness that the fact of having or not having children is not associated with marital success. What is associated with marital success is the attitude of husbands and wives toward having children. Persons with higher marital success scores tend to have a stronger desire for children, whether they have them or not, than those with lower marital success scores.[8]

Yet both of these sets of writers elsewhere recognized that disproportionately low marital adjustment goes along with having children that are not wanted.[9] Evidently the decisive factor is not number of children, in and of itself, but the extent to which children are desired.

Nevertheless, it is our contention that desires (or values) can be most productive of understanding on this problem if they are treated as an intervening variable, rather than as a separate independent variable. To say that couples who desire children tend to be better adjusted than those who do not is one thing; it supports the reasonable assumption that family-mindedness contributes to marital harmony. But what of the connection between desires and practice, and of the effect of *this combination* (balance of desires with practice) upon marital success? We would hypothesize that if the parental values of husband and wife were adequately taken into account and treated as intervening variables against which the relationships between family size and marital adjustment were studied, the research results of the various studies would be more consistent and the relationship sought would show up more clearly. Continuing research is likely to reveal that it is not either values (desires for children) or behavior (children actually born) considered alone that are the crucial variables affecting the marriage, but rather the "value-behavior discrepancy"[10] (or lack of it) which leaves married couples in varying states of harmony or dissonance.

Support for this view was offered in an article by Christensen and Philbrick published more than a decade ago.[11] From an interview study of married college students, it was demonstrated that, for the sample involved, a positive relationship existed between *desired* number of children and marital adjustment score, while a negative relationship (up to two children and for wives, especially) existed between *actual* number of children and marital adjustment score. This apparent contradiction is to be explained by the fact that, though family mindedness (desire for children) is normally associated with marital adjustment, when the desired children come before the couple is ready for them (because of the pressures of school in this case), values are violated and marital maladjustment results. Reinforcement of this interpretation was provided by several additional findings: disproportionately low marital adjustment scores were discovered for couples (a) with "unplanned" children, (b) who said they would have fewer children if starting over again, or (c) would wait until after college either to marry or to start their families if they had to do it over again, or (d) who regarded their dual activities of college attendance and parenthood as interfering with each other. In other words, by whichever measure used, marital adjustment was lowest where there was a discrepancy between what was desired and what actually happened. This was the overall conclusion, and it was presented as being in harmony with Reed's earlier finding, in the Indianapolis Fertility Study, that marital adjustment increases according to the ability of couples to control fertility in line with their desires.[12]. . . .

The Indianapolis Fertility Study also presented evidence to suggest that married couples are more successful in controlling the number of their children than the spacing of them. Regarding spacing, it was shown in that study that while some two-thirds of the wives in all groups thought the most desirable interval to first birth would be from two to three years, only a relatively small proportion of them actually had the first child at that time. The discrepancies between desire and practice were in opposite directions according to degree of planning success: about two-thirds of the "number-and-spacing-planned" wives waited longer than three years, while some three-fifths of the "number-planned" and the "too-many-pregnancies" groups (higher in the latter) had the first child in less than two years. And the same general patterns showed up for the spacing of second and subsequent children.[13] Thus, when planning is successful, child-spacing intervals tend to overshoot the couple's desires, whereas when planning is unsuccessful actual intervals turn out to be shorter than desired intervals.

But, though the Indianapolis Fertility Study demonstrated a clear relationship between marital adjustment and the ability to control *number* of children in line with desires, no evidence was presented on the possibility of a similar relationship between marital adjustment and the ability to *space* the children according to the couple's desires. It is to this latter problem that attention is now directed.

It will be recalled that, typically, American couples today space their first child about 18 months from the marriage, with second and subsequent births coming after progressively longer intervals and with the smaller families showing the larger intervals and vice versa. But the most important questions for our purposes have to do with the *effects* of the various alternative spacing patterns, and most especially their effects upon the marriage. Is it better to start the family as soon as possible or to postpone childbearing for awhile after the marriage? Is it better to have the children close together so that they can be companions to each other and so that parents can get their childrearing burdens over within a shorter but more concentrated period, leaving more time free later on for other things; or is it better to have them far apart to reduce sibling rivalry and strain on the mother and to permit parents to enjoy children at home at a more leisurely pace and for a longer portion of the family cycle?

Parents and prospective parents debate these questions, while at the same time being exposed to advice from physicians and varieties of child specialists. Obstetricians, with a primary concern for the mother's health, tend to recommend spacing intervals of from two to three years. Pediatricians and child development specialists look more toward what is best for the health and development of the offspring, but their counsel with reference to spacing seems less consistent. In neither instance has there been much concern with the effects of spacing patterns *upon the marriage;* and in both instances reliance for the positions taken has been more upon clinical experience and logical deduction than upon quantitative research. At any rate, there is a crying need for more and better research on this problem. And, it is our hunch that, when the necessary data are in, the crucial variable will be shown to be, not child-spacing pattern standing alone, but how successful parents are in controlling spacing to fit their desires. In other words, we hypothesize here, as we did earlier when dealing with family size, that values are an intervening variable and that it is value-behavior discrepancy that makes the difference.

There is at least some evidence to support this hypothesis. In their study, *Family Growth in Metropolitan America*,[14] Westoff and collaborators found the following: (1) Twenty-one percent of the wives said that the first child came too soon, and ten percent that it came too late according to their desires. (2) As one moves from very short to increasingly long intervals between marriage and first child, the percent thinking that this child came too soon decreases and the percent thinking it came too late increases. Where the interval was less than eight months, for example, 55 percent thought that the timing was too soon and none thought it was too late; whereas, with an interval of 42–53 months, none thought the timing was too soon and 31 percent thought it too late. A similar relationship was found to hold between the interval separating first and second child and percentages of couples thinking the timing was either too soon or too late. (3) Of those who thought the timing of the first child was too soon, 19 percent said that it interfered with marital adjustment, 26 percent with enjoying things with husband, and 41 percent with readying finances. Furthermore, with respect to each of these problems, the interference was deemed greatest by the wives experiencing the shortest intervals and smallest by the wives experiencing the longest intervals to first child. (4) Desired interval between first and second child involved a balancing of wanting children far enough apart to ease the burden of infant care with wanting them close enough together to insure that they become playmates. The tendency was to consider two to two and one-half years as the interval of optimum balance. (5) Preferred intervals to first, second, and third births showed considerable variation, which suggests a high degree of flexibility or adaptability regarding child-spacing. Respon-

dents perceived "a broad span of interval length as not causing serious inconvenience."[15]

It will be noted that the Westoff study of preferred birth intervals was based upon retrospective judgments and, furthermore, that it did not relate actual spacing patterns to any objective measure of marital success. The closest it came to our present problem is represented in the third point of the above paragraph, namely, that those who thought the first child came too soon saw this as interference with one or more aspects of marriage adjustment—subjectively decided. Nevertheless, this does support our notion of maladjustment resulting from value-behavior discrepancy.

The writer's previously reported cross-cultural research on timing of first pregnancy[16] throws some additional light upon the problem at hand. It was a record-linkage analysis of marriage, birth, and divorce files based on samples from sexually permissive Denmark, sexually restrictive Mormondom in the intermountain region of the United States, and midwestern United States, which is in between but was found to be nearer the restrictive than the permissive end of the continuum. Bringing the three sets of records together on a case-matching basis produced a neat longitudinal design having distinct methodological advantages. Since official vital records were used and the matching was done without the knowledge of subjects, problems of distortion through nonresponse and of falsification by respondents were largely eliminated, and other errors were confined to those already in the official records.

Child-spacing patterns were found to differ considerably across the three cultures studied. In the Danish sample some 24.2 percent of all first births came within the first six months of marriage (indicating premarital pregnancy), 36.5 percent within the first year of marriage, and 54.1 percent within the first two years of marriage. Comparable percentages for the Indiana sample were 9.4, 41.8, and 73.4, respectively; and for the Utah sample 3.4, 40.9, and 77.1, respectively. Thus, Denmark shows up disproportionately high on premarital conception and low on early postmarital conception, while in the United States samples—and especially Utah—the picture is just the reverse of this.

Of particular significance was the finding that the overall relationship between pregnancy timing and divorce rate is negative. Specifically, premarital pregnancy was more frequently followed by divorce than was postmarital pregnancy, and early postmarital pregnancy was more frequently followed by divorce than delayed postmarital pregnancy. Reasons for the association of divorce with premarital pregnancy seem to be, first, the fact that some premarital conceivers are pressured into marriage and lack either love or background preparation and, second, the probability that substantial numbers in this category harbor guilt feelings or fear discovery or disapproval, any of which can make for anxiety and interfere with adjustment. Similarly, there appear to be at least two good reasons for the association of divorce with early postmarital conception. In the first place, larger proportions of early conceivers may be presumed to have been unsuccessful in their birth-control attempts,[17] and there is strong evidence, as pointed out earlier in this paper, that couples with unplanned children have below-average marital adjustment.[18] In the second place, it may be tentatively assumed—though there is need for careful testing on this point—that the very early postmarital conceivers may be complicating their adjustments by having a child before there has been time for their own marital relationships to achieve stability.

Now, how do values intervene to qualify this picture of an overall negative relationship between length of interval to first birth and subsequent divorce rate? Since the vital records which provided the data told nothing of the couples' *desires* regarding the spacing of their children, the problem could not be approached on an individual case basis. But, since the differing fertility norms of the three societies are rather well known, it was possible to get at the problem by means of cross-cultural analysis. As to premarital pregnancy, it was expected that (though each of the three cultures showed somewhat higher divorce for these

cases than for the postmarital conceivers) the *difference* in premarital versus postmarital conceiver divorce rates would be least in the most permissive culture (Denmark) and greatest in the most restrictive culture (Utah), simply because premarital pregnancy is closer to the norm of Denmark and most divergent from the norm of Utah; hence, more easily coped with in the former while resulting in strains and dislocations in the latter. Research findings gave clear support to this hypothesis: *divorce-rate differentials* between premarital and postmarital conceivers turned out to be 62.2 percent in Denmark, 141.4 percent in Indiana, and 405.9 percent in Utah.[19]

As to early versus later postmarital conception, it was hypothesized that (though each of the three cultures showed somewhat higher divorce for the early starters) *divorce-rate differentials* would be greatest in the culture whose norm is to delay conception after marriage (Denmark) and least in the culture whose norm encourages early postmarital conception (Utah). Reasons for this expectation were similar to those relating to premarital pregnancy: it was thought that behavior which deviates from the norm would cause more difficulty than behavior which is in line with the norm of its group. Support for this hypothesis was only partial. Divorce-rate differentials between early (birth during 10–12 months of marriage) and later (birth during second year of marriage) postmarital conceivers turned out to be 17.1 percent for Denmark, 30.0 percent for Indiana, and 2.9 percent for Utah.[20] Why the differential was lower for Denmark than Indiana cannot be determined from the data. But at least it was lowest of all in Utah, where early postmarital conception has the most cultural support. . . .

This brings us to a resting place in our story, at least for now. Both number and spacing of children in the family have been seen as affecting the quality of the marriage. But they do not affect marriage in precisely the same way for all couples. Though most husbands and wives want at least one child, some are "allergic" to even that one; and, though most want some delay before starting the family and some control over the spacing of children after that, not all couples do. People vary considerably in their desires concerning both family size and child-spacing. Hence, number and spacing patterns may affect any given marriage either way, which can help explain why statistical studies that ignore the value variable are often inconclusive and/or contradictory.

The evidence we have strongly suggests that marital success is affected by both number and spacing of children, but that even more crucial than these factors, considered by themselves, is the degree to which couples are able to control number and spacing according to their desires. Values, in other words, are an important part of the equation; they constitute an intervening variable which cannot be ignored. The key questions then become, not: "How many children?" but: "Does the number one has line up with the number he wants?" not: "How are the children spaced?" but: "Does the spacing pattern conform with the desires of the couple?" It is value-behavior discrepancy that works against the marriage—more than either values or behavior considered alone. This was demonstrated for family size by taking into account in a limited sample the personal values of the respondents, and for child-spacing by taking into account differing social norms and comparing them cross-culturally. Both of these approaches, involving interpersonal comparisons on the one hand and cross-cultural comparisons on the other, offer promise for future research.

And more research is needed, both to verify present generalizations and to further develop the theory. Goals for extended study of this problem should include:

(1) A consideration of other types of value conflict. What, for example, happens when husband and wife differ on number and spacing preferences or when personal values in this regard conflict with cultural norms? Will these or other normative strains in any way modify the effects that we have found for value-behavior discrepancy?

(2) A testing of and/or control over other possibly relevant factors, such as age and health of the mother, economic status and security, family size and integration prior to the birth, educational level, religion, race, whether or not there is a sex preference, et cetera. How do these and other factors affect the marriage and—more to our present concern—how do they interrelate with value-behavior discrepancy over number and spacing of children in affecting the marital outcome?[21]

(3) A pinning down of the dynamics of the value and behavior variables. In other words, before the theory is firmly established, it will be necessary to take into account the changing nature of the variables and thus avoid relating values at one point in time with behavior at another. Though values must be reckoned with, we would hypothesize that it is *current* values that are most important in understanding current behavior and current behavioral consequences.

Where there is marital difficulty due to value-behavior discrepancy, one possibility for the couple is to control the behavior, but another is to adjust the values. Our partially formulated theory strongly suggests that marital success is made more probable if one or both of these lines of action is followed—to reduce the strain; to reestablish the balance.

NOTES

[1] Paul H. Jacobson, "Differentials in Divorce by Duration of Marriage and Size of Family," *American Sociological Review*, 15:2 (April 1950): 244.

[2] E. E. LeMasters, "Parenthood as Crisis," *Marriage and Family Living*, 19:4 (November 1957): 352–355.

[3] E. D. Dyer, "Parenthood as Crisis: A Re-Study," *Marriage and Family Living*, 25:2 (May 1963): 196–201.

[4] Cf. J. Richard Udry, *The Social Context of Marriage* (Philadelphia: Lippincott, 1966), pp. 360–361; 452–453; 489–495. In addition to his own discussion, this author cites the following research reports as bearing on the problem: Robert O. Blood and Donald M. Wolfe, *Husbands and Wives* (New York: Free Press, 1960); James H. S. Bossard, *The Large Family System* (Philadelphia: University of Pennsylvania Press, 1956); and several articles by David M. Heer, including "The Measurement and Bases of Family Power: An Overview," *Marriage and Family Living*, 35:2 (May 1963): 133–139.

[5] Brief reviews of these various studies can be found in: Udry, op. cit., pp. 488–489; Ernest W. Burgess and Paul Wallin, *Engagement and Marriage* (Philadelphia: Lippincott, 1953), pp. 713–715; and Harold T. Christensen and Robert E. Philbrick, "Family Size as a Factor in the Marital Adjustments of College Couples," *American Sociological Review*, 17:3 (June 1952): 306–312.

[6] Lewis M. Terman, *Psychological Factors in Marital Happiness* (New York: McGraw-Hill, 1938), pp. 171–173.

[7] Udry, op. cit., p. 489.

[8] Burgess and Wallin, op. cit., p. 722.

[9] Udry, op. cit., pp. 456, 488; Burgess and Wallin, op. cit., pp. 715–719.

[10] A phrase first used in the writer's (with George R. Carpenter) "Value-Behavior Discrepancies Regarding Premarital Coitus in Three Western Cultures," *American Sociological Review*, 27:1 (February 1962): 66–74. The concept is as relevant to the present analysis on family size and child-spacing as it was to the earlier one on premarital coitus; in fact, it *may be generally applicable* to problems of human behavior and its consequences.

[11] Christensen and Philbrick, loc. cit.

[12] Robert B. Reed, *Social and Psychological Factors Affecting Fertility*, VII, "The Interrelationship of Marital Adjustment, Fertility Control, and Size of Family" (New York: Milbank Memorial Fund, 1948), pp. 383–425.

[13] P. K. Whelpton and Clyde V. Kiser, *Social and Psychological Factors Affecting Fertility*, VI, "The Planning of Fertility" (New York: Milbank Memorial Fund, 1950), pp. 209–257.

[14] Charles Westoff, Robert G. Potter, Philip G. Sagi, and Elliot G. Mishler, *Family Growth in Metropolitan America* (Princeton, New Jersey: Princeton University Press, 1961), pp. 116–135.

[15] Ibid., p. 134.

[16] Harold T. Christensen, "Timing of First Pregnancy as a Factor in Divorce; A Cross-Cultural Analysis," *Eugenics Quarterly*, 10:3 (September 1963): 119–130. Several earlier articles are referenced in this one.

[17] Cf. S. Poffenberger, T. Poffenberger, and J. T. Landis, "Intent Toward Conception and the Pregnancy Experience," *Amercian Sociological Review*, 17:5 (October 1952): 616–620.

[18] Christensen and Philbrick, loc. cit.

[19] Christensen, op. cit., p. 126.

[20] Ibid., p. 126.

[21] Certainly values are not the only variables which may intervene to affect the relationships of family size and child-spacing to marital success. There is evidence, for example, that poverty-level families, not only have shorter intervals and more children, but that they have greater marital conflict, which in turn results in less effective contraception, and that early childbirth with them results in disproportionately greater marital strain because of their low statuses and insecure positions. A further relevant finding is that democratically oriented couples, who place high value on marital harmony, tend more than others to want small families. For an excellent summary treatment of some of these points, see Catherine S. Chilman, "Poverty and Family Planning in the United States: Some Social and Psychological Aspects and Implications for Programs and Policy," *Welfare in Review*, 5:4 (April 1967): 3–15.

54

THE FATHER IN CONTEMPORARY CULTURE AND CURRENT PSYCHOLOGICAL LITERATURE

John Nash

The aim of this review is to examine present day thought on the relationships between fathers and their children, and to consider the adequacy of present assumptions.

Much of the scientific literature in this field is sociological rather than psychological in content. While relatively few scientists write about the father, of those that do sociologists and anthropologists form a sizable proportion. Much of the literature is observational rather than experimental in character and, indeed, experimental studies meeting reasonable standards of methodological sophistication, including such refinements as control groups, are scarce; but this is a difficult area in which to practice sound method. Since the primary aim of this review is to survey the field as it is, some assertions that may or may not stand up to critical examination in the future will be cited. Certain of the ideas put forward both by this author and by others are nebulous at present and cannot at this stage of knowledge be made crisper; yet some of them may be productive of useful hypotheses, and in this belief the author does not wither them now with the criticisms that can admittedly be brought against them as they stand.

A majority of studies that will be quoted have been made in the United States of America: the fact that generalizations made about children in various parts of the United States may not be wholly applicable to children elsewhere must be borne in mind, though for present purposes it is perhaps legitimate to assume that the broad generalizations emerging from this review will be reasonably valid throughout the industrial Western world. Since there is a heavy predominance of American written texts among the standard works on child psychology, and since so much of the present knowledge of child development which is readily available for those who read English is based on studies of American children, psychologists throughout the English-speaking world must be strongly influenced by the American pattern. Careful perusal of the *Psychological Abstracts* and other sources have revealed only a few articles from non-English-speaking cultures, from Germany, Denmark, Norway, and France. One cannot say whether this reflects disinterest in the topic or merely the difficulties of covering the foreign literature, although the latter is a probable explanation. . . .

Child care in Western society, as perceived by some sociologists and psychologists, is mother-centered. Gorer (1948) epitomizes American society as the "Motherland," in which the American mother has "arrogated to herself, or has had thrust upon her, the dominant role in the rearing of her children." The father, he says, has become vestigial. He claims that this has affected American childhood, and in particular that of the American male, for "most boys reach and pass adolescence under almost undiluted female authority: their conduct has been regulated by female norms." Kluckhohn (1949) has made similar comments about the place of the woman and the mother in the United States. He claims that a large section of American women are freed from domestic chores by labor-saving devices and have nothing else to do but pamper their children. Many American men are, in his opinion, "so wrapped up in the pursuit of success that they largely abdicate control over their children's upbringing to their wives."

Elkin (1946) has claimed that the young American adult male has difficulty in accepting a mature and socialized concept of virility because his development in home and in school has been molded largely by women and "is less distinct from that of young girls than in any other country." For this reason virtues, such as politeness and tenderness, are associated in their minds with femininity, and they flee into coarseness and toughness in an overcompensatory endeavor to exert their ideas of masculinity, ideas which are derived mainly from the immature concepts of the preadolescent. . . .

The fact that such pronouncements do not appear to have excited criticism or strong protest is perhaps of significance, and the weight of informed opinion would seem to regard our culture as matricentric rather than giving equal importance to the two parents in their contribution to the psychological well-being of children: it certainly cannot be called patricentric as regards child-rearing, even if patriarchal in law.

There are no wide surveys or other experimental supports of these opinions, but it would seem reasonable to adopt as a hypothesis the assumption that Western society is matricentric in its child care, and perhaps one may even regard these opinions as having sufficient substance to throw the burden of proof on those who would argue otherwise. As will be mentioned later, there are some hints of the culture being less matricentric in fact than in the perception of the authorities quoted. . . .

The matricentric concept of child care is reflected in the psychological literature: in comparison with the large number of studies on mother-child interactions, and a very considerable literature discussing this topic, the attention given to fathers is scant indeed. A British book purporting (in the publisher's blurb) to give "a complete account of child development from birth to maturity," devotes two and a half pages out of nearly three hundred to the father. Sears, Maccoby, and Levin (1957), in their study of child-rearing practices in certain parts of the United States, open with the comment that because science is mostly a male prerogative it has failed to interest itself very much in children: note the assumption that interest in children is "unmasculine."

Fathers are, it is true, less accessible to study than mothers are, but it is pertinent that these authors feel satisfied in equating "mother's child-rearing practices" with "child-rearing practices." They mention that there were "a few questions directed toward the father's role in the family. Since it was not feasible to interview the fathers, all the information we gained about their child-rearing practices and attitudes was obtained from the mothers."

Carmichael's comprehensive *Manual* (1954) does not list "Father" in the index, and in an article by Nowlis (1952) which bears the title, "The Search for Significant Concepts in a Study of Parent-Child Relationships," the word "father" (or its synonyms) does not appear; the whole discussion centers on mother-child relationships. Such instances can be multiplied, and for many writers, "parent" means "mother."

Even among those who do give the father a mention, relatively few give him a role of any essential or crucial importance in child-rearing. Bowlby (1951) has left us in no doubt as to his views on the place of the father, at least during the infancy of the child. The father is, to him, "of no direct importance to the young child, but is of indirect value as an economic support and in his emotional support of the mother.". . .

The fact that books on child care are mother-directed tells us, of course, more about the perceptions of the authors than about the actual practice of society, but it is not unreasonable to suppose that these authors, who after all are products of the culture, reflect in some degree its assumptions. And, unless we are to accept the depressing belief that our writings have no influence, we must suppose that matricentric literature tends to reinforce matricentrism. . . .

Studies of the father-child relationships are not numerous. One of the earlier ones was by Gardner (1943) who investigated the attitudes of 300 fathers to their role by personal interview; these men were above average in education and socioeconomic status. As regards the hours spent at home, she notes that "they had ample time to do a lot of fathering" (though she does not analyze the amount of this time that may have been after the children's bedtime, or otherwise unproductive paternally), but she presents evidence that they did not use their opportunities to take any considerable role in child-rearing. This study does not cover a particularly representative sample (the men were mostly professional or semi-professional workers in Ithaca, New York), and it mirrors the father's reported behavior rather than actual behavior, but it does reflect the fact that the father was not in the center of child care in the home, at least in this group.

In a later study (1947), Gardner analyzed children's attitudes to their fathers, using a questionnaire given to groups. Three hundred and eighty-eight children were involved, mostly 10–12 years of age. Only 14 percent preferred the father to the mother, while 32 percent preferred the mother. Nine percent thought the father more understanding, and 35 percent the mother. "Bossiness" was a perceived attribute of the father in a large number of cases. In general, the children listed more attributes to the parent of like sex, but more positive ones to that of the opposite sex. (This could be regarded as an indication of the oedipal situation, or it may reflect the fact that on the whole the opposite-sex parent usually has less to do with punishment, which was generally administered by the like-sex parent.) The boys expressed a negative reaction to women's work and role, which was not found in the girl's reaction to men's work. In this study the fathers spent rather more recreational time with the daughters than with the sons. In the entire group 40 percent said that they wished the father would show more love, girls and boys equally.

The study by Tasch (1952) is a valuable one, being one of the few that have investigated the father directly. She interviewed 85 fathers who had a total of 160 children. They were drawn from the greater New York area, and covered a diverse range as regards nationality of origin, education, and occupation. She investigated such matters as the father's participation in routine daily care, recreational activities, and discipline. Her article contains data on many aspects of the parental role, but one of her most interesting conclusions is that from the reports of the fathers themselves. They did not see themselves as "vestigial," nor as merely secondary to the mother. They saw themselves instead as active participants in routine daily care, and they also saw child-rearing as an integral part of their role as father; they did not see support as their only or major function. She found that companionship with the children was highly valued by fathers, and where this companionship was good it was one of the major satisfactions. The comparatively few fathers who found their role unsatisfying often quoted lack of companionship from their children as one of the reasons of their discontent. Many of the fathers expressed enjoyment at spending time with their children and regret that their economic activities limited the time they could spend. It is interesting to note that few of the fathers mentioned providing a masculine model for their sons as an important function. . . .

Systematic and detailed studies of parents' own attitudes (as distinct from those of experts) on the father's role would seem to be an interesting and perhaps revealing exercise. There are indications of differences between socioeconomic groups in the "ideal" conception of his role which would merit closer investigation. Comparative studies of such matters as the incidence of sexual discord in societies which encourage mother-centered child care to those encouraging the father's active participation would also be of great interest. . . .

Bartemeier (1953) . . . sees one role of the father in the family as an emotional support of the mother, and points out that the father-mother relationship is one that often has profound effects on the mother-child relationship. While he does emphasize this indirect influence of the father, he [claims] that a boy's direct identification with his father may also be of significance. . . .

Although the relationship between the spouses has an obvious (and generally acknowledged) influence on the children, and there is no doubt a wealth of data in case discussions in the clinical literature on this topic, it does not appear to have received a great amount of systematic treatment.

Despite its relevance, it is not proposed to pursue this aspect of the matter in detail here. . . .

A number of the authors already quoted have mentioned anxiety and emotional disturbances as characteristic of father-deprived children, and particularly of father-deprived boys. This leads one to ask if maladjustment and delinquency are associated with defective paternal relationships. Once again the preoccupation with mothers on the part of psychologists has resulted in a dearth of information about fathers on the question, though there are a few relevant studies.

Winch (1950) studied (by questionnaire methods) the courtship behavior of over 1,000 college students. ("Courtship behavior" was measured by the attitude to marriage.) The sort of behavior tapped would be a measure of maturity and sexual adjustment. He found that men from a father-absent home situation scored significantly lower than those in which the father was present, whereas the absence of the mother produced no such effect. Among the women there was no significant finding in relation to the absence of either parent. Men who said they were most attached to the mother had significantly lower scores. While his findings showed a relationship between poor adjustment and mother-dependency in males, there was no such tendency in females who showed a preference for or dependency on the father, and his evidence, which is suggestive rather than conclusive owing to the nature of the study, seems to indicate that cross-sex dependencies of this kind are more harmful to males than to females. Johnson (1963) has gone so far as to suggest that the female, like the male, actually depends upon her identification with the father to produce her appropriate sex-role orientation. . . .

Mussen (1961) found a "high masculine" group of adolescents, who were all well identified with their fathers, to be better adjusted, "more contented, more relaxed, more exuberant, happier, calmer, and smoother in social functioning" than boys low in masculinity. Ostrovsky (1959) presents a number of case histories of behavior disorders in young school children, which

are related either to an unsatisfactory relationship with the father or to his absence. Stephens (1961) reports a study in which social workers were asked to compare boys from families with a father with boys from fatherless families: those from fatherless families were often judged to be anxious about sex and to be more effeminate than the boys with fathers. As the author himself says, only tentative conclusions from this study are justified, but since his findings are in line with others, they are strengthened. . . .

Much of the foregoing discussion has revolved around father-son relationships. The same economic factors that have prevented the father from having too much concern in the rearing of his children presumably prevent strong affectional relationships between father and daughter from being very common. Some studies . . . suggest that a number of fathers express a preference for their daughters rather than their sons. This is, of course, in line with psychoanalytic theory, but little empirical verification is to be found. Radcliffe Hall's autobiographical novel *The Well of Loneliness* is an instance from literature of the effects of an unduly strong father-daughter relationship, and the case histories suggest that such attachments are commonly found as an etiological factor in female homosexuality. On the whole, however, the presently available evidence, as reviewed elsewhere by Nash (1954), suggests that strong attachments between father and daughter are less inimical to the girl's normal development than are strong mother-son attachments to that of the boy. Johnson (1963) has brought up the same point and has indeed gone further than this in suggesting that the girl's normal development of sex-role orientation depends upon her identification with the father. This is obviously a point requiring a more definitive study.

An alternative line of argument is provided by Beach's (1961) suggestion that, even at the human level, females are less dependent on learning than are males for the emergence of sex-behaviors, but are more determined by innate factors. If this is so (and we are not, of course, by any means certain that it is), then it could be that girls are less dependent upon the learning provided by any identification process for the emergence of sex-appropriate orientations. Identifications with either parent can form the social responsiveness necessary to later more specifically sexual relationships. The data on girls from the Lynn and Sawrey (1959) study are contradictory to Johnson's hypothesis, but not inconsistent with the second viewpoint. Since the evidence is so scanty, either point of view is speculative at present, but an interesting area of research is suggested by the alternative suggestions. . . .

[Homosexuality] has some important bearings on understanding the father's place in child development. Little doubt remains that homosexuality is the result of psychological factors in a child's upbringing: it is rarely if ever the result of glandular abnormalities. . . . Constitutional factors may possibly make one child more prone and another less susceptible to adverse upbringing without being the arbitrary determinant of sexuality, and constitution cannot be ignored. But it may be doubted if constitution alone, in spite of satisfactory environment, can predetermine homosexual development.

A second point that needs to be mentioned is that seduction is apparently not an important cause. Where seductive incidents appear in homosexual case histories, they may be at the most precipitants of already existing tendencies; in many cases these tendencies can be shown to have been precursors of the "seduction" which the child has consciously or unconsciously invited (Bender & Blau, 1937).

Full documentation of the evidence on paternal roles in child-rearing cast by homosexuality would require considerable space, and for this reason is omitted here. Nash (1954) has discussed in some detail the question of paternal insufficiency as a causal factor, and, in brief, an examination of homosexual case histories reveals that in the male there is characteristically a lack of warm, affectionate relationships with the father. Brown (1957, 1958) has also discussed this as a major factor in determining the condition. These authors have developed a hypothesis that the crucial causal factor in male homosexuality is a failure to identify with the father. A variety of reasons contribute to this failure, some in one case, others in another. A recent study (Nash & Hayes, 1965) suggests that "passive" homosexuals (that is, those preferring the "female" role in erotic activities) have in addition to faulty paternal relationships a closer relationship with their mothers than have "active" homosexuals.

There is less evidence available on the question of female homosexuality, though there is some to suggest that failure to identify with the mother, and identification with the father instead, may be causal (Nash, 1954), but a complicating factor is discussed in the section on father-daughter relations. . . .

The social behaviors prescribed for males and females differ rather widely from culture to culture, though in general males are expected to be more active and aggressive than females and dominant in their relations toward females (Barry, Bacon, & Child, 1957). The universality of such cultural expectations could be due to biological substratum upon which the sex-differences rest. These norms for conduct pervade many kinds of social behavior and give rise to both gross and subtle distinction between the sexes. For instance, men are expected to speak with a deeper voice, and this has its biological basis; but they also use different intonations, phrases, and idioms, and a few cultures even go so far as having different languages for men and women (Jesperson, 1922). The social behaviors in which sex differences are prescribed include not only sex behaviors themselves, but such things as economic activity as well: in fact almost all phases of behavior show them, as in the feminine gestures, stance, manner of speech, which are distinct from masculine ones.

Cultures differ rather widely in the strictness with which these distinctions are insisted upon. It is sometimes said that our culture is confused in its sex-role expectations, and uncertain of its standards. This may be untrue: it could be argued that our culture still retains a fairly clear idea (or even ideal) of distinctive social sex roles and is insistent upon adherence to them, but what it does lack is the sort of child-rearing system which will communicate these to its boys and girls, more particularly the boys. Many of the stresses and strains afflicting young males in our society possibly arise from the circumstance that they are told that they must behave in an ill-defined masculine manner, but without the education that will enable them to do this effortlessly. . . .

In spite of being a widely used term, or perhaps because of it, "identification" is not precise, and it is difficult to say just what it means. Nevertheless, it does seem to refer to some thing or process recognized as important to psychological development; while much could be written in criticism of the concept, this does not seem to be the place to do this. With reservations, therefore, the term is used in this review as it is so widely in the literature.

Freud has stated that the child tends to identify with the parent that he fears most. Accordingly in the oedipal situation the boy sees the father as a rival in his affections for the mother, but fears him because of his greater power, and so allies himself with the father for safety's sake. In this Freudian view the boy's identification with the father is based on negative mechanisms and is fear-induced. In line with this view is the article by Collette (1957) which reported that children's earliest memories of the father do not go back earlier than 3 years of age, and are more often unpleasant than pleasant. After this (presumably due to the resolution of the oedipal conflict) the image of the father changes to a collaborative, protective one, though still frustrating.

As the present writer has pointed out elsewhere, this concept of identification is unsatisfactory, and gets Freud into logical difficulties when he comes to consider the problem of homosexuality. An alternative is to consider identification as a form of learning along the lines proposed by Stoke (1950) and Mowrer (1950). In this view, one of the more important conditions for identification is a warm, affectionate relationship with the person to be identified with. Some empirical support to this is found by Payne and Mussen (1956), who in adolescent boys found a significant relationship between identification with the father and perception of him as a highly rewarding, affectionate person.

Bandura and Huston (1961) have described identification as a process of incidental learning, and in an experimental situation in which the ostensible task was a discrimination problem, preschool children were shown to pattern their behavior on irrelevant as well as relevant aspects of an adult model's behavior. Moreover, this identification was in general closer with children having a "nurturant" relationship with the model than those having a "distant" initial experience.

Another factor to be considered important to this process of identification by the Stoke-Mowrer model is prolonged association. The above study would appear to be inconsistent with this, since imitation (which Bandura and Huston equate with identification) did occur on short association, but here only small segments of behavior were being acquired. Presumably sex-role acquisition involves a vast range of behaviors requiring considerable time for their attainment and practice. Scott (1963) has made the suggestion, based apparently on an unpublished animal study by Fisher, that prolonged contact is the only crucial factor in the forming of social relationships, and that the nature of the experience, whether rewarding or punishing, is immaterial. What relevance this may have for the theory of identification in humans is uncertain at this stage, though if confirmed it might modify the Stoke-Mowrer position. In the Bandura and Huston experiment, the imitation of aggressive patterns of behavior, unlike others, was independent of nurturant or nonnurturant relationships, so different behaviors may require differing conditions for their acquisition.

In the development of the self-concept one of the important aspects is that of the self as a male or a female person. It is commonly agreed in the psychological literature, both psychoanalytic and otherwise, that the boy's pattern for himself in the male role is obtained from his identification with the father, the girl's identification with the female role from the mother. This view has been held for many years, but yet the question of just how it happens has not been satisfactorily explained, though the Stoke-Mowrer approach offers a working hypothesis. This does not deny the possibility of other approaches, for example the "status envy" hypothesis of identification of Burton and Whiting (1961).

Whatever the mechanisms of identification may prove to be, it is evidently important to the acquisition of many patterns of behavior, including those involved in masculine and feminine social and sexual ones. Moreover, relationships with the parent of the same sex apparently play some significant role in this process. It would follow that in a society in which the conditions are not conducive to close father-son relationships, the developing boy may find difficulty in acquiring his self-concept as a male person. . . .

Sears, Pintler, and Sears (1946) made a study of the effects of the father's absence on the aggressive behavior of preschool children as reflected in doll play. It was found, among other things, that there was a reliable sex difference between boys and girls in the use of the father doll as an object of aggression, whereas there was little difference in the aggression shown the mother doll. They concluded that the father normally serves both as a more aggressive model and a more potent frustrator to the son than to the daughter. In a later study also using the doll-play technique, P. S. Sears (1959) confirmed these findings, and found the differences to increase up to 5 years (the oldest studied). Paternal absence, mostly on war service, she found to have a number of effects on the doll play of boy dolls. That is, they showed more girl-earlier years, boys whose fathers were absent differed less from girls than the controls in the frequency of aggression, and they emphasized less than boys whose fathers were present the common sex factor of the maleness of the father and boy dolls. That is, they showed more girl-like behavior and were less conscious of their masculinity. The differences between father-present and father-absent groups is reliable over the whole study. In the case of father-absent boys and girls, there was no difference at 4 years and a difference

reliable at the 2 percent level at 5 years, whereas in the father-present group there was a reliable difference at all ages. She concludes that "it appears either that the absence of the father delays the sex-typing process in 3- to 4-year-olds, or that those early years are more crucial for the development of phantasy aggression and the father's absence interferes with this process." These studies suggest that the father's influence on the boy's development begins in the preschool period.

Bach (1946) studied the father phantasies of father-separated children, aged 6 to 10 years. They were lower-middle-class children of average intelligence (10 boys, 10 girls) whose father had been away in the forces when the children were between 1 and 3 years. A control group with fathers at home, suitably matched, was used, and the investigation used the doll-play technique devised by Sears. The mothers' attitudes to the fathers were also obtained by interview. The father-separated children produced an idealistic and feminine phantasy picture of the father, as compared with that of the control group, and the influence of the mother's attitude was seen in this typing. The difficulties that might arise on the father's return to be matched against this distorted phantasy were pointed out.

Seplin (1952) made a study of the effects of the father's absence during military service on child behavior. She studied children from 43 families, and a methodological point in her research was that she used one child from the family as the subject and another as control. The experimental group had had the father absent during the formative years, whereas he was present during the corresponding years of the control siblings. The experimental group had an average age of 8 years at the time of the study, whereas the control group (which was, of course, younger since it involved siblings born after the father's return) had an average age of 4 years. (This introduces a methodological difficulty, which follow-up until the younger group reaches the age of the older would help resolve.) She noted that the children in the experimental group tended to have a closer relationship with the mother and also to show more signs of emotional disturbances than the controls. She noted that the experimental group was markedly retarded in its emotional development. She also noted that twice as many children in the experimental group showed behavioral disturbances, and that these problems were more apparent among boys than among girls. She concluded that the differences observed were directly attributable to the father's absence over these formative years.

One of the more extensive studies of the father is that of Stolz and her collaborators (1954) on the father relations of children born during the war. The subjects were the families of married veterans returning to their studies at Stanford University, who were housed in special units, a circumstance which aided the investigators. These families had children, some of whom were born during the war while the father was absent. A particular feature of this investigation was that the fathers were studied directly.

The primary focus of the investigation was on the relations of the father with his first child, born while he was away from home in the Armed Services, and the effects of these relations on the developing personalities of the children. A control group consisted of families in which there had been no separation from the father. The experimental model contained a number of general hypotheses: in brief these were that the absentee father would have difficulty in establishing his role as a father on return, and similarly the child would have difficulty in accepting him in that role: certain personality characteristics in the child were predicted to accompany this situation, including those resulting from an unusually high identification between mother and child.

Investigation consisted in an extensive study of a small sample, 19 families, in which the father was separated during the pregnancy of the mother and reunited after the first child was at least a year old. All the fathers were either students or faculty members. The 19 families had 35 children, 19 first born and 16 children born after the father returned. The children were of average or above average intelligence. Similar campus families in which there had been no separation of the father were used as controls. The families were matched for age and sex of children.

The method of investigation consisted of a series of intensive interviews with the fathers, two "semi-structured" interviews with the mother, an observation of the children in social situations with peers and adult leaders, and observation of children in five projective play situations. A considerable body of data was collected, and only the broad general conclusions can be quoted here.

They found that the war-separated father was faced on his return with major adjustments in assuming his role of head of the family: these included vocational as well as marital and family problems of adjustment. The first-born child had to adjust to an unknown man, who suddenly invaded the family, taking the dominant position from the mother and upsetting the intimate routines to which the child had become accustomed. Typically, the child's early relations to the father were shy, withdrawn, and unresponsive; the child was not affectionate toward him, and often refused his attentions. The father's reaction to this rejection by his child was liable to exacerbate the situation and result in the more complete alienation of the first-born child.

As might be expected, the first-born child was closer to the mother than to the father. The war-separated children also showed more serious behavior problems than the control children, were less independent, showed more fears of a serious nature and more overt expressions of tension. In group situations with other children, the war-separated children were less skilful in establishing or maintaining associations. The war-separated children were more dependent than the controls were on other adults, particularly female teachers. They showed more hostile aggression than the control-group children did, and there was consistent evidence of their having greater feelings of anxiety. The fathers complained that much of their behavior was unmasculine. The authors point out that this situation was very frustrating to the fathers, and in many cases increased their own feelings of inadequacy. It also had detrimental effects on the psychological development of the children.

Bach's (1946) study has shown that father-separated children tended to have an idealistic effeminized phantasy picture of the father. This idea of the father was related to the mother's own attitude to her absent husband, which she communicated to the children. We may assume that partially father-deprived children also experience some difficulty in identification with him.

To test the hypothesis that boys lacking a father-figure are handicapped in their masculine identification, the present writer undertook a study using a battery of tests of "masculinity" and "femininity" similar to those developed by Sears (1946) and others. A group of 41 boys in a Scottish orphanage (tested at a mean age of 8 years, 9 months, range 6–14), all of whom had entered in the first six months of life, and who had been brought up entirely by women in a baby home until the fifth year, were found to score toward the feminine pole. A control group of boys reared in normal families with a father-figure present made clearly "masculine" scores (the tests had been selected to discriminate highly between boys and girls). Support for ascribing this difference to the absence of a father-figure is given by further analysis: after the age of 5 years, 21 of these boys had gone to cottages run by a married couple, and hence had a father-figure present. Though significantly less masculine than the normal control group, these boys consistently made more masculine scores than the other 20 who continued after 5 years of age in cottages run only by women. The most feminine scores were found in this latter group. These results were interpreted as suggesting that boys reared for the first five years in the absence of a father-figure fail to acquire the masculine attitudes of boys reared under more normal conditions. On the Draw-a-Person Test, using the criteria of masculine and feminine drawings described by Goodenough (1926) and Geil (1944), the same group of boys also demonstrated a failure of masculine identification.

There is some evidence in these studies that the process of identification with the father may be seriously impaired if the father is not present in the preschool period, and that permanent deficiencies in identification may result; that is, this early period is critical. Furthermore, there is some evidence (in the case studies of Stolz, for instance), to suggest that this critical period may be quite early and that both acceptance of the child by the father and of the father by the child may be increasingly more difficult as the months pass. The phenomenon of imprinting, described by the ethologists, may be of relevance here.

Most of the studies so far made have concerned offspring imprinting the parents; the possibility of parents having to imprint their offspring is illustrated by the refusal of acceptance of a strange lamb by a ewe (Collias, 1953; Collias, 1956). Admittedly, the evidence is meager as yet, but the hypothesis is suggested that human infants have sign-stimulus properties to human adults (the "cupie-doll" sign-*gestalt* of Lorenz), and that fathers (no less than mothers, and possibly more so) have their acceptance of an infant facilitated by imprinting. A culture which discourages close contacts between father and infant may hinder this imprinting.

Similarly, it is at least feasible that infants are attached to parents by an imprinting phenomenon too, and that the early presence of the father may be necessary if this process is to include him. Possibly, the time of weaning may be a critical period in the boy's necessary transfer from mother to father. . . .

The foregoing discussion has emphasized the part of father-son relationships in the dynamics of sex-role identification and psychosexual development, and some indicators that early relationships are of crucial importance have been seen in the studies of boys deprived of a father-relationship in the preschool period. . . .

In the previous section it was suggested that *early* identification with the father is an essential part of the development of sex-role identifications. Hartup and Zook (1960) have produced experimental evidence that sex-role *preferences* do in fact occur early in life, being apparent in 3-year-old children: by the fourth year clearly defined preferences for the own-sex role are established. (These authors believe that this process is easier for boys because the cultural stereotype in American society is clearer for the masculine role than the feminine one: they offer no proof that this is in fact the case.) They distinguish sex-role *preference* from *identifications*.

Levin and Sears (1957) have made a study of the manner in which paternal characteristics tend to be incorporated by the child. Measuring by a doll-play technique the fantasy aggression of 5-year-old boys and girls, they found that the boys showing most fantasy aggression were those usually punished by the father, with whom they identified. Similarly, the most aggressive girls were those punished more severely by the mother. The punitive like-sex parent had provided the model for aggression. Similarly, boys identifying with nonaggressive fathers were low in aggressive fantasy. (It should be noted, however, that there was also a fairly high degree of aggression shown in those children more severely punished by the unlike-sex parent, so that one could invoke Anna Freud's concept of "identification with the aggressor": these authors are inclined to reject this explanation.) However, somewhat in contradiction to these results, Angrilli (1960) reports a study in which there was no significant relationship between the sex-identifications of fathers and those of their sons. He suggests some possible psychodynamic explanations of this; for instance, that low-masculine fathers may compensate by encouraging high masculinity in their sons. But one may also question whether the result is not an artifact of the necessity of using different tests for the adults and children. In 30 preschool boys, he found a wide range in the degree of psychosexual identification, but offers no data as to whether those more highly masculine identified with the father, or those less masculine with the mother.

Mussen and Distler (1960) interviewed the mothers of two small groups of boys of kindergarten age to obtain data about the child-rearing practices of their families, including father-son relationships. The two groups were selected from a large population by means of a projective test of sex-role preferences (Brown, 1956), one group being high masculine, the other low masculine. They found father-son relationships to be more directly related to sex-typing than mother-son relationships were, and the high masculine boys were reported to have stronger affectional ties to their fathers, who also took more part in their sons' upbringing than did the fathers of the low group. Mussen (1961), from a study of 68 high school boys, aged 17–18, concluded that adolescents who regarded their paternal relationships to be favorable and rewarding showed strongly masculine interests (as measured by the Strong V.I.B.), whereas those whose relationship with the father was less favorable showed more feminine interests. The group with good father relationships was also found to be emotionally more stable and superior in adjustment.

Poffenberger and Norton (1959) report that college freshmen's attitudes toward mathematics reflect the fathers' attitudes, but the data are ambiguous from our point of view, since those students who were close to their fathers were no more strongly like their fathers in attitude toward mathematics than those who were distant (Poffenberger, 1959). Since there is some evidence that numerical ability is inherited (Carter, 1932), this may be a confounding factor here, particularly as there seems to be some form of sex-linkage involved. Milton (1957) has shown that a positive relationship exists between masculine identification in both males and females and problem-solving skill. Again, genetic factors may play a part. An area for inquiry is pointed to by such studies. . . .

Because it is in relation to the development of boys that paternal factors are the most significant, this review has concentrated almost exclusively upon father-son interactions. It is not intended to imply that mother-son, or father-daughter, relationships are of no consequence, but the former is arbitrarily excluded as outside the scope of this review. To consider the latter, which has been extensively discussed in psychoanalytic literature but very little in more experimental studies, would greatly extend an already lengthy discussion. It is for convenience only, and not because they are judged unimportant, that these matters are not treated here. . . .

SUMMARY

From an over-all view of the literature on fathers and their place in child-rearing, it appears that:

1. In the opinion of some sociologists, American society in particular, and probably Western industrial society in general, can be epitomized as "mother-centered" in its philosophy of child care.

2. This is in contrast to certain primitive societies with a family cooperative economy, which have typically a way of child-rearing which emphasizes father-son and mother-daughter relationships.

3. The difference can be explained by the economic history of our industrial civilization, in which the primitive family cooperative economy has been supplanted by one in which the father is usually the sole support of the family. While engaged in this economic activity, he delegates his place in child-rearing to his wife.

4. Psychologists have adopted this cultural philosophy of child care, perhaps uncritically, and many appear to have assumed that it is both the only and the most desirable pattern of child care. In consequence, the majority of psychologists have not perceived the father as important in child-rearing, and this is reflected in their writings. Some psychologists have adopted the cultural assumption so thoroughly as to ignore the father entirely or even to deny him a position of any significance.

5. This culturally determined concept of child care has further removed the father by enhancing the assumption that the rearing of children is a specifically feminine duty.

6. Clinical studies and investigations of delinquents suggest that father-child relationships, and especially those between father and son, may be of considerable etiological importance to both social and psychological abnormality.

7. Psychosexual difficulties, such as homosexuality, apparently result when a child's major identification is with the parent of the opposite sex. If this is the case, a mother-centered system is peculiarly unsuited to the needs of the boy, for while he is under cultural pressure to act as a male, he is reared predominantly by women from whom he is likely to acquire a feminine pattern.

8. Identification of child with parent is significant in sex-role and psychosexual development, and can be understood in terms of learning theory: warm, affectionate relationships and prolonged associations (in contrast to the veiled hostility of the oedipal theory) are probably among the more vital requirements to successful identifications.

9. Though as yet little understood, critical periods may be found in human development, as they almost certainly are important in the acquisition of some animal behavior.

10. There is some evidence from the few available studies of early paternal deprivation that there is a critical period during which the kind of affectional relationship with the father necessary to identification can be built up. This critical period appears to be early, and has tentatively been described as lasting from the time of weaning to entering school.

11. The role of the peer culture as a factor in sex-role development has been discussed, and its possible limitations because of its immaturity.

REFERENCES

Angrilli, A. F. "The Psychosexual Identification of Preschool Boys." *J. Genet. Psychol.*, 97 (1960): 329–340.

Bach, G. R. "Father-Fantasies and Father-Typing in Father Separated Children." *Child Develpm.*, 17 (1946): 63–80.

Bandura, A., and Huston, Aletha, C. "Identification as a Process of Incidental Learning." *J. abnorm. soc. Psychol.*, 63 (1961): 311–318.

Barry, H., Bacon, Margaret K., and Child, I. L. "A Cross-Cultural Survey of Some Sex Differences in Socialization." *J. abnorm. soc. Psychol.*, 55 (1957): 327–332.

Bartemeier, L. "The Contribution of the Father to the Mental Health of the Family." *Amer. J. Psychiat.*, 110 (1953): 277–280.

Beach, F. A. "Sex Differences in the Psychological Bases of Mating Behavior in Mammals." In *The Physiology of Emotions,* Simon, Herbert, Strauss, eds. (Springfield, Ill.: Charles C Thomas, 1961).

Bender, L., and Blau, A. "The Reaction of Children to Sexual Relations with Adults." *Amer. J. Orthopsychiat.*, 7 (1937): 500–518.

Bowlby, J. *Maternal Care and Mental Health.* (Geneva: World Health Organization, 1951).

Brown, D. G. "Sex-Role Preferences in Young Children." *Psychol. Monogr.*, 1956, No. 14 (Whole No. 421).

Brown, D. G. "The Development of Sex-Role Inversion and Homosexuality." *J. Pediat.*, 50 (1957): 613–619.

Brown, D. G., "Inversion and Homosexuality." *Amer. J. Orthopsychiat.*, 28 (1958): 424–429.

Burton, R. V., and Whiting, J. W. M. "The Absent Father and Cross-Sex Identity." *Merrill-Palmer Quart.*, 7 (1961): 85–95.

Carmichael, L. *Manual of Child Psychology.* (New York: John Wiley & Sons, 1954).

Carter, H. B. "Family Resemblances in Verbal and Numerical Abilities." *Genet. Psychol. Monogr.*, 12 (1932): 1–104.

Collette, A. "Le Père et le Premier Souvenir d'Enfance" (The Father and the Earliest Childhood Memory). *Cah. Pedag. U. Liege*, 16 (1957): 111–126.

Collias, N. E. "Some Factors in Maternal Rejection of Sheep and Goats." *Ecol. Soc. Am. Bull.*, 34 (1953): 78.

Collias, N. E. "The Analysis of Socialization in Sheep and Goats." *Ecology*, 37 (1956): 228–239.

Elkin, H. "Aggressive and Erotic Tendencies in Army Life." *Amer. J. Sociol.*, 51 (1946): 408–413.

Gardner, L. P. "A Survey of the Attitudes and Activities of Fathers." *J. genet. Psychol.*, 63 (1943): 15–53.

Gardner, L. P. "Analysis of Children's Attitudes to Fathers." *J. genet. Psychol.*, 70 (1947): 3–38.

Geil, G. A. "The Use of the Goodenough Test for Revealing Male Homosexuality." *Crim. Psychopath.*, 6 (1944): 307.

Goodenough, F. *Measurement of Intelligence by Drawings.* (New York: World Book, 1926).

Gorer, G. *The American People: A Study of National Character.* (New York: Norton, 1948).

Hartup, W. W., and Zook, E. A. "Sex-Role Preferences in Three- and Four-Year-Old Children." *J. consult. Psychol.*, 24 (1960): 420–426.

Jesperson, O. *Language, Its Native Development and Origins.* (London: Allen & Unwin, 1922).

Johnson, M. M. "Sex-Role Learning in the Nuclear Family." *Child Develpm.*, 34 (1963): 319–333.

Kluckhohn, C. *Mirror for Man.* (New York: McGraw-Hill, 1949).

Levin, H., and Sears, R. R. "Identification with Parents as a Determinant of Doll-Play Aggression." *Child Develpm.*, 27 (1956): 135–155.

Lynn, D., and Sawrey, W. L. "The Effects of Father-Absence on Norwegian Boys and Girls." *J. abnorm. soc. Psychol.*, 59 (1959): 258–262.

Milton, G. A. "The Effects of Sex-Role Identification in Formation of Problem-Solving Skill." *J. abnorm. soc. Psychol.*, 55 (1957): 208–212.

Mowrer, O. H. *Learning Theory and Personality Dynamics.* (New York: Ronald Press, 1950).

Mussen, P., and Distler, L. "Child-Rearing Antecedents of Masculine Identification in Kindergarten Boys." *Child Develpm.*, 31 (1960): 89–100.

Mussen, P. "Some Antecedents and Consequences of Masculine Sex-Typing in Adolescent Boys." *Psychol. Monogr.*, 75 (1961): No. 2.

Nash, J. "The Psychology of Deprivation." Unpublished doctoral dissertation, Univer. of Edinburgh, 1954.

Nash, J. "Critical Periods in Human Development." *Bull. Maritime Psychol. Ass.*, 1954, 18–22.

Nash, J., and Hayes, F. In press.

Nowlis, V. "The Search for Significant Concepts in a Study of Parent-Child Relationships." *Amer. J. Orthopsychiat.*, 22 (1952): 286–299.

Ostrovsky, E. S. *Father to the Child.* (New York: G. P. Putnam, 1959).

Payne, D. E., and Mussen, P. H. "Parent-Child Relations and Father Identification among Adolescent Boys." *J. abnorm. soc. Psychol.*, 52 (1956): 358–362.

Poffenberger, T. "A Research Note on Father-Child Relations and Father Viewed as Negative Figure." *Child Develpm.*, 30 (1959): 489–492.

Poffenberger, T., and Norton, D. "Factors in the Formation of Attitudes Towards Mathematics." *J. educ. Res.*, 52 (1959): 171–176.

Scott, J. P. "The Process of Primary Socialization in Canine and Human Infants." *Monogr. Soc. Res. Child Develpm.*, 28 (1963): No. 1.

Sears, P. S. "Doll-Play Aggression in Normal Young Children: Influence of Sex, Age, Sibling Status, Father's Absence." *Psychol. Monogr.*, 65 (1951): No. 6.

Sears, R. R., Maccoby, E. E., and Levin, H. *Patterns of Child Rearing.* (New York: Row, Peterson, 1957).

Sears, R. R., Pintler, M. H., and Sears, P. S. "The Effect of Father Separation on Preschool Children's Doll-Play Aggression." *Child Develpm.*, 17 (1946): 219–243.

Seplin, C. D. "A Study of the Influence of the Father's Absence for Military Service." *Smith Coll. Stud. soc. Wk.*, 22 (1952): 123–124 (Abstract).

Stephens, W. N. "Judgments by Social Workers on Boys and Mothers in Fatherless Families." *J. genet. Psychol.*, 99 (1961): 59–64.

Stoke, S. M. "An Inquiry into the Concept of Identification." *J. genet. Psychol.*, 76 (1950): 163–189.

Stolz, L. M., and Collaborators. *Father Relations of War-Born Children.* (Stanford, Calif.: Stanford Univer. Press, 1954).

Tasch, R. J. "The Role of the Father in the Family." *J. exp. Educ.*, 20 (1952): 319–361.

Winch, R. "Some Data Bearing on the Oedipal Hypothesis." *J. abnorm. soc. Psychol.*, 45 (1950): 481–489.

55

CHILD-REARING IN FAMILIES
OF WORKING AND NONWORKING MOTHERS

Marian Radke Yarrow, Phyllis Scott, Louise de Leeuw, and Christine Heinig

In the history of research on child development and child rearing, social concerns have often stimulated particular areas of inquiry. An instance is the work of the 1930's and 1940's on the influences of early institutionalization upon children. Society's concerns about the impact of hospitalization, orphanage placement, and the like posed empirical questions which research recast and redefined as basic problems in socialization. In similar fashion the rapidly increasing employment of mothers has currently prodded investigation of the effects of this changed mother role on the rearing of children. Judged by frequency of occurrence in American family structure, maternal employment is a significant socialization variable: two out of five mothers of school age children were reported in the labor force in the 1957 survey.[1]

The initial questions directed to research on this problem, motivated from the social welfare concerns, were broad and atheoretical: "What happens to children whose mothers work?" The questions were framed with the strong suggestion that the working mother was a "problem," creating conditions of child neglect, juvenile delinquency, disorganized family life, etc. The studies resulting from the practical orientation produced a confusion of findings. In her review of the research literature on maternal employment, Stolz[2] suggests that the inconclusive nature of findings may be laid to the failure of investigators to specify the circumstances surrounding mothers' employment (whether in broken or intact families, motivated from economic stress or personal satisfactions in work, with young or older children, with or without good substitute care) and to the failure of investigators to include adequate control groups.

The inconclusive results can also be explained by the fact that most studies have failed to conceptualize maternal employment in terms of theoretically relevant variables. For example, inherent in the situation of a mother's work outside the home are mother-child separation, multiple mothering, and changed mother-father roles, all of which are familiar variables of developmental research. It is apparent that maternal employment is not a single condition or variable of mothering; it is rather a set of conditions which may vary greatly from case to case.

The research questions in the present investigation are two: (1) When structural variables of the family environment (such as family class and composition, presence of mother, father, and supplemental mother figures) are controlled, do working and nonworking mothers provide different child-rearing environments? (2) Do working and nonworking mothers who differ in their attitudes and feelings about their adult roles differ in their maternal roles?

Personal variables which characterize the mother as an individual have generally been ignored in studies of child rearing. It is hypothesized that the mother's gratifications and frustrations in her other adult (nonmother) roles, her achievement needs, and her feelings of self-fulfillment influence her functioning as a mother and affect what is mediated to the child by her child-rearing practices. Since employment status may be intimately bound up with the mother's self-attitudes and values, the study of employed and nonemployed mothers who differ in attitudes offers an opportunity for an initial test of the more general hypothesis concerning the significance of this class of variables in socialization studies. The particular personal factors studied are those relating to the meaning of working or not working, i.e., the woman's sex role ideology, her basic preferences regarding working or not, the motivations supporting her present work status, and her motivations in her role as mother.

Choice of dependent variables was made on the basis of existing opinion and theory concerning the possible consequences of maternal employment for the rearing of children. Working is presumed to result in "deficiencies" in mothering: less dedication and less effectiveness, deviations in supervision and control of the child, exaggeration of the child's dependency needs, greater stress on achievement, altered sex role training, and decreased participation of mother with child.[3] Mothers' reports of practices and philosophies constitute the data on child rearing. . . .

The subjects of this study are 50 employed and 50 nonemployed mothers. The classification of *working* required at least 28 hours of work per week in steady employment extending over the past year. To be classed in the *nonworking* group, the mother could not have engaged in any paid employment over the past year. Unfortunately the two groups have similar work histories: all having worked at some time. Half of the nonworking mothers had worked after marriage, before the birth of a child.

Subjects of the employed and nonemployed groups were matched in family characteristics. Families were white, intact, with a male wage earner present. There were one to four children per family, with at least one child (about whom the mother was interviewed) between four and eleven years of age. . . .

In selecting the sample it was the objective to choose social class groups in which employment is not a traditional role for married women, but in which both a traditional woman's role and a changed role exist and are tolerated, and in which differing values and sentiments about women's employment are held. We wished to have groups in which working or not working is more likely to be a matter of individual choice than of dire economic necessity. Narrowing the class range should also reduce variations in child-rearing values and practices, leaving remaining variations more clearly attributable to personal maternal factors or the maternal work role. Middle and upper middle class families and upper working class families living in middle class neighborhoods were included in the sample (Groups I, II, III, IV on the Hollingshead Index of Social Position).

Family structural variations associated with maternal employment (separation of mother from child, substitute "mothers," changes in father and mother roles) were greatly reduced in range. Substitute care was primarily for the out-of-school hours, when, for the great majority, paid help or a relative (grandmother, aunt, occasionally an older sibling) cared for the children. Fathers retained wage earner roles in the homes of both groups.

The subjects were located in the Greater Washington area, in twelve public schools selected in terms of social class criteria. The location of eligible families in eight of the schools was facilitated by data on family characteristics from another study.[4] For these families, a letter, followed by a telephone call, determined willingness to cooperate in the study. For the other schools, it was necessary to canvass each home (with knowledge only of the age of the children) to enlist interest and determine eligibility. After preliminary screening on race and social class, approximately 650 families were further screened on family characteristics, using a brief set of polling-type questions. An eligible mother who did not consent to an interview after she had been informed of the nature of the study was counted as a refusal. Twenty-one percent of the working mothers and 17 percent of the mothers not employed did not consent to participate. Illness, imminent moving, and the like, accounted for a few of the refusals. The other women indicated they preferred not to be research subjects. The social characteristics of the 100 interviewed mothers are presented in Table 1. . . .

The subjects were interviewed in their homes. A schedule was followed as closely as was consistent with the responses of the subject. The interview dealt, in sequence, with the mother's past and present employment status, her motives for working or not working, and her attitudes concerning role differences of men and women as these re-

TABLE 1. CHARACTERISTICS OF EMPLOYED
AND NONEMPLOYED MOTHERS

Characteristics		Working Mothers (N = 50)	Nonworking Mothers (N = 50)
Index of Social Position	I	16	13
	II	14	16
	III	8	14
	IV	12	7
Number of Children in Family	Mean	2.14	2.36
Sex of Children	Girls	27	27
	Boys	37	37
Age of Children*	9–11 years	36	38
	6–8 years	21	19
	4–5 years	7	7
Age of Mother	29–39	28	24
	40–50	22	26
Education of Mother			
Some college or college graduate		30	26
Some high school or high school graduate		20	24
Mother's Occupation			
Professional		13	—
Semiprofessional or managerial		12	—
Clerical or secretarial		19	—
Service trades		6	—

* Mothers were interviewed with regard to the children who met the criteria of the sample; i.e., keeping the age between 4 and 11 years, and having age and sex comparable in working and nonworking samples.

late to dependency and achievement needs and to primary responsibility to the home. Interview questions about child rearing included the kind of substitute care provided for the children in the mother's absence, mother's opinions about her own employment or nonemployment in relation to the rearing of her children, and mother's philosophy and practices in the areas of discipline and control, dependency and independency training, warmth and involvement with the child, and sex role training. . . .

FINDINGS

. . . The classification of mothers by whether or not they are employed is almost unrelated to child-rearing patterns. These working and nonworking mothers, who are of similar cultural background and family circumstances, are very much alike in philosophy, practices, and apparent relationships with their children. In only one comparison is the difference between the groups statistically significant at the 5 percent level. This difference is in the mother's confidence about her role as mother. Working mothers (42 percent) more frequently than nonworking mothers (24 percent) express misgivings and anxious concern about their role, often by explicit questioning and worry as to whether working is interfering with their relationships and the rearing of their children.

Absence of differences in certain of the variables is particularly interesting. The working and nonworking mothers do not express differing points of view on sex role training. About 40 percent of the total sample present opinions of philosophy which emphasize differences in the rearing of boys and girls in such respects as handling of aggression, activity, social relationships; 40 percent reject the idea of rearing differences; the others are uncertain. Using household responsibilities that are assigned to boys and girls as a measure of sex role typing, families of working and nonworking mothers again do not differ (40 percent in the working group, 42 percent in the non-working assign tasks in terms of traditional sex roles). It may seem reasonable to expect that a working mother will have greater need to schedule time carefully and may, therefore, inject more time-tension into family routines. There is only a suggestive difference in the expected direction; pressured scheduling is prominent among 26 percent of the working and 12 percent of the nonworking group. Working and nonworking mothers do not differ on the summary measure of adequacy of mothering. . . .

More important in differentiating mothers according to child-rearing practices than the fact of working or not working is how the work variable is combined with other maternal characteristics. When work (or nonwork) is analyzed according to whether it is a goal in itself or a means to certain goal attainments, associations with child rearing take on more meaningful patternings. The mothers clearly differed in their desires to work or not to work outside the home. Replies to two questions determined their classification as preferring or not preferring their present status: (1) if given the choice, would the mother want to work, and (2) how would she rank a number of alternatives involving job, marriage, and children. Seventy-six percent of the working mothers and 82 percent of the nonworking mothers indicated preference for their present situations. The resulting four subgroups were compared in their child-rearing characteristics.

The questions about these groups can be asked in two ways: (1) Do working and nonworking mothers who are similarly satisfied (or dissatisfied) with present status differ in child rearing? (2) How do working mothers who prefer to work and those who do not prefer to work compare, and, likewise, how do nonworking mothers who prefer to work and those who do not prefer to work compare on child rearing?

Dissatisfaction with present role appears to contribute to mothering functions, and especially among mothers who are not employed. The subgroups differ as follows. If mothers are in their *preferred* work or nonwork *roles*, working or not working makes little difference in their child rearing.

There are only two suggestive differences: Thirty-four percent of satisfied nonworking mothers and 11 percent of satisfied working mothers are rated as showing high sensitivity to children's needs. There is a difference of borderline significance giving the nonworking satisfied mothers higher scores on adequacy of mothering. When *dissatisfied* working and nonworking mothers are compared, differences appear in areas of control, emotional satisfaction, confidence in child rearing, and on scores on adequacy of mothering, favoring the dissatisfied working mothers. For example, 67 percent of dissatisfied nonworking mothers and 18 percent of dissatisfied working mothers report a more or less continuing "battle" for control between mother and child. High ratings in confidence in the mother role occur more often among the working than the nonworking dissatisfied mothers (50 percent and 11 percent, respectively). In the closely related measure of emotional satisfaction in relationships with the child there are similar differences favoring the working over the nonworking dissatisfied mothers. The sum of ratings shows significantly lower scores on adequacy of mothering for the dissatisfied nonworking mothers than for the dissatisfied working mothers.

The same data may be examined with work status controlled. Among *working* mothers there is some support for the idea that there are more internal inconsistencies in child rearing among the dissatisfied than among the satisfied mothers. Three-fourths of the dissatisfied mothers compared with two-fifths of the satisfied mothers report clear limit-setting for the child. At the same time, however, control is more often rated a continuing issue in the family for the dissatisfied than for the satisfied mothers. More dissatisfied working mothers describe their children as dependent while at the same time tending to exert more verbal pressure toward independent behavior and to assign more responsibilities to their children than do the satisfied mothers.

Among *nonworking* mothers, several dimensions of child-rearing behavior are clearly related to role preference. Clarity in limit setting is more characteristic of the satisfied mothers (61 percent of this group as compared with 22 percent in the dissatisfied group). A significantly higher proportion of dissatisfied mothers show extreme inconsistency between principles and practices (57 percent of the dissatisfied mothers as compared with 6 percent of the satisfied mothers). Control remains a continuing "issue" between mother and child for 67 percent of the dissatisfied and 32 percent of the satisfied mothers. Lack of emotional satisfaction in relationships with her child is more frequent among dissatisfied than satisfied mothers (78 percent and 35 percent, respectively). Similarly, high confidence in the mother role, expressed in 90 percent of the satisfied group, is rare (11 percent) among the dissatisfied mothers. The generally inferior mothering by the dissatisfied nonworking group is reflected in significantly lower summary scores on adequacy of mothering. . . .

Although it is understandable that a woman's career dissatisfactions may enter into her relationships with her child, it is not so clear why this should be more the case in the nonworking than in the working group. A possible explanation may lie in understanding why the women were working or not working, regardless of their expressed preference. The mothers in this sample were working either primarily as a means of achieving certain *family and child-rearing goals* that were not available without the mother's working, or as a means of *self-fulfillment*. Mothers (52 percent) who spoke of family goals were interested in cultural advantages, social status, educational and health goals for the family. They included both mothers who preferred and those who did not prefer to work. Mothers (48 percent) who found self-fulfillment through working referred to use of their educational training, feelings of contributing to society, needing to be with people, etc. These mothers preferred to work.

Since working but preferring not to is related to valued family benefits, the situation for these reluctant working mothers does not appear to represent great frustration. Certainly one would expect these mothers to be less frustrated than women who have reason to resent the necessity for their working as a circumstance forced upon them by their husbands' failures or as a circumstance in which the work itself involves personal hardship. The absence of differences in child rearing associated with family motivations and self-fulfillment motivation is, therefore, not surprising. . . .

Among nonworking women reasons for not working reflect either a *love of mothering* (48 percent), a *duty to mothering* (36 percent), or a desire for "freedom," or an "easier" life (15 percent). "Freedom" is for avocations and "volunteer" work but also, on the less noble side, it is freedom regarded selfishly. As one woman said, she "had it made"; now that husband and children could get their own breakfasts and get off to work and school, the day was for herself. Because of the heterogeneity of motives in the "freedom" group, it was not used in further analyses.

Mothers classified by "love" and by "duty" express different feelings toward the mother role. The "love" mothers are oriented entirely toward mothering; the "duty" mothers speak of child rearing as a responsibility that carries with it various hardships and deprivations. The classification of "love" and "duty" in general parallels the classification of satisfied and dissatisfied nonworking mothers, although "duty" mothers appear in both the satisfied and dissatisfied groups. Differences in child rearing are similar in both classifications; the less favorable qualities appearing in the "duty" and the dissatisfied mothers.

The data on the nonworking mothers support the position that the mother's motivations and fulfillments in nonmother roles are related to her behavior in the child-rearing role. It is necessary, in a sense, first to look at maternal employment and nonemployment as dependent variables before making predictions concerning associated child-rearing variables. . . .

If work status is ignored, college-trained and high school-trained mothers (within the class range of our sample) do not differ on child-rearing measures. But, when work status and educational level and child rearing are considered together suggestive interactions appear. *Nonworking* college mothers and nonworking high school mothers appear to differ in more ways in child rearing than do *working* college mothers and work-high school mothers. In the *nonworking* groups, college mothers are significantly more often rated high in independence training (30 percent and 8 percent for college and high school, respectively), in sensitivity (50 percent and 8 percent), in consistency between principles and practice (85 percent and 54 percent), and in clarity in limit setting (69 percent and 39 percent). The higher mean scores for the college mothers on "adequacy of mothering" summary score reflect the differences on the individual items. The *working* groups differ only on ratings of sensitivity to child's needs (40 percent and 10 percent of high school and college mothers, respectively, are rated low on sensitivity), and on the father's being the stricter parent (70 percent and 34 percent of high school and college groups are so rated). The data suggest that employment may be selective of certain kinds of mothers, or that working hàs the effect of "leveling" social class differences in child rearing. The mothers of high school background who are using working as a means of social mobility (more lessons, education, travel for family) may also be altering their child-rearing practices.

When working and nonworking mothers are compared within each educational group, it appears that families of different social class backgrounds make different types of adaptations to the mother's working. Mothers of high school background more often report the father as the stricter parent when these mothers work (70 percent) than when they do not work (33 percent). Children are less likely to be reported as rebellious by working mothers (10 percent) than by nonworking mothers (46 percent) in the high school group. Similarly, they are more likely to be assigned a heavy load of household responsibilities (30 percent as compared with 8 percent). The working mothers are more likely to stress independence training (80 percent as compared with 54 percent). In other words, children of the working mothers with *high school* backgrounds are under firmer control and are called upon to perform with more responsibility and independence.

The picture for the college-trained group is not the same. The college working mother compared with her nonworking peers is not more likely to describe the father as the stricter parent; there is instead a tendency in the opposite direction (the father is the stricter parent in 30 percent and 50 percent of the working and nonworking groups, respectively). Assignment of responsibilities and nurturance of independence are not stressed by the college-trained working mothers as they are by the working mothers with high school background. (The differences, though not significant, are in the opposite direction from the high school group.)

A variable which has not shown differences in any other comparisons but which appears in the working-nonworking comparisons of college-trained women is that of planned shared time and activities with the child. In the families of college working mothers both parents apparently attempt to compensate for out-of-the-home time by planned time together with the child. Forty percent of the college working mothers report giving planned time to the child. It is reported for 38 percent of the fathers. The nonworking college group have 16 percent and 8 percent in the comparable categories. In families of high school background there is no difference in this variable between working and nonworking groups.

Subcultural or social class analyses may be extremely important in attempting to pin down the kinds of influences that the widespread employment of mothers may have on the socialization of large populations of children. The present data suggest that rearing influences cannot be predicted across class and cultural boundaries (any more than they can be predicted across motivational differences among mothers), and that the nature of influences for different social groups will vary and will grow out of the values and needs of the particular groups.

SUMMARY AND CONCLUSIONS

Qualities of child rearing by mothers who are employed and those who are not employed outside the home have been studied.

One hundred mothers of intact families, of the middle and upper middle class white urban population were interviewed. Families of working and nonworking mothers were matched on family composition and social class.

Mothers' employment status is not related to child-rearing characteristics. The data, however, support the hypothesis that mothers' fulfillments or frustrations in nonmother roles are related to child rearing. When mothers' motivations regarding working are taken into account, the nonworking mothers who are dissatisfied with not working (who want to work but, out of a feeling of "duty," do not work) show the greatest problems in child rearing. They describe more difficulties in the area of control, less emotional satisfaction in relationships with their children, and less confidence in their functioning as mothers. They have lower summary scores on "adequacy of mothering." Working mothers who prefer to work and those who do not wish to work show few group differences in childrearing practices, probably because the working mothers (of this sample) who prefer not to work are nonetheless achieving certain valued family goals by means of their employment.

Among high-school trained mothers, differences between working and nonworking mothers appear in the following areas of rearing: firmer control over children, assignment of greater responsibilities to children, and delegation of the stricter disciplinary role to the father appear more frequently in families of working than nonworking mothers. In the college-trained working and nonworking groups, these differences do not appear. The college working parents tend to compensate for time away from children by more planned, shared activities with their children than is found in the college nonworking group. The data on educational groups suggest that maternal employment brings different kinds of familial adaptations depending on the value systems of the particular cultural subgroups in which the mother is combining mother and worker roles.

The findings of the present study confirm and elaborate observations by other investigators[5] of the importance of social, familial, and personal factors in determining the kind of success the mother achieves in her dual roles. The specific differences in childrearing practices reported in the present study are perhaps less important in our conclusions (until they are replicated) than is the general pattern of significant subgroupings of mothers in relation to child rearing.

The findings of this study have relevance for studies of child rearing more generally in pointing to the interplay of rearing practices (as they are usually defined) and maternal motivations within differing subcultures. These variables need further scrutiny in studies of child-rearing antecedents of child behavior and personality.

APPENDIX: DESCRIPTION OF DEPENDENT VARIABLES

Discipline

1. Mother's strictness. Mother's ratings on direct questions of how strict she regards her discipline. (3 point scale)

2. Father stricter than mother. Mother's statement of relative strictness of mother and father.

3. Disciplinary techniques. Mother's reports of control techniques used: Presence or absence of physical punishment, isolation or deprivation, reasoning, commanding, and scolding, manipulation by threat of loss of love or creating guilt, praise, and affection, distraction. It should be noted that none of the specific techniques differentiated among groups.

4. Mother's permissiveness of aggression. Ratings based on mother's descriptions of child's "temper" and aggression—its frequency, intensity, how she handles it: "All children feel angry now and then. How about ——, would you say he (she) has a temper? How does he show it? Over what things? With whom? How often? How bad before you step in? How do you handle it? How much does he get into fights? How do you handle these?" (5 point scale)

5. Child's rebellious behavior. (Based on same questions as 4 above. 5 point scale)

6. Control an issue between mother and child. Ratings of degree of "issue," based on mother's descriptions of child's reactions to questions: "Does child find it hard to obey? What ways of handling him do you find best, if he does have difficulty? Would you say child has a temper? How does he show it? How often? How do you handle this? In what ways does child sometimes get on your nerves?" (5 point scale)

Independence Training

1. Nurturing independence. Ratings of responses to questions: "In what kinds of things do you feel you can allow your child a fair amount of freedom and in what things do you feel you should keep firm control? What regular jobs or responsibilities does he have? How important is it to you that he carry these out?" (4 point scale)

2. Household responsibilities. Ratings of same questions for quantity of jobs and responsibilities assigned. (3 point scale)

3. Child's dependence on mother. Separate ratings of reports of child's responses to separations from mother, and child's seeking help and attention from mother, "How does —— act when you leave him with somebody else? How much help does —— ask from you in getting things done, with homework, with ideas, dressing, or to ask for information? Do you feel this is necessary, or that he could manage without it?" (3 point scale)

Emotional Relationships

1. Sensitivity to child's needs. Overall ratings of apparent communication between mother and child, how much mother has manifested awareness of child's feelings and her response to child's feelings, how mother has indicated "adjustments" in her actions to meet needs of child, mother's recognition of individuality in her children, mother's insight into her difficulties with her child. (3 point scale)

2. Emotional satisfaction in relationships with child. Overall ratings of mother's explicit expressions of enjoyment, satisfaction, frustration, rejection as well as the indirect display of enjoyment or lack of it. (4 point scale)

3. Planned activities with child by mother and father. Description of activities with child, when and how they occur. Who initiates? Any planning ahead? (3 point scale)

4. Confidence in child rearing. Responses to question "What has child gained or lacked because of your job, or because you have stayed at home?" Reactions to the difficulties experienced with her child with regard to control. Spontaneous expressions of "failure" and misgiving as well as of success and confidence. (3 point scale)

Rearing Environment

1. Formulated principles of rearing. Number of statements of rearing principles given spontaneously anywhere in interview, as well as evidence of formulated principles in response to questions regarding control-freedom and dependency-independency items. (3 point scale)

2. Clarity of limits set for child. Questions on giving or encouraging freedom and independence and on supporting dependence, and on handling aggression, obedience, and conformity (described under these headings). Clarity ratings are based on how explicit are the limits set for the child. (3 point scale)

3. Consistency between principles and practices. Consistency ratings compare philosophy or intention and described practices in these areas. Based on same questions as 2 above. (3 point scale)

4. Scheduling. Overall ratings of evidences of time-tension, concern about timing and schedule. (3 point scale)

5. Traditional philosophy regarding sex role training. Response to question "Do you (could you) bring up boys and girls in much the same way; or are there differences in the way they are reared?"

6. Traditional sex-typed household functions. Traditional sex typing of regular household tasks carried out or assigned to each parent and to child. (3 point scale)

7. Adequacy of mothering (summary rating). Summary ratings on eight variables; see text.

NOTES

[1] National Manpower Council, *Womanpower* (New York: Columbia University Press, 1957).

[2] Lois M. Stolz, "Effects of Maternal Employment on Children: Evidence from Research," *Child Development,* 31 (December 1960): 749–782.

[3] Ibid.

[4] Thomas L. Gillette, "The Working Mother: A Study of the Relationship Between Maternal Employment and Family Structure as Influenced by Social Class and Race," unpublished doctoral dissertation, University of North Carolina, 1961.

[5] Ibid.; Ruth E. Hartley, "What Aspects of Child Behavior Should be Studied in Relation to Maternal Employment?" in Alberta E. Siegel, ed., *Research Issues Related to the Effects of Maternal Employment on Children* (University Park, Pennsylvania: Social Science Research Center, 1961); Lois Hoffman, "Effects of Maternal Employment on the Child," *Child Development,* 32 (March 1961): 187–197; Alberta E. Siegel, "Characteristics of the Mother Related to the Impact of Maternal Employment or Nonemployment," in Alberta E. Siegel, ed., op. cit.

Part Eleven

Why Some Marriages Succeed and Others Do Not

The topics covered in this and the next two sections are difficult to place in the developmental sequence. Yet the success or failure of marriage must be treated at some point. It is known that the early years of marriage are the most risky, but since the actual timing of success or failure in marriage is impossible to place in a general way, these topics are placed somewhat arbitrarily as a unit following the discussions of getting married and having children.

Success in marriage is a controversial topic; it concerns us all, but it has rather nebulous characteristics to try to measure. Most often, the measures used have been happiness and stability, and these two criteria have frequently been used interchangeably as though they were one and the same. This is because many people assume that a couple stays together because they are happily married, or at least happy enough not to end their marriage. Recent research has made it pretty clear, however, that just staying together for a married lifetime does not necessarily mean that the couple has been happy in the relationship. Conversely, there are also marriages that report happiness for a period of time, months or even years, and then are disrupted either by changes in one or both partners or in the circumstances surrounding the couple. Sometimes forced separations, such as those created by military service, a job away from home, or even the birth of a child, will cause a harmonious relationship to be disrupted and perhaps come to an end.

There are degrees of stability ranging from that where the couple barely hangs on over the years to that where the couple has never even considered a separation. However, if stability is to be defined simply as staying together without considering the quality of the relationship, then if the couple does part, at least a clearly observable statistic is available. At the same time, those marriages that are simply existing in name only are termed a success because no divorce takes place. It is easy to see that as a measurement of a successful marriage, stability alone is not a very satisfactory criterion.

Similarly, the other measure, happiness,

is not one that gives very concrete evidence of success either. It is elusive, subjective, and therefore difficult to measure. Happiness in marriage must often be studied by interviewing the couple or by using questionnaires to measure their attitudes toward certain factors thought to predict happiness or satisfaction. These attitudes about happiness are as difficult to pin down as are the ones toward love and infatuation discussed in Part Six. The researcher on marital happiness must try to distinguish between the overall personal happiness of the partners as individuals and the happiness that each feels comes about as a result of the marriage. It is suspected that men and women who are basically satisfied with themselves and with other aspects of their lives will find marriage a more satisfying experience than will individuals who generally see life as negative. Furthermore, some men and women are disturbed enough that any marriage they enter would have trouble succeeding. Hence, since stability may be caused by factors other than satisfaction and happiness, and since the quality of happiness is so elusive to measure, there is clearly a need for better ways to study marital success.

With the current emphasis on individual growth and satisfaction, marriage is no longer seen as an institution which the partners must serve, but is instead seen as an institution to serve the needs of the husband and wife. Perhaps success of a marriage might more accurately be assessed by determining the individual and joint goals of the couple and how well the marriage is facilitating these goals. A marriage would then be pronounced a success if it could be shown to be conducive to helping the couple reach these goals, and a failure if it frustrates such growth.

One thing becomes apparent in the analysis of why some marriages are successful and others not—by whatever standards they are assessed—and that is that there are a variety of kinds of marriages which are deemed successful. The varieties seem to have as departure points the model of the traditional marriage on the one hand and the companionship or equalitarian marriage on the other. The types of marriage within

the more traditional framework emphasize roles and expected behavior of husbands and wives as defined by society as a whole. As might be expected, how much agreement the husband and wife have about how each shall play his or her own roles, and how much these roles are socially approved, correlate highly with the success of the marriage. The more traditional the marriage, the more the husband tends to define the roles and the more he is expected to be dominant, brighter, better educated, and usually older. In the first selection, Robert Stuckert examines role concepts and expectations and shows that marital happiness is more often reported when both partners agree on how the roles are to be played. His sample consists of newly married young couples—even at this early stage the picture is complicated.

Since people are dynamic and the life-cycle creates new needs and changing abilities, roles and behavior expectations can be expected to change over the years. Such change has been termed the "developmental adjustment in marriage," and in recent years a good deal of research has been completed in this area. It seems that marital problems continue through the life-cycle, but that not all people learn to cope with them successfully. Marital tension is often highest during the years when the children are growing up and, for some couples, levels off during the later stages of life. The low point for many couples comes during the children's adolescent years; but if the marriage survives, a rising trend of satisfaction begins.

Couples report tensions over the years concerning how each is carrying out his or her roles and about relationships with children and other family members, how the money is handled, what they do in their leisure time, and how their sexual life is faring. Still other life-cycle studies have indicated that there is a gradual decrease in marital satisfaction over the years even with couples who report they are happy. Although some couples seem to enjoy marriage more with each year, when the average is taken enough couples say satisfaction declines to cause the trend in this direction. Part of the reason the data conflict is that in many studies the information for males is not separated from that for females. Husbands and wives seem to view marriage with differing degrees of satisfaction over the years. Wives seem to be at low ebb during the child-rearing years, particularly if they stay at home to take the bulk of the responsibility. In the second reading, Boyd Rollins and Harold Feldman study the stages of the family life-cycle, showing the male-female differences and the changes in marital satisfaction.

Because the working wife is in many ways breaking away from the role of the traditional wife, many researchers have studied how her employment affects both her own satisfaction with her marriage and her husband's satisfaction. It has been suspected that a husband might be threatened in his traditional role of provider and that he may be forced to take more responsibility at home, thus causing conflict. A major factor in how the husband and wife react to her employment is tied to the life-cycle, since the concerns by both for the care of their children are very real. Families with mothers employed outside the home still seem to see the responsibility for the home and children as being primarily the wife's. To suggest that, if the sitter doesn't show up or if a child is ill, the husband may need to stay at home seems to be a solution few couples would even consider. The attitude that housework and child-care are the woman's province has led some observers to say that the working wife has gained the freedom to have two full-time jobs. The third article is a careful study by Susan Orden and Norman Bradburn on the tensions and satisfactions that result from the wife's employment. They show that, when the woman works out of necessity, both she and her husband are negatively affected.

In studies on the various types of companionate marriage, the emphases are on interpersonal involvement, communication, love, and those qualities symbolic of closeness. There is evidence that marriages of this kind are more apt to be viewed as happy by the partners because of their good personal interaction and because their concerns with situational factors, such as money, in-laws, and problems with children, are secondary. Such a relationship has a

great deal of importance to the emotional and even physical well-being of the partners. Since each partner has so much investment in the other partner and such a great ego-involvement in the marriage, personal happiness and health are seriously impaired if the marriage is not successful. Karen Renne reports an extensive study of marriage which indicates how marital satisfaction is correlated with emotional and physical health. An important finding in this study is that the blacks in the sample, as well as others in the low-income, low-education group, register more marital unhappiness than more affluent, better educated people. Renne's evidence supports the findings of other research that children do not add to the satisfaction of marriage, and that childless marriages or marriages after the children leave home report more satisfaction.

Another interesting aspect of the love and companionship approach to marriage is the sexual relationship between the couple. A great deal has been written about the lack of sexual gratification reported by many married couples, and the problems have been blamed on boredom, overfamiliarity, the unnaturalness of lifetime monogamy, opportunity for extramarital sex, and countless other factors. While these probably do play a part, important research has shown that the quality of the interpersonal relationship between husband and wife may hold the real answer. Husbands and wives who are unhappy in the marriage are low in sexual responsiveness; those who report love and respect for their partner grow in sexual responsiveness in the marriage as a result of positive sexual experiences with each other. Sex, then, is not a duty which goes with a role, but is a part of the interpersonal relationship.

It becomes increasingly clear that marital success is a complex phenomenon and that there are many durable and satisfying forms of marriage. The idea that marriages are made in heaven and that, if the couple is in love, all will be well is being dispelled by the research showing that individuals and their marriages change with the life-cycle. All marriages have imperfections, but there are good marriages that are more than merely stable ones. There is evidence that good and stable marriages depend on health and happiness and companionship. The final article in this chapter, by Lois Pratt, explores the equalitarian marriage versus the marriage of unequal power, rigid role casting, and lower companionship. Heterosexual friendship seems to be the core of most of today's successful marriages, and friendship can flourish best where both parties feel equally important and valuable. In today's world, most of the needs of the married couple center around companionship and caring. While roles will always be functional, the realization that the definition of roles should be mutually determined is a growing part of the marriage picture.

56

ROLE PERCEPTION AND MARITAL SATISFACTION— A CONFIGURATIONAL APPROACH

Robert P. Stuckert

The roles of husband and wife, like any set of culturally related roles, carry a complex pattern of expectations of the responses which are to come from the other. Adjustment to either role is influenced by the consistency with which the other responds by making the responses called for by the role pattern. Inconsistency in the responses of the other to the individual increases the insecurity of the person in either role since it makes him uncertain of the validity of his own role concept. This is particularly true when an individual first moves into a marital role. In this case, not only has he had no opportunity to test the validity of his role concept, it is also necessary for the other person in the role situation to make the changes in his responses and expectations called for by the new role.

Whether or not a marital partner responds consistently with the expectations of the other depends on his own performed concept of his role, his own expectations regarding the reciprocal role of his spouse, his perception of his mate's expectations of him, and the degree of correspondence between the two sets of role concepts and expectations. If these role concepts are similar, communication is easier and the relationship existing between the marriage partners is more satisfactory to both. If role perception is accurate, each partner is better able to anticipate the other's feelings and gear his own responses to the expectations of the other.

Previous studies of the relationship between role perception and marital satisfaction indicate there are at least four significant components of perception. The first is the degree of similarity between the role concepts and expectations of one partner and the other's own role concepts and expectations. The second is the degree of similarity between the way a person perceives the role expectations of his marital partner and the partner's actual role expectations. The third is the degree of congruence between his concept of the marital role in general and his concept of his specific role, i.e., does he view his marriage as being similar to or different from most marriages? The fourth is the degree of similarity between a person's role expectations and his perception of the expectations of his spouse.[1]

The results of these studies have not been in complete agreement as to the relationship between modes of perception and marital satisfaction. In some, congruent perception was found to be associated with marital success; in others, the relationship was not evident. One of the latest reported that ". . . satisfaction in marriage was related significantly to the congruency of the husband's self-concept and that held of him by his wife, but was found unrelated to the agreement of the concepts the wife holds of herself and that which her husband holds of her."[2]

The key to this may lie in an idea which everyone mentions but is seldom tested directly. Marital adjustment is not a function of any single component of perception or even of several taken independently. The major hypothesis of this study is that marital satisfaction is a function of the mutual interaction of these components. The way in which any one of these components is related to marital satisfaction may depend on the specific relationship of the others with this criterion. . . .

In order to study the effects of discrepancies in role expectations and perception on marital adjustment before other familial factors come into operation, a sample of newly married couples was used. The population consisted of all couples between the ages of 19 and 26 who were listed in the Milwaukee newspapers as having applied for marriage licenses during July and August, 1959. A random sample of 100 couples were selected. Locating these couples at the time of the study was a problem because the addresses given in the newspapers were those prior to marriage. To reduce the variability of the sample, only white, native-born persons were included. In addition, any couple with a child at the time of the interview was eliminated. The final sample consisted of 50 couples who had been married nine months or less. There was only one refusal. . . .

Role concepts and expectations were determined by means of a set of 30 questions incorporated into an interview schedule.

These questions involved the relative importance to the individual of selected personality factors in the husband and wife roles. The ten personality needs most frequently listed in a study of marital choice by Anselm Strauss were used in modified form.[3] These are:

1. Importance of love in marriage
2. Being able to confide in one's spouse
3. Showing affection
4. Respecting one's ideals
5. Appreciating the achievements of the other
6. Understanding the other's moods
7. Helping in making important decisions
8. Stimulating the other's ambition
9. Showing respect for the other
10. Giving self-confidence in relations with other people

During the interview, the respondent was asked to evaluate the relative importance of these factors in three different ways:

1. Their importance in marriage in general
2. Their importance in his own marriage
3. Their importance from the point of view of his spouse

In every case, the respondent was asked about his expectations with respect to both his role and the role of the other. The ten factors were rank-ordered on the basis of the respondent's evaluation of their relative importance. Husband and wife were interviewed separately. . . .

The individual's own evaluation of his marriage was used as the criterion of marital satisfaction. . . .

The accuracy with which the wife perceives the marital expectations of her husband is related to her marital satisfaction. The accuracy of her husband's perception of his wife's views is not associated with satisfaction in this early period of marriage. The degree of similarity between the views of husband and wife is related to the marital satisfaction of the husband but not to that of the wife. None of these five variables is correlated with any of the others. . . .

The total sample was divided into subsamples to develop a set of marital types. A set of factors was used to identify a distinct type if over 80 percent of the cases included were similar with respect to the criterion of marital satisfaction. . . . The procedure resulted in three husband types and three wife types.[4]. . .

Type H1 is defined by a single characteristic. He shares a common view of marriage with his wife. When other factors are examined, an interesting pattern emerges. On the one hand, there is no relationship between the accuracy with which he perceives his wife's role expectations and his marital satisfaction. Husbands in this category are about evenly divided between those who perceived their wives' expectations accurately (56 percent) and those who did not (44 percent). On the other hand, this is the only one of the three husband types in which the majority of the wives perceive their husbands' role expectations accurately. . . .

Type H2, as defined by two characteristics, is a dissatisfied type. His view of marriage is different from that held by his wife. He also perceives his wife's expectations correctly. In this case, accuracy of perception is inversely related to marital satisfaction. This is the only group in which the husband and wife differ as to whether or not they view their marriage as being typical of marriages in general. The wife tends to view their marriage as being typical; the husband views it as being different. The wives of these men tend to be dissatisfied with the marriage as well.

Although the role expectations of Type H3 are different from those of his wife, he does not perceive her expectations accurately. He defines his marriage as being typical of marriages in general. In these two characteristics, he is similar to his wife. This type of husband was the only one that stated in the interview that things did not run smoothly and that he was often unsure of himself when family decisions had to be made. This may be due to his not perceiving his wife's differing marital expectations accurately. Since he may define this as being characteristic of marriage, this type of husband is generally satisfied with his marriage.

Type W1 is the perceptive wife. She sees her husband's role expectations as he de-

fines them himself. Apparently this is sufficient because 84 percent of the 25 wives in this category have a "Satisfied" rating. It is interesting to note that these wives are not appreciably high on any of the other factors including similarity of the actual role expectations of the two marriage partners.

Although Type W2 does not perceive her husband's role expectations accurately, her expectations of both her own role and his are similar to those he has of the two roles. Her marital satisfaction score is also high. The husband may be the crucial factor because this is the only group of wives with husbands who perceive their wives' expectations accurately. Almost every one of these couples view their marriage as typical of marriages in general. Type W3, the dissatisfied category, not only has dissimilar views of marriage from her husband but also does not perceive her husband's views of the marital roles accurately.

CONCLUSIONS

This study reveals that the relation between the accuracy with which a recently married person perceives the role expectations of his spouse and marital satisfaction is not a simple one. For the wives in the sample, the extent to which their perception of their husband's expectations correlates with the husband's actual expectations is the dominant factor associated with marital satisfaction. In the case of the husbands, however, the actual similarity between their own role concepts and expectations and those of their wives is the most important single factor. Furthermore, in one-half of the cases studied, whether or not accuracy of perception is related to marital satisfaction depends on a configuration of factors of which it is a part.

The other factors included in the definitions of these configurations in this study are the individual's view of his marriage and the expectations each marriage partner has of the spouse. On the one hand, accurate perception may detract from marital satisfaction if the two marriage partners have widely differing expectations of the roles of husband and wife. On the other hand, inaccurate perception may not result in dissatisfaction if the person defines his marriage as being typical of marriages in general.

The data in this study support the thesis that the husband's role definitions and expectations may be more important to the early success of a marriage than the wife's. Family adjustment may be greatly affected by the extent to which the husband and wife are oriented toward both actual and potential role changes. Since American cultural patterns still generally define the husband as the dominant spouse, he may have a greater part in establishing the general structure of the new family.[5] A greater proportion of a woman's life is family-related. Her interests and activities tend to be family-centered to a greater extent than her husband's. Since our culture tends to define her role as centering around her family, there may be greater pressure on her to develop an accommodative pattern in relation to other members of the family. As Eleanor Luckey points out, if it is the wife who must make the greater adjustment in marriage, "it is to the benefit of the relationship if she knows what she's adjusting to! If she sees the husband as he sees himself, she is better able to make adjustments which bring more satisfaction to the marriage."[6]

NOTES

[1] Leland H. Stott, "The Problem of Evaluating Family Success," *Marriage and Family Living*, 13 (Fall 1951): 149–153; M. G. Preston and others, "Impressions of Personality as a Function of Marital Conflict," *Journal of Abnormal and Social Psychology*, 47 (April 1952): 326–336; Orville Brim and Nancy Wood, "Self and Other Conceptions in Courtship and Marriage Pairs," *Marriage and Family Living*, 18 (August 1956): 243–248; A. R. Mangus, "Family Impacts on Mental Health," *Marriage and Family Living*, 19 (August 1957): 256–262; Eleanor B. Luckey, "Marital Satisfaction and Congruent Self-Spouse Concepts," *Social Forces*, 39 (December 1960): 153–157; Nathan Hurvitz, "The Measurement of Marital Strain," *American Journal of Sociology*, 65 (May 1960): 610–615.

[2] Luckey, op. cit., p. 153.

[3] Anselm Strauss, "Personality Needs and Marital Choice," *Social Forces*, 25 (March 1947): 332–335.

[4] None of these types was related to either religious affiliation or occupational status of the husband.

[5] John Sirjamaki, "Cultural Configurations in the American Family," *American Journal of Sociology*, 53 (May 1948): 464–470.

[6] Luckey, op. cit., pp. 156–157.

57

MARITAL SATISFACTION OVER THE FAMILY LIFE CYCLE

Boyd C. Rollins and Harold Feldman

The concept of developmental adjustment in marriage has recently stimulated concern for patterns of change in marital interaction over the family life cycle. This approach contrasts sharply with the earlier attempts to predict adjustment in the early stages of marriage under the assumption that personal readiness for marriage, compatible mate selection, and early adjustment were the keys to marital success. Dovetailing with the interest in developmental adjustment is the concept of stages of the family life cycle. Both Loomis (1936) and Lansing and Kish (1957) have demonstrated that stages of the family life cycle are more highly correlated with family economic behavior than either age of head of household or length of time a couple had been married. . . . The issue of the meaning of marital success, its pattern over the family life cycle and its developmental antecedents and correlates is a primary issue in contemporary family sociology.

Burgess and Locke (1945) identified eight criteria of marital success that have been utilized in part in the evaluation of the strengths of marriages during the past three decades. These criteria are: (1) permanence, (2) social expectations, (3) personality development, (4) companionship, (5) happiness, (6) satisfaction, (7) adjustments, and (8) integration. By 1964 about 400 articles or books on some aspect of marital success had been published (Aldous and Hill, 1967). About one half of these dealt with marital satisfaction or of somewhat similar criteria of success; namely, happiness, adjustment, integration, or companionship. . . .

As a descriptive device the family life cycle has been used to compare structures and functions of marital interaction in different stages of development. A fairly simple scheme and the one used in this study was to classify couples into eight stages of the family life cycle in terms of the age of the oldest child. . . . The classification was as follows:

Stage I. Beginning Families (couples married 0 to 5 yrs. without children)

Stage II. Childbearing Families (oldest child, birth to 2 yrs. 11 mos.)

Stage III. Families with Preschool Children (oldest child, 3 yrs. to 5 yrs. 11 mos.)

Stage IV. Families with Schoolage Children (oldest child, 6 yrs. to 12 yrs. 11 mos.)

Stage V. Families with Teen-agers (oldest child, 13 yrs. to 20 yrs. 11 mos.)

Stage VI. Families as Launching Centers (first child gone to last child's leaving home)

Stage VII. Families in the Middle Years (empty nest to retirement)

Stage VIII. Aging Families (retirement to death of first spouse) . . .

The present study was done in an attempt to find answers to some of the discrepancies in the earlier studies, especially concerning the pattern of marital satisfaction following the "schoolage" stage of the family life cycle for wives and over the whole life cycle for husbands. The discrepancies in the previous studies were contaminated by extremely small samples in the later stages of the family life cycle or a failure to differentiate males and females in the data analyses. Also, it was hoped that a substantiated pattern of marital satisfaction would be described from this study and provide a basis for beginning attempts to construct a developmental theory of marital satisfaction. . . .

Data for this study were obtained through the use of an area survey sample of middle class residents of Syracuse, New York, in 1960. Dr. Charles Willie, a sociologist at the University of Syracuse had previously classified all the census tracts in the city of Syracuse, New York, into one of six "social areas" in terms of (1) percent of single family dwellings, (2) average monthly rental, (3) average market value of owned homes, (4) median number of school years completed, and (5) percent of operatives, service workers, and laborers in the census tract. The census tracts in the top two social areas were considered to include a large proportion of upper middle class and upper class residents.

The nine census tracts in the top two socioeconomic categories of the city were sampled in this study. Each of these tracts was arbitrarily divided in half taking the half closest to the center of the city for one and the half furthest away for the next until a geographical area in each tract was selected. Every third housing unit in the selected area was a target dwelling. If either one or both spouses were to be absent from the household during the data gathering period, were unable to complete the questionnaire (illiterate in English, mental or serious illness), or the husband was a full-time student, the household was eliminated from the study.

Fieldworkers stopped at each selected housing unit, left a questionnaire for each husband and each wife and made an appointment to pick them up within a few days. The questionnaire asked for information on family of orientation and family of procreation, marital history, occupation, marital satisfaction, communication, decision making, methods of handling conflicts, values, frequency of integrative and disruptive experiences, and satisfaction with stages of the family life cycle from each individual. Only the data used to classify couples by stage of family life cycle and marital satisfaction are analyzed in this paper. A high response rate of 85 percent usable questionnaires from both husbands and wives in the same households were collected from the target housing units. This provided data on a total of 852 married couples.

On religious preference 21 percent of the couples indicated Catholic, 35 percent Protestant, 27 percent Jewish, and 17 percent either mixed or none. Eighty-eight percent of the husbands were classified as white collar and only 12 percent as blue collar according to their occupation, and only 12 percent of the couples included a person

who had been married previously to another person. Sixty-eight percent of the husbands had received some college education and 24 percent had received post graduate education. The sample was predominantly caucasian, well-educated, middle- and upper-class persons in their first marriage with the wife not working outside the home.

Fifty-three of the initial 852 couples were married for more than five years and were still childless. They were eliminated from the analysis because they were considered atypical in terms of stages of the family life cycle. On the basis of length of time married, age of oldest child, and residence of children, the remaining 799 couples were classified into one of eight stages of the family life cycle. The distribution of these couples was as follows: 51 at Stage I ("Beginning"), 51 at Stage II ("Infant"), 82 at Stage III ("Preschool"), 244 at Stage IV ("Schoolage"), 227 at Stage V ("Teen-age"), 64 at Stage VI ("Launching"), 30 at Stage VII ("Empty nest"), and 50 at Stage VIII ("Retirement").

The data on marital satisfaction were taken from four questions on the questionnaire as follows:

1. General Marital Satisfaction—"In general, how often do you think that things between you and your wife are going well? — all the time, —most of the time, —more often than not, —occasionally, —rarely, — never."

2. Negative Feelings from Interaction with Spouse—"How often would you say that the following events occur between you and your husband (wife)? —never, — once or twice a year, —once or twice a month, —once or twice a week, —about once a day, —more than once a day." The combined responses of each individual in reply to "you feel resentful," "you feel not needed," and "you feel misunderstood" were used in the data analysis. In a factor analysis of the data these three events were equally highly loaded on a dominant factor.

3. Positive Companionship Experiences with Spouse —"How often would say that the following events occur between you and your husband (wife)? —never, —once or twice a year, —once or twice a month, — once or twice a week, —about once a day, —more than once a day." The combined responses of each individual in reply to "laugh together," "calmly discuss something together," "have a stimulating exchange of ideas," and "work together on a project" were used in the data analysis. In a factor analysis of the data these four events were equally and highly loaded on a dominant factor.

4. Satisfaction with Present Stage of the Family Life Cycle—"Different stages of the family life cycle may be viewed as being more satisfying than others. How satisfying do you think the following stages are? — very satisfying, —quite satisfying, —somewhat satisfying, —not satisfying." Data on this question were used in reply to "before the children arrive" for individuals in Stage I, "first year with infant" for Stage II, "preschool children at home" for Stage III, "all children at school" for Stage IV, "having teen-agers" for Stage V, "children gone from home" for Stages VI and VII, and "being grandparents" for Stage VIII. . . .

On only two of the four indices of marital satisfaction is there a consistent pattern over the family life cycle for both husbands and wives. Concerning the frequency of positive companionship experience, they both reported a substantial decline from the beginning of marriage to the "preschool" stage and then a leveling off over the remainder of the stages. The events used to form this scale, laughing together, calm discussions with each other, having a stimulating exchange of ideas with each other, and working together on a project are events to which they could both objectively report a frequency of occurrence. Since they were mutual events, we would expect a similar response from the husbands and wives in each couple, if they were objective in their evaluations. The pattern here seems to be very clear, that stimulating common activity in marriage decreases from the very beginning with no recovery. A similar result was found by Pineo (1961) from reports of both husbands and wives and by Blood and Wolfe (1960) from reports of wives only.

Concerning satisfaction with present stage of the family life cycle, both husband and wife rate highly the childbearing and early childrearing phases and are at a low point when launching the children from the home. Perhaps this is an indication of satisfaction with parenthood more than marriage.

The two indices of marital satisfaction in which husbands and wives follow different patterns over the family life cycle refer to the subjective affective state of each individual with reference to their marriage. In general, husbands seem to be much less affected by stage of the family life cycle in their subjective evaluations of marital satisfaction than are wives. The husbands vary little from the establishment through the childbearing and childrearing phases. However, the wives have a substantial decrease in general marital satisfaction and a high level of negative feelings from marital interaction during the childbearing and childrearing phases until the children are getting ready to leave home. After the childrearing phases both husbands and wives have a substantial increase in marital satisfaction through the "retirement" stage with an apparent temporary setback just before the husband retires.

These data suggest that experiences of childbearing and childrearing have a rather profound and negative effect on marital satisfaction for wives, even in their basic feelings of self-worth in relation to their marriage. Perhaps this is partly a consequence of the great reduction in positive companionship experiences with their husbands instigated by the pressures of childrearing responsibilities. On the other hand, the loss of companionship seems to occur for husbands without a decrease in marital satisfaction. The most devastating period of marriage for males appears to be when they are anticipating retirement. Marital satisfaction might be influenced more by occupational experiences for husbands than the event and developmental level of children in their families.

These data suggest that marriage has very different meanings for husbands than for wives and that very different events within or outside the marriage and/or family influence the developmental pattern of marital satisfaction in men and women. This might help explain the fact that some studies have found family life cycle differences for both men and women and some for women only. It seems that men are influenced more by events both before and after there are children in families while women are influenced more by the presence of children.

From a review of the literature and the data reported in this study it seems evident that marital satisfaction of husbands and wives is associated with stages of the family life cycle and a developmental theory of marital satisfaction is needed to explain this association. However, it is questionable that the same developmental theory would have utility for both husbands and wives. It is suggested that a developmental theory of marital satisfaction for wives would focus on the contingent role of parenthood while for husbands the contingent occupational role seems more relevant.

REFERENCES

Aldous, Joan, and Reuben Hill. *International Bibliography of Research in Marriage and the Family, 1900–1964.* Minneapolis: University of Minnesota Press, 1967.

Blood, Robert O., and Donald M. Wolfe. *Husbands and Wives: The Dynamics of Married Living.* Glencoe, Illinois: Free Press, 1960.

Burgess, Ernest W., and Harvey J. Locke. *The Family: From Institution to Companionship.* New York: American Book Company, 1945.

Lansing, John J., and Leslie Kish. "Family Life Cycle as an Independent Variable." *American Sociological Review,* 22 (October 1957): 512–519.

Loomis, Charles C. "The Study of the Life Cycle of Families." *Rural Sociology,* 1 (June 1936): 180–199.

Pineo, Peter C. "Disenchantment in the Later Years of Marriage." *Marriage and Family Living,* 23 (February 1961): 3–11.

58

WORKING WIVES AND MARRIAGE HAPPINESS

Susan R. Orden and Norman M. Bradburn

There have been dramatic changes in the participation of married women in the labor force in the United States. The rate of participation more than doubled from 1900 to 1940 and then doubled again from 1940 to 1960.[1] "In 1962, there were 23,000,000 women in the labor force and the forecast for 1970 is 30,000,000. [Editor's note: According to the Bureau of Labor Statistics of the U.S. Department of Labor, as of March 1972 there were 32,939,000 women in the labor force.] Approximately three out of five women workers are married. Among married women one in three is working; among nonwhite almost one in two. Many of these women, nearly a third, work part time; three-fifths of all part-time work is done by married women."[2]

This paper deals with the effects of a woman's work status on her marriage and suggests that a woman's freedom to choose among alternative life styles is an important predictor of her own and her husband's happiness in marriage. . . .

Other investigators have not disclosed any statistically significant relationships between a woman's work status and her adjustment in marriage.[3] They have found only some tendency for employment to increase the conflict a woman encounters in her relationship with her husband. Nye suggests that the net adverse effect of employment is less in the higher socioeconomic families than in the lower. Blood, on the other hand, suggests that there is some positive evaluation of marriage associated with the wife's employment for lower-income families and some negative evaluation when the husband's income is high. Feld reports no difference in evaluations of either marital problems or marital unhappiness between employed and nonemployed mothers and concludes that the woman's employment status is not an important variable in accounting for adjustment in marriage. Blood recommends that a more fruitful approach for future research would be to specify more precisely the conditions under which employment has positive or negative effects.

There are several important gaps in previous research. First, the husband has been completely neglected. Earlier studies have been based exclusively on interviews with women. The impact of a woman's participation in the labor market may be significantly different for the husband than it is for the wife.

Second, the concept of economic necessity used in previous studies is, at best, as Blood describes it, a "slippery term in an advertising-saturated culture."[4] While it is undoubtedly true, in general, that the need to work is related to income, previous research measuring need by husband's income alone ignores qualitative differences in the perception of need at different class levels. The middle-class woman's "need" to supplement her husband's income in order to acquire the numerous accoutrements of the good life may be as real to her as the lower-class woman's need to meet her family's basic requirements for food, clothing, and shelter.

Finally, the measures of marital adjustment in previous investigations have ignored the positive side of the marriage—the companionship and sociability that husbands and wives enjoy together. The measures of adjustment in these studies have dealt primarily with over-all evaluation and with the negative side of the marriage—the conflict or tension encountered in the relationship. Blood points out that no information exists on what he and Wolfe consider the purest form of companionship: "going out together just to have a good time."[5] It is not at all clear whether a woman's contribution to the family income increases the amount of money which can be budgeted for social activities or whether employment drains the woman's physical and psychic energies, making her content to join her husband with the proverbial pipe and slippers. . . .

This paper proposes to fill in some of the gaps in our knowledge of the relation between a wife's employment and marriage happiness. First, our sample includes husbands. There are 781 husbands and 957 wives, or a total of 1,738 married respondents. This analysis is concerned with 1,651 of these respondents who report the husband as the chief wage earner.[6] The men and women are not couples; but, since they both were selected on a probability basis, it seems reasonable to assume that, on the average, the distribution of responses is the same as it would have been if they had been couples.

Second, we distinguish between women who are impelled into the labor force by perceived economic necessity and those who enter the labor force by choice. This distinction is based on responses to the following question: "Would you [or your wife, if the respondent is a man] work if you [or she] didn't need the money?" As we shall see, the distinction between wives who are reluctant recruits to the labor force and those who enter the labor market as a preferred alternative has important consequences for the analysis of marriage happiness.

Ideally, it would be desirable to make a comparable distinction between women who choose to center their activities in the home and those who are there reluctantly. However, in the absence of data to make this distinction, we consider these women as a single group. We assume that, in general, women who are in the home are there by choice. In periods of high levels of economic activity and relatively low unemployment, it seems reasonable to assume that women who choose to will generally find employment opportunities and make the necessary arrangements. The year 1963, when our study was in the field, was a year of high economic activity. The gross national product was $583.9 billion, an increase of $27.7 billion over the 1962 level; the unemployment rate for women was 6.5 percent compared with 6.2 percent in 1962; factory sales of passenger cars totaled 7,638,000, an increase of 10 percent over 1962 levels.[7]

We recognize that the assumption that married women generally have free access to the labor force in a full-employment economy is an oversimplification. On the supply side, there are undoubtedly restraints to freedom of entry imposed by the woman's education, her stage in the life cycle, her own and her husband's attitudes toward "working wives," the availability of adequate substitute help, and her own personality disposition, needs, and desires. On the demand side, there may be restraints to free entry imposed by employers as well as by male incumbents in the labor force.[8] To the extent that wives in the home include reluctant recruits who would prefer to be in the labor market, they would tend to understate the marriage adjustment of the group as a whole.

The third addition this study makes to earlier research is to correct for omission of the positive side of the marriage. The analysis will use a conceptual framework that views marriage happiness as a two-dimensional model composed of a dimension of satisfactions and a dimension of tensions.[9] By means of a cluster analysis or responses to two checklists—one of recent pleasurable experiences in the marriage and another of disagreements—two clusters of marital experience were differentiated. One cluster reflects satisfactions—the companionship and sociability that husbands and wives enjoy together. The other cluster reflects tensions—the disagreements that husbands and wives encounter in the relationship. The items in the satisfactions cluster do not correlate, or correlate only moderately, with the items in the tensions cluster. Thus, satisfactions and tensions are not merely opposite ends of a single continuum of experiences but are separate and independent dimensions. Two indexes of satisfactions (companionship and sociability) and a single index of tensions were derived from responses to the batteries of items. These indexes correlate in the expected directions with the individual's own rating of his happiness in marriage: both indexes of satisfactions are positively related to marriage happiness, and tensions are negatively related to marriage happiness, while the two dimensions are virtually independent of each other. These characteristics of satisfactions and tensions suggest that the difference between an individual's scores on these separate dimensions, which we call the Marriage Adjustment Balance Scale (MABS), is a good indicator of happiness in marriage.

Finally, we propose that a study of married women's participation in the labor force cannot rely on the simple distinction made in studies of the male labor supply which view market work and leisure as the principal alternatives. For married women, there are three basic alternatives: work in the home, work in the labor market, and leisure activities.

When we speak of work for women, we must consider the woman who centers her life in the home and specializes in the production of home goods—principally child care, food preparation, and housekeeping. Adapting a distinction made by Cain,[10] we have designated women in the sample as either labor market workers or home market workers. Leisure can then be viewed as an alternative open to both groups of women.

This designation of women as labor market workers or home market workers should help to clarify the concept of work for women and eliminate some of the ambiguity in discussions of role conflicts. The designation, however, should not obscure the fact that home market work differs from labor market work in several important respects. First, there are no monetary rewards for tasks performed in the home; second, there are no job descriptions or universal standards of achievement for the production of home goods; third, the value of goods and services produced in the home is not included in the national income if the woman performs them herself but is included if they are performed by a substitute and then only at the lowest wage level; fourth, the home market worker reduces her responsibility if she performs well, while the labor market measures success by increase in responsibility. These differences undoubtedly create complex problems of prestige and achievement which cannot be resolved simply by designating all women as workers and then differentiating between women who work in the labor market and women who work in the home market. We do expect, however, that this distinction will prove useful as an operational concept.

In this study, the dependent variable—marriage happiness—is described by five measures. Satisfactions are measured by two indexes, one of companionship and the other of sociability, tensions by a single index; and over-all happiness in marriage by two measures, the individual's own assessment of his marriage and the MABS. The analysis will be done separately for husbands and wives in terms of three subgroups of the sample—marriages where the woman is in the labor market by necessity, those where the woman is in the labor market by choice, and those where the woman is in the home market by choice.

The data are from personal interviews by the NORC interviewing staff on the third wave of a longitudinal study of psychological well-being. Respondents were drawn from a probability sample of four communities, two within the Detroit metropolitan area and one each from the Chicago and the Washington metropolitan areas, as well as a fifth sample from the ten largest metropolitan areas in the United States.[11] . . .

In the aggregate, the women in the sample follow the national pattern of labor market participation. Of the 34 percent of the married women in the labor market, 25 percent work full time and 9 percent work part time.

A woman's education, her husband's education, the size of her family, and her stage in the life cycle are important predictors of her probability of entering the labor market. Table 1, which deals with educational attainment, shows how participation in the labor market increases from 35 percent among married women who have an eighth-grade education or less to 45 percent for college-educated women.

TABLE 1 WIFE'S WORK STATUS BY EDUCATION OF HUSBANDS AND WIVES

Education	Wife's Work Status				
	Labor Market			Total	
	Full Time	Part Time	Home Market	Percentage	N–NA
Wife's education:					
8th grade or less	23	12	64	99	146
Some high school	21	9	70	100	240
High school graduate	23	8	69	100	342
Some college	27	13	60	100	116
College graduate	40	5	55	100	58
Husband's education:					
8th grade or less	24	13	63	100	151
Some high school	26	7	67	100	175
High school graduate	26	6	67	99	199
Some college	38	7	55	100	85
College graduate	21	8	71	100	137
N–NA			1,649		
NA education			2		
Total N			1,651		

Although women who are themselves college graduates are most likely to enter the labor market, the wives of college-educated men are least likely to do so. Only 29 percent of these women are in the labor market. This probably reflects the fact that wives of many college graduates have less education than their husbands. In the 1960 Census, for example, there were 3,843,000 married men who had completed four or more years of college compared with only 2,020,000 married women who had done so.[12] Blood and Wolfe suggest, "If a wife has less education than her husband, the chances are she will be unusually satisfied with his income and less apt to go to work herself."[13] Another possible explanation is that the less educated woman can find employment only in low-status jobs which would be inconsistent with her husband's status and might prove as an embarrassment both to herself and to her husband.

As one would expect, children are an important factor in determining the labor market participation of married women. The proportion of women who are employed drops from 65 percent for those who have no children to 40 percent for those with one child. The proportion continues to decline as the number of children increases: 30 percent of the women who have two or more children and only 22 percent of those who have four or more children are in the labor market.

A married woman's life is less likely than her husband's to follow a continuous pattern. As she moves through the life cycle, the nature of her responsibilities changes, and she has the opportunity to choose among a new set of alternative ways of organizing her life. At the points of change, a woman reexamines her responsibilities and commitments to her husband, children, home, and self. The choice she makes when her children are infants is likely to be different from the choice she makes when her children move on to school, or when they finally leave the home to pursue independent lives. Participation in the labor force —movement both into and out of paid employment—is one way that women respond to changes in their life patterns. . . . During their children's infancy and early childhood, only 18 percent of the wives are employed. As children grow, there is a steady increase in the proportion of women entering the labor market. When the youngest child in the family is in the upper half of grade school, the proportion of women in the labor market reaches a peak of 49 percent and remains near this level as the youngest child moves on to high school and from there to independent activities.

The changing pattern of part-time and full-time employment . . . illustrates how women respond to changes in their responsibilities. After the period of infancy and early childhood when employment is minimal, women begin to move into both part-time and full-time employment at each successive stage of child rearing. This trend continues until the youngest child is in the upper half of grade school. At this stage in a woman's life cycle, part-time employment is at a peak of 18 percent. After the youngest child is in high school, mothers begin to move out of part-time and into full-time employment. At the stage when there are no longer any children under twenty-one in the home, only 6 percent of the mothers are employed part-time, while 44 percent are employed full time.

If the wife was employed, we asked the respondent (husband or wife) the main reasons for her presence in the labor market. The responses were 69 percent in order to earn money, 6 percent in order to pursue a career, 15 percent in order to get out of the house, 10 percent for other reasons. We found little difference in the responses given by women and by men to this question. We did find, however, that the opportunity to earn money was more likely to be given as the major motive for full-time employment than it was for part-time employment. Three-quarters of the women employed full time compared with only one-half of the women employed part time reported that the chance to earn money was their major objective.

Even though the opportunity to earn money is a major motive for employment for most women, it is essential to distinguish those women who are in the labor market out of economic necessity from those who are there by choice. Over half of the women in the labor market (55 percent) reported that they would work even if they did not need the money. This group was designated as women who have a commitment to their employment and are in the labor market by choice rather than by economic necessity. . . .

As one would expect, . . . the proportion of employed women who are in the labor market by choice increases with education from 34 percent among those with an eighth-grade education or less to 77 percent among college graduates. In terms of the husband's education, a somewhat smaller increase occurs, but it is in the same direction.

In summary, the data show that, while on the average one-third of married women participate in the labor market, this proportion increases with the woman's own education but declines with the husband's education. Participation in the labor market is responsive to the size of the family and to the woman's changing responsibilities as she moves through the life cycle. . . .

The crucial question to which this paper is directed is how a woman's labor market participation affects both her marriage happiness and that of her husband. The relative standing of each subgroup in the sample on the five measures of marriage adjustment will be expressed in terms of ridits.[14] This statistic measures the probability that a person chosen at random from a particular subgroup of the sample will be better or worse off on a measure than an individual chosen at random from an identified reference distribution. The ten metropolitan areas were the natural selection as the identified reference distribution, since they were included in the study to provide a basis for comparison. . . .

Both partners in a marriage are lower in marriage happiness when the wife is denied a choice and is in the labor market only because she needs the money than when the wife participates in the labor market by choice. When a married woman is in the labor market only out of economic necessity, there is a significant reduction in her happiness, measured both in terms of her perception of the balance of recent positive and negative experiences and in terms of her long-range evaluation of her marriage. The husband is also lower on both indicators of over-all happiness. . . .

The particularly interesting finding . . . is that the strain in the marriage stems from different sources for men and for women. When the wife is in the labor market only out of necessity, the husband perceives a significant increase in the negative side of the marriage in the tensions he experiences in the relationship. In the same situation, the wife perceives a significant reduction in the positive side of the marriage in the sociability she enjoys with her husband.

The questions which served as the bases for the indexes of tensions and satisfactions were phrased in terms of disagreements or enjoyable activities with the spouse during the past few weeks. Even though the men and women in the sample are not couples, we would expect, on the average, little difference between them in activities which involve them both. It seems safe to assume, therefore, that the differences observed here are largely perceptual in character. We shall see later, when we control for education, that these perceptual differences occur mainly among the less educated segments of society. Lower-class men are higher in tensions and lower-class women are lower in sociability if the woman is in the labor market out of necessity than if she is there by choice. Among the better educated, both husbands and wives are higher in tensions and lower in sociability.

The difference in the way men and women at lower socioeconomic levels perceive the level of sociability they enjoy in marriage may reflect differences in their psychological needs and expectations. In this group, wives more than husbands may look to the marriage partner to satisfy their need for sociability. The wife's lower perception of the sociability she enjoys may reflect a discrepancy between her needs and expectations, on the one hand, and her actual social experiences, on the other.

The perceptual difference on the tensions index probably reflects a basic difference in the way lower SES husbands and wives conceptualize their roles. The man whose wife is in the labor force out of necessity may feel derelict in the performance of his economic role as the income provider for his wife and children. A man interprets his marriage role in terms of his ability to provide for the economic needs of his family. The fact that he cannot support his family without his wife's help is a threat to his perception of himself as a husband and father. He appears to be more sensitive to disagreements in his marriage that loom as an additional threat to an already shaky ego.

The woman, on the other hand, is probably more capable of integrating her need to supplement her husband's income into her role of caring for her children. The woman who is in the labor market out of economic necessity is apparently, either intentionally or unintentionally, overlooking some disagreements in her marriage. They may not weigh as heavily on her, or she may not perceive them as disagreements at all.

Among women who are free to choose between the labor market and the home market, there is no evidence that the labor market choice creates a strain in the marriage either for the wife or for the husband. On the contrary, . . . if the wife chooses the labor market, husbands and wives both attain a higher balance in their perceived levels of tensions and satisfactions than they do if the wife chooses the home market. Both husbands and wives are lower in tensions and higher in sociability if the wife chooses the labor market than if she chooses the home market, but the difference for men is significant only on the tensions index and for women only on the sociability index.

The lower tension level for men whose wives choose the labor market over the home market may reflect something of the personality, outlook, and attitude of the husband as well as his relationship with his wife and children. It seems likely that the wife's choice to participate in the labor market indicates that both partners recognize, enjoy, and perhaps commit themselves to a marriage in which both will be relatively free and independent. Also, in a relationship as intimate and complex as marriage, the man whose wife chooses to participate in the labor market may experience some

relief from the pressures upon him as a person in the relationship. Our data are not sensitive enough to test these hypotheses directly.

The higher level of sociability in marriages in which the wife chooses the labor market over the home market may simply reflect the fact that the wife's income allows the husband and wife the means to enjoy a higher level of sociability together. The sociability index is composed of items which presuppose a certain level of discretionary income—going out to a sporting event together, eating out in a restaurant together, entertaining, and visiting friends. The wife's income may be an important factor in allowing the couple to fit these activities into the family budget.

This hypothesis can be tested by controlling for different income levels. Income is positively related both to labor market choice and to sociability. Among those women who have a choice, the proportion who choose the labor market increases from 10 percent to 14 percent to 31 percent as total family income increases in three categories: less than $5,000, $5,000–$7,999, and $8,000 or more. Sociability at these three income levels increases from an average ridit of .24 to .38 to .46. Thus, if income explains the difference on the sociability index between the labor market and the home market choice, we would expect this difference to disappear when we control for income. . . .

Income explains all of the difference on the sociability index when total family income is under $8,000 and some of the difference when family income is over $8,000. At the higher income levels, the wife's income may have an "extra" tag which frees the couple psychologically to enjoy higher levels of sociability than are enjoyed by the home market wife and her husband at the same income level.

We can make another comparison across income levels. A woman at one income level who chooses the labor market can be compared with a woman at the next lower level who chooses the home market, on the assumption that the employed woman would be at the lower income level had she not chosen to participate in the labor market.

Even though the woman is in the labor market by choice, the fact that she is gainfully employed places her in a higher income bracket than if she had not made this choice. We expect that her contribution to the total family income gives her an advantage on the sociability index compared with the woman who does not make the labor market choice.

When we compare women across income levels, we find that the woman who chooses the labor market is higher on marriage sociability than the woman who chooses the home market at the next lower income level. In comparing women in the $8,000 or higher group who choose the labor market with women in the $5,000–$7,999 income group who choose the home market, the average ridits on the sociability index are .49 against .38; and in comparing labor market wives in the $5,000–$7,999 income group with home market wives in the less than $5,000 income group, the average ridits are .38 and .24. In the first comparison the difference is significant, and in the second it is just short of significance. The same general argument holds for men whose wives are in either the labor market or the home market by choice.

It seems quite clear, then, that the woman's contribution to the family income is an important factor in explaining differences on the sociability index between marriages in which the wife chooses the labor market and those in which she chooses the home market. In addition, the woman who chooses the labor market may be involved with a new network of friends from among her work associates with whom then both she and her husband socialize.

Even though husbands and wives are both significantly higher on the MABS if the wife chooses to participate in the labor market than if she chooses the home market, there is no difference between these two groups in their own assessment of their marriage happiness. On this measure, there is only a slight tendency for husbands whose wives choose the labor market to report that they are happier than husbands whose wives choose the home market. There is no difference for the wives themselves. A woman who chooses the home market is just as likely to say her marriage is happy as the woman who chooses the labor market.

This suggests to us that home market workers entertain certain commitments and responsibilities that are as meaningful to them as the employment commitment is for women who choose the labor market, at least at certain stages of the life cycle. In the aggregate, there is no difference in over-all marriage happiness ratings associated with the choice between the home and the labor market. However, we shall see later, when we control for stages in the life cycle, that certain differences tend to emerge. When there are preschool children in the home, most women choose to focus their identity in the home as the center of the family. These women are more likely to assess their marriage as happy than are women who choose the labor market. As children enter school, the proportion of women who enter the labor market increases. At this stage, women in the labor market seem to have some advantage over those in the home market. Later, when children are of high school age or older, there appears to be no difference in the way women evaluate their marriage. Women who remain in the home apparently take on other commitments as a way of adapting to changes in their life patterns. They may commit themselves to volunteer, civic, or church activities, to artistic or intellectual pursuits, or simply to social activities. The woman who chooses the home market appears to find alternative ways to adapt to her life pattern which are as satisfying to her as employment is to the woman who chooses the labor market.

It should be noted, however, that there are undoubtedly important differences in the alternatives which are open to women in the home market at different levels of the social structure. The lower-class woman, for example, is probably limited by her own husband's traditional orientation toward the woman's role, by her educational attainment which affects the level of her expectations and aspirations, and by her reluctance and lack of aggression in moving out from the family clan to confront the problems of a larger society and to share in the pleasures of this society.[15]. . .

When a woman enjoys the freedom to choose among alternative life styles, there is some tendency for marriage adjustment to be more favorable for both partners if she chooses part-time employment over either full-time employment or the home market. . . .

For one thing, women making the part-time choice are more likely to report that they are happy in marriage than are women making either the full-time or the home market choice. For another, the husband whose wife chooses part-time employment is higher in companionship than are other husbands. This is striking because, generally, companionship remains remarkably stable in response to changes in a woman's work status. This case is one of the few times we observe any change on the companionship index. Also, the husband whose wife chooses part-time employment is significantly higher on the MABS than is the man whose wife chooses the home market. And finally, in all of the comparisons on the five marriage adjustment measures, part-time employment is more favorable than the home-market choice; and, in eight of the ten comparisons, part-time is more favorable than full-time employment.

These tendencies suggest that part-time employment may indeed be the way for a woman to combine the labor market and the home market to achieve optimum adjustment in the marriage relationship both for herself and for her husband. However, only a small proportion of women—just 6 percent of those who are free to make a choice—choose part-time participation in the labor market. This fact may reflect limited opportunities for part-time employment as well as social pressures to put in a "full day's work.". . .

In marriages where the wife is in the labor market out of economic necessity, there is also some tendency for adjustment to be more favorable if the woman is employed part time than if she is employed full time. Seven of the ten comparisons on the marriage adjustment measures favor part-time over full-time employment. The control for part-time and full-time employment does not explain the difference be-tween marriages where the wife participates in the labor market by necessity and those where she participates by choice. Participation in the labor market out of necessity, whether it is part time or full time, creates a strain in the marriage for both the husband and the wife. . . .

We noted earlier that, as one would expect, women are most likely to participate in the labor market out of economic necessity at lower socioeconomic levels. The proportion declines with steps up in education from 66 percent for women who have an eighth-grade education or less to 23 percent for women who are college graduates.

The interesting finding . . . is that the strain holds at all levels of education for both husbands and wives if the woman is in the labor market out of necessity. There are undoubtedly qualitative differences in the interpretation of need at different class levels. Yet, despite differences in standards of evaluation and in probabilities, marriages at all levels of the social structure are affected adversely when the woman is in the labor market only out of necessity. At each of three levels of education, husbands and wives are lower on both measures of over-all happiness—the individual's own assessment of his or her happiness in marriage and the MABS—if the woman is in the labor market by necessity rather than by choice.

The source of the strain on the marriage varies with the three educational groups. As we noted earlier, in the lowest educational group the strain in the marriage comes from different sources for men and for women. Here the women are lower in sociability and the men higher in tensions if the wife is in the labor market by necessity than if she is there by choice. In the high school graduate group, husbands and wives are both higher in tensions, but the impact is greater on the husband than on the wife. Even considering the small case base, this difference is significant for the husband. In the highest of the three educational groups —those who have at least some college education—husbands and wives are both lower in sociability and higher in tensions if the wife is in the labor market by necessity than if she is there by choice.

Differences in the way men and women

perceive the tensions and sociability they experience in marriage occur mainly among the less educated and tend to disappear at higher levels of education. We have already commented on the possibility that, at lower socioeconomic levels, differential perception of sociability enjoyed in marriage may reflect differences in psychological needs and expectations between men and women. Differences in their perception of tensions may indicate a basic difference in the way lower-class husbands and wives conceptualize their roles. The man whose wife is in the labor market only out of necessity may feel threatened in his primary role as the income provider for his family, while the woman may be better able to integrate her more diverse roles. At higher socioeconomic levels, the congruence between the man's and the woman's perception of the tensions and sociability they enjoy in marriage suggests that these marriages are more egalitarian than are marriages at lower levels of the social structure.

When we compare marriages in which the woman is free to choose between the labor market and the home market, . . . at the three educational levels there is little difference in the individual's own assessment of the marriage either for husbands or for wives. On the MABS, however, husbands and wives both achieve a higher positive balance of recent experiences if the wife chooses the labor market than they do if the wife chooses the home market. Even with the small case base, this difference is significant for college-educated men. With only one exception, there are less tensions and more sociability at every educational level for both men and women if the wife chooses the labor market over the home market.

Thus, we conclude that, in general, the relationship between a woman's work status and marriage happiness holds for different levels of the social structure, but the introduction of a control for education specifies that differences between men and women on the tensions and sociability which they perceive in marriage occur in the less educated segments of society. . . .

At every stage of the life cycle, differences in marriage adjustment persist for husbands and wives when we compare marriages where the woman is in the labor market out of economic necessity with those where she is free to choose between the labor market and the home market. In twenty-one out of twenty-four comparisons, . . . participation in the labor market by necessity is less favorable for the marriage adjustment of both the wife and the husband than is participation in either the labor market or the home market by choice.

Among those who are free to choose between the home market and the labor market, there are some differences at varying stages of the life cycle. When there are preschool children in the home, husbands and wives are both happier in marriage if the wife chooses the home market than if she chooses the labor market. Seven out of ten comparisons favor the home market choice. When there are grade school children in the family, all of the comparisons favor the labor market choice. When the youngest child in the family is of high school age or older, there is little or no difference in marriage adjustment between the labor market and the home market choice.

CONCLUSIONS

Since the freedom to choose among alternative life styles is clearly an important variable in predicting happiness in marriage, efforts to extend this freedom should have positive effects on the marriage happiness of both husbands and wives. A general upgrading and expansion of educational and employment opportunities for lower-SES men would allow them to fulfill their role as income providers for their families and, at the same time, would extend to their wives the freedom to choose between the home and the labor market.

However, even when the husband's income is adequate to meet his family's needs, there are undoubtedly other restraints on a woman's freedom of choice. On the supply side, there are restraints to freedom of entry into the labor market imposed by the woman's education, her stage in the life cycle, the availability of adequate substitute help, and her own personality disposition, needs, and desires. On the demand side, there may be restraints to free entry in the labor market imposed by employers and by male incumbents in the labor force. Any efforts that individuals and private and public institutions direct toward removing these restraints would extend women's freedom to choose between the home market and the labor market.[16] In the private sector, for example, an expansion of employment opportunities commensurate with a woman's talents and capabilities, on both a full-time and a part-time basis, would insure that the choice was a meaningful one. In the public sector, if society moves toward its national goal of better educational opportunities for all its members, there should be an increase in the proportion of women who choose to enter the labor force in prestigious occupations to which they have a real sense of commitment. We predict that this phenomenon will not be detrimental to the institution of marriage. On the contrary, there is evidence to support the contention that there might well be a strengthening of the marriage relationship both for the husband and for the wife.

NOTES

[1] Glen C. Cain, *Married Women in the Labor Force: An Economic Analysis* (Chicago: University of Chicago Press, 1966).

[2] U.S. President's Commission on the Status of Women, *American Women* (Washington, D.C.: Government Printing Office, 1963), p. 27.

[3] Harvey J. Locke and Muriel MacKeprang, "Marital Adjustment of the Employed Wife," *American Journal of Sociology*, 54 (May 1949); Robert O. Blood, Jr., and Donald M. Wolfe, *Husbands and Wives: The Dynamics of Married Living* (Glencoe, Ill.: Free Press, 1960); F. Ivan Nye, "Marital Interaction," in F. Ivan Nye and Lois Hoffman, eds., *The Employed Mother in America* (Chicago: Rand McNally & Co., 1963); Robert O. Blood, Jr., "The Husband-Wife Relationship," in Nye and Hoffman, op. cit., and Sheila Field, "Feelings of Adjustment," in Nye and Hoffman, op. cit.

[4] Blood and Wolfe, op. cit., p. 284.

[5] Ibid., p. 296.

[6] Out of the original sample of 1,738 married respondents, we have excluded eighty-seven deviant cases: wives who are chief wage earners, men who are not chief wage earners, retired respondents, persons on pension or on relief, and respondents for whom we have incomplete data.

[7] U.S. Bureau of the Census, *Statistical Abstract of the United States: 1965*, 86th ed. (Washington, D.C.: Government Printing Office, 1965), gross national product, p. 325; unemployment, p. 216; auto factory sales, p. 569.

[8] See Lee Rainwater, Richard P. Coleman, and Gerald Handel, *Workingman's Wife* (New York: Oceana Publications, 1959); Mirra Komarovsky, *Blue-Collar Marriage* (New York: Random House, 1964); Joseph D. Mooney, "Urban Poverty and Labor Force Participation," *American Economic Review*, 57 (March 1967): 104–19; and Robert W. Hodge and Patricia Hodge, "Occupational Assimilation as a Competitive Process," *American Journal of Sociology*, 71 (November 1965): 249–64.

[9] Susan R. Orden and Norman M. Bradburn, "Dimensions of Marriage Happiness," *American Journal of Sociology*, 73 (May 1968): 715–31.

[10] Cain, op. cit.

[11] The research design, the over-all research objectives, and the sampling techniques are described in detail in Norman M. Bradburn, *The Structure of Psychological Well-Being* (Chicago: Aldine Publishing Co., in press); and David Caplovitz and Norman M. Bradburn, *Social Class and Psychological Adjustment: A Portrait of the Communities in the "Happiness" Study—a Preliminary Report* (Chicago: National Opinion Research Center, 1964).

[12] U.S. Bureau of the Census, *U.S. Census of Population: 1960, Subject Reports Educational Attainment*, Final Report PC (2)–5B (Washington, D.C.: Government Printing Office,

1963). Data for married men are from Table 4, p. 54; for married women, from Table 5, p. 71.

[13] Blood and Wolfe, op. cit., p. 99.

[14] Irwin D. J. Bross and Rivkah Feldman, *Ridit Analysis of Automotive Crash Injuries* (New York: Cornell University Medical College, 1965); Irwin D. J. Bross, "How to Use Ridit Analysis, *Biometrics,* 14 (March 1958): 18–38; and Thomas S. Langner and Stanley T. Michael, *Life Stress in Mental Health* (New York: Free Press, 1963), pp. 87–101.

[15] See Rainwater et al., op cit., and Komarovsky, op. cit.

[16] For a discussion of policy proposals, see U.S. President's Commission on Status of Women, op. cit.; Eli Ginsberg and Associates, *Life Styles of Educated Women* (New York: Columbia University Press, 1966), chap. xii, pp. 179–95; and Hannah Gavion, *The Captive Wife* (London: Routledge & Kegan Paul, 1966), chap. xvi, pp. 141–48.

59

CORRELATES OF DISSATISFACTION IN MARRIAGE

Karen S. Renne

Satisfaction with one's marriage is, in our monogamous society, an important component of individual well being. The independence of each "nuclear" family (parents and dependent children) from its own kin, and the relative social isolation of urban households, makes the spouse the primary companion and source of emotional sustenance.[1] Relations with the spouse are so central a feature of an individual's social and emotional life that an unhappy marriage may impair the capacity of both partners for satisfactory relations with their children and others outside the family.

In an *adequate* marriage—not necessarily "happy," but certainly not "unhappy"— each partner is a source of emotional support, companionship, sexual gratification, and economic support or assistance for the other. Each spouse also supports the other in his roles as parent, friend, colleague, kinsman, and so on. To the extent that either partner's performance in any of these areas is inadequate, the other's emotional and social life is damaged.

One who invests much of his time and emotional energy in frustrating or unrewarding exchanges with the spouse is handicapped in his relations with people outside the marriage. And if the marriage fails as a partnership for rearing children, one spouse must take most of the responsibility for decision-making, nurturing, and caretaking, which also limits his capacity for satisfactory relationships outside the family. A marriage may fail as a partnership in other areas, too; for example, as a vehicle for promoting the interests or ambitions of one partner, so that he must carry on without the moral support and physical assistance or cooperation that a more satisfactory spouse would provide.

Involvement in an unhappy marriage is, then, analogous to functional disability: one who suffers from marital distress is limited in his relations with others, or socially "disabled," just as a person suffering from a chronic heart condition is limited in his physical activities, or physically disabled. Marital dissatisfaction is not a pathological condition, however, nor does it stem from a specific cause. On the contrary, some degree of dissatisfaction is inherent in the marital situation, for even the most compatible partners sometimes find their needs, impulses, or interests in conflict. The completely satisfactory marriage must be far more rare than its opposite, even more rare than "perfect health." Conventional discourse recognizes this, and accordingly, the term "unhappy" is usually reserved for acute cases, while the ordinary, not completely satisfactory marriage is considered "happy."

Ordinary marriages depend on compromise and accommodation, and though few husbands and wives find themselves entirely satisfied with their marriages, few abandon their families because of relatively minor discomfort. Even a frustrating and disappointing relationship may yield some rewards for at least one spouse, and marriage confers many benefits, even when the couple quarrels frequently. Moreover, separation and divorce are troublesome to initiate and expensive to carry out. A great many relatively unrewarding marriages persist for a combination of reasons: inertia, lack of money, a preference for the familiar, and, more significantly, each partner's commitment to spouse and children, an emotional investment difficult to renounce.

Thus, people tend to maintain unsatisfactory marriages longer than they might unsatisfactory business partnerships, or conflict-ridden friendships. At any given moment in a given population, we expect a certain proportion of marriages to be "unhappy," and accordingly, a certain proportion of individuals to be suffering from the kinds of deprivation an unsatisfactory marriage imposes.

Like other forms of disability, however, unhappy marriage is not evenly distributed throughout the population. The data to be reported here show that it is endemic in some subgroups, rare in others. (For instance, people with relatively low incomes are more likely than people with higher incomes to be dissatisfied with their marriages.) Of course, knowing *which* people are likely to be unhappily married is not equivalent to knowing *why* their marriages

are unsatisfactory, just as knowing which people have cancer does not, in itself, tell us what causes cancer. Nevertheless, epidemiology is useful, in both cases, because other information about the subgroups where the disease is prevalent provides clues to its causes. We assume, for instance, that economic deprivation imposes a strain on a marriage, not only because it is more difficult to live without enough money, but also because an inadequate income represents, for many couples, the husband's failure to perform satisfactorily as a provider. Regardless of the reasons for this failure, our culture is such that it affects the husband's self-respect, and his wife's regard for him, adversely. Thus, we infer that failure in a major aspect of the marital role often (not inevitably) leads to marital dissatisfaction.

This study differs from previous studies of marital happiness in a number of ways. First, it is really a by-product of the main research, which is an exhaustive investigation of the relation between health and way of life. No systematic effort was made to replicate previous studies of marital happiness, most of which aimed to "predict" marital success or failure by correlating a score on some index of marital happiness with various social, economic, and psychological factors. (Bowerman, 1964). While the present study does not aim to predict marital happiness, it resembles its predecessors in its focus on the relations between a composite index and various social, economic, and psychological variables. It differs from similar studies in its additional emphasis on physical health, which arises from the overall research objectives.

Second, the sample represents the entire population of a large metropolitan area (Alameda County, California). Previous studies have used small, nonrepresentative samples, sometimes because their means permitted no alternative, sometimes because the research was designed to be carried out with "extreme" groups (e.g., divorced couples and happily married couples).[2] With a large representative sample one can legitimately investigate the prevalence of marital unhappiness among married couples in various subgroups.

Third, this analysis treats marital dissatisfaction as analogous to illness. No previous study, to my knowledge, has taken this approach. Instead, the focus is usually on marital happiness, or "success," and divorce is taken as a sign of failure. In the present approach, however, divorce may be the only remedy for an ailing marriage which otherwise would have disastrous consequences for those involved, including the children. Thus, the dependent variable is not rate of divorce or separation, but rate of expressed dissatisfaction among people presently married. . . .

The data reported here are based on an area probability sample of households in Alameda County, California. A total of 4,452 households were sampled and enumerated, yielding 8,267 adults (i.e., persons age 20 and older, or 16–19 and ever married). Of these, 6,928 (84 percent) completed mail questionnaires or supplied the information in personal interviews.

An interviewer left a questionnaire for each potential respondent in the household, with instructions to fill it out and mail it back. Reluctant respondents received a reminder letter and later a telegram, and approximately 30 days after the initial contact an interviewer visited everyone who had not responded and attempted to retrieve their questionnaires. (Respondents who were unable to complete the questionnaire because of illness or language difficulty were interviewed at this time.) The majority of those who completed questionnaires (81 percent) returned them by mail.

Almost three-quarters (5163 or 74 percent) of those who returned questionnaires were married and living with spouse at the time of the survey. Since every adult in each household was asked to complete a questionnaire, most of these married people are couples. Only 60 wives and 143 husbands failed to complete questionnaires, while 2480 couples completed both questionnaires. . . .

This 1965 survey of health of Alameda County was not intended as a study of marital satisfaction, nor was it presented as such to the respondents. With his questionnaire, each respondent received a letter identifying the study as a "survey of health and ways of living" conducted by the California Department of Public Health. The 23-page questionnaire (in separate forms for men and women) began with questions about appetite, sleep, and energy and continued through several pages of questions about health and medical problems. Five questions about marital status and marital history appeared in the middle of the questionnaire, followed immediately by nine questions about the respondent's attitude toward his marriage (to be answered only by those who were currently married).

Six of these nine questions were used to construct the Index of Marital Satisfaction. These questions are shown in Table 1, in the order they appeared in the questionnaire, together with the percentage distribution of responses to each one. The 4,924 persons (95 percent of the married people in the sample) who answered all six questions were classified "satisfied" or "dissatisfied" according to their responses to these six questions.

The "dissatisfied" group consists of (1) the 502 people who gave the asterisked response to at least one of the last three questions in Table 1, plus (2) 506 people who gave none of these "extreme" responses but answered the questions in various ways that indicated dissatisfaction with their marriages. Approximately one third of the "dissatisfied" group had "seriously considered divorce recently," although they did not consider their marriages "unhappy," nor had they "often" regretted their marriages. Another two-fifths described their marriages as "somewhat happy" but gave other responses indicating dissatisfaction.

A large majority (80 percent) of the "satisfied" group had "never" regretted their marriages, and they considered their marriages "happy" or "very happy." Among the 785 others who admitted occasional regrets but were still classified as "satisfied," 623 said they had regretted their marriages "a few times" but nevertheless were "happy" or "very happy." Those who regretted their marriages "sometimes" or said they were only "somewhat happy" comprise only 4 percent of the satisfied group, and they gave no other dissatisfied responses.

TABLE 1 COMPONENT ITEMS OF THE INDEX OF MARITAL SATISFACTION

(Underlined response indicates dissatisfaction)

	Percent	
	Husbands (N=2413)	Wives (N=2511)
7. Does your husband (wife) give you as much understanding as you need?		
No, not really	8	15
Yes, but not completely	43	45
Yes, completely	49	40
8. Does your husband (wife) show you as much affection as you would like?		
More than I like	3	7
As much as I like	72	71
Less than I like	25	22
9. Even happily married couples sometimes have problems getting along with each other. How often does this happen with you?		
Often	5	8
Sometimes	38	43
A few times	45	40
Never	12	10
11. Do you ever regret your marriage?		
*Often	1	3
Sometimes	10	13
A few times	20	19
Never	70	66
12. Have you seriously considered separation or divorce recently?		
*Yes	6	9
No	94	91
13. All in all, how happy has your marriage been for you?		
*Very unhappy	1	1
*Unhappy	1	1
*Somewhat unhappy	2	5
Somewhat happy	12	13
Happy	38	37
Very happy	46	42

* An "extreme" response; see text.

Wives were more likely than husbands to be dissatisfied (23 percent were so classified by our index, compared with 18 percent of the husbands; this difference is statistically significant at the .05 level (t-test)). But from the point of view of either sex, about one marriage in five in Alameda County is "unhappy," or sufficiently unsatisfactory to evoke complaints from at least one spouse.

We could, of course, have used a single direct question about marital happiness instead of the multiple-item index. The last item in Table 1 is such a question; another is the last item in the series on marriage (not included in the index), in which the respondent was asked to recall what he had expected of his marriage:

Has your marriage turned out to be better or worse than you expected?

A few people who claimed their marriages were better than expected were nevertheless dissatisfied, according to the index, but almost everyone who said his marriage had failed to live up to expectation also expressed dissatisfaction in his answers to the index questions. At the same time, however, 67 percent of the men and 59 percent of the women classified as dissatisfied said their marriages were *better* than they had expected or about the same (data not shown). Although this question followed several specific questions about possible defects in the marriage, relatively few people, even among the "dissatisfied" said their marriages were worse than expected. Similarly, about 20 percent of the "dissatisfied" said their marriages were "happy" or "very happy.". . .

Evidently people were reluctant to make negative overall evaluations of their marriages; thus, if we had used a single direct question, substantial numbers of people who regretted their marriages or had seriously considered divorce would have been included in the "satisfied" group. The index *reduces* the risk of overlooking people who may be suffering acutely from an unsatisfactory marriage but whose standards prevent them from classifying it as "unhappy." At the same time, of course, it increases the risk of including people who find their marriages reasonably happy, on the whole, in spite of the occasional periods of doubt and ambivalence reflected in their answers to the index questions. . . .

Black people in our sample have much higher rates of marital dissatisfaction than whites do; among people under 45 the black rate is double the white. In part this difference is due to socioeconomic status: people who are less well educated, in lower-prestige occupations, or with lower income are more likely than others to express dissatisfaction with their marriages, as will be shown, and black people tend to be less well educated, in lower-prestige occupations, and earning less money than white people. Thus, the rate of dissatisfaction among black men as a group is almost double the rate for white men, but the difference is reduced to five percentage points or less among college-educated men, and the difference between black and white men with family income of $10,000 or more is also relatively small.

For women, however, neither education nor affluence compensates for being black. Younger black women especially are much more likely than white women at the same income or education level to express dissatisfaction.[3] Evidently the hostility and neglect that most black people encounter in white-dominated American society damage family life for women, particularly women raising children, more than for men.

Since E. Franklin Frazier published his *Negro Family in the U.S.* in 1939, the facts about black family life have been widely known. Most notably these include high rates of desertion, separation, and divorce, large proportions of children born out of wedlock, and large proportions of households headed by women.[4] Black women bear more than their share of the responsibility for family support, and evidently even those who live with their husbands find insufficient compensation in their marriages.

Black wives are far more likely than white to be working outside the home, in our Alameda County sample as in the U.S. population. The fact that the wife works is not in itself detrimental to marital adjustment, but black men have fewer alternatives than white men do to prove their manhood. Bernard (1966:95) reminds us that in the Jewish ghettos of Eastern Europe women were proud to support their scholar husbands, but "the Negro husband is not in the scholar's position, nor has the outside world allowed him to cultivate his masculine honor." Deprived by systematic discrimination and exclusion of the primary white means of expressing masculine competence—economic achievement—black men often exploit the women who bear their children.

The contrast between the white way of life and the black in Alameda County is represented most economically by the contrasting patterns of employment. . . . Black husbands in our sample were more likely than white to be unemployed, and black wives were far more likely than white to be working or looking for work. Older black people were also more likely than older whites to be employed on a part-time basis.

The circumstances surrounding black marriages differ so much from those surrounding white marriages that the two situations are virtually not comparable. For this reason black people were analyzed separately from white in the following report.[5] . . . Black people were almost twice as likely to be dissatisfied with their marriages as white people of the same age and sex.

Not surprisingly, husbands and wives of both races evaluated their marriages differently, as did young people and old. Wives were more likely to express dissatisfaction than husbands were, regardless of age and race; people over 45 were less likely to express dissatisfaction, except among white wives.

These differences reflect the fact that one's experience in marriage is conditioned by age and sex as well as race. Of more importance here, however, are the relations between race, sex, and age and other factors that affect marital satisfaction. To reduce the probability that age, sex, or race is actually responsible for an apparent correlation between marital dissatisfaction and health, income, education, etc., the data were analyzed within the eight subgroups, . . . that is, controlling for race, sex, and age.[6] . . .

People of higher status—better educated, in higher-prestige occupations, or with higher incomes—were less likely than others to express dissatisfaction with their marriages.[7] The various relationships involved are rather weak, however, and often irregular. This is partly because each one was considered within the *relatively* homogeneous subgroups formed by controlling for race and age. Black husbands, for example, had both a high rate of dissatisfaction and a low level of education. Had they been grouped with white husbands, the association between satisfaction and education would have appeared to be stronger than it actually is for either whites or blacks.

Nevertheless there is a definite tendency within these subgroups toward a positive relation between marital satisfaction and socioeconomic status. College-educated people under 45 were less likely to be dissatisfied than others in the same age range, among men and white women. But education had little effect on marital satisfaction among older whites, and older blacks who did not go beyond the eighth grade were less likely to be dissatisfied than those who did.

Occupation had a similar effect on marital satisfaction.[8] Blue-collar workers were more likely than others to express dissatisfaction, especially those in service occupations or unskilled labor, but again differences are small and exceptions occur.[9] Education alone does not account for the relation between occupation and marital satisfaction, for the lowest rates of dissatisfaction among white husbands were *not* among professional and technical workers, most of whom are college-educated, but among clerical and sales workers, who are less likely to have gone to college.[10]

The generally lower rates of dissatisfaction among white-collar workers may instead be due to their higher income. . . . People with an adjusted family income of less than $6,000 were most likely to be dissatisfied with their marriages, and people with $15,000 or more ($10,000 or more for blacks), least likely to be dissatisfied.

Income had a more substantial effect on marital satisfaction among black people than among white, probably because black men with low incomes were more likely than low-income whites to be unemployed or to work in very low-status jobs with no hope of advancement and no compensatory features such as intrinsic interest or enhancement of self-esteem. A high family income (i.e., $10,000 or more) sharply reduced the difference in rates of marital dissatisfaction between white husbands and black; at the lower income levels, however, race differences *exceeded* the overall differences between blacks and whites.

Evidently affluence is conducive to satisfaction in marriage, although it was not a critical factor for the majority of white respondents (older white wives are an exception). For most black couples income was very important: the . . . striking feature . . . is the reduction in rates of dissatisfaction among black people with an income of $10,000 or more.

Income is more closely related to marital dissatisfaction than is either education or occupation, probably because it has an independent and very concrete impact on a couple's daily life.[11] Other aspects of social status count for relatively little if the family's income is not adequate to its needs. The difference in marital satisfaction between white couples and black was reduced more for those with high incomes than for those with college educations or high-status occupations; thus, the domestic problems of black couples can be attributed primarily to economic deprivation. . . .

Contrary to popular belief, childless marriages are more satisfactory than others; parents, especially those currently raising children, were definitely less apt to be satisfied with their marriages. The *number* of children had no consistent effect on the rate of dissatisfaction.[12]

The sharp reduction in race differences among the childless suggests that an economic factor may be responsible: people without children have fewer financial problems. But . . . income is not the only or even the most important factor involved. Regardless of sex, race, age, or adjusted household income, people raising children were more likely to be dissatisfied with their marriages. Controlling income reduces, but does not eliminate, the difference between parents raising children and others.

A more adequate explanation is indicated by the relatively low divorce rate noted by others for parents of children under 18.[13] People without dependent children can divorce or separate more readily than those raising children; presumably the unhappiest marriages among childless couples and those whose children have grown up have already been dissolved, while the unhappily married with children remain married longer.

In addition, of course, parenthood makes special demands on people. A marriage that functions satisfactorily without children may be susceptible to acute problems after the children arrive. Rossi (1968) recently pointed out that parenthood is, particularly for women, one of the most abrupt and least well-prepared role transitions in our culture. Among other things it may drastically alter the relationship between husband and wife established during the early part of the marriage, not necessarily for the better. Motherhood may also deprive a woman of important sources of gratification outside the family (e.g., a career, higher education, outdoor recreation).

Parenthood is especially difficult for black people. Even when they have an adequate income they can do little to protect their children from the irrational restrictions, insults, and degradation black people encounter in this society. The restriction of all but a very few black men to poorly paid jobs without prestige, responsibility, or authority not only deprives most black men of an important basis for self-respect but also detracts from their ability to act as "heads" of their families. In a society with as strong a patriarchal bias as ours has, this is a serious handicap, and where there are children it may be devastating (Bernard, 1966:129). Hence race differences in marital satisfaction, in our sample, were larger among people with children than among people without children, regardless of income.

But the children themselves and the special problems they create probably do less damage to their parents' marriage than their parents' marriage does to them. Parents in our sample who reported problems

with their children were more likely to be dissatisfied with their marriages than those who reported no problems.

Parents who indicated a problem (or problems) with their children and also said they had talked with a professional person (school principal, minister, judge, policeman, social worker, or psychologist) about their children were decidedly more likely to be unhappy in their marriages than those who reported no problem, and somewhat more likely to be unhappy than those who reported a problem but no professional consultation. This suggests a "sick family" syndrome, in which the unsatisfactory marriage not only affects the child's behavior but also is made more unhappy by the apparent failure in childrearing.[14] . . .

Marital dissatisfaction is seldom an individual's sole complaint, but more often one of a number of physical and psychic symptoms, ailments, and disabilities. Because the state of his marriage, as he sees it, both influences and is influenced by his general feeling of well-being, marital satisfaction is strongly related to various indices of health and morale.

One such index is an evaluation of one's own general health. (This is also an index of morale, since "good health" is a relative concept, and no definite criterion for it exists in our culture). Each respondent was asked to rate his health "excellent," "good," "fair," or "poor." Those who said "fair" or "poor" were considerably more likely than others to be dissatisfied with their marriages.[15] This suggests that an unhappy marriage depresses an individual's estimate of his physical health. These self-evaluations were not without objective basis, however: people with some disability were far more likely to rate their health "fair" or "poor" than those without a disability, and those with no health problems were far more likely than others to rate their health "excellent."[16]

Healthy people were much less likely to be dissatisfied with their marriages than those with a disability, symptom, or chronic condition. Disabled people and those with a chronic condition *and* at least one symptom were more likely to be dissatisfied than people with no problem or only a chronic condition. In other words, the people with the most serious health problems were most likely to be dissatisfied with their marriages.

While it is quite likely that an unhappy marriage affects an individual's evaluation of his general health, it is less probable (though certainly not impossible) that an unhappy marriage leads to functional disability, symptoms, or chronic disease. Physical health should probably be regarded primarily as a "prior" variable, so far as it can be evaluated independently of the respondent's state of mind. As a *consequence* of his illness, the sick spouse may be unable to function adequately as a partner, or in a marriage already damaged by unresolved conflict, he may use his illness as a weapon, to harass, inconvenience, or otherwise injure the spouse. . . .

Black people, and others who live in poverty without hope of improvement; people who feel they must maintain an unhappy marriage for the sake of the children; people suffering from disability or chronic illness—these are the people one would expect to be depressed, lonely, and suffering from low morale and other symptoms of poor emotional health. Thus, various indices of morale and psychological health are very strongly related to marital satisfaction.

One of the most telling questions asked was:

"All in all, how happy are you these days?"

. . . A large majority of those who said they were "not too happy" also expressed dissatisfaction with their marriages; hardly any of those who said "very happy" did so. In all probability the respondent's view of his marriage influences his general feeling of well-being, or morale.[17]

Marital satisfaction affects morale in other areas, too. For example, people—men especially—who were satisfied with their jobs were also likely to be satisfied with their marriages.

Job satisfaction is undoubtedly affected by the income and prestige associated with the job, but the number of people who said they were "very satisfied" is so large (it is the modal category in every subgroup) that it must have included many individuals in low-status, low-paying jobs.[18] Answers to this question, like answers to the "general happiness" question, must depend partly on general morale and are therefore influenced by the respondent's marital situation.

Excessive drinking can also be regarded as an indicator of low morale, as well as a symptom of emotional illness. Respondents were asked, in separate questions, how often they drank wine, beer, and liquor, and how many drinks they usually had. Relatively heavy drinkers—those who reported at least three drinks at a sitting[19]—were more likely than others to be dissatisfied with their marriages. Among white husbands and wives and black husbands under 45, rates of dissatisfaction were much higher among the heaviest drinkers (five or more at a sitting), but older white people who reported only 3–4 drinks at a sitting were more likely to be dissatisfied with their marriages.

White husbands and younger black wives who said they did not drink at all were less likely to express their dissatisfaction with their marriages than those who reported any drinking, but black husbands and older black wives who reported one or two drinks at a sitting were less likely than teetotalers to be dissatisfied. Evidently it is not drinking as such that is associated with unhappy marriage, but rather heavy drinking.

Drinking may be, in part, a reaction to a tense or frustrating marriage, but because it is apt to create problems worse than those the drinker seeks to escape, it may also contribute to the circumstances leading the respondent to judge his marriage unsatisfactory. Heavy drinking is both cause and effect of marital dissatisfaction; both are parts of a syndrome of emotional illness.

Other items more directly indicative of psychic malaise were also closely associated with marital satisfaction. Nine of these, referring to loneliness, depression, general dissatisfaction, boredom, uneasiness, and meaninglessness of life, were combined to form an "Isolation-Depression" Index.[20] The relation between this index and marital satisfaction is very strong. . . . A majority of those who gave isolated or depressed responses to as many as four of these items were also dissatisfied with their marriages; the percentage dissatisfied declines consistently as the number of isolated or depressed responses declines, in all eight subgroups.

If unhappy marriage is a social disability, as argued, then a sense of isolation should be one of its chief symptoms, for the marital relationship is crucial to satisfactory relations with others. [There is] evidence that unhappily married people actually [are] socially isolated. . . . Under the heading "Your Activities," respondents were asked:

How many close friends do you have? (People that you feel at ease with, can talk to about private matters, and can call on for help.)

Immediately following was a similar question about "relatives that you feel close to," and another asking how many of these friends and relatives the respondent saw at least once a month.

People with few intimate associates were more likely than others to be dissatisfied with their marriages; in other words, marital satisfaction is related to the number of "close" relatives and friends claimed by the respondent.[21] Social isolates—those who claimed no more than two close friends and no more than two close relatives—were much more likely than others of the same race, sex, and age to be unhappily married.

A more objective criterion—number of friends seen, rather than felt close to—produces the same pattern. Those who saw fewer than three close friends or relatives monthly were distinctly more likely than others to be dissatisfied with their marriages.

The close relation between number of intimate associates and marital satisfaction suggests that people involved in unhappy marriages were unable to maintain satisfactory relations outside the marriage, and tended to withdraw. Feelings of isolation and depression ensued.[22] Having withdrawn, they found their problems exacerbated by lack of companionship and emotional support, and their dissatisfaction with the marriage increased.

SUMMARY

(1) Black people and others with low income or little education were more apt to be dissatisfied with their marriages than were white people or people with adequate income and education. This difference between white and black couples persisted regardless of other conditions, but it was sharply reduced for husbands at higher socioeconomic levels and for couples without children.

(2) The relation between marital satisfaction and socioeconomic status is stronger for blacks than for whites, but the following relationships between marital satisfaction and parental status, physical health, emotional health, and social integration hold for both blacks and whites.

(3) People currently raising children were more likely to be dissatisfied with their marriages than people who had never had children or whose children had left home, regardless of race, age, or income level.

(4) Physically ill people are less able than others to function in various social roles, including that of spouse. Thus people suffering from some chronic condition or physical symptom, or who described themselves as functionally disabled, were more likely than others to be dissatisfied with their marriages.

(5) Marital satisfaction is an integral part of emotional or psychic well-being. Thus, marital satisfaction was closely associated with general morale or "happiness," a positive view of own health, and satisfaction with job, and (negatively) with heavy drinking, feelings of isolation and depression, and an absence of intimate associates.

CONCLUSION

Black people and others with inadequate income or education are especially susceptible to marital unhappiness, as are persons suffering from physical disability, chronic conditions, impairments, or physical symptoms. Unhappily married people are socially and psychologically isolated, depressed, and prone to heavy drinking, not only because they are more likely to be ill or economically deprived, but also because the disability imposed by an unsatisfactory marriage is analogous to the disability imposed by minority race, chronic illness, or a missing limb.

For couples lacking economic or social resources, divorce is less feasible a solution to an unhappy marriage than it is for other couples, no more unhappy but better off occupationally or financially. This is especially true when children are involved; parents generally are less likely to be satisfied with their marriages than couples who have never had children or whose children have left home.

The follow-up study proposed for 1972 should either substantiate or radically alter these conclusions. For one thing, it will provide partial validation for our index of marital satisfaction: a higher rate of divorce and separation among those now classified as dissatisfied with their marriages is expected. People now married, but divorced or separated by 1972, should include a disproportionate number of parents whose children leave home during the interval, if the inference drawn above is correct.

The follow-up study should also establish the reliability of baseline relations between marital dissatisfaction and various forms of social and psychological malaise, and between marital dissatisfaction and various forms of social and economic deprivation. Should some of the presently "dissatisfied" couples become "satisfied" with their marriages, for example, we would expect to find that other aspects of their health and morale had also improved, or that their economic circumstances were more comfortable, and so on.

NOTES AND REFERENCES

[1] For an analysis of the effect of urban industrial life on marriage, see Goode (1963: Ch. 1).

[2] For example, Locke (1951:15–16) used a "representative" sample consisting of (1) all the couples divorced in a single Indiana county prior to 1944 (about 300), and (2) about 200 "happily married" couples recommended as such by the divorced couples and by a "random sample" of married persons in the same county. Since the procedure used to obtain the "random" sample could not have ensured randomness, and since no criteria for judging the happiness of couples were set, it is not clear what the happily married sample "represents."

[3] Black wives in the Detroit study were also less satisfied with their marriages than white wives. In particular, they were dissatisfied with their husbands' understanding of their problems and their feelings; the authors feel that this is "unusually striking in view of the fact that Negro husbands do not differ significantly from white husbands in their pattern of responding to (the wife's) troubles. . . . Hence, the wife's dissatisfaction may be due primarily to the severity of the problems she faces" (Blood and Wolfe, 1960:215).

[4] Summarizing and updating information compiled by Frazier and others, Jessie Bernard (1966) traces this pattern to the effects of slavery and its aftermath.

[5] Black-white comparisons should be made within categories of some index of socioeconomic status, but black people are so small a minority that a representative sample of a northern metropolitan area like Alameda County cannot yield sufficient numbers to permit such a control in a detailed analysis.

[6] The age division is close to the median for the whole sample, and it also creates two relatively homogenous groups. People 65 and over are less likely to be dissatisfied than people 45–64, but the differences are not significant. People under 30 differ very little in rates of dissatisfaction from people 30–44.

[7] Gurin, et al. (1961:107) report that among respondents in a national survey the percentage describing their marriages as "not too happy" or "average" was correlated with education. Blood and Wolfe (1960) used a composite index of marital satisfaction, based on scores on the wife's satisfaction with the family standard of living, with her husband's understanding of her "problems and feelings," and with the companionship, love, and affection she received from him. Scores on this index and its components were correlated with both husband's and

wife's education, and wives of white-collar workers scored higher than wives of blue-collar workers.

[8] About 60 percent of white wives and 37 percent of black wives were keeping house. Differences between these women and employed women are smaller and less consistent than those between women working in white-collar jobs and those working in blue-collar jobs. (Blood and Wolfe (1960:101) also found no difference between working and non-working wives in overall satisfaction scores.)

[9] Among blacks 45 and older, blue collar workers are *less* likely to be dissatisfied, and among white wives under 45, operatives (factory workers) are by far the most likely to express dissatisfaction, while service workers and laborers do not differ significantly from professional, technical, and managerial workers.

[10] In the Detroit study also, wives of "low white-collar" (clerical and sales) workers had higher satisfaction scores than wives of professional and managerial workers did (Blood and Wolfe, 1960:254). Gurin, et al. (1961:225) found that wives of salesmen (but not wives of clerical workers) were most likely to describe their marriages as happy.

[11] Mirra Komarovsky (1962:Ch. 13) concluded from her study of white Protestant "blue-collar" couples that those with low income (under $3500) were less likely to be happily married than the others because the "failure of the husband as provider disturbs the reciprocities inherent in conjugal roles," and because the "absence of future prospects" also deprives the couple of a common interest. Black couples are even more likely to experience this kind of strain.

[12] This finding directly contradicts the Detroit data (see Blood and Wolfe, 1960:262). Their mean satisfaction scores were lowest for people with five or more children, but highest for those with *three* children; people without children were *less* satisfied than those with any number under five. The different criterion used by Blood and Wolfe for marital satisfaction, the fact that they reported mean scores rather than pecentages, and perhaps also the fact that their study was done ten years earlier, may account for this contradiction. (In 1955 fewer wives were childless by choice, since oral contraceptives were not yet available, and it was more fashionable to have several children—birth rates among younger couples have been declining since 1958.) A more recent study reports results consistent with ours. Hurley and Palonen (1967) found that in a sample of 40 married-student couples at Michigan State University, marital satisfaction scores were negatively correlated with the ratio of number of children to number of years married ($r = -.39$) but not with number of children or years married.

[13] Jacobson (1959:133–134) reports that for all reporting states in 1955, the rate of divorce per thousand existing marriages without children was 11.9 compared with 7.4 for marriages with children under 18. The divorce rate declined as the number of children in the family increased.

[14] In the Detroit study (Blood and Wolfe, 1960:251) wives who reported more than the average frequency of disagreements with their husbands had, on the average, more children than those who reported fewer disagreements. Wives who reported that children were the chief source of disagreement also reported the most disagreements, and the authors comment: "In view of the fact that disagreements are most frequent among couples whose chief problem is children, it is difficult to escape the conclusion that children are a potent source of conflict between husbands and wives." They do not reconcile this comment with their finding that childless couples are less satisfied with their marriages than those with children.

[15] This is true regardless of the more objective health conditions recorded in their previous answers. . . .

[16] Less than 10 percent of people with no problems rate their health "fair" or "poor," and less than 10 percent of those with a disability rate their health "excellent." But at least half the sample rate their health "good," regardless of the nature of the health problems reported.

[17] Gurin, et al. (1961:31) report that respondents in their sample who said they were "very happy" mentioned marriage and family as the source of their happiness much more often than people who said they were "not too happy," and the "not too happy" were most likely to give marriage and family as the sources of their unhappiness. "When he is happy in these relationships he tends to be happy generally; when he is unhappy in these relationships he tends to be unhappy."

18 Respondents were also asked whether their jobs made full use of their training and experience, and whether they had ever had another job that made better use of their training and experience. Persons who replied "yes" to the first question and "no" to the second were most likely to be "very satisfied" with their jobs, but large proportions of those who said their job did *not* make full use of training and experience were also "very satisfied" (e.g., 18 percent, among white men under 45; 31 percent, among white men over 45; 23 percent, among black women under 45, etc.).

19 Four response categories were provided for each question about the number of drinks: none, 1–2, 3–4, and 5 or more. In general those who reported 3–4 drinks *or* 5+ drinks at a sitting were liquor drinkers—half of them said they drank liquor at least once a week, compared with about a quarter of those who reported only 1–2 drinks at a sitting.

20 The nine items were selected from a larger number of questions about feelings and attitudes, by factor analysis of data collected in an earlier pilot study. The two most closely related to marital satisfaction were "It often seems that my life has no meaning (True/False)" and "How often do you feel very lonely or remote from other people? (Never/Sometimes/Often)."

21 Rates of dissatisfaction are exceptionally high among white people who claim no more than two "close" relatives, even when they claim as many as nine close friends, and those who claim many "close" relatives are least likely to be dissatisfied, even when they have few close friends. But number of "close" relatives claimed is related rather closely to the number of close friends claimed. Approximately 50 percent of those claiming 0–2 relatives also claimed 0–2 friends (70 to 80 percent among younger blacks), and approximately 50 percent of those claiming 10+ relatives also claimed 10+ friends. "3–5" friends was the modal choice for those claiming 3–5 or 6–9 relatives, among whites; among blacks, there was a stronger tendency to make the number of friends match the number of relatives.

22 One could also argue that the "isolation-depression" index identifies people who lack the capacity to relate to others in a mutually rewarding way and hence can be neither happily married nor closely involved with others. But as will be shown in a subsequent paper, divorced people were less isolated than the unhappily married, and less likely to display the kinds of neurotic symptoms characteristic of the unhappily married.

Bernard, Jessie. *Marriage and Family Among Negroes.* Englewood Cliffs: Prentice-Hall, 1966.

Blood, Robert O., and Donald M. Wolfe. *Husband and Wives.* New York: Free Press, 1960.

Bowerman, Charles E. "Prediction Studies." In H. T. Christensen, ed., *Handbook of Marriage and the Family.* Chicago: Rand McNally, 1964.

California State Department of Public Health. *Alameda County Population 1965.* Human Population Laboratory Series A No. 7, 1966.

Goode, William J. *World Revolution in Family Patterns.* New York: Free Press, 1963.

Gurin, Gerald, et al. *Americans View Their Mental Health.* New York: Basic Books, 1961.

Hurley, John R., and Donna P. Palonen. "Marital Satisfaction and Child Density Among University Student Parents." *Journal of Marriage and the Family,* 29 (August 1967):483–84.

Jacobson, Paul H. *American Marriage and Divorce.* New York: Rinehart, 1959.

Komarovsky, Mirra. *Blue-Collar Marriage.* New York: Random House, 1962.

Locke, Harvey. *Predicting Adjustment in Marriage.* New York: Henry Holt, 1951.

Rossi, Alice. "Transition to Parenthood." *Journal of Marriage and the Family,* 30 (February 1968):26.

Waller, Willard. *The Family* (rev. by Reuben Hill). New York: Dryden, 1951.

60

CONJUGAL ORGANIZATION AND HEALTH

Lois Pratt

The specific hypothesis examined in this paper is that in marriages which are characterized by shared power, flexible division of tasks, and a high level of companionship the level of health and health behavior of husbands and wives will be higher than in marriages which are characterized by unequal power, rigid sex role differentiation, and a low level of companionship. The paper contributes to the general question of the relationship of patterns of family organization to the functioning of the family; particularly, whether "emergent" patterns of family organization are more or less effective than "traditional" patterns. While there are abundant and influential position statements regarding the desirability of one family form as opposed to another, little research has been directed at measuring the relative effectiveness of different family forms in performing various family functions.

The paper begins with a review of research literature concerning patterns of conjugal organization, family health functions, and the relationship of conjugal organization to health. . . .

A brief summary of evidence concerning patterns and trends of conjugal power, sex role differentiation, and companionship in American families will be presented here. A detailed analysis and documentation will be presented elsewhere. . . .

Distribution of conjugal power is defined as the extent to which the power to make decisions in the several areas of family life is concentrated in one spouse or shared between the two spouses. While there is a widespread tendency for husbands to exercise more power in the family than their wives, there is considerable diversity among contemporary American families in the pattern of conjugal power, ranging from high equality to high inequality. However, neither the fully patriarchal nor the fully equalitarian pattern is widespread in American families.

The couples in the sample on which the present study was based were distributed quite evenly along a 6-point index which measured the extent to which family decisions were concentrated in the husband or wife or were jointly made. . . .

Sex role differentiation refers to the extent to which there is a sharp distinction between the tasks and activities of men and women based on conventional definitions of male and female roles, or the extent to which there is interchangeability or flexibility in assignment of tasks to men and women. There are widely differing patterns of task assignment in American marriages, ranging from sharp traditional role segregation to liberal role crossing and little consensus about a preferred pattern. Few couples are found to practice no traditional sex-typing of activity. The division of labor in the household appears to be strongly influenced by practical circumstances, particularly the relative availability of the husband and wife to do various tasks.

The couples in the sample studied here were characterized by a diversity of practices, ranging from sharp differentiation to a high degree of overlap in task performance. . . .

Companionship is defined here as the extent to which a husband and wife share, communicate, participate together in activities, and enjoy each other's company. There is great diversity among American couples in their degree of companionship. Marital companionship is not evenly distributed among the socioeconomic status groups, apparently due to the sharper cleavage between the worlds of men and women and the more limiting life circumstances in the lower than in the middle and upper socioeconomic groups.

In the present sample, couples tended to

concentrate near the middle of a companionship scale, skewed slightly toward the companionship end. However, couples scored throughout the full range of the continuum, from almost no joint activities to joint participation in all the activities listed. . . .

The extent to which conjugal power, sex role differentiation, and companionship are interdependent has not been systematically investigated. There is suggestive evidence that at least in the modern American family, as men participate more in household and child care activities and as wives participate in the labor force, each gains the experience and right to share in decision-making in that task area.

Authoritarian power apparently sets limits to companionship, and intimate companionship may also tend to break down autocratic power. Sharp differentiation between sex roles also probably inhibits sharing and companionship, but a fairly high degree of companionship can exist with a fairly traditional division of labor between husband and wife.

While conjugal power, role differentiation, and companionship appear to be interrelated, couples may have a fairly high degree of one without the others. In addition, these patterns appear to respond to social forces differently and therefore to be emerging at different rates in various segments of the population. For example, companionship is closely and positively related to social class, while role flexibility and equalitarian power are not. Power and sex role differentiation are more closely related to the wife's employment than companionship is.

In the present study sample, significant correlations were found among the three conjugal patterns: high companionship was associated with equalitarian power, high companionship was associated with low sex role differentiation, and equalitarian power was associated with low sex role differentiation. . . .

While this is not a study of social change, it is important to inquire into the direction of change in family organization. It cannot be assumed that the family form that is most prevalent or that is emerging as the dominant form will necessarily be the one which functions most effectively to sustain health. On the contrary, family organization is influenced by many social forces other than the demand for individual good health, such as pressures from the economic and political systems, and those pressures may not contribute to the family's ability to sustain health. However, if the emergent patterns of family organization are found, as hypothesized, to be associated with better health and health behavior, then we may be moving in the direction of more effective health functioning by more families.

Review of research literature has shown that there has been a trend away from patriarchal power, sex role differentiation, and limited companionship between husbands and wives toward equalitarian power, sharing and flexibility in division of labor, and a higher level of companionship. . . .

There is fragmentary evidence concerning the relationship of conjugal power, role differentiation, and companionship to health and health behavior. Two studies give evidence suggesting advantages in the de-differentiated family pattern. Large differences in physical health were found between employed and nonemployed married women, favoring the employed women. This was true not only for major illnesses but also for minor neurotic symptoms. Couples with little role separation practiced contraception more effectively than couples with sharp role differentiation, although this held true only for the working class. Another study suggests that the equalitarian power pattern provides health advantages over the patriarchal form. Male domination was found to be related to neuroticism of both wives and husbands; female domination was not related to neuroticism. . . .

There appear to be no direct studies of the relationship between the level of conjugal companionship and health. Suggestive evidence may be derived from families with only one marriage partner present, for these represent persons who completely lack conjugal companionship. Physical illness was found to be significantly more prevalent among spouseless mothers than among mothers with husbands. However, a study found that mothers who lacked a husband obtained medical care of their families as readily as did women with spouses. It may be that spouseless women suffer more illness because of the loneliness and stress associated with spouselessness, but may be adept at coping with the world because of the independence asserted as a result of spouselessness. Two other studies provide contrary evidence. One study found that the lack of a husband was a major handicap in reaching families with a comprehensive health care program, and another reported that family stability was related to acceptance of modern medicine.

The evidence concerning health and health behavior associated with different patterns of conjugal organization tends slightly to favor the equalitarian, de-differentiated, companionship patterns over the traditional family form. The evidence is quite inconclusive, however, in part because existing evidence is conflicting and partly because there has been very little direct research concerning the hypothesis. . . .

The present study is based on information obtained from detailed interviews with a representative cross-sectional sample of families with children aged 9 to 13 from households having a husband in residence and living in a northern New Jersey city. Interviews were conducted by professionally trained interviewers using a standardized instrument with fixed-alternative questions concerning health and family behavior. All health measures are based on the respondents' self-evaluations and not on professional medical reports.[1] Separate interviews were conducted with the wife, the husband, and child in 273 families and with the wife and child in an additional 237 families. The present analysis is based on the interviews with the 273 paired husbands and wives and on the total sample of 510 wives. . . .

Separate indices were constructed for the wife and husband on three aspects of marriage organization:

1. Distribution of conjugal power. For seven areas of family decision-making, the respondents reported whether decisions were made by "husband entirely," "husband more," "both equally," "wife more," or "wife entirely." The index measures the extent to which family decisions are concentrated in the husband or the wife or are jointly made.

2. Sex role differentiation. Respondents were asked to indicate for four aspects of child and home care whether the activity was done by "husband entirely," "husband more," "both equally," "wife more," or "wife entirely." The index measures the extent to which the husband and wife participate in the same household activities.

3. Companionship. The index measures the extent to which the husband and wife engaged together in eleven types of activities and the extent to which he or she enjoyed companionship with the mate.

Seven indices of health and health behavior are used.

1. Present health level is based on the wife's or husband's rating of his or her present level of health and recent illnesses.

2. Lifetime health level includes self-ratings of health from childhood to the present.

3. Total symptoms index is based on the respondent's reports on whether or not he or she had ever had each of 15 health problems and whether or not he or she had had each within the preceding two weeks.

4. Personal health maintenance practices index represents the overall quality of personal health practices in sleep, exercise, elimination, dental hygiene, smoking, alcohol consumption, and nutrition. Responses to 76 questions were used.

5. Use of preventive medical services index is based on the respondent's use of immunizations and preventive tests and examinations.

6. Total use of services is based on 44 questions measuring use of a wide range of professional health services.

7. Health knowledge is based on the accuracy of responses to a nine-item true-false test of general health information. . . .

SUMMARY

All three aspects of conjugal organization which were examined here were found to be significantly related to certain aspects of health and health behavior. Companionship exhibited a more consistent and significant relationship to the health variables than did sex role differentiation or conjugal power.

Among the health variables, use of professional health services exhibited one of the strongest relationships to conjugal organization. Among both husbands and wives, all three aspects of conjugal organization were related significantly to the use of either preventive services or the total range of services. All three aspects of conjugal organization were also found to be related to health knowledge among husbands, while among wives companionship and sex role differentiation (but not power) were related to health knowledge. All three aspects of conjugal organization were related to the present and lifetime health level of wives, while only companionship was related to husbands' health level. The conjugal patterns were not found to be significantly related to personal health practices of husbands, but power and companionship were related to the health practices of wives. . . .

The present study was directed at the general problem of whether or not certain patterns of family organization function more effectively than other forms. The criterion of effectiveness was maintenance of family members' health. The data permit us to conclude that marriages characterized by a relatively equalitarian power pattern, flexible division of labor, and a high degree of companionship are associated with a higher level of health and health behavior among both husbands and wives than are marriages which are characterized by relatively unequal power, strict sex role differentiation, and lower companionship. While it has not been possible to demonstrate conclusively that the pattern of family organization directly affects members' health, the findings do call for a reexamination of an influential stream of family sociological theory which has presented the traditional sex-role differentiated family as the most effective form.

Recently there have been some attempts to formulate a theoretical statement concerning the effectiveness of an equalitarian, nondifferentiated, companionship family form. These statements suggest that it may have some functional advantages, primarily because of its greater flexibility and greater attention to the needs of individual members. Pollak (1967:288, 291) has stated that ". . . change has brought about a situation where neither husband nor wife can find satisfaction or security in a division of labor between the sexes." Given the fact that the modern family must above all fulfill the need for understanding and psychological relief, the traditional sex and age divisions are likely to appear absurd, "for in the realm of intimacy there are only equals."

Slater suggested: "It may be that the more highly differentiated family, despite its prevalence, is simply too unsophisticated a structure for a technologically advanced industrial society such as ours. Its apparent dependence on a stable social context imparts to it a rigidity analogous, in its effects on the family system, to the greater rigidity of inherited as opposed to learned responses in the individual organism" (Slater, 1961).

Hobart maintains that changes in the social structure have tended to make the traditional form of family obsolete. "It follows from this that the family of the future must not be defined in terms of more structure, but in terms of less explicit structure. It must at once be flexible enough for increasingly individuated people, yet a stable basic unit for human life. The family as a commitment implies freedom in the definition of the marital relationship in order to meet the demands of the particular way of life of the two people involved" (Hobart, 1963:410).

Clark Vincent has also pointed out that modern social and technological conditions require enormous adaptability of the family system. "The rapid and pervasive social changes associated with industrialization necessitate a family system that both structurally and functionally is highly adaptive externally to the demands of the other social institutions and internally to the needs of its own members" (Vincent, 1966:29).

These attempts to reformulate sociological notions concerning family form and functioning may turn out to be much more than idealistic ruminations about individual freedom, for if the present findings are any indication, research data may turn out to reveal an "emerging" family form or forms which outperform the "traditional" form within the contemporary social setting. Such families may be especially adapted to the task of obtaining the best health care for their members from the modern medical system.

NOTES AND REFERENCES

[1]The self-report method was chosen for this study because these reports constitute a more direct expression of the individual's experience of good or poor health than do physicians' reports. While there are difficulties in evaluating health data obtained by this method, weaknesses in the use of physicians' reports have also been documented. There have been found to be significant differences in the symptoms reported and diagnoses made by two physicians examining the same patient (Elsom et al., 1960; Schor et al., 1964), and doctors and patients have been found to disagree about what symptoms are significant (Koos, 1954).

Elsom, K. A., S. Schor, T. W. Clark, K. O. Elsom, and J. P. Hubbard. "Periodic Health Examination: Nature and Distribution of Newly Discovered Disease in Executives." *Journal of the American Medical Association,* 172 (January 1960):55–60.

Hobart, C. W. "Commitment, Value Conflict and the Future of the American Family." *Marriage and Family Living,* (November 1963): 405–414.

Koos, E. L. *The Health of Regionville.* New York: Columbia University Press, 1954.

Pollak, O. "Outlook for the American Family." *Journal of Marriage and the Family,* 29 (February 1967):193–206.

Schor, S., T. W. Clark, H. L. Parkhurst, J. P. Baker, and K. A. Elsom. "An Evaluation of Periodic Health Examinations: The Findings in 350 Examinees Who Died." *Annals of Internal Medicine,* 61 (1964):999–1005.

Slater, P. "Parental Role Differentiation." *American Journal of Sociology,* 67 (November 1961):296–311.

Vincent, C. "Familia Spongia: The Adaptive Function." *Journal of Marriage and the Family,* (February 1966): 29–36.

Part Twelve

*Searching for
New Ways to
Make Marriage Work*

So often, any deviation from the monogamous, sexually contained, "till death do us
part" marriage is judged as unhappy, deviant, or on the verge of divorce. Only
recently has it been acknowledged that
previously unapproved types of marriages
could be sound and satisfying to the partners. Anthropologists and historians tell us
that little of what is considered new today
has not already been tried successfully at
other places and in other times. Communal
living, group marriages, extramarital sex,
common-law marriage, marital counseling,
all are old remedies or dangers for marriage,
depending upon how they are viewed. According to the press and much of the popular literature, the number of couples currently trying one or more of these avenues
is what is suprising. But there may not be
so many more experimenters today; like the
so-called sexual revolution, the current popularity of new marital forms may be instead
a matter of how open the couples are about
their search for answers. For example, extramarital sex has been around since the
beginning of recorded history, at least, but
it has evolved for some couples into the
shared activity of mate-swapping in which
no attempt is made to be secretive about
the sexual relationships outside the marriage. Living together without being legally
married is nothing new either, but perhaps
what is different today is who the couples
are and their reasons for not being wed.
It is not uncommon for couples to be living
together for idealistic rather than financial
reasons and for the individuals involved to
be college-educated instead of mainly those
from the lower socioeconomic strata.

While some men and women are questioning the whole idea of marrying in the
first place, the majority of those searching
are not questioning marriage itself but the
form of marriage desirable for them. Most
are seeking ways to improve and strengthen
marriage and make it responsive to the
changing values of society as a whole.
Marriage and the family have traditionally
been very slow to change and have usually
lagged behind other institutions in adopting
change and adjusting to current needs of
family members.

The articles in this section present various

paths couples may try when their marriages are not satisfying and they wish for options other than divorce or separation. One such option is the increasing attempt to seek professional help from a person who is trained to see the marital relationship in an objective fashion and who offers help to the couple as they attempt to construct a workable plan for their marriage. For years the church has offered most of the marriage and family counseling that has been given. This help has ranged from prayer to counseling by professionally trained clergy. The family physician has been the second most commonly sought confidant; usually the couples bring up their problems as if they were medical problems. The quality of help has varied from medication to highly qualified aid given by a physician trained in marriage counseling. Today, a growing number of couples are turning for help to professional marriage and family counselors. These counselors try to help each couple achieve their own goals in life by helping them create a climate at home of harmony and satisfaction. In the first selection, Richard Meryman reports on the counseling process as it was used by one couple and their therapist. As insight into their problem grew and as communication improved, the couple became increasingly able to recognize the source of their problems and to begin to help themselves.

Sometimes as a result of counseling, but frequently on their own, couples arrive at unique ways of making a success of their marriages. Usually, the plan they choose will not last a lifetime, but it may be effective for a few years while the couple is in a particular stage of the life-cycle. On occasion, variations on the plan may stay with the couple through every stage of life; but even if it does not, the plan has helped them learn that flexibility is the key to a dynamic life together. One such plan—which is both controversial and helpful to many couples—is the drawing up of a contract between husband and wife. This kind of contract has nothing to do with the legal one they entered into at their wedding, but is instead one they draw up and agree to as a matter between themselves. Criticisms have been leveled at such contracts on the grounds that they freeze the partners into roles instead of freeing them. It is also said that marriage is not a cutthroat business, that it should be built upon trust where no written document is needed. It is probably true that contracts are only needed where there is evidence, or even just suspicion, that one or both partners will not live up to his or her side of the bargain. However, this is the case with many unsuccessful, unsatisfying marriages. If a contract will help, then the couple has every reason to draw one up and to use it to develop the kind of marriage each can agree to and profit from. Several marriages using such contracts have been publicized in recent years, and the idea seems to be catching on. The notion that an agreement of responsibilities can be used to liberate the marriage partners as well as to hold them to promises and guarantee a working relationship seems to appeal to many couples. Marriage and family counselors frequently suggest such an agreement to motivate the couple to communicate their role expectations to each other and to ensure an understanding of each other's position, energy, values, and interests. In the second article in this section, Norman Sheresky and Marya Mannes discuss the need for a contract and suggest that it should be developed in the premarital period to avoid later conflicts. Perhaps a number of couples would never marry if they sat down to work out such an agreement; but, as the authors point out, that is a good reason for doing just such a thing. In articles III, IV, and VII of the proposed contract, the couple anticipates future expectations, future support, and future property ownership. Such foresight is valuable, but the practicality may be questionable. Couples are dynamic and usually cannot forecast what their needs and exact situations will be in the future, so the likelihood that the existing contract will have to be rewritten at some future date to accomodate new circumstances is great. When the couple feels the contract is becoming limiting instead of liberating, perhaps it is time for them to reevaluate the terms. Many couples report that after living with a contract for a period of time, they depend upon it less and less because they cooperate and communicate their needs and trust each other not to shirk duties nor take more from the relationship than he or she gives to it.

The couple in the first article is one of many involved in extramarital affairs because they believe they will answer a personal need. Still others involve themselves in sex outside marriage as a way to keep their marriages viable, believing that an affair sends them home revitalized and satisfied to take up the pleasant but often routine life of a long-time married person. As with other marital plans, there is great controversy concerning the merits of this solution; and the majority opinion seems to be that couples will destroy a marriage this way rather than strengthen the relationship. However, many couples testify to the contrary; they have seemingly profited from such experiences. Extramarital sex appears to be a very individual thing—some profit, some don't. The role of extramarital sex in successful marriages is little studied, while its negative impact on marriage has been documented many times. Often, the evidence against sex outside marriage comes from therapists and counselors, who see persons troubled by their sex lives or other personal problems, and who are drawn to the conclusion, right or wrong, that it was the affair that hurt the marriage. Consequently, personal reports of married persons of their feelings about their adultery and some observations of their marriage by outsiders are all the evidence available about the positive impact such behavior may have. Certainly, more research needs to be done and many questions are yet to be answered. Some couples who have been studied and who do volunteer experiences suggest strongly that their extramarital affairs were not damaging to them personally, or at least have not damaged their marriages and may have added certain positive dimensions. Of course, we can question whether men and women who go outside marriage for sex do so because they are not sexually satisfied at home, or if there are other factors at the root of extramarital sex which motivate even those who have no complaint about their married sex lives.

A rather unique approach to extramarital sex, and perhaps a truly new phenomenon in marital life-styles, is the practice of mate-swapping. Couples involved in this practice defend it as marriage enrichment that gives variety to what has become overly familiar and provides for individual growth that makes each mate more satisfied with the marriage. Those who disapprove of mate-swapping do so for a variety of reasons, ranging from the usual moralistic ones to the criticism that it is too impersonal. The mate-swappers, of course, believe that the impersonal and casual nature of the sexual contacts—with full approval of their spouses—is the reason that it is no threat to the marriage. In the reading by Duane Denfeld and Michael Gordon, "swinging" is examined in its many dimensions, and the authors conclude that it may indeed help many marriages that otherwise would be unsatisfying or even end in divorce.

Communal living has come in for its share of attention in the last decade and has most commonly been associated with the young and unmarried; often it is considered to be an activity of the deviant population. Less publicized is the large number of serious married couples who believe that communal living is the answer to how their marriages and their family life can be made more rewarding. Communal living is certainly not new—the nineteenth century saw the rise of hundreds of such groups, most of which grew out of religious factions seeking a way to unify their membership. The contemporary commune movement has many faces; often it is religious in nature, or centers around an ideology such as returning to a simpler, agricultural life. Sometimes it is a part of a drug culture. All parts of the movement seem to have one unifying theme, however—the desire for intimacy and support from a family unit larger than the nuclear one. Some communal living arrangements include communal sex, but as many center around couples who are monogamous. The article by Joy Schulterbrandt and Edwin Nichols discusses the historical development of the commune and the problems facing communal groups.

Often confused with communal living

but quite a separate and distinct type of male-female relationship is the group marriage. At the present time, this is not a widespread phenomenon, and many predict it will never be popular because of its complexity. Larry and Joan Constantine have studied group marriages and think that it is too early to decide that such marriages won't work. Because the movement is less than ten years old, very little actual research has been done on group marriages; this particular article is the most comprehensive review of what is known presently.

61

A MARRIAGE IN TROUBLE

Richard Meryman

The marriage counseling hour was almost over. David and Lynn Maxwell were in their second month of therapy—and making little progress. The counselor, Marcia Lasswell, was talking. "David, what if five years from now Lynn still dislikes sex? Are you willing to live without it the rest of your life?"

"Absolutely not!" said David.

"Well, what will you do then, have an affair?" asked the counselor.

"No, by God, I want my sex with my wife."

"It sounds like you're saying you may get another wife."

"Well, I sure think about it a lot," answered David.

"Okay, how does that make you feel, Lynn?" asked the counselor.

"I don't want to lose my marriage," answered Lynn. "I guess I'll have to work on my problem. But don't *I* get anything? I want some emotion from him—and damn it, I want some freedom to be *me!*"

Such voices, such dilemmas, such angers sometimes seem to be beyond every doorstep. Forty percent of U.S. marriages now end in divorce. In southern California, the national trend barometer, the rate is over 50 percent. A federal study found that since last year the divorce rate for marriages of 20 years and over has shot up 38 percent. Is marriage an anachronism in today's America? What *has* happened?

There is an answer in the story of the Maxwells. They live—under a different name—in Pomona, Calif. At 40, David is a $20,000-a-year computer programmer. He is a curly-haired man of medium height, in top physical trim from volleyball and fencing at his local YMCA. Lynn, at 36, is a good-looking, solidly built blond woman a little taller than her husband. They have been married 12 years and have two boys, Peter, 10, and Duncan, 8. And though they do have occasional good times—camping, going to the beach, working on crossword puzzles—the Maxwells' marriage mostly is lacerated by battles.

Some of their quarrels are as old as the oldest marriage joke. But those ancient, almost reflexive collisions between two human natures are taking place in a new world. The Maxwells' struggles are occuring in this "age of self-fulfillment," in which selfless commitment to being the perfect wife and mother, the ultimate provider and father, the ideal son or daughter is just no longer the be-all of life.

So for Lynn Maxwell, like many, many women in every part of America, a new theme has been amplifying virtually all of her problems. "The inner me," it goes, "is more important than serving society's traditional commandments. If that 'me' can be fulfilled, I will be a better person, and everybody close to me will benefit. Therefore I am morally justified in doing whatever is necessary to liberate myself." Out of this philosophy has come, of course, the counterculture of the youth and the women's liberation movement.

The Maxwells' experience can be distilled in three periods of their marriage. In 1965 Lynn had an affair with a man in her amateur theatrical group. Her state of mind in that time is a classic description of how marriage can destroy a woman's self-confidence and self-esteem. In 1968 David had an affair with a secretary at his job. His behavior is an example of what often happens when a wife pushes hard for more freedom and identity, and a husband tries to recharge his ego. This past January, the Maxwells started counseling with . . . Marcia Lasswell. The understandings they arrived at through her questioning offer important insights into much of what troubles marriages in America today. . . .

Lynn got to know a married television executive when they were together in an amateur production of *Life With Father*. She saw him as "very sensitive, artistic. He wrote poetry and painted, and I felt there was a tremendous vulnerability, the need to be protected—you know, my compulsion to mother men. And wow, I jumped. I asked him out for coffee and, God, I floored him. I told him I felt very sexually attracted to him. I had figured out that the way you got a man was sex. Then I could go to what I really wanted, what I wasn't getting from David: emotional satisfaction. It was the first time that I really stood up on my own two feet and did what I wanted regardless of the consequences."

In her relationship with her husband, Lynn says, "The only use I felt David had for me was in bed. We had a social marriage. He could chat intellectually just delightfully—you know, from now till hell freezes over, about everything except what is really important. But there is no real warmth between people unless there is a sharing of emotion.

"If I tried to talk about how I felt in a situation between us, that immediately threatened him. Like I was trying to explain what I felt was the problem with our oldest boy, Peter, and how things in David's and my relationship were hurting him. David just closed up, and as soon as he could said, 'Well, you're probably right,' and made an excuse to leave.

"If he felt angry or upset or depressed, I could tell by little signs, but he'd never express his emotions. I used to fight so much and so hard to get a reaction out of him, and I so seldom did. He'd argue beautifully and on such a logical plane. And I'd get so emotional I'd be tongue-tied —or didn't even know what I was saying. Then I'd get frustrated, and I'd end up crying. That made me feel beneath him, very inadequate.

"After our fights I would always end up feeling miserable. I was sure it was my fault that the marriage was in the situation it was in. David wasn't happy; the kids weren't happy. I had been taught as a child that the perfect wife has a very happy husband and this in return is her fulfillment. And I was constantly aware that society expected me to be a good wife, a good mother, a good woman, active in the community. And I just didn't fit into that slot."

Before her marriage, Lynn had had a very successful college career: good grades, president of the drama club, a starter on the field hockey team. When David married her she was a research assistant at a local TV station. In those days she felt strong, confident, and herself. But like most girls getting married, Lynn was full of vague dreams. As usual, there had been no realistic, explicit discussion of marriage at school, at home, or with David. Many of her expectations came from the stereotypes of young people's books, the movies, and magazines. "I felt," says Lynn, "marriage would be some great romantic thing, a wonderful freedom from being under my mother's thumb—that I'd be able to do what I wanted and go where I wanted with somebody I wanted to share those things with."

Lynn found instead that she was often the lonely focus of tremendous pressures—decisions to be made, repetitive tasks stupefyingly tiresome. She felt wrung between her yearnings for an independent sense of self and all those weighty obligations drilled into her since childhood. "Of course, I was doing no worse than anybody else, but I always assumed that everybody else on the street had their house running and in order and were solving their problems creatively—and I'm not. I'm inadequate. I felt guilty feeling that housework wasn't challenging, wasn't productive. But it's true. I tried to tell myself, 'You can find dignity in anything you do.' I'd fix a special dish and spend hours at it. I'd put it on the table and the kids would say, 'Yuuuk! Are we having that?' Of course, I had set myself up. I should have been able to fix a meal and not see it as a love offering.

"I tried very hard to sell myself on the idea that what ultimately mattered was my family. But the other side of me still said, 'Okay, but when you started out all those years ago, here was this circle which was me as a person. And in came that big chunk which was wife. And in came another big chunk and that's mother. And now there's just a little itty-bitty sliver left of the circle that is still me.'

"It's pretty hard to be your own person when you're running the whole show for everybody else. It seemed like if I didn't nag David constantly, the bills didn't ever get paid. When the school principal called to say Peter was in trouble, I felt I didn't have anybody to depend on to help me decide what to do. And all the small things. God, if I left getting up in the morning to David, all three of them would still be in bed at noon. Even the cars were my job. I felt like nothing ever happened in that house unless I made it happen. I remember I would look at David and think, 'Who are you to place this burden on me and sit there smug, eating your meal and then reading a magazine afterwards?' And I

hated myself because I was letting it be done to me."

The parents, grandparents, aunts, uncles, cousins who might have been a sympathetic sounding board for Lynn were all in the East, where she grew up. And this type of isolation is among the most crucial of all factors affecting marriage today. In the past 70 years all the social forces surrounding marriage have drastically changed. When America was essentially rural and people stayed put, the values and voices of Lynn's larger family would have enveloped and supported her. And there was not the concern then about identity; on the farm the family was more of a team, working together on almost every aspect of living and survival, including education and religion.

But now, Lynn's marriage existed in an urban, anonymous mobile world. And today, aside from child-rearing, the prime job of marriage is to provide emotional contact. Isolated in their shifting, rootless world, the members of the nuclear family—mother, father, and children—are asked to answer every emotional need for each other.

"Just before I had my affair," says Lynn, "I was really desperate—seemed like every day there were moments when all I wanted to do was curl up into a little ball in a corner and escape everybody and everything. I guess one big reason I got involved with another man was that I thought it took another person to prove I was somebody. You know, a man is willing to lie or cheat because he finds me exciting and interesting.

"It was very important to discover that I wasn't frigid. I could be sure the problem came mainly from my mother. She was an extremely domineering woman and I spent an awful lot of my childhood doing things I hated because I was obliged to. Before we were married, David and I had a great sex life because then I thought I was being a person in my own right—doing something my mother didn't approve of. After we were married sex was one more obligation —you know, like it was right there in the marriage contract. And also, we had so little emotional contact that making love was a very empty thing, and afterwards I would get so depressed. I would get the feeling that what I was doing was really nothing more than masturbation, because he really wasn't there for me.

"There was this terrible paradox in me that I wanted to be normal; I hated feeling like a failure as a wife, and yet I didn't want to change. Looking back on my affair, I realize there really wasn't anything happy about that time—just two people not knowing how to swim, drowning and hanging onto each other for support. All the lying —I wasn't very good at it. I was terrified that David would wonder why I was going to such a lot of school meetings and why the drama club rehearsals were lasting so god-awful late. I'd get home and I'd be sure it showed on me somehow. It was like living on the edge of a cliff waiting for the wind to push you over. And it's pretty hard to feel guilty like that and good about yourself at the same time."

David never did learn about the affair until it was over—and Lynn never had to choose between the two men. The television producer got a job offer in another city and simply moved away with his family. "Lousy as things were at home," Lynn says, "being married was still better than being lost in a sea of people. It's funny, but just having another warm body in the house . . . I mean, even if you're fighting all the time—or maybe because you are—there's a kind of a connection you feel. And also, my ego was so shot, I felt I had to have somebody to provide for me, take care of me. Somehow, I felt as though my marriage created my identity, and without it, I'd just be a big zero. And when you think, 'I've got to stay in this marriage,' even that is debasing. It's more proof that you're nobody.

"When my affair was over, I felt devastated. It was like an adolescent in her first love—this feeling of longing and desperation and never seeing the person again. It must have been a year before I got over it. Of course, I didn't really want to get over it. I wrote him several times—and got one business letter back.". . .

"We always seemed to have our fights on Saturday mornings," says David, "and always about something trivial. On this particular Saturday afternoon we went sailing with friends and by then we weren't speaking. Lynn was steaming and I was like an iceberg. And . . . well, I happen to think marital problems should be kept strictly inside the home, so I tried to act natural.

"That evening, Lynn just ripped into me. You know, 'You lousy bastard. Big phony. Pretending like everything is just swell and I'm your dear little wife—sweetie—all that stuff—it makes me sick because it's such a lie.' She went on and on like that. She ended up saying I should start having some honest emotions and show them—or just get out.

"And suddenly I felt, 'Oh my God, here we are—the 9,000th argument and it's going to lead nowhere for the 9,000th time'—and it was like everything I'd ever felt at those moments came at me all at once. So I just walked out and went and stood alone in the garage to try to keep control of myself.

"Lynn followed me out there, and before she could lay something else on me I said, 'I want a divorce.' And I really meant it. She just kind of stood there and the skin all around her mouth got tight-looking. Then she said, 'Is there somebody else?' I guess I just smiled. 'Cause for six weeks I'd been in love with another woman.

"The girl I'd taken up with was my boss's secretary. We'd been in a car pool together, and I guess, compared to her husband, I was a literate, educated genius. We began having lunch and sharing a lot of feelings. And, you know, she hadn't heard all my stories before.

"One Saturday we both had to go to the office, and driving home she suddenly slid across the seat, put her head on my shoulder. And I felt, 'Oh, my God. Terrific. What's happening? What have I gotten myself into?' But, man, I was really ready for something like that!"

At that moment David was sure an affair would heal his unhappiness—but it is the experience of counselors that when people want to improve the quality of their lives, but are uncertain what they want from life, then their attempts at fulfillment are going to be confused and often destructive. They will try to reshape their worlds to fit their fantasies, laying all blame outside themselves.

"The marriage was bleak, really in a rut. I was closed up tight. Lynn was closed up tight. I really felt lonely. A man has to have a woman he can unload to, talk to, somebody who isn't always running him down and hassling him about things.

"It's amazing how important it is to come home and be welcomed, be greeted, you know, warmly. Mostly it was come home, go find Lynn, say, 'Hi, how are you? What's happened today?' She'd be sort of unresponsive—so then it was just find the newspaper, see what the mail was. And, I suppose, she was probably standing there thinking, 'That son of a bitch. He comes home and doesn't thank me for all the . . . practically doesn't see me.' But you expect to find your wife there. She's been there all day, you know."

A major friction which had readied David for his affair was Lynn's increasing involvement with women's liberation ideas. For six months before his affair, Lynn had been attending a weekly meeting with other restless wives at their church. It was, in effect, an informal women's liberation consciousness-raising group. They used as their "text" a special issue of their Methodist magazine devoted to the ideas of the movement. There were titles such as "The Dancing Dog" and "Women's Will to Fail." The tidal wave of popular literature describing what a good marriage ought to be is one of the modern stresses on marriage. It almost always insinuates that nobody should settle for less than total success.

Lynn would always deny she was in a women's liberation group; she feared belittling, crude remarks and jokes. And David frequently managed little digs at Lynn and her friends—like "Well, you liberated women, what's on for today?" He delighted in pumping Lynn for intimate details about the other women in the discussion group. But when he learned that one was having a secret affair, he was suddenly fearful that they might be urging Lynn to do the same again. He also began to won-

der what would happen if these women did indeed help make Lynn confident and self-reliant, which he had often silently disparaged her for not being.

As Lynn began to apply more and more of the liberationist doctrine to herself, housework, typically, became one of the tensest topics with David. "Sometimes," says David, "I'd come home tired out from my day at work and find her sitting there reading some book of plays, and see a sinkful of dirty dishes and the house a mess. And I'd think, 'Damn it, why doesn't she get about her business—which is *not* reading.' She'd see me look at the dishes and say, 'If you want the dishes clean—clean them.'

"I remember once Lynn was off at her meeting with those women, and I was up to my elbows in soapsuds. And I thought, "What the hell am I doing here? I'm a respected professional with a full-time job that brings in all our money—and Lynn is just off talking. Damn it, what I do is life, and what she's doing is amusement.'

"Somebody has to take the responsibility for the home, and since I'm gone at work and Lynn is home, she's the person. It's not that I didn't agree she should be fulfilled. I agreed that there are no socially redeeming features about housework. That's why I didn't want to do it either, and why I didn't see why I should be her only alleviation from drudgery. And I might add that things I was doing in my job were not an unmitigated joy. A lot of it was as crappy as laundry.

"My time is worth money. And that includes unaccounted time at home just staring out the window sort of recharging my batteries. If she thinks running the house is tough, she should try the whole financial responsibility for a while."

The confrontation in the garage—David's demand for a divorce—had a dramatic effect. Lynn was suddenly affectionate, and interested in sex. Simultaneously, tells David, "My girl friend said, 'This can't go on.' How's that for an original line?" Two weeks later, David and the woman he was having an affair with sat in his car at a vacant construction site in the woods. David told her he would stay with Lynn. "It was the hardest thing I've ever done," says David. "Whether it was guilt or fear, God knows. It wasn't chivalry."

A week after David's decision, Lynn's desire for sex disappeared as abruptly as it started. "It really was not conscious," says Lynn, "and I felt terribly, terribly guilty about it." A month later, Lynn woke David at one A.M. "Would it be all right with you," she said, "if I got a job?" "We'll talk about it in the morning," said David.

But they did not talk. And a week later Lynn announced that she had a part-time job at a real estate office, fitted in while David and the children were gone at school and work. "That meant," says Lynn, "that I had to move twice as fast and be twice as careful so I'd be working—but it would be like I wasn't working. See, I was willing to push for my freedom, but I was not ready to risk my marriage. And part of me was really hung up on guilt, on the idea that my real responsibility was still to David and the kids.

"But, wow, that job was great. I was very scared that I'd be incompetent. But I learned. And my boss trusted me and depended on me, which was terrific and really made me feel like a person again. And the other people in the office seemed to find me interesting and made me feel fun."

Though David was still making digs at Lynn—"Seems like all the career women I've ever met are always competing and arguing"—he also quite liked the idea that she was bringing in some money, even though he sometimes disapproved of how she spent it. Also, they now had more to talk about. Her mind and anger were not so concentrated on him and the household.

Perhaps out of guilt over his affair, David began helping more around the house—and feeling very virtuous about it. But he was also playing the politics of housework. "I never disagreed aloud with the principle," admits David, "but I sure dragged my feet. I'd agree the hell out of Lynn, but wind up saying something like, 'I don't have compulsive, middle-class

standards. I don't mind a dirty house.' Or I'd do jobs shoddily or wastefully so I wouldn't be asked to do them again."

David was playing the same game he always had. He never had talked Lynn into taking all the household responsibility, but had steered her into those responsibilities by the familiar strategem of default—an extremely common ploy among personality types like David, known as "passive-aggressives." Often such men learned to be dominated by women during boyhood, when mothers and female teachers and Cub Scout den mothers literally taught them passivity by forbidding roughhousing, fighting, and emotional outbursts. As adults, these men get their way by that subtle, infuriating monolithic aggression of passive resistance.

"I had a sort of British-type upbringing," says David, describing his childhood in Pennsylvania. "Where it was 'Don't show caring. Don't show feeling. Be the great stone face. Nothing fazes you.' So I had this mechanism that blocks out even thinking. When Lynn got mad at me, it was 'I'm in my own shell. Screw you. I've really got my wall up.' Then I'd sulk."

The marathon of job and home soon began to leave Lynn feeling almost as oppressed as before. And she put even more pressure on David to help. "What I couldn't understand," says David, "was why hiring help wasn't the perfect solution. But she just got all upset over that. Her point was that I should be willing to share, that we're homemakers together, parents together, everything together. But she wouldn't spend her salary on getting help—said having some money of her own was part of being free. I felt if she wouldn't sacrifice, I was damned if *I* was going to sacrifice."

It was a familiar marital contest, one of the most destructive attitudes in marriage: "Am I giving up more than I am getting?" One of Lynn's complaints was that David always got to do whatever he wanted. Once David asked Lynn, "Where do you want to go to dinner?" She said, "Oh, I don't care." David said, "Well, let's go to such and such." Suddenly Lynn was furious. "Jesus, we always go where you want to go."

"Society had pretty much spelled out

my role," David says, "and now I was being attacked for it on all fronts, the awful things I was supposedly doing were because I'd been trained to do them. But that didn't mean I wasn't likable, that I wasn't a good person—you know, good old . . . I really wanted to treat Lynn fairly. I really am a person of goodwill.". . .

One night early in January of this year, two policemen knocked on the Maxwells' door to quiz their son Peter about some vandalism in the neighborhood. Lynn suspected Peter was guilty, and she was overwhelmed by the feeling that their problems were out of control. Torn on one hand by her need for the same liberation at home she felt at work and on the other by her vision of herself as a bad mother and wife, Lynn was desperate for someone who might help. David, himself frustrated and embattled, acquiesced. Lynn chose as a marriage counselor a woman who seemed completely liberated: Marcia Lasswell, who is successfully married, a mother and, in addition to her private counseling practice, is a professor of psychology at California State University, Pomona.

To the counselor, the Maxwells were a very familiar case. When David and Lynn met, they had been drawn to each other by their differences—David's calm passivity meshing with Lynn's impatient strength. "But," says Marcia Lasswell, "people lose respect for differences, and begin to defend themselves against the differences. Then the qualities that made them different become their defense mechanisms." David got more and more passive as Lynn got more aggressive to overcome his passivity. So finally their behavior became so exaggerated that they were almost caricatures of where they started out. "They were poles apart," says the counselor, "with a battleground in between—and they'd ceased communicating."

So the first step was to teach David and Lynn to communicate with each other. And the counselor quickly found a classic sample of garbled communication. The tension between the Maxwells over sex would periodically build until Lynn felt so guilty that she would decide that, okay, she would give in tonight. And she would be furious at David when, after she had talked herself into it, he then misread her cues and stayed downstairs watching television.

"I was watching TV," David said in the second counseling session, "and I heard Lynn say, 'I'm tired! I'm going to bed.' And that meant to me, 'I'm going to sleep, don't bother me.' "

"Okay, Lynn," asked Marcia Lasswell, "what *did* you mean?"

"He should have known I wanted him to come upstairs pretty soon," answered Lynn.

"Now then, David, could Lynn have meant that?"

"Well, why didn't she *say* so?"

"Okay," said Marcia Lasswell, "suppose she did say, 'I'm going upstairs; are you coming up?' Then what would you have said?"

"I might have said, 'I'm going to wait until the news is over.' "

"What would that have meant to you, Lynn?"

"I'd have figured he wasn't interested and I'd have gone to sleep."

"No," said David, "I would have meant, 'I'll be up when the news is over. Don't go to sleep.' "

"You get the point?" finished the counselor. "I'm trying to show you how ambiguous you are most of the time and how everybody tries to read minds. People jump to conclusions and read meanings which are simply wrong, then act on the basis of those misinterpretations, and when their expectations are not delivered, they feel rejected and not loved.

The Maxwells met Marcia Lasswell one evening a week for an hour—at a cost of $25 per hour. For four weeks they detailed their complaints about each other, defended themselves, let Marcia Lasswell lead them through self-analysis of their motives and feelings. They did not, however, make any effort at home to use their new understandings to solve problems.

The counselor decided to take drastic action: the use of confrontation technique to jolt them into taking aggressive steps to help themselves. "I am willing to listen for a few weeks," she says, "to people playing that 'poor me' song over and over. But that's as long as I'll listen."

One night, Lynn got a bawling out from the counselor. "I am tired," Marcia Lasswell said, "of listening to you talk about how hard life is, and how rotten you feel about it. I'm trying to help you see through some of these problems and agree on some solutions. If you want to come in here and work, all right. But please don't come in here and take up my time sulking."

Lynn got up and stalked out. Out in the car, Lynn wept in David's arms. Several days later, Marcia Lasswell telephoned Lynn, and despite an icy reception they agreed that she would return to counseling. "I think that was the turning point in my therapy," says Lynn. "It was a revelation to me that somebody can get mad at you because they care about you, and it doesn't mean they have rejected you. It gave us a tremendous closeness."

The next confrontation came when David threatened Lynn with a divorce unless the sex problem eased, and Lynn in return demanded more emotions and more freedom from David. Shaken up, they then went to work on their sex difficulties.

The counselor felt that Lynn's disinterest in sex had always been present. Therefore, Lynn could use sex as a weapon to punish David, while getting out of sex herself. "Women who enjoy sex," says Marcia Lasswell, "rarely withhold sex because they are also depriving themselves. They'll find some other way to punish their husbands."

She applied a technique called "desensitization." Every other night would be "open" for sex or not as the Maxwells wished. But on the alternate nights no sex was allowed. Instead, they would have tender physical contact doing whatever they enjoyed such as hold each other close, rub backs, brush hair, bathe together. Hopefully, when Lynn did not have to worry that David was "trying to march me off to bed," she would be able to relax enough to rediscover sensual feelings with him. "They were so jittery with each other," says Marcia Lasswell, "that they couldn't even hold hands anymore. Lynn wouldn't

touch David because it might encourage him. And, unless he was desperate, David wouldn't touch her for fear of being rejected." Two weeks later, Lynn triumphantly announced they had made love very happily that Saturday night and again the next morning.

Each counseling session usually began with the question, "What do you want to talk about today?" Lynn for some time had wanted to attack the question of women's liberation directly. And she assumed that the counselor would be her eager ally in thumping David. But although Marcia Lasswell is in complete sympathy with the movement, she consciously avoids pushing those ideas on her clients, feeling that tackling their basic emotional conflicts will also tackle problems of liberation. "It could really mess up a couple," she says, "if I said, 'Hey look. Live the way I do and you'll be happy.'"

So the day Lynn brought up the subject, the counselor guided her into an analysis of just how much liberation she was actually ready for. Lynn was explaining that there was a rule that the boys had to put their dirty clothes into the hamper, or their laundry did not get washed. "I was telling myself," said Lynn, "that I'd be damned if I'd keep picking up after them. But then I feel terribly guilty when they don't have clean clothes." Ten questions and answers later, Marcia Lasswell said, "If you really, deep, deep down believe that a good mother always picks up the clothes and the child doesn't need to respond by putting laundry in a hamper, that if you are a good person you will do this—then how can I help you?"

"Well," said Lynn, "when you say it that way, I'm being ridiculous. But getting myself to believe it is a lot harder."

Trying to alter the emotional reflexes of a lifetime is obviously a slow process, but David and Lynn did feel they were learning about themselves. One evening Marcia Lasswell, probing David, steered him to an important insight into why he pushed all responsibilities onto Lynn. They concluded that David feared getting angry because he was afraid he might say unforgivably hurtful things to people. And he believed that getting angry was a necessary part of taking responsibility.

When the Maxwells were some three months into their counseling, it suddenly came out that their desensitization program had gradually drifted into disuse. They had fallen back into their old routines—watching TV until David, full of good intentions early in the evening, would often fall asleep on the couch, and Lynn would go up to bed.

Lynn was angry at David for being lazy about the program, which to her secret astonishment had been working so well for her. In fact, the counseling had eased the Maxwells' marriage a great deal—which is why they had become overconfident and momentarily lapsed. Lynn's guilt was much lighter, and there was not the steady, grinding tension between her and David. Even in public they held hands and would greet each other with a kiss and a one-arm hug. Lynn's anger was less frequent; David was taking a heavier hand with the children. Understanding themselves better, they were able to handle or head off collisions. And they would never again return to their original despair.

But what ultimately happens to the Maxwells depends on how hard they are willing to work—and they still have a distance to go to achieve a happy marriage. Still missing for the Maxwells is that crucial element lacking in virtually all troubled marriages today: Lynn must fulfill her potential as a woman, and David must fulfill his as a man. Only through an affectionate blend of independence and sharing can a couple and a marriage have the strength to withstand the awesome stresses of modern society. Otherwise, maintains Marcia Lasswell, David and Lynn will always depend on each other to satisfy every need—for gratitude, esteem, emotion, companionship, etc., etc.—and no one human being can supply another with all that.

"We are talking," says Marcia Lasswell, "not about women's liberation, but human liberation." She considers "human liberation" the key to the future of marriage in this changing society. Almost certainly, marriage will always be there in some form. And it is equally certain that men and women in marriages will always behave like hedgehogs, moving close to each other for warmth, pricking each other, moving apart into the cold, then back to closeness.

And it is certain, too, that the most illusive, indefinable, and unpredictable element in marriage will always be love. During her affair, Lynn kept a diary, recording all her activities and longings and aches and desperations. She left it in her top bureau drawer. A month after the affair ended, David inevitably found the small volume. He read it and was overcome with fury and humiliation. But when he came to the end, David took a pen and wrote after the last entry, "Lynn, I have read this. And I love you."

62

A RADICAL GUIDE TO WEDLOCK

Norman Sheresky and Marya Mannes

We marry in America with less knowledge of what we are doing than when buying a car. And a little knowledge goes a notably short way. According to the latest report on marriage issued by the National Center for Health Statistics in the Department of Health, Education, and Welfare, 455 out of every 1,000 marriages made in this country last year are destined to wind up in the bitter and unhappy toils of the divorce court. With our divorce rate now the highest in the world, obviously the time has come to ask what is wrong with the American way of marrying—with letting people in for the price of a state license and out only at the emotional cost of a heart transplant.

But is there an alternative? What if, for example, we made the tough part of marriage getting in instead of getting out? What if we obliged potential marriage partners to explore together in advance of marriage—and in writing—their motives for marrying, as well as the extent of their intended commitments with regard to children, property sharing, and future alimony, should the marriage fail? Some will argue that if we required couples to take such a deep look at their motives and potential obligations before marriage, a good many people would never go through with marriage at all. But that, in part, is just the point.

In the following pages we present a sample of a premarital contract between two fictitious but reasonably typical contemporary candidates for marriage. Before turning to it, however, let us glance briefly at the system it would improve upon—that is, at the way we marry now. Why *do* we marry? What undermines our chances of success? And what are some of the marital obligations we presently take on by law at the moment of marriage—whether or not we agree to them or even know about them?

We Americans are a mobile and unauthoritarian people, increasingly rootless, shedding our past, evading our future. We live for today and shut out the reality of tomorrow in the same way that we shut out the reality of death. In this context, a man and woman marry when there is a curious and too often strictly temporary alignment of their expectations and needs. We are attracted to our partners because they promise a fulfillment of ourselves, because they satisfy our sexual appetites, because they seem to enlarge our sense of living and loving—now.

Our vision entering marriage is not merely temporary, however. It is also still strongly affected by traditional social attitudes, ones that are concerned less with enduring love than with appearances. Ingrained in a great many women is the belief that marriage combines two opposite ideals: escape and security—escape from parents or the burden of creating a separate identity; security in the arms and home of the protector-provider. Nor is a man immune to the nudgings of social convenience and convention. A wife is good for business. A wife can supply comforts few bachelors bother with on their own. And sex? No lack of it anywhere, but men dream of not having to leave the beds of others at dawn and of feasting at will.

Besides seeking mates who seemingly are able to satisfy our present sexual needs or our present needs for familial substitution, we often have other individual needs that we more or less unconsciously seek to satisfy in marriage. If we are drug addicts, alcoholics, or people with other compulsive habits, we tend to find mates who will satisfy us either by punishing us for our habits or by continually trying to rescue us from them. If we are insecure self-doubters, we may seek the satisfaction of marrying mates whose frailties loom even larger and whom we may therefore criticize. If we are lonely and afraid, we may seek anybody who will give us the temporary relief of filling time and space. Very often we marry for the same reason that others take pills ("uppers" or "downers")—simply to change our state of being.

Marriages crumble, finally, when each partner blames the other for failing to embody the original visions that impelled their union: "I would have made something of myself if it hadn't been for you!" or, "I could have married anybody I wanted. Why did I have to choose you?" Why, indeed?

Even if we chose wisely in the light of an apparent meshing of respective strengths and requirements, however, the crack in the marriage foundation that can still split it wide open is, simply, ignorance—an appalling ignorance of the realistic obligations of marriage itself. Ironically, ignorance about the true nature of physical love often is a cause of major marital fission—ironically, because we now appear to know everything we ever wanted to know about sex and are bombarded with manuals on how to please everybody forever. How then does ignorance about sex continue to be responsible for the wreck of an enormous number of marriages?

Serious students of sex, such as Masters and Johnson, have made important and useful contributions to the knowledge of our sexual selves, contributions that have already saved foundering marriages and could, if translated into less abstruse language, rescue many more. That such information about sexual problems is not made available in simple terms may well reflect society's belief that we are not to be trusted with it. Deluged instead with nonbooks by nonwriters (e.g., *The Sensuous Woman, The Sensuous Man*), many marriage partners persist in believing that the sexual pleasures they enjoy before or anticipate when they marry will last forever, without further knowledge, effort, or growth on their part.

And what of our overwhelming ignorance of the obligations we take on by law when we marry? Any law student will tell you that a contract cannot exist between two people unless the parties to it agree to each of its essential terms. But we all know that when we say in a state of trembling euphoria, "I do," no contract detailing the terms we are agreeing to is ever presented.

If you are of sufficient age and mental capacity, free of specific diseases, not imprisoned, and not already married, the state will license you to marry anybody of the opposite sex—even if you hate babies, dote on rock music, and believe wholeheartedly in the overthrow of the government while your intended spouse loves large families, likes classical music, and sits on the Republican National Committee. But once married in the state of New York, for example, you are harnessed with several hundreds of sections of the Domestic Relations Law, the Family Court Act and Rules, and other related statutes and decisions that have the force of law. It seems that our legislators feel that marriages are not to be lightly discarded, even if they have been lightly contracted.

Marriage partners are obliged, by law, to divulge to each other some of the most essential facts about themselves. Concealing prior marriages, hereditary diseases, past imprisonments, unwillingness to become a parent, or affiliations with dubious organizations may be grounds for annulment or divorce on the basis of fraud. Married persons must also engage, at least occasionally, in sexual relations, although there is not the slightest obligation to enjoy such activities and no regulation involving frequency. No statutory obligation to love, honor, or obey exists, but wives may not refuse to cohabit with husbands in such reasonable places as the husband may designate. Each partner in a marriage must insulate the state against the cost of supporting the other and the children of the marriage. The state, for example, will not pay for the hospitalization of the husband if the wife can afford to foot the bill.

There are a host of other obligations involving the ownership of property that arise out of the marital relation. Husbands and wives may now own property separate and apart from each other. They may contract with each other and sue each other. But contracts between husbands and wives are minutely scrutinized by the courts and, since each is assumed to have a duty to treat the other fairly and openly, contractual agreements may be obliterated and "implied obligations" imposed by a judge if he feels the married partners have not been open and fair with each other.

It is an extremely common occurrence for husbands and wives, faced with impending divorce, to claim that all of the property, real or personal, standing in the name of one spouse was always intended by both parties to be joint property. A myriad of statutes and decisions exists for determining the status of real or personal property, whether held individually or jointly. But in matrimonial cases, laws and precedents are not applied with the same rigidity accorded to routine commercial transactions. Again, outcomes are often up to the judge.

The state maintains, finally, that a husband has a duty of which he may not relieve himself—that of supporting his wife and children. But what are the rules concerning alimony? They are incomprehensible—that's what they are. There are rules, decisions, and statutes instructing the judge that wives should not be permitted to become "alimony drones"—self-indulgent, indolent parasites. These compete with other rules, statutes, and decisions directing that the court take into consideration the length of the marriage, the age of the wife, the age of the children, and a preseparation standard of living.

What all this means is that the amount of alimony, if any, is no more certain than a roll of the dice in Las Vegas and the consequences to the litigants may be just as disastrous as they are to the gamblers. Yet, how often do engaged couples consider this crucial subject in advance? Or their feelings about child support? Or whether their assets and joint income should be divided or undivided? Why should a woman whose husband has permitted her and encouraged her to become a marital cripple with no economic potential be treated on a parity with a woman whose earning capacity has not been influenced or deterred by the marriage at all?

More importantly, why shouldn't the parties themselves make the rules before there is trouble? Why shouldn't the standard of support be agreed upon before it is imposed upon the couple? Why is it not just as sensible for newlyweds to agree on what standards they wish imposed rather than to rely upon a judge to whom marriage may have an entirely different meaning?

The following hypothetical agreement between a fictitious engaged couple, whom we shall call Donald Brown and Ina Jones, sets forth in advance of their marriage the sort of facts and beliefs that we think should be spelled out explicitly by persons entering into a hopefully lifelong relationship. It goes without saying that such an agreement as this would be invalid under existing laws in every state in the Union. Furthermore, we recognize, of course, that the very idea of such a contract goes against the grain of our romantic matrimonial tradition. Yet the notion of the fullest possible disclosure of relevant facts and viewpoints, the concept of the planned marriage, and the idea of facing the possibility of the dissolution of a union prior to entering into one should not threaten the institution of marriage in our society. Indeed, such frankness might well guarantee its future.

MEMORANDUM OF UNDERSTANDING AND INTENT made this twenty-eighth day of July, 1972, between *Donald Brown*, residing at 1142 Damon Avenue, City of Chicago, Cook County, and State of Illinois, herein called *Donald*, and *Ina Jones*, residing at 1602 North State Parkway, City of Chicago, Cook County, and State of Illinois, herein called *Ina*.

WHEREAS the parties about to marry desire to make full and fair disclosures to each other of significant facts and circumstances concerning their lives; and

WHEREAS the parties desire to make full and fair disclosures of their attitudes and expectations concerning their marital future and the future of any children born to them from the pending marriage; and

WHEREAS the parties desire to determine and fix by this antenuptial agreement the rights and claims that will accrue to each of them in the estate and property of the other by reason of the marriage,

IT IS MUTUALLY AGREED AS FOLLOWS:

ARTICLE I
DECLARATION OF MARITAL INTENTION

(a) *Donald* and *Ina* each declares to the other the intention to marry in the City of Chicago, Cook County, State of Illinois, on or before September thirtieth, 1972.

(b) This marriage is freely and voluntarily being entered into out of mutual love and respect held by the parties for each other. Neither party has agreed to enter this marriage under any threats, emotional or otherwise, nor has any relative of either of the parties exercised any undue influence upon either *Donald* or *Ina*.

(c) Each party assures the other that he or she has had sufficient time and information to make the decision to marry in accordance with the terms of this MEMORANDUM.

ARTICLE II
HISTORICAL REPRESENTATION

Donald hereby warrants to *Ina* and guarantees that she may act in reliance upon the following representations:

(a) He is twenty-nine years old. He attended the University of Chicago from which he graduated in 1965 with a bachelor of science degree and with acceptable but unexceptional grades.

(b) His mother and father are living; until February 1963 he resided with them and contributed toward their support. He still occasionally contributes toward their support and intends to continue to the extent that he is able during marriage. *Donald's* parents react favorably to the contemplated marriage. *Donald's* parents have not been divorced, nor has his sister, but his older brother has been divorced twice.

(c) *Donald* was previously married in April 1963, and that marriage ended in a divorce in June 1970. There is one child

of the marriage, *Michael,* age six. The decree of divorce was handed down by the Supreme Court, Cook County. It awarded custody of *Michael* to *Donald's* former wife, granted her alimony and child support in the sum of $140 weekly, and granted *Donald* visitation privileges every other weekend, holidays, and two weeks in summertime with *Michael.* A copy of the divorce decree has been shown to and read by *Ina*.

(d) There is no known history of mental illness in *Donald's* family. There are no hereditary or other diseases prevalent in *Donald's* family, and *Donald* is in excellent physical health.

(e) There is no history of any arrest or conviction of *Donald* for any criminal behavior, nor is there any history of compulsive addiction to drugs, alcohol, or gambling.

(f) *Donald* is presently employed as an assistant sales manager for Rugby Electronics Company at a salary of $20,500 annually, including bonuses and exclusive of certain travel and entertainment expenses, which are made available to him by his employer. His salary during the three previous years was as follows: 1969–$14,500, 1970–$17,500, 1971–$18,500.

(g) The relationship of *Donald* with his parents, his brothers, and sister has been explained fully to *Ina*.

Donald and *Ina* have discussed at length his family's "tradition" of a two-week sojourn every year at the Brown residence in Michigan and *Donald's* desire to continue that tradition. *Ina* has expressed a reluctance to adhere to the tradition but agrees to be bound by *Donald's* wishes. *Donald* has agreed that he will make no arrangements for other familial visitations without the consent of *Ina* and that such visitations should be no more frequent than twice monthly.

(h) *Donald* has disclosed to *Ina* that his relationship with his past wife continues to be strained. He has disclosed to her that on at least two prior occasions he and his former wife have been involved in legal proceedings relating to the custody and amount of support of *Michael.* The nature of such proceedings, the reasons therefore, and all other questions of *Ina's* concerning them have been fully explored by the parties.

Donald's relationship with *Michael* has been fully explored by the parties. It is *Donald's* present feeling that the time may arise when he would wish to gain custody of *Michael*. *Ina* is reluctant, however, to consider *Donald* having custody during the first two years of their marriage. It has been agreed by *Donald* and *Ina* that, barring an emergency, no attempt will be made by *Donald* to obtain such custody for two years from the date of marriage.

Donald has made known to *Ina* his concern over *Michael's* hostility toward her. Both parties have agreed that, while the welfare of *Michael* should continue to be a paramount consideration of both parties, the relationship between *Donald* and *Ina* should not be affected by *Michael's* attitude nor should their marriage be delayed by it. It has been agreed that the parties will make clear to *Michael* that his hostility will not be tolerated as a wedge between *Donald* and *Ina* and that his conduct will have to be reasonably acceptable to both *Donald* and *Ina*. The parties have agreed that in the event they cannot cope successfully with this problem they will seek professional guidance to help them overcome it.

(i) There has been nothing in the past sex life of *Donald* that requires further disclosure. There are no sexual acts that are important to him or an essential part of the sex life contemplated by him that are not presently practiced by the parties. *Donald* has been able to express himself sexually in all ways important to the parties, and such issues as frequency of intercourse, desire for periods of sexual abstention, positions of intercourse, etc., have been explored to *Donald's* satisfaction.

Ina hereby warrants to *Donald* and guarantees that he may act in reliance upon the following representations.

(a) She is twenty-one years old. She attended, but did not graduate from, the University of Michigan, which she left after her junior year in 1970. At that time her grades were passing but below average. The circumstances under which she left

college and the reasons therefore have been fully explained to *Donald*.

(b) Her mother and father are divorced, and she has no brothers or sisters. Until October 1970 she lived with her mother. She rarely sees her father, with whom she has an extremely disagreeable relationship. *Ina's* relationship with her mother is unusually close, and she visits with her as often as three or four times weekly. *Ina* and *Donald* have had many conversations concerning what *Donald* has protested to be far too close a relationship between mother and daughter. He has sought, but has been refused, permission from *Ina* to discuss the matter directly with her mother. *Ina's* view that her mother has been left "out on a limb" by her father and that *Ina*, as a consequence, has an obligation to her mother to visit more frequently than is customary, has been rejected by *Donald*. Although *Ina* has agreed to limit her visits to her mother to two afternoons weekly and has agreed that joint visitations with her mother by her and *Donald* be limited to twice monthly, *Ina* feels such concessions should not have been asked of her.

Donald has expressed considerable hostility toward *Ina's* mother and has openly displayed such hostility. For his part, he has agreed to discontinue such practices.

Each party agrees that the "mother-in-law" issue has not been fully resolved between them, but they agree that their marital relationship should have priority over the relationship between *Ina* and her mother.

(c) *Ina's* physical and mental condition is excellent, and there is no history of hereditary or mental diseases in the Jones family.

(d) During 1969 *Ina* had an illegal abortion under circumstances that have been fully disclosed to *Donald*. During *Ina's* senior year of high school she was suspended for three weeks after she and a group of fellow students were detained by juvenile authorities for the possession of marijuana cigarettes.

(e) There has been nothing in the past sex life of *Ina* that requires further disclosure. There are no sexual acts that are important to her or an essential part of the sex life contemplated by her that are not presently practiced by the parties. *Ina* has been able to express herself sexually in all the ways important to the parties, and such issues as frequency of intercourse, desire for periods of abstention, positions of intercourse, etc., have been explored to *Ina's* satisfaction.

(f) *Ina* is presently employed as an assistant interior decorator for Bon Marche Department Store, and her salary this past year was $6,300.

(g) There is no history of compulsive addiction to drugs, alcoholic beverages, or gambling.

ARTICLE III
FUTURE EXPECTATIONS

(a) *Donald* and *Ina* have discussed fully where they propose to reside during the course of their marriage. They agree that considerations relating to the location of their respective families should play no part in such determination. They agree their primary consideration shall be proximity to *Donald's* place of business. That factor should govern regardless of where *Ina* may be employed and regardless of whose earnings are greater.

(b) Neither party to this memorandum holds any formal religious beliefs that should in any way interfere with the marriage. Neither insists on, or has even expressed any preference concerning, the other's adherence to any particular religious belief. Neither will, without the consent of the other, impose any religious belief upon any children of the marriage.

(c) It is the parties' present intention that *Ina* continue to work, health permitting, until such time as she may become pregnant. The parties have no exact intentions concerning the employment of *Ina* after the birth of any child or children, although *Ina* has expressed the feeling that simply caring for children would not be sufficiently stimulating to her. *Donald's* inclination at the present time is that he would prefer for *Ina* to discontinue any full-time employment if she had a child,

but he would not insist upon it.

Both parties agree that any subsequent employment of *Ina* after the birth of a child should be such that it would permit her to spend reasonable periods of time with the child and that it should not entail any evening or weekend hours.

(d) Both *Donald* and *Ina* have expressed opposition to adultery. *Donald* has stated he would immediately divorce *Ina* if such an act occurred on her part, regardless of the circumstances. *Ina* has said that, although she does not wish to solicit such conduct on the part of *Donald*, nevertheless she is unable to determine her attitude toward adultery on *Donald's* part in advance of knowing what the circumstances might be. If the act were an isolated "meaningless" episode, *Ina's* opinion is that she would rather not know of it because she does not know how it would affect her relationship with *Donald*.

Both parties have agreed that in the event either engages in any serious or prolonged affair with anyone else, he or she is under an obligation to disclose that fact to the other.

Both *Donald* and *Ina* believe that their sex life together is sufficiently pleasurable and knowledgeable at present so that no serious adjustment need be made by either. *Ina* has expressed the belief that her sex life with *Donald* will soon become more pleasurable, and somewhat less tense, after marriage and after each party has had more "experience" with each other. She denied, however, having any apprehension concerning future sexual relations with *Donald*.

(e) The parties intend to have two or three children of their own. It is their desire to have such children sometime after the next two years, although the possibility of having a child prior to that time does not cause any particular anxiety in either of them. In the event *Ina* becomes accidentally pregnant, the parties' present inclination is to have such a child and not seek an abortion. Both parties feel, however, that any decision on abortion should be left entirely to the discretion of *Ina*.

(f) *Donald* and *Ina* have discussed and have rejected the following notions: marriage of limited duration, separate vacations, separate beds, divorce by reason of the physical incapacity of the other, divorce by reason of the inability of *Ina* to bear children.

(g) In the event *Ina* is unable to bear children, the parties are in conflict over whether or not to adopt a child. It would be *Ina's* desire under such circumstances to adopt, but it is *Donald's* strong feeling that he would not want to. Although the parties agree that this eventually would be of considerable importance to them, they feel it is better to leave resolution of the question of adoption undetermined prior to its arising.

ARTICLE IV
FUTURE SUPPORT

(a) In the event that either party desires a separation (by mutual agreement or legal decree) or a divorce during the first five years of marriage, provided there is no surviving child born of the marriage, neither party will request support from the other unless he or she is in dire need thereof, and then only for such temporary periods as may be deemed necessary in accordance with Article VIII hereof.

(b) If either party desires to separate after the first five years of marriage or if, at the time of a request for separation during the first five years, a child of the marriage is alive, either party may request support, which shall be granted or denied by arbitration in accordance with Article VIII hereof. In determining whether or not to grant support and, if so, in what amount, the arbitrator shall consider the following: the length of the marriage, the number of children, their ages, the ages and health of the parties; the ability of *Ina* to work, the number of years that *Ina* has been unemployed, the reasons therefore, and *Ina's* realistic chances of being productively employed; the disparity between the parties' incomes and income-earning potentials; the amount of property to be divided between them in accordance with this agreement; the question of which party desires such

separation or divorce and the reasons therefore; *Donald's* legal obligations to his former wife and to his son, *Michael;* and the parties' preseparation standard of living, provided such standard was reasonable. No factor shall be conclusive, and the award of support, if any, should be such as to do substantial justice between the parties after consideration of all factors.

ARTICLE V
DIVISION OF PROPERTY

(a) *Donald* presently has a checking account at the First National Bank of Chicago, One First National Plaza, the present balance of which is $1,685.50. He maintains a savings account at the same bank, (Account No. 104F–003), the balance of which is $3,750.

(b) *Ina* presently has a checking account in her own name at the Continental National Bank and Trust Company, 231 South La Salle Street, the present balance of which is $385. She maintains a savings account at the same bank (Account No. 1A24–72), the present balance of which is $950.

(c) *Donald* owns four hundred shares of Great Western United Corporation, which is traded on the New York Stock Exchange, having a present value of approximately $4,000; he owns no other securities. *Donald* is also the owner of a 1970 Buick Riviera, on which $650 in installment obligations is presently due.

(d) *Ina* owns no securities and does not own an automobile.

(e) Neither party presently owns any real property.

ARTICLE VI
FUTURE OWNERSHIP OF PROPERTY

(a) *Donald* and *Ina* have agreed that all property now standing in the name of either shall continue to be held in the individual names of the parties owning such property.

(b) Upon the marriage of *Donald* and

Ina, they will create a joint-checking account and a joint-savings account to which each shall contribute in the same proportion as their earnings shall bear to each other. In the event that either party decides to seek a separation or divorce within a period of thirty-six months from the date of their marriage or at any time prior to the birth of a child, the proceeds of such checking and savings accounts shall be divided in the same proportion in which such funds were contributed by the parties. If either party seeks a separation or divorce after the birth of a child or at the end of said thirty-six-month period, whichever is earlier, such proceeds shall be divided between the parties equally.

(c) In the event that *Ina* is unable to find employment or is involuntarily unemployed or is unable to work during a period of maternity or illness, her contributions to the joint funds during the period of such unemployment, illness, or maternity shall be deemed to have been made in direct proportion to the contributions previously made by her during the period immediately preceding such unemployment, illness, or maternity.

(d) All questions concerning the investment of the joint funds of *Donald* and *Ina* in securities or real estate shall be decided jointly by the parties, and the ownership and division of such real or personal property should be made in accordance with paragraphs (a) and (c) hereof.

(e) The parties do not contemplate a different division of property, real or personal, whether or not either or both may later be guilty of any marital misconduct as defined by the laws of the State of Illinois. Any property not held in accordance with the terms of this article by either of the parties shall be deemed to be held in trust for the other party, and no additional private or oral understanding between the parties concerning the division of property between them is to be deemed valid until agreed to in writing in accordance with paragraph (f) hereof.

(f) In the event that either *Donald* or *Ina* subsequently wishes to change the rules by which their property shall be divided, the party desiring such change shall notify the other in writing and by registered mail at least one hundred and twenty days prior to such proposed change. If the other party does not wish to make such change, he or she may notify the other party in writing within the one hundred and twenty days. The matter shall be resolved by arbitration in accordance with the terms of Article VIII hereof. In making a determination the arbitrator shall fully inquire into the facts and circumstances surrounding the reasons for the proposed change. No modification of existing financial arrangements shall be made if it is determined that a substantial reason for such proposed change is that the party seeking modification has the imminent expectation of coming into a sudden period of prosperity from which the other party is to be excluded. The arbitrator may consider such other factors as he wishes in order to do substantial justice between the parties, but he may not order that any modification of the rules by which the parties have agreed to divide the property be made retroactive to the period preceding the written request for modification.

ARTICLE VII
MATTERS OF ESTATE

After thirty-six months of marriage each party agrees to leave the other at least 40 percent of his or her entire estate, and each agrees to make no attempt to assign, transfer, or otherwise dispose of, without valuable consideration, any portion of his or her estate with the intention of depriving the other of the benefits of this agreement.

ARTICLE VIII
ABRITRATION

Any dispute that arises under the terms of this Memorandum shall be resolved in accordance with the rules and regulations then obtaining of the American Arbitration Association, and such arbitration shall be held in the City of Chicago, Cook County, State of Illinois, unless at the time of dispute both parties reside in some other state, in which event arbitration shall take place in that state.

ARTICLE IX
MODIFICATION

This Memorandum may not be changed or modified except in writing, signed by the party against whom such change or modification is sought.

IN WITNESS WHEREOF, the parties hereto have signed their hands and seals this 28th day of July 1972.

Donald Brown
Ina Jones

63

MATE SWAPPING:
THE FAMILY THAT SWINGS TOGETHER CLINGS TOGETHER

Duane Denfeld and Michael Gordon

In the early decades of this century, and to a certain extent still today, social scientists equated deviant behavior with disease and set about to find the cures. The tone of this early perspective is nicely illustrated by the following excerpt:

The study of social pathology is undertaken not to breed pessimism but to furnish a rational ground for faith in the future of the world. The diseases of society, like the diseases of the human body, are to be studied so that remedies may be found for them where they exist, but most of all, that by a larger wisdom the number of diseases may be reduced to the lowest terms and we may set ourselves to social tasks with the ideal of conquering them altogether.

So firm a commitment to the extirpation of "social pathology" obviously precluded consideration of any contributions its phenomena might make to the social order. More recently there has been a reap-praisal of the role of deviant behavior in society. Albert Cohen, for one, has admonished his colleagues for equating deviance with social disorganization, and other sociologists have begun to focus their attention on deviance as a societal process rather than as a social disease. Howard Becker, a leading proponent of this new position, has argued:

We ought not to view it [deviant behavior] as something special, as depraved or in some magical way better than other kinds of behavior. We ought to see it simply as a kind of behavior some disapprove of and others value, studying the processes by which either or both perspectives are built up and maintained.

Perhaps of greater significance for the viewpoint of this paper are the opinions of the students of deviance who claim that deviance may support, not undermine, social order; among the most eloquent of these is Kai Erikson:

. . . Deviant behavior is not a simple kind of leakage which occurs when the machinery of society is in poor working order, but may be, in controlled quantities, an important condition for preserving the stability of social life. Deviant forms of behavior, by marking the outer edges of group life, give the inner structure its special character and thus supply the framework within which the people of the group develop an orderly sense of their own cultural identity.

We shall maintain that only from the perspectives found in the writings of Becker, Erikson, and their associates can the social scientist understand mate swapping and the role it plays in American society.

In this country there has been a tradition of great ideological commitment to the importance of confining sexual behavior in general, but sexual intercourse in particular, to the sanctity of the marital bed. Concomitantly there has also been a rich history of institutionalized nonmarital sex. One of the foremost historians of colonial family life has noted that "the cases of premarital fornication [in colonial New England] by husband and wife were evidently numerous." Further, prostitution never appears to have been completely absent from these shores. However, it was not until the second half of the nineteenth century that sexual morality and prostitution especially became a national concern. David Pivar, in his history of the Social Purity Movement in the United States, claims that

during the nineteenth century many social evils existed, but the Social Evil was prostitution.

Prostitution, its development and spread, constituted the primary element in the moral crisis that shook Western civilization in the latter decades of the nineteenth century. A premonition that traditional morality was failing permeated the fabric of American life, and reformers increasingly expressed alarm over a general decay in morality. Religionists and moralists found decay manifestly evident in official life, but most strikingly in the man-woman relationship.

Attention to the destructive effects of prostitution did not cease with the coming of the new century, or even with the moral revolutions supposedly wrought by World War I; in a very much milder form it is present still.

Nevertheless, in 1937 Kingsley Davis published a paper that was to cause many social scientists, at least, to reappraise this great "Social Evil." He advanced what has since come to be known as the "safety-valve" model of deviance, developing with great insight and much cogency the idea that

. . . the attempt of society to control sexual expression, to tie it to social requirements, especially the attempt to tie it to the durable relation of marriage and the rearing of children, or to attach men to a celibate order, or to base sexual expression on love, creates the opportunity for prostitution. It is analogous to the black market, which is the illegal but inevitable response to an attempt to fully control the economy. The craving for sexual variety, for perverse satisfaction, for novel and provocative surroundings, for ready and cheap release, for intercourse free from entangling cares and civilized pretense—all can be demanded from the women whose interest lies solely in price.

A further point implicit in Davis' argument is that since the prostitute by "virtue" of her profession is, for the most part, excluded from the ranks of potential spouses, the risk of romantic involvement which may threaten a man's marriage is greatly reduced.

Let us stop at this point to look more closely at the underlying assumption of this "safety-valve" model of deviance: a society may provide certain institutionalized outlets for forms of behavior which are condemned by the prevailing legal and/or moral system. This is not to say that in every society all deviants will find some structured way of satisfying their proclivities with minimal danger of running afoul of the law. A good case in point here would be pedophilia. With the virtual disappearance of child brothels, the pedophile must, if he wishes to gratify his need, engage in acts which almost certainly will result in a confrontation with the police; in contrast is the man who frequents houses of prostitution for some unusual form of sexual activity. Therefore, the "safety-valve" model does not assume that *all* forms of deviant behavior will be provided with outlets; but rather that *some* of those forms for which "frustration and discontent may lead to an attack on the rules themselves and on the social institutions they support" will be provided with outlets. So, then, in the case of prostitution (or any other form of deviance), the "safety-valve" model does not explain why it exists, but why it is tolerated: presumably it is supportive of monogamous marriage. It should be emphasized that this idea is best thought of as an hypothesis, not as a law. Interestingly enough, one of the few other convincing applications of the "safety-valve" model also applies to sexual behavior.

Ned Polsky recently applied Davis' ideas concerning prostitution to pornography, and claimed that the latter was a functional alternative to the former:

In saying that prostitution and pornography are, at least in modern societies, functional alternatives, I mean that they are different roads to the same desired social ends. Both provide for the discharge of what the society labels antisocial sex, i.e., impersonal, nonmarital sex: prostitution provides this via real intercourse with a real sex object, and pornography provides it via masturbatory, imagined intercourse with a fantasy object.

He places particular emphasis on a point which Davis mentions but does not elaborate, *viz.*, that prostitution and pornography cater to a considerable amount of what, in the parlance of the prostitute, is known as "kinky" sex—oral, anal, masochistic, fetishistic, etc. To this extent pornography, more than prostitution, provides a safety valve for those sexual inclinations for which no institutionalized behavioral outlets exist, e.g., pedophilia, which we have already mentioned.

In both the Davis and Polsky papers the focus is almost exclusively, if not exclusively, on *male* nonmarital sex. Males prostituting themselves for females has never been common, perhaps merely because, apart from their economic positions, males are constitutionally less suited for frequent and prolonged intercourse. Drawing largely on the Kinsey studies, Polsky argues that pornography is largely produced for, and consumed by, males. Kinsey found that relatively few women are aroused by pornography, and even fewer use it as grist for the masturbatory fantasy mill. While no reliable systematic data are available, there is some indication that at least one form of pornography, the "stag" film, is migrating from the fraternity house and VFW lodges —though not abandoning them altogether —to the suburban home, i.e., it is now being viewed by heterosexual audiences. A replication now of the section of the Kinsey study dealing with female response to pornography might yield some surprising results.

If, in fact, pornography is now becoming more of a heterosexual item—and we must emphasize again that this is by no means documented—it provides support for the main argument of this paper: mate swapping (we will use the terms "mate swapping" and "swinging" synonymously) is an outgrowth of the dramatic changes that have taken place in this century in the position of women in American society and, more crucially, changes that have taken place in the conceptions of female sexuality and female sexual rights. While the contention that women are now seeing and enjoying pornography more than was so previously cannot be proved, there is no lack of documentation for the larger changes noted above. Evidence can be found both in the realm of sexual ideology and behavior.

One of the most vivid indicators of the degree to which American women have come into their own sexually since 1900 is the marriage manual. Michael Gordon has recently completed an extensive study of American marital education literature for the period 1830 to 1940. Perhaps the most striking finding to emerge from his work is that the transformation in the prevailing conception of female sexuality, and marital sex in general, took place in the first four decades of this century. The following passage is based on the Gordon article.

Throughout most of the nineteenth century the commonly held attitude toward sexual intercourse was that it was, unhappily, required for the perpetuation of the species. Not only was it an unfortunate necessity, but also a dangerous one at that. Frequent indulgence by the male in the pleasures of the flesh could lead to an enervating loss of the "vital fluids" contained in the sperm; for the female it could result in nervous and constitutional disorders. In short, sex was a seriously debilitating business. As the century drew to a close we begin to get rumblings of acceptance of marital sex as something which, apart from its procreative function, was beneficial to the marriage, but such views are very much in the minority even in the 1890s.

With the first decade of the twentieth century, however, and reaching—if the reader will pardon the expression—its climax in the 1930s, there is a growing belief not only in the fact that women experience sexual desire (which in its own way is held to be as strong as that of men), but also that this desire should be satisfied, most appropriately in intercourse resulting in simultaneous orgasm. What we observe in these decades, then, is sex moving, ideologically, from an act whose prime purpose is procreation to one whose prime purpose is recreation, a shift which has been commented on by others. Because this development has been extensively documented in the article by Gordon, there is no need to explore it further. Let it suffice to say that by 1930 the concern with marital sex, its "artistry" and technique, has reached such proportions as to allow characterization of the authors of marriage manuals of the time as proponents of a "cult of mutual orgasm."

The increasing acceptance of the pleasures of marital sex seems to have had an impact on a number of areas relevant to the theme of this paper; possibly the most important of these is prostitution. To the best of our knowledge there are no data available which support the contention that since 1900 prostitution has been a declining profession. However, it has been claimed that there has been a reduction in the num-

ber of brothels in American cities; furthermore, there is good evidence on which to base the opinion that premarital intercourse with prostitutes is declining:

The frequencies of premarital sexual relations with prostitutes are more or less constantly lower in the younger generations of all educational levels. . . . In most cases the average frequencies of intercourse with prostitutes are down to two-thirds or even one-half of what they were in the generation that was most active 22 years ago.

This, it could be reasoned, may well be related to a finding reported in the second Kinsey volume:

Among the females in the sample who were born before 1900, less than half as many had had premarital coitus as among the females born in any subsequent decade. . . . For instance, among those who were still unmarried by age twenty-five, 14 percent of the older generation had had coitus, and 36 percent of those born in the next decade. This increase in the incidence of premarital coitus, and the similar increase in the incidence of premarital petting, constitute the greatest changes which we have found between the patterns of sexual behavior in the older and younger generations of American females.

It should be noted, by way of qualification, that Kinsey also found that most women who did have premarital intercourse had it exclusively with the men they eventually married. These two phenomena—the decreasing amount of premarital contact with prostitutes for males and the increasing amount of premarital sex for women—give credence to our argument that the acceptance of female sexuality and the pleasures of marital sex has grown in this century. It is unusual now to find a man saying he has intercourse with prostitutes because his idealized wife-mother image of his spouse prevents him from carrying out the act with her. Furthermore, there are also attitudinal data on the breakdown of the double standard in this country.

It is implicit in our thesis that shifts in attitudes toward female sexuality, premarital sex, and, especially, marital sex, which we have been discussing, are crucial to the understanding of mate swapping as an institutionalized form of extramarital sex. Another factor which has undoubtedly also made a contribution to the development of mate swapping, or at least has facilitated its growth, is the revolution in contraceptive techniques that has occurred in the past decade. A study done in 1960, based on a national probability sample, found the following order of frequency for contraceptive techniques: condom, 50 percent; diaphragm, 38 percent; rhythm, 35 percent; douche, 24 percent; withdrawal, 17 percent; and others in small percentages. (The total exceeds 100 percent because many couples used more than one method.) Similar studies are yet to be made for the last years of the 1960s, but some comparative data are available. Tietze estimated that as of mid-1967 there were 6½ million women in this country on the pill, and somewhere between one and two million using the IUD. A recent Gallup poll estimated that 8½ million American women were on the pill (*Newsweek*, February 9, 1970). Figures such as these allow us to estimate that about 10 percent of the fecund American women take the pill and another 1 percent use the IUD.

The emergence of chemical and intrauterine birth-control methods is of significance on several counts. One, they are considerably more reliable than the previously available techniques, and thus, one would assume, dramatically reduce anxiety over unwanted pregnancy. Two, and the importance of this cannot be minimized, they separate the act of prevention from the act of sex. While the new methods insure against pregnancy resulting from failure to take contraceptive measures in the heat of spontaneous passion, they also improve what could be termed the aesthetics of sex, i.e., there need be no hasty retreat to insert a diaphram or roll on a "safe" (to use an antiquated but charming term). All in all, then, the new contraceptives allow sex to be indulged in with less apprehension and more pleasure.

We shall now try to summarize and more explicitly state the argument contained in what we have written up to this point. The current conception of female sexuality as legitimate and gratifying, coupled with enlarged opportunities for women to pursue sex without unwanted pregnancies, is likely to have greatly increased the incentive for women to seek—as men have always done—sexual variety outside marriage. Among the available ways for both husbands *and* wives to find such variety, mate swapping is the least threatening and the one most compatible with monogamy.

Of the alternatives to mate swapping, the one which comes to mind immediately is what might be called "bilateral prostitution" (a term suggested to us by Albert Cohen). We have already pointed out that constitutionally males seem less suited than females for prostitution, although there may be some homosexual hustlers who can turn "tricks" at a surprising rate, but nothing that compares with that of their female counterparts. There are, however, economic problems associated with bilateral prostitution. It might place a greater drain on the family's financial resources than swinging, and, more significantly, create conflict over budgeting for the extramarital sexual expression of the husband and wife, i.e., how is the decision on allotment of funds to be made? Perhaps of greater concern is that it would separate the husband and wife for recreation at a time when a great deal of emphasis is placed on "familistic" activity, especially of the recreational variety, e.g., couples play bridge together, bowl together, boat together, and so on. That is to say, bilateral prostitution would enlarge their private worlds at the expense of their common world.

Given such considerations, the advantages of mate swapping as a solution to the problem of marital sexual monotony become obvious, though in all fairness we must note that many of the points we are going to make cannot be fully appreciated until the reader has completed our description of mate swapping himself. To begin with, the cost is probably less than that of bilateral prostitution, and is much more easily integrated into the normal recreational or entertainment budget. Second, it keeps the couple together, or at least in the same house.

But further, it is an activity which involves common planning and preparation, and provides subject matter for conversation before and after; thus it could further consolidate the marriage. Finally, the sexual activity that takes place is, to a greater or lesser extent, under the surveillance of each; this means that each exercises control over the extramarital activity of the other, and the danger that the sexual relationship will become a romantic relationship is minimized. This, of course, is also facilitated by the brief and segmented nature of the relationship.

In summary, then, for the couple committed to the marital relationship and for whom it still performs important functions for which no other relationship exists, mate swapping may relieve sexual monotony without undermining the marriage. . . .

Swinging, or mate swapping, has been a subject that sells "adult reading" paperbacks, but few social scientists have analyzed it. Fortunately, there are a handful of serious studies of the swinging scene. This is not to maintain that we know all we need to know; the analyses available must be viewed as tentative. The findings of the research are problematic because designs have not been employed which allow generalization. Furthermore, some crucial aspects of the phenomenon have been neglected, e.g., what are the characteristics of those who drop out of swinging? We say this not by way of criticism of the research of our colleagues; they are pioneering in an area that involves great technical as well as ethical problems. Our statements are merely intended to qualify what we have to say in the rest of the paper.

Despite the problems cited above, there are studies . . . that provide excellent descriptive data based on participant observation and interviewing. We will use these ground-breaking papers to test the model presented earlier. It is hoped that the important contributions of Symonds, Bartell, the Smiths, and the Breedloves will encourage further research in this area. Before evaluating our model it is necessary to specify the term "swinging," to discuss the emergence and extent of swinging, and the swingers themselves. . . .

One definition of "swinging" is "having sexual relations (as a couple) with at least one other individual." Another definition, and more appropriate for our purposes, is that "swinging" is a husband and wife's "willingness to swap sexual partners with a couple with whom they are not acquainted and/or to go [to] a swinging party and be willing for both [him] and his mate to have sexual intercourse with strangers." The latter definition directs our attention to swinging as a husband-wife activity. The accepted term among mate-sharing couples is "swinging"; the term "wife swapping" is objectionable, as it implies sexual inequality, i.e., that wives are the property of husbands.

Swingers, according to Symonds, are not of one mold; she distinguishes "recreational" from "utopian" swingers. The recreational swinger is someone "who uses swinging as a form of recreation"; he does not want to change the social order or to fight the Establishment. He is, in Merton's typology of deviance, an "aberrant." The recreational swinger violates norms but accepts them as legitimate. The utopian swinger is "nonconformist," publicizing his opposition to societal norms.

He also tries to change them. He is generally acknowledged by the general society to be doing this for a cause rather than for personal gain.

Swinging, for the utopian, is part of a new life style that emphasizes communal living. The proportion of utopians within the swinging scene has not been determined. Symonds feels that their number is small. She found the utopians more interesting

because of their more deviant and encompassing view concerning the life that they desire to live if it ever becomes possible. In some respects, they fall close to the philosophy of some hippies in that they would like to retreat from the society at large and live in a community of their own kind.

In societal terms, the recreational swinger is a defender of the status quo; the utopian swinger is one who wants to build a new order.

We are most interested in the recreational swingers, because their deviation is limited to the sharing of partners; in other areas they adhere to societal norms. Couples who engage in recreational swinging say they do so in order to support or improve their marriage. They favor monogamy and want to maintain it. . . .

The swingers who advertise and attend swinging parties do not conform to the stereotypical image of the deviant. They have higher levels of education than the general population; 80 percent of one study attended college, 50 percent were graduates, and 12 percent were still students. They are disproportionately found in professional and white-collar occupations. They tend to be conservative and very straight.

They do not represent a high order of deviance. In fact, this is the single area of deviation from the norms of contemporary society. The mores, the fears, that plague our generation are evidenced as strongly in swingers as in any random sampling from suburbia.

Every study we looked at emphasized the overall normality, conventionality, and respectability of recreational swingers. . . .

The number of couples engaged in swinging can at best be roughly estimated. The Breedloves developed, on the basis of their research, an estimate of eight million couples. Their figure was based on a sample of 407 couples. They found that less than 4 percent of them placed or replied to advertisements in swinging publications, and in the year prior to publication (1962–1963) of their study, "almost 70,000 couples either replied to, or placed, ads as swinging couples." With this figure as a base they arrived at their estimate of the number of couples who have at one time or another sexually exchanged partners. They further concluded that, conservatively, 2½ million couples exchange partners on a somewhat *regular* basis (three or more times a year). . . .

The "swap" or swingers club is an institutionalized route to other swingers, but it is not the only method of locating potential partners. Bartell suggests four ways: (1) swingers' bars, (2) personal reference, (3) personal recruitment, and (4) advertisement. The last method deserves special attention.

Advertisements are placed in underground papers and more frequently in swingers' magazines. The swingers' publications, it has been claimed, emerged following an article in *MR.* magazine in 1956.

Everett Meyers, the editor of MR., *later claimed that it was this article which touched off a flood of similar articles on wife-swapping, or mate-swapping. In any event,* MR. *followed up its original article with a regular monthly correspondence column filled with alleged letters from readers reporting their own mate-swapping accounts.*

Publications began to appear with advertisements from "modern marrieds" or swingers who wished to meet other swingers. *La Plume,* established about 1955, has boasted in print that it was the first swingers' magazine. A recent issue of *Select,* probably the largest swingers' publication, had 3,500 advertisements, over 40 percent from married couples. *Select* and *Kindred Spirits* co-sponsored "Super Bash '70'" on April 11, 1970. It was advertised to be "the BIGGEST SWINGDING yet," and featured dancing, buffet dinner, go-go girls, and a luxurious intimate ballroom. Clubs such as Select, Kindred Spirits, Mixers, and Swingers Life have moved beyond the swingers' party to hayrides and vacation trips.

There are at least a couple of hundred organizations like Select throughout the country. Many of them are very small, some with only a few members, and many of them are fly-by-night rackets run by schlock guys less interested in providing a service than in making a quick buck. Most, however, are legitimate and, as such, very suc-

cessful. They have been a major factor influencing the acceleration of the swapping scene.

Our review of the swinging club and magazine market located approximately fifty nationally sold publications. The "couple of hundred" figure reported above may include some lonely hearts, nudist directories, homosexual, and transvestite organizations, some of which serve the same purpose as swingers' publications. They bring together persons with the same sociosexual interests.

A person's first attendance at a swingers' party can be a difficult situation. He must learn the ideologies, rationalizations, and rules of swinging. These rules place swinging in a context that enables it to support the institution of the family. We turn to these rules in the next section. . . .

Our model views swinging as a strategy to revitalize marriage, to bolster a sagging partnership. This strategy can be seen in the following findings of the empirical research. Evidence to support the model is divided into four parts: (1) the perception of limitation of sex to the marital bond, (2) paternity, (3) discretion, and (4) marital supportive rules.

1. *"Consensual adultery": the perception that sex is limited to the marital bond.* Swingers have developed rules that serve to define the sexual relationship of marriage as one of love, of emotion. Some of the Smiths' respondents would answer "no" to questions pertaining to "extramarital sexual experience," but would answer "yes" to questions pertaining to "mate-sharing or comarital relations." Sharing, for the swingers, means that the marriage partners are not "cheating." Swingers believe that the damaging aspect in extramarital sex is the lying and cheating, and if this is removed extramarital sex is beneficial to the marital bond. In other words, "those who swing together stay together." Swingers establish rules such as not allowing one of a couple to attend a group meeting without the other. Unmarried couples are kept out of some groups, because they "have less regard for the marital responsibilities." Guests who fail to conform to rules are asked "to leave a party when their behavior is not appropriate."

For one group of recreational swingers, it is important that there be no telephone contact with the opposite sex between functions. Another group of recreational swingers always has telephone contact with people they swing with, although they have no sexual contact between functions.

2. *Swinging and children.* "Recreational swingers are occasionally known to drop out of swinging, at least temporarily, while the wife gets pregnant." By not swinging, the couple can be assured that the husband is the father of the child; unknown or other parentage is considered taboo. This reflects a traditional, middle-class view about the conception and rearing of children.

Swinging couples consider themselves to be sexually avant-garde, but many retain their puritan attitudes with respect to sex socialization. They hide from their children their swinging publications. Swingers lock their children's bedrooms during parties or send them to relatives.

3. *Discretion.* A common word in the swingers' vocabulary is discretion. Swingers desire to keep their sexual play a secret from their nonswinging or "square" friends. They want to protect their position in the community, and an effort is made to limit participation to couples of similar status or "respectability."

Parties in suburbia include evenly numbered couples only. In the area of our research, singles, male or female, are discriminated against. Blacks are universally excluded. If the party is a closed party, there are rules, very definitely established and generally reinforced by the organizer as well as other swingers . . . Stag films are generally not shown. Music is low key fox trot, not infrequently Glenn Miller, and lighting is definitely not psychedelic. Usually nothing more than a few red or blue lightbulbs. Marijuana and speed are not permitted.

The swinging suburban party differs, then, from the conventional cocktail party only in that it revolves around the sexual exchange of mates.

4. *Swingers' rules.* We suggest that the above rules on sex and paternity are strategies to make swinging an adjunct to marriage rather than an alternative. Another set of rules or strategies that is relevant is that dealing with jealousy. Swingers recognize the potentially disruptive consequences of jealousy, and are surprisingly successful in minimizing it. The Smiths found that only 34 percent of the females and 27 percent of the males reported feelings of jealousy. Some of the controls on jealousy are: (1) that the marriage commands paramount loyalty, (2) that there is physical but not emotional interest in other partners, (3) that single persons are avoided, and (4) that there be no concealment of sexual activities. The sharing couples

reassure one another on this score by means of verbal statements and by actively demonstrating in large ways and small that the marriage still does command their paramount loyalty. Willingness to forego an attractive swinging opportunity because the spouse or lover is uninterested or opposed is one example of such a demonstration.

Developing a set of rules to control potential jealousies demonstrates the swingers' commitment to marriage.

CONCLUSION

In this paper we have attempted to account for a new form of extramarital sexual behavior in terms of a sociological model of deviance. We have contended that swinging may support rather than disrupt monogamous marriage as it exists in this society. A review of the volumes of the *Reader's Guide to Periodical Literature* and *The New York Times Index* failed to reveal any articles dealing with this phenomenon in the United States. This would suggest that swinging has not as yet been defined as a social problem in the traditional sense of the word. Thus swinging, like prostitution, despite its violation of the social and, in many cases, legal norms, is permitted a degree of tolerance which would appear to demonstrate the appropriateness of our model.

Finally, it should be said that we make no pretense to having touched upon all the changes that have played a role in the emergence of swinging. Restrictions of space prevented our looking at the larger societal trends that may have been at work here, e.g., feminism, the changing occupational position of women, suburbanization, and so on. Nevertheless, we do feel that we have delineated those issues which are most directly related to it. The validity of our model will be tested by time.

64

ETHICAL AND IDEOLOGICAL PROBLEMS FOR COMMUNAL LIVING: A CAVEAT

Joy G. Schulterbrandt and Edwin J. Nichols

If one agrees with the proposition that traditional family forms, despite their historical contributions, no longer meet significant needs of a growing number of their members, then maintaining an open mind toward emerging alternative family forms becomes essentially a spontaneous and non-threatened response. Information on the emerging family life styles is scanty, and because at this stage many people are unsure of what consequences these new forms will have on the young and upon society in general, the tendency in established society is to suppress rather than to support the development of these experiments in family living. Undeniably and unfairly, too, many of the early emerging experiments in communal living received a bad press. This was particularly true for the unsophisticated, poorly organized communes formed by so-called "hippies" and the under-30 flower children. Consequently, even today many communal families still have to deal with the stigmata of being "deviant."

The traditional nuclear family and its legitimate spin-offs, i.e., one-parent families, nuclear dyads, and second-career families, are comprehensively discussed by Sussman and Cogswell (1972), Sussman (1971), and Ramey (1971). Discussed here instead will be some of the ethical, ideological, and survival problems which face the new communes. The intent will be to raise questions more than to furnish answers, since without "hard" data as to the consequences of this life style, any conclusions at this point would have to be speculative.

A number of authorities in the field of the family, Ogburn, Sorokin, and Watson, have proposed that under the impact of technology, inventions, and ideologies, the traditional family has lost its most important functions and that this loss in turn has led to decay (Vincent, 1967).

Still another group, Goode, Parsons, and Mannheim, has insisted that it is only the traditional functions and methods of socialization which the family has lost, and because of its adaptive and mediating characteristics, it is differentiating itself to offer a better "fit" between the needs of a given family system and changing larger society (Vincent, 1967).

Whatever the fears, the family is not dead. Above all other social institutions it is pivotal in the civilization of man. It is the social agent with the earliest and most sustained access to children's minds and behavior, and it is no accident that it is the family which is held most responsible for the process of socialization and humanization.

Communal living as a family life style is not new. For centuries there have been communes organized around a unifying principle of religion such as the Hutterites, Mennonites, Shakers, Mormons, and the Bruderhofs, a German group of more recent origin. What is new in this country has been the emergence of communal groups, many of them only loosely organized, whose central purpose is to seek out new and more meaningful forms of social and interpersonal relationships. Their binding principle is humanism, and they seem to be motivated by a fervent conviction that the fulfillment they seek can only be satisfied ultimately by an investment of unconditional love in their fellowmen. Historically, humanism was a cultural and intellectual movement in both the Greek and Latin cultures and was one of the factors which gave rise to the Renaissance in Europe between the fourteenth and sixteenth centuries.

In 1969, a journal, *Modern Utopian,* issued by the Alternatives Foundation of Berkeley, California, published a directory of 300 or more communes in the United States. California, New York, and Pennsylvania led in the number of established communes. The communes vary widely in types as well as subsistence. Some are small urban groups that share living quarters and raise their families together but hold outside jobs. Others are rural farming communes that combine work and living. Some communes are agricultural, some religious, some produce arts and crafts, but generally most are diversified.

The communes or social development movement began as experiments around the 1960s, led originally by "hippie" tribal juveniles and the under-30 generation. Since then the movement has grown, attracting many over 30 from the more traditional and "respectable" professions and walks of life. Some groups are well organized while others [are] simply small groups of persons who know each other well, like each other, and decide to live together. The structures of these new styles are embryonic at this stage of development and range from a communal type of living where monogamous relationships and personal property ownership are maintained, such as Twin Oaks in Virginia, to the other extreme, such as The Family near Taos, New Mexico, which encourages the sharing of husbands, wives, and children.

There is no question that the search for more humane ways of self-expression and interaction is legitimate and socially responsible. The pervasive destructiveness of racism, which is as damaging to whites as it is to blacks, and the growing psychosocial and interpersonal deprivation of the young, particularly middle and upper income families (Ad Hoc Committee on Child Mental Health, 1971), attest to the justification for some urgency to explore the potential contribution of alternative family forms. Additional contributing factors are increases in child abuse, alcoholism, and drug dependency among adults; depression among married couples (Raskin, Schulterbrandt, Reatig, and McKeon, 1969); and reported estimates by marriage specialists that 40 to 60 percent of all marriages are "subclinical" or in need of counseling and support (Otto, 1970). And it could hardly be more fitting for these experiments than to have originated within the family, the social system which has first crack at establishing "right" and "wrong" for the child. The question

here is not whether the traditional family has failed, but whether or not the system of values from which it evolved has led it today to fall short of fulfilling specific human needs for which a growing number of its members are now "ready."

Admittedly, there are signs that the traditional forms of the family and marriage are changing, at least peripherally and in a pragmatic way to meet the demands of its members. Witness the new liberalized abortion law (probably catalyzed by the advent of the "pill"), and emerging changes in the law, i.e., "no fault" divorce. The metamorphosis of this latter changeling is of special interest, because under the traditional family forms marriage—even if it were a bad one—was preferable to divorce.

With these pieces of evidence of its responsiveness, there remains still a sense that in the traditional family system, the change is not emanating from the core or from a philosophy or system of values which is responding sympathetically to the needs of its members. Perhaps it is because the leadership for change is coming from the courts, traditionally considered the more dispassionate of our social institutions, rather than from the other social-oriented agencies which work daily with families and know intimately the feeling component of a "bad" marriage. Maybe also the uneasiness springs out of the observation reported by Ramey (1971) that "changes do not move into the main stream of society until approximately seven to ten percent of the population adopt them." There is undeniably a sort of chilling coldness and a sense of mindlessness that emanates from a social system which gauges its decision to change or to reduce human anguish on the basis of frequency of occurrences.

The issue is what are the chances for survival among these varied experimental groups in communal living? The thesis is that at the present developmental stage their survival is directly related to how compatible they are with the dominant traditional form and the type of confrontation strategies employed. Some support for this hypothesis is provided by Ramey (1971), who described the relative failure of the "Utopian" type of communal living forms which made the decision to withdraw from society and migrate into the country. According to Ramey, their strategy to withdraw into the country created the handicap of high visibility. Furthermore, since this specific group had been previously, if unfairly, labeled "hippie" types by the established society, they became easy prey to a social order which viewed them as anathema, and which capitalized on their lack of organization by creating diffusion and insurmountable legal and social obstacles.

At this point it is necessary to explore the assertions made heretofore—that value systems, degree of compatibility between existing and emerging family forms, and strategies are significant variables in understanding the driving power behind the commune movement and its survival potential.

During the 1970 White House Conference on Children, conferees expressed that they were disturbed by the observation that although we had the knowledge and technology, we lacked the "will" to provide a better environment for families and children (Chandler, 1971). While this explanation for our resistance to implementing change may be partially true, it does not go far enough in identifying what the causes might be. For this explanation, it is necessary to turn attention toward the umbilical alliance among the dominant ethic (puritanism), ideology (pragmatism), and psychology (Skinnerian or operant conditioning) in American life. It is precisely upon these three bases that the measure of compatibility between existing and emerging family forms is to be determined. It seems an important measure to assess since an accurate reading of the implied threat to the established family forms would offer to the emerging forms guidelines for strategies most likely to succeed.

To return to the concept of compatibility, it might serve well to recall the function of a set of ethics, ideology, and psychology. The first determines what is to be done; the second provides the justification for doing it; and the latter, with its behavior modification emphasis, demonstrates how to do it. The elements of this triad of puritanism, pragmatism, and Skinnerian psychology are

highly intercorrelated and would have to be complimentary to each other in order to function as a whole. A conspicuous absence at the core of all three forces is some provision for maintaining feed-back between people and their environment and regard for human dignity and feeling. The achievement of the physical or material "goal" is sacrosanct and nowhere are people a focus for concern.

Thus, take work as a simple example. Under the puritan ethic it is a virtue of itself with implicit moral underpinnings. This work value is justified by the fact that it earns money which purchases conspicuous material goods and is a measure of success, moral standing, and power. Since work accomplishes the intended end, i.e., success in material things, then it is good and the original premise about work is confirmed. To increase one's standing it is necessary to have an abundance or more than what one and his family can use. To obtain that glut of consumer goods within a short time, it is necessary to structure the environment so that "success" is more likely to "happen" to some than to others. The task, then, is to program certain people for failure and others for success without having to get hung-up with conscience and feelings. Operant conditioning, according to the Skinnerians and behaviorists, can do this cheaply and unobtrusively, simply by positive reinforcement schedules. Moreover, this methodology is consonant with the aforementioned ethical and ideological systems because, like them, its thrust is goal-oriented and quite successfully bypasses the complexity of feelings of others and fairness. In fact, in his latest book, *Beyond Freedom and Dignity*, Skinner made it quite clear that feelings and conscience were irrelevant constructs both to science and society (Fair, 1971). Furthermore, he could validate that point by demonstrating that "goodness" was simply a product of positive reinforcement.

"Explanations" such as those mentioned above dealing with ethics, ideology, and psychology make seemingly incongruent behavior coherent. Who will ever forget the drama of the 1960s with white "men of the cloth" pushing and manhandling black would-be parishioners out of the doors of churches, white women and men with children of their own flailing six- and seven-year-old black children with sticks and stones, and more recently in 1970 parents sacrificing their children by siding with the law in the Kent State massacre. It is hardly a comfort to their children to know that their parents love law and order more than they love them.

All these events, as well as the model described earlier in the work example, are obviously incompatible with the emerging ethic and ideology of the communal living groups. Certainly, these behaviors are incongruent with establishing a sense of community and community love, unconditioned love, a society where one man's gain is not another's loss, a society in which people come first, and a society where there is a realization of the self by having one's central purpose outside the self. These are some of the sentiments within the evolving ethical and ideological systems of the new communal family forms (Roy and Roy, 1970). The psychology for the communal family form has not been developed as yet. The charismatic personalities and leadership roles that characterize the communal movement will probably be a factor in determining the substance of the psychology. Sometimes, as in Tom Wolfe's *Electric Kool-Aid Acid Test*, it has been difficult to escape a feeling of elitism.

It has been pointed out that the focus in traditional family forms is goal pursuit oriented, and the goals are consumer products. In the emerging forms, the focus is humanism and the goal is a realization of the self through highly developed socio-interpersonal relationships with others. Thus, it would appear that since a basic fundamental incompatibility exists, both on ethical and ideological grounds, between the traditional and emerging communal forms of family living, attention to strategy is all important. According to Ramey, some communal groups which he calls evolutionary have been doing just that (1971). While sympathetic to the "back to the country" movement, these other groups avoid the mistakes of earlier communes (high visibility) by remaining in the urban areas, work-

ing at their regular professions, and forming highly organized social networks which they feel will make the existing environmental social system work better for them. It is too early at this time to evaluate either of the exact criteria being used to measure success.

Finally, one last point should be made regarding the difference in directions of the impetus between the traditional and new communal family forms. It seems to be a reasonable hypothesis that the direction of drive under traditional family forms is outward; to aggress, to fulfill, and to imprint its mark upon the physical environment.

In contrast with the emerging communal forms, the impetus is to receive by giving; to be fulfilled, or to be through receiving. In one sense, the distinction could be made that in traditional family forms, the drive was to find a mission in life. In the communal family form, the drive is to find a meaning to life.

In traditional structures, tasks were well defined, concrete, and tangible. For example, the objective of subduing the Indians, establishing frontiers and developing the land, exploiting blacks, making money, acquiring consumer goods, determining cost-ratio indices, and minimum requirement guidelines are fairly concrete and managerial tasks. On the other hand, the tasks for communal groups are difficult to define because they are more intangible and abstract and because there have been so few successful models in the past.

In some ways, these new communal groups read almost like a blueprint of the people whom one would expect to find on the upper levels of Maslow's hierarchy of needs: those searching for a sense of belonging and self-actualization.

Some support for this hunch is accorded by the profile of who tends to seek out and experiment with these new forms of family living. They are usually persons from the upper middle class strata, college trained, and capable, if they choose, of "making it" in the financial sense. In many ways, they also resemble Ramey's "committed" type (1971).

Using knowledge learned from experiences of earlier communal trials, one might predict that evolutionary communal groups, at this stage at least, will compromise, paying close attention to strategies, organization, and selection of members. Americans on the whole do not seem to relish revolutions in the historical sense of radical overthrow. Instead, whatever social revolution we are presently undergoing is more within the frame of reference that Charles Reich (1970) alluded to: a gradual heightening of consciousness and awareness.

According to Chekov, whatever course a group of people take, a price is exacted of them. Some of those costs which traditional ethics and ideology have placed on their adherents have been examined. Critics of the newly emerging communal family forms can also point to some costs that will accrue to their adherents. Nevertheless, if these communal forms are given a chance to explore and develop their potential, the price they pay will be substantially different from Faust's.

REFERENCES

Chandler, Barbara A. "The White House Conference on Children: A 1970 Happening." *The Family Coordinator*, 20 (1971): 195–207.

Fair, Charles M. "The World as a Huge Skinner Box." *The Washington Post Book Section*, September 1971.

Otto, Herbert. "Has Monogamy Failed?" *Saturday Review*, April 25, 1970.

Ramey, James W. "Emerging Patterns of Behavior in Marriage." Presented at Groves Conference on Marriage and the Family, San Juan, Puerto Rico, May 1971.

Raskin, A., J. Shulterbrandt, N. Reatig, and J. McKeon, Jr. "Replications of Factors of Psychopathology in Interview, Ward Behavior, and Self-Report: Ratings of Hospitalized Depressives." *Journal of Nervous and Mental Diseases*, 148 (1969).

Reich, Charles. *The Greening of America*. New York: Bantam Books, 1970.

Roy, Rustum and Della Roy. "Is Monogamy Outdated?" *The Humanist*, March/April 1970.

Sussman, Marvin B. "Family Systems in the 1970s: Analysis, Policies, and Programs." *Annals of the American Academy of Political and Social Science*, 396 (1971): 40–56.

Sussman, Marvin B. and Betty E. Cogswell. "Changing Families in Changing Environments: Implications for Population Growth and Human Service Systems." *Ohio Welfare Conference Bulletin*, March 1972.

Vincent, Clark E. "Mental Health and the Family." *Journal of Marriage and the Family*, 29 (1967): 18–38.

65

THE GROUP MARRIAGE

Larry L. Constantine and Joan M. Constantine

The family is society's most ubiquitous group—and probably its oldest. Its origins indeed predate man and may well form part of our heritage from primate predecessors. From primordial beginnings, the family, and marriage, the relationship on which it is based, have changed and evolved in many ways but never so rapidly as in the past few generations. Though the pace of change is almost a world-wide phenomenon, the details vary.

The trends have been widely observed and discussed—with alarm, hope, or indifference. In general, the family has become increasingly unstable in various ways. The high and increasing divorce rate is common knowledge, though Department of Health, Education, and Welfare figures indicate it may be stabilizing in the United States. And desertion may well be more common than divorce. The very pace of events in the family history has been increasing. Leaving home, marriage, first child, last child, and the children's leaving in turn, are occurring on a compressed time scale.

Concomitantly, the family has undergone a progressive loss of function. Its purposes as an economic unit, socializing institution for children, even recreational facility have been seen by Nimkoff[1] and others as being partly and progressively surrendered to (or usurped by) society. Even in its (historically) recently stressed function in the personal fulfillment of its members, it is seen as seriously deficient. The gradual decay of the husband-wife relationship, the onset of boredom, the "seven year itch," the "thirty-sixth year crisis," and the disenchantment with marital age discussed by Pineo[2]—all are part of the picture of contemporary marriage. The almost pandemic extramarital affair and the rapid advent of mate-swapping are social phenomena that are pathognomonic of the failure of marriage and the family to fulfill many personal needs.

One of the most persistent and dramatic processes has been the gradual reduction in size of the family unit, not only in number of children but also in terms of extensions of the core family—the husband, wife, and children. While the progression from extended to nuclear family structure is not entirely unambiguous (some nuclear family orientation has characterized the United States almost from the outset), it is crucial. Loss of function and functional diversity, failure in need satisfaction, instability—these are properties of a unit whose size has been reduced below critical levels.

Today's family is almost completely autonomous and nuclearized. Only the core of a man and wife and their children is left as a family unit. The autonomous nuclear family has advantages in a rapidly changing technological age. It is mobile and comparatively plastic. In keeping with the changed pace of family events, it reduces the ideological and stylistic conflicts of its predecessor, the multigeneration, or *extended*, family, which today would juxtapose generations whose culture and ideologies are separated by major discontinuities. But the nuclear family exacts a price of its members as well. The smaller group has a shorter, more uncertain lifetime. Its members are provided with ready opportunities for intimate interaction with one or at best a few others. Its children have limited models for adult roles and behavior and for sexual identification.

In diagnosing the statistical failure of modern marriage, we must go beyond divorce to other, less terminal, behavioral manifestations of degeneration. We must ask of the marriages and families that provide no happiness, or providing some measure, do not facilitate the personal growth of either children or adults.

It does not take an alarmed intuitive leap to recognize that the problem may not lie so much in marriage as practiced—in our culture's interpretation of the model—as in the model itself. If there are shortcomings in the model, no "return to normalcy" is possible.

If we look at marriage and the family (but not too closely), we find a single, constant idealized definition, a romantic love, one-man-one-woman, lifetime model which fits only some fraction of real marriages. The actual underlying model demands homage to the idealized form while being based on monogyny (one wife at a time) rather than monogamy (one lifetime mate). And, without real provision in either model, the majority of these monogynous marriages will at some time become involved with extramarital relations. This unitary design for marriage is what Cuber and Harroff[3] have termed "the monolithic code."

If we look at marriage more closely, as Cuber and Harroff have done in their study of the marriages of "successful" people, we find a variety of functional bases operative within the single structure. The typology they developed is broadly useful, for it recognizes that marriage must satisfy an impressive array of varying human needs. Thus the passive-congenial relationship, while lacking vitality and romance, may well best fit the casual companionship needs of its members. Even the conflict-habituated marriage of Virginia Woolf may satisfy important, even if neurotic, needs of both partners. . . .

Many concerned individuals want to build a stronger, more secure, more vital, more cohesive, more productive family, one that provides an enlarged framework for personal growth and an enriched environment for the nurture of their children. Some of these have been led to question the basic contemporary models of marriage and family structure. A few, among them popular utopian novelist Robert Rimmer[4] and science fiction writer Robert Heinlein, have proposed a new set of models based on multiperson marriages. A group marriage, through a larger "community of intimates" is offered as potentially providing exactly the size and diversity fundamentally lacking in autonomous, nuclear monogyny.

Of the many attracted by intellectual or endocrinological bent to the poetry and polemics of group marriage proponents, a small number have begun to put into practice a fundamentally new form of marriage. Their unusual relationships differ in concept and execution from most historically and anthropologically related forms of marriage. They are each trying to build a laterally expanded family, a marriage of equals tied together by deep bonds of love and caring, into a many-sided structure. We might properly call this *multilateral* marriage. As such, their present functioning and future potential depends on the nature and contributions of all bonds, including especially the bonds between members of the same sex.

Ten such families scattered across the United States are cooperating in an initial descriptive investigation of multilateral marriages today. Our experience in trying to locate functioning group marriages suggests that this is still an exceptional form of marriage. Pressed for an estimate, we would guess there may be fewer than a hundred, almost certainly less than a thousand group marriages in the United States. Nevertheless, interest in and speculation concerning such innovations in marriage and family relations have been considerable, as evidenced by *Psychology Today's* recent sex survey.[5] Most of this interest has surfaced in fictional accounts which, necessarily, idealize and simplify the nature of group marriage. Little of professional caliber has appeared beyond Herb Otto's collection on alternate models for the American family structure.[6] The formulations in both bodies of literature are, as might be expected, misleading. Practice is sufficiently divergent from theory that the potential participant basing his entrance on the experience of Rimmer's characters is in for genuine surprises if not serious difficulty.

It is important to differentiate what these groups are involved in from other, more widespread and better known social anomalies. Swinging, or organized mate-swapping, has an extensive participation, especially on the West Coast. As a whole, swinging has been found to emphasize purely sexual, temporary liaisons, often carefully structured to avoid *personal* involvement. (Symonds[7] has, however, identified a minority subgroup, the utopian or ideological swingers, who emphasize interpersonal relations.) Clearly, too, the ubiquitous extramarital affair is a different phenomenon, being based on secrecy and isolation of the spouses rather than openness and mutual participation. Ironically, though mate-swapping and affairs are better known, they are in almost as sad a state as group marriage when it comes to formal study.

Our study emerged over a year's time from a desire to substitute understanding of the actual phenomenon for the surfeit of conjecture and argument. Locating active groups and devising a productive plan and philosophy for investigation have been the largest problems. An initial series of interviews with three families, when combined with our prior knowledge of attempted formations, suggested factors of prime interest and guided the study design.

The highest priority has been given to developing a primarily descriptive understanding of what group marriage in modern America is. The most basic questions are being investigated. Who is in it? Why? Does it work at all? Up to expectations? What are the special problems and difficulties? How can these be dealt with? The initial contacts suggested that a broad, comparatively unstructured approach to data gathering was needed. We chose to continue to rely on in-depth, face-to-face contact as our primary tool, supplemented with paper-and-pencil instruments where appropriate. The twenty odd historical, structural, and functional factors chosen for closer study have been divided between interview and reply schedule through several rounds of revision and trial using one group with whom close contact could be maintained. . . .

Respondents in the current study are located in six states with "concentrations" in New England and California. They are not exclusively young; more than half are over thirty, with two distinct clusters, one in the midtwenties, another in the midthirties. The youngest participant is twenty-two; the oldest, sixty.

All but two groups have children, none more than three. If this is truly a general indication, the implications for population stabilization are substantial. The children range from infants through age thirteen. In every case, the children are an integral part of the expanded relationship. They are fully aware of their parents' involvement.

Unfortunately, most central tendencies are fictions in a sample of this size. The problem is exacerbated by the multidimensional diversity of the known participants. Among our respondents are group incomes ranging from below $10,000 per annum to in excess of $100,000, for example. Ten more unique marriages could hardly be found through deliberate search.

Occupationally, the respondents are so diverse that there are no duplications except in the category student in which there are four full time, and housewife, of which there are three. A physician, a high-school teacher, a commercial artist, and a rehabilitation aide have all chosen group marriage. Others are self-employed in small businesses, work as custodians, as postal letter carriers, teach ballet, or are unemployed. About one-third of the present participants entered as single individuals. If there is a pattern among the present respondents, however, it is for one married couple to act as a nucleus around which other couples or single individuals are drawn. . . .

It is interesting to ask why individuals would choose to enter group marriages. A multilevel interpretation of the psychology of participation is required. The public arguments offered are as important as the private ones, the surface reasons as interesting as underlying causes. How an individual perceives the origins of his involvement says much of the individual and the group marriage. . . .

Public justifications, that is, the readiest answers and reasons given on casual acquaintance, most often make reference to "community" and to "extended family." Participants seek a restoration of a lost sense of community, of family identification that is expanded. It is also evident that these are reasons with which the average person readily identifies. Benefits to children are often also cited. Similarly, the sexual dimension is often publicly *deemphasized*, and this happens to be the element that the majority of people find the most threatening.

While these indications are not surprising, it *is* somewhat surprising that love is infrequently mentioned at this public level. The capacity for and benefits of multiple love relationships are important elements of the theoretical and fictional justifications of multilateral marriage. . . .

In deeper investigations, verbal and written, sex emerges as fairly central to participation in group marriages. It certainly does not appear to be a driving force for initial entry, but it is very frequently discussed as a retrospective benefit.

At this level, discussions of personal growth potential are dominant. The role of the group marriage as growth catalyst will be discussed in a later section.

Love still is relatively unimportant in these private responses. This may result from a special property of our sample. Our respondents include only one group in which the group marriage *began* with love relationships which later grew into sexual intimacy and finally cohabitation. All the others originated at more practical or intellectual levels, based on ideas of community, sexual freedom, economic efficiency, or admiration of the *concept* of group marriage. In many cases, these initially nonemotional relationships have *grown* into deep affection. . . .

Lacking more penetrating study, it appears that people enter group marriage for the same reasons as people enter two-person marriage—love, security, sex, child-rearing, companionship, an almost endless list. The reasons are almost completely unique to the individuals and to the marriages. Our tiny sample includes passive-congenial relationships, marriages-of-convenience, even relationships based, apparently, on strong neurotic needs. . . .

The majority of the group marriages involve four partners, a few include only three, and one has six. These sizes *may* reflect very fundamental processes. Triads appear to be especially easy to form. This is true of triads involving either two men or two women. They seem to be functionally stable but psychologically metastable; there is always a push to equalize the sex ratio.

This makes four the first potentially stable point. But our respondents find numerous arguments for expansion, and most are actively trying. One group even deliberately experimented over a period of years with various sizes up to twelve. Now a fairly stable foursome, their conclusion is that six is maximal (and probably optimal). The limiting factor seems to be the capacity to build and maintain simultaneously a number of substantially equivalent, very deep, intimate relationships. While conclusions cannot be reached, a trend for four- and six-person groups is indicated by a number of independent factors.

As the size rises much beyond six, the group appears increasingly like a commune. Because the commune or small intentional community is the group that is most readily confused with a multilateral marriage, it provides a convenient contrast. It is difficult, however, to give a rigorous and non-circular set of definitions. We find that there are indeed two phenomena, differing in many dimensions, which are conveniently labeled as "group marriages" and "communities." Probably the definitive characteristic is the nature of commitment. The individual in a community either makes no commitment or commits himself to the community, its purpose, or its philosophy. Marriage is a fairly long-term commitment to other *individuals*. We have found it adequate to accept the individual's perception as an operational criterion. If he says he is married to all the others, we can assume he is. We also require a group to have confronted and creatively dealt with sexual sharing to be included. A "joint family" consisting of several monogamous couples, though an interesting alternate family structure, is simply not a group *marriage*.

Communes are short-lived, according to Rick Margolies,[8] averaging less than a year, and the population within is highly variable. Almost all respondents are seeking permanent or long-term associations. While they may not succeed, their intentions are the same as the typical couple at the altar. Because a group would have to last for some time to reach our attention, our respondents may well represent a biased sample. They have averaged twenty months together, and one is nearly four years old. None has broken up since the start of our study a year ago.[9]

The interaction within a group marriage is typically intense and intimate, many times more so than one would encounter in any other group of comparable size. From our investigations, communities seldom reach this level of intimacy. It is often like an encounter group, the closest comparison, and one used by many of our respondents. It differs from the typical encounter group in being leaderless and exitless.

Coming from psychologically sophisticated segments of the population, most participants have first-hand experience in encounter groups and sensitivity training. This fact, coupled with the absence of trained leadership, may frequently contribute to dysfunctional intensity of interaction. This can be circumvented, as has been done, by bringing in an outside group therapist whose function `is to facilitate *constructive* interaction. . . .

Marriage takes on many forms. Of Murdock's 554 societies, only 135 had monogamy as the cultural norm.[10] At the same time, no society has ever been catalogued in which group marriage was the cultural norm, leading Nimkoff[11] to conclude that this form, while presenting special problems, possesses no special advantages. This leads us to conclude that Nimkoff and others never really looked at group marriage.

We shall resist the temptation of apologists who deemphasize the sexual element of multilateral marriage. The temptation originates with the opponents, who immediately pounce upon what they see primarily as legitimized promiscuity, evidencing further moral decline. The proponents then counter by playing down sex, emphasizing that it is but one dimension of any marriage. . . .

No (other) formalized type of marriage provides for a variety of sexual partners for both sexes within the marriage. The provision of group marriage is important. It has often been argued that the cross-cultural preponderance of polygyny and rarity of polyandry evidences a higher male need for a variety of partners. In view of the

historical importance of the family as economic and work unit and nearly universal male ascendancy (even often in polyandrous cultures), this conclusion is unwarranted. It much more likely simply reflects male dominance. At this juncture, there is no a priori reason to assume a greater drive for multiple partners by either sex, and considerable behavioral basis for assuming they are biologically comparable.

What we find is that the majority of both the men and women in group marriages particularly enjoy the element of secure sexual variety afforded by their marriage. The criterion of responsibility and interpersonal involvement appears to be preeminent over sexual involvement. Thus, while some individuals engage in sexual activities outside the group marriage, these too tend to reflect interpersonal criteria and none would properly be described as promiscuous.

It is important not to confuse sexual variety, in the form of varied techniques and positions for intercourse, and varietism, in the form of different partners. The extent to which multiple partners are incorporated, by violation, into conventional marriage patterns is the best evidence that these represent distinct needs.

Reflected in reasons for entering group marriage, we find emphasized the dual aspect of sex in the group. At once, a depth of emotional commitment and involvement incongruent with most extramarital relations is possible, while a variety of partners are even more readily accessible. The group marriage seems to satisfy participants' needs for sexual varietism without the high emotional cost of clandestine affairs or impersonal swapping.

Early sexual involvement has been a pattern in all but one group, where one pair, after 18 months, have not had intercourse. The sexual involvement of many participants is not exclusively limited to their group marriage; intimate relations do also occur with close friends and in a few instances, in casual encounters.

The mechanisms by which groups resolve the issues of sexual sharing and sleeping arrangements vary but have certain elements in common. Most multilateral families aspire to natural, spontaneous sexual relations. This has been difficult to achieve, and some have had to retreat occasionally to the dependability of formal rotation. Even after possessive jealousy recedes into the background, insecurity is manifest in the difficulty of deciding the sleeping arrangements. Unfortunately, immediate preference for one partner is too easily read as sexual rejection of another, and in our society that is tantamount to personal rejection. We would not describe the sexual sharing of any of the groups as truly spontaneous, though clear progress toward this is evident.

As a typical example, a group may spend a significant portion of its collective energy on this one decision, that is, who sleeps with whom. The decision-making time itself may be of short duration, but by observing other activities, it may be seen that this question arises early in the day, and there may be considerable tentative sounding and maneuvering prior to the actual confrontation. This may be the price of informality if not spontaneity. One can, hopefully, expect more efficiency with practice.

The fixed rotation scheme, say switching partners every week, so enthusiastically espoused by Rimmer[12] does not work well in practice. It may, as he suggested, assure (artificially) equal sexual demand for all partners; unfortunately, it not only utterly destroys spontaneity but avoids confrontation on an issue the facing of which is vital. Fixed rotation has generally been abandoned early, though it may serve as a useful transitional solution.

A novel compromise has evolved in one group which frequently begins by collecting unbiased, isolated, unprocessed preferences. Giving honest, purely personal first choices, without regard to the processing of the preferences of others, is a valuable general skill for group participation, and this framework is a good practice ground. If a conflict occurs in unprocessed choices of partners (which is not always), a group arbiter is selected who, while attempting to do best by the group as a whole, nevertheless makes a binding decision. Role of arbiter rotates, giving decision-making practice to all. Here is one way

to turn a hassle into a learning experience.

Assignments of bedrooms vary. Groups with ample room give each individual his own bedroom, leaving a "your-place-or-mine" decision to each pair, at the same time solving the territoriality problem. Both primarily matricentric and patricentric sleeping have been tried. While assigning bedrooms permanently to the women may compensate somewhat for historical wrong-doing and residual male chauvinism, it has had no distinct advantages in practice.

Group sex, with possible bisexual participation, is another area in which espoused or aspired directions diverge from practice. Multiperson and bisexual activities are generally either accepted as permissible or advanced as desirable despite the fact that very little has taken place. In only one group do three people consistently sleep together; in some others, group sex, though a live option, is rare. Consistent with reports from other sources, notably mate swappers and the sexual freedom movement, instances of three person participation with one man and two women account for the vast majority of those that do occur.

Multiple couple sex is quite rare, in contrast to its predominance among mate swappers. It has been found to be particularly conducive to triggering destructive jealousy. It also facilitates competition, especially male competition, which has sometimes been particularly destructive, in minimal cases manifesting temporary impotence. . . .

Operationally, what most distinguishes multilateral marriage from a conventional dyadic one, is the potential for and necessity to deal with jealousy, possessiveness, and competition as an intrinsic part of group functioning. Two consistent and definite patterns emerged. First, the classic argument that jealousy is an inherent, irreversible quality of man's psychological makeup *seems* not to hold. While it would be difficult to prove now, there appear to be individuals who not only do not manifest behavior suggestive of jealousy but who also appear to have outgrown the feelings of jealousy that precipitate the behavior. . . .

What will happen in the long run, we do

not know, but at present the vast majority of group marriage participants have largely outgrown or found effective ways of dealing with jealousy. On the other hand, no group reports being completely free of *some* residual problems. This is not surprising in view of the tremendous backlog of cultural conditioning which supports and even promotes jealousy and its variants. . . .

In every aspect of group functioning, we find a recurrent theme—coping with complexity. All the mechanics of living are more complicated. Money, discipline, food, personality conflicts, all are multiplied in terms of problem potential. Fortunately, tradition, formal rules, and habit set in to reduce the continued level of complexity; unfortunately, this effect is only partial and the individual participant probably must be of that temperament that makes for the good member of a large family or a commune.

It can be surprising how important seemingly trivial aspects of life style can be. What may appear to be surface elements—brand of toothpaste, preferences in meat, which side of the bed to sleep on—emerge as being a persistent, ingrained, often intensely personal complex. These infinitely varied combinations of generally conflicting patterns have to be resolved in some way in every marriage. Needless to say, toothpaste can be more of a problem with six "newlyweds" than with two. This appears to be more of a problem with groups exclusively formed of previously married couples. What seems to be operative is a tendency, once having made such adjustments in one marriage, to resist further accommodation, even if unconsciously.

The complexity which must be dealt with successfully is not only a product of particular individual personalities, but a fundamental property of the enlarged, intimate group. Between two people there are two interrelationships which must be built and maintained in a satisfactory manner. (An interrelationship is always directed; A can love B without B loving A, for example.) Among four there are twelve such interrelationships; among six there are thirty. While compatibility may be facilitated by initial selection, the basic mathematics of group structure cannot be countered. . . .

The family based on a group marriage involves potentially new dimensions of interactions with children and of roles assumed by the parents. Some distinct patterns have emerged here. . . .

For the most part, all adults assume parental roles in rearing children in the group. These tend to be somewhat less sex-differentiated than in many conventional marriages. The husbands, as a rule, take very active roles in child care, in some cases rotating all such duties, from diaper changing on, with the wives. In terms of most mechanical aspects of child care, little distinction is made between biological parents and other members of the group marriage.

Most groups intend for the children to come to regard all the adults as parents, though all who are old enough are aware of their biological parents. In watching groups form, we find it takes very little time for children of any age to adjust and to accept new adults in parental roles, even if differentiated from those of their actual parents. Indeed, we have been impressed by the manner in which children have responded to an expanded family situation. The effects include behavioral manifestations such as increased self-confidence and, in one case, improved performance in school.

One child has been born into a group marriage. The fatherhood is in doubt, though believed to be the nonlegal co-husband rather than legal husband of the mother. Unrelated factors result in no other groups planning such "cross-couple" children. The effect of such children on group marriages is unknown as yet. In some cases young children have grown to employ relational forms of address like "Mommy" for other than actual parents.

A markedly differentiated pattern emerges in terms of discipline. While discipline may generally be administered by all adults, most groups report that the character of discipline is largely set by biological parents. In one group the patterns of child rearing for the two couples are very distinct, one being considerably more authoritarian and formalized. The resolution takes the form of general consistency among the four adults for each child, with the inconsistency between the two children. It is a source of friction. . . .

One of the central hopes of group marriage and other forms of expanded or extended families is greater flexibility in the assumption of specific roles. In a family with several breadwinners and several potential sources of child care, it should be easier for a man to become a "househusband" (or *hemman* as he is referred to in Denmark) or for a woman to pursue a full-time career.

We find *some* reduction in traditional sex roles. In general, participants are highly equalitarian in principle. In practice, the most noticeable manifestation is in terms of greater than average involvement by the men in child rearing and some household duties. On the other hand, much of the potential here has been unrealized as yet. Participants themselves feel their hopes for greater role freedom (and freedom in general) have been largely unfulfilled. One family intends in the future for one of two women to be principal wage-earner and the man involved will retire, but no such arrangements exist now. . . .

What is the prognosis for the group marriages considered here and others like them? This is an involved issue, for it incorporates not only the intrinsic qualities of each groups' own relationships but also exogenous elements—the social milieu in which they are pioneering a new form of marriage. Very little of this environment is indifferent to their attempt; most, if their marriages were known, would be openly hostile.

A surprisingly large percentage of people have shown exceptionally strong negative reactions to even the abstract concept of multiperson marriage, appearing to be deeply threatened by it. In view of the inevitable increase in other potential "cultural shocks," this phenomenon is worthy of investigation in itself. Most such reactions give every appearance of either guilt over extramarital involvement or resentment over the greater freedom of others.

In itself, multilateral marriage is beginning to appear to be a viable alternative for some members of our society. We can absolutely assert short-to-intermediate-term success in the sense of continued existence.

This is a stronger assertion than a similar one for dyadic marriage. For a conventional marriage to last four years only implies that the relationship is not so bad as to justify to its members the difficulty and disruption of an early divorce. In contrast, all exogenous forces (and perhaps more crucially, many culturally preconditioned internal personality forces) are working to disintegrate the multilateral marriage, making a four-year continuing commitment somewhat remarkable.

Moreover, we do see progress, if not what could be legitimately called success, in terms of meaningful self-insight and personal growth achieved through participation in group marriage. To the limited depth we have explored filiocentric factors, the conclusion is unmistakably in favor of the multilateral marriage as an improved child-rearing institution. In most families, we find committed, highly motivated individuals building a community of mutual trust and love, though this process is neither rapid, monotonic, nor universal.

But even if the observed variables were uniformly positive in terms of the internal processes of the multiperson marriage—and they are not—the laterally expanded family would have to be reconciled with contemporary society for it to be genuinely viable. In part, the currently active group marriages have remained viable through anonymity and their quiet minority position.

Open, direct, perhaps explosive confrontation with society seems all but inevitable. Rising interest in alternative family structures serves, in part, to release further xenophobic responses vectored on a moral scapegoat for current social dilemmas. Indeed, Nimkoff[13] has observed that pointing to family decline as a scapegoat for diverse social ills is a cross-cultural norm.

But we must not lose sight of the immense, psychological price paid by a society that espouses a single, monolithic conception of marital structure. While it remains unproven whether innate human needs are more congruent with nuclear or compound families, with monogamous or polygamous relations, it is certain that man's psychological polymorphism guarantees that anything short of cultural pluralism in marriage must deny, in sum, many intrinsic needs of many individuals.

Looking beneath superficial idealism in the *form* of modern monogamous marriage, and beyond ultimate emotional gains possible in the nonexistent perfect dyadic relationship, we see a forest of human needs and desires laid waste by our society's idolatry. The luckiest of conventionally married people will have one fully trusted confidant, one secure supportive relationship, one selective mirror of his or her self-reality, one intimate relationship with an autonomous equal. If he is in any other way a product of our age, he will long for a sense of community long lost, for an identification in more than a familial microcosm, for extended intimacy without guilt.

Our respondents continue to explore an uncertain answer to these needs. At present, not all are even in agreement among themselves about the likelihood of a continued relationship. Their mood fluctuates, although for most their ability to function cohesively increases fairly steadily. For groups having problems, there are no multilateral-marriage counselors to help them with the problems they and we see. It is essential to recognize that, as with conventional marriage, a break-up is not necessarily a total loss. Most participants themselves have stated that they regard their involvement as worthwhile regardless of final outcome. We concur in most instances. They will not necessarily have failed—only chosen not to choose each other permanently. Irreversible positive effects of their difficult commitment are already evident.

NOTES AND REFERENCES

[1] M. F. Nimkoff, ed., *Comparative Family Systems* (Boston: Houghton Mifflin, 1965).

[2] Peter C. Pineo, "Disenchantment in the Later Years of Marriage," *Marriage and Family Living*, 23 (February 1961):3–11.

[3] John F. Cuber and Peggy Haroff, *The Significant Americans* (New York: Appleton-Century-Crofts, 1965).

[4] Robert H. Rimmer, *Proposition 31* (New York: New American Library, 1968).

[5] *Psychology Today*, 4, no. 2 (July 1970).

[6] Herbert A. Otto, *The Family in Search of a Future* (New York: Appleton-Century-Crofts, 1969).

[7] Carolyn Symonds, "Pilot Study of the Peripheral Behavior of Sexual Mate Swappers." Unpublished Master's thesis, University of California, Riverside, 1968.

[8] Rick Margolies, "Life in Urban Communes." Plenary address, 1969 meeting of the National Council on Family Relations.

[9] In the short period of ten days, while final manuscript revisions were being prepared, two of the groups in the study have disintegrated. One dissolved in the midst of an attempted transition from three to four participants, the other broke up apparently as the result of latent instabilities in a prior marriage. We have not had adequate time to analyze these dissolutions, but report them here in the interest of accuracy and currency. Intensive follow-ups in both cases are planned.

[10] George P. Murdock, "World Ethnographic Sample," *American Anthropologist*, 59 (1957):686.

[11] Nimkoff, op. cit.

[12] Rimmer, op. cit.

[13] Nimkoff, op. cit.

Constantine, Larry L. "Personal Growth in Multiperson Marriages," *Radical Therapist*, 2, no. 1 (April–May 1971).

Constantine, Larry L., and Joan M. "Multilateral Marriage: Alternate Family Structure in Practice," in Robert H. Rimmer, *You and I for Tomorrow* (New York: Dell, 1971), pp. 157–173.

——. "The Pragmatics of Group Marriage—Year One," *The Modern Utopian*, 4, no. 3 (Summer 1970).

——. "Where is Marriage Going?" *The Futurist*, 4, no. 2 (April 1970):44–46.

Part Thirteen

Marriage Dissolution and Multimarriage Families

Although many marriages are troubled, nearly three fifths of them are stable enough to stay together until the death of one partner. The average husband dies seven years before his wife, and the average age at widowhood in the United States is about fifty-five. The death of a marriage partner is the end of a stable marriage, perhaps a happy one as well. The surviving partner is not as apt to remarry as is the divorced person, probably because the survivor is usually an older woman, who has less choice due to the shortage of older men and the proclivity of American men to marry women younger than they.

In the case of an unhappy marriage, there is a growing trend among younger persons not to wait until death ends the marriage but to seek a divorce instead. As a result of this trend, the divorce rate for the United States ranks highest in the world at the present time, followed closely by Japan, Russia, Algeria, Israel, and Egypt. The overall United States figure is estimater to be about 40 percent; in some sections of the United States, the rate of divorce is even higher—in 1971 it was reported to have reached 70 percent in one county in California. Of course, this overall figure includes those who marry and divorce more than once, thus obscuring the fact that the rate for first marriages is a much lower figure of around 25 percent.

Divorce and annulment statistics are easy to keep, but separations and desertions are not officially recorded. It has been estimated that for every legally ended marriage there is probably another marriage that has been broken without court proceedings. Separated and deserted men and women do not remarry, of course, but face lives complicated by problems resulting from their undefined marital status.

It is speculated that in the future most marriages will end by means other than death. An important factor in the rising divorce rate is that the life expectancy has increased to over seventy years of age, which means that people are now expected to remain married about fifty years. This is a long time to expect things to go well, especially when men and women expect so much happiness and fulfillment from the marriage relationship.

The rising divorce rate has alarmed many people. Some see it as the herald of decay of the family; while others feel that the divorce process itself needs to be revamped. Recommendations have been made and instituted in a few states to change divorce from an adversary system to one of mutual consent. No longer must one party be guilty and thus sued for divorce, while the other partner is claimed innocent and awarded the divorce, the children, and the larger share of joint resources. Similarly, the grounds for divorce also are undergoing changes, so that in California, for instance, only two grounds are recognized—incurable insanity and the one that is used in nearly every case, irreconcilable differences. The aim is to simplify the divorce process so as not to add to the suffering of the unhappy pair and their children. At its simplest, divorce is a complicated, painful matter because of the ego-involvement of the partners, the financial problems, child custody, and the adjustment to being single again. Other family members and friends often react in unpredictable ways, and loneliness is not an uncommon problem to combat. The first reading, by Felix Berardo, is an overview of widowhood status in the United States, as well as a discussion of the effects of bereavement on other family members. In the second selection, Jack Westman and David Cline discuss problems resulting from divorce and the implications for children. Since divorce most frequently occurs with couples who have children, the stresses on children become an important consideration in the total picture.

In most cases of divorce, the mother receives custody of the children, but this practice is changing somewhat as a result of a more enlightened view on the part of the judiciary about the best interests of the child. In the past, it was assumed that the mother was likely to be the better parent for the children and that she could stay at home with them while her ex-husband sent child support. Actually, however, the mother frequently goes to work out of desire or necessity and the children do not receive her maternal care as intended.

Hence, the courts are now awarding the children to the partner who, in their opinion, is best able to provide proper care.

The responsibility is great on the parent with custody who must also work; and "parents without partners" often seek each other out for support and companionship. Organizations offering help and recreation to parents who are alone have grown rapidly. In the third reading, E. E. LeMasters examines the types of one-parent families and concludes that, despite the problems, many single parents are managing to survive and are perhaps providing a better home than some still married couples. It is tragic that in too many cases, when the parent has to work, adequate child-care facilities are not available and the children are not well cared for.

Although divorce is often considered a tragedy, it can also mark the start of a new and more satisfactory life for persons who are unhappily married. But adjustments must be made to a single life, and frequently the problems of finances, companionship, and loneliness, feelings of rejection, and society's reaction leave the divorced person feeling damaged. Generally, the person who suffers the most in a divorce is the partner with the fewest alternatives for making a new and rewarding life. Often this is the woman, who may have few marketable skills and who may be bound to the children whose custody she has. Divorce often means that she must jump from an identity as wife and mother to that of almost total responsibility as head of the household. This is particularly difficult for young mothers who married before they had much education or a sense of identity. Middle-aged women, divorced after their children have left home, but with no skills or identity aside from housewife, face different problems; and they frequently suffer from lack of confidence and feelings of uselessness. Men, too, have a unique set of problems, which result from having to move away from their homes and children, often to a small apartment and meals at the corner coffee shop. Some recent studies have indicated that the mate most damaged by a divorce is the *rejected* husband—who moves out of the home to a life of depression and often suicide.

Paul Bohannan, in the fourth article, takes a careful look at six types of experiences that often go along with divorce. Divorce is becoming an everyday experience in our society, and its magnitude reflects the many reasons that people currently have for instituting the proceeding. In the past, adultery may have been the only recognized grounds. The variety of reasons for divorce produce a variety of reactions, and to formulate some kind of framework in which to analyze the reactions, as the author has done, is a much needed contribution to understanding the impact of a broken marriage.

Most persons who divorce remarry within two or three years, and they usually marry a person who also has been divorced. This statistic indicates that it is not the idea of marriage with which men and women are disillusioned, but the particular marriage in which they are mired. In fact, our high divorce rate and societal pressures to be married have made plural marriage more popular in the United States—although we still have only one mate at a time—than it is in some polygamous societies. Indeed, it has been suggested that in the near future almost everyone will be married more than once in a lifetime and a broken marriage may be a necessary experience on the way to finding marital success. The next article, by Betty Rollin, is a discussion of remarriage in our society. As Rollin indicates, for most persons remarriage is a good adjustment to divorce, and most remarriages are better than the prior marriage—although there are some people who seem to be divorce-prone.

Remarriages do not follow a particular model any more than do first marriages but there are usually more complications in second marriages, for it is probable that children will be involved and that a "ready-made" family will accompany the marriage. Much has been written about the adjustment of children in remarriage homes versus those who live with a parent who does not remarry. The general conclusion is that remarriage is not detrimental to the children involved, particularly when they are in the custody of their mother and a stepfather. Stepmothers fare somewhat worse, but this may be due to their more intensive relationship as the mother substitute. There are doubtless more strains and ambivalent feelings in the average remarried family, for there are two sets of parents, often two sets of stepparents, multiple grandparents, and an assortment of stepsiblings and half-siblings. The final selection, by Charles Bowerman and Donald Irish, is both a review of the literature on stepchildren and their parents plus a report of two studies on different aspects of mingling two families by remarriage of the parents. The argument that children may benefit from the remarriage because it offers stability and harmony seems to hold if, indeed, the remarriage is successful and the children's parent finds the marriage satisfying and an improvement over the last one.

66

WIDOWHOOD STATUS IN THE UNITED STATES: PERSPECTIVE ON A NEGLECTED ASPECT OF THE FAMILY LIFE-CYCLE

Felix M. Berardo

Widowhood is rapidly becoming a major phenomenon of American society. National census data indicate that there are close to 11 million widowed persons among our population today, the large majority of whom are women. Over the past several decades the widowed female has, in fact, been outdistancing her male counterpart by a continually widening margin. Whereas the number of widowers has remained relatively constant from 1930 to the present, female survivors have shown a substantial rise during this period. Thus, in 1940 there were twice as many widows as there were widowers. During the following decade widows increased by more than 22 percent while the number of widowers rose by only 7 percent. By 1960 the ratio of widows to widowers had risen to more than 3½ to 1, and throughout the decade has continued to climb to a present ratio of more than 4 to 1. Currently, there are well over eight and three-quarter million widows in the nation, and their total is expected to continue expanding.[1] Widowhood then is emerging as an important area for sociological inquiry because of the growing and extensive population involved. (Unless specified otherwise, the term widowhood as used in this paper will have reference to female survivors and their families only.) . . .

Widowhood has long been known to entail a variety of social problems at the local level, being related to adult and child dependency, poverty, unemployment, illness, and the more significant facts of family disorganization and of women's insecure industrial status. In order to more fully portray the magnitude of the problem in contemporary society it is necessary to present a concise but somewhat abbreviated demographic profile on American widowhood. In addition to serving as a point of information regarding certain baseline data, the picture to be presented hopefully will also provide proper amplification of the current social conditions surrounding female survivors and will set the stage for exploring the sociological dimensions of their status for both the family and society.

It should be noted at the outset that from a statistical standpoint widowhood is largely a problem of the aged woman. As a result of the impact of advances in medical technology, pervasive health programs, etc., on decreasing mortality prior to midlife, widowhood for the most part has been postponed to the latter stages of the family life-cycle. Around the turn of the twentieth century about 1 in 25 persons was 65 years old or older, as compared to 1 in 11 in the present decade. Since the gains in longevity have been more rapid for females than for males, the growing proportion of elderly women in our population is accentuating the problem of widowhood. Thus, currently more than three-fifths of the widows in the United States are 65 years of age or over (almost another fourth are between 55–64) and "unless the trends in male and female mortality are sharply reversed, the excess of women over men at the upper ages will increase, and our older population will contain a larger proportion of widows." . . .

Because the majority of widows are aged, their economic circumstances are usually below average. A special survey of widows 55 years of age or older, for example, revealed that almost two-thirds of the husbands left a sum total of assets (including cash, savings, life insurance, property value of the home, and other assets) of less than $10,000 to their families; 44 percent left assets of less than $5,000. Equally significant, the median income of the wives in the year preceding the survey was less than $2,000 (Institute for Life Insurance, 1964). These figures are comparable to some extent with census data on the aged which shows the median income of the widowed as a group to be less than $1,200 per year, in comparison to almost $3,000 for the aged married. The census data also indicate that widows have substantially lower assets than non-widows in all age groups.

One thing is clear—the available evidence on income levels lends little support to the occasional stereotype of "the wealthy widow," as a statistically prevalent type among our aged population. In this connection, it is frequently stated that women, as a consequence of outliving their husbands, control a great deal of the inherited wealth in the United States. It is said, for example, that they are beneficiaries of 80 percent of all life insurance policies (National Consumer Finance Association, 1963). It is true that as beneficiaries, women in the United States received more than two-thirds of the nearly $5 billion paid in 1965 following the death of a policyholder. Such gross figures, however, can be misleading. In the study cited earlier, for example, almost three-fourths of the husbands owned *less* than $5,000 in life insurance at the time of their death, and an additional 20 percent owned less than $10,000. Moreover, many of these women have to use what small amounts of insurance their husbands did carry to pay for funeral expenses, medical bills, taxes, mortgages, and so on, leaving them with only small savings on which to survive.

There is no doubt that life insurance has become a principal defense against the insecurity and risk of widowhood in our urban, industrial society with its attendant nuclear family system. It is a concrete form of security which in some instances may help the bereaved family to avoid an embarrassing and reluctant dependence on relatives and/or the state in the case of untimely death. Nevertheless, it has been the experience of investment bankers and the like that few female survivors are capable of handling the economic responsibilities brought about by the husband's death, inasmuch as they know very little about matters of real estate, titles, mortgage, contracts, stocks, bonds, and matters of property.[2]. . . .

Because they frequently encounter serious economic problems soon after their husbands have passed away, many wives find it necessary to seek employment. This is particularly the case where dependent children are involved; approximately 900,000 female survivors carried this responsibility in 1960. Moreover, at that time over half of all widows under age 35 were either employed or else seeking work. At ages 35–54, this proportion rises to nearly two-thirds (Metropolitan Life, 1966).

While women entering widowhood at the older ages are not as likely to have dependent children in the home, they are nevertheless often faced with a similar problem of self-support, since Social Security benefits provide for the minimum necessities only. Moreover, the obstacles to securing employment at this stage of the life-cycle are often rather difficult to overcome. Typically, these women have been absent from the labor market for several years and are, therefore, at a disadvantage with respect to the educational and occupational demands of current employment. In addition, they are frequently confronted with a subtle but pervasive discrimination on the part of the employers who are not in favor of hiring older persons, let alone older women. Since the majority of all widows, but in particular the aged widows, are unemployed, they are unable to support themselves and consequently are partly or wholly dependent on the assistance of children or relatives, and on public or private funds. While the 1965 amendments to Social Security Act broadened and substantially increased benefits available to widows and their dependent children, their economic circumstances still remain far from satisfactory.

Female survivors who have obtained employment are heavily concentrated in the low-paying jobs. Over one-third are private household or other service workers; one-fifth are clerical and kindred workers, and one-seventh are operatives and kindred workers. Less than one-tenth of all widows are engaged in professional or technical occupations. In any event, research indicates that playing a role in the productive economy is predictive of favorable adaptation to widowhood. . . . An employed widow in later life tends to be better adjusted, that is, to have higher morale, than both a housewife who has never worked or a retired widow. The acts of preparing for work, carrying out one's tasks, and returning home are viewed as being intimately connected to feelings of personal worth, self-esteem, and significance in life. This has led to the suggestion that "for widowed women, there is a need for a service that will provide occasional jobs, such as baby-sitting, service as companions for bedridden persons, and occasional light housekeeping tasks. Many widows have never been in the labor force and have never acquired skills in any other line. These kinds of jobs frequently coincide with their experience as homemakers."[3] . . .

The proportion of children in the United States under 18 years of age who have lost one or both of their natural parents through death has declined markedly since the turn of the century, due to modern advances in medicine and improved health conditions. Nevertheless, orphanhood remains a social problem of considerable magnitude in this country and one that necessitates a variety of services and assistance to accommodate the families affected.

Currently there are approximately 3.4 million orphans in the nation and they represent about 4.8 percent of all children under age 18. Among these are more than 2 million "paternal orphans," that is, children who have lost their fathers through death. The most recent estimates indicate that of all orphans in the nation today, approximately 71 percent have lost their fathers only and about 27 percent have lost their mothers only. Less than 3 percent have lost both parents. Thus, the burdens of orphanhood are borne primarily by women.

Children who have experienced the trauma of bereavement and/or who have been reared in a one-parent household have been typically depicted as occupying a particularly disadvantageous position due to purported family disruption engendered by such circumstances. The dysfunctional consequences for the personality development of children involved have been especially emphasized. Researchers sharing this perspective have often "assumed as a working hypothesis that the young person in the broken home who does not go to the extreme of delinquency may still experience problems in his adjustment with peers and teachers, in school relationships, and in the community which are not experienced by young people living in families with both parents present." The broader assumption underlying this viewpoint, particularly in the case of the paternal orphan, is that the absence of a proper sex-role model represented by the parent results in inadequate socialization. Similarly, it is assumed that because the mother is forced to shoulder dual parental role obligations, she is not able to adequately supervise and control her children. These circumstances are said to result in a variety of negative consequences, such as delinquency, mental illness, and the like.

The major sociological opinion, then, has endorsed the attributes of a complete family environment. This somewhat traditional viewpoint, however, has been challenged by a number of investigators who stress that the presence of both parents does not automatically guarantee a better child-rearing situation. Rather, it is argued, "the crucial factor in the adjustment of children is the social-psychological success or failure of the family, not whether or not it is legally and physically broken" (Nye, 1957, p. 356). Current research evidence appears to support this contention (Burchinal, 1964). Nye, for example, found that the adjustment of adolescents from *broken* homes was more successful than that of children from *unhappy unbroken* homes. That is, they showed less psychosomatic illness, less delinquency, and better adjustment to parents. Moreover, he found no evidence of greater adjustment problems in "mother only" homes than in remarried or unhappy unbroken homes. As a matter of fact, parent child relationships were superior in the "solo" mother homes in almost every area of adjustment measured. Perry and Pfuhl (1963) similarly found no significant differences between adolescents in homes broken by death or divorce and those in remarried homes in terms of delinquent behavior, psychoneurotic tendencies, and school grades. The results of these and similar studies throw into question the assumption that the effects of family dissolution on children are adverse and they suggest that family dissolution, per se, is not the most important factor influencing the lives of the adolescents studied. The issue, of course, is by no means settled, and more research is needed which focuses specifically on the social adjustment of children in homes dissolved through the death of a parent. . . .

That widowhood presents serious problems of personal adjustment and mental health is rather well established. Empirical research has consistently demonstrated that the widowed typically have higher death rates, a greater incidence of mental disorders, and a higher suicide rate than their married counterparts. More specifically:

The Widowed Die Sooner. Analyses of National Vital Statistics and Census data for the United States reveal that the widowed have a significantly higher mortality rate than married persons of the same age, and that among young widowed people there is a particularly high excess of mortality. Additional investigations in this country and abroad have supported these findings. Moreover, recent research by Rees and Lutkins (1967) has provided rather dramatic statistical confirmation of the long-standing hypothesis that a death in the family produces an increased post-bereavement mortality rate among close relatives, with the greatest increase in mortality risk occurring among surviving spouses. At present, little is known of the primary causative agents underlying this association between bereavement and mortality. Homogamy, common affection, joint unfavorable environment, and loss of care have all been suggested as possible influences. Moreover, "personality factors, social isolation, age (old people withstand bereavement better than young), and the nature and magnitude of the loss itself all seem to be important factors. When the bereaved person is supported by a united and affectionate family, when there is something left to live for, when the person has been adequately prepared for the loss, and when it can be fitted into a secure religious or philosophical attitude to life and death there will seldom be much need for professional help. When, however, the bereaved person is left alone in a world which is seen as hostile and insecure, when the future is black and the loss has not been prepared for, help may be needed" (Rees and Lutkins, 1967, p. 3).

Widowhood and Suicide. Durkheim is generally recognized as the first well known sociologist to stress the connection between widowhood and suicide. "The suicides, occurring at the crisis of widowhood . . . are really due to domestic anomie resulting from the death of husband or wife. A family catastrophe occurs which affects the survivor. He is not adapted to the new situation in which he finds himself and accordingly offers less resistance to suicide" (Durkheim, 1951, p. 259). Numerous investigations have since demonstrated that within a given age group, the suicide rates of the widowed are consistently higher than the married. A review of these studies indicates that suicide—whether attempted or actual—frequently tends to be preceded by the disruption of significant social interaction and reciprocal role relationships through the loss of a mate (Rushing, 1968). Moreover, these studies further reveal that the death of one or both parents in childhood is common among attempted and actual suicide victims; that the incidence of suicide among such persons when they attain adulthood is much greater than that for comparable groups in the general population.

Widowhood, Social Isolation, and Mental Health. That a high correlation exists between marital status and mental illness has been repeatedly noted in the scientific literature. While considerable professional controversy prevails over identification of the exact sequence of the antecedent-consequent conditions which predispose individuals toward various forms of organic and psychogenic disorders, there is little disagreement with the general hypothesis that "the emotional security and social stability afforded by married life makes for low incidence of mental illness" (Adler, 1953, p. 185). Again, the evidence is quite consistent that the widowed experience a substantially higher rate of mental disorders than the still married, particularly among the older populations.

The association between marital status and mental disorders has been shown to be a function of several intervening factors, including age, socioeconomic status, physical condition, and the degree as well as duration of social isolation. Problems of social isolation, often accompanied by distressing loneliness, are especially germane to the personal adjustment of aged female survivors, a very high proportion of whom are residing alone as occupants of one-person households. Fried and Stern (1948), for example, found that almost two-thirds of the widowed in their study were dissatisfied with the single state and were lonesome even after 10 years of widowhood. The loss of a husband not only creates many practical problems of living alone, but also produces a social vacuum in the life of the aged widow which is difficult to fill. She may find herself "marooned" in an environment which generally requires paired relationships as a prerequisite to social participation. Consequently, various researchers have found that, compared to married women, widows are more apt to feel economically insecure, unhappy, to suffer from fears of being alone and from loss of self-esteem as women, to exhibit undue anxiety and emotional tensions, and to lack self-confidence. In the case of widows who are still mothers: "There are the objective problems of limited income and the need to find the time and energy for a job to augment it and still be the kind of mother children need in the circumstances—a mother who can maintain a home, discipline and educate young people, and insure their positive emotional growth. Then there are the countless problems of guilt, fear, frustration, and loneliness, ever-present and always threatening" (Illgenfritz, 1961, p. 41). . . .

Anthropologists, of course, for some time have been describing various facets of death and bereavement and the ritualistic customs and behavior associated with such phenomena among different societies around the world. Unfortunately, while there appears to be considerable information in the anthropological literature regarding the status of widows, it is scattered among the pages of voluminous monographs which generally focus on larger units of social organization. A library search of various anthropological journals revealed a similar situation. There are apparently no articles devoted *exclusively* to the theoretical or practical aspects of widowhood, although many contain anywhere from a paragraph to two pages of commentary on the subject. Moreover, the relevant data on widowhood tend to be highly descriptive in nature and lacking in systematic treatment. . . . It appears that past anthropological analyses of widowhood have concentrated rather exclusively on its relationship to the economic and kinship systems. Particular emphasis seems to have been placed on patterns of widowhood inheritance, as reflected through the ancient practices of the levirate and sororate marriage arrangements. . . .

Widowhood must be viewed as a pervasive social problem directly encompassing increasing numbers of women and their families and indirectly affecting many others. Within this context, the husband's demise creates a crisis situation which, to adapt Waller's definition, "strains the resources which families possess, cannot be solved by the repertory of ready-made answers provided by the mores or built up out of the family's previous experience with trouble, and requires the family to find new (and usually expedient) ways of carrying on family operations." Moreover, "once family habits are threatened successfully the influence of the event travels through the family like a bowling ball through a set of tenpins—as one set of habits is disrupted, other sets are affected and there arises the objective possibility of family paralysis" (Waller and Hill, 1951, pp. 456–457). If this type of disruption is to be avoided, and if a successful and long-term adaptation is to be executed, the family must be reorganized as an ongoing social system—roles must be reassigned, status positions shifted, and values and goals reoriented. Although the bereaved family may receive initial support from its kin group in the immediate period just prior to or following the husband's death, thereafter it must usually fend for itself both socially and psychologically. Major attention, therefore, needs to be directed toward answering the question: What kinds of social relationships with non-familial persons and groups in the environment need to be developed or maintained which will establish social support for the widow and her family and enable the family to continue functioning despite its loss?

At the more personal level, widowhood requires the development of alternative patterns of behavior if the female survivor is to maintain satisfactory relations with the family, the kin group, and the community, and if she is to establish and sustain an acceptable self-conception—one that will receive approval and which may be appropriately expressed. Women occupying widowhood status experience varying degrees of role ambiguity emanating from vague and contradictory normative expectations concerning appropriate behavior. As a result, the American widow frequently experiences considerable uncertainty and anxiety over reaching decisions concerning such matters as when to terminate the mourning period, how to make others aware of this, when to begin dating again, how long she should wait before considering remarriage, etc. Sociologically, then, the period of widowhood necessitates a reorganization and reintegration of social roles suitable to a new status. The diverse ways through which such role modifications are effectively accomplished, and the manner in which the ambiguous social situation in which the widow finds herself is eventually resolved, represent important areas for empirical inquiry. . . .

Sociologists have long known that "few events in the life cycle require more extensive changes in activities, responsibilities, and living habits (or cause greater alterations in attitudes, reranking of values, and alterations of outlook on life) than does a change from one marital status to another"

(Bogue, 1959, p. 212). More specifically, and in terms of the present discussion, they have recognized that the disruption of marriage by the death of a husband has profound repercussions for the widow, her family, and the community. Yet our review of the literature reveals that the special problems that confront the widow both at the time of bereavement and beyond have not undergone extensive *sociological* research. Certainly a rapidly growing population of elderly women, an ever mounting proportion of whom are widowed, would call for a systematic study of their lives, problems, and modes of adaptation. A knowledge of the variations in successful adaptation to widowhood status would have pragmatic consequences with the framework of action-oriented sociologists for educating and preparing individuals and families for dealing with this common experience with better understanding and insight. "Death, even when expected for a long time, is always a shock to the family which has been broken by it. The pain of grief cannot be avoided; but proper preparation will help in facing the work of grief, will lessen the disruption of family life, and will prevent the making of unfortunate decisions during this period of strain. Above all, this preparation will give members of the family insight into ways of helping each other" (Peniston, 1962, p. 16).

In this paper we have concentrated on the widow in American society. The same type of inquiry, however, needs to be undertaken with respect to the widower, about whom scientific information is even less adequate. Currently, there are well over 2 million widowers in our population, and it can be assumed that the structuring of their adaptation would be different from that of their female counterparts (Berardo, 1967). Unless or until extensive and systematic investigations of widowhood and widowerhood are undertaken and completed, the sociology of isolation will exhibit an unnecessary lag in its development.

NOTES AND REFERENCES

[1] Three *major* factors are generally cited to account for the growing excess of widows in the United States, namely: (a) mortality among women is lower than among men and, therefore, larger numbers of women survive to advanced years; (b) wives are typically younger than their husbands and, consequently, even without the sex differences in mortality have a greater probability of outliving their husbands; (c) among the widowed, remarriage rates are considerably lower for women than men. Other major factors which also have an impact on widowhood status are the effects of war casualties, depressions, and disease pandemics (Jacobson, 1959, pp. 24–27).

[2] Actually, the economic dilemma in which widows often find themselves is frequently brought about as a direct result of the failure of husbands to plan their estates and advise their wives. "The truth is that most men leave their affairs in a jumble. This is not because their lives are unduly complicated, but simply because they can't seem to get around to the task of setting up a program for their families that would automatically go into operation upon their death. Death is unpleasant to think about and always seems remote. The tendency is to put the problem off and plan 'to get to it one of these days' " (*Changing Times*, 1961, pp. 9–14). Moreover, many husbands themselves are incapable of making sensible financial decisions and preparations.

[3] A federally sponsored program which dovetails rather nicely with the employment needs of older widows who lack specialized technical skills is the recently initiated Foster Grandparent Project developed by the Office of Economic Opportunity. Under this project, the federal government awards grants of money to the states to be used to employ older people as "foster grandparents" to work with and serve as companions for the mentally retarded, physically handicapped, delinquent, emotionally disturbed, and dependent and neglected children in institutions, day care centers, and homes (*Look*, 1966, pp. 67–71).

Adler, Leta M. "The Relationship of Marital Status to Incidence and Recovery from Mental Illness," *Social Forces*, 32 (1953):185–194.

Berardo, Felix M., *Social Adaptation to Widowhood Among a Rural-Urban Aged Population*, Washington Agricultural Experiment Station Bulletin 689, 1967, College of Agriculture, Washington State University.

Bogue, Donald T., *The Population of the United States*, Glencoe, Ill.: The Free Press, 1959.

Burchinal, Lee G., "Characteristics of Adolescents from Unbroken, Broken, and Reconstituted Families," *Journal of Marriage and the Family*, 26 (1964):44–51.

Durkheim, Emile, *Suicide: A Study in Sociology*, Glencoe, Ill.: The Free Press, 1951.

Fried, Edrita G. and Karl Stern, "The Situation of the Aged Within the Family," *American Journal of Orthopsychiatry*, 18 (1948):31–54.

"How to Help Your Widow," *Changing Times*, November 1961, 9–14.

Illgenfritz, Marjorie P., "Mothers on Their Own—Widows and Divorcees," *Marriage and Family Living*, 23 (1961): 38–41.

Institute for Life Insurance, *Some Data on Life Insurance Ownership and Related Characteristics of the Older Population*, 1964, (Mimeographed).

Jacobson, Paul H., *American Marriage and Divorce*. New York: Rinehart and Co., Inc., 1959.

"Love is Being Needed," *Look*, August 23, 1966, 67–71.

Metropolitan Life Insurance Company. "Orphanhood—A Continuing Problem," *Statistical Bulletin*, 47 (1966):3–5.

Nye, F. Ivan, "Child Adjustment in Broken and in Unhappy Unbroken Homes," *Marriage and Family Living*, 19 (1957):356–361.

National Consumer Finance Association, *Finance Facts*, Educational Service Division, Washington, D.C., January, 1963, 1.

Peniston, D. Hugh, "The Importance of 'Death Education' in Family Life," *The Family Life Coordinator*, 11 (1962):15–18.

Perry, Joseph P., Jr., and Erdwin H. Pfuhl, Jr., "Adjustment of Children in 'Solo' and 'Remarriage' Homes," *Marriage and Family Living*, 15 (1963): 516–540.

Rees, W. Dewi and Sylvia G. Lutkins, "Mortality of Bereavement," *British Medical Journal*, 4 (1967): 13–16.

Rushing, William A., "Individual Behavior and Suicide," in Jack P. Gibbs (Ed.) *Suicide*, New York: Harper and Row, 1968, Ch. 4.

Waller, Willard. *The Family: A Dynamic Interpretation* (rev. ed. by Reuben Hill), New York: The Dryden Press, 1951.

67

DIVORCE IS A FAMILY AFFAIR

Jack C. Westman and David W. Cline

For most people, divorce is a step two adults take when their marriage fails. Although others obviously are affected, the impact of divorce is seen largely through the eyes of the man and woman. Actually, the penetrating roots of marriage are exposed through the effect of its disintegration on children, relatives, and friends. The fact is that most American divorces occur in families with children. As a result, one out of six youngsters grow up today in homes either anticipating, experiencing, or reverberating to divorce.

Much misunderstanding arises from the popular view of divorce as an *event*, as something that happens crisply and changes everything drastically. Divorce is commonly seen as the end of a relationship, the beginning of a "new life"—as a final closing of an unfruitful marriage—as a correction of error that sets the "books straight." Actually divorce is an *adjustment of relationship* that does not erase the past nor create an unrelated future. For the departing husband it may mean a major change, living alone. For the wife and children life may be much the same, only more difficult. Divorce legally dissolves the marriage, but it only realigns the material and intangible bonds between the affected parties.

As those who have gone through it know, divorce really is a *process* consuming a few or many years, not just the months required to legalize the step. People rarely enter marriage with the expectation that divorce will occur. First there is a period of *disillusionment* that precedes thought and discussion of divorce. During this period, the marriage relationship is strained and the children receive the backwash, even when open conflict has not occurred. At the very least, the rift between the parents creates an atmosphere in which their children lack an image of emotional honesty between adults.

After the disillusionment phase, parents often vacillate in reaching a decision to separate, with or without recourse to counseling. The decision to *separate* then follows. This occurs most commonly about five years after marriage, when children are young. The legal steps involved in *finalizing* the divorce action follow, occurring from 7 to 10 years after marriage. Thereafter, the *aftermath* of divorce consists of the years during which custody, visitation, and financial arrangements are tested and adjusted. Feelings persisting after divorce can be powerful as shown by Goode's sociological study (2), which disclosed that half of a typical group of divorcees either wished to remarry or punish their ex-husbands years after the divorce occurred. All of these things illustrate that divorce is a long, drawn-out experience having its repercussions for the participants in many obvious and subtle ways.

In order to learn more about the actual experiences people have in connection with divorce, we must look beyond the available statistics. We know that divorce occurs 50 percent more frequently today than in 1940, but we know very little about the experience of living through divorce. Some people stress its pain; others its relief. For those concerned with divorce, it would be helpful to know more about typical things that occur. . . .

In order to answer the questions of parents regarding the impact of divorce on their children, a University of Wisconsin research team studied a series of divorces affecting people from all walks of life in Dane County, Wisconsin (4). Information was obtained about what transpired before, during, and after the divorce. All of the cases had received varying degrees of mandatory counseling, a fact that ensured that the divorce was not impulsive. Social work services were also available to help minimize the adverse effects of the divorce. In spite of these efforts, one-third of the divorces involving children were followed by legal contests raised by one of the parties, either regarding the financial settlement, visitation rights, arrears in payments, or custody disputes. Since these disputes came to the attention of the court through litigation, one can only assume that there were other conflicts that did not reach the level of legal action. This evidence clearly points out that divorce did not end the marital conflict in many situations. On the contrary, it affirms that if two people cannot agree before divorce, the likelihood is that they will fare no better after it.

The high incidence of post-divorce litigation indicates that the aftermath of divorce is frequently a turbulent experience for the affected adults and children. By examining each individual case with a turbulent course following the divorce, we sought to uncover the human situation underlying the legal suits. Our study disclosed that each situation was unique in its own right, but that variations occurred on several central themes. We clustered the patterns of divorce experience under the following headings:

1) *Parent-centered post-divorce turbulence*—In these cases the parents after divorce appeared to continue the same conflicts and relationships that existed beforehand. Sometimes one parent tries to use the power and authority of the court to punish or harrass the other spouse by continuing to discredit that spouse in the eyes of the court. As an extreme example, the parents of a 12-year-old girl continually quarreled over her management. Although custody had been awarded to the mother who had fulltime employment, the father continued regular visits and found fault with his former wife's housekeeping, cooking, and control of their daughter. He ultimately initiated court action to obtain custody of his daughter. Study of the court staff disclosed that neither parent was adequately able to meet the needs of the child. Placement in a foster home was arranged.

2) A second pattern was identified in which the post-divorce conflict was *child-centered* in origin. In these situations it appeared that the affected children manipulated the parents to perpetuate continued conflict or to promote reuniting the parents. The effect was to continue an intense relationship between the parents.

Although most children of divorce wish that their parents would reunite under ideal circumstances, these children took active steps to either repair the marriage or return it to its conflict-ridden pre-divorce state. For example, a 9-year-old boy visited his father on weekends and told him stories about the harsh treatment he was receiving from his mother. When he returned home to his mother, he told her about the idyllic existence of his father, leading her to believe that her son was being overindulged by his father. The parents developed exaggerated pictures of what went on in their respective homes. Each parent filed action in court complaining about the adverse influences of the other. When they were brought together and had an opportunity to obtain a more realistic picture of their son's role in exaggerating their concerns, they dropped their complaints and established regular contact to discuss plans for their son. They previously had decided to avoid direct conversation. In effect, their son was trying to bring them together in the only way available to him.

3) Another pattern was found in which *one parent and a child* teamed up to produce an effect on the other parent. Not infrequently a child sided with one parent or the other, though feeling ambivalent underneath. In these cases one parent appeared to deliberately undermine the other through a child. As an illustration, the father of a 13-year-old girl frequently saw her both at home and away on what assumed the form of "dates." He deliberately provoked jealousy in his former wife and promoted his daughter's defiance of her mother. The mother petitioned the court to stop the father's visitation. Investigation of the case led the court to honor the mother's request and help the daughter recognize that her mother bore the responsibility for her upbringing and that her own interests were being subverted by her father.

4) Sometimes the perpetuation of post-divorce turbulence arose from the influence of *relatives*. This pattern confirmed the popular image of "meddling in-laws." In one case the wife's parents always had disapproved of their son-in-law, promoting the divorce obtained by their daughter. After the divorce they encouraged her to demand an increase in support payments. On the other hand, the man's parents also had held longstanding antipathy for their daughter-in-law and her parents. They supported the husband in resisting an increase in alimony. They provoked his concern about the adverse effect of the maternal grandparents on the grandchildren. An active competition actually existed between the grandparents over the favor of the grandchildren. The court ultimately arranged to bring the feuding grandparents together to show them the effect their struggle was having on the grandchildren. This was unsuccessful, but the husband and wife could see more clearly their need to free themselves from their own parents' influence and resist the undermining influence of the grandparents.

5) Other cases defied categorization aside from being so *bizarre* that the truth was stranger than fiction. In these situations the divorce was incidental to continued and pervasive irrational behavior by the adults concerned. A case in point was a couple who had separated from each other 17 times with 3 divorces and 18 reconciliations. . . .

With an appreciation of the turbulence associated with divorce, several general principles about the child's side of divorce merit attention (4). From the point of view of the affected children, divorce requires a number of important adjustments: 1) to the anxiety, confusion, and strife of the conflict-ridden marriage, 2) to the absence of an image of adults with mutual affection and respect, 3) to the compromise of routine child-rearing responsibilities accompanying the disintegrating marriage, 4) to the prospect of change in parent relationships, and 5) to the parents' preoccupation with rearranging their own emotions and lives, leading to a reduction in attention to the children, or, in some cases, to an over-reliance on the children for support. If divorce were an event that occurred quickly, these associated repercussions would be minimized. The process of divorce is lengthy, however. These side-effects are important and persistent realities for the affected children.

The specific ideas children entertain about the causes of divorce warrant special consideration. Because of their immaturity and natural tendency to see the world only through their own eyes, children generally exaggerate their own roles in causing the divorce. Frequently the cost of supporting children and the general burdens of raising children are reasons husbands give for leaving home. In addition, arguments between parents often revolve around the misbehavior and management of children. There ordinarily are many "proofs," such as these, in the minds of children that they are, in fact, the villains causing the divorce. Furthermore, children understandably feel that the departing parent is rejecting or abandoning them, perhaps, because they have not been "good" sons or daughters. All of these "half-truths" are exaggerated by inner negative feelings that children have about their parents' marriage. On one hand, they rely heavily upon the preservation of their parents' marriage. But on the opposite side the children feel jealousy at being excluded from the intimacy of their parents' relationship. Every child has moments when he feels like "running away" and finding an ideal home, when he wishes for better parents. These moments are more common in homes prone to divorce. All of these fantasies lead children, particularly the young, to automatically assume that the fracture of their parents' marriage has something to do with their hidden wish that it might occur.

The fact that the parents have mixed feelings before, during, and after the divorce inevitably contributes to uncertainty and confusion in the minds of their children. But frequently, a divorced woman may be unable to recognize her own wish for reunion, or her own hurt over her husband's remarriage, only to find that her 8-year-old son can speak these thoughts openly.

Turning to suggestions about handling divorce with children, the uniqueness of each situation highlights the folly of generalization. Much can be done to clarify the constructive management of the divorce experience for concerned parents through professional counseling with a psychiatrist, social worker, or psychologist. Although it is too early to document the specific effects, it is realistic to view divorce as potentially disadvantageous to children, and to give thought to minimizing adverse outcome.

Generally speaking, the hazards of divorce for children result not only from stressful events but because of misunderstandings (3). Every effort should be made to help the children understand the realities of the divorce experience. The keynote is to provide knowledge about what is happening and promote acceptance of it. All of this may take years and may be quite difficult, because many divorced couples themselves are not sure about what is going on. This leads to a series of simple, yet often overlooked, considerations:

1) The responsibility for making the decision to divorce belongs with the adults and not the children.

2) It is important for the children that the divorcing couple agree upon the realistic reasons for the divorce. Counseling can be used not only to prevent divorce but also to more adequately clarify why it is taking place.

3) Then, if the adults concerned know what they are doing and have a reasonable idea about why, this information can be shared realistically with the children. Paradoxically, it is difficult for many divorcing parents to admit to their children that they don't like each other, and that the divorce is a result of their being "bad" for each other. These parents prefer to say the divorce is occurring under "friendly" terms. This approach only mystifies children, who may have witnessed the opposite, or, if they haven't, may only conclude that the parents are withholding the truth, namely that they are getting divorced because of the children. It is also helpful for the children to know that the divorce is calculated to make each of the parents happier than they would be if they remained together. Nothing burdens the children more than feeling that their parents are going to continue to be unhappy, or unhappier, following what ought to be a problem-solving action. Facing these issues openly, although difficult to do, is profitable for the divorcing couple. When parents try to discuss their situation with their children, they discover their own irrational, and poorly understood, motivations in the divorce action. For the same reason many parents find themselves avoiding discussions with their children in order to hide their own uncertainty.

4) It is most important for parents to tailor the divorce settlement to their own situation. Many settlements are made in moments of desperation, indifference, or vengeance. The financial settlement should be enough, but not too much, so that it becomes unrealistic for the father to continue payments. Many children lose contact with their fathers because of excessive alimony and child support that may even cause the father to leave the state in order to avoid prosecution. This is particularly meaningful because many fathers remarry

and assume the cost of raising two families. Visitation should be flexible and responsive to the children's needs: enough contact, but not impractically and rigidly prescribed. Sometimes fathers feel obliged to take their children for a whole weekend, spending more time together than fathers and children ordinarily need or desire. Older children may be much more interested in their own friends and resent an obligation to see their equally ambivalent parent.

5) Often feelings of embarrassment, shame, or inadequacy stand in the way of a needed and still potentially rewarding relationship between parent and child. The father is still "my Dad" and needed by the child as an image. Sustained interest in the child on the part of the parent, however small, is treasured. Whatever defects the parents have are readily forgiven by a youngster who naturally tends to idealize his parents. The departing parent will help his child if he has something special to symbolize their bond. Today we [tend] to underestimate the importance of family possessions and heirlooms that are particularly important when homes are broken and families dispersed.

6) Direct, continued planning by the separated parents around matters of child management is essential. Pride and bitterness frequently intrude, but the children's interests are best served if they are being mutually protected by the parents. Intermediaries between the parents on these matters cannot substitute for direct discussion. Misunderstandings and conflict are heightened when others are interposed, especially if the intermediaries stand to benefit from perpetuated conflict.

7) Discussing and working-through the divorce, its causes, and sequelae are a lifelong matter for affected children and their parents. One should not overlook the character building aspects of having lived through a stressful and painful experience. Many basic lessons in life can be learned through being the child of a divorced couple. One adult said she did not really understand why her own parents divorced each other until she became married herself. Only then could she understand why her parents separated.

8) The age of the child inevitably arises as a consideration in talking about divorce. Families have children of different ages, and each one has a unique capacity to understand and accept. Generally divorce has the greatest impact between the ages of 3 and 7 and runs the greatest risk of being misunderstood during those years. And this is the age span of most children experiencing divorces. During these early years the tendency to blame oneself and infer rejection by the departing parent are the greatest and the ability to understand the complexities the least. An important guideline is to stress simple facts, for example, that the parents don't like each other anymore, that they have changed their minds about being married, that they fight and argue, if they do. Whatever the child has heard and observed should be confirmed. If the child knows another woman is in Daddy's life, he deserves to know that his own Mommy has been hurt. The details of what will happen are also important: that Daddy will leave, and come back to visit; that he will have another place to live; that he will see the children and have birthday and Christmas celebrations or whatever the agreed-upon arrangements are; and that Mommy and Daddy are sad about this, if they are, but also that they are glad, if they are.

9) During the elementary years it is possible to emphasize for the child the human frailties of the parents. The child's questions will provide cues as to how much he wishes to know. During preadolescent years the child's self-esteem and standing with his peer group are the most vulnerable, so he will profit from awareness of the advantages of the divorce. Adolescents have more direct experience to go by since they have been with the situation longer. They have the mental and emotional maturity to understand, and they can handle all of the details. But the adolescent is still too young to be burdened with participation in making the decision to divorce.

The increasing availability of child psychiatrists and community mental health services for children offers further aid in handling problem situations and providing preventive counseling to concerned parents.

Divorce is a fact of American life and deserves objective study rather than indifference, condemnation, or neglect. It may have redeeming features, but from the point of view of children divorce remains a stressful experience both because of the disruption of the home and the way of life caused by the disillusionment, separation, finalizing, and aftermath of the divorce action itself. Divorce is expensive in cost, energy, and repercussions. The adverse impact can be minimized by realistic and sensitive attention to its effects on children. We should recognize that divorce does not end anything. It is merely an alteration in the living arrangements of affected families.

REFERENCES

1. Gardner, R. A. *The Boys and Girls Book About Divorce.* New York: Science House, Inc., 1970.
2. Goode, William J. *Women in Divorce.* New York: Free Press Paperback, 1965.
3. Steinzor, B. *When Parents Divorce.* New York: Pantheon Books, 1969.
4. Westman, J. C., Cline, D. W., Swift, W. J. and Kramer, D. A. "The Role of Child Psychiatry in Divorce." *Archives of General Psychiatry,* 23 (November 1970):416–420.

68

PARENTS WITHOUT PARTNERS

E. E. LeMasters

In thinking about parents it is easy to assume a model of what might be termed "the biological parent team" of mother and father. In this model two parents act as partners in carrying out the parental functions. Furthermore, both of the parents are biological as well as social parents. It is this parent team model that is analyzed in most of the chapters in this book.

What is not realized by many observers, especially by parent critics, is the fact that a considerable proportion of contemporary American parents do not operate under these ideal conditions. These parents include "parents without partners" (mostly divorced or separated women, but including a few men also); widows and widowers with children; unmarried mothers; adoptive parents; stepparents; and, finally, foster parents.

Some of the groups in the list above are amazingly large—Simon, for example, reports that in the 1960s in the United States there were about *seven million* children living with a stepparent. This means that approximately one out of every nine children in modern America is a stepchild.

MOTHERS WITHOUT FATHERS

One of the by now familiar parental types in our society is the mother rearing her children alone. As of 1960 about one household out of ten in the United States was headed by a woman. In an earlier, more innocent America, this mother without father was seen as a heroic figure—a brave woman whose husband had died who was struggling to rear her brood by scrubbing floors, taking in family laundry, and so on. This was the brave little widow of an earlier day.

After the end of World War I, as the divorce rate began to climb, this picture—and this woman—underwent a radical change. With the rapid improvement of American medicine, marriages in the early and middle decades of life were no longer broken primarily by death; now the great destroyers of marriages came to be social and psychological, not biological.

With this shift the public's attitude toward the mother with no father by her side changed drastically—it became ambivalent. In some cases she might be viewed with sympathy and understanding, if she happened to be your sister or a close friend, but more often she was perceived as a woman of questionable character—either the gay divorcee of the upper-social class levels or the ADC mother living off of the taxpayers at the lower social-class levels. In either case the image was a far cry from that of the heroic little widow of the Victorian era.

Statistically, and otherwise, these mothers without fathers fall into five different categories: divorced, separated, deserted, widowed, and never married. All of these categories overlap, so that some mothers might at some point in their lives occupy all five positions in the list.

Our procedure in discussing these mothers in their parental role will be to identify the generic patterns and problems shared by all of these mothers, and then to look at the relatively unique patterns that cluster about any specific position. . . .

1. *Poverty.* It has been estimated that while households headed by a woman comprise only about 10 percent of all U.S. households, they constitute about 25 percent of the families in the so-called poverty group in American society.

In the best study yet published on divorced women, Goode found financial stress to be a major complaint. At any given time approximately 40 percent of the divorced husbands in this study were delinquent in their support payments, a pattern that seems to be nationwide.

Poverty is extremely relative, as is deprivation. A divorced woman receiving even $1,000 a month in support payments may have to reduce her standard of living from what it was before her divorce.

The reasons for the financial difficulties of these mothers are not mysterious or difficult to identify. Most American men cannot afford to support two living establishments on a high level. This is one reason why some support payments are delinquent. The man usually gets involved with at least one other woman, and this costs money. Often his new woman is not well off financially and the man may find himself contributing to her support also.

Since a considerable proportion of divorced women are apparently employed at the time of their divorce, they had what is commonly called a two-income family. The mother may continue to work after the father has left the home, but with two living establishments to maintain, two cars, and so on, the financial situation tends to be tight.

In a study of ADC mothers in Boston, it was discovered that these women faced financial crises almost monthly. They coped with these difficult situations by accepting aid from members of their family; by pooling their resources with neighbors and women friends in the same plight; and by occasional aid from a boy friend.

In several counseling cases with divorced women, the writer was impressed with the annoying feature of the relative poverty experienced by these women—one woman didn't have the money to get her television set repaired and this created tension between herself and her children. Another woman, who lived in an area with inadequate bus service, could not afford an automobile. Any person in our society can understand how frustrating problems of this nature can be.

2. *Role conflicts.* Since these women have added the father role to their parental responsibilities, they tend to be either

overloaded or in conflict over their various role commitments. The presence of a husband-father provides more role flexibility than these women now have—if the mother is ill, or has to work late, the husband may be able to be home with the children.

When these mothers are employed outside of the home, as a sizable proportion are, the work hours usually conflict with those of the school system. Children leave for school too late, get home too early, and have far too many vacations for the employed mother. There are also childhood illnesses that must be coped with.

It is true that the termination of the marriage has reduced or eliminated the mother's role as wife, but she is still a woman in the early decades of life and men will be in the picture sooner or later. Thus she may not be a wife at the moment but she will soon be a girl friend, and the courtship role may be even more demanding than that of wife.

It is the writer's belief, based on numerous interviews with divorced women, that being the head of a household is, for most women, an 18-hour day, seven days a week, and 365 days a year job. It would seem that only the most capable, and the most fortunate, can perform all of the roles involved effectively.

3. *Role shifts.* Since the vast majority of the mothers being discussed here—80 to 90 percent—will eventually remarry, they face the difficult process of taking over the father role and then relinquishing it. This is not easy for most of us; once we have appropriated a role in a family system, it is often difficult to turn it over to somebody else.

Furthermore, these mothers operate in an unusual family system in that, for an indefinite period, they do not have to worry about what the other parent thinks. They are both mother and father for the time being.

This is not entirely true, of course, in the case of the divorced woman, but it seems to be largely true, even for this group. The departed father starts out with the best intentions of "not forgetting my kids," but a variety of factors tend to reduce his parental influence as time goes on. . . .

4. *Public attitudes.* These mothers are operating in deviant family situations, and for the most part the community tends to regard them and their children as deviants. Except for the widow, all of these mothers are viewed with some ambivalence in our society. They receive some sympathy, some respect, and some help, but they are also viewed as women who are not "quite right" —they did not sustain their marriage "until death do us part."

The unmarried mother, of course, never had a marriage to sustain and the public has no ambivalence about her; they simply condemn her and that's that.

If these mothers require support from public welfare they will find the community's mixed feelings reflected in their monthly check—the community will not permit them and their children to starve, but it will also not allow them to live at a decent level.

We have now examined some of the generic problems of the one-parent family system, except for the system in which the one parent is a father, which will be looked at later. Now let us analyze the specific features of the subsystems in the one-parent family. . . .

1. *The divorced mother.* The divorced mother has several advantages over the deserted mother: she at least has had the help of a domestic-relations court in spelling out the financial responsibility of the father, also the legal arrangements for custody. In this sense divorce is a lot less messy than desertion in our society.

The divorced mother is also legally free to associate with other men and to remarry if she finds the right person—advantages the deserted woman does not have.

The divorced father, it seems to us, is not in an enviable position in his role as father. He may be happy not to be married to his children's mother any more but he often hates to be separated from his children. In a sense he still has the responsibility of a father for his minor children but few of the enjoyments of parenthood. To be with his children he has to interact to some degree with his former wife—a process so painful that he was willing to have the marriage terminated.

In an unpublished study of 80 divorced

men, one of the most frequent regrets expressed by the men was their frustration and concern about their relationship to their children.

The divorced mother has one parental advantage that she shares with all other parents without partners; she does not have to share the daily parental decisions with a partner who might not agree with her strategy. In the Goode study of divorced women, the mothers seemed to think this was an advantage. The parental partner can be of great help if the two parents can agree on how their children should be reared, but when this is not the case one parent can probably do a better job going it alone.

2. *The deserted mother.* It has already been indicated that desertions in our society are more messy than divorces. There are two reasons: (1) desertion is more apt to be unilateral with the decision to pull out being made by one party alone; and (2) there is no court supervision of the desertion process—it is unplanned from society's point of view.

The deserted mother is likely to have more severe financial problems than the divorced mother because support payments have not been agreed upon.

Psychologically, desertion is probably more traumatic than divorce, partly because it is more unilateral but also because it is less planned. To the extent that this is true—and we recognize that the evidence on this point is not conclusive—then the deserted mother is handicapped in her parental role by her emotional upheaval or trauma.

This woman also has other problems; she is legally not free to remarry and in a sense not even free to go out with other men since she is technically still a married woman. These feelings, of course, will tend to reflect the social class and the moral subculture of the particular woman.

3. *The separated mother.* If we assume that most marital separations in modern America have been arrived at by mutual agreement, then this mother has certain advantages over the deserted mother. One disadvantage is that her courtship status is ambiguous; another is that she is not free

to remarry. Psychologically, the separated mother should reflect patterns similar to those of the divorced mother: her marriage has failed but she has done something about it and now has to plan for her future life.

4. *The widowed mother.* The one big advantage of this parent is the favorable attitude of her family, her friends, and the community toward her. This tends to be reflected in her self-image, thus giving her emotional support. Once she emerges from the period of bereavement, however, she has to face about the same problems as the women discussed previously—she probably will have financial problems; she will have to be father as well as mother. . . .

5. *The unmarried mother.* This is not the place to review the status and problems of the unmarried mother in our society—the literature on this woman is quite voluminous. It only needs to be said here that this mother has all of the problems of the women discussed before plus a few of her own. She is more likely to be a member of a racial minority—one of the extra burdens she has to shoulder. She is also more likely to be on public welfare—a major burden in itself in our society. Her chances for marriage are not as gloomy as some people once thought, but her chances for a successful marriage may be more dubious. . . .

FATHER-ONLY FAMILIES

It has been estimated that approximately 600,000 U.S. families have only a father present in the home at any given time. This figure seems large but is small compared to the 4 to 5 million American families in which only a mother is present.

There seems to be relatively little research data available on these "father-only" families. Since custody of minor children is awarded to the mother in our divorce courts in 90 to 95 percent of the cases, it seems logical to assume that the bulk of these "fathers without mothers" represent either desertion or the death of the mother.

It seems likely that these fathers do not continue indefinitely to rear their children alone, that the majority of them remarry, in which case they would experience the same problems of role shifts discussed earlier for mothers on their own.

It also seems likely that these men experience role conflicts between their jobs, their social life, and their parental responsibility.

It is doubtful that these solo fathers would suffer from poverty to the extent found among solo mothers—but the writer has no data to cite in support of this statement.

The rat race experienced by mothers rearing families without the help of a father would likely be found among these men also; it simply reflects what might be termed "role overload."

Psychologically, . . . these men probably suffer from the same syndrome found among mothers who have lost their husbands—loneliness, sorrow, perhaps bitterness, often a sense of failure, plus a feeling of being overwhelmed by their almost complete responsibility for their children. About the only effective treatment for feelings of this nature is to find a new partner and get married—the solution most adult Americans rely on for whatever ails them. These fathers are no exception to this statement.

It would appear that these men have a few problems that would be less likely to bother mothers: the physical care of preschool children and the tasks of home management, such as shopping for food and clothes, preparing meals, doing the family laundry, and cleaning the house. Some men become quite adept at this women's work after awhile, but for others a stove or an iron remains a mystery forever. . . .

Most of us probably assume that the one-parent family is inherently pathological—at least for the children involved. It seems only logical to assume that two parents are better than one—the old adage that two heads are better than one.

In his text on the American family, Bell summarizes several studies that question the assumption that two parents are better than one—judging by the adjustment of the children. This, however, does not say anything about the impact of solo child rearing on the parent, which is the major concern of this book.

If one wishes to debate the number of adults required to socialize children properly the question can be raised: who decided that *two* parents was the proper number. Biologically this is natural enough, but this does not prove its social rightness.

As a matter of fact, a good family sociologist, Farber, has asked the question—"Are two parents enough? . . . In almost every human society *more* than two adults are involved in the socialization of the child."

Farber goes on to point out that in many societies a "third parent," outside of the nuclear family, acts as a sort of "social critic" of the child.

In a recent review of the literature on the one-parent family by Kadushin, the data did not seem sufficient to support the hypothesis that the one-parent family is inherently dysfunctional or pathological. It has been demonstrated by Schorr that the one-parent family is considerably overrepresented in the American poverty population and also on our public welfare rolls. This does not prove, however, that these families are inherently dysfunctional; it merely proves that our economic, political, and social welfare systems are not properly organized to provide an adequate standard of living for the one-parent family. A casual drive through many rural areas in America, especially Appalachia and the rural South, will soon demonstrate to an unbiased observer that the mere presence of *two* parents does not assure a decent standard of living for a family in our society.

To prove that the one-parent family is inherently pathological one would have to demonstrate that the system generates a disproportionate amount of personal disorganization. Kadushin's search of the literature did not reveal enough firm research data to support such a conclusion. This, of course, does not prove that one parent in the home is as good as two—it simply says that the research to date is not adequate to answer the question.

It is obvious to any clinician that the two-parent system has its own pathology—the two parents may be in serious conflict as to how their parental roles should be performed; one parent may be competent but have his (or her) efforts undermined by the incompetent partner; the children may be caught in a "double bind" or crossfire between the two parents; both parents may be competent but simply unable to work together as an effective team in rearing their children; one parent may be more competent than the other but be inhibited in using this competence by the team pattern inherent in the two-parent system.

The writer happens to believe that one *good* parent is enough to rear children adequately or better in our society. It seems to us that enough prominent Americans have been reared by widows or other solo parents to prove the point.

It is interesting to note that adoption agencies are taking another look at the one-parent family and that some agencies are now willing to consider single persons as potential adoptive parents.

69

THE SIX STATIONS OF DIVORCE

Paul Bohannan

Divorce is a complex social phenomenon as well as a complex personal experience. Because most of us are ignorant of what it requires of us, divorce is likely to be traumatic: emotional stimulation is so great that accustomed ways of acting are inadequate. The usual way for the healthy mind to deal with trauma is to block it out, then let it reappear slowly, so it is easier to manage. The blocking may appear as memory lapses or as general apathy.

On a social level we do something analogous, not allowing ourselves to think fully about divorce as a social problem. Our personal distrust of the emotions that surround it leads us to consider it only with traditional cultural defenses. Our ignorance masquerades as approval or disapproval, as enlightenment or moral conviction.[1]

The complexity of divorce arises because at least six things are happening at once. They may come in a different order and with varying intensities, but there are at least these six different experiences of separation. They are the more painful and puzzling as personal experiences because society is not yet equipped to handle any of them well, and some of them we do not handle at all.

I have called these six overlapping experiences (1) the emotional divorce, which centers around the problem of the deteriorating marriage; (2) the legal divorce, based on grounds; (3) the economic divorce, which deals with money and property; (4) the coparental divorce, which deals with custody, single-parent homes, and visitation; (5) the community divorce, surrounding the changes of friends and community that every divorcee experiences; and (6) the psychic divorce, with the problem of regaining individual autonomy.

The first visible stage of a deteriorating marriage is likely to be what psychiatrists call emotional divorce. This occurs when the spouses withhold emotion from their relationship because they dislike the intensity or ambivalence of their feelings. They may continue to work together as a social team, but their attraction and trust for one another have disappeared. The self-regard of each is no longer reinforced by love for the other. The emotional divorce is experienced as an unsavory choice between giving in and hating oneself and domineering and hating oneself. The natural and healthy "growing apart" of a married couple is very different. As marriages mature, the partners grow in new directions, but also establish bonds of ever greater interdependence. With emotional divorce, people do not grow together as they grow apart —they become, instead, mutually antagonistic and imprisoned, hating the vestiges of their dependence. Two people in emotional divorce grate on each other because each is disappointed.

In American society, we have turned over to the courts the responsibility for formalizing the dissolution of such a marriage. The legislature (which in early English law usurped the responsibility from the church, and then in the American colonies turned it over to the courts) makes the statutes and defines the categories into which every marital dispute must be thrust if legal divorce is possible. Divorce is not "legalized" in many societies but may be done by a church or even by contract. Even in our own society, there is only one thing that a divorce court can do that cannot be done more effectively some other way—establish the right to remarry. As long as your spouse lives, you cannot legally remarry until you are legally divorced. Because of the legal necessity of this one aspect, several other aspects of divorce are customarily taken care of by lawyers and judges. However, legal divorce itself does nothing but create remarriageability.

The economic divorce must occur because in Western countries husband and wife are an economic unit. Their unity is recognized by the law. They can—and in some states must—own property as a single "legal person." While technically the couple is not a corporation, they certainly have many of the characteristics of a legal corporation. At the time the household is broken up by divorce, an economic settlement must be made, separating the assets of the "corporation" into two sets of assets, each belonging to one person. This is the property settlement. Today it is vastly complicated by income tax law. A great deal of knowledge is required to take care of the tax positions of divorced persons—and if the lawyer does not have this knowledge, he must get assistance. Although the judges may ratify the property settlement, they usually do not create it unless the principals and lawyers cannot do so.

The coparental divorce is necessary if there are children. When the household breaks up, the children have to live somewhere. Taking care of the children requires complex arrangements for carrying out the obligations of parents.

All divorced persons suffer more or less because their community is altered. Friends necessarily take a different view of a person during and after divorce—he ceases to be a part of a couple. Their own inadequacies, therefore, will be projected in a new way. Their fantasies are likely to change as they focus on the changing situation. In many cases, the change in community attitude— and perhaps people too—is experienced by a divorcee as ostracism and disapproval. For many divorcing people, the divorce from community may make it seem that nothing in the world is stable.

Finally comes the psychic divorce. It is almost always last, and always the most difficult. Indeed, I have not found a word strong or precise enough to describe the difficulty or the process. Each partner to the ex-marriage, either before or after the legal divorce—usually after, and sometimes years after—must turn himself or herself again into an autonomous social individual. People who have been long married tend to have become socially part of a couple or a family; they lose the habit of seeing themselves as individuals. This is worse for people who married in order to avoid becoming autonomous individuals in the first place.

To become an individual again, at the center of a new community, requires developing new facets of character. Some people have forgotten how to do it—some never learned. The most potent argument against teen-age marriages is that they are likely to occur between people who are searching for independence but avoiding autonomy. The most potent argument against hurried remarriage is the same: avoidance of the responsibilities of autonomy.

Divorce is an institution that nobody enters without great trepidation. In the emotional divorce, people are likely to feel hurt and angry. In the legal divorce, people often feel bewildered—they have lost control, and events sweep them along. In the economic divorce, the reassignment of property and the division of money (there is *never* enough) may make them feel cheated. In the parental divorce they worry about what is going to happen to the children; they feel guilty for what they have done. With the community divorce, they may get angry with their friends and perhaps suffer despair because there seems to be no fidelity in friendship. In the psychic divorce, in which they have to become autonomous again, they are probably afraid and are certainly lonely. However, the resolution of any or all of these various six divorces may provide an elation of victory that comes from having accomplished something that had to be done and having done it well. There may be ultimate satisfactions in it.

Divorce American style is a bewildering experience—so many things are happening at once. We have never been taught what we are supposed to do, let alone what we are supposed to feel. I know a divorced man who took great comfort in the fact that one of his business associates asked him, when he learned of his divorce, "Do I feel sorry for you or do I congratulate you?" He thought for a moment and said—out of bravado as much as conviction—"Congratulate me." It was, for him, the beginning of the road back.

THE EMOTIONAL DIVORCE AND THE PROBLEMS OF GRIEF

One of the reasons it feels so good to be engaged and newly married is the rewarding sensation that, out of the whole world, you have been selected. One of the reasons that divorce feels so awful is that you have been deselected. It punishes almost as much as the engagement and the wedding are rewarding.

The chain of events and feelings that lead up to divorce are as long and as varied as the chain of events that lead up to being selected for marriage. The difference is that the feelings are concentrated in the area of the weak points in the personality rather than the growing points of the personality.

Almost no two people who have been married, even for a short time, can help knowing where to hit each other if they want to wound. On the other hand, any two people—no matter who they are—who are locked together in conflict have to be very perceptive to figure out what the strain is really all about. Marital fights occur in every healthy marriage. The fact of health is indicated when marital disputes lead to a clarification of issues and to successful extension of the relationship into new areas. Difficulties arise only when marital conflict is sidetracked to false issues (and sometimes the discovery of just what issue is at stake may be, in itself, an adequate conclusion to the conflict), or when the emotional pressures are shunted to other areas. When a couple are afraid to fight over the real issue, they fight over something else—and perhaps never discover what the real issue was.

Two of the areas of life that are most ready to accept such displacement are the areas of sex and money. Both sex and money are considered worthwhile fighting over in American culture. If it is impossible to know or admit what a fight is all about, then the embattled couple may cast about for areas of displacement, and they come up with money and sex, because both can be used as weapons. Often these are not the basis of the difficulties, which lie in unconscious or inadmissible areas.

These facts lead a lot of people to think that emotional divorce occurs over money or over sexual incompatibility just because that is where the overt strife is allowed to come out. Often, however, these are only camouflage.

Money and the Emotional Divorce

One of the most tenacious ideas from our early training is "the value of a dollar." When in the larger society the self is reflected in possessions, and when money becomes one mode of enhancing the self—then we have difficulty with anybody who either spends it too lavishly or sits on it more tightly than we do.

Money is a subject about which talk is possible. Most middle-class couples do talk about money; most of them, in fact, make compromises more or less adequate to both. But in all cases, money management and budgeting are endlessly discussed in the American household. If communication becomes difficult, one of the first places that it shows up is in absence of knowledge about the other person's expenditures.

I interviewed one divorced woman who blamed her ex-husband's spending practices and attitude toward money as a major factor in their divorce. She said that he bought her an expensive car and asked her to leave it sitting outside the house when she was not driving it. *She* announced that *he* could not afford it. He asked her to join a golf club. She refused, although she was a good golfer and liked to play—because *she* told him *he* could not afford it. Whenever he wanted to use her considerable beauty and accomplishments to reflect a little credit on himself for being able to have captured and kept such a wife, she announced that he could not afford it. After the divorce, it continued. Then one day, in anger, she telephoned him to say that she was tired of making sacrifices—this year she was going to take the children on a transcontinental vacation and that he would simply have to pay for the trip. He did not explode; he only thought for a minute and said that he guessed that would be all right, and that he would whittle down his plans for the children's vacation with him, so that it would come within the budget.

This woman told this story without realizing what she had revealed: that her husband was not going to push himself or them into bankruptcy; that he did indeed know how much things cost, and that he could either afford or otherwise manage what he wanted to give her. There was doubtless a difference of opinion about money—she, it appears, preferred to save and then spend; he preferred, perhaps, to spend and then pay. She, for reasons I cannot know

from one extended interview, did not recognize his feelings. She *did* announce to him, every time that he wanted to spend money on her, that he was inadequate. I suspect it was her own fear that she would let him down. Without knowing it, she was attacking him where it hurt him and where her housewifely virtue could be kept intact, while she did not have to expose herself or take a chance.

I am not saying that there are not spendthrift husbands or wives. I am saying that if differences that lie beyond money cannot be discussed, then money is a likely battleground for the emotional divorce.

Sex and the Emotional Divorce

Among the hundreds of divorcees I have talked to, there is a wide range of sexual attitudes. There were marriages in which sexual symptoms were the first difficulties to be recognized by the couple. There were a few in which the sexual association seemed the only strong bond. I know of several instances in which the couple met for a ceremonial bout of sexual intercourse as the last legitimate act before their divorce. I have a newspaper clipping that tells of a man who, after such a "last legal assignation," murdered his wife before she became his ex-wife. And I know one divorce that was denied because, as the judge put it, he could not condone "litigation by day and copulation by night."

Usually, when communication between the spouses becomes strained, sexual rapport is the first thing to go. There are many aspects to this problem: sexual intercourse is the most intimate of social relationships, and reservations or ambivalences in the emotions are likely to show up there (with unconscious conflicts added to conscious ones). The conflicts may take the extreme form of frigidity in women, impotence in men. They may take the form of adultery, which may be an attempt to communicate something, an unconscious effort to improve the marriage itself. It may be an attempt to humiliate the spouse into leaving. Adultery cannot sensibly be judged without knowing what it means to a specific person and to his spouse in a specific situation. Adultery is a legal ground for divorce in every jurisdiction in the United States, and indeed in most of the record-keeping world.

Because sexuality is closely associated with integration of the personality, it is not surprising that disturbance in the relationship of the spouses may be exposed in sexual symptoms. Except in some cases in which the marriage breaks up within a few weeks or months, however, sexual difficulties are a mode of expression as often as they provide the basic difficulty.

Growing Apart

Married people, like any other people, must continue to grow as individuals if they are not to stagnate. Only by extending themselves to new experiences and overcoming new conflicts can they participate fully in new social relationships and learn new culture. That means that no one, at the time of marriage, can know what the spouse is going to become. Moreover, it means that he cannot know what he himself may become.

Some of this growth of individuals must necessarily take place outside of the marriage. If the two people are willing and able to perceive and tolerate the changes in one another, and overcome them by a growing relationship directly with the other person, then the mutual rewards are very great, and conflicts can be resolved.

Inability to tolerate change in the partner (or to see him as he is) always lies, I think, at the root of emotional divorce. All marriages become constantly more attenuated from the end of the honeymoon period probably until the retirement of the husband from the world of affairs. That is to say, the proportion of the total concern of one individual that can be given to the other individual in the marriage decreases, even though the precise quantity (supposing there were a way to measure it) might become greater. But the ties may become tougher, even as they become thinner.

When this growing apart and concomitant increase in the toughness of the bonds

does *not* happen, then people feel the marriage bonds as fetters and become disappointed or angry with each other. They feel cramped by the marriage and cheated by their partner. A break may be the only salvation for some couples.

In America today, our emotional lives are made diffuse by the very nature of the culture with which we are surrounded. Family life, business or professional demands, community pressures—today all are in competition with one another for our time and energies. When that happens, the social stage is set for emotional divorce of individual couples, because the marriage relationship becomes just another competing institution. Sometimes emotional divorce seems scarcely more than another symptom of the diffuseness.

Emotional Divorce and Grief

Emotional divorce results in the loss of a loved object just as fully—but by quite a different route of experience—as does the death of a spouse. Divorce is difficult because it involves a purposeful and active rejection by another person, who, merely by living, is a daily symbol of the rejection. It is also made difficult because the community helps even less in divorce than it does in bereavement.

The natural reaction to the loss of a loved object or person (and sometimes a hated one as well) is grief. The distribution of emotional energy is changed significantly; new frustration must be borne until new arrangements can be worked out. Human beings mourn every loss of meaningful relationship. The degree depends on the amount of emotional involvement. Mourning may be traumatic—and it may, like any other trauma, have to be blocked and only slowly allowed into awareness. Mourning may take several months or years.

Divorce is even more threatening than death to some people, because they have thought about it more, perhaps wished for it more consciously. But most importantly—there is no recognized way to mourn a divorce. The grief has to be worked out alone and without benefit of traditional rites, because few people recognize it for what it is.

When grief gets entangled with all the other emotions that are evoked in a divorce, the emotional working through becomes complicated—in a divorce one is very much on his own.

THE LEGAL DIVORCE AND THE PROBLEM OF GROUNDS

Judicial divorce, as it is practiced in the United States today, is a legal post-mortem on the demise of an intimate relationship. It originated in Massachusetts in the early 1700s as a means for dealing with the problems that emotional divorce caused in families, at the same time that all going households could continue to be based on holy matrimony. Legal divorce has been discovered and used many times in the history of the world, but this particular institution had no precursors in European history. The historical period in which it developed is important. In those days it was considered necessary that the state could profess its interest in the marriage and the family only in the guise of punishing one of the spouses for misconduct. Thus, the divorce itself was proclaimed to be the punishment of the guilty party. Whether divorce as a punishment was ever a common-sensical idea is a moot point—certainly it is not so today. Yet, our law still reflects this idea.

Thus, if the state is to grant divorces to "innocent" spouses as punishment to offending spouses, it must legalize certain aspects of the family—must, in fact, establish minimal standards of performance in family roles. Marriages break down in all societies; we have come, by state intervention, to solve some of these breakdowns with the legal institution of divorce. Until very recently, no country granted its citizens the clear right to divorce, as they have the clear right to marry. The right is always conditional on acts of misbehavior of the spouse, as misbehavior has been legally defined and called "grounds." Whatever the spouse does must be thrust into the categories that the law recognizes before it can be grounds for divorce.

This way of handling divorce has some strange and unintended effects. It has made lawyers into experts in several aspects of divorce; there are no recognized experts in other aspects of divorce. Therefore, lawyers are called upon to assume responsibility for more and more aspects of the institution—and in many they have no training, in others there is no possible legal base from which they can operate. The difficulty in legal divorce in America seems to lie in two related situations: the uncertainty of the population and even of the legal profession about what the lawyers are supposed to do, and the absence of institutions paralleling the legal institutions to handle the nonlegal problems.

Divorce Lawyers and What They Do

If you want a physician, you look in the yellow pages and find them noted, most of them with their specialties spelled out. With lawyers it is not so—there is only a list. It is an unfortunate by-product of the ethical commitment of the American Bar Association not to advertise that attorneys cannot list their special competences. It is my opinion that, at least as far as family lawyers are concerned (the only exception now allowed is patent law), this ruling should be changed.

The legal profession is committed to the proposition that any lawyer—or at least any firm of lawyers—should be able to handle any sort of problem. Legally, divorce is indeed a simple matter; that is part of the trouble. Any competent lawyer can indeed write the papers and make the necessary motions. The difficulty comes in the counseling aspect of divorce practice.

Every divorcing person must find his lawyer—and it may be difficult. It may be done through friends, business associates, clergymen, but it is surprisingly often done in the yellow pages. Perhaps there is no other situation in our country today in which a person in emotional distress is so faced with buying a pig in a poke. Clients who are inexperienced may not realize that they can fire a lawyer faster than they can hire him. They worry along with a lawyer they neither like personally nor trust professionally.

Because lawyers are for the most part untrained in family psychology and sociology, and because there is no practice—not even the criminal law—in which they are dealing with people in such states of emotional upset, divorce becomes a "messy" or "dirty" kind of practice—these are their words. In the hierarchy of lawyers by specialties (and there is a rigid and fairly overt hierarchy), the divorce lawyer and criminal lawyer rank approximately at the bottom—allowing, of course, for such considerations as ethics, financial success, social rank, and the like. My own opinion is that the more emotional the problems a lawyer handles, the further down the lawyers' pecking order he ranks. Corporation lawyers are at the top; corporations have no emotions. Divorcees and criminals have little else.

Lawyers also dislike divorce practice because it is not lucrative. Many divorcees think lawyers take advantage and overcharge them. In most divorce cases, the legal fees—both of them—are paid by the husband, and are set by the judge at the time of the divorce hearing. Many lawyers think that the fees that the court sets are ridiculously low—another reason that they do not like to take divorce cases. Many lawyers make additional charges for the many other services they perform for divorcees. Divorce lawyers tend to work on an hourly rate, though probably all of them adjust the rate to the income of their client.

Most divorcees, on the other hand, do not appreciate how much work their lawyers actually put in. Because the court hearing seldom takes more than a few minutes, and because the papers are often not a thick bundle, the assumption is that comparatively little effort went into it. The divorce lawyers I know earn their fees; the good ones always contribute a lot of personal advice, care, and solace without charge.

Many divorce cases do not end when the decree is final. Money must be collected; ex-husbands may use nonpayment of alimony as the only sanction they have

over ex-wives; financial positions and obligations change. For these and many other reasons, the divorcee may come back to the lawyer sooner or later. One divorced woman summed it up, "Every divorcee needs a good firm of lawyers."

But the greatest difficulty arises from the fact we started with: divorce lawyers are forced, in the nature of the law, to put the "real situation," as they learn it from their clients, into language that the law will accept. If a divorce action is to go to court, it must first be couched in language that the courts are legally permitted to accept. Both marriage counselors and lawyers have assured me that reconciliation is always more difficult after grounds have been discussed and legal papers written than when it is still in the language of "reasons" and personal emotion. Legal language and choice of grounds are the first positive steps toward a new type of relationship with the person one of my informants called "my ex-to-be." Discussion of grounds often amounts, from the point of view of the divorcing person, to listing all the faults that the spouse ever committed, then picking one. Since everyone has faults, this is not difficult to do. (There is an old joke that goes the rounds of divorce lawyers about the conscientious young man who came to his lawyer and said he wanted a divorce, but was not sure he had grounds. The cynical lawyer raised his eyes and asked, "Are you married?")

We all know that grounds and reasons may be quite different. The divorcing person usually feels that he should not "tattle" and selects the "mildest" ground. Yet, every person who institutes a suit for divorce must wonder whether to use "adultery" if in fact it occurred, or to settle for the more noncommittal "mental cruelty." Does one use drunkenness when divorcing an alcoholic? Or desertion? Or does one settle for "incompatibility?"

What the Court Does

The judges in a divorce court are hardworking men who must become accustomed to a veritable chaos of emotional confusion.

Some of them do the job well, with great knowledge and commitment. Others feel that they have themselves been sentenced, that no human being should be asked to stand very much of it, and hope to be in some other court soon.

The usual divorce in court takes only a few minutes—sometimes as little as two or three and seldom more than fifteen or twenty. Many divorcees are disturbed to discover this fact, having thought all their grievances would be heard and, perhaps, they would "get some justice." Many report, "It's a weak-kneed system. I don't feel that it really did the job." Others are constantly aware that they perjured themselves —about grounds, about residence, perhaps about facts. Some divorcees feel virtuous for using "mental cruelty" as a ground and tell all their friends "the real reason"— thereby alienating friends. Others take a pragmatic attitude about the legal proceedings: "What do I care? I got what I wanted, didn't I?"

The court action seems short and ineffective at the time—not traumatic. Most divorcees, in retrospect, cannot remember the details of it; in part, I think, because there is little to be remembered. Divorce dockets are crowded in all American cities. Judges do not have time to give each case the thought and time the divorcing parties think it deserves—realizing that one's monumental troubles are not worth the court's time can often act as a restorative, but sometimes as a depressant. Many judges agree that they would like to have more time to make specific investigations and suggestions in each case—to convince themselves that attempts have been made to discover whether these two people should in fact be divorced—whether divorce is a reasonable solution to their problems. Though judges do take time with some cases, most would like to be able to take more.

One of the reasons that the divorce institution is so hard on people is that the legal processes do not provide an orderly and socially approved discharge of emotions that are elicited during the emotional divorce and during the early parts of preparation for the legal processes. Divorces are "cranked out" but divorces are not "cooled out."

THE ECONOMIC DIVORCE AND THE PROBLEM OF PROPERTY

The family household is the unit of economic consumption in the United States. As such, middle-class households must have a certain amount of domestic-capital equipment besides personal property such as cars and television sets. In most households, these items "belong to the family," even though they may be legally owned in the name of one of the spouses. There are (at the time of writing) six states in the United States that declare all property owned by either spouse to be "community property" except for what they owned before the marriage and what they inherit. California is the most thorough and noteworthy example of a community-property state; many states are in process of changing their laws—some of them toward stricter community-property principles, some for a "better break" for one partner or the other. Any list is soon out of date.

Behind the idea of fair settlement of property at the time of divorce is the assumption that a man cannot earn money to support his family if he does not have the moral assistance and domestic services of his wife. The wife, if she works, does so in order to "enhance" the family income (no matter how much she makes or what the "psychic income" to her might be). Therefore, every salary dollar, every patent, every investment, is joint property.

In most states, the property settlement is not recorded in the public records of divorce, so precise information is lacking. However, in most settlements, the wife receives from one-third to one-half of the property. As one sits in a divorce court, however, one realizes that in many divorces the amount of property is so small as to need no settlement or even to cause any dispute. Judges regard settlement as the province of lawyers, and generally agree that the lawyers have not done their jobs if the matter comes to court.

Many wives voluntarily give up their

rights to property at the time they become ex-wives. Some are quite irrational about it—"I won't take *anything* from *him!*" Sometimes they think (perhaps quite justly) that they have no moral right to it. Others, of course, attempt to use the property settlement as a means of retaliation. The comment from one of my informants was, "Boy, did I make that bastard pay." It seems to me that irrational motives such as revenge or self-abnegation are more often in evidence than the facts of relative need, in spite of all that judges and lawyers can do.

The property of the household is never, in the nature of household living, separable into two easily discernible parcels. Even in states that lack common-property laws, the *use* of property is certainly common within the household and subject to the rules of the household, of course, but (except for clothes or jewelry or tools) usually not the exclusive property of any specific member of the household. Whose, for example, is the family car? Whose is the hi-fi? Whose is the second-best bed? And whose is the dog?

Alimony

The word "alimony" is derived from the Latin word for sustenance, and ultimately from the verb which means "to nourish" or "to give food to." The prevailing idea behind alimony in America is that the husband, as head of the family, has an obligation to support his wife and children, no matter how wealthy the wife and children may be independently.

At the time of divorce, the alimony rights of the wife are considered to be an extension of the husband's duty to support, undertaken at the time of marriage. Therefore, alimony means the money paid during and after the divorce by the ex-husband to the ex-wife (rarely the other way around).

There is, however, another basis on which some courts in some American jurisdictions have looked on alimony—it can be seen as punishment of the husband for his mistreatment of the wife. Where this idea is found, the wife cannot be entitled to alimony if she is the "guilty party" to the divorce. In most states, the amount of alimony is more or less directly dependent on whatever moral or immoral conduct of the wife may come to the attention of the court. A woman known to be guilty of anything the court considers to be moral misconduct is likely to be awarded less than the "innocent" wife. The law varies widely on these matters; practice varies even more.

The most important thing about the award and payment of alimony is that it is done on the basis of a court order. Therefore, if it is not paid, the offending husband is in contempt of court. The institution of divorce is provided, as we have seen before, with only one formal sanction to insure the compliance of its various parties. And that is the court.

The amount of alimony is set by the court, on the basis of the wife's need and the husband's ability to pay. Both her education and training may be taken into account; the state of health may be relevant. Sometimes the length of the marriage is a consideration—a short period entitling the wife to less alimony. The age of the children, the moral behavior of each spouse, the income tax position—all these things and undoubtedly many more will affect the court's decision about alimony.

Either ex-spouse may petition the court to have alimony arrangements changed, upon any change in either the ex-wife's need or the ex-husband's ability to pay. It cannot, however, be changed on the basis of the postmarital behavior of either party. Some courts listen with sympathy to an ex-husband's request to reduce alimony at the time of his remarriage; almost all alimony is arranged so that it stops entirely at the time of the ex-wife's remarriage.

Child Support

Courts and citizens are both much clearer about child support than they are about alimony. The principle is obvious to all: as long as he is able to do so, the responsibility for supporting children lies with their father. Whether a man is morally and legally obliged to support his children depends only on one factor: his ability to do so. In assessing child support payments, the court looks simply at his ability to pay, including his health, and the needs of the child. The amount may be set by the court; it is always ratified by the court.

The principles behind the idea of child support are simple. However, the functioning of the child support aspects of the divorce institution are anything but simple. The difficulty arises, again and as usual, because of the lack of sanctions aside from the court, and from the further fact that court action is expensive and usually slow. The father who does not pay the stipulated child support is in contempt of court, and can be brought back into court on that basis. In order to avoid clogging the courts, some states have found various ways in which the payments can be made to the state and forwarded to the mother or other guardian of the children. This, too, is expensive. There seems to bè no really adequate means, as yet, of dealing with men who do not make support payments.

Some mothers try to stop the visitation of fathers who do not make support payments—and some courts uphold them. Although most divorced parents realize that "fighting through the children" is harmful to the children, not all succeed in avoiding it.

THE COPARENTAL DIVORCE AND THE PROBLEM OF CUSTODY

The most enduring pain of divorce is likely to come from the coparental divorce. This odd word is useful because it indicates that the child's parents are divorced from each other—not from the child. Children do not always understand this: they may ask, "Can Father divorce *me?*" This is not a silly or naive question; from the standpoint of the child what was a failure in marriage to the parents is the shattering of his kinship circle.

The children have to go somewhere. And even when both parents share joint legal custody of the child, one parent or the other gets "physical custody"—the right to have the child living with him.

The word "custody" is a double-edged

sword. It means "responsibility for the care of" somebody. It also means "imprisonment." The child is in the custody of his parents—the criminal is in the custody of the law. When we deal with the custody of children in divorces, we must see to it that they are "in the care of" somebody, and that the care is adequate—we must also see that the custody is not punitive or restricting.

Legal custody of children entitles the custodial parent to make decisions about their life-styles and the things they can do which are developmentally important to them—educational and recreational and cultural choices. In the common law, the father had absolute property rights over the child —the mother had none, unless she inherited them at the death of the father. About the time judicial divorce was established in America, custody preferences shifted until the two parents were about equal. With the vast increase in the divorce rate in the early third of the twentieth century, the shift continued, giving the mother preference in both legal and physical custody. We rationalize this practice by such ideas as mother love, masculine nature, or the exigencies of making a living.

Custody of the children, once granted to the mother, will be taken away from her by the courts *only* if she can be shown to be seriously delinquent in her behavior *as a mother*. Her behavior *as a wife* may be at stake in granting the divorce or in fixing the amount of the alimony—but not in granting custody. A woman cannot be denied her rights as a mother on the basis of having performed badly as a wife, or even on the basis of her behavior as a divorcee if the children were not threatened physically or morally. Similarly, a man cannot be penalized as a father for his shortcomings as a husband.

The overriding consideration in all cases is that the court takes what action it considers to be "in the best interests of the child." The rights of children as human beings override, in our morality and hence in our law, all rights of the parents as parents, and certainly their rights as spouses. We have absolutely inverted the old common law.

It is generally considered that a child's best interests lie with his own parents—but if they do not, what is called "third-party custody" can be imposed by the court. Courts do not like to separate children from at least one parent—but sometimes there is no alternative "in the best interests of the child."

A man is always, either by statute law or by common law, obliged to take financial responsibility for his minor children. If there are overriding circumstances that make it impossible for him to work, then that responsibility devolves on their mother. Sometimes a mother refuses her ex-husband the right to support his children as a means to deny him the right to see them—some men accept this, but few would be forced by a court to accept it if they chose to question its legality.

The rights of the parent who has neither legal nor physical custody of the child are generally limited to his right of visiting the child at reasonable times. This right stems from parenthood and is not dependent on decrees issued by a court. The court may, of course, condition the rights of visitation, again in the best interests of the child.

Children and One-Parent Households

Children grow up. The association between parent and child and the association between the parents change with each new attainment of the child. The child grows, parents respond—and their response has subtle overtones in their own relationship. In divorce, their responses must necessarily be of a different nature from what it is in marriage. In divorce, with communication reduced, the goals of the spouses are less likely to be congruent—the child is observed at different times and from different vantage points by the separated parents, each with his own set of concerns and worries.

Coparental divorce created lasting pain for many divorcees I interviewed—particularly if the ex-spouses differed greatly on what they wanted their children to become, morally, spiritually, professionally, even physically. This very difference of opinion about the goals of living may have

lain behind the divorce. It continues through the children.

The good ex-husband/father feels, "My son is being brought up by his mother so that he is not my son." A divorced man almost always feels that his boy is being made into a different kind of man from what he himself is. Often, of course, he is right. The good ex-wife/mother may be tempted to refuse her ex-husband his visitation rights because, from her point of view, "He is bad for the children." This statement may mean no more than that the children are emotionally higher strung before and after a visit, and therefore upset her calm. But the mother may think the father wants something else for the children than she does, thus putting a strain on her own efforts to instill her own ideals and regulations.

It is difficult for a man to watch his children develop traits similar, if not identical, to those he found objectionable in their mother and which were among those qualities that led to the emotional divorce. The child becomes the living embodiment of the differences in basic values. A man may feel that "she" is bad for the children even when he has the objectivity to see also that the children will not necessarily develop unwholesome personalities, but only different personalities from those they might have developed through being with him.

The problem for the mother of the children is different—she has to deal with the single-parent household, making by herself decisions, which she almost surely feels should be shared. She does not want somebody to tell her what to do, as much as somebody to tell her she is right and make "sensible suggestions." Like most mothers, she wants support, not direction.

There is a traditional and popular belief that divorce is "bad for children." Actually, we do not know very much about it.

Although social scientists no longer put it this way, there is still in the general population a tendency to ask whether divorce "causes" juvenile delinquency. Obviously, if the child's way of dealing with the tensions in the emotional divorce of his parents is to act out criminally, he has turned to delinquency. But other children react to similar situations with supercompliance and perhaps ultimate ulcers. The tensions in divorce certainly tell on children, but the answers the children find are not inherent in the institution of divorce.

The more fruitful question is more difficult: "How can we arm children to deal with themselves in the face of the inadequacies and tensions in their families, which may lead their parents to the divorce court?" At least that question avoids the scapegoating of parents or blaming it all on "society"—and it also provides us a place to start working, creating new institutions.

Telling Children About Divorce

It is a truism today that parents should be honest with their children, but parents apparently do not always extend this precept to being honest with their children about divorce. One of the most consistent and discouraging things found in interviewing American divorced persons came in response to my question, "What have you told your child about the nature of divorce in general and your own in particular?" The question was almost always followed by a silence, then a sigh, and then some version of, "I haven't told them much. I haven't had to. They know. You can't kid kids."

It is true, generally, that children are not easily deceived. But it is not true that they know instinctively why something is happening. Children today are comparatively sophisticated about divorce—until they are involved in it.

Children who live in and with the institution of divorce have a lot to learn that other children may never have to learn. The most important ideas to be communicated to them deal with the nature of the new life they will lead. It may be reasonable, in some cases, not to acquaint them with the facts of the emotional and legal divorces. But the new situation—custody, visitation, the new division of labor in the household —can be explained quite clearly so that the child can do his adjusting to a fairly predictable situation.

Of equal importance, they must be taught purposefully and overtly some of the culture of the family that does not occur in the ex-family. That is to say, children in divorce must pick up by instruction what they would have learned by habituation or osmosis in an unbroken healthy home.

The children must learn how to deal with the "broken orbit" of models for the roles they will play in life. A boy cannot become fully a man—or a girl a woman—if they model themselves only on the cues they pick up from one sex alone. A woman cannot teach a boy to be a man, or a girl a woman, without the help of men. And a man cannot either teach a boy to be a man or a girl to be a woman without the help of women.

All of us interact with members of both sexes. Our cues about the behavior of men come from the responses of women, as well as from the responses of men. Children—like the rest of us—must have significant members of both sexes around them.

Obviously, children of even the most successful homes do not model themselves solely on their parents, in spite of the importance parents have as models. There are television models (boys walk like athletes or crime busters); there are teachers, friends, storekeepers, bus drivers, and all the rest. But the child who lives in a one-parent home has to adjust to a different mixture of sex-role models. The big danger may be not so much that a boy has no father model in his home, but that his mother stops his walking like Willie Mays or a television cowboy because she doesn't like it. And worst of all, she may, without knowing it, try to extinguish in him the very behavior patterns he has learned from his father: especially, if she does not want to be reminded of his father.

Children who live in one-parent homes must learn what a husband/father is and what he does in the home—and they have to learn it in a different context from children of replete homes. They must learn what a wife/mother is in such a home. Children are taught to be husbands and wives while they are still children. In the one-parent home the children have to be taught actively and realistically the companionship, sexual, coparenting, and domestic aspects of marriage.

It is important to realize that these things can be taught. Yet, it is in this very process of teaching the child that the parent may reveal a great deal of bitterness and hostility toward the ex-spouse. The good parent has to teach the child without denigrating or idealizing the other parent.

A noted psychoanalyst has told me that in her opinion there are only two things children learn in two-parent homes that cannot be taught in one-parent homes; one is the undertone of healthy sexuality that is present in a healthy home. Nothing appears on the surface save love—but the sexual tone of married love permeates everything. Even in the most loving one-parent home this is something that can, perhaps, be explained to children, but something that they will have trouble feeling unless they experience it elsewhere. The other thing that is difficult to teach, she says, is the ambivalence of the child toward both parents. When the relationship of father-child is none of the business of the child's mother, or the relationship of mother-child outside the ken and responsibility of the child's father, then the illusion can be maintained by the child that father is wholly right and mother wholly wrong, or father wholly unjustified and mother completely innocent. It is seldom true.

In short, the ex-family must do many of the things that the family ordinarily does, but it does them with even more difficulty than the family. It is in the coparental aspects of the divorce that the problems are so long-lasting—and so difficult. And the reason, as we have seen, is that a child's mother and father are, through the child, kinsmen to one another, but the scope of activities in their relationship has been vastly curtailed.

THE COMMUNITY DIVORCE AND THE PROBLEM OF LONELINESS

Changes in civil status or "stages of life" almost invariably mark changes in friends and in significant communities. We go to school, and go away to college. We join special-interest groups. When we are married, we change communities—sometimes almost completely except for a few relatives and two or three faithful friends from childhood or from college.

When we divorce, we also change communities. Divorce means "forsaking all others" just as much as marriage does, and in about the same degree.

Many divorcees complain bitterly about their "ex-friends." "Friends?" one woman replied to my question during an interview, "They drop you like a hot potato. The exceptions are those real ones you made before marriage, those who are unmarried, and your husband's men friends who want to make a pass at you." The biggest complaint is that divorcees are made to feel uncomfortable by their married friends. . . .

Like newly marrieds, new divorcees have to find new communities. They tend to find them among the divorced. Morton Hunt's book, *The World of the Formerly Married*, provides a good concise report on these new communities. Divorcees find—if they will let themselves—that there is a group ready to welcome them as soon as they announce their separations. There are people to explain the lore that will help them in being a divorcee, people to support them emotionally, people to give them information, people to date and perhaps love as soon as they are able to love.

America is burgeoning with organizations of divorced people. The largest, and a vastly admirable organization, is *Parents Without Partners*, which has many branches throughout the country. Here . . . a divorced person can find information and friends. The character of this organization varies from one of its chapters to another. I know one chapter—over a third of its membership widows—that is quiet to the point of being sedate. I know other chapters that devote themselves to public works, large-scale picnics and parties that include all their children, and the kind of "discussion" of their problems that enables people "to get to know each other well enough to date seriously rather than experimentally."

There are, of course, some people who avoid other divorcees. Such people tend to disappear into the population at large, and hence are more difficult to find when we study their adjustments.

But the community divorce is an almost universal experience of divorcees in America. And although there are many individuals who are puzzled and hurt until they find their way into it, it is probably the aspect of divorce that Americans handle best.

THE PSYCHIC DIVORCE AND THE PROBLEM OF AUTONOMY

Psychic divorce means the separation of self from the personality and the influence of the ex-spouse—to wash that man right out of your hair. To distance yourself from the loved portion that ultimately became disappointing, from the hated portion, from the baleful presence that led to depression and loss of self-esteem.

The most difficult of the six divorces is the psychic divorce, but it is also the one that can be personally most constructive. The psychic divorce involves becoming a whole, complete, and autonomous individual again—learning to live without somebody to lean on—but also without somebody to support. There is nobody on whom to blame one's difficulties (except oneself), nobody to shortstop one's growth, nobody to grow with.

Each must regain—if he ever had it—the dependence on self and faith in one's own capacity to cope with the environment, with people, with thoughts and emotions.

Why Did I Marry?

To learn anything from divorce, one must ask himself why he married. Marriage, it seems to me, should be an act of desperation—a last resort. It should not be used as a means of solving one's problems. Ultimately, of course, most people in our society can bring their lives to a high point of satisfaction and usefulness only through marriage. The more reason, indeed, we should not enter it unless it supplies the means for coping with our healthy needs and our desires to give and grow.

All too often, marriage is used as a shield against becoming whole or autonomous individuals. People too often marry to their weaknesses. We all carry the family of our youth within ourselves—our muscles, our emotions, our unconscious minds. And we all project it again into the families we form as adults. The path of every marriage is strewn with yesterday's unresolved conflicts, of both spouses. Every divorce is beset by yesterday's unresolved conflicts, compounded by today's.

So the question becomes: How do I resolve the conflicts that ruined my marriage? And what were the complementary conflicts in the spouse I married?

Probably all of us marry, at least in part, to defend old solutions to old conflicts. The difficulty comes when two people so interlock their old conflicts and solutions that they cannot become aware of them, and hence cannot solve them. Ironically, being a divorced person has built-in advantages in terms of working out these conflicts, making them conscious, and overcoming them.

Why Was I Divorced?

Presumably the fundamental cause of divorce is that people find themselves in situations in which they cannot become autonomous individuals and are unwilling to settle for a *folie à deux*. Divorcees are people who have not achieved a good marriage—they are also people who would not settle for a bad one.

A "successful" divorce begins with the realization by two people that they do not have any constructive future together. That decision itself is a recognition of the emotional divorce. It proceeds through the legal channels of undoing the wedding, through the economic division of property and arrangement for alimony and support. The successful divorce involves determining ways in which children can be informed, educated in their new roles, loved and provided for. It involves finding a new community. Finally, it involves finding your own autonomy as a person and as a personality.

Autonomy

The greatest difficulty comes for those people who cannot tell autonomy from independence. Nobody is independent in the sense that he does not depend on people. Life is with people. But if you wither and die without specific people doing specific things for you, then you have lost your autonomy. You enter into social relationships—and we are all more or less dependent in social relationships—in order to enhance your own freedom and growth, as well as to find somebody to provide for your needs and to provide good company in the process. Although, in a good marriage, you would never choose to do so, you *could* withdraw. You could grieve, and go on.

These are six of the stations of divorce. "The undivorced," as they are sometimes called in the circles of divorcees, almost never understand the great achievement that mastering them may represent.

NOTES

1. The parts of this book that were written by Paul Bohannan are based on research carried out between 1963 and 1966 under grants MH 06551–01A1 and MH 11544–01 of the National Institute of Mental Health, and grant No. GS–61 from the National Science Foundation.

70

THE AMERICAN WAY OF MARRIAGE: REMARRIAGE

Betty Rollin

Item: An old friend, a small, brown-haired girl, ordinary, except for her extreme good nature, calls up with news of her impending divorce. "I guess we're the last to go," she says. And I know what she means—that, of all our friends who got married between five and ten years ago, almost everyone is divorced. Item: I go to a party and run into a man I haven't seen for a long time, who, as they used to say about young brides, is all aglow. It seems he has just remarried, and he is so ecstatic, he is boring. I think about this man later and realize something key—that of all the marriages I can think of that are either intact and/or seemingly happy, most are *re*marriages. I know perfectly well that tens of millions of people live within the traditional marriage-for-life framework, and live within it happily. But I also know that there are growing millions of those who do not, and that they are not, to say the least, all misfits. There are now so many people of all kinds who live within the divorce/remarriage framework—and there is so much evidence of their success —that it is probably time to call their way of marriage (remarriage) just that: another way.

Anyhow, remarriages, from where I sit, and for whatever reason, look pretty good.

The question is, since my seat is in New York, is it just my remarried friends that seem both plentiful and OK? Or do they speak for some kind of national condition?

So I call Washington and start checking numbers. Yes, divorces are up, with almost 30 percent of them still going to the young (teen-agers and early twenty-ers), and there's a new peak: among marriages that have lasted 20 to 24 years, the divorce rate is up 28 percent, and 36 percent for couples married 25 to 29 years. But guess what else is up? In the 1960's, there were, it seems, 300,000 more marriages a year than in the previous decade and, catch this, an unprecedented half of these were remarriages. More than three-fourths of all divorcing men remarry, explains Dr. Paul Glick, chief of the Population Division of the Census Bureau, "and about two-thirds of all divorcing women." And both of those figures are on the rise. From another angle, one out of six male and female I do-ers did it before. Altogether, there are, in this country, about ten million marital unions in which one or both partners have been married before, and eight million of these involve children.

Time for a hard-cover check: "Instead of wedding 'until death do us part,'" says Alvin Toffler in *Future Shock*, "couples will enter into matrimony knowing from the first that the relationship is likely to be short-lived. . . . Serial marriage—a pattern of successive temporary marriages—is cut to order for the Age of Transience in which all man's relationships, all his ties with the environment, shrink in duration." Bloodless, but sort of convincing. Less bloodless and just as convincing is the overwhelming evidence indicating that second marriages are not only pretty good, they are better than first marriages. In all the books on the subject—Jessie Bernard's *Remarriage*, William Goode's *Women in Divorce*, Paul Bohannan's *Divorce and After*, Harvey Locke's *Predicting Adjustment in Marriage*, Morton Hunt's *The World of the Formerly Married*—not to mention opinions, based on studies and interviews, of assorted sociologists, psychologists, demographers, marriage counselors, and journalists, there is surprising concurrence as to the success of the Second Leap.

Many studies show that people who have divorced once are more likely to divorce again than people who have never divorced. But, statistics are distorted by the chronic divorcers, whereas, actually, says Paul Glick, "those who remarry are much more likely to remain married until death intervenes than they are to become divorced." Moreover, data imply "that persons who remarry are more likely to remain in their second marriage than persons married only once are to remain in their first marriage."

So much for remarriages lasting; what of their quality? Dr. Locke's study of 146 chiefly middle-class remarried folk found only one out of nine unhappy, by their own estimate, and Dr. Bernard, who studied over 2,000 remarriages (in the Northeastern part of the country), found that seven-eighths rated their marriages anywhere from satisfactory to extremely so. In Dr. Goode's study of divorced women, 92 percent reported that their second marriages were much better than their first, and felt their children were either the same or better off.

The divorced or remarriageable population used to mean young, non-Catholic, third-generation Americans, low on the socioeconomic ladder. (I am not saying much about the widowed remarriers because there are many fewer of them than the divorced, and because, in a sense, they do not remarry entirely by choice.) Today, it can mean just about anyone—like about one-third of those who marry. One of the most striking statistics on divorce is that marriages between young persons (men, under 22; women, under 20) are more than twice as likely to end in divorce than marriages of persons of a more mature age.

Nothing is easier than trying to figure out why young marriages don't work out. Motivation is a big clue: Again and again one hears, "I was pregnant," or, "She got pregnant"; "All my friends were getting married"; "I don't have anything else to do"; "I wanted to get out of the house"; "I slept with him, and since I was a good girl, I thought I should marry him."

Add to that group, the reality-ignoramuses (however better motivated). "I just didn't realize what the day-to-day thing would be like!" Or "I just couldn't handle my problems [in this case, job] *and* hers." Or "The trouble really started when the baby came" (as it usually does—too soon).

The quotes above, picked up across the country, are from young marriers who got young divorces. When they remarry (99 percent of women who are divorced by age 25 remarry), the new marriage is bound to be somewhat better even if they are still young. They are, at least, a little older, and they have had, after all, *some* experience.

There are, to be sure, plenty of people who marry and remarry and don't get any better at it—"divorce prone," they are called, or, if you like, neurotic. But there are a lot of buts to this point. Like, but there are multiple marriers who *do* learn. It just takes them a couple of extra mates to do it. (I know one man, blissfully married for ten years to a fourth wife. The first two marriages were brief teen-age follies; the third, more mature, longer-term, not horrendous, nevertheless unsatisfactory.) But No. 2: multiple remarriers may be more neurotic than others, but having divorced once—or twice—and not died from it, they find divorce preferable to dissatisfaction. Also, maybe they're neurotics, but neurotics are capable of change too, particularly if they've been psychoanalyzed. Besides, divorcers aren't the only neurotics. There are plenty of married ones who don't get divorced because they're *too* neurotic or just more conservative. Divorce is difficult and painful, but, as anyone who has done it and come out ahead in a good remarriage will tell you, it can be a terrifically positive and healthy step.

"My first marriage," says one Connecticut woman, "was like a dead fish. It took me two years to get the courage to do something about it. For a long time I thought, well, that's just how life is—dull. Then I thought, it's my fault. I'll just try harder. But, finally, I just couldn't take it. It's the best, most creative thing I ever did. . . . My ex-husband isn't a bad person. He was just bad for me, and I, him."

The Women's Liberation movement has made its mark on the divorce and remar-

riage movement too. There are no statistics yet, but there are increasing numbers of women who are getting out of marriages that won't tolerate their new, less compliant, less domestic selves. These women do not rush to remarry, necessarily, but if they do, one hears comments like: "With my first husband, I was a bathroom cleaner. With my second, I'm a person—who cleans the bathroom sometimes."

Personal growth may be the biggest marriage killer of all—another reason why marriages that started early are so often doomed. People change and grow at different rates, and in different ways. If a couple is compatible at 20, and they still are compatible at 30, 40, or 50, it is, nowadays, more lucky than likely.

Of course, sometimes "growth" is a euphemism for a rise in status, fame, or wealth. Not that male movie stars are the only wife-shedders. Among executives making over $25,000, the rate of divorce has increased almost threefold in the last decade. Eugene E. Jennings, a social scientist at the University of Michigan who has studied this group, says, "Once you separate and attach in the corporate world, it's easier to do it in the married world." Interestingly, companies, like society in general, are much more tolerant of divorced men than they used to be. "Probably," says Jennings wryly, "it's because corporations have discovered that their best men are divorced."

When these men remarry, they remarry younger—and richer—women. Whereas their marriages might be better—more pleasing to them—their ex-wives face little that is pleasing to *them*. These are women whose lives have centered on their husbands and children. They are women, in other words, whom Women's Liberation *and* their husbands (and their grown children) have left behind. Their chances of remarrying are small, and their chances of achieving what we think of as happiness are smaller. They are probably the most serious casualties of the divorce/remarriage phenomena.

The increased number of middle-aged marital breakups has a lot to do with, simply, time. "Until death do us part" was easier when death parted people sooner. In

1900, for example, people who married at 20 were likely to be dead by 47. Today, people who marry at 20 are still alive at 70. Contrary to the myths, numerous studies show that two factors make a bad marriage worse—children and time. Time not only aggravates personality conflicts, it can kill sex. That didn't matter much when everyone thought that sex and romance and, perhaps, certain kinds of joyousness in general were prerogatives of the young. If sex was dirty, it was doubly dirty for older people. Masters and Johnson changed all that when they reported that men and women could have a fine time in bed into their eighties (and did!). When older people remarry, by the way, "the effect [on sex] of a new partner," says Jessie Bernard, "is favorable in almost every case." No doubt this is true, not just because of sexual mechanics, but because in the previous marriage bad sex was an integral part of a bad relationship.

Desperate efforts to spark new life into bad or gray marriages have led to a recent spurt of group sex. But for the majority, this kind of shot in the sexual arm is not about to displace divorce and remarriage (now they're calling it "serial monogamy") as a solution to marital mortality.

Although divorce is prevalent, and more culturally accepted, it is still, needless to say, painful. And that goes for almost everyone who gets one. Not to mention children. It is also, as everyone knows, expensive. Many a divorced male has been financially crippled for life by a stiff alimony sentence. Almost no one gets divorced without some feelings of real or imagined loss and failure, and guilt. So why do so many put their hands in a flame that has already burnt them?

People get remarried, it turns out, for many of the same reasons they marry. One reason, lest we forget, is love—the wish to give it, get it, and cement it. Marriage is still what we do to cement and even define love in this culture. Even though de-cementing (divorce) is frequent, marriage is still with us. And it is still more of a commitment—public and private—than living together. And it's not just a matter of legiti-

mizing offspring, because many of the young people marrying today—and they *are* marrying, they're just living together *first*—are not planning on offspring. And homosexual couples, some of whom are marrying too, surely are not. But, the point is, they're getting married anyway. Ask some marrying-after-living-together students, and you get answers like: "He didn't really want to, but *I* did"; "We thought, why *not?*" "My parents were getting upset"; "I dunno. We just felt like it." "Feeling like it" can mean, simply, wishing to formalize contractually the *intention* of exclusivity and permanence, even if neither is achieved. "Marriage," says sociologist William Goode, "*feels* permanent and that's the important thing. It's buying, instead of rental. It's even-if-you're-acting-like-an-s.o.b.-we'll-stick-it-through. It's going home at night to somebody you don't have to keep winning. It's having *decided*. In a way, you know, the happiest people in prison are the lifers."

The social pressures to marry—and remarry—go without saying. Particularly for women. Despite the current advances towards self-reliance, a woman without a man in our society is, more often than not, a woman who wants a man—probably to marry. And if she is divorced with children, she wants a man—definitely to marry. Not that she's alone. According to Dr. Pauline Bart, who is working on a study of divorced men, *they* wish to marry as well. Not right away, maybe, but most of them have it in mind. Also, surprising numbers of divorced fathers, says Dr. Bart, hope, somehow, to get their children back, and want a wife as a "new mother" for their children. In any case, they soon tire of the "swinging" bachelor life, which is either not that swingy, or, if it is, palls before too long. Similarly, the "other woman" (or man) who might have broken up the marriage may become less desirable when available. Some of the heaviest swinging-bachelor fantasizers are, of course, young marriers, who, after they play their fantasies out, go right back to the same woman—every year in the United States, there are 10,000 remarriages to the same person.

So, with few exceptions, most people who

have married once want to again—either to the same person, or, much more often, to someone new. And, thanks to the increasing numbers of divorced men and women at all ages, they probably will.

"It's funny," says a slow-talking, languid woman, six years into a second marriage, "the first time I married, I was really in love. It was a very high feeling. Then, like the cliché, love turned into hate and the feeling went very, very low. The second time I was in love, it was not as 'high' a feeling to start with, but it has stayed pretty much on the same level. I think it's just that I knew better what I was getting into. I was more confident in myself, my second husband was more confident in himself. I don't know, we were both grown-ups. We've been quite happy. There are problems, dumb things like he still calls me by his first wife's name sometimes, and there are things about him I just don't like and never will, but we ride over them, somehow. If nothing else, my first marriage taught me what *not* to expect, what *not* to do."

That's an older, wiser woman talking. It's also a more accepting woman. ("The older bride," Jessie Bernard reminds us, "is less likely to try . . . to remake the man she loves.") It's also a woman with more at stake. That is, one of the most severe losses in a divorce can be one of self-esteem—particularly if the divorce is the other person's doing. Such people want to make a second marriage work, among other reasons, to regain their sense of self. They want to be able to say to themselves, "Someone is happy with me. I am happy with someone. I am OK." Although ex-mates can be troublesome, in one sense, the *more* troublesome, the better the new and different partner seems by comparison. It's also true that the new someone is often like the old someone, and that the only change is an improved adjustment.

"The most distinguishing characteristic of second marriages," says a New York marriage counselor, "is sweat." "They really work at it." It's not only working at it, but having better equipment—e.g., more mature, experienced, confident selves—to work

with. By the time most people remarry (three-fourths do, within nine years), they know themselves better, both personally and professionally. The older they are, the more likely it is that they have found themselves, and the less they will look to the other person for support or definition. The intermediary span between marriages itself can swing people—especially women—from roles of previously dependent housewifery to self-reliant, self-respecting individuality. "The trouble with my first marriage," says one of these, "was me. I just didn't like myself, but I didn't have the courage to do anything about it. Besides, I didn't know what to do about it. I had gone from home to school to husband. There was always somebody around telling me what to do and who to be. Being divorced forced me to develop myself. Boy, it was rough at first. But I made it." (She went back to school and is now teaching in Boston.) Dr. Bernard says that older men, who are more professionally established, are freer to enjoy their wives and families. "It wasn't my wife's fault," says one male self-blamer. "I just didn't want to be married at that time. I was nowhere in my work. I was anxious about it all the time—then she pushed for a child and that made it worse. . . ."

In most people's minds, children loom as the dark side of the divorce-remarriage picture. It is undeniable that they suffer in such shake-ups. But we know now that a bad marriage kept intact for the sake of the children is a specious idea at best. It is common knowledge that what's bad for the children is a bad marriage, not the *end* of a bad marriage. And as far as remarriage goes, although it may be rough going at first—particularly with adolescents—remember Goode's study, for one, in which 92 percent of remarried women said that their children were either better off or the same. "My children wanted me to remarry from the start," reports one small, peppy divorcée. "Not that they weren't choosy. My daughter became a seven-year-old Jewish mother. Every man that came to the house, she'd ask, 'Are you married? What do you do?' "

Generally, children adjust more easily to stepfathers than to stepmothers—the "step" term doesn't help—but, since real mothers almost always have custody, the children normally do not *live* with the stepmother. Still, at first, the remarital situation can be emotionally trying for kids. And that can make things trying, in turn, for the new couple. Some kids, for example, may have trouble adjusting to the idea of their parent's sexuality with a new person. And depending on the behavior of the newlyweds, children may feel left out—or, just as bad, rushed into an intimacy they're not ready for.

In *Divorce and After*, Bohannan tells of a new wife greeting her husband's daughter for the first time: "I am your new mother!" she cooed. "The hell you are," said the daughter. Children generally resent stepparents, both when they try to replace a living parent, or when they are, actually, replacing a dead one. But the new parent is, after all, not a replacement of a parent, but an additional parent, and, apparently, that's how most kids come to feel about it. "At first I rejected her wanting me as a daughter," says a 20-year-old California college girl of her stepmother. "She has two sons of her own. . . . But she was so lovely to me—even when I was mean to her. I rejected her at first because of my mother. But now I can really accept her. It took a while, but now I guess I love her."

Similarly, step-siblings become either rivals or friends, and there is no evidence that rivalry is prevalent. It depends largely, of course, on the behavior of the adults. If the principle and practice of addition rather than replacement is carried out successfully, it will work against the problem of conflicting loyalties.

As long as there are children, ex-wives and ex-husbands remain not only linked to each other as parents but as part of each other's family. Bohannan calls such relationships "divorce chains," but they are not, he maintains, the bitter connections one would expect. Not after a while, anyway. He tells of many divorce-chain families where exes and exes are not only civil, but friendly.

Probably it's the "sweat" factor that operates when remarriages with kids work out. Part of making the new marriage work is making it work with, and for, them. Like the new marital partner, the child of that partner needs to be wooed too. If the wooing is genuine, and if the wooer is patient, the child is usually won. Kids have great resilience and flexibility; after all, they want the "gap" filled, and they respond, like their parents, to love. "The divorce," says one mother, "was very hard on Erica. She was very attached to her father, and he used to put me down. When I married again, Erica was five. At first she was frightened of Ted. He is such a silent man compared to her father. It was a long, hard row for both of them. But, finally, he won her over."

Washington psychiatrist Dr. William Davidson thinks that children involved in divorce/remarital shake-ups can emerge not only with their mental health intact, but the better for it. "This kind of ambiguous, expanded experience," he says, "moves kids to better adjustment in a society that is highly ambiguous and expanded. I've discovered that people who have grown up in these situations cope better with the ambiguities of life. . . ." Davidson says, too, that parental guilt can "help" children feel victimized, even when they are not.

To point out remarital success is not to suggest that one should change spouses like partners at a dance, and then dance away until the next little tap on the shoulder. Even with the sensible no-fault divorce idea, it is unlikely, as some fear, to make passing fancies out of marriage and divorce. The beginnings and ends of marriages are still among the most important and emotionally charged events in a lifetime. But there are certain new realities—like longevity, like more mobility, like more willingness, healthy willingness, I think—to change and grow and then do something about the change and growth. One would hope that marital choices will become even broader, broad enough to include monogamous forever marriages *and* unlimited remarriages, and a whole lot in-between. It would be nice, for example, if it were more socially and psychologically comfortable not to be married at all, or to be married very late, or not to have children, or not to have those ill-conceived, ill-worked out young marriages be legal marriages at all. Of course, many kids who live together know perfectly well that it is better not to marry young. (In one sense, their living together in what used to be called sin suggests they take marriage more seriously—and more thoughtfully—than their parents.) It should be more possible for older women whose husbands have died or divorced them to marry and/or enjoy younger men, if necessary. It should certainly be more possible for them to be more independent, so that, if/when they are left out of the twilight marriage market, they won't dissolve into useless misery.

And how about more leeway within the institution of marriage, itself? Institutions should serve individuals, after all, and individuals are different.

Of course, the cornerstone of individuality is choice. But from society's viewpoint, it is more orderly and efficient to have conformity, not choice. All right, things must work, but why not a more joyous and individualistic pragmatism? To act on choices well made is, after all, what it's all about, isn't it?

71

SOME RELATIONSHIPS OF STEPCHILDREN TO THEIR PARENTS

Charles E. Bowerman and Donald P. Irish

The "wicked stepmother" of folklore has long existed in our legends. The concept of the "neglected stepchild" occurs commonly in our linguistic usage. The multifarious and presumably negative results of broken homes have received abundant popular comment. But no comprehensive analyses of the problems involved in step-relationships have yet been made. A thorough examination of the research literature for the past forty years reveals that there have been relatively few systematic inquiries concerned with the stepchild. Excluding discussions of individual cases, the scholarly literature yields fewer than forty published articles or books which analyze empirical data. . . .

William C. Smith has published a comprehensive review of the literature, summarizing the data and insights with regard to step-relationships. His major volume,[1] supplemented by additional articles,[2] presents exploratory views and advances some thoughtful hypotheses, most of which remain yet to be tested.

More recently, in an extensive study of 2009 remarriages, many of which involved stepchildren, Jessie Bernard considered the attitudes of stepparents toward their spouse's children, the patterns of adjustment which newly married pairs developed with regard to the children, and the validity and relevance of the folk myths about step-relationships.[3] Although the data she used were the responses of *friends* of the couples involved and not of the principals themselves, the investigation was useful in suggesting many hypotheses for direct inquiry. Bernard's study also serves to provide data from the parent generation to complement inquiries, like the present ones, in which the data were secured from the children involved.

William J. Goode has made a significant contribution to the understanding of step-relationships. He reached 425 divorced respondents, all mothers of children, through a thorough and quite effective procedure to secure a representative sample within a county.[4] Many of these women had remarried since their divorce. The data he provides illumine the processes and phases of adjustment through which divorced mothers of varied situations may go and the manner in which stepfathers are introduced into the family group.

A number of scholars have examined the differences in adjustment of children in broken and unbroken homes. Few, however, have attempted to discern "whether children are better adjusted in homes psychologically broken but legally and physically intact, compared with legally broken homes." Ivan Nye, in a study similar in method and problem to the present research, found within a sample of almost 800 high school youth that, as a group, "adolescents in broken homes show . . . better adjustment to parents than do children in unhappy unbroken homes." He pointed out that "reconstructed" families, those into which a stepparent had been incorporated, often brought about enhancement of the child-parent adjustments as a result of remarriage.[5] . . .

The findings reported in this paper stem from two separate, though related, studies. Data for the first were collected in the State of Washington in the spring of 1953, while the data for the second and larger study were secured in North Carolina and Ohio in the spring of 1960. In both inquiries, questionnaires were administered by classroom teachers to junior and senior high school students. The analyses being presented here are derived from those portions of the data provided by the 2145 stepchildren found among the almost 29,000 teen-agers who were involved in these two endeavors. The total number of subjects comprised about 90 percent of all the white pupils enrolled in the 7th through 12th grades within the selected cities and counties.[6] . . .

For those subjects who resided with both real parents, it is evident that the average level of affection in every combination is higher toward mothers than toward fathers. The extent of this difference, however, varies considerably according to the age and sex of the respondents. The younger children (7th through 9th grades) were considerably closer to each parent, according to our indices, than were the older subjects (10th through 12th grades). Within each of the two age groups, males were more intimately related to fathers than were females, and the latter were closer to mothers than were the males. Among the possible dyadic combinations, the closest in degree was that between younger females and their mothers; while the most "distant" occurred between older females and their fathers.[7]

When the scores toward stepparents are contrasted with those toward real parents of the same sex, it is quite apparent that for the majority of our subjects stepparents had not been able to attain the same level of affection and degree of closeness as had real parents. However, in this regard, it is evident that the differences in magnitude between males and females or between the younger or older adolescents in our populations are neither large nor consistent. "The general consensus among remarried parents," Bernard asserts, "seems to be that very young or quite grown-up children tend to assimilate a new parent more easily than do adolescents."[8] . . .

Since they have more distant relationships to stepparents, one might expect that stepchildren would compensate by developing exceptionally close ties to their real parents. Although children in homes with a mother and stepfather have slightly lower scores, on the average, toward their mothers than do those youngsters who live in homes that have remained unbroken, the level of affection toward stepfathers is usually markedly lower than toward real fathers. Thus, the *difference* in attitudes toward parents is greater in this type of step-home than in homes containing both real parents. Perhaps any tendency to compensate for the attenuated relationship toward stepfathers by establishing even closer than customary bonds with the mother is partially offset by the effect on the relationship of a greater amount of discord in the home. Other evidence from these studies makes this assumption tenable.[9]

For the father-stepmother families the situation was somewhat different. Generally, the relationships with fathers in such homes were close slightly more often than toward fathers in unbroken homes. Since the affectional level toward stepmothers was quite low, adolescents in these homes tended to have closer bonds with the real father than with the stepmother. However, the average levels of the relationships toward the two parents tended to be lower than occurred in either of the other parent patterns.

The recurring implication in Smith's discussions of the stepchild is that the adjustment of the stepchild to his parents, singly and jointly, is more difficult and at a less harmonious level than is that of the child in a normal home. Our data substantiate his contention. Over-all, the adjustment toward stepparents is usually poorer than toward the real parent of the same sex, for both boys and girls and with regard to both stepmothers and stepfathers. Further, in most of the parent-child and age-sex combinations the stepfather appears to fare better in comparison with the real fathers than do stepmothers in contrast with mothers in normal homes. Nonetheless, the identity of sex roles does tend to place the girls closer to their mothers and the boys closer to their fathers, whether they be real or stepparents.[10]. . . .

Presumably numerous influences interact to bring about the seemingly complicated result that children of the divorced may tend more often to adjust to their stepparents *both better and worse* than those who have experienced bereavement before a remarriage. Among those factors which may be involved, several can be suggested: the younger age and smaller number of children, on the average, who acquire a stepparent after a divorce, contrasted with a death experience; differentials in the timing before remarriages and, thus, in the intensity and content of the children's memories; factors which operate in a divorce situation to select the parent that will retain custody of given children; differences in personal attributes and the probability of remarriage; the comparative facility of the stepfather role in contrast to the difficulty of the stepmother role, and the probability of each following divorce or death of parents; disruptive influences of former spouses in the aftermath of divorce; and even class differentials in death and divorce frequencies and consequences. Precise and representative data related to children involved in remarriages in this country are lacking. Furthermore, little is known of the consequents of remarriage following divorce or death of one's spouse. Consequently, our discussion of these factors must be recognized as merely suggestive.

Why might a larger proportion of children of divorce adjust *better* to stepparents than is the case with children of bereavement? First, on the average, children who acquire a stepparent following divorce probably do so more promptly after the event, at an earlier age, and in fewer numbers (per family) than do those who have experienced the death of a mother or father. Not only do the differentials in mortality and remarriageability by age contribute to this result, but also often the ready availability of a prospective partner (if a "triangle" were involved), and the proprieties surrounding bereavement, are factors which introduce a stepparent into families earlier when divorce rather than death has broken the home. Presumably younger children, particularly if very young, and more youthful parents, too, establish step-relationships more readily than will older ones. In addition, a remarriage in some respects may be less disruptive for those that have had a shorter experience in a post-marriage one-parent milieu than for those who have undergone a lengthier period with but one parent as an influence and confidant.

Furthermore, assuming that the average initial number of children involved in a post-divorce remarriage is slightly smaller and that the sibling and child-parent patternings are in some ways then more often simpler than in a post-bereavement remarriage (for example, more frequent parent-child combinations of the same sex), these influences, too, would accentuate the proportion of those making "good" adjustments.

Those who have experienced pre-divorce tensions may tend to reject the parent now out of the home and to anticipate and experience a stepparent as an improvement; whereas the tendency to idealize a deceased parent, and the presence of accumulated and, presumably, positive residues on the part of both the children and the surviving parent may impede the acceptance of a surrogate. The contrasting content in the memories of children in these two circumstances, coupled with the different degrees of flexibility linked to the time-lapse factor, could also increase the number who achieved satisfying relationships with their stepparents, when a divorce rather than a parental death figured in the family background.

A cluster of factors also operates to affect the selection of a new marriage partner, to whom the child is to adjust: which partner, when there are children, is more apt to select or be selected, and what attributes may be more likely to "survive" to interact in a second marriage. Some persons who have been divorced benefit by the experience, gain in "maturity," develop a determination to succeed in marriage and parenthood, and consequently engender improved relationships. Bereavement, which strikes persons generally without regard to their marital or parental fitness, perhaps serves less well to spur new approaches to family living and may actually hinder the acceptance of new patterns in the subsequent marriage.

Moreover, although customary custody arrangements following divorce leave the children with the mother, or sometimes with the parent of the same sex, the traditional patterns are sometimes altered to provide that the "more competent" parent retains the children, thereby leaving the decision concerning a remarriage and the selection of a stepparent to the more adequate partner, increasing to some degree the probability of success.

On the other hand, why might a greater proportion of children from divorced homes also be found to adjust *less well* to step-

parents than do those who lost a parent by death? Divorce often is symptomatic of those personalities who have failed to achieve an adequate adjustment to their spouses, and perhaps also occurs more often among those parents who were less competent as parents. The inadequacies of those persons then influence the decision to bring a stepparent of certain qualities into the family circle, and their marital attributes continue to operate within the new setting as well. Furthermore, the influence of previous tensions and deep conflicts may carry over directly or covertly into the personality, marital, and parental patterns brought to a new marriage. Often-times, an implication of failure and inadequacy may be directed toward a divorced parent, even a preferred one, and may militate against adequate child-parent adjustment; whereas such a qualification or imputation is not a factor in the child's assessment of a bereaved parent.

In addition, the difficulties engendered by the custody of children being split between the two parents or the intrusions otherwise of a former spouse produce disruptive effects upon some children of divorce not experienced by those with a parent deceased.

It is recognized that the social significance and psychological meaning of the behaviors and expectations implied or specified in the scale items probably are not the same for families of diverse socioeconomic statuses. However, while divorce now accounts for more stepparent-stepchild relationships than death, both death and divorce proportionately more often break homes in the lower economic segments of our population. Differentials in model behavior patterns; remarriageability rates by sex, age, previous marital status; value systems and levels of expectation; educational achievement; and economic security may serve to alter the consequences and thereby tend to polarize the results of divorce by class. . . .

Stepchildren are more likely to express a preference for one parent or the other than are those who live with both real parents. Girls and the older adolescents are more apt to express a preference than are the boys and our younger respondents. Stepchildren more often prefer the real parent over the stepparent.

The data show also that the frequency of preference is greatest when the adult is of the same sex as the child. Since these relationships occur whether the adult is a real or stepparent, for both the younger and older respondents, the tendency to identify with the parent of one's own sex is apparent. The sharing together of attitudes, interests, and activities of a subculture, by each sex, is presumably a prominent factor in producing these patterns.

However, while these influences usually prove insufficient to swing the affectional preference of the majority of the children to the *step*parent of the same sex, there is usually enough leverage involved to increase the proportion who indicate that they feel "the same" toward both parents. This "balanced" emotional position may represent a "way station" or intermediate position for these children, who can remain loyal and close to their natural parent of the opposite sex while yet signifying an affinity for the stepparent of the same sex and showing that the latter has been able to win at least an equal place in their affections. As the usual pattern is one of divergence in emotional attachment to the parents separately, equivalent affection for parents on the part of a child is an indication of achievement for a father in competition with a mother or for a stepparent in relation to a real parent, assuming that such equivalence is a status to be valued. . . .

Bearing on the topics already discussed are a number of other aspects of child-parent interactions related to adjustment and parent-preferences: namely, parental discriminations felt by stepchildren who have siblings; feelings of rejection or acceptance; and the presence, absence, and directionality of desires to emulate parents or to identify with them. Quite comparable data have been secured for these factors in both investigations. Although the analyses and interpretations will be extended in later reports, a résumé of the relationships is included.

Felt discrimination.—The Cinderella story and others in our folklore provide tradi-

tional illustrations of discriminatory practices and attitudes that stepparents may manifest. Folk beliefs portray stepparents as particularly prone to discriminate unfairly among children. The responses reported herein represent the *perceptions of the children* concerning the presence or absence of parental discrimination. These feelings are an important factor psychologically whether or not an objective appraisal would show that the parents charged with discrimination actually practiced it.

The items most pertinent to this concern were not the same in the two samples.[11] Since the Washington State question elicited the feelings more directly and avoided qualifications due to age, differences in sibling patterns, and so on, the following conclusions are from that sample. For each of the parent-child age-sex combinations, stepparents were believed to discriminate more often than were natural parents; and children in step-homes were more often "not sure" than were those living with both real parents. Stepparents of the opposite sex were more often suspected of discrimination than were those of the child's own sex. Stepchildren of both sexes believed that the stepmother discriminated more than did stepfathers. These differences were all significant at the .01 level.

Thus, these findings further substantiate that the relationships of stepchildren to their stepparents, particularly, but toward their natural parents as well, are marked by greater levels of uncertainty of feelings, insecurity of position, and strain than are those to be found in normal homes. Further analyses will control for varied types of sibling patterns, using the larger sample.

Feelings of rejection.—Closely parallel to feelings about discrimination are children's feelings that they may be or are rejected by one or both of their parents. The items utilized in the samples were quite comparable.[12] The results again were very similar; and the relationships proved to be significant at the .01 level.

Children residing with both natural parents least often felt rejected by either or both parents. Both boys and girls felt somewhat more often rejected by the natural parent in a stepparent home and felt much more often rejected by the stepparent than they did with natural parents, of their own sex, in a normal home. Boys generally expressed such feelings of rejection less often than the girls, within each parent pattern. Again, among the Washington respondents, those who were "unsure" regarding being wanted were found with greater frequency in the homes with step-relationships, for each parent-child sex combination. Very parallel findings resulted from questions closely similar in content: "Do your parents ever compare you unfavorably with other young people?" and "Do your parents seem to go out of their way to hurt your feelings?"

An inverse question was asked of the Washington teen-agers, and their responses provide corroborative evidence: "Do you ever wish you were living in a different family?" Children of both sexes least often rejected their own family when they resided with both natural parents, rejected it somewhat more frequently in a mother-stepfather home, and rejected it most often in father-stepmother families. The data once again highlight the greater difficulties faced by stepparents, particularly stepmothers.

Desire to emulate parents.—Also related to affections toward, and preferences for, parents are the wishes of children to emulate their parents.[13] Consonant with the assumptions underlying the foregoing analysis, it was expected that a greater proportion of stepchildren would wish to emulate their biological parent in more or most ways than would desire to imitate their stepparent in comparable fashion. The highest proportion of respondents wishing to emulate either or both parents was found among those living with both natural parents. In the homes involving step-relationships, as anticipated, children of both sexes wished more often to emulate their natural parent, rather than the stepparent. However, each parent, regardless of relationship, had greater influence with the children of his own sex.

SUMMARY

In all the aspects thus far examined, homes involving step-relationships proved more likely to have stress, ambivalence, and low cohesiveness than did normal homes. The reactions of adolescent children indicate that stepmothers have more difficult roles than do stepfathers, with the consequent implications for interactions within the family. Stepdaughters generally manifested more extreme reactions toward their parents than did stepsons. The presence of stepparents in the home affected also the adjustment of the children to their natural parents, usually somewhat diminishing the level of adjustment.

NOTES

1 William C. Smith, *The Stepchild*, Chicago: The University of Chicago Press, 1953.

2 William C. Smith, "The Stepchild," *American Sociological Review*, 10 (1945):237–42; "Remarriage and the Stepchild," in Morris Fishbein and Ernest W. Burgess (eds.), *Successful Marriage*, New York: Doubleday and Company, 1947, pp. 339–55; "Adjustment Problems of the Stepchild," *Proceedings* of the Northwest Annual Conference on Family Relations (1948):87–98; and "The Stepmother," *Sociology and Social Research*, 33 (May–June 1949): 342–47.

3 Jessie Bernard, *Remarriage: A Study of Marriage*, New York: Dryden Press, 1956. Chapter 8: "Establishing Dynamic Equilibrium: Remarriages with Children," pp. 210–26 and Chapter 12: "The Success of Remarriage: Children of the First Marriage," pp. 301–29.

4 William J. Goode, *After Divorce*, Glencoe: The Free Press, 1956. Chapter XXI, "The Children of Divorce," pp. 307–30.

5 F. Ivan Nye, "Child Adjustment in Broken and in Unhappy Unbroken Homes," *Marriage and Family Living*, 19 (November 1957):356–61.

6 Greensboro and Lexington cities and Chatham, Harnett, and Lee counties of North

Carolina; the cities of Hamilton and Urbana and Delaware and Morrow counties in Ohio; and Kitsap County, Washington. The parochial schools also participated in Ohio. Only white, public schools were included in North Carolina. Herein, the Negro respondents in Ohio and Washington are excluded from the data analyzed, and only white subjects are involved in all three areas.

[7] If one extended this finding to speculate about the relationship between family composition and family unity, the most "emotionally homogeneous" families would be those with all male children whose affection for mother and father were approximately equal; while the least "homogeneous" affectional ties would be expected in those families with all female children whose relationships with their mother and father were most widely divergent in intensity.

[8] Bernard, op. cit., page 216.

[9] Using data from this project, Earle found the level of marital discord to be higher in stepparent homes than in first marriages. See John R. Earle, *Parental Conflict in First Marriages and Remarriages as Reported by a Sample of Adolescents*, Chapel Hill: The University of North Carolina, unpublished master's thesis, 1961.

[10] For a more extended, though earlier, consideration of the affectional relations toward stepparents for the Washington sample see: Charles E. Bowerman, "Family Background and Parental Adjustment of Stepchildren," *Research Studies of the State College of Washington*, 24 (June 1956):181–82. Abstract.

[11] Washington State sample: "Have your parents favored other children over you?" ("yes," "not sure," "no" response categories toward each parent). North Carolina-Ohio sample: "How does the amount of discipline you get compare with what your brothers and sisters get?" ("I get much more," "I get a little more," "Some get more, some get less," "I get less," "have no brothers and sisters").

[12] Washington State sample: "Have you ever felt that your parents wished you were not in the family?" ("yes," "not sure," and "no" for each parent). North Carolina-Ohio sample: "Do your parents ever make you feel like you are not wanted?" ("Both parents do," "mother does," "father does," "neither does").

[13] The same question was used in the two samples, though with slightly different response categories: "Would you like to be the kind of person your mother (father) is?" Since the replies to this item by the North Carolina-Ohio subjects have not yet been machine-processed, the generalizations are based on the data from the Washington sample only.

Part Fourteen

A Changing View of Grandparents

A few generations ago in this country, a young person had a rather slim chance of knowing his or her grandparents for more than a very brief period, if at all. Life expectancy for a person born in 1900 averaged 47.3 years; today the average person lives to be over 70. One reason for the low average in times past was the high infant mortality rate; so there were some older grandparents around. But persons over 65 years of age comprised less than 3 percent of the population, a far cry from today's more than 20 million persons over 65, which is approximately 10 percent of the population. Nearly every child has living grandparents today, and some have living great-grandparents as well. In 1900, living great-grandparents were a rarity, since only a fraction of the population lived to be over 75 years of age; today about 6 million people have reached that age. All together, grandparents and great-grandparents may comprise as much as 30 percent of our population, if the over-45 population is counted. Since couples are now in their twenties, on the average, when their first child is born, there are plenty of 45-year-old grandparents. Furthermore, since the general trend has been toward continuing to marry in the early twenties and toward having fewer children, grandparents are likely not to have any small children of their own at home to compete with their grandchildren, but instead are classified as postparental.

Contrary to what may be believed by many, grandparents are usually not ignored by their children and grandchildren. Recent research shows that there is a great deal of visiting, contact by telephone and mail, and financial and emotional support going in both directions—from parents to children and from children to parents. While older people seem to prefer to maintain their own homes, especially while they are still married, over 30 percent of the over-sixty-five age group live with a child, and an overwhelming majority (84 percent) live within an hour's drive of a child. In fact, as grandparents grow older, they seem to "sell the old home" and move closer to their children, even if this means moving across the country. Younger grandparents, however, are often geographically distant and are self-sufficient enough not to be upset when their children must move away to school and jobs. Usually, when the move is made, it is to the vicinity of a daughter and her family, for the women in our society generally keep up the family contacts. And older women who become widows frequently move in with a daughter's family, perhaps because their own daughter will be more tolerant of having her in the house than would a daughter-in-law.

With the extension of the life-cycle, the postparental stage for couples now involves one quarter to one half of their married life. Indeed, the years of being a grandparent and great-grandparent are generally longer than the child-rearing years. Consequently, the significance of the grandparent role has changed and the style with which a grandparent plays the role is often closely connected to which part of the postparental period is being enjoyed. Almost all of the younger grandfathers are still busily employed, and about 45 percent of the younger grandmothers are also employed outside the home. In the first selection in this part, Bernice Neugarten and Karol Weinstein present data on seventy pairs of middle-class grandparents concerning their degree of comfort in their roles, what meaning the roles have for them, and the styles of grandparenting they display.

The heterogeneous nature of the grandparent population is striking not only from the point of view of age, but also from that of life-style. A third of them live in urban ghettos and one fourth in poverty. Advancing age brings problems with physical and emotional health, finances, and companionship. For the younger people in this group, life may be reaching a peak of enjoyment with fewer responsibilities, more money to spend on themselves, and more leisure time. There is no "typical" grandparent: some are married and living in their own homes and some are living with a child after losing a mate. For purposes of discussion and study, it has proven useful to divide the postparental generation into two groups: the younger couples who are still married, living in their own homes, and employed, but who have no children living at home; and the older, retired persons who may be

moving into the vicinity of their children and who are beginning to face problems of advanced age. Members of both groups must make the shift from a child-centered relationship to a relationship more centered on each other. In addition, the second group must deal with the problems of retirement and of reintroducing the husband—and wife, if she has been employed—back into the home on a full-time basis. These changes are usually made gradually, and couples may prepare for them in advance by slowing down their work schedules, spending more time alone as a couple, traveling, or otherwise engaging in leisure-time pursuits. Some couples begin such preparations during the last few years the children are at home.

In the second article, Irwin Deutscher discusses the quality of postparental life. It becomes clear that the family is still a very important part of the older person's life and that, while the "empty nest" is an important milestone in the life-cycle, it marks a new kind of family involvement, not the end of family involvement.

Several studies have concentrated on the marital, affectional, and sexual relationships of older couples and have stressed the growing disenchantment with marriage as the life-cycle progresses. However, recent information indicates that satisfaction increases once the children are launched. Many couples wait until the children grow up and leave to end the marriage, so the divorce rate peaks. For those who stay married, however, there seems to be an increase in companionship and congenial relations.

Unfortunately, as the couple gets older, the husband, who is usually older and has a shorter life expectancy, leaves his wife a widow; by age seventy, half the women are widowed. In 1970, for the more than six million widows over sixty-five in the United States, there were only a million and a half widowers. In an attempt to solve the problem that results from the shortage of potential remarriage partners, it has been proposed by some that an older man be encouraged to marry more than one widow, if he should so choose; also suggested has been a plan for communal living arrangements, so that older people can live together without marrying and yet receive love and companionship.

Nevertheless, despite the shortage of partners, remarriage in the later years is very common. Often, the decision to remarry at an advanced age meets with disapproval from friends, family, and society in general, for the notion that the couple is "acting foolish" and that sex ought to be a thing of their past is still prevalent. Those who do remarry seem to have a high success rate, probably because they have had years of experience and their expectations of what marriage can offer are more realistic. The article by Marcia Lasswell is an overview of what it means to reach fifty in terms of seeking affection and companionship and satisfying sexual needs, which can last as long as good health and a willing partner are a part of one's life.

The crisis at retirement usually marks for the husband and wife the entry into the second phase of postparental life. This phase offers the advantages of leisure; for those who are financially secure, there may be travel, rest, and time for hobbies. For most people, however, retirement means a drastic cut in income and a depressing loss of status. The once important and respected employed person may become a "has-been" who no longer receives attention when speaking of his or her area of expertise. Many people really begin to feel old and displaced when they retire. Although most of the studies have concerned themselves with the retirement of men, the growing number of women in the labor market makes this a very real issue for both sexes. Perhaps most affected are single men and women whose work has often been their life and who have no family to act as a buffer. Unless the retirement is of a voluntary nature and income remains adequate, the death rate sharply increases during the first year of retirement.

It is imperative that the retired find interesting activities other than hobbies, which seem to wear thin after a few months. Well-educated persons seem to find it easier to occupy their time than do unskilled or even skilled workers. Clubs and organizations, as well as day centers, have been developed to fill the hours for the retired. Hawaii has been the first state to provide licensed day-care centers for "senior citizens" whose previously empty days may have been marked only by an occasional visit, sleeping, television, and a lonely meal. These centers stimulate older persons to leave their feelings of uselessness behind by giving them activities and, more important, contact with others. Furthermore, the centers relieve the uneasiness or unhappiness of the older people's children, who now know that life is interesting and varied for their parents.

In the fourth article in this section, James Peterson discusses retirement and the necessary role changes that take place at this time. He believes that a person's past and his or her earlier attitudes toward old age are crucial to later adjustment. Old people have a long history behind them and a very limited one ahead—memories, experience, and the resulting attitudes have much to do with how the elderly survive.

In attempting to analyze how older persons cope with the society in which they live, it becomes important to determine the resources that are available. Obviously, health and income are basic to freedom from a troubled life. Old people suffer from a wide variety of health problems, ranging from arthritis to heart disease. Psychosomatic problems hit hard at this time too, since the adjustment mechanisms of the aged are ripe for the reaction to psychological disturbances. Accidents increase because of diminished sensory acuity, indifference, and disorientation. Health factors become increasingly important at this time, for, as goes without saying, old-age health problems invariably lead to death. Finances, too, imperil millions of old people in the United States. Poor people are often in poor health because of their living standards and poor medical care. It is a paradox that a country as advanced and affluent as the United States can produce such a large older population through advanced health care and diet, but cannot seem to use this knowledge to make the plight of the aged more humane. In the next reading, Gordon Streib discusses older persons and their troubles. He concludes that the elderly are remarkably resourceful in coping with life's difficulties and that they are helped by their children more than is generally realized. However, the thousands who have no family need programs that will enrich and sustain their lives at a higher level.

Some people do "grow old gracefully" and refuse to be defined as uninteresting and obsolete. For these people, old age is a period of freedom and actualization—a time of self-indulgence or delightful inactivity. They have no particular goals except to enjoy each day and they must impress no one. In some societies, the elderly are venerated and given a special place, but this is rare in the United States.

If the older men and women in this society feel special, it is usually due to good health and financial security and to some inner strength and peace of mind that allow them to see these years as the crown of life. In her recent bestseller on growing old, *The Coming of Age*, Simone de Beauvoir has written a short description of the hundred-year-olds, those hearty souls who may be the models of all who hope to live to an old and vigorous age. Finally, this section—and the book—close with a sonnet by Emory Bogardus, a man of ninety-one who is looking forward to being a centenarian and to whom this volume is dedicated.

72

THE CHANGING AMERICAN GRANDPARENT

Bernice L. Neugarten and Karol K. Weinstein

Despite the proliferation of investigations regarding the relations between generations and the position of the aged within the family, surprisingly little attention has been paid directly to the role of grandparenthood. There are a few articles written by psychoanalysts and psychiatrists analyzing the symbolic meaning of the grandparent in the developing psyche of the child or, in a few cases, illustrating the role of a particular grandparent in the psychopathology of a particular child. Attention has not correspondingly been given, however, to the psyche of the grandparent, and references are made only obliquely, if at all, to the symbolic meaning of the grandchild to the grandparent.

There are a number of anthropologists' reports on grandparenthood in one or another simple society as well as studies involving cross-cultural comparisons based on ethnographic materials. Notable among the latter is a study by Apple[1] which shows that, among the 51 societies for which data are available, those societies in which grandparents are removed from family authority are those in which grandparents have an equalitarian or an indulgent, warm relationship with the grandchildren. In those societies in which economic power and/or prestige rests with the old, relationships between grandparents and grandchildren are formal and authoritarian.

Sociologists, for the most part, have included only a few questions about grandparenthood when interviewing older persons about family life, or they have analyzed the grandparent role solely from indirect evidence, without empirical data gathered specifically for that purpose. There are a few noteworthy exceptions: Albrecht[2] studied the grandparental responsibilities of a representative sample of persons over 65 in a small midwestern community. She concluded that grandparents neither had nor coveted responsibility for grandchildren; that they took pleasure from the emotional response and occasionally took reflected glory from the accomplishments of their grandchildren.

An unpublished study by Apple[3] of a group of urban middle-class grandparents indicated that, as they relinquish the parental role over the adult child, grandparents come to identify with grandchildren in a way that might be called "pleasure without responsibility."

In a study of older persons in a working-class area of London, Townsend[4] found many grandmothers who maintained very large responsibility for the care of the grandchild, but he also found that for the total sample, the relationship of grandparents to grandchildren might be characterized as one of "privileged disrespect." Children were expected to be more respectful of parents than of grandparents. . . .

The data reported in this paper were collected primarily for the purpose of generating rather than testing hypotheses regarding various psychological and social dimensions of the grandparent role. Three dimensions were investigated: first, the degree of comfort with the role as expressed by the grandparent; second, the significance of the role as seen by the actor; and last, the style with which the role is enacted.

The data came from interviews with both grandmother and grandfather in 70 middle-class families in which the interviewer located first a married couple with children and then one set of grandparents. Of the 70 sets of grandparents, 46 were maternal —that is, the wife's parents—and 24 were paternal. All pairs of grandparents lived in separated households from their children, although most lived within relatively short distances within the metropolitan area of Chicago.

As classified by indices of occupation, area of residence, level of income, and level of education, the grandparental couples were all middle class. The group was about evenly divided between upper-middle (professionals and business executives) and lower-middle (owners of small service businesses and white-collar occupations below the managerial level). As is true in other middle-class, urban groups in the United States, the largest proportion of these families had been upwardly mobile, either from working class into lower-middle or from lower-middle into upper-middle. Of the 70 grandparental couples, 19 were foreign born (Polish, Lithuanian, Russian, and a few German and Italian). The sample was skewed with regard to religious affiliation, with 40 percent Jewish, 48 percent Protestant, and 12 percent Catholic. The age range of the grandfathers was, with a few exceptions, the mid-50's through the late 60's; for the grandmothers it was the early 50's to the mid-60's.

Each member of the couple was interviewed separately and, in most instances, in two sessions. Respondents were asked a variety of open-ended questions regarding their relations to their grandchildren: how often and on what occasions they saw their grandchildren; what the significance of grandparenthood was in their lives and how it had affected them. While grandparenthood has multiple values for each respondent and may influence his relations with various family members, the focus was upon the primary relationship—that between grandparent and grandchild. . . .

Degree of comfort in the role. . . . The majority of grandparents expressed only comfort, satisfaction, and pleasure. Among this group, a sizable number seemed to be idealizing the role of grandparenthood and to have high expectations of the grandchild in the future—that the child would either achieve some special goal or success or offer unique affection at some later date.

At the same time, approximately one-third of the sample (36 percent of the grandmothers and 29 percent of the grandfathers) were experiencing sufficient difficulty in the role that they made open reference to their discomfort, their disappointment, or their lack of positive reward. This discomfort indicated strain in thinking of oneself as a grandparent (the role is in some ways alien to the self-image), conflict with the parents with regard to the rearing of the grandchild, or indifference (and some self-chastisement for the indifference) to caretaking or responsibility in reference to the grandchild.

The significance and meaning of the role. The investigators made judgments based upon the total interview data on each case with regard to the primary significance of grandparenthood for each respondent. Recognizing that the role has multiple meanings for each person and that the categories to be described may overlap to some degree, the investigators nevertheless classified each case as belonging to one of five categories:

1) For some, grandparenthood seemed to constitute primarily a source of *biological renewal* ("It's through my grandchildren that I feel young again") and/or *biological continuity* with the future ("It's through these children that I see my life going on into the future" or, "It's carrying on the family line"). . . . This category occurred significantly less frequently for grandfathers than for grandmothers, perhaps because the majority of these respondents were parents, not of the young husband but of the young wife. It is likely that grandfathers perceive family continuity less frequently through their female than through their male offspring and that in a sample more evenly balanced with regard to maternal-paternal lines of ascent, this category would appear more frequently in the responses from grandfathers.

2) For some, grandparenthood affords primarily an opportunity to succeed in a new emotional role, with the implication that the individual feels himself to be a better grandparent than he was a parent. Frequently, grandfatherhood offered a certain vindication of the life history by providing *emotional self-fulfillment* in a way that fatherhood had not done. As one man put it, "I can be, and I can do for my grandchildren things I could never do for my own kids. I was too busy with my business to enjoy my kids, but my grandchildren are different. Now I have the time to be with them."

3) For a small proportion, the grandparent role provides a new role of teacher or *resource person.* Here the emphasis is upon the satisfaction that accrues from contributing to the grandchild's welfare—either by financial aid, or by offering the benefit of the grandparent's unique life experience. For example, "I take my grandson down to the factory and show him how the business operates—and then, too, I set aside money especially for him. That's something his father can't do yet, although he'll do it for *his* grandchildren."

4) For a few, grandparenthood is seen as providing an extension of the self in that the grandchild is one who will *accomplish vicariously* for the grandparent that which neither he nor his first-generation offspring could achieve. For these persons, the grandchild offers primarily an opportunity for aggrandizing the ego, as in the case of the grandmother who said, "She's a beautiful child, and she'll grow up to be a beautiful woman. Maybe I shouldn't, but I can't help feeling proud of that."

5) . . . Twenty-seven percent of the grandmothers and 29 percent of the grandfathers in this sample reported feeling relatively *remote* from their grandchildren and acknowledged relatively *little effect* of grandparenthood in their own lives—this despite the fact that they lived geographically near at least one set of grandchildren and felt apologetic about expressing what they regarded as unusual sentiments. Some of the grandfathers mentioned the young age of their grandchildren in connection with their current feelings of psychological distance. For example, one man remarked, "My granddaughter is just a baby, and I don't even feel like a grandfather yet. Wait until she's older—maybe I'll feel different then."

Of the grandmothers who felt remote from their grandchildren, the rationalization was different. Most of the women in this group were working or were active in community affairs and said essentially, "It's great to be a grandmother, of course—but I don't have much time. . . ." The other grandmothers in this group indicated strained relations with the adult child; either they felt that their daughters had married too young, or they disapproved of their sons-in-law.

For both the men and the women who fell into this category of psychological distance, a certain lack of conviction appeared in their statements, as if the men did not really believe that, once the grandchildren were older, they would indeed become closer to them, and as if the women did not really believe that their busy schedules accounted for their lack of emotional involvement with their grandchildren. Rather, these grandparents imply that the role itself is perceived as being empty of meaningful relationships.

Styles of grandparenting. Somewhat independent of the significance of grandparenthood is the question of style in enacting the role of grandmother or grandfather. Treating the data inductively, five major styles were differentiated:

1) The *Formal* are those who follow what they regard as the proper and prescribed role for grandparents. Although they like to provide special treats and indulgences for the grandchild, and although they may occasionally take on a minor service such as baby-sitting, they maintain clearly demarcated lines between parenting and grandparenting, and they leave parenting strictly to the parent. They maintain a constant interest in the grandchild but are careful not to offer advice on childrearing.

2) The *Fun Seeker* is the grandparent whose relation to the grandchild is characterized by informality and playfulness. He joins the child in specific activities for the specific purpose of having fun, somewhat as if he were the child's playmate. Grandchildren are viewed as a source of leisure activity, as an item of "consumption" rather than "production," or as a source of self-indulgence. The relationship is one in which authority lines—either with the grandchild or with the parent—are irrelevant. The emphasis here is on mutuality of satisfaction rather than on providing treats for the grandchild. Mutuality imposes a latent demand that both parties derive fun from the relationship.

3) The *Surrogate Parent* occurs only, as might have been anticipated, for grandmothers in this group. It comes about by initiation on the part of the younger generation, that is, when the young mother works

and the grandmother assumes the actual caretaking responsibility for the child.

4) The *Reservoir of Family Wisdom* represents a distinctly authoritarian patricentered relationship in which the grandparent—in the rare occasions on which it occurs in this sample, it is the grandfather—is the dispenser of special skills or resources. Lines of authority are distinct, and the young parents maintain and emphasize their subordinate positions, sometimes with and sometimes without resentment.

5) The *Distant Figure* is the grandparent who emerges from the shadows on holidays and on special ritual occasions such as Christmas and birthdays. Contact with the grandchild is fleeting and infrequent, a fact which distinguishes this style from the *Formal*. This grandparent is benevolent in stance but essentially distant and remote from the child's life, a somewhat intermittent St. Nicholas.

Of major interest is the frequency with which grandparents of both sexes are either Fun Seekers or Distant Figures vis-a-vis their grandchildren. These two styles have been adopted by half of all the cases in this sample. Of interest, also, is the fact that in both styles the issue of authority is peripheral. Although deference may be given to the grandparent in certain ways, authority relationships are not a central issue.

Both of these styles are, then, to be differentiated from what has been regarded as the traditional grandparent role—one in which patriarchal or matriarchal control is exercised over both younger generations and in which authority constitutes the major axis of the relationship.

These two styles of grandparenting differ not only from traditional concepts; they differ also in some respects from more recently described types. Cavan, for example,[5] has suggested that the modern grandparent role is essentially a maternal one for both men and women and that to succeed as a grandfather, the male must learn to be a slightly masculinized grandmother, a role that differs markedly from the instrumental and outer-world orientation that has presumably characterized most males during a great part of their adult lives. It is being suggested here, however, that the newly emerging types are neuter in gender. Neither the Fun Seeker nor the Distant Figure involves much nurturance, and neither "maternal" nor "paternal" seems an appropriate adjective.

Grandparent style in relation to age. A final question is the extent to which these new styles of grandparenting reflect, directly or indirectly, the increasing youthfulness of grandparents as compared to a few decades ago. (This youthfulness is evidenced not only in terms of the actual chronological age at which grandparenthood occurs but also in terms of evaluations of self as youthful. A large majority of middle-aged and older persons describe themselves as "more youthful than my parents were at my age.")

To follow up this point, the sample was divided into two groups: those who were under and over 65. . . . The Formal style occurs significantly more frequently in the older group; the Fun Seeking and the Distant Figure styles occur significantly more frequently in the younger group. (. . . The same age differences occur in both grandmothers and grandfathers.)

These age differences may reflect secular trends: this is, differences in values and expectations in persons who grow up and who grow old at different times in history. They may also reflect processes of aging and/or the effects of continuing socialization which produce differences in role behavior over time. It might be pointed out, however, that sociologists, when they have treated the topic of grandparenthood at all, have done so within the context of old age, not middle age. Grandparenthood might best be studied as a middle-age phenomenon if the investigator is interested in the assumption of new roles and the significance of new roles in adult socialization.

In this connection, certain lines of inquiry suggest themselves: as with other roles, a certain amount of anticipatory socialization takes place with regard to the grandparent role. Women in particular often describe a preparatory period in which they visualize themselves as grandmothers, often before their children are married. With the presently quickened pace of the family cycle, in which women experience the emptying of the nest, the marriages of their children, and the appearance of grandchildren at earlier points in their own lives, the expectation that grandmotherhood is a welcome and pleasurable event seems frequently to be accompanied also by doubts that one is "ready" to become a grandmother or by the feelings of being prematurely old. The anticipation and first adjustment to the role of grandmother has not been systematically studied, either by sociologists or psychologists, but there is anecdotal data to suggest that, at both conscious and unconscious levels, the middle-aged woman may relive her own first pregnancy and childbirth and that there are additional social and psychological factors that probably result in a certain transformation in ego-identity. The reactions of males to grandfatherhood has similarly gone uninvestigated although, as has been suggested earlier, the event may require a certain reversal of traditional sex role and a consequent change in self-concept.

Other questions that merit investigation relate to the variations in role expectations for grandparents in various ethnic and socioeconomic groups and the extent to which the grandparent role is comparable to other roles insofar as "reality shock" occurs for some individuals—that is, insofar as a period of disenchantment sets in, either early in the life of the grandchild or later as the grandchild approaches adolescence when the expected rewards to the grandparents may not be forthcoming.

When grandparenthood comes to be studied from such perspectives as these, it is likely to provide a significant area for research, not only with regard to changing family structure but also with regard to adult socialization.

NOTES

[1] Dorrian Apple, "The Social Structure of Grandparenthood," *American Anthropologist,* 58 (August 1956):656–663. See also S. F. Nadel, *The Foundations of Social Anthropology,* Glencoe, Ill.: Free Press, 1953; A. R. Radcliffe-Brown, *African Systems of Kinship and Marriage,* London: Oxford University Press, 1950.

[2] Ruth Albrecht, "The Parental Responsibilities of Grandparents," *Marriage and Family Living,* 16 (August 1954): 201–204.

[3] Dorrian Apple, "Grandparents and Grandchildren: A Sociological and Psychological Study of Their Relationship," unpublished Ph.D. dissertation, Radcliffe College, 1954.

[4] Peter Townsend, *The Family Life of Old People,* London: Routledge and Kegan Paul, 1957.

[5] Ruth Shonle Cavan, "Self and Role in Adjustment During Old Age," in *Human Behavior and Social Processes,* ed. Arnold M. Rose, Boston: Houghton Mifflin, 1962, pp. 526–536.

73

SOCIALIZATION FOR POSTPARENTAL LIFE

Irwin Deutscher

The span of time from the beginning of a family with the marriage of a young couple, the bearing, rearing, and marrying of their children, through the time when they are again alone together, until the ultimate death of one or both of them, is referred to as the family cycle. Cavan has described as thoroughly as anyone variations in family organization through the family cycle. She sees the cycle as "significant in that with each stage, changes occur in the family membership and consequently in family organization, roles, and interpersonal relationships." (3, pp. 262–263; 4, pp. 28–38) This paper focuses on the transition from the phase during which children are being launched into the adult world to the phase Cavan calls postparental: "The postparental couple are the husband and wife usually . . . in their forties and fifties. . . . The most obvious change is the withdrawal of adolescent and young children from the

family, leaving husband and wife as the family unit." (3, p. 573)

In the family career pattern of a large segment of our adult urban population, this appears to be emerging as a new phase of the family cycle, largely as a result of two demographic shifts: the fact that these people can expect to live considerably longer than their parents or grandparents and the fact that they averaged fewer children over a shorter span of years than their parents or grandparents.[1] The typical couple of two generations ago had a life expectancy which enabled them to survive together for 31 years after marriage, two years short of the time when their *fifth* child was expected to marry. But, "the decline in size of family and the improved survival prospects of the population since 1890 not only have assured the average parents of our day that they will live to see their children married but also have made it probable that they will have one-fourth of their married life still to come when their last child leaves the parental home." (11) . . .

Theoretically, it might be expected that the transition to postparental life would be a difficult one for the middle-aged spouses to make. Since this is an emerging phase of the family cycle, few of those entering it can find role models: in most cases one of their own parents was dead before the last of their own siblings was launched. This lack of anticipatory socialization—the absence of an opportunity to take the role of a postparental spouse, to rehearse the part before having to play the role themselves —ought theoretically to make for an extremely difficult situation after the children leave home. Much of the descriptive literature indicates that this, indeed, is a dangerous time of life (2, p. 626; 5, p. 404; 9, p. 3; 16, pp. 353–354; 17; 18, p. 79; 21, p. 7; 22, p. 43). *Nevertheless, despite expectations based on both theory and clinical experience, when urban middle-class postparental couples describe their life, the hurdle does not appear to have been insurmountable and the adaptations are seldom pathological.*

In discussing postparental life, middle-aged spouses clearly reveal that it is not sound to assume that anticipatory socialization is absent because this is a new stage of the family cycle—that is, because middle-aged couples of today have not had the experience of observing their parents make such a transition. In spite of the fact that the identical situation could not be observed and rehearsed—that there was no opportunity to learn to take the role of the other by observing others—*analogous* situations exist in one's own life. Sussman recognizes this when he suggests that "most parents are gradually prepared to some degree for the day when their children marry and leave home by their periodic absences away at school or elsewhere." (20) Such periodic absences do not, however, represent the full extent to which such socialization by analogy can occur.

Situations such as these provide an opportunity for the parent to rehearse in his own mind what life will be like when his children are gone. . . . Even though these practice situations may not be considered as permanent, important, or serious (they are more nearly instances of "playing-at-roles" than "role-playing") it will be seen that they provide the continuity in role conditioning—the socializing opportunity—that is needed. The word "opportunity" is used advisedly. Individuals react to the socialization process in different ways; on some it "takes" and on others it doesn't. The simple fact that an individual is provided with a potentially socializing experience does not necessarily result in his defining it as such or in his being socialized as a result of the experience. The remainder of this paper will be devoted to an examination of what these socializing opportunities are and the manner in which they appear to facilitate the transition to postparental life. . . .

One of the underlying cultural values of our contemporary society is the focus on change for its own sake. In a sense all Americans are socialized from early childhood to believe that change is both inevitable and good. The notion that things will not remain the same—politically, economically, or socially—is an integral part of our national ethos. . . .

In our interviews, we find evidence that middle-class urban Americans have internalized this value and are able logically to relate it to the family cycle. One mother observes philosophically that "it seems like life spaces itself. You look forward to finishing up one space but then another space always pops up. When this is accomplished something else comes along." The clearest statements, however, come from two of the fathers. One of them, when asked how it felt to become a grandfather responded that "like most things in my life, it's just a matter of course. Things can be expected, like you expect changes in jobs and expect children to be married. Natural events come afterward and you take those things as a matter of course." This process, felt to be "natural" in our society, is described in full detail by the other father:

Of course you hate to give up your daughter, but I think we all understand that is the way of life; you can't stand still; you can't be the same forever. Life moves on and that is the most natural thing. You see them grow. You see them graduate from high school. Then you see them graduate from college—you follow along. It is changing all the time. First it is childhood. You hold them on your lap then you go walking with them. Then you see them through high school. I was her chauffeur, all the time taking her to social functions. She went through music school, then she got a bachelor of arts, then we sent her for four years to Juilliard and she got her bachelor's and master's there. Then she comes out and teaches in college for one year and then she gets married and settles down.

It is clear that at least some people are aware of a life cycle and a family cycle and are resigned (if not committed) to a philosophy of change. Whether or not one is willing to accept the conditioning effect of a basic cultural emphasis on change *per se*, there remain several more specific types of experiences which provide parents with an opportunity of anticipatory socialization. . . .

Opportunities for middle-class parents at least to play at a postparental role frequently occur when the children leave home for college. However, such opportunities are exploited to varying degrees, or, to put it another way, the experience is defined differently by different couples. Some parents make no mention of the possibility of college as a socializing experience for themselves. Presumably many of these do not see that possibility. On the other hand, there are others who see clearly what is happening. A mother claims that, "The breaking point is when your children go away to college. After that you grow used to it. By the time they get married you're used to the idea of their being away and adjust to it."

The question, "Do you think your child was ready to marry when he did?" brought out the functionality of the college experience. One father responded, "Yes, I thought she was. She had already gone through college—those five years of college and two years working. She was ready to get married." More important is that the college experience meant that he was now ready

for her to get married. This kind of projection—the notion that college is training for the child to get away rather than training for the parent to release him—is expressed most clearly by a mother:

It's only natural, when you have a family of three without any relatives near by, to notice a gap when she gets married. Of course, the first adjustment is when they go away to school; that's the first break. It's healthy for an only child to go far away to school. It makes them more self-sufficient. She had been in school away from home since she was 16 and I think she was very well adjusted. Being away like that she learned to be independent, and make her own decisions and take responsibilities on her own. It was a sort of training period which prepared her [sic; "us"?] for leaving us [sic; "her"?].

Another mother says of her recently married son, "We had gotten used to just being by ourselves while he was in the Navy and away at college." This brings us to another frequently occurring opportunity for parents to play at the postparental role: the departure of children for military service. Life experiences tend to be evaluated in comparison with other experiences. They are not just good or bad; they are better or worse. Apparently it is better to lose a child through marriage than through war: "My most unhappy time was around the war years when my boy was in service. I worried over him coming back; he was missing several times." This is the kind of socialization that gives a parent a sense of relief to have a child home and married. We learn from another mother that, "When he was sent overseas, I was so worried about him over there that it was a relief when he got married and settled down." The importance of this as a learning experience is illustrated by the mother whose three children are now married, but who says of the time when her son went into service and she still had two others at home, "I think that the lonesomest part of my life I ever had was when my son was in service. We missed our boy." Her husband, interestingly enough, explicitly states that the

Army experience serves as preparation for marriage. When asked if he thought his children were mature enough to get married, he responded: "Well, I thought more so about the boy because he was in the Army, but I did think that she (the daughter) should have waited."

Being in the armed forces serves both to wean the parents away from the children and the children away from the parents. Still another mother reports that:

After he came out of the service he had aged a lot. He used to confide in us about life and to tell us about everything that was happening in school. But after he went into service he changed. We always spent our afternoons together—both the children. We'd go out for drives or picnics or something like that. But after he came home from service he didn't do that anymore. He wasn't contented to be at home.

But then, after the anguish of wartime separation, another woman implies that it is good just to know that the child is safe and is in this country:

He was in the Second World War and he was overseas. And after having been so far away from home he feels like he's practically right here, because we can telephone and it's just 50 miles. After having been in Europe a couple of years, you know 50 miles away is "at home."

There are other experiences which, like college or service in the armed forces, give parents an opportunity to practice living without their children. Nearly a quarter of the families interviewed had parted with their children for extended periods of time while they were still in their teens. For example, there is the son who couldn't get along with his father: "My son used to say that as much as he would like to stay here, he couldn't take things off of his dad any longer. So I never insisted on him staying. He left a couple of times and would come back." Then there is the child with the wanderlust: "That boy wasn't interested in anything except to hitchhike—just to get as far as he could and to see what he could see.

He was walking when he was eight months old and has been walking ever since." More common than either of these two experiences is the departure of children prior to marriage in search of work. Although this sometimes occurs with daughters, it is more frequently the sons who leave for this reason:

(Do you remember how you felt when you first found out he was going to get married?) Yes, he was the first one. Both of them are married now. It was all right. He was able to take care of himself. He was away from home a lot. He and the oldest boy were up in Detroit on defense work. They have really been away from home a long time—ever since 1940.

(How did you find it when the children left? Did you have a lot of time on your hands?) Well, that came gradually. The war had something to do with that. They were both in the war before they got married and we were alone then. And the youngest one went to aviation school. He was just barely 18 when he got his first job in Texas. Then he went to Phoenix and then he came home and then he went into service. And the other boy was at home for awhile and then he had to go. So with their coming and going it kinda eased off gradually.

Finally, in connection with these temporary departures of children prior to marriage, a word should be said about the modern middle-class urban high school complex. In some cases it results in the home being little more than a place to sleep and certainly in infrequent contacts with the parents. This reaction was obtained only from fathers. Possibly mothers maintain closer contacts with their children—especially with daughters—during the high school years. Be this as it may, one father reports that:

There is a difference when they grow older —particularly when they went to high school. Naturally they got their own friends and you saw less of them than you did before. They'd come home from school late and then they'd have a game or maybe the girl would have a date and you might see them at dinner time, but you probably wouldn't see them until breakfast—or maybe after the game or date.

Another father stated that the "best years" were when his boys were around nine or ten: "(When they started to grow up did you feel that they were growing away from you?) No, but when they go to high school they have different ideas and interests than the people at home have." There is, however, another side to this coin. The proud father of a high school athlete was asked when was the happiest time of his life: "Oh—that kid of mine—the things he did when he was in high school. It was like living your life over again. I guess I really enjoyed that period."

On the basis of such observations, there is reason to believe that there are bridges— transitional learning experiences which aid parents in adapting themselves to postparental life. These appear to provide continuity in role conditioning. Such "rehearsals" are not as difficult as "opening night," the real and permanent departure of the children which will come later. They are defined as temporary and are broken by regular visits home or the expectation that the children will at some time again return to live at home. But the "temporary" can gradually shift into the permanent without any traumatic transition: "My daughter went to California, to Berkeley, to go to school. Then she decided to work there a while and then she got married out there and she has lived there ever since." The fact that these socializing experiences occur at a time when the parents are still extremely active with their own affairs should not be ignored. It is probably easier to prepare for and accept such a transition in early middle age than in later years when it will actually occur. When one mother was asked how she made out at home with the children all off to college, she shrugged off the question with, "Oh, I don't know. I was just too busy to be bothered about anything.". . .

Even when father is at home, he may be so in body only, being engrossed in his work day and night whether on the road or in town. When this kind of commitment to work evolves, men whose work never takes them out of town may see less of their families than some who, like the railroader, travel a great deal. One mother generalizes: "I think most men are so occupied with their work that they sort of leave that (rearing of children) to the mother." A father whose work has never taken him out of town concurs: "I'm afraid I left most of bringing him up to his mother. Lots of times when he was growing up I had to work late. I wouldn't get home till 9:30 or 10:00 at night and I'd be out to the office at 5:00 in the morning."

It is important, however, that this parental detachment not be overemphasized. Not all middle-class fathers orient themselves to the work role so strongly. There are certainly some who leave their work at the office: "I have no night work. My work is at the office and when I leave the office I'm through until the next day, regardless of what I've got. I've never made a practice of bringing work home." There are others who emphasize that, in spite of many temptations, they have steadfastly refused to take their work out of the office.

It would seem that there are a good many cases among urban middle-class families where life goes on without father during the years when the child is growing up. As dysfunctional as this may be to the family at that stage, it does provide the fathers with continuity in role conditioning which can stand them in good stead at the later postparental stage when the time comes for the children to depart permanently. . . .

If the work role helps to condition fathers for the departure of their children, at least some mothers appear to be provided with a conditioning device which is the distinctive property of their sex. That device is the cultural myth of the mother-in-law: "As soon as my youngsters were born I made up my mind that I was not going to be a mother-in-law like you read about." Such a resolution, if intended seriously, could go far in preparing a mother to accept the departure of her children. In addition to the folklore on the mother-in-law, there is the reality of experience:

My son got married before he even finished his education. He was only 17 years old, but I did not say a word! I don't think it's good policy. That can be a very tender spot. I know because I went through it. I had a mother-in-law—well, she was just butting into everything all the time. I just resolved never to act like that myself. The Bible says something about to hold your peace. And that's not prose. That's just the way it should be. People when they get married should get away from relatives. Far enough away so that it takes three days for a postcard to get to them and three more for it to get back.

The following mother expresses the same opinion even more vehemently:

I'll go to the county home before I'll live with any of my children. I have very definite ideas on that. Because I had his mother with us every winter for 20 years whether I had room for her or not and it doesn't work and I very definitely *will* not *do a thing like that! If I have to take a dose of strychnine first, I won't!*

Humor is, of course, an effective form of social control—especially in an increasingly other-directed society. Mothers, like everyone else, are sensitive to the pleas of the mass media for conformity. They want to be "good" mothers-in-law and Evelyn Duvall's study indicates that they are—that the mother-in-law is not nearly the center of conflict in America that she is often thought to be (7). It is very possible that a more accurate statement would be that the mother-in-law is not nearly the center of conflict that she *used* to be. The pressures of experience and folklore as indicated in the passages cited above may have brought about a shift in the self-conception of mothers-in-law and in the role which they play. In any event, at least in some cases, these myths and experiences provide an opportunity for mothers to anticipate and prepare themselves for postparental life—a socializing opportunity. . . .

The postparental phase of the family cycle was described earlier as a newly emerging phenomenon resulting from increasing longevity and decreasing fertility. No longer is it true, as it was at the turn of the century, that both parents will have died before the last of their children was launched. However, as with any emerging phenomenon, fragmentary survivals of the earlier pattern remain. In such cases, there is, in effect, no transition to make—these people have no postparental period. Take, for example, the couple with six children ranging in age from 31 to 44, with three of them married and residing in the metropolitan area and a fourth divorced and living at home. Their daily life remains essentially the same as it has always been, although the work is somewhat lighter and the economic situation somewhat more secure:

(Tell me just how you spend a typical day nowadays?) Well, I do my housework in the morning and then I get meals again, and the children will come in once in a while and sometimes I go down to one of my daughters'. That is all I do. I have a fine family. They are all good Christian children and I am just as proud of them as I can be.

Life has changed so little for this couple that they even argue about the same kinds of trivialities they did 30 years ago:

. . . take that rug there in the dining room. I didn't like the color but he bought it anyway because it was a good buy. It was a remnant. But it seemed to me that a rug is something you have to live with for a long time and it ought to satisfy you. But he said that I had had my way with the wallpaper so he went ahead and bought it.

An extended family need not be one of procreation; even with few children, postparental couples may refer themselves to a large family of orientation. This older pattern manifests itself in the case of a couple one of whose two married children is now living in Minneapolis. In spite of this, there is a plethora of parental siblings, in-laws, nephews, nieces, and grandchildren

—all part of a second- and third-generation Irish clan residing in the Kansas City area:

(Tell me what do you do with your time these days?) Well, we are quite home people, that is, with the grandchildren, the daughter, and his (husband's) people. He has seven brothers and they are all living in Kansas City, and we are very close to one another—the husbands and wives. We have picnics, and we go from home to home for little parties and then I have my sisters too and they live here. You know, we just enjoy family. I have brothers and sisters and he has all brothers. So that gives me a lot of sister-in-laws too. So we are very family people—very home people.

This kind of extended family support appears to lessen the trauma of the disintegration of the family of procreation. Most families, however, find themselves far more isolated from "kinfolk" in the modern American city.

SUMMARY AND CONCLUSIONS

We have seen that several conditioning situations present themselves as potential aids in the socialization of parents for postparental life. These situations provide an opportunity to anticipate postparental roles, not by taking the role of the other in the usual sense, but by experiencing analogous situations which are quasi-postparental and which enable the parents to play at anticipated roles. There is the underlying value in our society on change for its own sake —a value which can be applied to the particular case of change in the family structure; there are the temporary departures of children during the adolescent years for college, service in the armed forces, and a variety of other reasons; there is the modern complex of urban high school life, which can move the children into a world which is foreign to their parents; there are the exigencies of the work situation which often remove the middle-class father from the family during the years when the children are growing up; there is the myth and the

reality of the mother-in-law which some mothers internalize as lessons for themselves. In addition, remnants of the older extended family pattern which tend to reduce the impact of the transition cannot be ignored.

It was stated earlier that *theoretically* this could be assumed to be a difficult transition to make, largely because of the absence of role models—the absence of socialization to play postparental roles. However, the middle-aged couples whose children have left home indicate that there are opportunities for them to learn these new roles before they are thrust upon them.

It was also stated earlier that much of the descriptive literature indicates that this is a difficult period of life. By and large such observations are based on clinical experiences with persons who have so much difficulty in making the transition that they must seek outside help. The small group of postparental spouses interviewed by the present writer represent a random sample of such people who discussed their lives in their own living room. Although definite conclusions cannot be drawn from the responses of this small fragment of the population, they have managed to provide us with some notion of the variety of alternative modes of anticipatory socialization available to their ilk. It would appear from their comments that it is reasonable to assume that people do have opportunities to prepare for postparental life and, in addition, that most of them take advantage of these opportunities.

This phase of the family cycle is seen by the majority of middle-aged spouses as a time of new freedoms: freedom from the economic responsibilities of children; freedom to be mobile (geographically); freedom from housework and other chores. And, finally, freedom to be one's self for the first time since the children came along. No longer do the parents need to live the self-consciously restricted existence of models for their own children: "We just take life easy now that the children are grown. We even serve dinner right from the stove when we're alone. It's hotter that way, but you just couldn't let down like that when your children are still at home."

NOTES AND REFERENCES

[1] Although it may appear that, in terms of average number of children, the offspring of the current crop of postparental couples are reverting to the patterns of older generations, this reversion is more apparent than real: "The fact that the crude birth rate has been higher in the postwar period than in the 1930's is due primarily to the operation of two factors: a larger proportion of women have been marrying at younger ages, and more of those marrying have started their families relatively soon after marriage. These factors may have only a minor effect on the final average number of children that women will have borne by the end of the child-bearing period. . . ."

1. Benedict, Ruth. Continuities and discontinuities in cultural conditioning. *Psychiatry*, 1938, *1*, 161–167.

2. Burgess, Ernest W., and Locke, Harvey. *The family: from institution to companionship*. New York: American Book Co., 1945.

3. Cavan, Ruth S. *The American family*. New York: Thomas Y. Crowell Company, 1953.

4. Cavan, Ruth S. *Marriage and family in the modern world*. New York: Thomas Y. Crowell Company, 1960.

5. Christensen, Harold. *Marriage analysis*. New York: The Ronald Press Company, 1950.

6. Deutscher, Irwin. Married life in the middle years: a study of the middle class urban postparental couple. Ph.D. dissertation, Department of Sociology, University of Missouri, 1958.

7. Duvall, Evelyn M. *In-laws: pro and con*. New York: Association Press, 1954.

8. Duvall, Evelyn M. Implications for education through the family life cycle. *Marriage and Family Living*, November, 1958, *20*, 334–342.

9. Duvall, Evelyn M., and Hill, Reuben. *The dynamics of family interaction*. National Conference on Family Life, Inc., 1948 (mimeographed).

10. Freedman, Ronald, Whelpton, Pascal K., and Campbell, Arthur A. *Family planning, sterility and population growth*. New York: McGraw-Hill Book Company, 1959.

11. Glick, Paul C. The family cycle. *American Sociological Review*, April, 1947, *12*, 164–169.

12. Glick, Paul C. The cycle of the family. *Marriage and Family Living*, February, 1955, *17*.

13. Hiltner, Helen J. Changing family tasks of adults. *Marriage and Family Living*, May, 1953, *15*, 110–113.

14. House, Floyd N. The natural history of institutions. In *The development of sociology*. New York: McGraw-Hill Book Company, 1936, 141–157.

15. Hughes, Everett C. *Men and their work*. New York: The Free Press, 1959.

16. Kinsey, Alfred, Pomeroy, Wardell B., Martin, Clyde E., and Gebhard, Paul H. *Sexual behavior in the human female*. Philadelphia: W. B. Saunders Company, 1953.

17. Lowrey, Lawson G. Adjustment over the life span. In George Lawton (ed.), *New goals for old age*. New York: Columbia University Press, 1943, 8–9.

18. Pollak, Otto. *Social adjustment in old age*. New York: Social Science Research Council, Bulletin 59, 1948.

19. Sirjamaki, John. *The American family in the twentieth century*. Cambridge, Mass.: Harvard University Press, 1953.

20. Sussman, Marvin B. Parental participation in mate selection and its effect upon family continuity. *Social Forces*, October, 1953, *32*, 76–77.

21. Tibbitts, Clark. National aspects of an aging population. In Clark Tibbitts and Wilma Donahue (eds.), *Growing in the older years*. Ann Arbor, Mich.: The University of Michigan Press, 1951.

22. Waller, Willard, and Hill, Reuben. *The family: a dynamic interpretation*. New York: The Dryden Press, 1951.

74

LOOKING AHEAD IN AGING: LOVE AFTER FIFTY

Marcia E. Lasswell

Living beyond the age of fifty is a new phenomenon. A few generations ago very few people lived to be over sixty-five; but today there are over 20 million people over sixty-five in the United States, and this number is constantly growing. A person who is between fifty and sixty-five is considered to be *young;* yet many people go into a mild state of shock on their fiftieth birthdays. Although people react differently to hitting the middle and later years, most find themselves taking stock and reevaluating their lives as they discover new opportunities and new ways of experiencing.

One thing does not change when an individual passes the fifty-year mark—his or her need for love and affection does not diminish. Most people find ways to satisfy the need to love and be loved, but often the patterns built during the first fifty years cease to be effective during the last few decades of their lives. One of the chief complaints of the "over fifties" is that they are lonely and seem caught up in a search for meaning which leads them into many blind alleys.

MARRIAGE AND THE NEED FOR AFFECTION

Since most Americans marry at least once—currently about 95 percent—and six out of seven who divorce remarry, the marital relationship, as well as the bonds of affection set up with children, provide the major avenues for affectional needs in our society. Usually some contact is maintained with extended family members over the years, but most often, the major bonds of affection are transferred from our original family to the new family which we create by marriage.

Many studies have indicated that married people are far happier and healthier than single, widowed, or divorced persons, and this is true of the couples over fifty as well as of younger people. There is a great deal of security in a good marriage, for each partner receives love and affection from a person who means a great deal to him or her. Happily married people don't have to pretend to be what they are not; they can relax and feel settled with each other. If the couple is supportive of each other, life is easier and problems don't have to be met alone. In spite of the fact that their circle of friends may have grown smaller, they still have each other; the years of devotion and caring for their children can now be replaced by strengthening bonds between husband and wife. Their habits grow more alike—sometimes they seem to look alike. A good marriage, thus, solves most of the affectional needs of the mature couple; and the children and grandchildren may provide still another welcome dimension in many cases. And if the children fail to contribute to the couple's affectional needs, they still have each other. Of course, a couple may come to rely on each other too much, but such a problem is generally avoided if they have outside interests.

A worrisome part of this rather ideal solution to love after fifty is that, if a couple has been truly happy throughout their years together, the death of one partner makes the adjustment for the other difficult. Often the death of the other partner quickly follows (which must make even the most unromantic of us suspect that there may be such a thing as dying of a broken heart).

Perhaps the problem of the death of a spouse is compounded by the fact that the couple has had more time together than was previously thought possible. An average couple of fifty years ago could expect to live together about thirty years. A typical marriage of four generations ago lasted only twenty years. Thus, when one of the partners died, there was at least a child at home to give the other a reason to go on. Life expectancy was much shorter for both men and women; and people married, had a good-sized family, and, before the last child left home, one or both of them died.

Today, however, young couples marry in their early twenties and live to be well over seventy, on the average. Fifty years of marriage to one person—or to a series of people—is quite common today and may be the rule of tomorrow. Recently, for example, the newspapers carried a story about an Iowa couple who had been married for eighty years and were both hale and hearty at 103 years of age. I am sure we will begin to hear more of these stories in the future, since there are already over 160,000 golden anniversaries each year.

To further complicate the problem of old age, today's average parents not only live longer but have fewer children. Consequently, they often have roughly one quarter of their married lives still to come when the last child leaves home. This is the first time in the history of the world that such a situation has existed, and it gives a new dimension to marriage that has been little explored at this point.

Most people are still married when, near their fiftieth birthdays, their last child leaves home. However, for people between fifty and sixty-five, both divorce—the incidence of which sharply rises when the last child leaves home—and death increase; only about half of the population aged sixty-five and older still lives with a spouse. Although, as was mentioned earlier, there are more older married couples today than there were a few generations ago, still a couple married when they are at a truly advanced age are almost considered deviant —they are the exception rather than the rule. Such a couple, furthermore, may not have as many friends as they once did, for most of their past friends are no longer married and there is less in common in their lives.

Divorce and death take their toll on the marriages of the "over fifties," but many widows and widowers who know the comforts of a good marriage seek to remarry—

to find a companion with whom to share life. However effective marriage is as a solution to loneliness and needs for affection, remarriage too has its drawbacks. Because the age span for women is greater than for men, and there are more widows than there are men to marry, the difficulty of such an undertaking increases for women as they grow older. (Perhaps polygamy is a solution to this problem.) Many times, the children of an older person disapprove of his or her remarrying—for reasons ranging from fear of losing their inheritance to general disapproval of anything short of celibacy from their aging parents. Also, many people over sixty-five live on Social Security and pensions, which widows stand to lose upon remarriage. Since it is difficult for two to live on one Social Security check, they may be discouraged from marrying. Over one fourth of the persons in the United States over sixty-five live at the poverty level. Some 5 million of them were at this economic level to begin with, but the other 15 million are the "newly poor," of whom 2 million live on Social Security checks alone and only 10 percent receive pension benefits from jobs they have held. Aside from health and loneliness, lack of money is probably the most pervasive worry of those over sixty-five, and it has resulted in hundreds of older men and women living together without being married.

Because of the numerous financial and social problems accompanying old age, and because the number of older people has increased steadily in the last half century and is increasing at an even faster rate today, some solutions to these problems for persons who desire to reestablish themselves in marriage during their later years must be found. A good marriage is health-and-happiness insurance; those who have such a relationship are fortunate, and those who desire to find this relationship again should be encouraged—not discouraged. As one gets older, the warmth and sharing found in marriage become even more important, for there are few people who are willing to or can provide this for them. The older person who is cut off from touching and physical contact (not necessarily sexual contact) when this has been an important part of his or her life often has a real physical reaction to the deprivation. Older people are often left very much alone physically, and their hunger for contact may account in large measure for the depression and stress which lead to physical and mental problems in old age.

Of course, many people over fifty are not happily married or are not married at all. They may more often be portrayed as having a "crisis of passing fifty," as suffering from problems caused by the changes in their bodies and psyches. "Over fifties" are often characterized as unemployed, introspective, depressed, and heavy users of drugs—much like some descriptions of *young* people today. Certainly, not all of these problems can be attributed to lack of love, but there is no doubt that many, if not most, of the problems would be helped by being loved by someone who matters. The adjustment problems of these years, which are caused by the interaction of several physical, psychological, and environmental factors, produce deeply disturbing life situations for some people, are taken in stride by others, and provide real enjoyment for many others. What seems to make the difference?

THE CRISIS OF PASSING FIFTY

Two major theories have been advanced to explain the different behaviors resulting from aging. The first is the *disengagement theory,* which says that aging is accompanied by an inner process that makes loosening of social ties a natural process. According to this theory, the healthiest and happiest older people learn to accept each day as a gift and realize that the basic meaning of life is now to conserve and enjoy rather than to accumulate and accomplish. Losses begin to mount more quickly than new interests and friends can be gained. Every day seems to bring the death of an old friend or the realization that an activity is out of reach due to age and energy; memories must suffice as the older person becomes resigned to the losses of life. This theory is largely the philosophy be-

hind retirement communities—the "Leisure Worlds" and "Sun Cities." For many, this way of life is not only desirable but so satisfactory that they encourage their friends to come to join them.

The second theory says that *engagement* with life is the way to contribute the most to psychological well-being, no matter how old one is—not disengagement. According to this philosophy, disengagement theory is a rationale for the "I-haven't-a-damn-thing-to-do-and-nothing-to-do-it-with" attitude. Since most people don't have many financial resources, and, certainly, not everyone can afford retirement homes that provide the "good life" (almost a third of the older people never leave their block), they have been forced into disengagement. The engagement theory postulates that with age the type of engagement changes from the aggressive, driving-to-achievement kind to one concerned with people and ideas; the involvement in social bonds—not the loosening of these bonds—is seen as the key to successful aging.

Rather than side with one theory or the other, it is logical to draw them together. One way of synthesizing them is to consider aging as a time when roles can either change or remain the same. A few people stay engaged in the same roles they have always had all of their lives—they never retire nor do they slow down very much. These people, who may be self-employed, craftsmen, farmers, and some housewives, continue nearly the same routine day after day, until they die. At eighty, they work every day, are healthy and happy, and look sixty. Mental responses are mostly slowed by anxiety as we grow older—it is our attitude toward old age, not so much old age itself, that causes most slowing down of mental processes. Rarely are these actively engaged older people lonely, since they are busy and interesting and draw people to them. Married or not, they seem to find affection and a rewarding life. However, the number of such persons is small in our society, for we do not provide this opportunity for many over sixty-five. And if we lower the retirement age to fifty-five, we will eliminate a source of adjustment for millions of people who are vitally engaged in lifelong roles.

Another, larger, group of older people, who fit the disengagement theory, are disengaged from work that they have done over the years and are delighted to be free. Some have been anticipating and planning for disengagement for years and would welcome retirement at age fifty-five because they have so many things they have been waiting to do. For those who have planned for their retirement wisely and who stay healthy, these years may be among their best—a chance to start over on long-postponed activities that is earned through the years of hard work. Carl Jung, the eminent psychoanalyst who lived a full and rewarding life to the age of eighty-five, spoke of aging as a process of continuous inward development; he felt that being able to adjust to a new life-style was the sign of good health.

However, if we are to believe what we read about aging, the third group consists of most of the "over fifties." In this group are disengaged persons who don't like giving up valued roles and for whom growing older is unpleasant. Both men and women are in this third category, but women in our society generally reach this stage first—particularly those who have devoted twenty-five or thirty years to motherhood. Taking care of a family has for most of her life constituted the woman's major interest and shaped her activities; now it has come to an end. Concern for her children is likely to stay high on her list of priorities; but her children don't need her as much, and she may feel that her major function in life has been completed. While she may in many ways be relieved, the loss of her role is difficult to adjust to, and she must make a definite shift in her way of life. Her adjustment is made more difficult by menopause, which brings physical and, for many, psychological changes. Of course, only about 40 percent of women have significant menopausal symptoms of a physical variety; given good health and an interesting life, most women have a minimum of difficulty. Also, hormone replacement can reduce or even eliminate menopausal symptoms, and the woman may even welcome menopause as a freedom from the years of menstruation and from the possibility of pregnancy.

For the man, the critical aspect of being over fifty usually concerns coming to terms with his level of accomplishment, carrying the load of responsibilities before he faces retirement, and facing what he will do when he retires. He has probably been striving for goals which he has either reached or has recognized are beyond his reach. He, too, is undergoing physical changes; while they may not be as readily noticeable as the cessation of menstruation is in women, there is the realization that things just aren't the same as they used to be. Some men even have physical changes and swings in mood and temperament similar to those reported by women at the climacteric. The climacteric in men stems from changes in the gonads similar to the hormonal changes that cause menopause in women. But, whereas the menopause is a comparatively quick shutdown of the ovaries and of the estrogen hormone they secrete, in males the activities of the testicles slowly decrease. Unlike women, men probably never grow too old to reproduce, although the likelihood diminishes as age advances. Nor does the output of sex hormones of the male gland stop—it is merely reduced. Still, middle age often means a sexual slowing down in men; however, if sexual *interest* lags, it is either psychological or possibly atrophy due to nonuse (which stems from psychological doubts). Some men panic when they begin to slow down, and either give up—feeling that they are "over the hill"—or go to an outside interest to reaffirm their youth.

Thus, physical changes need not complicate the problems caused by growing older. But often, other emotional problems can be involved. A person's life and marriage may not have been happy or may have ceased to be really satisfying. Couples sometimes stay together despite their problems, although the estrangement which has occurred during the child-rearing years causes them to resign themselves to a life of increasing loneliness or to look elsewhere for companionship. They lose their enthusiasm for each other—even their sexual relationship is no longer satisfying—and they begin to blame each other for the general disenchantment with life that results. They are tired and may feel that life has passed them by. Often, instead of trying to work out the problems—because it seems hopeless, or just too much trouble—one or both of the partners may begin to look outside the marriage for what seems to be missing. The fact that the affectional bonds have not been transferred from the children to the spouse may cause the individual to be dependent on the children. The husband and wife, whose relationship may become devitalized and uninspired, become unwilling, uncomfortable housemates. Once so much alive and in love, they find themselves drifting apart; knowing they are left alone with each other, they feel empty and as strangers. Each needs the other more than ever, but, hesitating to admit such needs, they turn away from demonstrations of affection or intimacy. They need to get reacquainted and to recognize the advantages of making something of the relationship in which so many years and so much effort have already been invested.

AGING AND SEXUALITY

Many middle-aged men and women report that another sex partner has "made me feel alive again." Since sexual organs respond to use and atrophy with disuse, the most important factor in maintaining effective sexuality for the over-fifty male and female is an active sexual life. The sex drive is stimulated by sexual activity; giving it up may spell the end of sex forever. A person —especially a male—who responds to changing sexual functions with fear will grow unable to respond. It is often found that, when any change occurs in how a man responds sexually that he does not understand, he apparently tends to feel that the change means the end, and he worries about possible loss of masculinity. Many older men really believe they are "over the hill" sexually, yet they are not quite sure when it happened or what made them think this was the case. Since a male never loses the facility for erection, he is a potentially effective sex partner after age

fifty. Men's interest in sex only changes a little from seventy to eighty, even though there is a slight drop in activity—a *gradual* widening in the "interest-activity gap." Women older than seventy are usually much less interested, and their "interest-activity gap" is not as wide as that of men. Effective sexual functioning for women after fifty depends in part on their knowledge of male sexual physiology as well as of their own physiology in the declining years. Sex-steroid treatment for women, or sexual exposure, can overcome the influence of sex-steroid inadequacy, so that men and women can have a close and very satisfying physical relationship.

Overwork, tranquilizers, sedatives, and other drugs vastly interfere with normal sexual response, and excessive smoking may reduce potency in even the young. Since these kinds of things are a big part of life for many "over fifties," they may contribute significantly to sexual inadequacy. But sexual failure during later years is largely psychological, sometimes due to plain boredom. Sexual response depends on sexual stimuli, especially in the later years, and the same stimulus repeated too often gradually loses its effect. Couples often get into a sexual routine lacking in excitement, and they don't realize that habit dulls interest. A couple needs new experiences to provide needed stimuli during the long years of marriage.

Some couples will have abandoned sex altogether by midlife and may hardly miss it, although totally avoiding sex may point to something much deeper than a mere lack of sex drive. Sex is a highly symbolic act; couples do not ignore it through oversight. Sex helps people keep a reasonably good body image and becomes symbolic of caring and being cared for. For married couples, sexual success symbolizes a relationship of two people who have invested a great deal in each other—an affirmation of their love. And it can help the unmarried or unhappily married accept and adjust to sexual changes that are taking place in the body, and can become an affirmation that the person is still sexually alive.

The fact that older men and women have not previously had good sex lives may make it more difficult to start, but it is no reason for them to give up. The comedian who said that sex after fifty is something like taking the *Glenn Campbell Good Time Hour* and trying to turn it into *Mission: Impossible* was not at all accurate. Couples who re-marry in later life often find the sexuality they felt was long dead reawakened. Men and women who care about each other, who have made good emotional and physi-cal adjustments to each other, who do not come to the bed fatigued, worried about their business, and full of three martinis can continue vigorous sexual activity as long as they live.

The new knowledge that we have about both male and female changes in sexual functioning is going to cause a new kind of sexual revolution—that of the "over fifties!" We now know that menopause has no ef-fect on sexual drive unless the woman thinks it will have such an effect, and then she is only responding to her own negative expectations. And with men, the decrease in testosterone production plays a very small role in decreasing sexual interest, if any. It does increase the time between peri-ods of sexual tension buildup and does de-crease the amount of seminal fluid, but it does not affect the erection—only the need and the capacity to ejaculate. And orgasm and ejaculating are not the same things, which many of us often forget and many others do not even know. In many ways, the older man is a more satisfactory sexual partner than those young men who lack experience or may suffer from premature ejaculation, for, with aging, the man in-creases his capacity to maintain an erection prior to ejaculation—a cause for rejoicing for both men and women.

Many middle-aged and older people do not know what is happening to their bodies, despite the fact that they may be quite aware that changes are occurring. This lack of understanding may result in many nega-tive attitudes; and the reaction of a person to these changes may affect the rest of his or her life. The individual must realize that physical changes do occur, but that these changes do not mean he or she is "falling apart." Instead, they mark the beginning of a second "prime of life"; making the most

of the changes and achieving the maximum in good health and loving relationships takes adjustment. They must accept grow-ing older as a time to value warmth and understanding above passion and excite-ment.

PERSONAL GROWTH IN AGING

For most of us, finding out who we are and what we want to do with our lives should be a lifelong search, and the search itself a satisfying and significant part of the experience of living. One thing is clear about persons who make good adjust-ments to their aging—they never quit grow-ing. At the same time that we look for-ward with comfortable anticipation to *do-ing,* it is equally important to learn to *be* —to have a deep inner sense of aliveness and contentment in just being with onself. We need to have a meaningful and satisfy-ing friendship with ourselves to be able to give and receive love. In order to "love thy neighbor as thyself," we must begin by feel-ing love for ourselves. Yet many older people dislike themselves so much that they give up. One million old people are in nurs-ing homes, another 10 percent are in in-stitutions or are bedridden at home. And sickness in old age is more often due to stress and diet than to age. Hence, what-ever gives us a greater understanding and allows us to be more sensitive is the nour-ishment we need. Most of us would agree that the most unhappy aging people are those who are afraid of being alone be-cause they do not feel that they are very good company; they are those who seem to have little to share with others in their lives.

Not only do the "over fifties" sell them-selves short when they do not understand their aging and believe they are on the downhill grade, but they fail those around them who need their wisdom and perspec-tive. The old have a responsibility to try to transmit to the next generations some words of advice on how to enjoy the long life that medical research has given us. Older persons have a responsibility to show the next generations how to face the problems of old age: what to do, where to live, how to find love, and how to give love.

Finding love, being attractive to others, will be difficult in our youth-oriented society. The "over fifties" may have to give a little more than when they were younger. They may need to broaden their horizons, not narrow them, so as to see things a bit more objectively and so as to be more interesting to others. But if they do these things, with all of the living they will have behind them, how can they help but be nicer to have around than when they were young and not so mellow?

75

ANTICIPATION OF THINGS TO COME

James A. Peterson

If the loss of children precipitates a crisis in family life, there is another to follow which must be faced by all men. The work life is one day over and retirement confronts the man who has organized his last forty years around his occupation. This change inevitably creates still another problem of adjustment for both husband and the wife. . . .

The end of a work career brings with it a number of role shocks. One of the most severe is the readjustment of the relationship of husband and wife, who have become used to seeing each other a limited number of hours a day. Some marriages persist only because opportunity for contact is limited. When the partners in such marriages face continuous confrontation, misery results. Another role shock has to do with the sudden end of enforced routine, with the new freedom to invest one's efforts in one's own way, with the relief from the tensions and demands associated with any career. But with this shock comes another, for the end of the occupation means the swift reduction in financial resources and generally a change in status.

All of these may serve to confuse both the man and his wife, say gerontologists Wilma Donahue, Harold Orback, and Otto Pollack, and to produce a "shock effect on the physiology and personality organization of the individual."[1] They conclude that this presents a "major challenge" to all the individual's resources. The disorganizing aspects of this crisis will be less if "the individual has taken anticipatory measures."[2] Thus the ideal time to prepare for retirement is in those years of middle age when a couple have the time and resources to plan effectively for their last years.

In one sense the need for anticipatory planning for an older age may make a significant contribution to middle-age adjustment. If individuals take the long view that middle age provides more leisure time and more freedom than the period of child raising, then the development of interests which will make the retirement years significant also cushions the transition experienced in the child-launching period. Every person's life is at all times incomplete and fragmentary in terms of the totality of his wishes and needs. If he utilizes the mid-years to take some steps in the expansion of life space by cultivating new friends, new mental horizons, new interests, he has provided that type of foundation which makes the advent of retirement less of a shock than it might otherwise have been. We are suggesting that planning may well be for the last half of life and not simply for middle age or, later, for old age. If couples do make such enlargements, they will certainly benefit both periods. . . .

The emphasis here has been on couples because we have already suggested some knotty developments that plague couples with retirement. The suggestions regarding role reversal between husband and wife may be normal for most couples, but they are not at all inevitable. Certainly the turbulence that such role reversal occasions can be rather completely avoided when the husband and wife are aware of the nature of those changes.

Why does the wife become domineering and the husband submissive? Part of the explanation is probably endocrinological. The wife loses more and more of her estrogenic hormones that influence her feminine behavior and produces more testosterone. The husband on the other hand is constantly producing less testosterone. From a psychological point of view there is the whole reaction formation on the part of the wife to the fear of disruption of her habits and household management by a husband who is now going to be underfoot all the time.

A woman once said to me when I was interviewing her on the television show, "Houseparty": "I don't know what has gotten into my husband. All our lives he was content. Now that he is home he complains all the time that I am a rotten housekeeper. Why is that?" I had to explain to her that "This is the first time he really has had a look at your housekeeping, and could know how bad you are!" After that facetious remark I went on to explain that the man was not really complaining about her housekeeping. He was merely expressing his irritation at his own unemployment and lack of things to do. Many women steel themselves for the moment when their husbands are going to be permanently home. There is a sociological aspect, too, in the sudden drop of status when a man leaves work.

Hitherto he has earned his place in the family as the provider. What is he when he quits work? He contributes little. It is true that a couple live because he earned and saved, but his main function as the instrumental leader is gone. It is perhaps precisely because of this that his wife now becomes the leader and he recedes into the background. In many families this reversal of role leads to disastrous quarreling and unhappiness. But such a catastrophic conclusion to a lifetime of togetherness does not have to happen. If a couple have, at middle age, taken the opportunity afforded by that transition to build new communication and to develop new ways of sharing, by the time they reach retirement these patterns will be well established and no great new adjustment will need to be made or damage suffered. . . .

One of the most significant insights which has come from the series of cases studied by Otto Pollack, a prominent sociologist and gerontologist, is that marital adjustment is the critical issue. For instance he found that no activity, no matter how engaging and rewarding, contributes to good adjustment in aging unless it is accepted by the marital partner.

The increased importance of the marriage relationship in this phase of life makes harmony with the spouse apparently a conditio sine qua non *of positive adjustment.*[3]

This comment means far more to us than simply a comment on retirement interests. It highlights the increasing significance of good marital relationships for life satisfaction as the years pass. It is a common finding of all gerontological studies that marital pairs are far happier than individuals who are single, widowed, or divorced. Again the significance of this fact for middle-aged persons is obvious. If, at the critical juncture of the prime of life, behavior is such as to sow seeds of suspicion or to infer neglect of the other, the deterioration of the relationship will have disastrous results later on in life. On the other hand, the couple who at this point in time renew their vows of fidelity and concern lay an important foundation for the type of union that is decisive for later happiness. When I have urged attention in great earnestness to new emphasis on marriage I have been also discussing preparation for success during the retirement years. Couples who renew their concern for their marriages will still have adjustments to make when the husband's work role is over, but they will know few of the calamitous repercussions experienced by those who have been increasingly alienated during the middle years. . . .

There are other relationships which need attention during the middle years if there is to be a payoff later on. [It is necessary] to bridge the generational gap with sons and daughters and [there are] problems of dealing with parents. But not far in the future is the time when we will be the elderly parents and our present adolescents and young adults will be middle-aged. They too will face the problems with us that we are facing with our parents! We too, in need of some warmth from them, will resent their lack of attention and concern. But the resolution of this problem can also be made in this period if we can transcend our growing rigidity and make the rapprochement with our young people. . . . *Much of the difficulty between middle-aged persons and their parents is the final statement of their failure to work out closeness earlier in life. . . .*

Pollack also discovered that the need for recognition, or "social approval," increases with age. Having given up the prime method for gaining approval in our society —working—the retired person covets acceptance. For instance, individuals who had taken up a new interest, such as painting, want to see their works admired. Recently when I had finished a lecture outlining in detail all the ways retired persons could enjoy new activities, one man expressed the group's response: "That's all very good, Dr. Peterson, but what can we do that has *meaning* to others. We don't simply want to amuse ourselves."

Those activities encountered in the middle years that bring one into close contact with others and that can be continued until the end of life are more apt to be useful to the ego than some novel concern developed after retirement. By retirement, one ought to have some skill and some achievement in the interest so that he is not defeated in trying a new pursuit for the first time. It is this continuity of at least part of a person's life that prohibits him from that "roleless role" described by Ernest Burgess, a top sociologist at the University of Chicago. . . .

Retirement is unattractive only to those who have not learned the "equivalence of work and play" or who have not already established competence in the leisure arts, provided that they can afford it.

Provided that they can afford it—this is one of the critical determinants of adjustment in the later years. The possibility of travel, hobbies, adequate housing, visiting family, and health care are all dependent on whether the man who has left his job has provided sufficient means to live well. Whether he will be comfortable or not in his retirement years depends on the skill with which he previously planned his financial life.

The life cycle presents different financial demands at each stage. It is one of the ironies of our system that the period of maximum expense in bearing and raising and educating children usually comes before a man has reached his maximum earning capacity. Furthermore, most families in America are buying a home and making other payments constantly while they are in these earlier phases of earning capacity. By the time a man is earning his maximum, his home may be paid for and his children through college. He has fifteen years or more of employment to go at maximum pay and lower expenses. While he should have been saving some all along, this is the period when he can make maximum investments for his retirement.

Al and Susan illustrate a life cycle financial plan geared to the differential demands of different needs in their life together. When they were first married, they put off child bearing for three years and saved all of her salary to make a down payment on a home, to pay off their automobiles, and to lay aside money for doctor bills and hospital expenses when she became pregnant. They conscientiously added one bit of furniture after another to the nursery until at the end of three years their room for the baby was ready; so was their savings account. In the meantime Al carried term insurance, which was the cheapest he could buy. When Susan quit work, they did not need to reduce their living habits because they had been living on his salary.

During the next fifteen years they consistently raised the amount of insurance they carried and every year invested in a savings bond and a mutual fund program so that when their first child was ready for college a generous sum was available. At the time their second child entered college, the twenty-year mortgage on their house was paid off and they were able to divert some of the income that had been used for those payments to ease the strain caused by having two children in college. With payments eased, normal increments in salary, and the use of savings designated for educational expenditures, they were able to maintain three children in college and still live well.

When the last child graduated from college, they entered the third phase of their economic plan. They then invested for their retirement the income they had previously used as payments on their home and for the children's education. They also began to enlarge their interests by investing in photographic equipment, extension courses, and a program of travel, which they had carefully planned in earlier years. Travel was possible because they had more means and Al had earned longer and longer vacations due to his increasing years with his company. But programs change and needs sometimes take sudden turns. On a trip to Mexico this particular couple became greatly intrigued with the early history of that country, and they longed to spend a good deal of time in exploring the excavation of early pyramids and towns. As they could not afford this, Susan decided to go back to work for several years to provide them a longer "sabbatical" in Mexico. Like hundreds of thousands of other middle-aged women, she found that employment was available and that she enjoyed the work. At the end of three years Al was granted a leave, and they made their ex-

pedition. Susan's salary, as it had been in the first years of marriage, was carefully earmarked for these special goals, and their savings program for the future was not impaired.

By the time they were ready for retirement they had accumulated sufficient funds to enable them to carry on their lives in a rewarding way.

Financial planning for retirement is often superficial because the couple asks the wrong questions. It is not enough to save money to sustain life: to pay the rent, insurance policies, clothing, food, and other necessities. The wise person will accumulate enough to provide, beyond the necessities, for (1) underwriting those hobbies, travel plans, books, etc., which are essential for a full life, and (2) any large catastrophic event, such as a fire, long illness, or injury to a loved one, that may occur. No scale has ever been devised which would help families in specifically anticipating their future needs because each couple have grossly different needs. Nevertheless many hours of discussion and pencil work will pay large dividends in contentment later on in life. It is now obvious that middle age is the time when these concerns become a paramount interest and when there is a real opportunity to implement them.

In looking at retirement income there are some specific facts which can be recorded. The income from Social Security can be projected with fair accuracy. The income from a company retirement program can be ascertained without difficulty. Income from savings and loan accounts can be estimated within certain limits. The income from stocks and bonds is not so easily estimated because their value fluctuates from year to year. However the value of money in banks and savings and loan associations or in retirement funds tends to become less because of inflation, while money invested in real estate or stocks and bonds rises as the market rises. The Federal Government has tried to introduce a compensatory program to inflation by raising Social Security payments to match the decrease of dollar value. Probably a varied type of savings and retirement investment which considers both safety and hedges against inflation is the wisest course. Some retirement programs now split their investments between straight savings, on the one hand, and stocks and bonds, on the other. This field is more complex than it may appear to an average husband and wife so that taking a course in investments or employing an investment counselor would be an intelligent way to make retirement investment sound and safe.

The retirement income of retired persons shows some improvement, but not much. The following table is included, not for academic reasons, but to emphasize the seriousness of our recommendation that middle-aged persons plan diligently for their future. This table is adapted from one put out by the Administration on Aging, of the Department of Health, Education and Welfare, and summarizes the latest available data.

TABLE I   TRENDS IN MEDIAN FAMILY INCOME[4]

Year	Families				
	Head 14–64		Head 65 and over		
	Amount	Percent Change	Amount	Percent Change	Percent of 14–64
1960	$5,905	%	$2,897	%	%
1961	6,099	3.3	3,026	4.4	49.1
1962	6,336	3.9	3,204	5.9	49.6
1963	6,644	4.9	3,352	4.6	50.6
1964	6,981	5.1	3,376	0.7	50.4
1965	7,352	5.3	3,460	2.5	47.1

Some 23 percent, or about one fourth, of the families whose head was over the age of sixty-five had an income of less than $2,000 a year; 10 percent had an income over $10,000 a year. The plight of single persons over sixty-five was greater because one third of them had incomes of less than $1,000 and 57.9 percent had incomes of less than $1,500. If we consider that a person or a family (where both parents work) earns on the average today $7,353 a year for forty years, almost $300,000 will have passed through a typical checking account by the time retirement arrives. Careful budgeting should make it possible to add enough to Social Security and company retirement plans to prevent impairment of plans for a full and happy involvement during the retirement years. This is primarily a middle-age task. . . .

Of course money does not alter the fact of aging and it cannot buy freedom from the aches and pains of our last years; 80 percent of our current population sixty-five and over report one or more chronic health conditions or impairments. Still, half of these

report that these conditions do not impose any limitations on their activities, but one out of five (20 percent) report that they are unable to carry on what they designate as their major activity at all. Of those older persons who report that impairments do limit their activities, the most frequently reported problems are heart conditions (21.8 percent), arthritis and rheumatism (20.7 percent), and visual impairment (9.5 percent). Thirty-six percent of all persons in the middle-age group of ages fifty-five to sixty-four have lost all of their permanent teeth. This figure goes up to 56 percent by ages sixty-five to seventy-four. Evidence is fairly conclusive that a great many individuals are not enjoying optimum health because of dental deficiencies. Mental illness reaches its peak during the middle-age period of ages thirty-five to fifty-five and then declines. The total number of commitments to mental hospitals increases after fifty-five through seventy because of the large number of older persons who suffer from cerebral arteriosclerosis and senile psychosis. The incidence of the psychosis falls rapidly during the period fifty-five and older.

It has been said that there are no diseases of old age. What occurs to the cells and tissues then is the direct result of insults to them throughout the course of life by disease, malnutrition, and neglect. We have suggested that death rates in the United States for the forty-to-sixty age group appear higher than in almost any other country. Remember that part of this may simply mean that the science of medicine has already added many years to the lives of those who in other cultures would be dead much earlier. But it may also be a product of our "good living," in which we can afford to eat and drink too much. Whatever the cause, more adequate care would reduce mortality. What can be done during middle age to make those years more comfortable and to lay a foundation for a relatively healthy old age?

Dental care is one of the most important factors. During middle age much of the problem resides in pyorrhea and other diseases of the gums and mouth. Cavities do not pose such an important problem as overall oral health. For this reason strict adherence to a program of dental inspection may mean the difference between health and poor health. If one recalls the loss of permanent teeth during and after this period and the comments about the importance of oral hygiene to general health, such a regime is indispensable.

Nutrition is of optimum importance. Poor nutrition affects both mental and physical vigor. Malnutrition may make the difference between heart compensation and heart failure. Adequate diet has been related to mental health. For middle-aged persons one might add that there is a problem not so much of malnutrition as of overnutrition, the tendency to eat oneself to death.

A third aspect of preventive health care is the maintenance of consistent levels of exercise. Vascular tissues are almost always found to be in better condition in those who exercise. It is instructive to note that the more a diabetic exercises, the less supportive insulin he needs. Most of us are acquainted with the fact that the heart spe-

cialists who have treated our Presidents have insisted that they add more than the rocking chair to their daily movements! This does not apply when the illness is far advanced. In fact all of these general recommendations are to be modified by the specific instructions of one's physician.

There is the fourth matter of preventive medicine. Long ago several surveys including thousands of subjects under scrutiny discovered that about one third of the respondents had undetected disease and that a large number of them improved under treatment. Eugene Confrey and Marcus Goldstein, students of aging, list diseases of the heart, malignant neoplasm, and vascular lesions affecting the central nervous system as accounting for three of every four deaths above the age of forty-four. They go on to relate this to middle age: "On the other hand, many of the premature deaths from disease might have been averted had appropriate preventive measures been followed."[5]

They state two cases, cancer of the uterus and obesity leading to fatal cases of heart disease, that might have been prevented by earlier care. The implication for making consistent preventive visits to the physician is evident. Middle-aged men and women can assure themselves of not only a longer but also a healthier second half of life by utilizing their medical contacts for prevention as well as cure. The proliferation of preventive immunization for influenza and other conditions is part of this program.

While the research material does not yet give a clear picture of the relationship of morale to illness, most gerontologists conclude such studies by indicating that they feel that a "sense of purpose and of continuing participation in life" is essential to good mental and physical health. No individual is just a mind, or just a physique. All of these combine in a psychosomatic way to determine morale and satisfaction. What we have indicated in these paragraphs is the critical importance of paying attention to dental, mental, and physical health in such a way that we may reap the advantages of recent and current medical research. No other course of action seems sensible when we contemplate the dividends. . . .

Middle age is a period to develop new organizational contacts and experiences. . . . This enlargement of contacts is viewed in this chapter as a prerequisite to adjustment after retirement, but it has as much promise for the middle-age period as it does for the later one. We take our clue from Robert Havighurst, who says that the changes in role that are required of workers when they retire demand role flexibility and that ". . . probably the best assurance of role flexibility in later years is a reasonably successful experience in a variety of roles during the middle years, the emphasis being on *reasonable* and *variety*, for outstanding success in certain roles in middle age sometimes makes for rigidity."[6]

Some writers have felt that role flexibility can be deliberately cultivated during this middle period of life, and they have developed programs to help men and women in this period develop new interests which lead to "useful and creative roles."

The scope of opportunity for new roles in new formal and informal organizations is unlimited. One may decide either to intensify participation in religious or educational groups or to invade new fields. The critical point in decision must consider two dimensions: (1) Does this new interest contain future rewards that will be emotionally satisfying over a long period of time? (2) What opportunity does this venture provide for long-term human contact? One can collect buttons and bows or he can study the philosophy of the Greeks. He can hunt mushrooms or agates, become a deacon in his church, or take golf lessons. What seems essential is that middle-aged persons recognize this period as a pivotal time for change. "In order to build an effective program at older age levels," says J. E. Anderson, "we must build it as a new product, even though it is based on past interests and activities."[7]

It is this renewed interest in life beyond the family circle that would make the contribution and capacity of middle-aged persons available for the guidance of society. On the other hand the sense of worth and new stimulation that comes to both men and women by participation means much to them. Women in their forties tend to increase the time they give to voluntary organizations, sometimes to the extent that this becomes a major aspect of these lives. Men likewise serve as members of boards of directors or as trustees of the same groups in which their wives are active. Women participate more often than men, but that is understandable because men are more often employed. Voluntary organizations can be divided into two types: those aimed primarily at ameliorating some problem faced by society (these may serve such large purposes as those included in the Red Cross or they may be very specific in limiting their interest to a specific disease), and those which bring together individuals for the purpose of enhancing their own interests (an example would be a philatelic club where the members focus on learning about and trading stamps). Many individuals belong to both types of groups; one contributes to their sense of adding something to the common wealth and the other to the individual's specific leisure-time interests. Men find status and spiritual return in contributing their knowledge of administrative skills to worthwhile community endeavors. They may contribute through religious, political, or community groups. Whatever they do, they are laying a foundation of information and experience which will stand them in good stead in the later years when they can give more time and energy to the organization. This enables them in later years to be a part of life even though they are retired. But unless this is done during the middle years the person will not have the contacts, the interest, the skill, or the opportunity to do so later.

SUMMARY

It is now evident in discussing the relationships of the middle-aged person that whatever he does will have repercussions in the later years. He is inevitably laying the foundations for retirement during that period from forty to sixty when he has the mental and energy levels to achieve role change and to develop new interests. The way he treats his health during this period will determine his health later. The manner in which he solves his problems in relation to his spouse and his children will be mirrored in happiness or unhappiness during his last years. The wisdom of his investment program will greatly affect the scope of his opportunities in the later period of his life. His participation in an amplified group of activities and organizations will determine the richness of his experience when he is no longer working. The surprising thing is that whatever he does to insure a fuller experience in his years after work will also enrich the mid-years of his life.

NOTES

[1] Wilma Donahue, Harold Orback, and Otto Pollack, "Retirement: The Emergent Social Pattern," in *Handbook of Social Gerontology*, Clark Tibbits, ed. (Chicago: University of Chicago Press, 1960), p. 378.

[2] Ibid.

[3] Ibid., p. 390.

[4] Memorandum (Washington: Administration on Aging, Department of Health, Education, and Welfare, 1966), p. 1.

[5] Eugene A. Confrey and Marcus S. Goldstein, "The Health Status of Aging People," in Tibbits, op. cit., p. 187.

[6] Robert J. Havighurst, "Flexibility and Social Roles of the Retired," *American Journal of Sociology*, 59:311.

[7] J. E. Anderson, "Psychological Aspects of the Use of Free Time," in *Free Time: Challenge to Later Maturity*, Wilma Donahue, Dorothy Coons, and Helen Maurice, eds. (Ann Arbor: University of Michigan Press, 1958), p. 41.

76

OLDER FAMILIES AND THEIR TROUBLES: FAMILIAL AND SOCIAL RESPONSES

Gordon F. Streib

The assertion is frequently made that the American family is declining. One piece of evidence offered is that the American family is not meeting its traditional obligations, particularly in the care of its older members. The idea that the family alone should be primarily responsible for the health and welfare of older persons is a vestigial attitude from an earlier historical period. The conception of the family as an autonomous social unit which is supposed to solve all of the basic problems of living is, in some ways, a carry-over of thinking about the family retained from the agrarian [period] and early phases of industrialization.

Many families do have considerable autonomy, and this is a goal desired by most family units. However, when we consider the family in the latter part of the life cycle, there is a need to rethink the notion of the autonomous family—independent, self-regulated, and able to take care of itself as a group. Family autonomy and independence are very congruent with American goals and values in the spheres of the political, the economic, and the educational. But family autonomy must be more than a shibboleth, particularly when one studies families in trouble at any stage of the life cycle. Independence and autonomy may be desired by families, but in reality they are sometimes hard for some families to attain, particularly under conditions of economic or medical crisis at the end of life. It is during the latter phases of the life cycle that some notion of shared function must be brought into the analysis of the situation of older families and into the thinking of persons involved as practitioners with older families.

What is the theory of shared functions? It is the notion that formal organizations and families must coordinate their efforts if they are to achieve their goals. The idea of shared functions was developed by Eugene Litwak who with several colleagues explicated and tested the implications of the theory in a series of stimulating papers. (Litwak, 1965; Litwak and Meyer, 1966; Litwak and Figueira, 1968; Litwak and Szelenyi, 1969)

The ways in which bureaucratic structures and family groups are articulated is a crucial matter in urban-industrialized societies. Although the theoretical analysis is still incomplete and many of the applications must be worked out, the basic idea of shared functions is sound.

This paper will explore some of the ways in which various kinds of primary groups and bureaucratic organizations may share functions in meeting problems or crises which older families face. Bureaucracies are social structures which have an instrumental basis for operation, emphasize impersonality, are organized on the basis of formal rules, and stress professional expertise. On the other hand, a family as a prototype of primary groups is characterized by face-to-face contacts, employs affective

bases for judgments, stresses diffuse demands and expectations, and so on.

One primary assumption which needs to be emphasized is that family groups and bureaucratic organizations are not to be considered in competition with each other. The two types of structures have multiple goals and tasks which in many instances may overlap. Furthermore, it is assumed that the family has not "failed" when it utilizes formal organizations for assistance. There is a range or a continuum of groups from a "pure" primary group—the nuclear family—to the monocratic bureaucracy, and there is a variety of mixed types of groups or organizations which may be located on the continuum.

There are writers who describe the United States as a post-industrial society, and there are others who write about American society as being in the mature—not the developmental—phase, of industrialization. Clearly a society whose urban-industrial structure is as developed as is that of the contemporary United States is markedly different from the society emerging at the turn of the century or even the society which America's senior citizens lived in just a generation ago at the beginning of World War II. Technology has changed; some phases of private and governmental bureaucracies have changed, and primary groups—such as the family—are changing. But as Litwak and Szelenyi state: "It would be an error to say that, because a primary group structure changes from one stage of historical development to another, it is moving to destruction." (Litwak and Szelenyi, 1969, 480) . . .

One of the first steps which is necessary in order to understand the notion of shared functions is to clarify what is meant by the family. A major distinction must be made between: (1) the residential family or the family in which one lives, and (2) the extended family or the kin network to which a person belongs by blood ties or marriage.

Residential families are diverse because of their intrinsic structure and also because of two other important considerations, age and sex. Whether a person is 65 or 85 makes a great deal of difference in terms of family relations and the need for assistance.

Sex is a factor because of the differential death rates; the proportion of widowhood is much greater among women than among men. About ten percent of the men in the age category 65 to 69 are widowed, in comparison to 38 percent of the women. Considering all persons over 65, about a fifth of the males are widowers and about half of the women are widows. This means that a man is much more likely to have another person in his household to help in times of trouble or crisis, while a woman is more likely to need to turn to outsiders or bureaucratic organizations for assistance.

Most older people—70 percent of men and women over 65—live in families (living arrangements) with two or more members. Twenty-one percent of older persons over 65 live alone and only four percent live in institutions or other kinds of group quarters.

A more detailed examination of the kinds of persons who live in a household of one person accentuates the differentiation by sex: only sixteen percent of the males compared to 32 percent of the women live in households entirely alone or with nonrelatives. These proportions increase for subcategories of the older persons, for living alone is a characteristic of the later rather than the earlier phases of the life cycle.

An examination of the facts about kin networks . . . shows that the great majority of older persons in the United States belong to kin networks of three or four generations. A nationwide survey conducted by Shanas and her associates revealed that about one older person in five was a part of a one generation kin network and almost one-third of the older persons in the United States were members of three or four generation networks.

Thus the analysis of the older family in situations of trouble and stress encompasses a tremendous variety of family structures based on the variation in residential types of families and the way they are or are not tied in with kin networks of varying complexity. There are, for example, three generation families living in one household, older couples with young children, single-person families, and newlyweds in postretirement families, to mention a few of the variations. Thus it is important to stress:

there is no "typical family" in later life, for there are many patterns.

This great variation in family structures and relations is the result of a complicated set of factors and of decisions which go back much earlier in the life cycle. To understand those families which are most vulnerable, have the fewest resources to draw upon, and probably require the most attention from health and other helping agencies, one must realize that many of these families have been limping along through most of life. In addition, there are some families which are in trouble for the first time in later life. Many families which have met the vicissitudes of child rearing, have dealt successfully with intermittent economic distress, and have been able to solve previous medical emergencies now find the dilemmas of later maturity too much of a challenge to cope with. . . .

Attention to the major factors that create problem families in later maturity follows. There are four major resources which contribute to the strength of older families. They are:

1. Physical health
2. Emotional health
3. Economic resources
4. Social resources—family, kin, friends.

The interrelationship between these four factors is very complex, . . . and the absence of one or more can bring about severe dislocation in the life of the older person. On the other hand, an abundance of any of the resources can greatly alleviate the stress caused by the absence of the others. For example, a warm, supportive family can help to ease the crises caused by failing physical and emotional health, and assist in supplying economic resources.

An examination of five types of families in terms of these major resources follows. Type I, the Golden Sunset Family has all of the four resources. Fortunately, they constitute a significant number of older families in this society. These are the people in good health and spirits with a comfortable pension, warm family relations and friends.

At the other extreme are Type V, the "unfortunate families" who end their years in misery—the Totally Deprived. These families are the ones who present the most serious crisis in old age—indeed, many of them are in institutions for they lack *any* of the four basic resources needed to meet their needs. When people talk about the family and a care crisis, it is this type of "family" that they have in mind, and from their knowledge or acquaintance of such tragic types, they may assume that there are more of these families than really exist. Between these two polar types there is a variety of combinations: in all there are sixteen different combinations considering the four resources.

An important and interesting question is how many families are there of the various types? . . . At the present time only a rough estimate can be made of the numbers and proportions of the various types by fitting together items of information on single variables and isolated characteristics. A crude estimate is that about a quarter of the older population are "privileged aged" and about a half are "typical aged" and the remaining proportion, roughly 25 percent, are the "needy aged."

These estimates are based upon facts of the following kind: About 95 percent of the United States' older population lives in the community, and of those who do about nine out of ten are ambulatory and perhaps two percent are bedfast. Moreover, among the older persons living at home almost two-thirds scored zero on an incapacity scale; that is, they could perform six basic tasks without difficulty.

The economic resource variable is probably the one that has been surveyed more often and with greater precision than the others. For example, a recent U.S. Senate Committee reported that one out of every four individuals 65 and older lives in poverty. Poverty, like other characteristics, is differentially distributed in the population, for the same Senate document reported that among the elderly women who live alone about one-half fall below the poverty line; and the nonwhite older females are especially disadvantaged.

Another way to index economic resources is by the ownership of property. About two-thirds of the aged own their own homes, and of these thirteen million plus older American homeowners about 80 per-

cent own their homes free and clear. Moreover, over six and half million (about 50 percent of the homeowners) have an equity of $25,000 or more in their homes.

Social resources are more difficult to ascertain than financial resources. What indices of social resources should one utilize? Presence or absence of children? Siblings? Neighbors? Membership in organizations? The presence of facilities like the telephone, radio, or television which may increase one's social contacts with the wider world? . . .

The psychic or emotional resources are probably the most difficult resource to estimate. Gurin and associates in a nationwide survey of America's mental health, using five questions, found that among persons 55 and over about 27 percent reported themselves as "very happy," 55 percent as "pretty happy," and 18 percent as "not too happy." (Gurin et al., 1960) The same national survey found that if one employs "worry" as an index of emotional health, the elderly report themselves as not worrying any more than younger categories of the population. About a third of the persons over 55 years of age say they "worry a lot" or "worry all the time."

How can these complicated variables be grouped together into clusters or types? In a nationwide urban survey of males 60 and over conducted some years ago, four variables were grouped together in order to determine how health, socioeconomic status, and whether a person was working or retired were related to morale. (Streib, 1956) The three independent variables had a cumulative effect upon morale. For example, among those who were retired, in poor health, and had a low socioeconomic status 71 percent had low morale. Conversely, among the men who were employed, in good health, and had a high socioeconomic status, only 25 percent had low morale. And between the extreme categories low morale varied according to whether a positive or negative factor was present.

Some persons have argued that the way to solve the problems of families in old age is to give them more money. Yet they forget that some people can be rich in economic resources and poor in some of the other factors that make life meaningful. Some readers will recall the news accounts of the "richest girl in the world" who spent a recent Christmas sick in a luxury hotel suite in San Francisco and alone except for an entourage of servants. If one is to believe news reports, her circle of friends and relatives is small, she is in poor physical health, and she is unhappy. Yet she has tremendous economic resources at her command.

The most elusive and most difficult resource to identify and measure is the emotional or psychological health of the individual. Just as one person may have immense financial resources and lack the other three, these are some old persons who are lacking in health, financial, and social resources and yet have sufficient psychological and emotional resources. These are the kinds of older people whom Dr. George Reader of the Cornell Medical School has described as performing the Indian rope trick for they seem to be able to function without any visible means of support. (Reader, 1969, 312) These people who sometimes come to the attention of public and private agencies are in very poor physical health, exist in dire poverty, have no family or friends—in fact, seem to be totally lacking in resources. Yet they seem to be able to remain cheerful and can cope with life—in short, they possess an abundance of the elusive factor of emotional resource which somehow enables them to integrate their lives. Dr. Reader said it was a source of amazement to some medical students that such people could even survive. Just as the Indian *fakir* seems to defy the laws of gravity, so these deprived persons seem to defy all the rules and generalizations of social workers and sociologists about the basic resources needed to maintain an integrated life, for somehow they are able to cope.

This schematic presentation obviously leaves out the variations in resource level which must be considered in analyzing the diverse kinds of families. The easiest resource to measure in an objective sense is money; however, the way in which a given set of financial resources are perceived and utilized by older people varies considerably. Streib and Schneider summarized the situation in their longitudinal study of 2000 retirees: "Thus a given amount of income might be considered plentiful by one retiree while the same amount would represent dire poverty to another. The amount of income an individual receives may not be as important as whether he thinks it is 'enough.'" (Streib and Schneider, 1971, 82) . . .

In the following sections the discussion will focus on the forms of intervention and the way in which resources are employed in meeting troubles. The analysis of the intervention process illustrates how the theory of shared functions works out in practice. The articulation of family and other groups and organizations is very intricate and thus the following discussion will only highlight a few aspects as they pertain to older families.

The forms of intervention can be classified into three broad categories: (1) help and intervention by family and kin; (2) quasi-family or pseudo-family forms of intervention; (3) institutional or bureaucratic forms of intervention.[1] These categories are not mutually exclusive, but there is utility in considering them separately. The principal criterion employed to distinguish the three forms of intervention is the nature of the relationship between the person offering help and the recipient. Does the intervention agent have an ascribed kin relationship to the recipient? Or does he assume a pseudo-family role in the relationship? Or is the intervention agent acting as a bureaucrat?

The kinds of resources which the three forms of intervention may offer can encompass all of the four resources referred to earlier in the paper, namely, (1) health and medical, (2) emotional and psychological, (3) economic and financial, (4) social or interactional. For example, kinsmen may render nursing care; they may give financial help; and they may also be a source of social interaction and emotional support. Similarly, a government agency or several agencies can and do intervene and offer help which involves one or more and sometimes all of the four resources. . . .

There is a great deal of popular writing and public discussion about the inadequacy and breakdown of the American family and its failure to meet the needs of older people in an industrialized society. An examination of documented studies presents a picture that is not as bleak or as dysfunctional as some persons assert.

For example, many Americans were moved by the studies made by Ralph Nader's investigators who reported the sad plight of many old people who seemed to be abandoned and forgotten in nursing homes, and perhaps the more so because the investigators were young females. But it would be inaccurate for Americans to hold a stereotyped picture that many older Americans are abandoned by their children. It will be recalled that eight percent of persons over 65 have never married. Not all married persons have surviving children, for of the noninstitutional population over 65 about 25 percent do not have any living children.

What do research studies show concerning interaction of older families and their adult children? One almost universal finding from family studies in western society is summarized in the phrase offered by Rosenmayr and Kockeis, "intimacy at a distance." (Rosenmayr and Kockeis, 1963) Again and again in surveys, case studies, and from clinical observations one learns that old people wish to have continuous meaningful contact with their children and other kin, but they do not wish to reside in the same household. This is what is meant by "intimacy at a distance."

The form in which intimacy at a distance manifests itself has been clearly demonstrated in numerous studies which show that the great majority of older Americans who have children live within one-half hour driving distance of at least one child. Moreover, they see one another quite frequently. In the nationwide study conducted by Ethel Shanas and her associates, 65 percent of the elderly in the sample had seen at least one child in the 24 hour period prior to the interview. (Shanas et al., 1968)

George Rosenberg found in his recently published book about Philadelphians that 90 percent of his respondents had at least one primary or secondary relative living outside their household in metropolitan Philadelphia. (Rosenberg, 1970) And over 80 percent received a visit from at least one such relative in the seven days preceding the interview.

One aspect of the kin network interaction patterns of older persons is the well documented observation that there are mutual help patterns present in many older families. In the Cornell Study of Retirement, for example, it was found that more help in the form of baby sitting, home repairs, and help during illness flowed from the older generation to the adult child than vice versa. (Streib, 1958)

Another aspect of parent-child relations in old age which is rarely brought to public attention is the way in which *some* older parents exploit and tyrannize their adult children. An example is a case study known to the author. Mr. Jones, father of five children, is 82 and comfortably situated financially. As a businessman, he was accustomed to giving orders. When his wife died five years ago, he demanded that his 45-year-old bachelor son give up his job and move in to take care of him (he is in a wheel chair). This seemed a reasonable solution to all the children as Buddy did not like his job anyway. Thus he became Dad's nurse, being given an allowance of $50 a week, a new car, and free board and room. Now, five years later the arrangement is still continuing. Dad is completely satisfied and refuses to consider any other arrangement. *But what about Buddy?* When his father does finally die, what chance will he have to get a job again? To some old people this may sound like an ideal arrangement for Mr. Jones, but the cost to Buddy must be considered also.[2]

The crucial variable in this case is that the older person has enough money to buy this life style. A combination of an authoritarian personality and sufficient money enables him to enforce his wishes. Also, it must be emphasized that this example reveals as much about Buddy's personality as Dad's. Gerontological studies have tended to overlook the rights and needs of the adult children and have seemed to blame them if they do not work out an arrangement that keeps the aged parent happy and comfortable. There has not been enough attention to the needs of the adult children when a "crisis" extends for ten or fifteen years. But as medical advances extend life, there will be more and more persons living for several years when they are not necessarily "happy." And no amount of care and sensitive arrangements by a loving and concerned family can really solve this problem. . . .

A further illustration of how the theory of shared functions operates in regard to older families is shown by the development of quasi- or pseudo-family types of intervention. Some of these programs may be supported by private or governmental agencies or organizations, but the nature of the relationship between the persons involved—usually older and younger—is that of a quasi-family relationship. The persons act toward one another and assume the role of family members during the period of social contact. But they are not genuine family members. The name of one of the best-known of these programs indicates the quasi-family nature—Foster Grandparents. This program employs persons 60 and older to work in close association, on a one-to-one basis, with children in orphanages, schools for mentally retarded persons, and other institutional settings. There are other volunteer programs, such as SERVE, which are similar in their operation. The important aspect to stress here is the dual benefits through the creation of a warm family kind of relationship between the older persons and the children and young people they serve. The program gives the older person a role in the community as a quasi-family member and at the same time the child receives the kind of love and attention that is essential for development.

There are a number of other programs which have been initiated in the last few years in which younger persons—usually teen-agers—take on a quasi-family role in relation to the older person. Some of these have been started by Girl Scout troops. One program in New York State is operated in connection with a state training school for girls. In this instance the girls from the training school visit as "granddaughters"

the residents of a nursing home who become "grandparents" to the girls. These programs, like those in which the initiative was taken by older persons, seem to have a very positive and enriching benefit for all who take part.

There are also a number of programs in some states which are operated in connection with the discharge of patients from mental hospitals. While these programs do not have a specific concern for the elderly, they often help older persons. In these programs a person may become a quasi-relative for the former patient so he can make a more satisfactory adjustment upon his return to his home community. . . .

The theory of shared functions involves the notion that both primary groups and bureaucratic organizations are important for achieving a variety of tasks in American society. There are thousands of bureaucratic groups which are concerned with the health and welfare of older families in the United States. It would be a formidable task to even list the many public and private bureaucracies which offer services to older Americans. The Social Security Administration is the one bureaucracy which contacts the most older persons; the Veterans Administration, the Social and Rehabilitation Service, and the numerous health and welfare agencies which are in contact with thousands of older persons at the local, state, and national levels of government also offer a wide variety of services. In addition, the bureaucracies affiliated with educational, religious, health, and private charitable organizations provide hundreds of programs. It is clear why the problem of referral and coordination of bureaucratic services is a major need of older persons which must receive more attention in the near future.

In this section of the paper it is proposed to focus upon the ways in which the mass media of communication, particularly television and radio, may play a greater role in coordinating the work of bureaucracies by serving as information and referral agencies, and also by assuming a new role of offering emotional and interactional resources to older persons.

Why should the mass media be singled

out as possible means of increasing the so-cial resources and particularly the emotional health of older people? It is because these powerful omnipresent communications media of modern society already permeate the residential units of almost all Americans. A variety of statistical information points to the high degree of participation of per-sons over 65 years of age in the use of tele-vision and radio. For example, in a typical 24 hour day in which an older person spends approximately nine hours in sleep and six to seven in obligated time (eating meals, housekeeping, personal care), the next largest segment of time is devoted to leisure. Of this 6.5 hours of leisure, 2.8 [are] devoted to television.

Another way to obtain a picture of the leisure activities of older people is by a survey of 5000 OASI beneficiaries in four urban areas. In this survey it was found that 70 percent of the 5000 persons had watched TV a median · number of three hours on the day preceding the survey. (Riley et al., 1968) In terms of the total number of hours involved, this activity en-gaged more time than any other leisure ac-tivity reported. No other leisure activity was reported by such a large percentage of older persons.

The attitude of many gerontologists is to deplore the fact that housebound older people spend so much time with the mass media. The author thinks that more atten-tion should be given instead to making the media a positive mechanism for enriching their lives.

From many surveys that were conducted the last few months preceding the Second White House Conference on Aging, it was found that one of the prime needs of older citizens is the provision of transportation so they can attend meetings, religious services, go visiting, etc. Indeed it is important to develop cheap public transportation for old and young in this society. Given the fact, however, that local, state, and na-tional legislative bodies are reluctant and even recalcitrant to take steps to deal with the complex problems in urban transporta-tion, an auxilliary approach can be the more imaginative use of mass media—par-ticularly local stations—as a means of in-forming and involving older people in pro-grams and activities which are specifically geared to their needs and stage of the life cycle.

What kinds of programs might be devel-oped which would offer a meaningful and realistic fare for America's older families?[3] These are suggestions based on limited present-day knowledge of the older popula-tion and which may be modified with in-creasing knowledge of the wishes of older viewers and a more precise understanding of the impact of various kinds of programs and services transmitted by television. For example, the content of more programs could be devoted to health and nutrition of the aged; the problems of inflation as it re-lates to social security, medical insurance, taxation—local, state, and national. There is a great range of programs which could be specifically geared to older ethnic, regional, and language audiences. Hobby shows and displays of arts and crafts could be offered. Reminiscing—what Dr. Robert Butler has called the "life review"—could be attempted. Interviews and life stories of a wide variety of older persons could be more widely pre-sented and also "meet the traveler" and his-torical programs. These are a few things which an amateur suggests. If the vast tal-ents of the mass media were utilized, many other kinds of subjects could be discovered and developed into attractive programs. Lo-cal programs which involve the concept of a "Help Column," now found in many newspapers, might be used on television. Closely related to this kind of program would be some kind of ombudsman pro-gram which would mediate grievances of the elderly. There should be more attempts to involve the viewer into the local pro-grams. In many places a large percentage of the aged have telephones so they could call in and easily participate in various kinds of programs.

It is essential to stress the nature of the electronic communication media in Ameri-can society in their broadest social context —in their structure, their control, and their operations. In the minds of most people, the mass media are viewed only as an entertainment device and the main empha-sis is upon programming to maximize the audience of viewers and listeners. It is necessary to broaden our expectation of what television can provide. . . .

Perhaps the primary reason for the studied neglect of America's older viewing families is the obvious fact that television and radio are primarily geared to selling goods and gadgets which America's older population either cannot afford or do not want. This tremendous concern with the huckstering of products to the maximum numbers of the youthful audience is a misuse of the airwaves which belong to all Americans, including its 20 million senior citizens. The very fact that older people do not have the money to purchase the products does not mean that their needs should be neglected. Older people are less mobile and thus cannot have the social contacts enjoyed by other segments of the population. This makes it even more imperative that relevant and useful materials are offered them—not merely to entertain them but to inform, to educate, and to give them some feeling of importance, worth, and dignity. The mass media can be their lifeline to the outside world and its more imaginative use can serve to inform them, inspire them, raise their spirits, and perhaps develop more feeling of community with other older persons. It can also direct them to the available bureaucratic services which are already provided but which, too often, they do not know about. . . .

Both the analyst and the practitioner who [are] concerned with older families must be cognizant of the diversity of older families and their varying access to four major resources; physical health, emotional health, economic resources, and social resources. The accessibility and management of these resources may involve family members, kinsmen, and outsiders and for this reason the theory of shared functions is a useful analytical tool.

Generally speaking, older families are resourceful in coping with troubles. Available evidence indicates that younger family members also provide a great deal of help and assistance for older families. The picture of abandonment and neglect is not as bleak as is sometimes portrayed. However, a realistic assessment requires an understanding of the complexity of the troubles and their long-term nature and that individuals and family groups can only deal with *some* of the problems. For those who have no immediate kin or whose family members are too far away to help, the possibility for raising the level of family integration can be increased by quasi-family members. There are a number of exciting programs of this kind exemplified by Foster Grandparents, Foster Grandchildren, SERVE, and other kinds of quasi-family projects which are being developed in many communities. The present programs could be greatly expanded for they are still very limited in the number of persons who are involved, and their financial support is minimal.

Other developments which might contribute new psychic and social resources to older families involve better utilization of bureaucratic structures. One of the most challenging possibilities is to find new ways for the mass media of communication, particularly television and radio, to enrich the lives of older people who have less mobility and decreased social contacts than formerly. It can also inform them of the services available from the many agencies and organizations already designed to serve them.

Part of the neglect of ten percent of America's population, its older citizens, is due to the fact that commercial television is oriented to maximizing the sales of youth-oriented products and services. Older populations are neglected. There is little doubt but that the commercial networks and their affiliated stations should be made aware of their responsibilities to serve older families. The great amount of time and talent which is devoted to promoting products to young buyers can be rechanneled to serving older persons. Governmental bodies share some of the responsibility for the continued wasteland nature of television as it relates to older Americans.

There are also increasing opportunities—presently untapped—for educational television and for cable television to be more sensitive to the listening and viewing needs of older Americans. More attention should be given to using technology to serve *all* citizens—not just the youth. There is little doubt that many older people are in trouble and their burdens can be eased and their lives enriched—psychologically and socially —if the imagination, resources, and skills of the society are shifted to helping more older families.

There is now greater understanding that care of older families in trouble is not merely a private family burden. Other persons—non-family, quasi-family members, can visit and help on a volunteer basis as pseudo-family members. Finally, there must be greater recognition and utilization of the many services of bureaucratic organizations by older families if the United States is to become a more humane industrialized society.

NOTES AND REFERENCES

[1] A fourth form of intervention is that initiated by the person himself. Psychotherapy and counseling with the individual person is, of course, an important kind of intervention.

[2] A side issue to be mentioned in the kinship patterns is that research has shown that daughters give much more attention and support to their parents than do sons. Hence, the burden of care in crisis situations in most instances falls to the daughter in families with children of both sexes.

[3] Some years ago a series of 20 educational TV programs sponsored by the State University of New York was developed. The series was called "Living for the Sixties," and topics such as diet, exercise, social security benefits, etc., were included. The series was shown by Station WPSX of University Park, Pennsylvania, and a few other educational TV stations. See *Aging*, No. 143, September 1966. For a description of a local radio program for older persons produced by a retired person see: *Aging*, Nos. 176–177, June–July 1969.

Gurin, Gerald, et al. *Americans View Their Mental Health: A Nationwide Interview Study.* New York: Basic Books, 1960.

Litwak, Eugene. "Extended Kin Relations in an Industrial Society." In *Social Structure and the Family: Generational Relations,* Ethel Shanas and Gordon F. Streib, eds. Englewood Cliffs, N.J.: Prentice-Hall, 1965, pp. 290–323.

Litwak, Eugene, and Henry J. Meyer. "A Balance Theory of Coordination Between Bureaucratic Organizations and Community Primary Groups." *Administrative Science Quarterly,* 11 (1966): 31–58.

Litwak, Eugene, and Josefina Figueira. "Technological Innovations and Theoretical Functions of Primary Groups and Bureaucratic Structures." *American Journal of Sociology,* 73 (1968): 468–481.

Litwak, Eugene, and Ivan Szelenyi. "Primary Group Structures and Their Functions: Kin, Neighbors, and Friends." *American Sociological Review,* 34 (1969): 465–481.

Reader, George. "Group Discussion. Seminar: Geriatrics and the Medical School Curriculum." *Journal of the American Geriatrics Society,* 17 (1969): 312.

Riley, Matilda W., et al. *Aging in American Society.* New York: Russell Sage Foundation, 1968.

Rosenberg, George S. *The Worker Grows Old.* San Francisco: Jossey-Bass, 1970.

Rosenmayr, Leopold, and Eva Kockeis. "Propositions for a Sociological Theory of Aging and the Family." *International Social Science Journal,* 15 (1963): 410–426.

Shanas, Ethel, et al. *Old People in Three Industrialized Societies.* London: Routledge and Kegan Paul, 1968.

Streib, Gordon F. "Morale of the Retired." *Social Problems,* 3 (1956): 270–276.

Streib, Gordon F. "Family Patterns in Retirement." *Journal of Social Issues,* 14 (1958): 46–60.

Streib, Gordon F., and Clement J. Schneider. *Retirement in American Society.* Ithaca, N.Y.: Cornell University Press, 1971.

77

THE HUNDRED-YEAR-OLDS

Simone de Beauvoir

I must say a few words about one very particular category of old people: the centenarians. There were between six and seven hundred in France in 1959 and the majority of these were to be found in Brittany. Most were under a hundred and two, and between 1920 and 1942 none was over a hundred and four at the time of death. There are many more women than men: Dr Delore, who directed the 1959 inquiry, estimates that the proportion is more than four out of five. He counted twenty-four women out of a total of twenty-seven individuals. These women had had a great variety of jobs. They had been retired for thirty or forty years; and they were then living in the country with their children or grandchildren, or in some cases in institutions or rest-homes. They had lost their husbands twenty to forty years earlier. They had very little money; they were all thin, not one of them weighing more than 9 stone 7 lbs. [133 lbs.]. They loved their food but ate little. Many of them were strong and well, and this also applied to the men—there was one who played billiards at over ninety-nine. Some of the women were slightly shaky, they were a little hard of hearing, and their sight was dim, but they were neither blind nor deaf. They slept well. They passed their time reading, knitting, or taking short walks. Their minds were clear and their memories excellent. They were independent, even-tempered, and sometimes gay; they had a lively sense of humor and they were very sociable. They were high-handed towards their seventy-year-old children and treated them as young people. Sometimes they complained of the present-day generation, but they were interested in modern times and kept in touch with what was going on. Heredity appeared to be one of the factors in their longevity: they none of them had any pathological history and had never

suffered from any chronic illness. They did not seem to be afraid of death. In the main, they behaved very differently from old people junior to them. Had they survived because of their exceptional physical and mental health? Or did their satisfaction in having lived so long give them their serenity? The inquiry has no answer to this question.

Dr Grave E. Bird gave the Society of Oriental Psychology the results of his twenty years' research on four hundred people of more than a hundred years old. His conclusions are in agreement with those of Dr Delore: "Most of the people in this group make careful plans for the future; they are interested in public affairs and are capable of youthful enthusiasm. They have their little fads and a sharp sense of humor; their appetites are good and they have great powers of resistance. They usually enjoy perfect mental health; they are optimistic, and they show no sign of being afraid of death."

Those centenarians who have been under observation in the United States gave the same impression: they were active and happy. Visher studied two men of over a hundred who were active, happy, and seemingly in good health, although later their postmortems showed that several of their organs were diseased.

In 1963 the Cuban newspapers devoted a whole page to some people of over a hundred. Among them was the particularly interesting case of a former black slave; an ethnologist recorded his recollections on tape. Historical evidence showed that he really was a hundred and four years old, as he claimed to be. He had an excellent memory which, although it was a trifle confused over certain periods, allowed him to recapitulate his entire life. His hair was white, his health good. He was a little suspicious at the beginning of the series of interviews, but later he listened willingly to his interviewer's questions and replied at great length. He was in full possession of his intellectual faculties.*

In remote parts of the world many of those who claim to be a hundred obviously are not; as there are no birth certificates they can claim an extraordinary longevity in all good faith. But those who really are more than a hundred years old are almost always quite exceptional beings.

NOTES

* *Esclave à Cuba,* by Miguel Barnet, published by Gallimard.

78

TOWARD A HUNDRED YEARS

Emory S. Bogardus

What new and stirring days are coming soon:
When humans live a hundred useful years,
A hundred years of healthful happiness
Amid companions of inspiring peers.

Then scientific rules will overcome
The ailments now defying human kind;
The pace that kills will be subdued, outlawed,
And to the ages of the past consigned.

Snuffed out will be excesses day and night;
And folks will space their work with restful roles,
Construct a world of vibrant social worth,
A world with valid common sense controls.

Hail to a hundred fruitful years! Salubrious day!
Alive with love, creative work, relaxing play!

Index

29-303